Mathematical Modelling and Optimization of Service Supply Chain

Editor
Yong He
Southeast University
Nanjing
China

Editorial Office
MDPI AG
Grosspeteranlage 5
4052 Basel, Switzerland

This is a reprint of articles from the Special Issue published online in the open access journal *Mathematics* (ISSN 2227-7390) (available at: https://www.mdpi.com/journal/mathematics/special_issues/Mathematical_Modelling_Optimization_Service_Supply_Chain).

For citation purposes, cite each article independently as indicated on the article page online and as indicated below:

Lastname, A.A.; Lastname, B.B. Article Title. *Journal Name* **Year**, *Volume Number*, Page Range.

ISBN 978-3-7258-1793-1 (Hbk)
ISBN 978-3-7258-1794-8 (PDF)
doi.org/10.3390/books978-3-7258-1794-8

© 2024 by the authors. Articles in this book are Open Access and distributed under the Creative Commons Attribution (CC BY) license. The book as a whole is distributed by MDPI under the terms and conditions of the Creative Commons Attribution-NonCommercial-NoDerivs (CC BY-NC-ND) license.

Contents

About the Editor . . . . **vii**

Preface . . . . **ix**

Yong He
Preface to the Special Issue "Mathematical Modelling and Optimization of Service Supply Chain"
Reprinted from: *Mathematics* **2024**, *12*, 2292, doi:10.3390/math12142292 . . . . **1**

Zhongxiu Peng, Cong Wang, Wenqing Xu and Jinsong Zhang
Research on Location-Routing Problem of Maritime Emergency Materials Distribution Based on Bi-Level Programming
Reprinted from: *Mathematics* **2022**, *10*, 1243, doi:10.3390/math10081243 . . . . **6**

Peng Zhang, Sisi Ju and Hongfu Huang
Can a Restaurant Benefit from Joining an Online Take-Out Platform?
Reprinted from: *Mathematics* **2022**, *10*, 1392, doi:10.3390/math10091392 . . . . **29**

N. Anbazhagan, Gyanendra Prasad Joshi, R. Suganya, S. Amutha, V. Vinitha and Bhanu Shrestha
Queueing-Inventory System for Two Commodities with Optional Demands of Customers and MAP Arrivals
Reprinted from: *Mathematics* **2022**, *10*, 1801, doi:10.3390/math10111801 . . . . **46**

Xiaotong Guo and Yong He
Mathematical Modeling and Optimization of Platform Service Supply Chains: A Literature Review
Reprinted from: *Mathematics* **2022**, *10*, 4307, doi:10.3390/math10224307 . . . . **58**

Liu Liu, Ying Yuan, Xiaoya Wang and Hongfu Huang
Strategic Licensing of Green Technologies to a Brown Rival: A Game Theoretical Analysis
Reprinted from: *Mathematics* **2022**, *10*, 4433, doi:10.3390/math10234433 . . . . **77**

Komeyl Baghizadeh, Nafiseh Ebadi, Dominik Zimon and Luay Jum'a
Using Four Metaheuristic Algorithms to Reduce Supplier Disruption Risk in a Mathematical Inventory Model for Supplying Spare Parts
Reprinted from: *Mathematics* **2023**, *11*, 42, doi:10.3390/math11010042 . . . . **98**

Lei Song, Qi Xin, Huilin Chen, Lutao Liao and Zheyi Chen
Optimal Decision-Making of Retailer-Led Dual-Channel Green Supply Chain with Fairness Concerns under Government Subsidies
Reprinted from: *Mathematics* **2023**, *11*, 284, doi:10.3390/math11020284 . . . . **117**

Shan Lu, Peng Wu, Lei Gao and Richard Gifford
Are State-Owned Enterprises Equally Reliable Information Suppliers? An Examination of the Impacts of State Ownership on Earnings Management Strategies of Chinese Enterprises
Reprinted from: *Mathematics* **2023**, *11*, 814, doi:10.3390/math11040814 . . . . **133**

Yonit Barron
Integrating Replenishment Policy and Maintenance Services in a Stochastic Inventory System with Bilateral Movements
Reprinted from: *Mathematics* **2023**, *11*, 864, doi:10.3390/math11040864 . . . . **159**

Xiao Zhou and Xiancong Wu
Decisions for a Retailer-Led Low-Carbon Supply Chain Considering Altruistic Preference under Carbon Quota Policy
Reprinted from: *Mathematics* **2023**, *11*, 911, doi:10.3390/math11040911 . . . . **194**

Yuling Sun, Xiaomei Song, Yihao Jiang and Jian Guo
Strategy Analysis of Fresh Agricultural Enterprises in a Competitive Circumstance: The Impact of Blockchain and Consumer Traceability Preferences
Reprinted from: *Mathematics* **2023**, *11*, 1090, doi:10.3390/math11051090 . . . . **217**

Cong Wang, Zhongxiu Peng and Wenqing Xu
Robust Bi-Level Optimization for Maritime Emergency Materials Distribution in Uncertain Decision-Making Environments
Reprinted from: *Mathematics* **2023**, *11*, 4140, doi:10.3390/math11194140 . . . . **235**

Yuling Sun, Xiaomei Song, Xiang Fang and Jian Guo
Self-Built or Third-Party Blockchain Traceability Strategy in a Dual-Channel Supply Chain Considering Consumers' Traceability Awareness
Reprinted from: *Mathematics* **2023**, *11*, 4312, doi:10.3390/math11204312 . . . . **265**

Golnaz Hooshmand Pakdel, Yong He and Sina Hooshmand Pakdel
Multi-Objective Green Closed-Loop Supply Chain Management with Bundling Strategy, Perishable Products, and Quality Deterioration
Reprinted from: *Mathematics* **2024**, *12*, 737, doi:10.3390/math12050737 . . . . **286**

About the Editor

Yong He

Yong He is a Professor at the School of Economics and Management, Southeast University, China. He has published over 80 papers in international journals, including the *European Journal of Operational Research*, *International Journal of Production Economics*, *Naval Research Logistics*, *OMEGA*, *International Journal of Production Research*, and *IISE Transactions*. His research interests are mainly supply chain management, information management, service management, and E-commerce.

Editorial

Preface to the Special Issue "Mathematical Modelling and Optimization of Service Supply Chain"

Yong He

School of Economics and Management, Southeast University, Nanjing 211189, China; hy@seu.edu.cn

Citation: He, Y. Preface to the Special Issue "Mathematical Modelling and Optimization of Service Supply Chain". *Mathematics* **2024**, *12*, 2292. https://doi.org/10.3390/math12142292

Received: 15 July 2024
Accepted: 18 July 2024
Published: 22 July 2024

Copyright: © 2024 by the author. Licensee MDPI, Basel, Switzerland. This article is an open access article distributed under the terms and conditions of the Creative Commons Attribution (CC BY) license (https://creativecommons.org/licenses/by/4.0/).

1. Introduction

In recent years, as the world economy has grown, increasingly, service-oriented systems play a more significant role in the supply chain. Therefore, the optimization of service supply chains has become crucial for organizations aiming to achieve strategic advantages. Unlike traditional product-based supply chains, service supply chains are characterized by their intangible outputs, variable demand patterns, and the significant influence of human resources. In the meantime, the application of advanced analytical methods, ranging from various programming models and stochastic optimization to game-theoretical models, is essential to help service supply chain members make better decisions.

In this context, this Special Issue, "Mathematical Modelling and Optimization of Service Supply Chain", aims to look for innovative approaches to realize the modeling and optimization of service supply chains, as well as high-quality research solicited to address both theoretical and practical issues in the service supply chain. This Special Issue is intended for a diverse audience, including students, researchers, and practitioners in the fields of supply chain management, operations research, industrial engineering, and business management. Our goal is to equip readers with both the theoretical foundations and practical tools necessary for optimizing service supply chains in various industries.

2. Overview of the Published Papers

The present Special Issue contains 14 papers accepted for publication after a conscientious review process.

Zhongxiu Peng, Cong Wang, Wenqing Xu, and Jinsong Zhang (Contribution 1) investigate the location-routing problem within the context of multi-agent participation in maritime emergency materials distribution decision-making. Based on deterministic scenarios, an overall layout of the maritime emergency logistics system is examined. Utilizing a bi-level programming approach, a model considering the time windows of accident points and the priority of multiple types of emergency materials distribution is constructed. A hybrid algorithm combining ant colony optimization and tabu search was devised to solve the model, with a case study conducted in the Bohai Sea area. The method proposed in this study achieves the coordinated optimization of onshore emergency material reserves and multi-level emergency material distribution routes in maritime emergency logistics systems. It can assist decision makers at different levels of maritime emergency logistics systems in making more scientifically rational decisions, thereby enhancing the service capability of maritime emergency logistics systems.

Peng Zhang, Sisi Ju, and Hongfu Huang (Contribution 2) focus on restaurants' take-out model choice and the take-out platform and how to set the commission rate and coordination mechanisms to attract more restaurants. By adopting mathematical modeling methods, they first derived the restaurant's optimal price and/or platform's commission rate. Then, by comparing the profits of restaurants under different models, they obtained the optimal take-out model for restaurants in different situations. Lastly, they designed a sales reward contract that could achieve price and model choice coordination as well as win–win outcomes for the restaurant and platform.

found that introducing blockchain techniques in the traceability system could shift demand from traditional enterprises to blockchain enterprises when the blockchain influence factor meets a certain range. Moreover, it was found that both consumer traceability preferences and the blockchain influence factor could significantly affect optimal pricing. Finally, some management suggestions are provided to improve fresh supply chain performance.

Cong Wang, Zhongxiu Peng, and Wenqing Xu (Contribution 12) explore the location-routing problem of emergency materials distribution (MEMD-LRP) in uncertain maritime environments from the perspective of joint decision-making by multiple decision-making agents, leveraging methods such as bi-level programming and robust optimization. Uncertainty in the problem mainly consists of uncertain sailing times and uncertain emergency material demands at accident points during the planning horizon. A robust optimization bi-level model was constructed to address this uncertainty, with a hybrid algorithm combining the ant colony and tabu search utilized to solve a case study in the Bohai Sea area. With the method proposed in this paper, decision-makers can be empowered to flexibly formulate emergency material reserve locations and distribution decisions that can effectively cope with uncertainties in maritime emergencies while ensuring rapid responses. This study aids in achieving a more optimized and flexible emergency logistics system, thereby enhancing the capability to respond to maritime emergencies.

Yuling Sun, Xiaomei Song, Xiang Fang, and Jian Guo (Contribution 13) investigate the strategic implications of blockchain technology to trace products in dual-channel supply chains composed of a manufacturer and an e-retailer. They analyzed how a monopoly manufacturer chooses between a self-built blockchain traceability system (SBT) and a third-party blockchain traceability system (TBT). Game analysis is developed to depict the pricing decision for the manufacturer and e-retailer. Our results demonstrate that the manufacturer will prefer to adopt a TBT when the fee paid to the blockchain service provider is low. Moreover, they found that consumers' traceability awareness, the cost of adopting TBT, the blockchain traceability technology level, and the research and development cost factor of blockchain technology could affect the decisions of supply chain members. Practical guidance for supply chain managers is also put forward for determining the optimal blockchain adoption strategy.

Golnaz Hooshmand Pakdel, Yong He, and Sina Hooshmand Pakdel (Contribution 14) present a model with four main goals to improve environmentally friendly closed-loop supply chain management. The model focuses on cutting costs, reducing risks, lowering emissions, and speeding up deliveries in uncertain demand conditions. It takes into account factors like goods and quality degradation that were overlooked in models. By using a customized NSGA II algorithm with a selection tournament method, the study effectively balanced conflicting priorities, surpassing the MOPSO algorithm in both solution quality and efficiency. This model is especially useful for supply chain managers working with perishable products as it offers a decision-making framework that supports sustainability efforts. The results indicate a cost decrease of around 2.38% compared to previous methods, demonstrating improved solution discovery and efficiency. The study highlights the value of objective optimization in refining theoretical concepts and real-world applications, recommending that decision-makers adopt these sophisticated techniques to enhance sustainability practices in supply chain management regulations.

3. Conclusions

The 14 published papers cover a wide range of topics connected to the theory and applications of advanced analytical methods in the service supply chain. To be specific, these topics include the following: (1) the study of customer preferences and behaviors, e.g., environmental consciousness, traceability preferences, and optional demand; (2) the optimization of service supply chain members' decisions, e.g., operational strategies, revenue management, and sustainability practices; (3) the proposal of coordination mechanisms in service supply chains, e.g., sales reward contracts and carbon trading mechanisms; and (4) the effects of the external environment, e.g., risks, government subsidies and innovative technology. In addition, these topics have been studied under some special service scenarios, including maritime logistics, food services, and green innovation.

These papers present new theoretical results, structural investigations, new models, and algorithmic approaches, as well as empirical research on the service supply chain. These studies can, to some extent, assist academics and practitioners to better address current issues and potential challenges in service supply chains. As a result, the performance and efficiency of the service supply chain can be enhanced.

Funding: This work is supported by the National Natural Science Foundation of China (Nos. 72171047).

Conflicts of Interest: The authors declare no conflicts of interest.

List of Contributions:

1. Peng, Z.X.; Wang, C.; Xu, W.Q.; Zhang, J.S. Research on Location-Routing Problem of Maritime Emergency Materials Distribution Based on Bi-Level Programming. *Mathematics* **2022**, *10*, 1243. https://doi.org/10.3390/math10081243.
2. Zhang, P.; Ju, S.S.; Huang, H.F. Can a Restaurant Benefit from Joining an Online Take-Out Platform? *Mathematics* **2022**, *10*, 1392. https://doi.org/10.3390/math10091392.
3. Anbazhagan, N.; Joshi, G.P.; Suganya, R.; Amutha, S.; Vinitha, V.; Shrestha, B. Queueing-Inventory System for Two Commodities with Optional Demands of Customers and MAP Arrivals. *Mathematics* **2022**, *10*, 1801. https://doi.org/10.3390/math10111801.
4. Guo, X.T.; He, Y. Mathematical Modeling and Optimization of Platform Service Supply Chains: A Literature Review. *Mathematics* **2022**, *10*, 4307. https://doi.org/10.3390/math10224307.
5. Liu, L.; Yuan, Y.; Wang, X.Y.; Huang, H.F. Strategic Licensing of Green Technologies to a Brown Rival: A Game Theoretical Analysis. *Mathematics* **2022**, *10*, 4433. https://doi.org/10.3390/math10234433.
6. Baghizadeh, K.; Ebadi, N.; Zimon, D.; Jum'a, L. Using Four Metaheuristic Algorithms to Reduce Supplier Disruption Risk in a Mathematical Inventory Model for Supplying Spare Parts. *Mathematics* **2023**, *11*, 42. https://doi.org/10.3390/math11010042.
7. Song, L.; Xin, Q.; Chen, H.L.; Liao, L.T.; Chen, Z.Y. Optimal Decision-Making of Retailer-Led Dual-Channel Green Supply Chain with Fairness Concerns under Government Subsidies. *Mathematics* **2023**, *11*, 284. https://doi.org/10.3390/math11020284.
8. Lu, S.; Wu, P.; Gao, L.; Gifford, R. Are State-Owned Enterprises Equally Reliable Information Suppliers? An Examination of the Impacts of State Ownership on Earnings Management Strategies of Chinese Enterprises. *Mathematics* **2023**, *11*, 814. https://doi.org/10.3390/math11040814.
9. Barron, Y. Integrating Replenishment Policy and Maintenance Services in a Stochastic Inventory System with Bilateral Movements. *Mathematics* **2023**, *11*, 864. https://doi.org/10.3390/math11040864.
10. Zhou, X.; Wu, X.C. Decisions for a Retailer-Led Low-Carbon Supply Chain Considering Altruistic Preference under Carbon Quota Policy. *Mathematics* **2023**, *11*, 911. https://doi.org/10.3390/math11040911.
11. Sun, Y.L.; Song, X.M.; Jiang, Y.H.; Guo, J. Strategy Analysis of Fresh Agricultural Enterprises in a Competitive Circumstance: The Impact of Blockchain and Consumer Traceability Preferences. *Mathematics* **2023**, *11*, 1090. https://doi.org/10.3390/math11051090.
12. Wang, C.; Peng, Z.X.; Xu, W.Q. Robust Bi-Level Optimization for Maritime Emergency Materials Distribution in Uncertain Decision-Making Environments. *Mathematics* **2023**, *11*, 4140. https://doi.org/10.3390/math11194140.
13. Sun, Y.L.; Song, X.M.; Fang, X.; Guo, J. Self-Built or Third-Party Blockchain Traceability Strategy in a Dual-Channel Supply Chain Considering Consumers' Traceability Awareness. *Mathematics* **2023**, *11*, 4312. https://doi.org/10.3390/math11204312.
14. Pakdel, G.H.; He, Y.; Pakdel, S.H. Multi-Objective Green Closed-Loop Supply Chain Management with Bundling Strategy, Perishable Products, and Quality Deterioration. *Mathematics* **2024**, *12*, 737. https://doi.org/10.3390/math12050737.

Disclaimer/Publisher's Note: The statements, opinions and data contained in all publications are solely those of the individual author(s) and contributor(s) and not of MDPI and/or the editor(s). MDPI and/or the editor(s) disclaim responsibility for any injury to people or property resulting from any ideas, methods, instructions or products referred to in the content.

delivery. The solution methods of LRP-related research mainly include staged solutions and global solutions. In [16], the green LRP is decomposed into two sub-problems, namely the cumulative LRP (CumLRP) and the speed optimization problem (SOP), and each sub-problem is solved hierarchically. The solution results of the cumulative location routing and speed optimization algorithm (CLRSOA) are compared with the iterated local search algorithm. Reference [18] proposed a hybrid heuristic algorithm based on a tabu search to solve the LRP with simultaneous pick-up and delivery. The algorithm is divided into three stages: initialization, location, and routing. References [15,17] used a hybrid genetic algorithm (HGA), and [19] proposed a multi-start hybrid heuristic algorithm with path relinking (MHH-PR) composed of local search and a variable neighborhood descent algorithm to solve the LRP as a whole.

The research on the combination of LRPs and emergency logistics has also become a hot issue considered by scholars at home and abroad. The relevant research on LRPs of emergency logistics by domestic and overseas scholars in recent years is summarized in Table 1.

Table 1. Summary of main features of related research on emergency logistics LRPs.

Author	Uncertainty	Maritime Emergency	Multiple Types of Emergency Materials	Time Window	Improved Algorithm
Liu et al. [13]				√	√
Tavana et al. [20]			√		√
Wei et al. [21]				√	√
Vahdani et al. [22]			√		
Xue et al. [23]			√		
Li et al. [24]		√	√		
Ai et al. [25]		√			√
Ai et al. [26]		√			√
Shen et al. [14]	√				√
Zhang et al. [27]	√	√			√
Bozorgi-Amiri et al. [28]	√		√		
Chang et al. [29]	√			√	
Veysmoradi et al. [30]	√				√
Wu et al. [31]	√				
Zhang et al. [32]	√				√
Hu et al. [33]	√		√		√
Liu et al. [34]	√		√		
Xiong et al. [35]	√		√		√
Qin et al. [36]	√			√	√
Liu et al. [37]	√				
Liu et al. [38]	√				√
This paper		√	√	√	√

Emergency rescue needs the joint action of multiple units and multiple departments. Government-led, functional departments cooperate, communicate, and coordinate with each other to carry out emergency rescue operations more reasonably and efficiently. Therefore, emergency logistics should be a joint decision-making activity with the participation of multi-level decision-makers. In the existing research on LRP with emergency logistics, some scholars consider the characteristics of multi-participation and multi-decision of emergency logistics by the government and enterprises and use the bi-level programming method to solve the problem from the perspective of multi-agent decision. To solve the problem of lack of road condition information increasing the uncertainty of disaster relief work within 72 h after an earthquake, Xu et al. [39] proposed a bi-level model based on a random fuzzy environment and designed an interactive genetic algorithm based on random fuzzy simulation to search the optimal solution of the bi-level model. Lou [40] studied (a) the expression of emergency logistics with the participation of the government and enterprises and (b) the post-disaster LRP. Lou [40] then established a bi-level programming model and designed a hybrid simulated annealing algorithm combined with tabu search technology. Safaei et al. [41] proposed a bi-objective, bi-level optimization model under an uncertain environment to design a complete disaster relief logistics operation framework, and the proposed nonlinear model was transformed into a single-level linear problem to solve. Chen et al. [42] established a bi-level programming model considering minimum allocation time and maximum allocation fairness and designed an improved differential evolution algorithm to solve the problem. Li et al. [43] established a multi-period, bi-level programming model for post-disaster road network emergency repair scheduling and disaster relief logistics problems and designed genetic algorithms to solve the problem. Considering the various characteristics of the two-level logistics emergency system, Zhou [44] studied transfer facility location and relief material transportation in the initial period after the earthquake. The grey mixed integer bi-level nonlinear programming model was established, and the genetic algorithm was designed. At present, few researchers have examined how to solve the LRP in emergency logistics using a bi-level programming method; the above research is all based on land disasters and emergencies.

Generally speaking, the research on the LRP of emergency logistics is rich and in-depth, and stochastic programming, robust optimization, and bi-level programming decision-making methods have also been applied to different forms of the LRP of emergency logistics. However, there are still some aspects worthy of further exploration. First, most of the existing studies focus on land disasters and emergencies, and few scholars consider using maritime emergencies as the background to optimize the overall layout of the maritime emergency logistics system. Among the above-mentioned references, only [24–27] explored the background of maritime emergencies. Second, most of the existing studies only consider a single kind of emergency material, and few scholars consider many kinds of emergency materials and the priority in distribution. Although many kinds of emergency materials are considered in [20,22–24,28,33–35,41,42], the priority of emergency materials distribution is only considered in [23]. However, the limitation of [23] is that it did not detail the joint decision-making of location and routing, and the location is not considered in the study. Third, most of the existing studies focus on the use of multi-objective models, without considering multiple decision-making agents and the application of bi-level programming methods. Different decision-making agents will lead to different decision-making problems. Location and route selection are activities at different levels that require a combined decision. The single-level programming method will separate the things that are originally related, and it cannot comprehensively analyze and solve the problems. References [39–44] adopt a bi-level programming method to solve the LRP of emergency logistics with the participation of multiple decision agents, but [40–44] do not consider that location and route selection are activities at different levels, making location decisions at the upper level and planning the route at the lower level. The biggest difference between maritime emergencies and other emergencies is that the environment is different. A dangerous situation at sea is sudden and harmful and can easily cause mass deaths and injuries. Maritime emergency operations are often carried out in harsh conditions, making rescue difficult. Therefore, the LRP of the maritime emergency network has higher requirements on time, which can deliver maritime emergency materials to the accident points in the shortest time as soon as possible. Due to the different environments, MEMD-LRP often needs a variety of professional emergency materials. There are many units and departments involved in the maritime emergency network, and problems in any link may lead to missing the best rescue opportunity. Therefore, the task of maritime rescue and coordination is also relatively heavy. The MEMD-LRP will definitely involve multiple decision-makers.

3. Problem Description and Model Construction

3.1. Problem Description

MEMD-LRP decisions require scientific and reasonable location selection of shore-based emergency materials reserves and distribution route planning of maritime emergency materials to achieve efficient scheduling of emergency materials and improve the overall operational efficiency of the maritime emergency logistics system. The problem can be described as follows: There are several shore-based candidate emergency materials reserves and several potential maritime accident points. Several suitable reserves are selected as distribution centers from the shore-based candidate emergency materials reserves. According to the information such as the location of potential accident points and the demand for emergency materials, under the constraints of meeting the time windows and other constraints, the commercial rescue unit reasonably plans the routes to distribute emergency materials with different priorities from the reserves to the accident points. The maritime logistics system and related elements studied in this paper are shown in Figure 1.

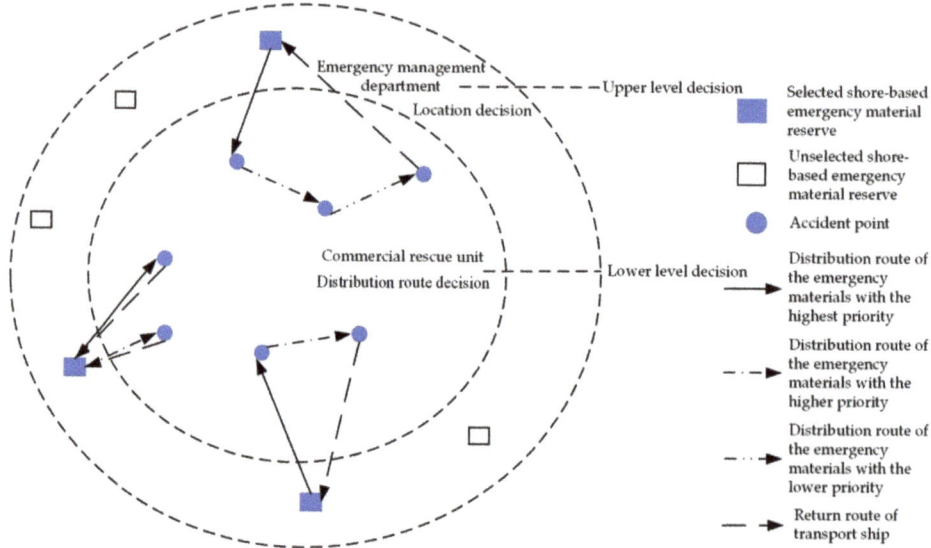

Figure 1. Schematic diagram of the maritime logistics system and related elements.

MEMD-LRP is a multi-level decision agent participation and joint decision problem. The bi-level programming method can be used to solve the practical problem of two-level decision-makers in the decision-making system; this problem can be described by bi-level programming. First, the upper decision-maker gives their decision. Then, under the decision given by the upper level, the lower decision-maker determines the optimal lower-level decision and feeds it back to the upper level. Next, the upper-level decision-maker adjusts the upper-level decision based on feedback from the lower-level decision-maker to make the best decision for the whole. The upper- and lower-level decision-makers influence each other but do not completely restrict each other; the upper-level decision is considered from a more overall point of view. In the research of this paper, the upper decision-maker is a member of the emergency management department. This upper decision-maker makes overall planning decisions on the location of emergency materials reserves while considering both the minimum total construction costs and the minimum loss costs of time satisfaction at the accident points. The lower decision-maker is a member of the commercial rescue unit. According to the location scheme given by the upper level, the lower level reasonably plans the distribution routes of emergency materials to minimize the cost of emergency materials distribution, ship transportation, ship dispatch, and time punishment. The upper decision-maker first makes the location decision; then, the lower decision-maker must respond to this decision. The lower decision-maker has a certain degree of independent decision-making power, and the rescue unit provides feedback on the distribution plan to the emergency management department. Then, the upper decision-maker must make another decision according to the response of the rescue unit to make the optimal decision for the whole emergency logistics system.

This paper has the following assumptions:

1. Multiple candidate emergency materials reserves with known locations and unlimited capacity.
2. Multiple potential accident points with known locations and the drift and diffusion of the accident points are not considered.
3. Multiple levels of emergency materials with known priorities; the transportation order of materials is in the order of priority, and the unit distribution cost of different levels of emergency materials is different.
4. The number of ships is sufficient, the transport ships are of the same type and capacity, and different levels of emergency materials can be mixed and loaded under the limitation of the time window of the accident point.
5. The emergency materials in the candidate reserves are sufficient, the emergency material demand at the accident point is known, the emergency materials storage capacity of each reserve meets the rescue needs of multiple accident points, and the demand at each accident point does not exceed the storage capacity of a single emergency material reserve.
6. Each accident point is rescued by only one emergency material reserve, and only one ship passes through the accident point in the process of emergency material distribution at each level, with time window restrictions.
7. Each ship belongs to an emergency material reserve. Starting from the warehouse and returning to the warehouse after transporting the materials, each ship can serve multiple accident points under the condition of meeting the time window limit.

Variables and symbols are described as follows:

$I = \{i|i = 1, 2, \cdots, |I|\}$ is the set of all candidate shore-based emergency material reserves;
$J = \{j|j = 1, 2, \cdots, |J|\}$ is the set of all accident points;
$B = I \cup J$ is the set of all nodes in the network;
$K = \{k|k = 1, 2, \cdots, |K|\}$ is the set of all ships;
$W = \{w|w = 1, 2, \cdots, |W|\}$ is the set of emergency materials priority number;
f_i is the fixed construction cost of the i candidate material reserve;
S_k is the transportation cost per unit distance of the k ship;
c_0 is the fixed dispatch cost per ship;
G is the fixed capacity per ship;
When $u_{jw} = 1$, the accident point j needs emergency materials of level w, and when $u_{jw} = 0$, the emergency materials of level w are not required at the accident point j;
D_{jw} is the demand for emergency materials of level w at accident point j;
C_{ijw} is the unit transportation cost of emergency materials of level w transported from reserve i to accident point j;
V_{pqk} is the actual average velocity of ship k from node p to q considering the influence of wind and water current;
v_{pqk} is the average velocity of ship k from node p to q in still water;
v_1 is the influence of the wind;
v_2 is the influence of the water current;
d_{pq} is the shortest sailing distance from node p to q;
T_k is the time of ship k loading and unloading unit materials;
T_{Ejw} is the expected arrival time of emergency materials of level w at accident point j;
T_{Ljw} is the latest arrival time of level w emergency materials that can be tolerated at the accident point j;
T_{jw} is the actual arrival time of level w emergency materials at accident point j;
c_1 is the time penalty cost caused by the arrival of emergency materials of level w earlier than T_{Ejw};
c_2 is the time penalty cost for the arrival of emergency materials of level w later than T_{Ejw} and earlier than T_{Ljw};

$F(T_{jw})$ is the time satisfaction function of the accident point j in the transportation of emergency materials of level w;

$f(F(T_{jw}))$ is the time satisfaction loss cost penalty coefficient function of the accident point j in the transportation of emergency materials of level w;

A is a sufficiently large positive number;

Decision variables:

$x_i = \begin{cases} 1, \text{Construct an emergency material reserve at the point} \\ 0, \text{Otherwise} \end{cases}$;

$y_{ij} = \begin{cases} 1, \text{Emergency materials reserve } i \text{ rescue the accident point } j \\ 0, \text{Otherwise} \end{cases}$;

$q_k = \begin{cases} 1, \text{The ship } k \text{ put into use} \\ 0, \text{Otherwise} \end{cases}$;

$z_{pqk} = \begin{cases} 1, \text{The ship } k \text{ sails from node } p \text{ to } q \\ 0, \text{Otherwise} \end{cases}$.

3.2. Model Construction

3.2.1. The Time Penalty Cost Description of MEMD-LRP

The maritime emergency rescue has the characteristic of strong time-effectiveness, so this paper improves the time penalty cost function in [21,40,45] to obtain the time penalty cost in MEMD-LRP. When the ship k transports a certain level of emergency materials to the accident point j, if it does not arrive at the expected time T_{Ejw} of the accident point j, the time penalty cost will be incurred. Under no circumstances shall the time taken to arrive at the accident point j exceed T_{Ljw}; otherwise, the ship k cannot transport materials to the accident point. The relationship between time and the cost of time penalty is shown in Figure 2.

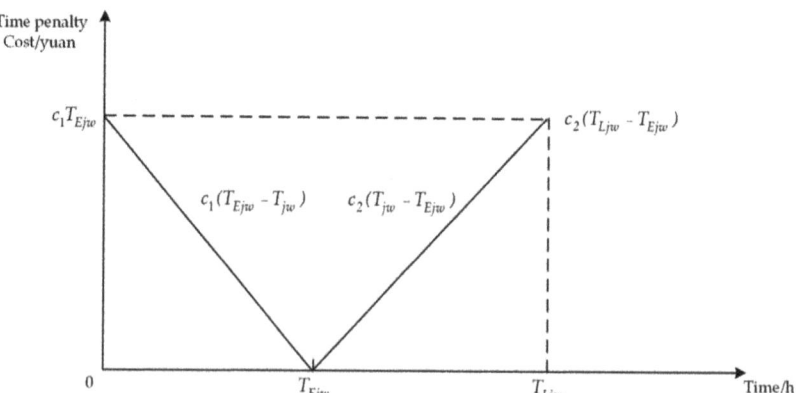

Figure 2. Relationship curve between time and time penalty cost.

3.2.2. The Time Satisfaction Loss Cost Description of at Accident Points of MEMD-LRP

In this paper, the decision-making problem of the emergency management department is that of selecting a suitable shore-based emergency material reserve to meet the needs of all potential accident points, from the overall point of view. Both the construction cost and the time satisfaction of the accident points should be considered. To facilitate calculation, time satisfaction is converted into time satisfaction loss cost into the goal of upper-level decision-makers. When the ship k transports a certain level of emergency materials to the accident point j and does not arrive at the expected time T_{Ejw} of the accident point j, the time satisfaction of the accident point j will be lost. The greater the difference between the time when the emergency materials arrive at the accident point j and T_{Ejw}, the greater the loss of time satisfaction is. According to the research results of [46], this paper selects the linear time satisfaction function to discuss the time satisfaction of the maritime accident points to the arrival time of emergency materials, and the functional relationship is set to $F(T_{jw})$, and the loss cost of time satisfaction at the accident point is related to the demand for emergency materials at the accident point. The penalty coefficient of the loss cost of time satisfaction at the accident point is a piecewise function corresponding to time satisfaction, and the functional relationship is set to $\phi(F(T_{jw}))$.

The time satisfaction function expression of the accident point j for the arrival time of a certain level of emergency materials is as follows:

$$F(T_{jw}) = \begin{cases} 1, T_{jw} = T_{Ejw} \\ \frac{T_{Ejw} - T_{jw}}{T_{Ejw}}, 0 \leq T_{jw} < T_{Ejw} \\ \frac{T_{Ljw} - T_{jw}}{T_{Ljw} - T_{Ejw}}, T_{Ejw} < T_{jw} \leq T_{Ljw} \\ 0, T_{Ljw} < T_{jw} \end{cases}, \forall j \in J, w \in W \quad (1)$$

The function expression of the penalty coefficient of the time satisfaction loss cost of the accident point j is as follows:

$$\phi(F(T_{jw})) = \begin{cases} 0, F(T_{jw}) = 1 \\ 1, F(T_{jw}) = \frac{T_{Ejw} - T_{jw}}{T_{Ejw}}, \forall j \in J, w \in W \\ 1, F(T_{jw}) = \frac{T_{Ljw} - T_{jw}}{T_{Ljw} - T_{Ejw}}, \forall j \in J, w \in W \\ +\infty, F(T_{jw}) = 0 \end{cases} \quad (2)$$

The total cost of the loss of time satisfaction at the accident points is as follows:

$$\sum_{i \in I} \sum_{j \in J} \sum_{w \in W} x_i \phi(F(T_{jw})) y_{ij} D_{jw} \quad (3)$$

3.2.3. The Bi-Level Programming Model of MEMD-LRP

Upper model:

$$\min f_1 = \sum_{i \in I} f_i x_i + \sum_{i \in I} \sum_{j \in J} \sum_{w \in W} x_i \phi(F(T_{jw})) y_{ij} D_{jw} \quad (4)$$

$$\text{s.t. } 1 \leq \sum_{i \in I} x_i \leq I \quad (5)$$

$$y_{ij} - x_i \leq 0, \forall i \in I, j \in J \quad (6)$$

$$x_i \in \{0, 1\} \quad (7)$$

The objective function (4) represents the minimization of the construction cost of emergency materials reserves and the loss cost of time satisfaction at the accident points. Constraint (5) indicates that the actual construction number of the emergency materials reserves cannot exceed the number of candidate emergency materials reserves. Constraint (6) indicates that materials can be transported only if they are selected as emergency materials reserves, and constraint (7) is the upper-level decision variable.

Lower model:

$$\min f_2 = \sum_{i \in I} \sum_{j \in J} \sum_{w \in W} u_{jw} d_{jw} C_{ijw} y_{ij} + \sum_{p,q \in B} \sum_{k \in K} z_{pqk} d_{pq} S_k + \sum_{k \in K} c_0 q_k + \\ \sum_{w \in W} \left(\sum_{i \in I} \sum_{j \in J} y_{ij} (c_1 \max\{T_{Ejw} - T_{jw}, 0\} + c_2 \max\{T_{jw} - T_{Ejw}, 0\}) \right) \quad (8)$$

$$\text{s.t.} \sum_{i \in I} y_{ij} = 1, \forall j \in J \tag{9}$$

$$\sum_{k \in K} \sum_{j \in J} z_{ijk} \geq x_i, \forall i \in I \tag{10}$$

$$\sum_{i \in I} \sum_{j \in J} z_{ijk} \leq 1, \forall k \in K \tag{11}$$

$$z_{pqk} \leq q_k, \forall p,q \in B, p \neq q, k \in K \tag{12}$$

$$\sum_{k \in K} \sum_{p \in B} z_{pjk} u_{jw} = 1, \forall j \in J, w \in W \tag{13}$$

$$\sum_{p,q \in B} \sum_{i \in I} \sum_{j \in J} D_{jw} u_{jw} y_{ij} z_{pqk} \leq G, \forall k \in K \tag{14}$$

$$\sum_{k \in K} z_{pqk} = 0, \forall p, q \in I \tag{15}$$

$$\sum_{p \in B} z_{pqk} - \sum_{p \in B} z_{qpk} = 0, \forall k \in K, q \in B \tag{16}$$

$$\sum_{j \in J} z_{ijk} + \sum_{j \in J} z_{jrk} \leq 1, \forall i, r \in I \tag{17}$$

$$y_{ij} D_{j(w+1)} \leq u_{jw} A, \forall i \in I, j \in J, w = 1, \cdots, |W| - 1 \tag{18}$$

$$T_{jw} \leq T_{j(w+1)}, \forall j \in J, w = 1, \cdots, |W| - 1 \tag{19}$$

$$\sum_{j \in J} T_{jw} \leq \sum_{j \in J} T_{j(w+1)}, w = 1, \cdots, |W| - 1 \tag{20}$$

$$y_{ij} T_{jw} \leq T_{Ljw}, \forall i \in I, j \in J, w \in W \tag{21}$$

$$T_{iw} + T_k D_{iw} z_{ijk} + \frac{d_{ij}}{V_{ijk}} \leq T_{Ljw}, \forall i, j \in J, w \in W, z_{ijk} = 1 \tag{22}$$

$$y_{ij} \in \{0,1\}, q_k \in \{0,1\}, z_{pqk} \in \{0,1\} \tag{23}$$

In the bi-level programming model, the constraints of the upper model are also applicable to the lower model. The objective function (8) is the minimum sum of the distribution cost of different levels of emergency materials, ship transportation cost, ship dispatch cost, and time penalty cost. Constraint (9) indicates that each accident point is rescued by only one emergency materials reserve. Constraint (10) means that each selected emergency materials reserve is assigned to ships. Constraint (11) means that each ship is assigned to a selected emergency materials reserve. Constraint (12) indicates that only ships put into use can transport, and constraint (13) means that there is only one ship passing by each accident point during the distribution of emergency materials at each level. Constraint (14) means that the emergency materials demand at the accident points on the distribution route of each ship is less than or equal to the ship capacity. Constraint (15) indicates that any two emergency materials reserves cannot be transported, and constraint (16) means that ships entering from that point also sail out from that point. Constraint (17) means that the ship departing from the emergency materials reserve will finally return to the emergency materials reserve. Constraint (18) indicates that the emergency materials transported from the emergency material reserve i to the accident point j can be transported only after the transportation of the emergency materials of the previous level is completed. Constraints (19) and (20) indicate that the actual delivery time of high-priority emergency materials is strictly less than that of low-priority emergency materials. Constraint (21) indicates that the actual arrival time of the level w emergency materials transported from the emergency material reserve i to the accident point j is less than or equal to the latest delivery time of the level w emergency materials that can be tolerated at the accident point j.

Constraint (22) represents the time window constraint of the ship in the process of serving multiple accident points, and constraint (23) is lower-level decision variables.

The calculation formula of the time when the ship k arrives at the accident point j is as follows:

$$T_{jw} = T_{iw} + T_k D_{iw} z_{ijk} + \frac{d_{ij}}{V_{ijk}}, \forall i, j \in J, w \in W, z_{ijk} = 1 \quad (24)$$

The speed of ship k will be affected by wind and water current, so the actual average velocity of ship k is the vector superposition of the ship k still water average velocity, wind velocity, and water current velocity. Because the research of this paper is in the prevention stage, it represents the overall layout of the maritime emergency logistics system. Therefore, it is assumed that the still water velocity of the ship, the wind velocity, and the water current velocity between nodes are constant [25,26]:

$$V_{ijk} = v_{ijk} + v_1 + v_2 \quad (25)$$

The bi-level programming model established in this paper has a bi-level hierarchical structure. The objective function and constraints of the upper-level optimization problem are not only related to the upper-level decision variable but also depend on the optimal solution of the lower-level optimization problem. At the same time, the optimal solution of the lower-level optimization problem is affected by the upper-level decision variable. The upper decision variable is x_i, the location decision that should be made, and the lower decision variables are y_{ij}, q_k, z_{pqk}. According to the location decision, accident points should be assigned to each selected emergency materials reserve, and appropriate rescue routes should be designed. The lower-level decision variables depend on the upper-level decision variable. Once the upper-level variable is determined, the corresponding lower-level variables can be determined. Each upper solution $\{x_i\}$ corresponds to a lower solution $\{y_{ij}, q_k, z_{pqk}\}$. It is only after the location decision of the upper level is completed that the lower level can allocate the accident points and plan the distribution routes of each emergency materials reserve to serve each accident point. The location decision of the upper level should be re-adjusted according to the response of the route decision of the lower level. Bi-level programming is used to emphasize the influence between upper and lower levels of decision-making; thus, bi-level programming usually cannot be solved independently.

4. Algorithm Design

The bi-level programming model is very difficult to solve. The model belongs to the NP-Hard problem, and there is no accurate solution algorithm [39,40]. The bi-level programming model constructed in this paper not only considers multiple emergency materials reserves, multiple accident points, and multiple types of emergency materials, but also considers factors such as emergency materials distribution priority, accident point time window, and accident point satisfaction loss cost. At the same time, the upper-level location result is the premise of lower-level route planning, which greatly impacts route planning. There are many model variables and constraints, which makes the model more difficult to solve. Ant colony algorithm is an approximate algorithm, which is used to solve a problem that no accurate algorithm has been found to solve so far. The algorithm has the characteristics of positive feedback, multi-point parallel search, and strong robustness, and it can be used to solve the problem in this paper. Although the ant colony algorithm has a strong global optimization ability, the local search ability is poor and the convergence speed is slow; the tabu search algorithm can jump out of the local optimal solution, and it is a global iterative optimization algorithm with strong local search ability. The combination of the two algorithms can avoid the algorithm falling into the local optimization and obtain the global optimal solution [47,48]. Therefore, according to the characteristics of bi-level programming in this paper and the existing algorithms for solving similar models [14,40,45], a hybrid algorithm of the ant colony and tabu search is designed.

4.1. Coding and Decoding

Suppose that there are I candidate emergency materials reserves and J accident points. First, the candidate emergency materials reserves and accident points are coded by real number coding. The ship's route begins at the emergency materials reserve, then passes through the accident points, and finally returns to the emergency materials reserve. For example, the scheme code of starting from reserve 1 and passing through accident points 2, 3, 5, and 6 is 123561. Secondly, the double-level coding method is used to encode the ants. The first level code is the access priority code of the accident points, the real number coding with the code length J, and the change interval is $[0, 1]$. The code is sorted in ascending order to obtain the access order code S_1 of the accident point. The second-level code is the assigned code of the reserves, the real number coding with the length J, and the interval is $[1, I + 0.999]$. After rounding down this code, the assigned reserves code S2 is obtained, indicating which reserve serves the accident point. For example, when $I = 4$ and $J = 6$, a randomly generated ant code can be x = (0.3,0.5,0.2,0.41,0.6,0.7,1.8,2.3,1.5,3.6,4.1,4.2), and the first level code is x_1 = (0.3,0.5,0.2,0.41,0.6,0.7). The code is sorted in ascending order to obtain S_1 = (3,1,4,2,5,6), which means that accident point 3 is accessed first, then the priority is to visit incident point 1, then the priority is to visit incident point 4, then the priority is to access incident point 2, then the priority is to access incident point 5, and then priority is to access incident point 6. The code of the second level is x_2 = (1.8,2.3,1.5,3.6,4.1,4.2), rounded down to obtain M = (1,2,1,3,4,4), indicating that accident point 3 is served by reserve 1, accident point 1 is served by reserve 2, accident point 4 is served by reserve 1, accident point 2 is served by reserve 3, accident point 5 is served by reserve 4, and accident point 6 is served by reserve 4. After ant colony decoding, the location and division of the accident points and distribution routes can be determined. A possible distribution route scheme real number coding is 4564. It is not possible to determine whether the resulting solution is feasible during the encoding and decoding process. Only when the optimal coding is obtained after several iterations of the algorithm and the optimal scheme and objective function values are obtained by decoding can we judge whether the scheme is feasible or not.

4.2. Ant Colony Movement

The core idea of the ant colony algorithm is that the ant colony moves in the direction of the maximum pheromone. For the current ant i, first randomly select t other ants and identify the ant with the largest corresponding pheromone among the t ants. This ant represents the maximum direction of the pheromones. Move the position of the current ant i according to the following equation: $xnew = (1 - speed) \times xi + speed \times xmax$, where $xnew$ is the new location of the ant, $speed$ is the movement speed of the ant, xi is the location of the current ant i, and $xmax$ is the ant location in the maximum direction of pheromones. The above movement is carried out for each ant such that the whole ant colony moves simultaneously in the maximum pheromone direction.

4.3. Pheromone Update

Ants will leave a certain amount of pheromones as they move forward, and at the same time, all pheromones will volatilize at a certain rate. The ACO-TS algorithm designed in this paper uses the equation $\tau_i(gen + 1) = (1 - \rho)\tau_i(gen)$ to describe the volatilization of pheromones, where $\tau_i(gen + 1)$ is the pheromone corresponding to the i ant of the $gen + 1$ generation, ρ is the pheromone volatilization coefficient, and $\tau_i(gen)$ is the pheromone corresponding to the i ant of the gen generation. Equation $\tau_i(gen + 1) = \tau_i(gen + 1) + \Delta\tau_i(gen + 1)$ is used to describe the enhancement of pheromones, where $\Delta\tau_i(gen + 1) = Q\frac{maxyj - yi}{maxyj - minyj}$ is the pheromone increment of the i ant of the $gen + 1$ generation, Q is the pheromone enhancement factor, $maxyj$ is the maximum sum of the upper and lower objective function values corresponding to all ants after dimension elimination, $minyj$ is the minimum sum of the upper and lower objective function values corresponding to all ants after dimension elimination, and y_i is the sum of the upper and lower objective function values corresponding to the i ant after dimension elimination.

4.4. Neighborhood Movement

The neighborhood moving method of the tabu search part is similar to the mutation operation of the genetic algorithm. It randomly generates a natural number r, changes the r bit of the coding of the current solution, rearranges the coding, and generates a neighbor of the current solution. Then, it checks whether the current neighbor is in the tabu table.

4.5. Tabu Table Length

The length of the tabu table affects the search time, local search strategy, and wide search strategy. The long table is suitable for wide search and the short table has good locality. The tabu length of the tabu search algorithm designed in this paper is fixed, and the fixed constant is selected according to the scale of the problem.

4.6. Stop Criterion

The stop criterion of the tabu search algorithm is to set the maximum number of iterations, which is equal to the maximum number of iterations of the whole algorithm.

4.7. Specific Steps

The specific steps of the hybrid algorithm proposed in this paper can be summarized as follows, and the flow chart of the algorithm is shown in Figure 3.

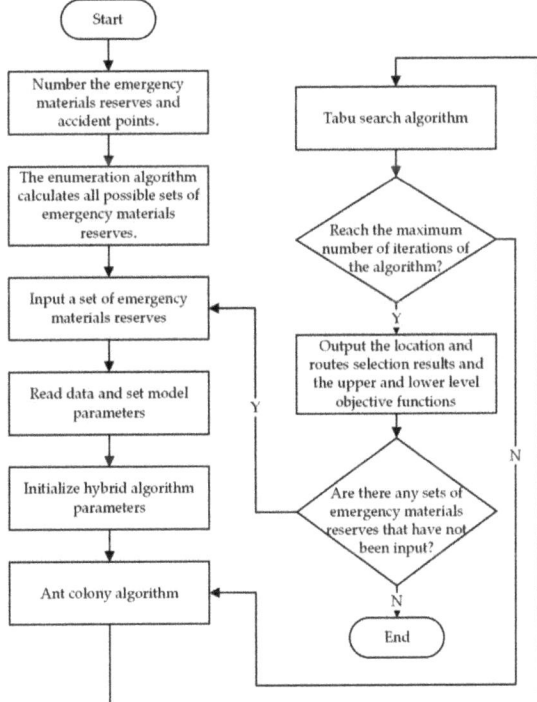

Figure 3. Algorithm flow chart.

Step 1: All candidate emergency materials reserves and accident points are numbered, and all different emergency materials reserve sets are calculated by the enumerating algorithm.

Step 2: Input a set of emergency materials reserves in which the initial number of reserves is equal to the number of candidate emergency reserves. Under the constraints of the time window and shipload, considering the priority of emergency materials distribution and the demand for each level of emergency materials at the accident points, the ant colony–tabu search algorithm is used to plan the routes. Then, the lower objective function is calculated, and the time satisfaction loss cost is returned to the upper objective function. Record the results of this location and route selection, as well as the values of the upper and lower level objective functions.

Step 2.1: Read the data and set the model parameters, the ant colony–tabu search algorithm parameters, and the number of iterations of the algorithm.

Step 2.2: Initialize the encoding and pheromone and decode to calculate the initialized lower-level objective function value, return the time satisfaction loss cost to the upper level to calculate the upper-level objective function value, and generate a tabu table.

Step 2.3: The ant colony moves in the direction of the maximum pheromone; decode to obtain the accident point served by each emergency materials reserve; divide the routes according to the time window, load, and priority constraints. The rules for dividing routes according to loads are as follows: the demand of the accident point is accumulated from the reserve, and when the cumulative demand is less than or equal to the ship capacity, the visited accident points are added to the current route; when the demand of the cumulative accident point is greater than the ship capacity, the front accident points join the route, allocate new ship to the current accident point, re-accumulate the demand of the accident point, and generate a new route. Calculate the time window constraints; calculate the lower objective function value, feed the time satisfaction loss cost back to the upper level, and calculate the upper objective function value. Update pheromones.

Step 2.4: The feasible solution generated by the ant colony algorithm is re-optimized as the initial solution of the tabu search algorithm.

Step 2.5: The candidate solution set is generated by neighborhood movement. If the generated domain is in the tabu table, it is regenerated until it does not exist in the tabu table. Decode and calculate the objective function values.

Step 2.6: The upper objective function is used as the evaluation function to evaluate the advantages and disadvantages of the candidate solution and update the solution.

Step 2.7: Update the tabu table, randomly select a feasible candidate solution to add to the tabu table, and remove the tabu of the first solution in the tabu table.

Step 2.8: Judge whether the maximum number of iterations of the algorithm is reached. If not, return to Step 2.3. If so, output and record the location and route selection results as well as the upper and lower level objective functions.

Step 3: Keep the number of emergency materials reserves in the set unchanged, update the set of emergency materials reserves, and return to Step 2. If there is no unselected set of emergency materials reserves containing the same number of reserves, then reduce the number of emergency materials reserves from the set of emergency materials reserves by 1, and return to Step 2.

Step 4: If the number of emergency materials reserves in the set is reduced to 1 and there is no unselected set of emergency materials reserves, the algorithm stops. The recorded results of location and route selection as well as the values of upper and lower objective functions are compared and analyzed, and the optimal location scheme and route selection scheme are obtained.

5. Results and Discussions

5.1. Introduction of a Numerical Example

To verify the effectiveness of the model and algorithm proposed in this paper, based on the real historical cases of the Bohai Sea, the example of this paper is designed according to the accident level, adding different priority emergency materials, accident point time windows, and other related information. Dalian Port, Yingkou Port, Tianjin Port, Qinhuangdao Port, Weifang Port, and Yantai Port are selected as candidate points for the construction of shore-based emergency materials reserves, and 40 collision and shipwreck accident points in the real historical cases in the Bohai Sea are selected as potential accident points. The attributes of the above two types of maritime accidents are similar, and collisions may lead to shipwrecks; thus, the types of materials needed are generally similar. Three levels of emergency materials are selected for rescue consumption, and some data are selected based on the optimal scheduling problem of emergency materials for major maritime accidents in [47]. Some of the information on the historical cases is shown in Table 2; the relevant data of candidate shore-based emergency materials reserves and accident points are shown in Tables 3 and 4. Due to space constraints, the relevant data of accident points only give the first-level emergency material demand and time windows of 20 accident points, and the distribution maps of candidate emergency materials reserves and potential accident points are shown in Figure 4. The main parameters of the model are set as $G = 30$ units/ship, $V_{pqk} = 25$ kn, $S_k = 1$ CNY/n mile, $c_0 = 900$ CNY/ship, $T_k = 0.05$ h/unit, $c_1 = 10$ CNY/h, $c_2 = 20$ CNY/h, $C_{ij1} = 5$ CNY/unit, $C_{ij2} = 4$ CNY/unit, and $C_{ij3} = 3$ CNY/unit. When solving the problem, the relevant software is used to convert the longitude and latitude of the actual port location and the location of the accidents into Cartesian coordinates.

Table 2. Information on some historical cases in the Bohai Sea area (data source: Maritime Safety Administration of the People's Republic of China).

Date	Accident	Number of People Involved	Economic Loss (CNY 10,000)	Accident Level
9 November 2016	Collision accident between "Xiangping River Cargo 0306" and "Jihuanggang Fishing Boat 19"	3	92	Larger
18 December 2017	Collision accident between "Yongyue 66" and "Lushouyu 60687"	8	100	Larger
13 April 2017	Collision accident between "Haiyang 207" and "NanDongting 6"	2	625	General
18 September 2018	Collision accident between "C" and "W9099"	0	600	General
3 September 2019	Collision accident between "K" and "L23626"	1	200	General
22 September 2020	Collision accident between "XCH" and "Jileyu XXXXX"	0	30	Small

Table 3. Data of candidate shore-based emergency materials reserves.

Number	Port	Longitude	Latitude	f_i (CNY10,000)
1	Dalian Port	121°39′17″	38°55′44″	20
2	Yingkou Port	122°06′00″	40°17′42″	18
3	Tianjin Port	117°42′05″	38°59′08″	20
4	Qinhuangdao Port	119°36′26″	39°54′24″	20
5	Weifang Port	120°19′05″	36°04′	18
6	Yantai Port	121°23′46.9″	37°32′51.8″	20

Table 4. Accident point data.

Number	Longitude	Latitude	D_{j1} (Units)	T_{Ej1} (h)	T_{Lj1} (h)	Accident Level
1	118°06′1″	38°52′2″	8	1	7	Larger
2	119°13′.7	38°52′.3	6	2	8	General
3	119°29.6′	38°43.3′	6	2	8	General
4	117°51′.6	38°55′.5	5	2	8	General
5	119°08′.1	38°47′.3	0	0	0	Small
6	118°31′.9	38°42′.3	0	0	0	Small

Table 4. *Cont.*

Number	Longitude	Latitude	D_{j1} (Units)	T_{Ej1} (h)	T_{Lj1} (h)	Accident Level
7	120°25′.78	40°02′.95	7	1	7	Larger
8	120°50′.23	38°37′.44	8	1	7	Larger
9	121°33′15.54″	40°05′13.86″	7	1	7	Larger
10	121°48.80′	40°12.24′	6	1	7	Larger
11	120°10′.98	39°13′	8	1	7	Larger
12	120°07′.211	40°01′.560	7	1	7	Larger
13	121°12′.88	40°08′.59	5	2	8	General
14	120°48′00.96″	39°02′46.56″	6	2	8	General
15	121°08′49″.17	39°35′49″.18	5	2	8	General
16	120°35′48.42″	38°35′34.92″	4	2	8	General
17	121°09′	39°27′	5	2	8	General
18	121°01.08′	40°42.31′	5	2	8	General
19	122°01′.3	38°46′.2	6	2	8	General
20	118°11.39′	38°26.19′	8	1	7	Larger

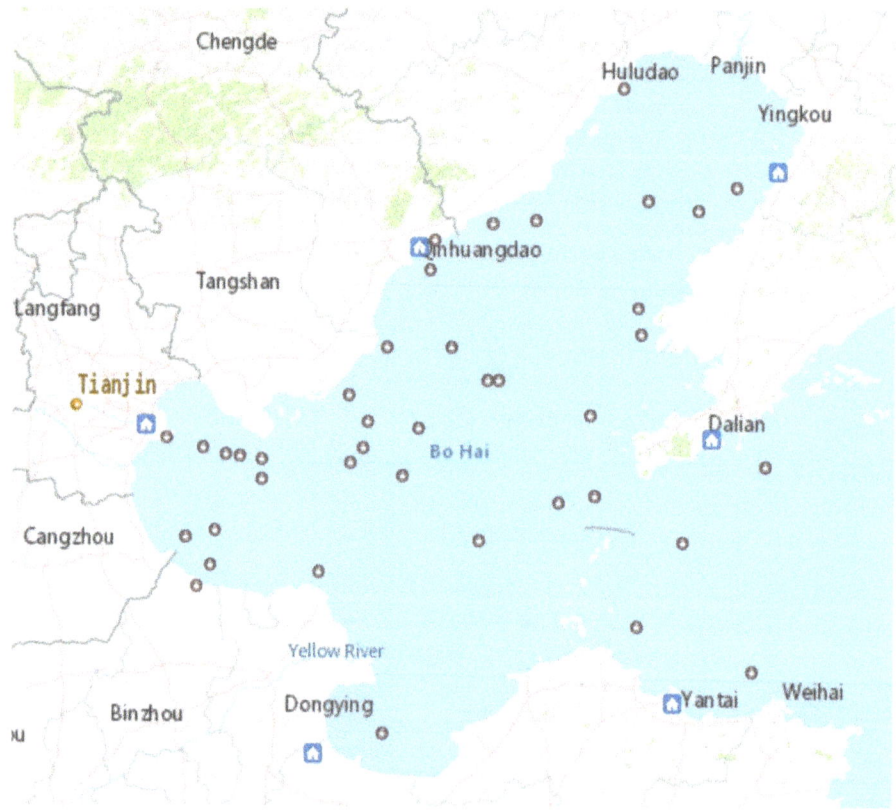

Figure 4. Distribution map of candidate emergency materials reserves and potential accident points.

MATLAB R2017a (MathWorks Inc., Natick, The United States of America) was used to solve the model and algorithm designed in this paper and was run on a computer with an Intel(R) Core (TM) i7-10510U processor at 1.80 GHz with 16 GB RAM. The main parameters in the algorithm are the number of iterations N, ant population m, ant crawling speed *speed*, pheromone volatilization coefficient ρ, pheromone enhancement factor Q, tabu table length L, and so on. According to the characteristics of the numerical example in this paper and the results of multiple tests, the main parameters are set as $N = 200$, $m = 200$, $speed = 0.05$, $\rho = 0.5$, $Q = 1$, and $L = 10$.

5.2. Solution Result and Analysis

5.2.1. Algorithm Analysis

To verify the effectiveness of the proposed algorithm, the ant colony–tabu search algorithm and the ant colony algorithm without tabu search algorithm are used to solve the examples in this paper. The main parameters in the ant colony algorithm without tabu search algorithm are the number of iterations N, ant population m, ant crawling speed $speed$, pheromone volatilization coefficient ρ, pheromone enhancement factor Q, and so on, making $N = 200$, $m = 200$, $speed = 0.05$, $\rho = 0.5$, and $Q = 1$.

When using the hybrid algorithm to experiment, it is found that when the number of shore-based emergency materials reserves is 1 under the current parameters, in all cases, three levels of emergency materials cannot be distributed to 40 accident points according to the priority of emergency materials within the specified time window, which can neither complete the distribution task nor accord with the actual situation of the Bohai Sea. When the number of shore-based emergency material reserves is 2–6, in most cases, the materials can be distributed to 40 accident points according to the priority of emergency materials within the specified time window. The sets of feasible emergency materials reserves and their results are shown in Table 5.

Table 5. Ant colony–tabu search algorithm to obtain feasible set and its results.

Number of Reserves Constructed	Feasible Reserve Set	Upper Objective Function Value (CNY)	Lower Objective Function Value (CNY)
2	(1,4)	400,621	88,388.13
2	(1,5)	380,621	90,357.17
2	(2,3)	380,621	85,030.14
2	**(2,5)**	**360,621**	**89,078.48**
2	(3,6)	400,621	93,957.46
2	(4,6)	400,621	94,432.83
3	(1,2,3)	580,621	94,031.79
3	(1,2,4)	580,621	87,522.29
3	(1,3,4)	600,621	87,095.50
3	(1,3,5)	580,621	92,320.94
3	(1,3,6)	600,621	93,290.49
3	(1,4,5)	580,621	81,984.93
3	(1,4,6)	600,621	85,566.20
3	(2,3,4)	580,621	88,886.87
3	(2,4,5)	560,621	93,514.44
3	(2,4,6)	580,621	94,088.88
3	**(2,5,6)**	**560,621**	**88,560.94**
3	(3,4,6)	600,621	84,988.67
3	(3,5,6)	580,621	91,868.98
4	(1,2,3,4)	780,621	79,176.22
4	**(1,2,3,5)**	**760,621**	**83,445.32**
4	(1,2,3,6)	780,621	91,623.80
4	(1,2,4,5)	760,621	86,400.66
4	(1,2,5,6)	760,621	89,852.23
4	(1,3,4,5)	780,621	83,745.40
4	(1,3,4,6)	800,621	86,068.29
4	(1,3,5,6)	780,621	91,003.71
4	(1,4,5,6)	780,621	82,959.10
4	(2,3,4,5)	760,621	88,423.75

Table 5. Cont.

Number of Reserves Constructed	Feasible Reserve Set	Upper Objective Function Value (CNY)	Lower Objective Function Value (CNY)
4	(2,3,4,6)	780,621	83,243.21
4	(2,3,5,6)	760,621	89,076.61
4	(2,4,5,6)	760,621	95,240.82
4	(3,4,5,6)	780,621	84,848.72
5	(1,2,3,4,5)	960,621	85,884.94
5	(1,2,3,4,6)	980,621	85,426.08
5	(1,2,3,5,6)	960,621	86,749.95
5	**(1,2,4,5,6)**	**960,621**	**84,223.97**
5	(1,3,4,5,6)	980,621	88,462.68
5	(2,3,4,5,6)	960,621	91,765.69
6	**(1,2,3,4,5,6)**	**1160,621**	**86,693.65**

Table 6 shows the feasible sets of emergency materials reserves obtained by the ant colony algorithm and the results. In the course of the experiment, it is found that when the number of emergency materials reserves constructed is 1–2, the result obtained by the ant colony algorithm cannot distribute three levels of emergency materials to the accident points within the specified time window. When the number of emergency materials reserves constructed is 4, the ant colony algorithm cannot find the optimal solution under the current number of iterations. When the number of emergency materials reserves constructed is 3, 5, or 6, the number of feasible sets obtained by the ant colony algorithm is much less than that obtained by the ant colony–tabu search algorithm. When the set of feasible reserves is the same, the value of the lower objective function obtained by the ant colony–tabu search algorithm is smaller than that obtained by the ant colony algorithm.

Table 6. Ant colony algorithm to obtain feasible set and its result.

Number of Reserves Constructed	Feasible Reserve Set	Upper Objective Function Value (CNY)	Lower Objective Function Value (CNY)
3	(1,2,4)	580,621	99,227.50
5	(1,2,3,5,6)	960,621	103,418.47
6	(1,2,3,4,5,6)	1,160,621	87,152.38

Figure 5 shows the comparison of the average iterative times of the ant colony algorithm and ant colony–tabu search. It can be seen from the figure that the average iteration times are independent of the running times. In most cases, the average number of iterations of the ant colony–tabu search algorithm is larger than that of the ant colony algorithm. The figure shows that the ant colony algorithm combined with the tabu search algorithm has stronger optimization ability and effectively avoids the problem of falling into the local optimal solution. Based on the above analysis, the ant colony algorithm combined with the tabu search algorithm has stronger optimization ability than the ant colony algorithm and can avoid falling into local optimization and obtain a better global optimal solution quickly.

5.2.2. Solution Analysis

In bi-level programming, the upper and lower decision-makers influence each other, and the upper decision is considered more overall. The upper level gives the decision first; then, within the allowable scope of the upper-level decision, the lower level has the right to make independent decisions. Next, the upper level makes decisions in line with the overall interests according to the response of the lower level. The optimal decision is made based on the above principles. When the number of shore-based emergency materials reserves is 2, the optimal decision of the emergency management department is (2,5), that is, to build shore-based emergency material reserves in Yingkou

Port and Weifang Port; the total cost of the upper level is CNY 360,621; and the total route planning the cost of commercial rescue unit is CNY 89,078.48. When the number of shore-based emergency materials reserves is 3, the optimal decision of the emergency management department is (2,5,6), that is, to build shore-based emergency materials reserves in Yingkou Port, Weifang Port, and Yantai Port, and the total cost of the upper level is CNY 560,621. The total cost of independent route planning by the commercial rescue unit is CNY 88,560.94. When the number of shore-based emergency materials reserves is 4, the optimal decision of the emergency management department is (1,2,3,5), that is, to build shore-based emergency materials reserves in Dalian Port, Yingkou Port, Tianjin Port, and Weifang Port; the total cost of the upper level is CNY 760,621; and the total cost of independent route planning of the commercial rescue unit is CNY 83,445.32. When the number of shore-based emergency materials reserves is 5, the optimal decision of the emergency management department is (1,2,4,5,6), that is, to build shore-based emergency materials reserves in Dalian Port, Yingkou Port, Qinhuangdao Port, Weifang Port, and Yantai Port; the total cost of the upper level is CNY 960,621; and the total cost of independent route planning of the commercial rescue unit is CNY 84,223.97. When the number of shore-based emergency materials reserves is 6, the optimal decision of the emergency management department is (1,2,3,4,5,6), that is, to build shore-based emergency materials reserves in Dalian Port, Yingkou Port, Tianjin Port, Qinhuangdao Port, Weifang Port, and Yantai Port; the total cost of the upper level is CNY 1,160,621; and the total cost of independent route planning of the commercial rescue unit is CNY 86,693.65. Among the above five decisions, when the number of emergency materials reserves constructed is 4, the total cost of the rescue unit planning routes is the lowest; however, when making its decision, the emergency management department should consider the maximization of its interests as a priority and choose the decision that minimizes total cost of the upper level. When the construction number of emergency materials reserves is 2, although the total cost of route planning of the lower rescue unit has increased, it is far less than the reduction of the construction cost of the upper location, which still achieves the goal of overall optimization of the emergency logistics system. Therefore, the optimal decision of the emergency management department is to build shore-based emergency materials reserves in Yingkou Port and Weifang Port. The location-routing result is shown in Table 7, the location-routing map is shown in Figure 6, and the emergency materials distribution route table (part) is shown in Table 8. The longest time for the commercial rescue unit to complete the distribution of first-level emergency materials is 7.8 h, the longest time for the second-level emergency materials is 14.6 h, and the longest time for the third-level emergency materials is 18.5 h.

The location of emergency materials reserves and the route optimization of emergency materials distribution are two important factors in the whole maritime emergency logistics system. The organic combination of the two to achieve overall optimization can avoid the limitation of considering only a single problem and realize the optimization of the whole maritime emergency logistics system. Maritime emergency logistics is jointly participated in and jointly decided by the emergency management department and commercial rescue unit. There is a game relationship between them, and their decisions affect each other. The emergency management department should give priority to maximizing its interests when considering the number and location of emergency materials reserves. Within the allowable range, the rescue unit will independently plan the routes to achieve the distribution goal, and the emergency management department will make decisions in line with the overall interests according to the route feedback of the rescue unit.

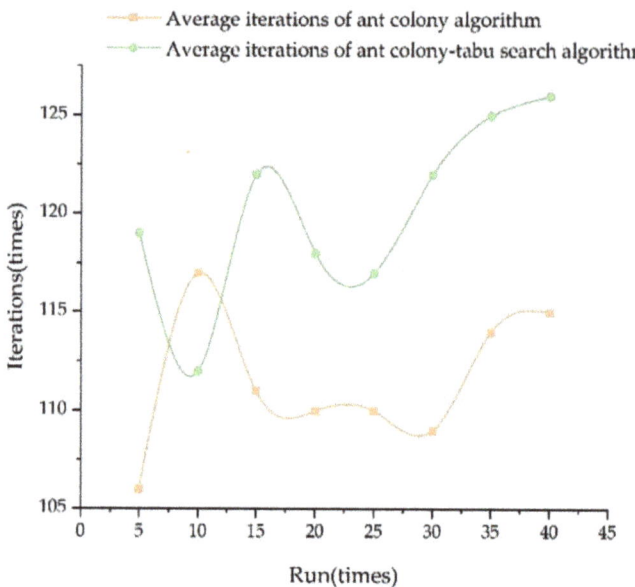

Figure 5. Comparison of average iteration times of two algorithms.

Table 7. Location-routing result.

Reserves	Upper Total Cost (CNY)	Time Satisfaction Loss Cost (CNY)	Lower Total Cost (CNY)	Emergency Materials Distribution Cost (CNY)	Ship Dispatch Cost (CNY)	Shipping Cost (CNY)	Time Penalty Cost (CNY)
(2,5)	360,621	621	89,078.47	2494	64,800	7330.37	14,454.11

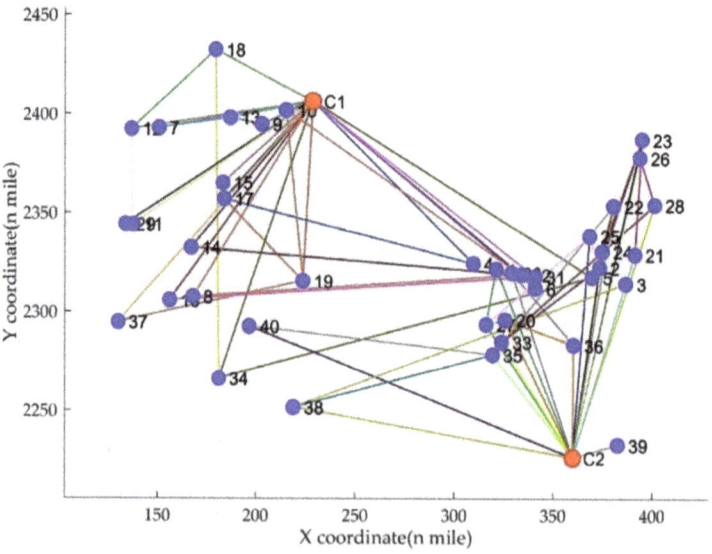

Figure 6. Location-routing map.

Table 8. Emergency materials distribution route table (part).

Reserves	Accident Points of Reserves Service	Ship	Distribution Routes (Emergency Materials Level in Parentheses)
2	4,5,6,7,8,9,10,11,12,13, 14,15,16,17,18,19,29, 31,32,34,37	1	0-7(1)-0
		2	0-15(1)-0
		3	0-37(1)-0
		4	0-11(1)-12(1)-0
		5	0-17(1)-19(1)-0
		6	0-13(1)-7(2)-0
		7	0-4(1)-17(2)-0
		8	0-34(1)-5(2)-0
		9	0-10(1)-19(2)-37(3)-0
		10	0-8(1)-32(1)-10(2)-0
5	1,2,3,20,21,22,23,24,25, 26,27,28,30,33,35,36, 38,39,40	1	0-1(1)-0
		2	0-24(1)-0
		3	0-26(1)-0
		4	0-39(1)-0
		5	0-35(1)-38(1)-0
		6	0-33(1)-20(1)-36(1)-30(1)-0
		7	0-3(1)-21(1)-23(1)-0
		8	0-27(1)-25(1)-2(1)-0
		9	0-22(1)-35(2)-40(2)-0
		10	0-28(1)-33(2)-2(2)-23(2)-24(3)-0

When the construction number of the emergency materials reserves is the same and the construction cost is the same, the emergency management department directly considers the interests of the rescue unit and selects the decision with the lowest cost at the lower level. When the number of emergency materials reserves constructed is the same and the construction cost is not much different, the emergency management department will consider the interests of the rescue unit and choose the option with the lowest lower and upper costs as small as possible to achieve overall optimization. For example, when the number of emergency materials reserves constructed is 4 in Table 5, the decision is made between the reserve sets of (1,2,3,4) and (2,4,5,6). When the number of emergency material reserve construction is different, the construction cost will vary greatly. However, the lower cost difference is not large at this time; therefore, the emergency management department gives priority to the decision to maximize its interests (such as the optimal decision with the number of reserves constructed being 2 and 4 in Table 5).

The maritime emergency rescue has strong regional characteristics, as can be seen from Figure 6. When the rescue unit plans the routes, they often distribute emergency materials according to the nearest principle. However, because different levels of emergency materials in this study can be mixed, cross-regional distribution can also exist on the premise of meeting the time window limit. The results show that the distribution cost of the rescue unit can be reduced as much as possible. The goal of this paper is to optimize the location of the emergency materials reserves and the distribution routes of emergency materials cooperatively. The overall layout of the maritime emergency logistics system should be carried out. The situation of cross-regional distribution is also conducive to the effective development of maritime emergency work. It can ensure that those accident points can also be effectively rescued when the emergency materials reserve nearest to the accident point is busy.

5.3. Management Implications

This study presents the following management implications and recommendations for relevant policies:

1. For the emergency management department of the upper decision-maker, the emergency management department has the priority decision-making power. This department's decision should consider the benefits of the commercial rescue unit of the lower-level decision-makers while maximizing their benefits to achieve global optimization. Under the premise of meeting the needs of the accident points, the construction number of emergency materials reserves does not need to be high; otherwise, excessive construction of emergency materials reserves will lose the significance of centralized distribution and increase unnecessary construction costs. When there is little difference in the lower cost and there is a large difference in the upper cost, priority can be given to the benefit maximization of the upper level. When the upper cost is the same or there is little difference, while the lower cost is significantly reduced, priority can be given to the benefits of the lower level to achieve global optimization.
2. For the commercial rescue unit of the lower-level decision-maker, within the scope permitted by the emergency management department, the rescue unit independently plans the distribution routes of emergency materials to (a) distribute multi-level emergency materials to the accident points within the specified time window and (b) feed the route scheme back to the emergency management department in time. When planning the routes, priority should be given to the regionality of the accident points, and emergency materials should be distributed according to the principle of proximity; however, there can also be a cross-regional distribution within the scope of the time window.
3. All participating units in the maritime emergency logistics system shall communicate and coordinate to (a) scientifically and reasonably select the location of the maritime emergency materials reserves and (b) plan the distribution routes of emergency materials to ensure that, in case of a maritime accident, the emergency materials can be delivered to the accident point in time and reliably, provide rescue capacity, control the impact of the accident to the minimum, reduce various losses caused by sudden maritime disasters, and effectively improve the emergency service capability of the maritime emergency logistics system.

6. Conclusions

This paper studies the problem of joint participation and joint decision-making of multi-level decision agents in MEMD-LRP. Using the method of bi-level programming, under the conditions of considering the time window and the priority of emergency materials distribution, the collaborative optimization of the location of shore-based emergency materials reserves and multi-level emergency materials distribution routes in the maritime emergency logistics system is realized, and the optimal decision for the maritime emergency logistics system is obtained.

This study is based on the scenario of parameter determination. In the future, it is planned to further consider the uncertainty of accident point demands and the uncertainty of maritime transportation time under the influence of wind and waves for modeling and analysis. In addition, based on a single type of ship transport, the mixed transport of multiple types of ships and the multimodal transport environment including aircraft and ships can be studied. In addition, future research can consider the scenario of the coexistence of public welfare relief and commercial rescue.

Author Contributions: Conceptualization, C.W. and Z.P.; methodology, C.W. and Z.P.; writing—original draft preparation, C.W. and Z.P.; writing—review and editing, C.W., Z.P., W.X. and J.Z. All authors have read and agreed to the published version of the manuscript.

Funding: This research was supported by the Social Science Planning Fund Program of Liaoning Province (L19BJL005), Natural Science Foundation of Liaoning Province (2020-BS-068), Jiangsu Planned Projects for Postdoctoral Research Funds (2021K347C), Humanities and Social Sciences Fund of Chinese Ministry of Education (21YJAZH070), and Fundamental Research Funds for the Central Universities (3132022281).

Institutional Review Board Statement: Not applicable.

Informed Consent Statement: Not applicable.

Data Availability Statement: Not applicable.

Conflicts of Interest: The authors declare that they have no conflict of interest.

References

1. Pang, H.; Ma, Y.; Mao, T.; Liu, S.; Zhang, Y. Evaluation of Maritime Emergency Rescue Capability Based on Network Analysis. In Proceedings of the 1st International Global on Renewable Energy and Development (IGRED), Singapore, 22–25 December 2017.
2. Wang, Z.; Lin, B. Q-Learning Based Delay Sensitive Routing Protocol for Maritime Search and Rescue Networks. In Proceedings of the 92nd IEEE Vehicular Technology Conference (IEEE VTC-Fall), Victoria, BC, Canada, 4–7 October 2020.
3. Jiang, M.; Lu, J. Maritime accident risk estimation for sea lanes based on a dynamic Bayesian network. *Marit. Policy. Manag.* **2020**, *47*, 649–664. [CrossRef]
4. Safety and Shipping Review 2020. Available online: https://www.agcs.allianz.com/news-and-insights/reports/shipping-safety.html (accessed on 15 July 2020).
5. European Maritime Safety Agency Preliminary Annual Overview of Marine Casualties and Incidents 2014–2020. Available online: http://www.emsa.europa.eu/publications/item/4378-preliminary-annual-overview-of-marine-casualties-and-incidents-2014-2020.html (accessed on 19 April 2021).
6. Statistical Bulletin on the Development of Transportation Industry in 2020. Available online: https://xxgk.mot.gov.cn/2020/jigou/zhghs/202105/t20210517_3593412.html (accessed on 19 May 2021).
7. Luo, M.; Shin, S.-H. Half-century research developments in maritime accidents: Future directions. *Accid. Anal. Prev.* **2019**, *123*, 448–460. [CrossRef] [PubMed]
8. Weber, A. *Theory of the Location of Industries*; The University of Chicago Press: Chicago, IL, USA, 1929.
9. Dantaig, G.B.; Ramser, J.H. The truck dispatching problem. *Manag. Sci.* **1959**, *6*, 80–91. [CrossRef]
10. Cooper, L. The transportation-location problem. *Oper. Res.* **1972**, *20*, 94–108. [CrossRef]
11. Laporte, G.; Nobert, Y. An exact algorithm for minimizing routing and operating costs in depot location. *Eur. J. Oper. Res.* **1981**, *6*, 224–226. [CrossRef]
12. Duan, S.Y.; Lan, H.J. Location-Routing Problem in Post Earthquake Emergency Logistics with Priority Grade. In Proceedings of the 6th International Symposium on Project Management (ISPM), Chongqing, China, 21–23 July 2018.
13. Liu, C.; Kou, G.; Peng, Y.; Alsaadi, F.E. Location-routing problem for relief distribution in the early post-earthquake stage from the perspective of fairness. *Sustainability* **2019**, *11*, 3420. [CrossRef]
14. Shen, L.; Tao, F.; Shi, Y.; Qin, R. Optimization of location-routing problem in emergency logistics considering carbon emissions. *Int. J. Environ. Res. Public Health* **2019**, *16*, 2982. [CrossRef]
15. Wang, S.; Tao, F.; Shi, Y. Optimization of location-routing problem for cold chain logistics considering carbon footprint. *Int. J. Environ. Res. Public Health* **2018**, *15*, 86. [CrossRef]
16. Dukkanci, O.; Kara, B.Y.; Bektas, T. The green location-routing problem. *Comput. Oper. Res.* **2019**, *105*, 187–202. [CrossRef]
17. Yu, X.; Zhou, Y.; Liu, X.-F. A novel hybrid genetic algorithm for the location routing problem with tight capacity constraints. *Appl. Soft. Comput.* **2019**, *85*, 105760. [CrossRef]
18. Wang, X.F.; Yang, F.; Lu, D.W. Multi-objective location-routing problem with simultaneous pickup and delivery for urban distribution. *J. Intell. Fuzzy. Syst.* **2018**, *35*, 3987–4000. [CrossRef]
19. Fan, H.M.; Wu, J.X.; Li, X.; Jiang, X. Presenting a multi-start hybrid heuristic for solving the problem of two-echelon location-routing problem with simultaneous pickup and delivery (2E-LRPSPD). *J. Adv. Transport.* **2020**, *2020*, 9743841. [CrossRef]
20. Tavana, M.; Abtahi, A.R.; Di Caprio, D.; Hashemi, R.; Yousefi-Zenouz, R. An integrated location-inventory-routing humanitarian supply chain network with pre- and post-disaster management considerations. *Socio-Econ. Plan. Sci.* **2018**, *64*, 21–37. [CrossRef]
21. Wei, X.; Qiu, H.; Wang, D.; Duan, J.; Wang, Y.; Cheng, T.C.E. An integrated location-routing problem with post-disaster relief distribution. *Comput. Ind. Eng.* **2020**, *147*, 106632. [CrossRef]
22. Vahdani, B.; Veysmoradi, D.; Shekari, N.; Mousavi, S.M. Multi-objective, multi-period location-routing model to distribute relief after earthquake by considering emergency roadway repair. *Neural Comput. Appl.* **2018**, *30*, 835–854. [CrossRef]
23. Xue, H.; Wang, Y.; Liao, Z.; Xu, R.; Xu, Z. Research on emergency material optimization scheduling and importance decision in cluster supply chain. In Proceedings of the Chinese Control and Decision Conference (CCDC), Hefei, China, 22–24 August 2020.
24. Li, S.; Grifoll, M.; Estrada, M.; Zheng, P.; Feng, H. Optimization on emergency materials dispatching considering the characteristics of integrated emergency response for large-scale marine oil spills. *J. Mar. Sci. Eng.* **2019**, *7*, 214. [CrossRef]
25. Ai, Y.-F.; Lu, J.; Zhang, L.-L. The optimization model for the location of maritime emergency supplies reserve bases and the configuration of salvage vessels. *Transport. Res. E-Log.* **2015**, *83*, 170–188. [CrossRef]
26. Ai, Y.; Zhang, Q. Optimization on cooperative government and enterprise supplies repertories for maritime emergency: A study case in China. *Adv. Mech. Eng.* **2019**, *11*, 1687814019828576. [CrossRef]
27. Zhang, L.; Lu, J.; Yang, Z. Optimal scheduling of emergency resources for major maritime oil spills considering time-varying demand and transportation networks. *Eur. J. Oper. Res.* **2021**, *293*, 529–546. [CrossRef]

28. Bozorgi-Amiri, A.; Khorsi, M. A dynamic multi-objective location-routing model for relief logistic planning under uncertainty on demand, travel time, and cost parameters. *Int. J. Adv. Manuf. Technol.* **2016**, *85*, 1633–1648. [CrossRef]
29. Chang, K.; Zhou, H.; Chen, G.; Chen, H. Multiobjective location routing problem considering uncertain data after disasters. *Discrete Dyn. Nat. Soc.* **2017**, *2017*, 1703608. [CrossRef]
30. Veysmoradi, D.; Vahdani, B.; Sartangi, M.F.; Mousavi, S.M. Multi-objective open location-routing model for relief distribution networks with split delivery and multi-mode transportation under uncertainty. *Sci. Iran.* **2018**, *25*, 3635–3653. [CrossRef]
31. Wu, X.H.; Cao, Y.R.; Xiao, Y.; Guo, J. Finding of urban rainstorm and waterlogging disasters based on microblogging data and the location-routing problem model of urban emergency logistics. *Ann. Oper. Res.* **2020**, *290*, 865–896. [CrossRef]
32. Zhang, B.; Li, H.; Li, S.G.; Peng, J. Sustainable multi-depot emergency facilities location-routing problem with uncertain information. *Appl. Math. Comput.* **2018**, *333*, 506–520. [CrossRef]
33. Hu, S.; Han, C.; Dong, Z.S.; Meng, L. A multi-stage stochastic programming model for relief distribution considering the state of road network. *Transport. Res. B-Meth.* **2019**, *123*, 64–87. [CrossRef]
34. Liu, J.; Guo, L.; Jiang, J.; Jiang, D.; Liu, R.; Wang, P. A two-stage optimization model for emergency material reserve layout planning under uncertainty in response to environmental accidents. *J. Hazard. Mater.* **2016**, *310*, 30–39. [CrossRef]
35. Xiong, X.; Zhao, F.; Wang, Y.; Wang, Y. Research on the model and algorithm for multimodal distribution of emergency supplies after earthquake in the perspective of fairness. *Math. Probl. Eng.* **2019**, *2019*, 1629321. [CrossRef]
36. Qin, X.; Liu, X.; Tang, L. A two-stage stochastic mixed-integer program for the capacitated logistics fortification planning under accidental disruptions. *Comput. Ind. Eng.* **2013**, *65*, 614–623. [CrossRef]
37. Liu, Y.; Lei, H.; Zhang, D.; Wu, Z. Robust optimization for relief logistics planning under uncertainties in demand and transportation time. *Appl. Math. Model.* **2018**, *55*, 262–280. [CrossRef]
38. Liu, Y.; Yuan, Y.; Chen, Y.; Ruan, L.; Pang, H. A Chance Constrained Goal Programming Model for Location-Routing Problem under Uncertainty. In Proceedings of the 3rd International Conference on Logistics, Informatics and Service Science (LISS), Beijing Jiaotong Univ, Sch Econ & Management, Reading, UK, 21–24 August 2013.
39. Xu, J.P.; Wang, Z.Q.; Zhang, M.X.; Tu, Y. A new model for a 72-h post-earthquake emergency logistics location-routing problem under a random fuzzy environment. *Transp. Lett.* **2016**, *8*, 270–285. [CrossRef]
40. Lou, Z. Bi-level programming model and algorithm of LRP for emergency logistics system. *Chin. J. Manag. Sci.* **2017**, *25*, 151–157.
41. Safaei, A.S.; Farsad, S.; Paydar, M.M. Emergency logistics planning under supply risk and demand uncertainty. *Oper. Res.-Ger.* **2020**, *20*, 1437–1460. [CrossRef]
42. Chen, Y.-X.; Tadikamalla, P.R.; Shang, J.; Song, Y. Supply allocation: Bi-level programming and differential evolution algorithm for natural disaster relief. *Clust. Comput.* **2020**, *23*, 203–217. [CrossRef]
43. Li, S.; Teo, K.L. Post-disaster multi-period road network repair: Work scheduling and relief logistics optimization. *Ann. Oper. Res.* **2019**, *283*, 1345–1385. [CrossRef]
44. Zhou, Y.F.; Zheng, B.; Su, J.F.; Li, Y.F. The joint location-transportation model based on grey bi-level programming for early post-earthquake relief. *J. Ind. Manag. Optim.* **2022**, *18*, 45–73. [CrossRef]
45. Wang, D.P.; Xu, Z.; Yang, C. Study on location-routing problem of logistics distribution based on two-stage heuristic algorithm. *Oper. Res. Manag. Sci.* **2017**, *26*, 70–75+83.
46. Zhang, L.Y.; Lyu, J.; Liang, X.; Fan, H.W. Optimal scheduling of emergency supplies for major maritime accidents considering multiple demand sites. *Syst. Eng.* **2021**, *39*, 103–114.
47. Chen, J.; Gui, P.; Ding, T.; Na, S.; Zhou, Y. Optimization of transportation routing problem for fresh food by improved ant colony algorithm based on tabu search. *Sustainability* **2019**, *11*, 6584. [CrossRef]
48. Li, Q.; Tu, W.; Zhuo, L. Reliable rescue routing optimization for urban emergency logistics under travel time uncertainty. *ISPRS Int. J. Geo.-Inf.* **2018**, *7*, 77. [CrossRef]

Article

Can a Restaurant Benefit from Joining an Online Take-Out Platform?

Peng Zhang [1,2,*], Sisi Ju [1] and Hongfu Huang [3]

[1] Business School, Yangzhou University, Yangzhou 225127, China; jusisi_g@163.com
[2] Jiangsu Modern Logistics Research Base, Yangzhou University, Yangzhou 225127, China
[3] School of Economics and Management, Nanjing University of Science and Technology, Nanjing 210094, China; huanghf@njust.edu.cn
* Correspondence: 007400@yzu.edu.cn

Abstract: In this paper, we study a restaurant's take-out model choice and the coordination of an online take-out supply chain. To this end, we first derive the restaurant's optimal price and/or platform's commission rate under the restaurant's three possible take-out models: do not provide online take-out service (NTO model), provide take-out service by joining an online take-out platform (TOF model), or provide online take-out service by itself (TOH model). We investigate the restaurant's optimal take-out model choice. We then derive the optimal decisions of price and the take-out model under centralization, and study the online take-out supply chain coordination problem. We find that, first, the restaurant may not always benefit from providing online take-out service. It will be beneficial only if the incremental demand generated by take-out service is high. Second, under the centralized supply chain, the TOF model is always better than the TOH model. Meanwhile, when the incremental demand is high, the restaurant should choose the TOF model; otherwise, the NTO model is better. Third, we find that the restaurant's take-out price and model choice decisions under a decentralized supply chain are both inconsistent with that under the centralized supply chain. Last, we design a sales reward contract which can achieve the price and model choice coordination as well as win-win outcomes for all supply chain members.

Keywords: online take-out service; take-out model choice; coordination; platform

MSC: 90B06

Citation: Zhang, P.; Ju, S.; Huang, H. Can a Restaurant Benefit from Joining an Online Take-Out Platform? *Mathematics* **2022**, *10*, 1392. https://doi.org/10.3390/math10091392

Academic Editor: David Carfì

Received: 22 March 2022
Accepted: 19 April 2022
Published: 21 April 2022

Publisher's Note: MDPI stays neutral with regard to jurisdictional claims in published maps and institutional affiliations.

Copyright: © 2022 by the authors. Licensee MDPI, Basel, Switzerland. This article is an open access article distributed under the terms and conditions of the Creative Commons Attribution (CC BY) license (https://creativecommons.org/licenses/by/4.0/).

1. Introduction

With the popularity of mobile Internet, the market scale of online take-out is growing rapidly. According to the statistics of the ZhiYan consulting company [1], the market scale of China's online take-out grew to $88.6 billion in 2019, an increase of 30.8% compared with 2018. By 2020, the number of online take-out users in China had reached 397.8 million. More and more restaurants started to provide online take-out service by joining some online take-out platforms (TOF model in short), such as Meituan, Ele.me and Delivery Hero. According to a financial report by Meituan, the number of restaurants that have joined the Meituan platform had reached 6.2 million by 2019. It is also reported that Delivery Hero has 150,000 restaurant partners across 40 countries [2].

In recent years, with the improvement of the industry concentration of online take-out platforms, some platforms have gradually increased their commission rate (or revenue share ratio). For example, Meituan's commission rate has increased from 5 to 22%. At the high commission rate, some restaurants find it difficult to benefit from online take-out service. In addition, with the reduction of a restaurant's take-out profit margin, the quality of food materials will be difficult to guarantee, which may cause food safety problems. Subsequently, some of them choose not to provide online take-out service (NTO model in short), while others choose to provide online take-out service by themselves (TOH model in short). As some restaurants leave the online take-out platform, the potential revenue of the platform will also be negatively affected.

Therefore, the following questions are of great practical importance. For online take-out platforms, how to set the commission rate and coordination mechanisms to attract more restaurants and to achieve win-win outcomes are key questions that need to be addressed. For restaurants, how to choose an optimal take-out model according to its own situation is equally important. To address these questions, we model a take-out supply chain with one restaurant and one online take-out platform (platform in short). We first derive the restaurant's optimal price (dine-in and take-out) and/or platform's commission rate under the TOF model, NTO model and TOH model. Then, we compare the restaurant's profit under the three models and analyze the restaurant's optimal take-out model under decentralization. Subsequently, we derive the optimal decisions of price and take-out model under centralization. By comparing these optimal decisions in the centralized and decentralized situations, we propose a sales reward contract and prove that it can coordinate the price and model choice simultaneously and achieve a win-win outcome.

Our main findings are as follows. First, we derive the optimal commission rate for the take-out platform. Second, the restaurant can benefit from providing the online take-out service only when the incremental demand generated by take-out service is high. In addition, the TOF model is always better than the TOH model under the centralized supply chain. Lastly, we find that the take-out price and the model choice under the centralized situation are not consistent with that under the decentralized situation. To coordinate the supply chain, we then propose a sales reward contract.

This paper makes three major contributions. First, to the best of our knowledge, there is scant literature on online take-out supply chain coordination. It is important that we fill this research gap, as this kind of supply chain structure is common in practice. Second, the existing relevant literature mainly focuses on the price and service effort level decisions of the platform. However, in practice, the commission rate has important effects on the platform and a restaurant's profits and take-out model choice. This paper not only considers the optimal commission rate decision, but also analyzes the impact of parameters on it. Lastly, although some scholars study the restaurant's take-out model choice, they mainly analyze whether the restaurants join the platform or not. But in real life, some restaurants provide online sales service through instant messaging software (e.g., QQ, WeChat and Skype) and online payment tools (e.g., Alipay, PayPal and WeChat), and then deliver the food to consumers by themselves. Therefore, we also consider this model when we study a restaurant's take-out model choice.

The rest of this paper is organized as follows. Section 2 provides a literature review. Section 3 describes the models and notations. Section 4 derives the optimal price and/or commission rate under the three take-out models. Section 5 studies the restaurant's take-out model choice. Section 6 proposes a sales reward contract which can coordinate the supply chain. Section 7 provides concluding remarks and suggests future research directions.

2. Literature Review

We classify the relevant literature into two streams. The first research stream includes papers on the restaurant industry; The second research stream includes papers on supply chain coordination.

The recently published papers in the first research stream are reviewed as follows. With the rapid development of e-commerce and the popularity of mobile Internet, many restaurants begin to open online sales channels or O2O channels by joining some platforms. Whether to join and how to price after joining has become a major issue for restaurants. Heo [3] studied the impact of joining in group-buying platforms on restaurant profits. Through an empirical study, he found that if restaurants can attract many new patrons by participating in group-buying platforms, they should cooperate with the platform; if many regular patrons shift to discount customers, joining the platform will damage restaurants' profits. Zheng and Guo [4] further consider a number of competing restaurants and examine the optimal pricing strategy of them. They also find that joining the platform is not always beneficial to the restaurant. They suggest that if the number of offline loyal customers is relatively small, the restaurants can join the platform and provide a discount for the online price. The above studies do not consider the game relationship between the restaurant and the platform.

In practice, the price subsidy will be provided in the initial stage to attract restaurants to join the platform. Xu et al. [5] study online price strategies of a restaurant, as well as the optimal service effort level of a take-out platform and further propose optimal cooperative strategies in different scenarios. Some scholars further analyzed whether restaurants should join the take-out platform. Zhang et al. [2] study the impacts of adding a take-out platform channel on firms' offline and total sales and profits based on the data of a Chinese fast-food restaurant chain. They find that although joining the platform will hurt offline and total profits in the short run, it improves offline and total sales and profits in the long run. In addition, they also find that joining more take-out platforms is not necessarily conducive to the improvement of a restaurant's profit. Zhang et al. [6] establish a Stackelberg game model between a take-out platform and a restaurant and study the optimal price subsidy of the platform and/or take-out price of the restaurant under the price subsidy and no price subsidy. By comparing the benefits in different cases, they propose the optimal strategy for the restaurant. In some of the above-mentioned papers, although the game relationship between restaurants and platforms is considered, the decision-making problem of platform commission is not studied. However, in practice, the commission is an important factor to affect the profit of platform and restaurant. This paper studies the commission decision of the platform. Meanwhile, in addition to study whether the restaurant should join the take-out platform, this paper also considers the situation that the restaurant provides online take-out service by itself. In addition, some scholars study the optimization of delivery network [7–9], quality of food supply chain [10,11], the purchasing behavior of consumers [12,13], and the recommendation system of take-out platform [14,15].

Papers in the second research stream are related to supply chain coordination. There is a large amount of literature in this field. The most literature mainly focuses on the traditional supply chain structure. In this field, scholars design a variety of contracts to coordinate the supply chain. For example, there are quantity discount contracts [16,17], buyback contracts [18,19], revenue sharing contracts [20,21], and sales rebate contracts [22]. Some scholars study the supply chain coordination under dual-channels (online and offline). Chen et al. [23] find that the manufacturer's contract with a wholesale price and an online sale price can coordinate the dual-channel supply chain, but does not achieve the win-win situation. They then combine this contract with a complementary agreement to solve the problem. He et al. [24] further consider a unidirectional transshipment policy between the online channel and offline channel and develop a quantity-discount contract to the dual-channel supply chain. Zhu et al. [25] establish a dual-channel supply chain in which the Conditional Value-at-Risk criterion is considered. They design a buyback with a revenue sharing contract to coordinate the dual-channel supply chain. In the above literature, companies set up the online channels by themselves. In reality, most companies establish online channels through online platforms. Zha et al. [26] establish a model where a hotel established an online channel through Ctrip.com (online platform) and propose a cost sharing contract that achieves channel coordination. Different from ordinary online platforms, the take-out platform not only provides online sales service, but also provides delivery service. Meanwhile, in the above literature, the study of supply chain coordination does not consider the mode choice of companies, that is, to join or not to join the platform. In practice, the restaurant has three modes to choose: NTO, TOF and TOH. This paper will study how the take-out platform can coordinate take-out price and model choice simultaneously, i.e., it makes the take-out price and model choice decision of restaurant under both decentralized and centralized situations.

3. The Models and Notations

In this paper, we consider a supply chain with one take-out platform (she) and one restaurant (he). The restaurant provides a single catering product at per unit cost c. The take-out platform provides the take-out service (online sale and delivery) at per unit cost c_t. Simultaneously, she charges a delivery fee c_d from consumers for unit product and a commission from the restaurant based on a certain percentage of turnover λ. λ is also called the commission rate. We assume the demand function is linear in price effects, and then analyze the demands under the NTO, TOF and TOH models.

Case 1: the demand under NTO model.

In this case, the restaurant just provides the dine-in service and sells to dine-in consumers at unit price p_r. Following Kurata et al. [27] and Hua et al. [28], we assume that the demand functions are linear in self-price effects. Hence, the dine-in demand q_r under the NTO model is formulated as follows:

$$q_r = a - b_r p_r \quad (1)$$

In (1), a represents the base demand. b_r denotes the coefficient of price elasticity of dine-in demand q_r.

Case 2: the demand under TOF model.

In this case, the restaurant not only provides the dine-in service, but also provides the take-out service through an online take-out platform. In reality, take-out and dine-in are often applicable to different consumption situations. For example, when consumers order take-out, they often have no time to go to the restaurant or don't want to go out. Consumers who adopt dine-in often want to enjoy better food and environment, or have extra social needs. Therefore, this paper does not consider the price competition between take-out and dine-in. This is different from the previous studies (e.g., [27,28]), because the restaurant can reach more potential consumers through the platform, and the base demand increases from a to $(a+s)$, where s denotes the incremental demand. In addition, consumers need to pay a delivery fee c_d for ordering meals through the take-out platform, so we further consider the impact of delivery fee on demand in our model. We then use p_r^j and p_e^j to denote the dine-in price and take-out price under the TOF model, respectively. The dine-in demand q_r^j and take-out demand q_e^j under TOF model are formulated as follows:

$$q_r^j = (1-\theta)(a+s) - b_r p_r^j \quad (2)$$

$$q_e^j = \theta(a+s) - b_e p_e^j - b_e c_d \quad (3)$$

In (2) and (3), θ ($0 \leq \theta \leq 1$) and $(1-\theta)$ denote the percentage of the base demand divided by take-out and dine-in when p_e^j and p_r^j are zero. θ can also be used to measure the preference degree of take-out. b_e denotes the coefficient of price and delivery fee elasticity of dine-in demand q_e^j.

Case 3: the demand under TOH model.

In this case, the restaurant provides the take-out service by itself. Because the restaurant lacks the support of platform traffic, his incremental demand drops to βs ($0 \leq \beta \leq 1$), where β denotes the consumer's retention rate. In real life, if the restaurant distributes take-out by itself, consumers generally do not need to pay the delivery fee. Therefore, in the TOH model, we do not need to consider the impact of delivery fees on demand. We then use p_r^i and p_e^i to denote the dine-in price and take-out price under TOH model, respectively. The dine-in demand q_r^i and take-out demand q_e^i under the TOH model is formulated as follows:

$$q_r^i = (1-\theta)(a+\beta s) - b_r p_r^i \quad (4)$$

$$q_e^i = \theta(a+\beta s) - b_e p_e^i \quad (5)$$

4. Price and/or Commission Rate Decision

To analyze which model is better for the restaurant, we need to obtain the restaurant's profit under a different model. To this end, in this section, we will study how the restaurant and/or the take-out platform decide the price and commission rate, respectively, to maximize their own profits.

4.1. The NTO Model

In this scenario, the restaurant decides the dine-in price to maximize its own profits. The retailer's profit, denoted as Π_R, is determined by

$$\Pi_R = (p_r - c)(a - b_r p_r) \tag{6}$$

In (6), $(p_r - c)$ denotes the restaurant's margin. $(a - b_r p_r)$ denotes the dine-in demand of restaurant.

Taking the first-order and second-order conditions of Equation (6) with respect to p_r:

$$\frac{d\Pi_R}{dp_r} = a - 2b_r p_r + b_r c \tag{7}$$

$$\frac{d^2 \Pi_R}{dp_r^2} = -2b_r < 0 \tag{8}$$

From (7) and (8), we then can obtain the following proposition:

Proposition 1. *Under the NTO model, the restaurant's profit is concave in p_r, the optimal dine-in price p_r^* is given by*

$$p_r^* = \frac{a + b_r c}{2 b_r} \tag{9}$$

Substituting p_r^* into (6), we then obtain the maximal profit of the restaurant Π_R^* under NTO model

$$\Pi_R^* = \left(\frac{a - b_r c}{2 b_r}\right)^2 \tag{10}$$

4.2. The TOF Model

In this scenario, the take-out platform, as Stackelberg leader, decides the commission rate λ first, and then the restaurant as the follower determines dine-in price and take-out price. By backward induction, we first analyze the restaurant's best response, and then study the platform's commission rate decision.

Stage 1: Restaurant's best response.

In this subsection, the restaurant will decide the best response to a commission rate to maximize its own profits. The restaurant's profit, denoted as Π_R^j, is determined by

$$\Pi_R^j = \left(p_r^j - c\right)\left[(1-\theta)(a+s) - b_r p_r^j\right] + \left[(1-\lambda)p_e^j - c\right]\left[\theta(a+s) - b_e p_e^j - b_e c_d\right] \tag{11}$$

In (11), the first and second terms denote the profit of dine-in and take-out, respectively. We then can get the restaurant's best response

$$p_r^j = \frac{(1-\theta)(a+s) + b_r c}{2 b_r} \tag{12}$$

$$p_e^j = \frac{\theta(a+s) - b_e c_d}{2 b_e} + \frac{c}{2(1-\lambda)} \tag{13}$$

Stage 2: Take-out platform's commission rate decision.

The take-out platform's profit, denoted as Π_f^j, is determined by

$$\Pi_f^j = \lambda p_e^j \left[\theta(a+s) - b_e p_e^j - b_e c_d\right] + c_d \left[\theta(a+s) - b_e p_e^j - b_e c_d\right] - c_t \left[\theta(a+s) - b_e p_e^j - b_e c_d\right] \quad (14)$$

In (14), the first term denotes the platform's revenue from the restaurant's commission, the second term denotes the platform's revenue from the consumer's delivery fee, and the last term denotes the total take-out service cost. c_t denotes the unit take-out service cost, specifically including the platform's operating cost and delivery cost. Substituting (13) into (14) and simplifying, we can obtain

$$\Pi_f^j = \left[\lambda\left(\frac{\theta(a+s) - b_e c_d}{2b_e}\right) + \frac{c}{2(1-\lambda)}\right) + c_d - c_t\right]\left[\frac{\theta(a+s) - b_e c_d}{2} - \frac{b_e c}{2(1-\lambda)}\right] \quad (15)$$

From (15), we can obtain the following proposition. For clarity, all the proof is provided in the Appendix A.

Proposition 2. *Under the TOF model, the take-out platform's profit is quasi-concave in λ, the optimal commission rate λ^* is given by*

$$\lambda^* = 1 - \sqrt[3]{A + \sqrt{A^2 + \left(\frac{A[c + 2(c_t - c_d)]}{3c}\right)^3}} - \sqrt[3]{A - \sqrt{A^2 + \left(\frac{A[c + 2(c_t - c_d)]}{3c}\right)^3}} \quad (16)$$

where $A = \frac{b_e^2 c^2}{[\theta(a+s) - b_e c_d]^2}$.

For clarity, all proofs, if not provided in the main text, are detailed in the Appendix A. Proposition 2 implies that the restaurant will only benefit from the increase of the commission rate if it is accompanied by additional revenues that more than compensate for the commission cost. The main reason is that the increased commission rate will prompt the restaurant to increase the take-out price, which will reduce the take-out demand.

We next study how system parameters (θ, s, c_t, c_d) impact the optimal commission rate. However, the expression of the commission rate is too complex. Thus, we conduct numerical studies to show the results, which are depicted in Figure 1. In the numerical studies of this paper, if not specified otherwise, the parameter values are: $a = 1000$, $\theta = 0.35$, $s = 600$, $b_r = 4$, $b_e = 6$, $\beta = 0.6$, $c_o = 10$, $c_t = 5$, $c_d = 3$ and $c = 30$. In practice, the platform or restaurant generally provides take-out service through the online mode, so it is easy for consumers to compare prices with other take-out prices. Therefore, the demand price elasticity of take-out b_e is generally greater than that of dine-in b_r. Based on it, we set $b_e = 6 > b_r = 4$. According to a financial report by Meituan, the delivery fee charged by Meituan to its customers does not cover wages paid to delivery staff. Hence, we set $c_d = 3 < c_t = 5$. In addition, based on the assumptions of this paper, we set $0 \leq \theta = 0.35 \leq 1$ and $c_o = 10 > c_t = 5$.

Observation 1. *The commission rate λ^* increases in the preference degree of take-out θ and incremental demand s, and decreases in the take-out service cost of platform c_t and the delivery fee c_d.*

The higher preference degree of take-out and incremental demand means that the restaurant can get higher revenues through take-out. Therefore, the take-out platform will also set a higher commission rate to share this part of the revenue. From (3) and (13), we can find that both commission rate and delivery fee have a negative impact on the take-out demand. Hence, the optimal commission rate will decrease as delivery fee increases. In practice, the take-out platforms provide take-out services for many restaurants and charge commissions at the same rate. However, different types of restaurants have different degrees of preference for take-out and incremental demand. From Proposition 2 and Observation 1, we know that the same commission rate for all restaurants is not a good strategy. The platform should set different commission rates according to the actual situation of different restaurants. For example, in the initial stage of joining the platform, due to the lack of historical sales and consumer reviews, this restaurant's ranking on the platform search page is generally lower, which will lead to a lower incremental demand. In this case, the platform should set a lower commission rate. Generally, consumers are more acceptable of hamburger or pizza take-out than hotpot take-out. Therefore, the commission rate of a burger or pizza restaurant can be higher than that of a hotpot restaurant.

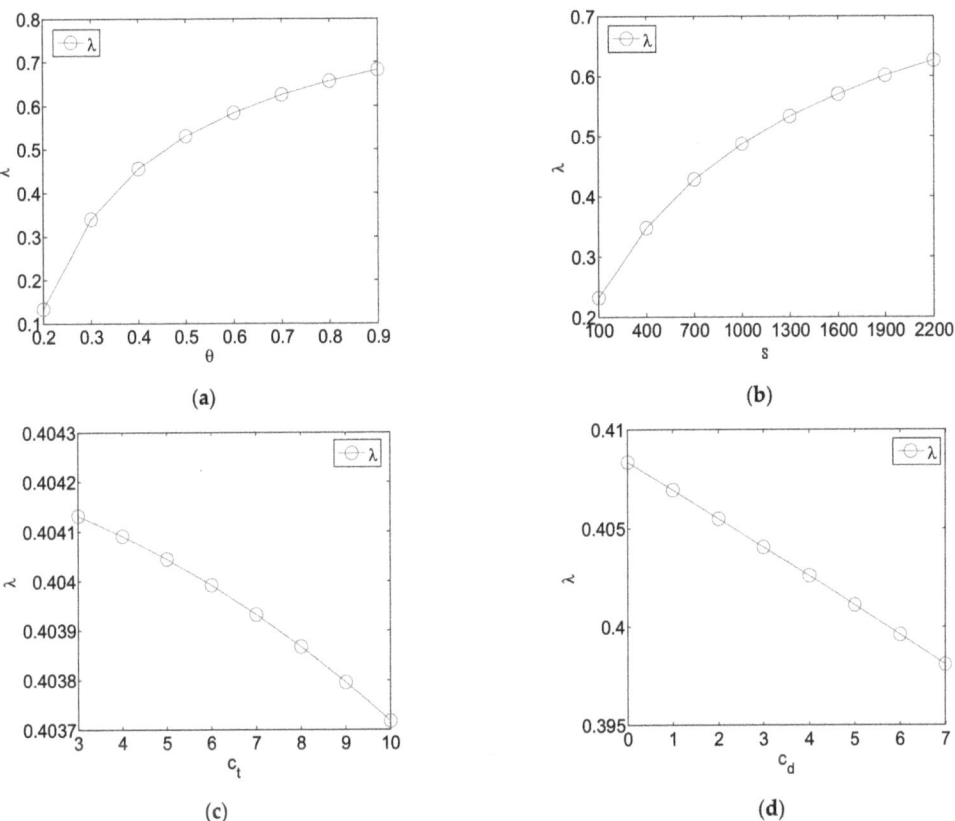

Figure 1. The impacts of system parameter on the commission rate λ^*. (**a**) The impact of θ on the commission rate. (**b**) The impact of s on the commission rate. (**c**) The impact of c_t on the commission rate. (**d**) The impact of c_d on the commission rate.

Substituting (16) into (13), we can obtain the following proposition:

Proposition 3. *Under the TOF model, the restaurant's optimal dine-in price p_r^{j*} and take-out price is p_e^{j*} are given by*

$$p_r^{j*} = \frac{(1-\theta)(a+s) + b_r c}{2b_r} \qquad (17)$$

$$p_e^{j*} = \frac{\theta(a+s) - b_d c_d}{2b_e} + \frac{c}{2\left(\sqrt[3]{A + \sqrt{A^2 + \left(\frac{A[c+2(c_t-c_d)]}{3c}\right)^3}} + \sqrt[3]{A - \sqrt{A^2 + \left(\frac{A[c+2(c_t-c_d)]}{3c}\right)^3}}\right)} \qquad (18)$$

Substituting p_r^{j*}, p_e^{j*} and λ^* into (11) and (15), we then obtain the maximal profit of the restaurant and take-out platform under TOF model.

$$\Pi_R^{j*} = \left[\frac{(1-\theta)(a+s) - b_r c}{2b_r}\right]^2 + \frac{[(1-\lambda^*)\theta(a+s) - (1-\lambda^*)b_e c_d - b_e c]^2}{4b_e(1-\lambda^*)} \quad (19)$$

$$\Pi_f^{j*} = \left[\lambda^*\left(\frac{\theta(a+s) - b_e c_d}{2b_e} + \frac{c}{2(1-\lambda^*)}\right) + c_d - c_t\right]\left[\frac{\theta(a+s) - b_e c_d}{2} - \frac{b_e c}{2(1-\lambda^*)}\right] \quad (20)$$

We then study the how system parameter (θ, s, c_t, c_d) impact the take-out platform's profit. We conduct numerical studies and plot the results in Figure 2.

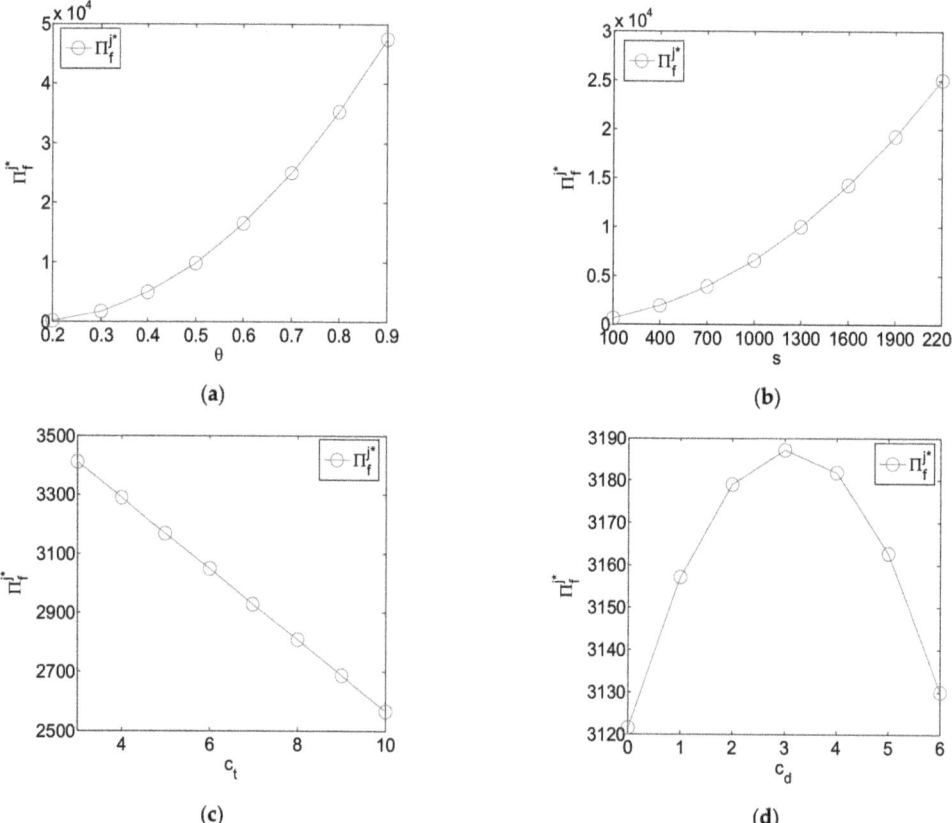

Figure 2. The impacts of system parameter on the take-out platform's profit Π_f^{j*}. (**a**) The impact of θ on the platform's profit. (**b**) The impact of s on the platform's profit. (**c**) The impact of c_t on the platform's profit. (**d**) The impact of c_d on the platform's profit.

Observation 2. *The preference degree of take-out θ, incremental demand s, delivery fee c_d and take-out service cost of platform c_t affects the take-out platform's profit Π_f^{j*} as follows:*

(1) *The take-out platform's profit Π_f^{j*} increases in the preference degree of take-out θ and incremental demand s, and deceases in the take-out service cost of platform c_t.*
(2) *The take-out platform's profit Π_f^{j*} is concave in the delivery fee c_d.*

Observation 2 implies that the take-out platform can increase its profit by increasing the preference degree of take-out and incremental demand and decreasing the take-out service cost of the platform. In practice, the preference degree of take-out of consumers mainly depends on the delivery speed and food quality. The platform can improve the delivery speed by optimizing the delivery task allocation and delivery path. The improvement of delivery speed can not only shorten the delivery time, but also reduce the difference in taste between take-out food and dine-in food, which will help to enhance the preference degree of take-out. The production process of take-out is not visible, and compared to dine-in, it also needs to be packaged and delivered, so some consumers are worried about the take-out food's quality. Therefore, the platform should strengthen the supervision of food quality throughout the entire process.

At present, due to the delivery cost, the delivery range provided by the take-out platform for restaurants is generally within 3 km. Expanding delivery range is the key to increase incremental demand. Simultaneously, the delivery cost is also the main expenditure of the platform. For example, in 2020, Meituan's delivery cost accounted for 74.8% of its total revenue. Therefore, reducing delivery cost is the key to increasing incremental demand and reducing the service cost of a platform. In addition to optimizing the delivery task allocation and delivery path, increasing the delivery scale and the delivery density are two main ways to reduce delivery cost. Therefore, the platform should open her delivery system to provide delivery service for more non-restaurant enterprises. In addition, different take-out platforms should strengthen cooperation and try to carry out joint delivery.

From Observation 2, we also find that either charging a higher or lower delivery fee is not a good choice for the platform. The main reason is that the lower delivery fee reduces the unit income, while the higher delivery fee greatly reduces the demand. Therefore, only moderate delivery fees benefit the platform.

4.3. The TOH Model

In this scenario, the restaurant decides the dine-in price and take-out price to maximize its own profits simultaneously. We use c_o to denote the take-out service cost of the restaurant. Generally, the scale and specialization of the take-out platform is higher than those of the restaurant, so we assume $c_o > c_t$. The restaurant's profit, denoted as Π_R^i, is determined by

$$\Pi_R^i = \left(p_r^i - c\right)\left[(1-\theta)(a+\beta s) - b_r p_r^i\right] + \left[p_e^i + c_d - c - c_o\right]\left[\theta(a+\beta s) - b_e p_e^i - b_e c_d\right] \quad (21)$$

In (21), the first term denotes the restaurant's revenue from the consumer's dine-in demand, the second term denotes the restaurant's revenue from the consumer's take-out demand.

From (21), we can then obtain the following proposition:

Proposition 4. *Under the TOH model, the restaurant's profit is jointly concave in (p_r^i, p_e^i), and the optimal dine-in price p_r^{i*} and take-out price p_e^{i*} are given by*

$$p_r^{i*} = \frac{(1-\theta)(a+\beta s) + b_r c}{2b_r} \quad (22)$$

$$p_e^{i*} = \frac{\theta(a+\beta s) + b_e(c+c_o) - 2b_e c_d}{2b_e} \quad (23)$$

Substituting p_r^{i*} and p_e^{i*} into (21), we then obtain the maximal profit of the restaurant Π_R^{i*} under the TOH model.

$$\Pi_R^{i*} = \left[\frac{(1-\theta)(a+\beta s) - b_r c}{2b_r}\right]^2 + \left[\frac{\theta(a+\beta s) - b_e(c+c_o)}{2b_e}\right]^2 \quad (24)$$

5. The Take-Out Model Choice

In this section, we focus on the main research questions of this paper: how does the restaurant choose the take-out model? Therefore, we need to compare the restaurant's profit among the NTO model, TOF model and TOH model. To this end, we first compare the profit between the NTO model and the TOH model. We then have the following proposition.

Proposition 5. When $s \geq \frac{D+\sqrt{D^2-4Bb_e^2[b_r^2c^2+b_r^2(c+c_o)^2-(a-b_rc)^2]}-2Ba}{2B\beta}$, the restaurant's profit under the TOH model is higher than that under the NTO model, where $B = (1-\theta)^2 b_e^2 + \theta^2 b_r^2$ and $D = 2b_e b_r [b_e c(1-\theta) + b_r(c+c_o)\theta]$.

Proposition 5 implies that when the incremental demand brought by take-out is large, the TOH model is better than the NTO model. Otherwise, the NTO mode is a better choice for the restaurant. The main reason is that the take-out service is a double-edged sword for the restaurant. On the one hand, the take-out service increases the total base demand, which will help increase the restaurant's profit. On the other hand, the take-out service transforms a part of the original dine-in consumption into take-out consumption. The take-out service requires an additional service cost, such as a delivery fee. As a result, the service cost to the consumers increases, which leads to lower profits for the restaurant. If the take-out service adds more demand to the restaurant, the former plays a greater role than the latter so that the retailer's profit increases. Otherwise, the latter will dominate. The restaurant' profit function under the TOF model is too complicated. Thus, we also conduct numerical studies to compare the results. Our results are depicted in Figure 3.

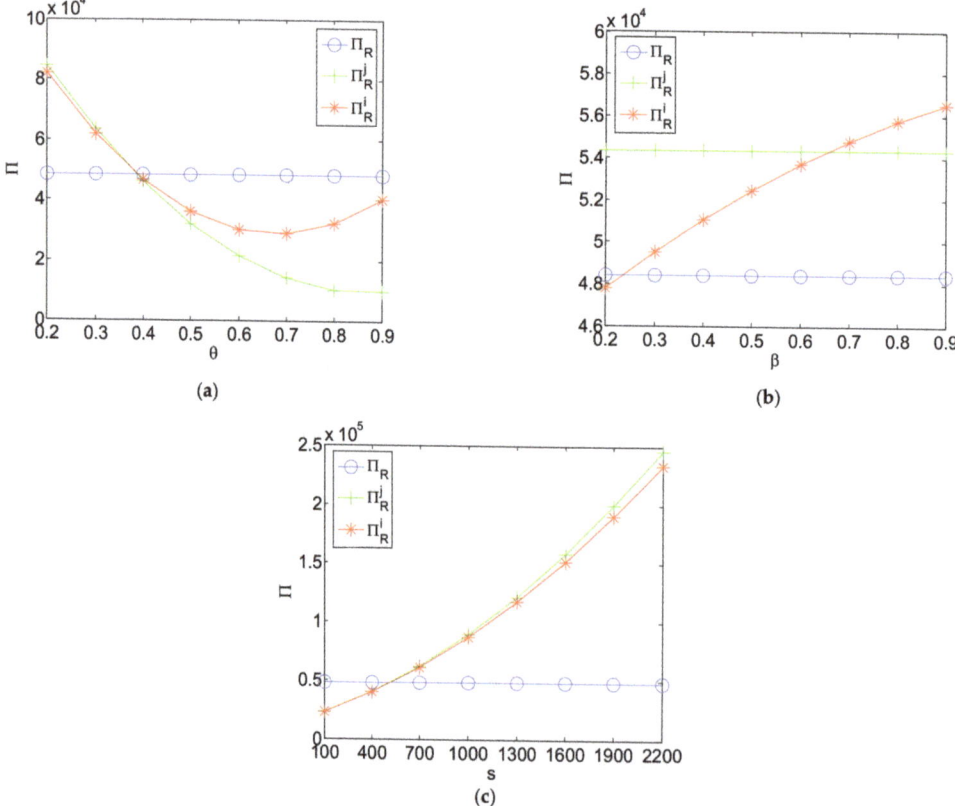

Figure 3. The impacts of system parameter on the model choice. (**a**) The impact of θ on the model choice. (**b**) The impact of β on the model choice. (**c**) The impact of s on the model choice.

Observation 3. *The preference degree of take-out θ, incremental demand s and retention rate β affect the restaurant's optimal model choice as follows:*

(1) *When the preference degree of take-out θ is low, the restaurant's optimal model choice is TOF. Conversely, the NTO model is the better choice.*
(2) *When the incremental demand s is high, the restaurant's optimal model choice is TOF. Conversely, the NTO model is the better choice.*
(3) *When the retention rate β is high, the restaurant's optimal model choice is TOH. Conversely, the TOF model is the better choice.*

The increased preference degree of take-out means that if the take-out service is provided, some dine-in consumption will transform into take-out consumption. Under this condition, the average unit cost will increase, which will lead to a decline in restaurant profits under the TOF and TOH model. Similar to the analysis of Proposition 5, when the incremental demand is low, the increased revenue cannot compensate for the increased cost, so the NTO mode is the best choice for restaurants.

From Figure 3a, we find that when the preference degree of take-out is lower, the restaurant's profit under the TOF model is higher than that under the TOH model. Compared with the TOF model, the advantage of the TOH model is that the restaurant does not need to pay commissions to the take-out platform, i.e., it does not need to share the take-out revenue with the take-out platform. The disadvantage of the TOH model is that the promotion ability is weaker than the take-out platform, i.e., incremental demand under the TOH mode is lower than that under the TOF model. When the preference degree of take-out is lower, more consumers who search for the restaurant through the take-out platform chooses dine-in, i.e., more traffic from the take-out platform is transferred to dine-in. The dine-in revenue does not need to pay commission, and the incremental demand under the TOF model is higher, so the restaurant should choose the TOF mode under this condition. When the preference degree of take-out is higher, the take-out revenue accounts for a larger proportion of the restaurant's total revenue. In addition, from Observation 1, we know that the commission rate also increases with the preference degree of take-out. It means that a large part of the restaurant's revenue will be transferred to the take-out platform as a commission fee. Therefore, under this condition, the restaurant's profit under the TOH model is higher than that under TOF model.

From Observation 1, we know that the commission rate increases as the incremental demand increases. It means that when the incremental demand is higher, the restaurant needs to pay a higher commission under the TOF model. Therefore, the take-out revenue under the TOH model will be higher than that under the TOF model. However, the higher incremental demand also brings higher dine-in consumption. Due to higher incremental demand under the TOF model, the dine-in revenue under the TOF model will be higher than that under the TOH model. When the incremental demand is higher, the latter plays a greater role than the former so that the restaurant should adopt the TOF model.

From Figure 3b, we find that when the consumer's retention rate is higher, the restaurant's profit under the TOH model is higher than that under the TOF model. Higher consumer retention rate means that when the restaurant leaves the platform to provide take-out service on its own, the loss of demand is not large. Simultaneously, the restaurant does not need to pay any commission. Therefore, under this condition, the TOH model is a better choice.

6. The Price and Model Choice Coordination

In this section, we mainly focus on these questions: From the perspective of a centralized supply chain, what is the optimal price and model choice decision? For the take-out platform, how do we establish a coordination mechanism to make the decisions under the decentralized supply chain consistent with those under the centralized supply chain?

In the centralized supply chain, the purpose of price and model choice decisions are to maximize the entire supply chain's profit. For clarity, we add superscript $()^k$ to the notation. Hence, for benchmark purposes, we first derive the supply chain's total profit Π_T^k as follows:

$$\Pi_T^k = \left(p_r^k - c\right)\left[(1-\theta)(a+s) - b_r p_r^k\right] + \left(p_e^k + c_d - c - c_t\right)\left[\theta(a+s) - b_e p_e^k - b_e c_d\right] \quad (25)$$

In (25), the first and second terms denote the profit of dine-in and take-out, respectively. From (25), we then can obtain the following proposition:

Proposition 6. *Under the centralized supply chain and TOF model, the supply chain is jointly concave in (p_r^k, p_e^k), the optimal dine-in price p_r^{k*} and the take-out price p_e^{k*} are given by*

$$p_r^{k*} = \frac{(1-\theta)(a+s) + b_r c}{2b_r} \quad (26)$$

$$p_e^{k*} = \frac{\theta(a+s) + b_e(c+c_t) - 2b_e c_d}{2b_e} \quad (27)$$

Comparing (27) and (18), we find that the take-out price under a centralized supply chain is not consistent with the price under the decentralized. The take-out platform charges the commission, which causes the double-marginal effect. This is the main reason for the price difference.

Substituting p_r^{k*} and p_e^{k*} into (25), we then obtain the maximal profit of the supply chain Π_T^{k*} under the TOF model.

$$\Pi_T^{k*} = \left[\frac{(1-\theta)(a+s) - b_r c}{2b_r}\right]^2 + \left[\frac{\theta(a+s) - b_e(c+c_t)}{2b_e}\right]^2 \quad (28)$$

Comparing the results in (28) and (24), we find that the profit of the centralized supply chain under the TOF model is always higher than the restaurant's profit under the TOH model. It means that from the perspective of the centralized supply chain, the TOF model is better than the TOH model. The main reason is that there is no commission under the centralized supply chain and TOF model. Meanwhile, the incremental demand and take-out service cost under the TOF model is lower than that under the TOH model. Therefore, we just need to compare the TOF model and NTO model. Comparing (28) and (10), we can get the following proposition:

Proposition 7. *Under the centralized supply chain, if* $s \geq \frac{E+\sqrt{E^2 - 4Ab_e^2[b_r^2 c^2 + b_r^2(c+c_t)^2 - (a-b_r c)^2]} - 2Ba}{2B}$, *the optimal model choice of supply chain is the TOF. Otherwise, the NTO model is better for the supply chain. Where* $E = 2b_e b_r [b_e c(1-\theta) + b_r(c+c_t)\theta]$.

Comparing Propositions 5 and 7, we can find that the optimal model choice under the centralized model is also not consistent with that under the decentralized one. We then can easily check that

$$\frac{E+\sqrt{E^2 - 4Ab_e^2[b_r^2 c^2 + b_r^2(c+c_t)^2 - (a-b_r c)^2]} - 2Ba}{2B} \leq \frac{D+\sqrt{D^2 - 4Bb_e^2[b_r^2 c^2 + b_r^2(c+c_o)^2 - (a-b_r c)^2]} - 2Ba}{2B\beta} \quad (29)$$

Based on (29), Propositions 5 and 7, we can draw a comparison figure of model choice, which is shown in Figure 4.

To achieve coordination, we design a sales reward contract. Under this contract, the take-out platform sets up a sales target for the restaurant. If the restaurant's take-out sales (turnover, i.e., $p_e q_e$) are beyond the target, the platform will give the retailer a rebate, G. In order to ensure that the price decision under the decentralized model is consistent with that under the centralized model, the sales target should be set as $p_e^{k*} q_e^{k*}$.

$$p_e^{k*} q_e^{k*} = \frac{\theta^2(a+s)^2 - b_e^2(c+c_t)^2 - 2b_e c_d[\theta(a+s) - b_e(c+c_t)]}{4b_e} \quad (30)$$

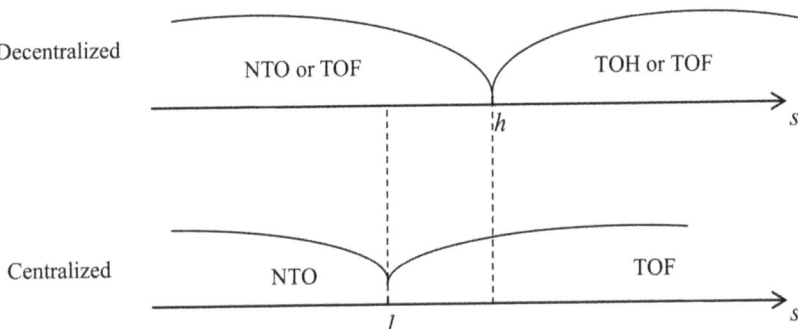

Figure 4. The comparison of mode choice between Decentralized and Centralized. (where $h = \frac{D+\sqrt{D^2-4Bb_e^2[b_r^2c^2+b_r^2(c+c_o)^2-(a-b_rc)^2]-2Ba}}{2B\beta}$ and $l = \frac{E+\sqrt{E^2-4Ab_e^2[b_r^2c^2+b_r^2(c+c_t)^2-(a-b_rc)^2]-2Ba}}{2B}$).

In practice, the platform and restaurant are willing to accept the coordination mechanism only when it can benefit all of them. Hence, an appropriate rebate G should be adopted to ensure that everyone's expected profit can improve under the sales reward contract. We next analyze the value range of the rebate G.

Case 1: $l \leq s \leq h$.

In this case, if $\Pi_R^{j*} \geq \Pi_R^*$, the restaurant will adopt the TOF model under the decentralized scenario. Under this condition, the restaurant's optimal profit is equal to Π_R^{j*}, and the platform's optimal profit is equal to Π_f^{j*}. In order to ensure that the platform and restaurant accept this sales reward contract, the rebate G needs to meet the following conditions

$$\Pi_R^j\left(p_r^{k*}, p_e^{k*}, \lambda^*\right) + G \geq \Pi_R^{j*} \tag{31}$$

$$\Pi_f^j\left(p_r^{k*}, p_e^{k*}, \lambda^*\right) - G \geq \Pi_f^{j*} \tag{32}$$

If $\Pi_R^{j*} < \Pi_R^*$, the restaurant will adopt the NTO model under the decentralized scenario. Under this condition, the restaurant's optimal profit is equal to Π_R^*, and the platform's optimal profit is equal to zero. To ensure that both of them can accept this contract, the rebate G needs to meet the following conditions

$$\Pi_R^j\left(p_r^{k*}, p_e^{k*}, \lambda^*\right) + G \geq \Pi_R^* \tag{33}$$

$$\Pi_f^j\left(p_r^{k*}, p_e^{k*}, \lambda^*\right) - G \geq 0 \tag{34}$$

Case 2: $s > h$.

If $\Pi_R^{j*} \geq \Pi_R^{i*}$, the restaurant will adopt the TOF model under the decentralized scenario. Under this condition, the restaurant's optimal profit is equal to Π_R^{j*}, and the platform's optimal profit is equal to Π_f^{j*}. To ensure that both of them can accept this contract, the rebate G needs to satisfy (31) and (32).

If $\Pi_R^{j*} < \Pi_R^{i*}$, the restaurant will adopt the TOH model under decentralized. Under this condition, the restaurant's optimal profit is equal to Π_R^{i*}, and the platform's optimal profit is equal to zero. To ensure that both of them can accept this contract, the rebate G needs to meet the following conditions

$$\Pi_R^j\left(p_r^{k*}, p_e^{k*}, \lambda^*\right) + G \geq \Pi_R^{i*} \tag{35}$$

$$\Pi_f^j\left(p_r^{k*}, p_e^{k*}, \lambda^*\right) - G \geq 0 \tag{36}$$

To sum up, we can get the following Proposition:

Proposition 8. *The take-out platform can provide the retailer with a rebate: a reward of G for the retailer's take-out turnover $(p_e q_e)$ above $\frac{\theta^2(a+s)^2 - b_e^2(c+c_t)^2 - 2b_e c_d[\theta(a+s) - b_e(c+c_t)]}{4b_e}$, which can make the price decision and model choice under the decentralized supply chains consistent with that under the centralized supply chains. The value range of G is as follows:*

(1) *When $l \leq s \leq h$, $G \in \left[\Pi_R^{j*} - \Pi_R^j\left(p_r^{k*}, p_e^{k*}, \lambda^*\right), \Pi_f^j\left(p_r^{k*}, p_e^{k*}, \lambda^*\right) - \Pi_f^{j*} \right]$ if $\Pi_R^{j*} \geq \Pi_R^*$, and $G \in \left[\Pi_R^* - \Pi_R^j\left(p_r^{k*}, p_e^{k*}, \lambda^*\right), \Pi_f^j\left(p_r^{k*}, p_e^{k*}, \lambda^*\right) \right]$ if $\Pi_R^{j*} < \Pi_R^*$.*

(2) *When $s > h$, $G \in \left[\Pi_R^{j*} - \Pi_R^j\left(p_r^{k*}, p_e^{k*}, \lambda^*\right), \Pi_f^j\left(p_r^{k*}, p_e^{k*}, \lambda^*\right) - \Pi_f^{j*} \right]$ if $\Pi_R^{j*} \geq \Pi_R^{i*}$, and $G \in \left[\Pi_R^{i*} - \Pi_R^j\left(p_r^{k*}, p_e^{k*}, \lambda^*\right), \Pi_f^j\left(p_r^{k*}, p_e^{k*}, \lambda^*\right) \right]$ if $\Pi_R^{j*} < \Pi_R^{i*}$.*

Proposition 8 implies that both the restaurant and the take-out platform will be happy to enter this sales reward contract when the take-out platform chooses a proper rebate G.

7. Conclusions

In this paper, we study the take-out model choice and the coordination of an online take-out supply chain. To this end, we model a supply chain with one restaurant and one platform. We then derive the optimal decisions of the price and/or commission rate under each of the three possible take-out models: the TOF model, NTO model and the TOH model. By comparing the restaurant's profit under these models, we find that under the decentralized supply chain, the restaurant should adopt the NTO model if the incremental demand is low; otherwise, the TOF model and TOH model are better choices. Next, we conduct numerical studies to further compare the restaurant's profit under TOF and TOH, and find that when the incremental demand is high, the restaurant's optimal model choice is TOH only if the retention rate is high. Subsequently, we derive the optimal decisions of price and take-out model under centralization. We find that the TOF model is always better than the TOH model. From the perspective of a supply chain, when the incremental demand is high, the restaurant should choose the TOF model; otherwise, the NTO model is better. Lastly, by comparing centralization with decentralization, we propose a sales reward contract and prove that it can coordinate the take-out supply chain.

Furthermore, our study provides some managerial insights. First, the restaurant may not always benefit from continuously increasing the commission rate. Second, as the preference degree of take-out and incremental demand increases or the take-out service cost of the platform deceases, the platform can increase the commission rate. Lastly, charging a higher or lower delivery fee from consumers will have a negative impact on the profit of the platform.

There are a few interesting topics for further research. First, in this paper, we do not consider competition between restaurants or platforms. Therefore, how competition affects price decisions, commission rate decisions, take-out model choices and coordinating mechanism design are worthy of future investigation. Second, this paper considers a single-period setting. However, in practice, the take-out price and commission rate are often set dynamically, which can also be a future research direction. Third, in the model of this paper, we consider a deterministic demand function. However, in business practice, the demand is often uncertain. Hence, modeling this more realistic but complicated setting is a worthwhile research direction. Lastly, in this paper, we assume that the delivery service is provided by the platform. In reality, there are also some third-party logistics companies that provide delivery services. Research opportunities abound in this supply chain which consists of restaurant, platform and logistics service providers.

Author Contributions: Conceptualization, S.J. and P.Z.; methodology, H.H.; validation, P.Z. and H.H.; formal analysis, S.J.; investigation, H.H. and P.Z.; resources, S.J.; writing—original draft preparation, S.J.; writing—review and editing, P.Z.; visualization, H.H.; supervision, P.Z.; project administration, P.Z.; funding acquisition, H.H. and P.Z. All authors have read and agreed to the published version of the manuscript.

Funding: This work was supported by the National Natural Science Foundation of China (Nos. 71801170, 72101117 and 72103178), Natural Science Foundation of Jiangsu Province of China (Grants BK20200485), the Humanity and Social Science Youth Foundation of Ministry of Education of China (No. 18YJC630246).

Institutional Review Board Statement: Not applicable.

Informed Consent Statement: Not applicable.

Data Availability Statement: Not applicable.

Conflicts of Interest: The authors declare that they have no conflict of interest.

Appendix A

Proof of Proposition 2. The second-order conditions of Π_R^j with respect to p_r^j and p_e^j, respectively, are

$$\frac{\partial^2 \Pi_R^j}{\partial p_r^{j2}} = -2b_r < 0 \tag{A1}$$

$$\frac{\partial^2 \Pi_R^j}{\partial p_r^{j2}} = -2b_e < 0 \tag{A2}$$

Based (A1) and (A2), we can get the restaurant's best response by taking the first-order conditions.

The first- and second-order conditions of Π_R^j with respect to p_r^j and p_e^j, respectively, are

$$\frac{d\Pi_f^j}{d\lambda} = \left[\frac{\theta(a+s)-b_e c_d}{2b_e} + \frac{c}{2(1-\lambda)} + \frac{\lambda c}{2(1-\lambda)^2}\right]\left[\frac{\theta(a+s)-b_e c_d}{2} - \frac{b_e c}{2(1-\lambda)}\right] \\ - \left[\lambda\left(\frac{\theta(a+s)-b_e c_d}{2b_e} + \frac{c}{2(1-\lambda)}\right) + c_d - c_t\right]\frac{b_e c}{2(1-\lambda)^2} \tag{A3}$$

$$\frac{d^2\Pi_f^j}{d^2\lambda} = \left[\frac{c}{(1-\lambda)^2} + \frac{\lambda c}{(1-\lambda)^3}\right]\left[\frac{\theta(a+s)-b_d c_d}{2} - \frac{b_e c}{2(1-\lambda)}\right] \\ - \left[\frac{\theta(a+s)-b_e c_d}{2b_e} + \frac{c}{2(1-\lambda)} + \frac{\lambda c}{2(1-\lambda)^2}\right]\frac{b_e c}{(1-\lambda)^2} - \left[\lambda\left(\frac{\theta(a+s)-b_e c_d}{2b_e} + \frac{c}{2(1-\lambda)}\right) + c_d - c_t\right]\frac{b_e c}{(1-\lambda)^3} \tag{A4}$$

Substituting $\frac{d\Pi_f^j}{d\lambda} = 0$ into (A4), we can get

$$\frac{d^2\Pi_f}{d^2\lambda} = \left[\frac{c}{(1-\lambda)} + \frac{\lambda c}{(1-\lambda)^2}\right]\left[\frac{\theta(a+s)-b_d c_d}{1} - \frac{b_e c}{(1-\lambda)}\right] \\ - \left[\frac{\theta(a+s)-b_d c_d}{b_e} + \frac{c}{(1-\lambda)} + \frac{\lambda c}{(1-\lambda)^2}\right]\frac{\theta(a+s)-b_d c_d}{1} < 0 \tag{A5}$$

From (A5), we can obtain that Π_f^j is quasi-concave in λ and the unique optimal λ^* should satisfy the first-order condition. Hence, we can get the proposition. □

Proof of Proposition 5.

$$\Pi_R^{i*} - \Pi_R^* = \left[\frac{(1-\theta)(a+\beta s)-b_r c}{2b_r}\right]^2 + \left[\frac{\theta(a+\beta s)-b_e(c+c_o)}{2b_e}\right]^2 - \left(\frac{a-b_r c}{2b_r}\right)^2 \tag{A6}$$

43

By rearranging, we can get that when $\Pi_R^{i*} > \Pi_R^*$, the following inequality must be satisfied

$$(1-\theta)^2 b_e^2 (a+\beta s)^2 + b_e^2 b_r^2 c^2 - 2b_e^2 b_r c(1-\theta)(a+\beta s) + \theta^2 b_r^2 (a+\beta s)^2 + b_e^2 b_r^2 (c+c_o)^2 \\ -2b_e b_r^2 (c+c_o)\theta(a+\beta s) - (a-b_r c)^2 b_e^2 > 0 \quad (A7)$$

We then can get that when $s \geq \frac{D+\sqrt{D^2-4B b_e^2 [b_r^2 c^2 + b_r^2(c+c_o)^2 - (a-b_r c)^2]} - 2Ba}{2B\beta}$, $\Pi_R^{i*} \geq \Pi_R^*$. □

Proof of Proposition 7.

$$\Pi_R^{k*} - \Pi_R^* = \left[\frac{(1-\theta)(a+s) - b_r c}{2b_r}\right]^2 + \left[\frac{\theta(a+s) - b_e(c+c_t)}{2b_e}\right]^2 - \left(\frac{a-b_r c}{2b_r}\right)^2 \quad (A8)$$

By rearranging, we can get that when $\Pi_R^{i*} > \Pi_R^*$, the following inequality must be satisfied

$$(1-\theta)^2 b_e^2 (a+s)^2 + b_e^2 b_r^2 c^2 - 2b_e^2 b_r c(1-\theta)(a+s) + \theta^2 b_r^2 (a+s)^2 + b_e^2 b_r^2 (c+c_t)^2 \\ -2b_e b_r^2 (c+c_t)\theta(a+s) - (a-b_r c)^2 b_e^2 > 0 \quad (A9)$$

We then can get that when $s \geq \frac{E+\sqrt{E^2 - 4A b_e^2 [b_r^2 c^2 + b_r^2(c+c_t)^2 - (a-b_r c)^2]} - 2Ba}{2B}$, $\Pi_R^{j*} \geq \Pi_R^*$. □

References

1. ZhiYan Consulting Company. Analysis of China's Take-Out Industry Market Transaction Volume, Industry Market Penetration, Online Takeout User Scale and Industry Development Trend from 2019 to 2020. Available online: http://www.chyxx.com/industry/202005/865307.html.2020 (accessed on 1 January 2020).
2. Zhang, S.; Pauwels, K.; Peng, C. The Impact of Adding Online-to-Offline Service Platform Channels on Firms' Offline and Total Sales and Profits. *J. Interact. Mark.* **2019**, *47*, 115–128. [CrossRef]
3. Heo, C.Y. Exploring group-buying platforms for restaurant revenue management. *Int. J. Hosp. Manag.* **2016**, *52*, 154–159. [CrossRef]
4. Zheng, X.; Guo, X. E-retailing of restaurant services: Pricing strategies in a competing online environment. *J. Oper. Res. Soc.* **2016**, *67*, 1408–1418. [CrossRef]
5. Xu, J.; Hu, L.; Guo, X.; Yan, X. Online cooperation mechanism: Game analysis between a restaurant and a third-party website. *J. Revenue Pricing Manag.* **2020**, *19*, 61–73. [CrossRef]
6. Zhang, H.; Luo, K.; Ni, G. The effects of price subsidy and fairness concern on pricing and benefits of take-away supply chain. *J. Comb. Optim.* **2020**. [CrossRef]
7. Liu, Y.; Guo, B.; Chen, C.; Du, H.; Yu, Z.W.; Zhang, D.Q.; Ma, H.D. FooDNet: Toward an Optimized Food Delivery Network based on Spatial Crowdsourcing. *IEEE. Trans. Mobile. Comput.* **2019**, *18*, 1288–1300. [CrossRef]
8. Wang, L.; Yu, Z.; Han, Q.; Guo, B.; Xiong, H.Y. Multi-objective Optimization based Allocation of Heterogeneous Spatial Crowdsourcing Tasks. *IEEE. Trans. Mobile. Comput.* **2018**, *17*, 1637–1650. [CrossRef]
9. Yan, L.; Xu, F.; Liu, J.; Teo, K.L.; Lai, M.Y. Stability strategies of demand-driven supply networks with transportation delay. *Appl. Math. Model.* **2019**, *76*, 109–121. [CrossRef]
10. Bai, L.B.; Shi, C.M.; Guo, Y.T.; Du, Q.; Huang, Y.D. Quality risk evaluation of the food supply chain using a fuzzy comprehensive evaluation model and failure mode, effects, and criticality analysis. *J. Food Qual.* **2018**, *2018*, 2637075. [CrossRef]
11. He, Y.; Huang, H.F.; Li, D.; Shi, C.M.; Wu, S.J. Quality and operations management in food supply chains: A literature review. *J. Food Qual.* **2018**, *2018*, 7279491. [CrossRef]
12. Young, J.A.; Clack, P.W.; Mcintyre, F.S. The web as an e-commerce medium: An exploratory study of consumer perceptions in a restaurant setting. *J. Mark. Channels* **2006**, *14*, 5–22. [CrossRef]
13. Tahir, M.; Guru, P. What factors determine-satisfaction and consumer spending in e-commerce retailing. *J. Retail. Consum. Serv.* **2017**, *39*, 135–144.
14. Wang, L.; Yi, B. Research on O2O take-away restaurant recommendation system: Taking ele.me APP as an example. *Cluster. Comput.* **2019**, *22*, 6069–6077. [CrossRef]
15. Hatami, M.; Pashazadeh, S. Enhancing prediction in collaborative filtering-based recommender systems. *Int. J. Comput. Sci. Eng.* **2014**, *2*, 48–51.
16. Yu, X.Q.; Ren, X.X. The Impact of Food Quality Information Services on Food Supply Chain Pricing Decisions and Coordination Mechanisms Based on the O2O E-Commerce Mode. *J. Food Qual.* **2018**, *2018*, 8956820. [CrossRef]

17. Wu, S.S.; Li, Q. Emergency Quantity Discount Contract with Suppliers Risk Aversion under Stochastic Price. *Mathematics* **2021**, *9*, 1791. [CrossRef]
18. Becker-Peth, M.; Katok, E.; Thonemann, U.W. Designing buyback contracts for irrational but predictable newsvendors. *Manag. Sci.* **2013**, *59*, 1800–1816. [CrossRef]
19. Guo, P.; Jia, Y.L.; Gan, J.W.; Li, X.F. Optimal Pricing and Ordering Strategies with a Flexible Return Strategy under Uncertainty. *Mathematics* **2021**, *9*, 2097. [CrossRef]
20. Nosoohi, I.; Nookabadi, A.S. Approaches to designing the revenue sharing contract under asymmetric cost information. *IMA. J. Manag. Math.* **2018**, *29*, 69–97. [CrossRef]
21. Taboubi, S.; Zaccour, G.; Leopoldwildburger, U. Pricing decisions in marketing channels in the presence of optional contingent products. *Cent. Eur. J. Oper. Res.* **2020**, *28*, 167–192.
22. Zhang, P.; He, Y.; Shi, C.M. Transshipment and coordination in a two-echelon supply chain. *RAIRO-Oper. Res.* **2017**, *51*, 729–747. [CrossRef]
23. Chen, J.; Zhang, H.; Sun, Y. Implementing coordination contracts in a manufacturer Stackelberg dual-channel supply chain. *Omega-Int. J. Manag. Sci.* **2012**, *40*, 571–583. [CrossRef]
24. He, Y.; Zhang, P.; Yao, Y.L. Unidirectional transshipment policies in a dual-channel supply chain. *Econ. Model.* **2014**, *40*, 259–268. [CrossRef]
25. Zhu, B.L.; Wen, B.; Ji, S.F. Coordinating a dual-channel supply chain with conditional value-at-risk under uncertainties of yield and demand. *Comput. Ind. Eng.* **2020**, *139*, 106181. [CrossRef]
26. Zha, Y.; Zhang, J.H.; Yue, X.H.; Hua, Z.S. Service supply chain coordination with platform effort-induced demand. *Ann. Oper. Res.* **2015**, *235*, 785–806. [CrossRef]
27. Kurata, H.; Yao, D.Q.; Liu, J.J. Pricing policies under direct vs. indirect channel competition and national vs. store brand competition. *Eur. J. Oper. Res.* **2007**, *180*, 262–281. [CrossRef]
28. Hua, G.; Wang, S.; Cheng, T.C.E. Price and lead time decisions in dual-channel supply chains. *Eur. J. Oper. Res.* **2010**, *205*, 113–126. [CrossRef]

Article

Queueing-Inventory System for Two Commodities with Optional Demands of Customers and MAP Arrivals

N. Anbazhagan [1,†], Gyanendra Prasad Joshi [2,*,†], R. Suganya [1], S. Amutha [3], V. Vinitha [1] and Bhanu Shrestha [4,*]

1. Department of Mathematics, Alagappa University, Karaikudi 630003, India; anbazhagann@alagappauniversity.ac.in (N.A.); suganya@alagappauniversity.ac.in (R.S.); vinitha@alagappauniversity.ac.in (V.V.)
2. Department of Computer Science and Engineering, Sejong University, Seoul 05006, Korea
3. Ramanujan Center for Higher Mathematics, Alagappa University, Karaikudi 630003, India; amuthas@alagappauniversity.ac.in
4. Department of Electronic Engineering, Kwangwoon University, Seoul 01897, Korea
* Correspondence: joshi@sejong.ac.kr (G.P.J.); bnu@kw.ac.kr (B.S.)
† These authors contributed equally to this work.

Abstract: This research analyses the performance of a perishable queueing-inventory system for two commodities with optional customers demands. We assume in the article that all customers who come to the system can only purchase the first item or the second item or service (they do not purchase both items). This is the original aspect of the paper. We show the significance of the impact of optional demands on the system's performance, which is the purpose of the paper. In this system, customers arrive, using the Markovian arrival process (MAP), to a demand for a single unit. The system is composed of a waiting hall with a limited capacity of F. The arriving customer observes the waiting hall is filled to capacity or the stock stage is zero, and they decide to leave the system. In the steady-state case, the joint probability distribution for the first commodity, the second commodity, and the number of customers in the system are computed using matrix geometric methods. We evaluate diverse system performance measures. Finally, we provide a numerical illustration of the optimal value for diverse parameters of the system, which highlights the results and implications of the article.

Keywords: two commodity; (s, Q)-policy; Markovian arrival process; optional demands; perishable inventory

MSC: 60J27; 90B05; 90B22

Citation: Anbazhagan, N.; Joshi, G.P.; Suganya, R.; Amutha, S.; Vinitha, V.; Shrestha, B. Queueing-Inventory System for Two Commodities with Optional Demands of Customers and MAP Arrivals. *Mathematics* 2022, 10, 1801. https://doi.org/10.3390/math10111801

Academic Editor: Yong He

Received: 24 April 2022
Accepted: 22 May 2022
Published: 25 May 2022

Publisher's Note: MDPI stays neutral with regard to jurisdictional claims in published maps and institutional affiliations.

Copyright: © 2022 by the authors. Licensee MDPI, Basel, Switzerland. This article is an open access article distributed under the terms and conditions of the Creative Commons Attribution (CC BY) license (https://creativecommons.org/licenses/by/4.0/).

1. Introduction

One of the critical problems in an inventory system is having a large number of items which can affect its integrated functioning. To avoid this problem, multiple commodity systems are used. To manage such systems numerous models have been proposed with various sorts of ordering policies. The joint ordering policy was introduced by [1] and developed by [2]. A two commodity inventory system with zero lead time and with the same demand process were inspected by [3,4], respectively. The authors of [5,6] analyzed a joint ordering policy with a substitutable inventory system. A queueing-inventory system can be manipulated according to a number of factors, such as arrival/service processes, waiting hall capacity, service interruption, and vacation assumptions. See [7,8] review articles and [9–19] articles for discussion of a two commodity queueing-inventory system.

A system needs to satisfy different kinds of customer demands to achieve profit. Sometimes customers need only service without purchasing an item. For example, in a mechanic shop, customers may come to repair their vehicle. Some customers come to the system with a required item—they only need service. Some customers come to the system without items—they need service with the item. In a similar way, we can observe this sort of circumstance in a tailoring shop, card printers, etc. In this circumstance, the system provides the same services for both demands.

Motivated by practical situations that arise, we consider how arriving customers may choose either service with or without an item. The present article also considers a perishable (s, Q) queueing-inventory system for two commodities in which customers arrive according to a Markovian arrival process (MAP) to a single unit or for service at a certain time.

A MAP is a type of tractable class of the Markov renewal process. The arrival process can be modified to be a renewal process by adjusting the MAP's parameters. The MAP is a diverse class of point processes that also includes the Poisson process. The purpose of MAP is to generalize the Poisson process and create more flexibility for modeling purposes. MAP may be used for both discrete and continuous time frames, but this paper focuses only on continuous-time frames. An explanation of MAP is provided by [20]. The states of the Markov chain are $\{1, 2, \ldots y\}$. When the chain goes into the state u, $1 \leq u \leq y$, it remains with parameter m_u for an exponential time. When the sojourn period is over, the chain may shift to a transition until arrival occurs; then the chain goes into the state v with the probability c_{uv}, $1 \leq v \leq y$, or if transition occurs without arrival, then the chain goes into the state v with probability d_{uv}, $1 \leq v \leq y$, $u \neq v$. When an arrival occurs, the chain might return to the same state. We describe the square matrices D_f, $f = 0, 1$, of size y by $[D_0]_{uu} = -m_u$ and $[D_0]_{uv} = m_u d_{uv}$, $u \neq v$, $[D_1]_{uv} = m_u c_{uv}$, $1 \leq u, v \leq y$. χ represents the continuous time Markov chain's unique probability vector with an infinitesimal generator matrix $D(=D_0 + D_1)$, and χ is obtained from $\chi D = 0$, $\chi \mathbf{e} = 1$.

Let φ represent the initial probability vector of the underlying MAP-based Markov process. We have an independent arrival, the end of an interval with minimum k arrivals, and the moment at which the system enters or exits a certain state, such as when a busy period begins or ends, etc.; by choosing a suitable φ, we can obtain the kind of time. The main purpose is that we obtain the unique probability vector of MAP by $\varphi = \chi$. The average arrival rate $\lambda = \chi D_1 \mathbf{e}$ provides the mean number of customers occurring per unit time. The MAP-described point process is a special category of semi-Markov processes with a transition probability matrix provided by

$$\int_0^x e^{D_0 t} dt D_1 = [I - e^{D_0 x}](-D_0)^{-1} D_1, \ x \geq 0.$$

For more information on MAP, readers can refer to [21–23]. Table 1 summarizes the overview of literature review.

Table 1. Literature review overview.

Author(s)	Poisson Arrivals	MAP Arrivals	Joint Replenishment	Optional Demand	Exponentially Distributed Lead Time	Perishable Inventory
Balintfy [1]	✓		✓			
Silver [2]	✓		✓			
Krishnamoorthy [3]	✓				✓	
Anbazhagan [4]	✓		✓		✓	
Anbazhagan [5]	✓		✓		✓	
Anbazhagan [6]	✓		✓		✓	
Karthikeyan [7]	✓					✓
Krishnamoorthy [8]	✓					
Sivakumar [9]	✓		✓		✓	✓
Benny [10]	✓					
Ozkar [11]		✓	✓	✓	✓	
Senthil Kumar [12]	✓					

Table 1. Cont.

Author(s)	Poisson Arrivals	MAP Arrivals	Joint Replenishment	Optional Demand	Exponentially Distributed Lead Time	Perishable Inventory
Sinu Lal [13]	✓				✓	
Senthil Kumar [14]	✓		✓			
Yadavalli [15]	✓	✓				✓
Nahmias [16]						✓
Murthy [17]				✓		
Uzunoglu Kocer [18]	✓			✓	✓	✓
Jacob [19]		✓		✓	✓	
Lucantoni [20]		✓				
Latouche [21]		✓				
Lee [22]		✓				
Chakravarthy [23]		✓				
This paper		✓	✓	✓	✓	✓

✓ Factors included in the research.

The findings of the above survey inspired our research, since, to our knowledge, there has been little study into two commodities with three forms of service, which is a common occurrence in business administration. Section 2 discusses the detailed description of our model. In Section 3, we provide an analysis of our prescriptive model. Analysis of the model's steady-state is described in Section 4. In Section 5, we develop several aspects of system performance for the steady-state case. In Section 6, the total expected cost rate (TCR) is calculated. In Section 7, numerical examples are provided.

2. Model Narrations

A two-commodity perishable queueing-inventory system is considered. The system has a maximum capacity of S_1 items for the first commodity, and S_2 items for the second commodity. The system provides the finite waiting room size of F along with one getting service. The customers show up as per MAP, with demand for a single unit. A single item of the first commodity is required by the customer (i.e., a high quality and high price item) with probability b_1 or the second commodity (i.e., a normal quality and cheap price item) with probability b_2 or service only with probability b_3. The server's service is the same for each demand. With parameter $b_i \mu$, $(i = 1, 2, 3)$, three different kinds of service times are exponentially distributed. We take the parameter γ_1 as the lifetime of the first commodity and γ_2 for the second commodity follows an exponential distribution. If both stock levels are close to their respective reorder levels $s_i (i = 1, 2)$, then an order is made for both commodities. $Q_i (> s_i, i = 1, 2)$ units are considered the ordering quantity for the i-th commodity. The lead time follows an exponential distribution with parameter $\beta (>0)$. The customer arrives during a stock-out period and the full system is considered to be lost. Customers leave the system after receiving the required service performances of the item.

3. Analysis

We consider $I^{(1)}(t)$ to represent the number of items in the first commodity at time t, $I^{(2)}(t)$ to represent the number of items in the second commodity at time t, $N(t)$ to represent the number of customers in the system at time t and $J(t)$ to represent the phase of the arrival process at time t. The Markov process $\left\{ \left(I^{(1)}(t), I^{(2)}(t), N(t), J(t) \right); t \geq 0 \right\}$ with discrete state space $\mathbf{E} = E_1 \times E_2 \times E_3 \times E_4$, where $0 \leq E_1 \leq S_1$, $0 \leq E_2 \leq S_2$, $0 \leq E_3 \leq F$, $1 \leq E_4 \leq y$.

The infinitesimal generator matrix $[\mathbb{W}]_{ij} = \begin{cases} \mathbb{O}_i, & j = i \times 1, & i = 1, 2, \ldots S_1 \\ \mathbb{P}_i, & j = i, & i = 0, 1, \ldots S_1 \\ \mathbb{R}, & j = i + Q_1, & i = 0, 1, \ldots s_1 \\ 0, & \text{otherwise} \end{cases}$

where
$[\mathbb{R}]_{kl} = \begin{cases} \beta I_Z \otimes I_y, & l = k + Q_2, \quad k = 0, 1, \ldots s_2, \\ 0, & \text{otherwise.} \end{cases}$

where, $Z = F + 1$

Here, $i = 1, 2, \ldots S_1$ and $A_Z = [a_{ij}]_{Z \times Z} = \begin{cases} 1, & \text{if } j = i - 1, i = 1, 2, \ldots F \\ 0, & \text{otherwise} \end{cases}$

$[\mathbb{O}_i]_{kl} = \begin{cases} (i\gamma_1 I_Z + b_1 \mu A_Z) \otimes I_y, & l = k, \quad k = 0, 1, \ldots S_2, \\ 0, & \text{otherwise.} \end{cases}$

Here, $B_Z = [b_{ij}]_{Z \times Z} = \begin{cases} 1, & \text{if } j = i + 1, i = 0, 1, \ldots F - 1 \\ 0, & \text{otherwise} \end{cases}$

$C_Z = [c_{ij}]_{Z \times Z} = \begin{cases} 1, & \text{if } j = i, i = F \\ 0, & \text{otherwise} \end{cases}$

$G_Z = [g_{ij}]_{Z \times Z} = \begin{cases} 1, & \text{if } j = i, i = 0, 1, \ldots F - 1 \\ 0, & \text{otherwise} \end{cases}$

$H_Z = [h_{ij}]_{Z \times Z} = \begin{cases} 1, & \text{if } j = i, i = 1, 2, \ldots F \\ 0, & \text{otherwise} \end{cases}$

For $i = 0$,

$[\mathbb{P}_i]_{kl} = \begin{cases} (k\gamma_2 I_Z + b_2 \mu A_Z) \otimes I_y, & l = k - 1, \ k = 1, 2, \ldots S_2, \\ (b_3 \mu A_Z \otimes I_y) + (B_Z \otimes D_1) + (((G_Z \otimes D_0) \\ \quad + (C_Z \otimes D)) - ((I_Z \otimes \beta I_y) + (H_Z \otimes (b_3\mu)I_y))), & l = k, k = 0, \\ (b_3 \mu A_Z \otimes I_y) + (B_Z \otimes D_1) + (((G_Z \otimes D_0) + (C_Z \otimes D)) \\ \quad - ((I_Z \otimes (\beta + k\gamma_2)I_y) + (H_Z \otimes (b_3\mu + b_2\mu)I_y))), & l = k, k = 1, 2, \ldots s_2, \\ (b_3 \mu A_Z \otimes I_y) + (B_Z \otimes D_1) + (((G_Z \otimes D_0) + (C_Z \otimes D)) \\ \quad - ((I_Z \otimes (k\gamma_2)I_y) + (H_Z \otimes (b_3\mu + b_2\mu)I_y))), & l = k, \\ & k = s_2 + 1, s_2 + 2, \ldots S_2, \\ 0, & \text{otherwise.} \end{cases}$

For $i = 1, 2, \ldots s_1$,

$[\mathbb{P}_i]_{kl} = \begin{cases} (k\gamma_2 I_Z + b_2 \mu A_Z) \otimes I_y, & l = k - 1, \\ & k = 1, 2, \ldots S_2, \\ (b_3 \mu A_Z \otimes I_y) + (B_Z \otimes D_1) + (((G_Z \otimes D_0) + (C_Z \otimes D)) \\ \quad - ((I_Z \otimes (\beta + i\gamma_1)I_y) + (H_Z \otimes (b_3\mu + b_1\mu)I_y))), & l = k, k = 0, \\ (b_3 \mu A_Z \otimes I_y) + (B_Z \otimes D_1) + (((G_Z \otimes D_0) + (C_Z \otimes D)) \\ \quad - ((I_Z \otimes (\beta + i\gamma_1 + k\gamma_2)I_y) + (H_Z \otimes (b_3\mu + b_1\mu + b_2\mu)I_y))), & l = k, \\ & k = 1, 2, \ldots s_2, \\ (b_3 \mu A_Z \otimes I_y) + (B_Z \otimes D_1) + (((G_Z \otimes D_0) + (C_Z \otimes D)) \\ \quad - ((I_Z \otimes (i\gamma_1 + k\gamma_2)I_y) + (H_Z \otimes (b_3\mu + b_1\mu + b_2\mu)I_y))), & l = k, \\ & k = s_2 + 1, \ldots S_2, \\ 0, & \text{otherwise.} \end{cases}$

For $i = s_1 + 1, \ldots S_1$,

$$[\mathbb{P}_i]_{kl} = \begin{cases} (k\gamma_2 I_Z + b_2\mu A_Z) \otimes I_y, & l = k-1, \\ & k = 1, 2, \ldots S_2, \\ (b_3\mu A_Z \otimes I_y) + (B_Z \otimes D_1) + (((G_Z \otimes D_0) + (C_Z \otimes D)) \\ \quad - ((I_Z \otimes (i\gamma_1)I_y) + (H_Z \otimes (b_3\mu + b_1\mu)I_y))), & l = k, k = 0, \\ (b_3\mu A_Z \otimes I_y) + (B_Z \otimes D_1) + (((G_Z \otimes D_0) + (C_Z \otimes D)) \\ \quad - ((I_Z \otimes (i\gamma_1 + k\gamma_2)I_y) + (H_Z \otimes (b_3\mu + b_1\mu + b_2\mu)I_y))), & l = k, \\ & k = 1, 2, \ldots S_2, \\ 0, & \text{otherwise.} \end{cases}$$

4. Steady State Analysis

From the structure of $\mathbb{W}$, the Markov process $\left\{I^{(1)}(t), I^{(2)}(t), N(t), J(t); t \geq 0\right\}$ on the state space $\mathbf{E}$ is irreducible, and the limiting distribution $Y(i_1, i_2, i_3, i_4) = \lim_{t \to \infty} Pr[I^{(1)}(t) = i_1, I^{(2)}(t) = i_2, N(t) = i_3, J(t) = i_4; I^{(1)}(0), I^{(2)}(0), N(0), J(0)]$, exists.

The limiting distribution $Y(i_1, i_2, i_3, i_4)$ is independent of the starting condition. Take

$$\begin{aligned} \mathbf{Y} &= (\mathbf{Y}(0), \mathbf{Y}(1), \ldots, \mathbf{Y}(S_1)), \\ \text{where } \mathbf{Y}(i_1) &= (\mathbf{Y}(i_1, 0), \mathbf{Y}(i_1, 1), \ldots, \mathbf{Y}(i_1, S_2)), i_1 = 0, 1, \ldots, S_1 \\ \mathbf{Y}(i_1, i_2) &= (\mathbf{Y}(i_1, i_2, 0), \mathbf{Y}(i_1, i_2, 1), \ldots, \mathbf{Y}(i_1, i_2, F)), i_2 = 0, 1, \ldots, S_2 \\ \mathbf{Y}(i_1, i_2, i_3) &= (\mathbf{Y}(i_1, i_2, i_3, 1), \mathbf{Y}(i_1, i_2, i_3, 2), \ldots, \mathbf{Y}(i_1, i_2, i_3, y)), i_3 = 0, 1, \ldots, F \end{aligned}$$

The steady-state probability vector $\mathbf{Y}$ obtained from $\mathbf{Y}\mathbb{W} = 0$, $\mathbf{Y}\mathbf{e} = 1$.

Theorem 1. *The steady-state probability vector $\mathbf{Y}$ for the Markov process whose rate matrix $\mathbb{W}$ is given by*

$$\mathbf{Y}(i_1) = \mathbf{Y}(Q_1)\Omega_{i_1}, \quad i_1 = 0, 1, \ldots, S_1$$

where

$$\Omega_{i_1} = \begin{cases} (-1)^{Q_1 - i_1} \mathbb{O}_{Q_1} \mathbb{P}_{Q_1 - 1}^{-1} \mathbb{O}_{Q_1 - 1} \ldots \mathbb{O}_{i_1 + 1} \mathbb{P}_{i_1}^{-1}, & i_1 = 0, 1 \ldots, Q_1 - 1; \\ I, & i_1 = Q_1; \\ (-1)^{2Q_1 - i_1 + 1} \sum_{j=0}^{S_1 - i_1} \left\{ (\mathbb{O}_{Q_1} \mathbb{P}_{Q_1 - 1}^{-1} \mathbb{O}_{Q_1 - 1} \ldots \mathbb{O}_{s_1 + 1 - j} \mathbb{P}_{s_1 - j}^{-1}) \\ \mathbb{RP}_{S_1 - j}^{-1} (\mathbb{O}_{S_1 - j} \mathbb{P}_{S_1 - j - 1}^{-1} \mathbb{O}_{S_1 - j - 1} \ldots \mathbb{O}_{i_1 + 1} \mathbb{P}_{i_1}^{-1}) \right\}, & i_1 = Q_1 + 1, \ldots, S_1; \end{cases}$$

The following two equations can be used to arrive to $\mathbf{Y}(Q_1)$:

$$(i.e)\mathbf{Y}(Q_1)\left((-1)^{Q_1}\sum_{j=0}^{s_1-1}(\mathbb{O}_{Q_1}\mathbb{P}_{Q_1-1}^{-1}\mathbb{O}_{Q_1-1}\ldots \mathbb{O}_{s_1+1-j}\mathbb{P}_{s_1-j}^{-1})\mathbb{RP}_{S_1-j}^{-1}\right.$$

$$(\mathbb{O}_{S_1-j}\mathbb{P}_{S_1-j-1}^{-1}\mathbb{O}_{S_1-j-1}\ldots \mathbb{O}_{Q_1+2}\mathbb{P}_{Q_1+1}^{-1})\mathbb{O}_{Q_1+1} + \mathbb{P}_{Q_1} +$$

$$\left.\left\{(-1)^{Q_1}\mathbb{O}_{Q_1}\mathbb{P}_{Q_1-1}^{-1}\mathbb{O}_{Q_1-1}\ldots \mathbb{O}_1 \mathbb{P}_0^{-1}\right\}\mathbb{R}\right) = 0$$

and

$$\mathbf{Y}(Q_1)\left(\sum_{i_1=0}^{Q_1-1}\left\{(-1)^{Q_1-i_1}\mathbb{O}_{Q_1}\mathbb{P}_{Q_1-1}^{-1}\mathbb{O}_{Q_1-1}\ldots \mathbb{O}_{i_1+1}\mathbb{P}_{i_1}^{-1}\right\} + I + \right.$$

$$\sum_{i_1=Q_1+1}^{S_1}\left\{(-1)^{2Q_1-i_1+1}\sum_{j=0}^{S_1-i_1}\left\{(\mathbb{O}_{Q_1}\mathbb{P}_{Q_1-1}^{-1}\mathbb{O}_{Q_1-1}\ldots \mathbb{O}_{s_1+1-j}\mathbb{P}_{s_1-j}^{-1})\right.\right.$$

$$\left.\left.\left.\mathbb{RP}_{S_1-j}^{-1}(\mathbb{O}_{S_1-j}\mathbb{P}_{S_1-j-1}^{-1}\mathbb{O}_{S_1-j-1}\ldots \mathbb{O}_{i_1+1}\mathbb{P}_{i_1}^{-1})\right\}\right\}\right)\mathbf{e} = 1$$

Proof. We know that
$$\mathbf{YW} = 0 \text{ and } \mathbf{Ye} = 1.$$

The equation $\mathbf{YW} = 0$ can be written as

$$\begin{aligned}
\mathbf{Y}(i_1+1)\mathbb{O}_{i_1+1} + \mathbf{Y}(i_1)\mathbb{P}_{i_1} &= 0, i_1 = 0, 1, \ldots Q_1 - 1 \\
\mathbf{Y}(i_1+1)\mathbb{O}_{i_1+1} + \mathbf{Y}(i_1)\mathbb{P}_{i_1} + \mathbf{Y}(i_1-Q_1)\mathbb{R} &= 0, i_1 = Q_1 \\
\mathbf{Y}(i_1+1)\mathbb{O}_{i_1+1} + \mathbf{Y}(i_1)\mathbb{P}_{i_1} + \mathbf{Y}(i_1-Q_1)\mathbb{R} &= 0, i_1 = Q_1+1, Q_1+2, \ldots S_1-1 \\
\mathbf{Y}(i_1)\mathbb{P}_{i_1} + \mathbf{Y}(i_1-Q_1)\mathbb{R} &= 0, i_1 = S_1.
\end{aligned} \quad (1)$$

The equations, except (1), can be solved recursively, yielding
$$\mathbf{Y}(i_1) = \mathbf{Y}(Q_1)\Omega_{i_1}, \quad i = 0, 1, \ldots, S_1$$

where

$$\Omega_{i_1} = \begin{cases}
(-1)^{Q_1-i_1}\mathbb{O}_{Q_1}\mathbb{P}_{Q_1-1}^{-1}\mathbb{O}_{Q_1-1}\ldots\mathbb{O}_{i_1+1}\mathbb{P}_{i_1}^{-1}, & i_1 = 0, 1\ldots, Q_1-1; \\
I, & i_1 = Q_1; \\
(-1)^{2Q_1-i_1+1}\sum\limits_{j=0}^{S_1-i_1}\{(\mathbb{O}_{Q_1}\mathbb{P}_{Q_1-1}^{-1}\mathbb{O}_{Q_1-1}\ldots\mathbb{O}_{s_1+1-j}\mathbb{P}_{s_1-j}^{-1}) & \\
\mathbb{RP}_{S_1-j}^{-1}(\mathbb{O}_{S_1-j}\mathbb{P}_{S_1-j-1}^{-1}\mathbb{O}_{S_1-j-1}\ldots\mathbb{O}_{i_1+1}\mathbb{P}_{i_1}^{-1})\}, & i_1 = Q_1+1, \ldots, S_1;
\end{cases}$$

After placing the value of Ω_{i_1} in (1) and in the normalizing condition, we acquire $\mathbf{Y}(Q_1)$

$$(i.e)\mathbf{Y}(Q_1)\left((-1)^{Q_1}\sum_{j=0}^{s_1-1}(\mathbb{O}_{Q_1}\mathbb{P}_{Q_1-1}^{-1}\mathbb{O}_{Q_1-1}\ldots\mathbb{O}_{s_1+1-j}\mathbb{P}_{s_1-j}^{-1})\mathbb{RP}_{S_1-j}^{-1}\right.$$
$$(\mathbb{O}_{S_1-j}\mathbb{P}_{S_1-j-1}^{-1}\mathbb{O}_{S_1-j-1}\ldots\mathbb{O}_{Q_1+2}\mathbb{P}_{Q_1+1}^{-1})\mathbb{O}_{Q_1+1} + \mathbb{P}_{Q_1} +$$
$$\left.\left\{(-1)^{Q_1}\mathbb{O}_{Q_1}\mathbb{P}_{Q_1-1}^{-1}\mathbb{O}_{Q_1-1}\ldots\mathbb{O}_1\mathbb{P}_0^{-1}\right\}\mathbb{R}\right) = 0$$

and

$$\mathbf{Y}(Q_1)\left(\sum_{i_1=0}^{Q_1-1}\left\{(-1)^{Q_1-i_1}\mathbb{O}_{Q_1}\mathbb{P}_{Q_1-1}^{-1}\mathbb{O}_{Q_1-1}\ldots\mathbb{O}_{i_1+1}\mathbb{P}_{i_1}^{-1}\right\} + I + \right.$$
$$\left.\sum_{i_1=Q_1+1}^{S_1}\left\{(-1)^{2Q_1-i_1+1}\sum_{j=0}^{S_1-i_1}\left\{(\mathbb{O}_{Q_1}\mathbb{P}_{Q_1-1}^{-1}\mathbb{O}_{Q_1-1}\ldots\mathbb{O}_{s_1+1-j}\mathbb{P}_{s_1-j}^{-1})\right.\right.\right.$$
$$\left.\left.\left.\mathbb{RP}_{S_1-j}^{-1}(\mathbb{O}_{S_1-j}\mathbb{P}_{S_1-j-1}^{-1}\mathbb{O}_{S_1-j-1}\ldots\mathbb{O}_{i_1+1}\mathbb{P}_{i_1}^{-1})\right\}\right\}\right)\mathbf{e} = 1$$

□

5. System Performance Measures

In this division, we surmise a few performance measures in the system.

5.1. Mean Inventory Level

Let $M^{I^{(1)}}$ and $M^{I^{(2)}}$ be the mean inventory levels of the first and second commodities, respectively, in a steady state, which can be expressed as

$$M^{I^{(1)}} = \sum_{i_1=1}^{S_1} i_1 \left(\sum_{i_2=0}^{S_2}\sum_{i_3=0}^{F} \mathbf{Y}(i_1, i_2, i_3)\right)\mathbf{e}$$

$$M^{I^{(2)}} = \sum_{i_2=1}^{S_2} i_2 \left(\sum_{i_1=0}^{S_1} \sum_{i_3=0}^{F} Y(i_1, i_2, i_3) \right) \mathbf{e}$$

5.2. Mean Reorder Rate

In a stable state, the M^R represents the mean reorder rate. The joint inventory level decreases to (s_1, s_2) or $(s_1, i_2), i_2 < s_2$ or $(i_1, s_2), i_1 < s_1$ if once service is performed, or if any of the $(s_i + 1), i = 1, 2$ items are perishable.

$$M^R = (s_1 + 1)\gamma_1 \sum_{i_2=0}^{S_2} \sum_{i_3=0}^{F} Y(s_1+1, i_2, i_3)\mathbf{e} + (s_2+1)\gamma_2 \sum_{i_1=0}^{S_1} \sum_{i_3=0}^{F} Y(i_1, s_2+1, i_3)\mathbf{e}$$
$$+ b_1\mu \sum_{i_3=1}^{F} \sum_{i_2=0}^{S_2} Y(s_1+1, i_2, i_3)\mathbf{e} + b_2\mu \sum_{i_3=1}^{F} \sum_{i_1=0}^{S_1} Y(i_1, s_2+1, i_3)\mathbf{e}.$$

5.3. Mean Perishable Rate

Let M^{P_1} and M^{P_2} be the mean perishable rates of the first and second commodity, respectively, in a steady state and are given by

$$M^{P_1} = \sum_{i_1=1}^{S_1} \sum_{i_2=0}^{S_2} \sum_{i_3=0}^{F} i_1 \gamma_1 Y(i_1, i_2, i_3)\mathbf{e}$$

$$M^{P_2} = \sum_{i_1=0}^{S_1} \sum_{i_2=1}^{S_2} \sum_{i_3=0}^{F} i_2 \gamma_2 Y(i_1, i_2, i_3)\mathbf{e}.$$

6. Cost Analysis

For the total expected cost function per unit time, we have evaluated the cost aspects listed below.

C^{C_i}: Carrying cost of i-th commodity per unit time ($i = 1, 2$)
C^S: Setup cost per order
C^{P_1}: First-commodity perishable cost per item per unit time
C^{P_2}: Second-commodity perishable cost per item per unit time

The total expected cost function is given by

$$TC(S_1, s_1, S_2, s_2, F) = C^{C_1} M^{I^{(1)}} + C^{C_2} M^{I^{(2)}} + C^S M^R + C^{P_1} M^{P_1} + C^{P_2} M^{P_2}$$

where $M^{I^{(i)}}$, M^R and M^{P_i} ($i = 1, 2$) are given in Section 5.

7. Numerical Illustration

The convexity of the TCR is demonstrated using numerical examples. We presume the below numerical example: The arrival process is hyper-exponential. As a MAP, its parameters are given by (D_0, D_1) where

$$D_0 = \begin{pmatrix} -10 & 0 \\ 0 & -1 \end{pmatrix} \text{ and } D_1 = \begin{pmatrix} 9 & 1 \\ 0.9 & 0.1 \end{pmatrix}$$

Let $F = 6, s_1 = 3, s_2 = 2, \beta = 0.45, \mu = 1.6, \gamma_1 = 0.7, \gamma_2 = 0.5, b_1 = 0.4, b_2 = 0.32, b_3 = 0.28$; $C^{C_1} = 1.4, C^{C_2} = 1.35, C^{P_1} = 1.28, C^{P_2} = 2.7, C^S = 1$;

Furthermore, let $TC'(S_1, S_2) = TC(S_1, 3, S_2, 2, 6)$.

This gives the expected cost rate for different values of S_1 and of S_2.

In Table 2, we present the $TC'(S_1, S_2)$ values. Here, the row minimum is represented in boldface and the column minimum is underlined. A convex function of (S_1, S_2) is $TC'(S_1, S_2)$, and the optimum at $(S_1, S_2) = (21, 16)$.

Table 2. TCR as a function of S_1 and S_2.

S_1/S_2	13	14	15	16	17
20	0.95816	0.93312	0.91461	**0.91429**	0.99542
21	0.93239	0.78797	0.66773	**0.56698**	0.68216
22	0.92900	0.86021	0.85043	**0.84890**	0.90087
23	0.98022	0.94679	0.90740	**0.90105**	0.90133
24	1.10383	0.96021	**0.94100**	1.48230	1.49438

Let $S_2 = 12$, $s_1 = 2$, $s_2 = 1$, $\beta = 1.4$, $\mu = 1.7$, $\gamma_1 = 1.01$, $\gamma_2 = 0.05$, $b_1 = 0.4$, $b_2 = 0.32$, $b_3 = 0.28$; $C^{C_1} = 1.1$, $C^{C_2} = 0.35$, $C^{P_1} = 1.28$, $C^{P_2} = 2.78$, $C^S = 1.76$;
Furthermore, let $TC'(S_1, F) = TC(S_1, 2, 12, 1, F)$.
This provides the TCR for different values of S_1 and of F.
In Table 3, we present the $TC'(S_1, F)$ values. Here, the row minimum is represented in boldface and the column minimum is underlined. A convex function of (S_1, F) is $TC'(S_1, F)$, and the optimum at $(S_1, F) = (7, 6)$.

Table 3. TCR as a function of S_1 and F.

S_1/F	5	6	7	8	9
5	0.8065	0.7642	**0.7512**	1.1471	1.3590
6	0.7631	**0.6991**	0.7172	1.1319	1.3489
7	0.8025	**0.6944**	0.7081	1.1281	1.3487
8	0.8277	**0.7062**	0.7073	1.1225	1.3438
9	0.8376	0.7136	**0.7114**	1.1232	1.3430
10	0.8413	0.7165	**0.7137**	1.1246	1.3434
11	0.8426	0.7176	**0.7146**	1.1254	1.3439

Let $S_1 = 6$, $s_1 = 2$, $s_2 = 3$, $\beta = 1.4$, $\mu = 1.7$, $\gamma_1 = 1.01$, $\gamma_2 = 0.05$, $b_1 = 0.4$, $b_2 = 0.32$, $b_3 = 0.28$; $C^{C_1} = 1.1$, $C^{C_2} = 0.35$, $C^{P_1} = 1.13$, $C^{P_2} = 2.78$, $C^S = 2.5$;
Furthermore, let $TC'(S_2, F) = TC(6, 2, S_2, 3, F)$.
This provides the TCR for different values of S_2 and of F.
The $TC'(S_2, F)$ values are presented in Table 4. The optimal cost for each S_2 and F are displayed in boldface and underlined, respectively. A convex function of (S_2, F) is $TC'(S_2, F)$, and the optimum takes place at $(S_2, F) = (13, 8)$.

Table 4. TCR as a function of S_2 and F.

S_2/F	5	6	7	8	9
12	0.76205	0.72886	0.72567	**0.71925**	0.84315
13	0.69172	0.63563	0.63280	**0.58965**	0.61770
14	0.73478	0.65798	0.64908	**0.59718**	0.61275
15	0.81303	0.69213	0.66818	**0.60717**	0.62222
16	0.81599	0.76243	0.73614	**0.71850**	0.73127

Let $F = 4$, $S_2 = 18$, $s_2 = 2$, $\beta = 0.3$, $\mu = 1.7$, $\gamma_1 = 1.01$, $\gamma_2 = 0.05$, $b_1 = 0.4$, $b_2 = 0.32$, $b_3 = 0.28$; $C^{C_1} = 1.09$, $C^{C_2} = 0.35$, $C^{P_1} = 1.28$, $C^{P_2} = 2.78$, $C^S = 1.77$;
Furthermore, let $TC'(S_1, s_1) = TC(S_1, s_1, 18, 2, 4)$.
This provides the TCR for different values of S_1 and of s_1.

In Table 5, we present the $TC'(S_1, s_1)$ values. Here, the row minimum is represented in boldface and the column minimum is underlined. A convex function of (S_1, s_1) is $TC'(S_1, s_1)$, and the optimum takes place at $(S_1, s_1) = (19, 5)$.

Table 5. TCR as a function of S_1 and s_1.

S_1/s_1	2	3	4	5	6	7	8
18	0.67208	0.66955	0.65955	0.65436	0.65222	**0.65190**	0.65216
19	0.65650	0.65287	0.65073	**0.64893**	0.64894	0.65007	0.65168
20	0.66838	**0.65296**	0.65385	0.65768	0.66257	0.66786	0.67321
21	0.70294	0.70154	**0.66367**	0.66487	0.67006	0.68021	0.69014
22	0.78844	0.77510	0.76728	0.76571	**0.68173**	0.68243	0.69431

Let $F = 5$, $S_1 = 12$, $s_1 = 2$, $\beta = 0.37$, $\mu = 0.3$, $\gamma_1 = 1.01$, $\gamma_2 = 0.05$, $b_1 = 0.4$, $b_2 = 0.32$, $b_3 = 0.28$; $C^{C_1} = 1.1$, $C^{C_2} = 0.35$, $C^{P_1} = 1.28$, $C^{P_2} = 2.78$, $C^S = 1.77$;
Furthermore, let $TC'(S_2, s_2) = TC(12, 2, S_2, s_2, 5)$.
This provides the TCR for different values of S_2 and of s_2.
The $TC'(S_2, s_2)$ values are presented in Table 6. The optimal cost for each S_2 and s_2 are displayed in boldface and underlined, respectively. A convex function of (S_2, s_2) is $TC'(S_2, s_2)$, and the optimum takes place at $(S_2, s_2) = (16, 3)$.

Table 6. TCR as a function of S_2 and s_2.

S_2/s_2	2	3	4	5	6
15	0.58260	**0.57920**	0.57942	0.58109	0.59306
16	0.58204	**0.57138**	0.57226	0.58004	0.58615
17	0.58123	0.58038	0.58045	0.59580	0.60113
18	0.59235	0.58550	0.58857	0.59855	0.60828
19	0.67502	0.59628	0.59979	0.60156	0.60891

The impact of the second commodity perishable rate (γ_2) on the TCR is shown in Figure 1 via three curves which relate to $\gamma_1 = 1, 1.03, 1.05$. We discovered that the TCR diminishes whenever the perishable rate of the first commodity (γ_1) and the perishable rate of the second commodity (γ_2) increase.

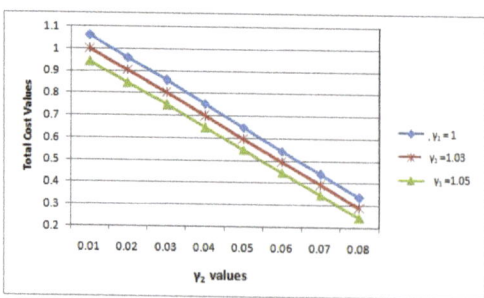

Figure 1. TC versus γ_2. $S_1 = 19$, $S_2 = 18$, $F = 4$, $s_1 = 5$, $s_2 = 2$, $\beta = 0.3$, $\mu = 1.7$, $\alpha = 0.01$; $b_1 = 0.4$, $b_2 = 0.32$, $b_3 = 0.28$, $C^{C_1} = 1.09$, $C^{C_2} = 0.35$, $C^{P_1} = 1.28$, $C^{P_2} = 2.78$, $C^S = 1.77$.

The outcome of the replenishment rate (β) on the TCR is depicted in Figure 2 via three curves which relate to (μ) = 1.75, 1.8, 1.85. We discovered that the TCR diminishes whenever the service rate (μ) and the replenishment rate (β) increase.

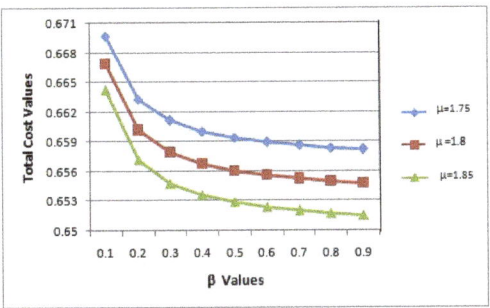

Figure 2. TC versus μ. $S_1 = 19$, $S_2 = 18$, $F = 4$, $s_1 = 5$, $s_2 = 2$, $\gamma_1 = 1.01$, $\gamma_2 = 0.05$, $\alpha = 0.01$; $b_1 = 0.4$, $b_2 = 0.32$, $b_3 = 0.28$, $C^{C_1} = 1.09$, $C^{C_2} = 0.35$, $C^{P_1} = 1.28$, $C^{P_2} = 2.78$, $C^S = 1.77$.

In Tables 7–9, we demonstrate the outcome of the setup cost C^S and the carrying cost of the first commodity C^{C_1}, and, similarly, the second commodity C^{C_2} on the optimal point (S_1^*, s_1^*) and the corresponding TCR TC'. The other parameters and cost values are $S_1 = 19$, $S_2 = 18$, $F = 4$, $s_1 = 5$, $s_2 = 2$, $\gamma_1 = 1.01$, $\gamma_2 = 0.05$, $\alpha = 0.01$; $b_1 = 0.4$, $b_2 = 0.32$, $b_3 = 0.28$, $C^{C_1} = 1.09$, $C^{C_2} = 0.35$, $C^{P_1} = 1.28$, $C^{P_2} = 2.78$, $C^S = 1.77$;

Table 7. Impact of C^{C_1} and C^{C_2} costs on the optimal values.

C^{C_1}/C^{C_2}	0.33		0.34		0.35		0.36		0.37	
	21	5	21	5	21	5	21	5	21	5
1.07	0.50896		0.54967		0.59039		0.63110		0.67181	
	21	5	21	5	21	5	19	5	19	5
1.08	0.54520		0.58592		0.62663		0.66310		0.69720	
	19	5	19	5	19	5	19	5	19	5
1.09	0.58074		0.61483		0.64893		0.68303		0.71713	
	15	5	15	5	15	5	15	5	15	5
1.10	0.60066		0.63476		0.70296		0.73706		0.76484	
	15	5	15	5	15	5	15	4	15	4
1.11	0.64349		0.71233		0.72289		0.78482		0.81679	

Table 8. Impact of C^{C_1} and C^S costs on the optimal values.

C^{C_1}/C^S	1.75		1.76		1.77		1.78		1.79	
	20	5	20	5	20	5	20	5	20	5
1.07	0.59257		0.59342		0.59426		0.59510		0.59594	
	20	5	20	5	20	5	20	5	20	5
1.08	0.62292		0.62377		0.62461		0.63245		0.64230	
	20	5	20	5	19	5	19	5	19	5
1.09	0.63327		0.63412		0.64893		0.66241		0.67195	
	19	5	15	5	15	5	15	5	15	5
1.10	0.68520		0.68919		0.69501		0.69591		0.69821	
	18	5	15	5	15	5	15	4	15	4
1.11	0.68663		0.69770		0.69877		0.69950		0.70116	

Table 9. Impact of C^{C_2} and C^S costs on the optimal values.

C^{C_2}/C^S	1.75		1.76		1.77		1.78		1.79	
0.33	20	6	20	6	20	6	20	6	20	5
	0.57182		0.57566		0.57950		0.58934		0.59919	
0.34	20	5	20	5	20	5	20	5	20	5
	0.61555		0.61629		0.61723		0.62607		0.62692	
0.35	19	5	19	5	19	5	19	5	19	5
	0.65187		0.65578		0.64893		0.66758		0.67748	
0.36	19	5	15	5	15	5	15	5	15	5
	0.69012		0.69336		0.70359		0.71081		0.73876	
0.37	18	5	15	5	15	5	15	4	15	4
	0.73502		0.75162		0.78509		0.79530		0.79741	

From the Tables 7–9, we discover the monotonic behavior of (S_1^*, s_1^*) as detailed below:

In Table 7, the TCR increases whenever both the carrying cost of the first commodity C^{C_1} and the second commodity C^{C_2} increases. In Table 8, the TCR increases when the carrying cost of the first commodity C^{C_1} and C^S both increase. Similarly, Table 9 shows that the TCR increases whenever the carrying cost of the second commodity C^{C_2} and C^S both increase. In addition, (S_1^*, s_1^*) monotonically decrease for all the Tables 7–9. The carrying cost, as well as the set-up cost, are components of the TC function, so, whenever the holding cost and setup cost increase, the total cost value also increases.

Furthermore, acquiring a significant amount of inventory increases a company's carrying costs, whereas ordering smaller amounts of items more regularly increases a company's setup costs. However, we want to minimize both costs so the TC is determined to do this work.

8. Conclusions

In this article, we studied a two-commodity inventory system that consists of a finite waiting hall. We investigated performance analyses of a perishable (s, Q) queueing-inventory system of two commodities with optional demands from customers. To obtain either a single item or only service without items, customer arrivals are analyzed using the MAP. We also obtained a steady-state vector. Furthermore, the outcomes were exemplified with numerical patterns to determine the convexity of the TCR. Similarly, we provided a numerical illustration that depicts the effect of the service rate on the inventory system's TCR. In the numerical illustration, it is shown that the TCR diminishes because the service rates and replenishment rates are increased. The model describes the contribution of customers' optional demands to the two-commodity system. We believe that the model portrayed and the investigation described have implications for a range of modern organisations since there are various kinds of customer demands, such as service requests without items. In the future, our proposed model can be used to explore more conditions, such as service and lead times under PH distribution, to assess whether customer arrivals might follow a batch Markovian arrival process, and to determine whether the server might also work under a vacation policy.

Author Contributions: Conceptualization, N.A.; data curation, R.S. and V.V.; formal analysis, N.A. and S.A.; funding acquisition, G.P.J. and B.S.; methodology, R.S.; project administration, B.S.; resources, B.S.; software, V.V.; supervision, G.P.J. and B.S.; validation, S.A.; writing—original draft, N.A.; writing—review and editing, G.P.J. All authors have read and agreed to the published version of the manuscript.

Funding: The present research has been conducted by the Research Grant of Kwangwoon University in 2022.

Institutional Review Board Statement: Not applicable.

Informed Consent Statement: Not applicable.

Data Availability Statement: The data presented in this study are available within the article.

Acknowledgments: Anbazhagan and Amutha would like to thank RUSA Phase 2.0 (F 24-51/2014-U), DST-FIST (SR/FIST/MS-I/2018/17) and DST-PURSE 2nd Phase programme (SR/PURSE Phase 2/38), Govt. of India.

Conflicts of Interest: The authors declare no conflict of interest.

Notations

$\mathbf{0}$	Zero matrix with appropriate dimension.
e	Column vector of 1's with appropriate dimension.
I	Identity matrix of appropriate order.
$[\mathbb{W}]_{ij}$	Entry at (i,j)th position of a matrix $\mathbb{W}$.

References

1. Balintfy, J.L. On a basic class of multi-item inventory problems. *Manag. Sci.* **1964**, *10*, 287–297. [CrossRef]
2. Silver, E.A. A control system for coordinated inventory replenishment. *Int. J. Prod. Res.* **1974**, *12*, 647–671. [CrossRef]
3. Krishnamoorthy, A.; Iqbal Basha, R.; Lakshmy, B. Analysis of a two commodity inventory problem. *Inf. Manag. Sci.* **1994**, *5*, 127–136.
4. Anbazhagan, N.; Arivarignan, G. Analysis of two commodity Markovian inventory system with lead time. *Korean J. Comput. Appl. Math.* **2001**, *8*, 427–438. [CrossRef]
5. Anbazhagan, N.; Arivarignan, G.; Irle, A. A Two-commodity continuous review inventory system with substitutable items. *Stoch. Anal. Appl.* **2012**, *30*, 1–19. [CrossRef]
6. Anbazhagan, N.; Goh, M.; Vigneshwaran, B. Substitutable inventory systems with coordinated reorder levels. *J. Stat. Appl. Prob.* **2015**, *2*, 221–234.
7. Karthikeyan, K.; Sudhesh, R. Recent review article on queueing inventory systems. *Res. J. Pharm. Technol.* **2016**, *9*, 1451–1461. [CrossRef]
8. Krishnamoorthy, A.; Lakshmy, B.; Manikandan, R. A survey on inventory models with positive service time. *Opsearch* **2011**, *48*, 153–169. [CrossRef]
9. Sivakumar, B.; Anbazhagan, N.; Arivarignan, G. A two commodity perishable inventory system. *Orion* **2005**, *21*, 157–172. [CrossRef]
10. Benny, B.; Chakravarthy, S.R.; Krishnamoorthy, A. Queueing-Inventory System with Two Commodities. *J. Indian Soc. Probab. Stat.* **2018**, *19*, 437–454. [CrossRef]
11. Ozkar, S.; Uzunoglu Kocer, U. Two-commodity queueing-inventory system with two classes of customers. *Opsearch* **2020**, *58*, 234–256. [CrossRef]
12. Senthil Kumar, P. A finite source two commodity inventory system with retrial demands and multiple server vacation. *J. Phys. Conf. Ser.* **2021**, *1850*, 012101. [CrossRef]
13. Sinu Lal, T.S.; Joshua, V.C.; Vishnevsky, V.; Kozyrev, D.; Krishnamoorthy, A. A Multi-Type Queueing Inventory System: A Model for Selection and Allocation of Spectra. *Mathematics* **2022**, *10*, 714. [CrossRef]
14. Senthil Kumar, P.; Mayil Vaganan, B. Two commodity inventory system with variable ordering quantity. *AIP Conf. Proc.* **2020**, *2261*, 030026.
15. Yadavalli, V.S.S.; Adetunji, O.; Sivakumar, B.;Arivarignan, G. Two-commodity perishable inventory system with bulk demand for one commodity. *S. Afr. J. Ind. Eng.* **2010**, *21*, 137–155. [CrossRef]
16. Nahmias, S. *Perishable Inventory Systems*; Springer: New York, NY, USA, 2011.
17. Murthy, S.; Ramanarayanan, R. Two (s, S) Inventory Systems with Binary Choice of Demands and Optional Accessories with SCBZ Arrival Property. *Int. J. Contemp. Math. Sci.* **2009**, *4*, 397–417.
18. Kocer, U.U.; Yalcin, B. Continuous review (s, Q) inventory system with random lifetime and two demand classes. *Opsearch* **2020**, *57*, 104–118. [CrossRef]
19. Jacob, J.; Shajin, D.; Krishnamoorthy, A.; Vishnevsky, V.; Kozyrev, D. Queueing-Inventory with One Essential and m Optional Items with Environment Change Process Forming Correlated Renewal Process (MEP). *Mathematics* **2022**, *10*, 104. [CrossRef]
20. Lucantoni, D.M.; Meier-Hellstern, K.S.; Neuts, M.F. A Single Server Queue with Server Vacations and a Class of Non-renewal Arrival Processes. *Adv. Appl. Probab.* **1990**, *22*, 676–705. [CrossRef]
21. Latouche, G.; Ramaswami, V. *Introduction to Matrix Analytic Methods in Stochastic Modelling*; SIAM: Philadelphia, PA, USA, 1999.
22. Lee, G.; Jeon, J. A New Approach to an N/G/1 Queue. *Queueing Syst.* **2000**, *35*, 317–322. [CrossRef]
23. Chakravarthy, S.; Dudin, A. Analysis of a Retrial Queueing Model with MAP Arrivals and Two types of Customers. *Math. Comput. Model.* **2003**, *37*, 343–363. [CrossRef]

Review

Mathematical Modeling and Optimization of Platform Service Supply Chains: A Literature Review

Xiaotong Guo and Yong He *

School of Economics and Management, Southeast University, Nanjing 210096, China
* Correspondence: hy@seu.edu.cn

Abstract: With the increasing importance of the platform service supply chain (PSSC) in creating economic value, academic research is paying more and more attention to it. The current literature's research topics and problems cover broad areas. This review adopts bibliometric analysis and thematic analysis to review the related literature systematically and comprehensively. We divided the literature about PSSC into six groups according to the literature's research topic and research question. Each literature's research problem and research method are categorized and summarized. Our review results demonstrate that the supply chain's members' operational decisions and the supply chain's coordination are two main types of research questions. Pricing decisions have received the most attention. In terms of the research method, game models are the most common method used in research to achieve the optimization of the PSSC.

Keywords: platform; service supply chain; mathematical modeling; optimization

MSC: 00-02

Citation: Guo, X.; He, Y. Mathematical Modeling and Optimization of Platform Service Supply Chains: A Literature Review. *Mathematics* **2022**, *10*, 4307. https://doi.org/10.3390/math10224307

Academic Editor: Ripon Kumar Chakrabortty

Received: 31 October 2022
Accepted: 15 November 2022
Published: 17 November 2022

Publisher's Note: MDPI stays neutral with regard to jurisdictional claims in published maps and institutional affiliations.

Copyright: © 2022 by the authors. Licensee MDPI, Basel, Switzerland. This article is an open access article distributed under the terms and conditions of the Creative Commons Attribution (CC BY) license (https://creativecommons.org/licenses/by/4.0/).

1. Introduction

With the development of technology, innovation in the supply chain has developed rapidly and reached unprecedented heights [1]. Online platform services are the critical outcomes of innovation in the supply chain [1]. An increasing number of companies from different industries are joining online platforms or building their platforms to provide more value-added services for customers to obtain more profits. Platform modes have occupied all kinds of markets, like retail, tourism, accommodation, transportation, and so forth [2]. People become used to enjoying services like purchasing, ordering food, booking hotels, and sharing things with others through different platforms. The famous representatives include Alibaba.com, JD.com, Amazon.com, Airbnb, etc. [3]. Official statistics showed that the size of China's digital platform economy has surpassed USD 6 trillion in 2021. In this context, the platform economy has gained momentum, and supply-chain management has connected with it more closely [2].

With the increasing prevalence of platforms in the enterprise operation process, the platform service supply chain (PSSC) has become the mainstream of economic and social development. The commercial value and technological innovation promotion brought by PSSC has drawn a great deal of researchers' attention [2]. Many researchers studied firms' operation strategies under the platform mode and were concerned about different subjects' different decisions under various conditions. Meanwhile, some literature analyzed the dilemma and conflicts in the PSSC. Therefore, it is necessary to analyze and classify the research on the PSSC and to identify current research trends.

Some researchers have already conducted related reviews. Song et al. (2022) and Zhang and Zhao (2021) reviewed green and sustainable supply-chain management in platform economies [1,4]. Kuhzady et al. (2021) reviewed sharing platforms in hospitality and tourism [5]. Shroff et al. (2022) reviewed the development of online food delivery platforms and identified potential future research themes [6]. Although these papers have reviewed the PSSC-related studies, the majority of them only concerned one specific area. Furthermore, these reviews seldom paid attention to the research methods and mathematical models that papers used to conduct research. Unlike these reviews, we do not limit our review to one specific area but consider every area that PSSC covers, and we analyze the models that the paper used in research.

As noted briefly above, despite the academic community and researchers having a growing interest in PSSC, a systematic and organized overview of the current state of the literature is missing. Although some attempts have been made in this problem, their research content does not cover all of the extensive fields involved in the PSSC. Works specifically targeting PSSC are still unavailable. Secondly, owing that different research backgrounds require different approaches to mathematical modeling, the examination of research methods in PSSC is important, yet the extent reviews of PSSC only concentrated on research topics and research problems. The exact analytical models that the paper conducted are neglected by researchers.

In light of these premises, the purpose of this review is to identify what kinds of PSSC can be divided into. What problems are researchers concerned about in each area? What mathematical modeling methods were used to research? Were there research gaps? In order to answer these questions, we will adopt bibliometric analysis to conduct a quantitative analysis to identify the research trend of the PSSC. Meanwhile, the most researched keywords will be analyzed, too. After that, we will analyze the research content clearly by thematic analysis. The favorite PSSC sectors will be identified. The contributions of this review are as follows. First, to the best of our knowledge, this paper is the first to analyze and categorize research topics and research contents on the PSSC systematically and comprehensively. We reviewed broad areas that the PSSC covers. Secondly, we reviewed the mathematical modeling and optimization of the PSSC comprehensively, which few papers concerned. We identify the normal models that researchers used to analyze their research questions.

2. Methodology

In order to identify the research trend and emergent themes in PSSC nowadays, we conduct a bibliometric analysis first. Through the bibliometric analysis, we in-depth analyze the correlations among papers and keywords and conduct a quantitative analysis of the literature of the PSSC to identify the research status. To answer the questions of what research problems researchers are concerned with and what methods were used, we conduct a thematic analysis to make a structured and comprehensive view of existing literature. To be specific, our review follows three steps.

Firstly, we research related literature from scholarly databases to determine the scope of papers for the review. Secondly, we carry out a bibliometric analysis of the collected articles to identify the characteristics of the current status of the PSSC. We subsequently delve into the content of each paper and organize them based on different topics. Finally, we summarize the corresponding results of the research contents and research methods.

2.1. Data Collection

We search the relevant research papers from the largest scholarly database Scopus and the Web of Science database through titles, keywords, and abstracts [7]. We define some keywords including platform, service, and supply chain to extract the papers that are broadly related to our research topic for the first step. Based on the reality of the emergency and development of PSSC, we only analyze the English articles that were published in journals from 2000 to 2022. Similar to Kuhzady et al. (2021) [5], this review focuses on academic journals to guarantee the academic value of this review, and conference papers and review articles are not included. This is because that academic journals are considered the main source for research results. For the first study, we obtain 630 papers by setting platform, supply chain, and service as keywords. In the second step, we screen the papers and limited the subject areas to business, management, decision sciences, mathematics, economics, and finance. Then 348 papers related to our review topic were selected. After that, we conducted descriptive statistics and bibliometric analysis taking these 348 papers as data to analyze the overall research situation in PSSC.

2.2. Descriptive Statistics

An analysis of the articles published during the review period indicated that research on the PSSC literature has increased significantly year by year (as indicated in Figure 1). We can find that the first paper was published in 2001, and the number of published papers surged until 2020, which is in accordance with reality. In 2020, with the development of electronic business and the outbreak of the COVID-19 epidemic, more platform services were developed. Given the increasing economic value and academic attention on the topic of the PSSC, it is possible that such research will continue to preoccupy scholars in the upcoming years.

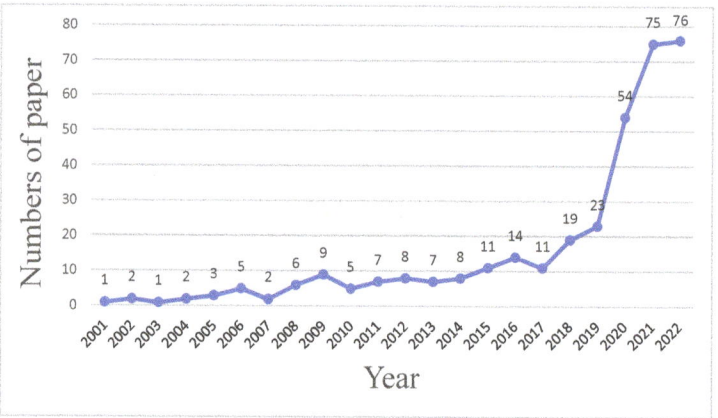

Figure 1. Number of articles published per year.

The distribution of articles published in journals indicates that over half of the related literature comes from five major journals, which are *the International Journal Of Production Economics, International Journal Of Production Research, Transportation Research Part E Logistics And Transportation Review, Annals Of Operations Research*, and the *European Journal Of Operational Research*. The *International Journal Of Production Economics* published 22 papers alone. Details can be seen in Figure 2.

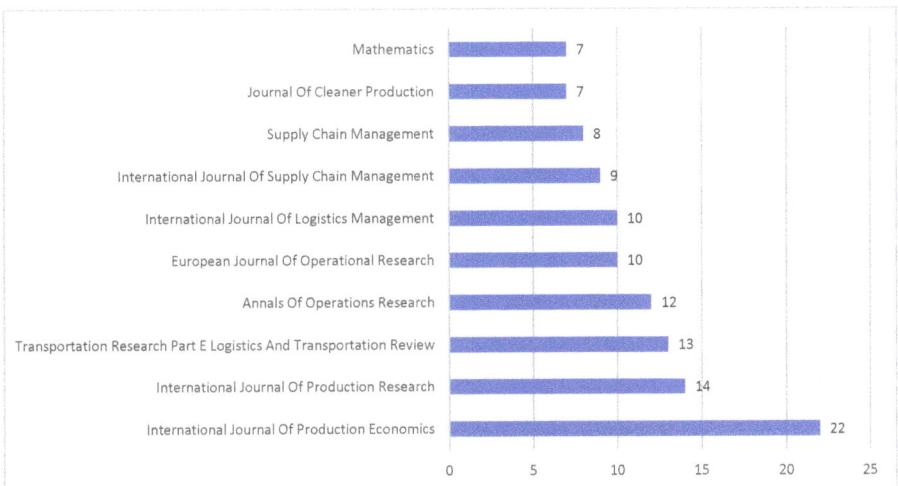

Figure 2. Number of articles published in major journals.

2.3. Bibliometric Analysis

In this part, we used Citspace to conduct the bibliometric analysis, which can establish a scientific network and image by using the literature information in the publication academic database [3]. According to Kuhzady et al. (2021) [4], the keyword describes the main topic of an article and is usually used to analyze emerging trends in research. Therefore, based on the keywords in the selected articles, which reflect the salient information contained in them, we performed content analysis by using CiteSpace to generate the complex relationship between keywords of PSSC through co-word analysis.

To be specific, we studied the temporal evolution of the key intellectual foundations of the PSSC literature to examine the research on this topic. Through the co-word analysis, we identify the evolution of PSSC along with the timeline. Meanwhile, we conducted the cluster analysis. These keywords are clustered based on their frequency of co-occurrence. The word represents the key thematic areas researched. The line between word bubbles indicates the relationship between thematic areas. We examined and ranked the frequency of keywords in the reviewed papers. The top ten keywords are shown in Table 1.

Table 1. Top 10 most frequent keywords.

Keywords	Number of Papers	Percentage
supply chain	154	44.25%
supply-chain management	77	22.13%
electronic commerce	38	10.92%
sale	33	9.48%
manufacture	32	9.20%
cost	31	8.91%
blockchain	28	8.05%
decision making	24	6.90%
profitability	21	6.03%
competition	17	4.89%
game theory	17	4.89%

Through analysis, the most frequently used keywords were 'supply chain', 'supply chain management', 'electronic commerce', 'sale', and 'manufacture'. These keywords show the main research interest of PSSC concerns supply-chain members' operational decisions. E-commerce is the main area that researchers are concerned about, which is consistent with the reality that e-commerce platforms are booming. Furthermore, we can find that research problems concern economic aspects like operation costs and sales activities. With the development of technology, blockchain and other Internet technologies are playing an increasing role in PSSC. Our results also show the main method to solve research problems: game theory, which we will analyze in detail in the later section.

Through Figure 3, cluster 0 (sale) was the basement of the early research on the PSSC since 2001. Clusters 1, 2, 3, and 6 demonstrated that the research on PSSC was related to novel technology, which is in accordance with the development of PSSC. Cluster 4 (Stackelberg game) pointed out the main research method that researchers adopted. Clusters 9, 10, and 11 indicated that the main research questions in PSSC are decision-making and supply-chain integration. What is more, through the cluster results, we found that supply-chain finance in PSSC attracted many researchers' attention after 2018.

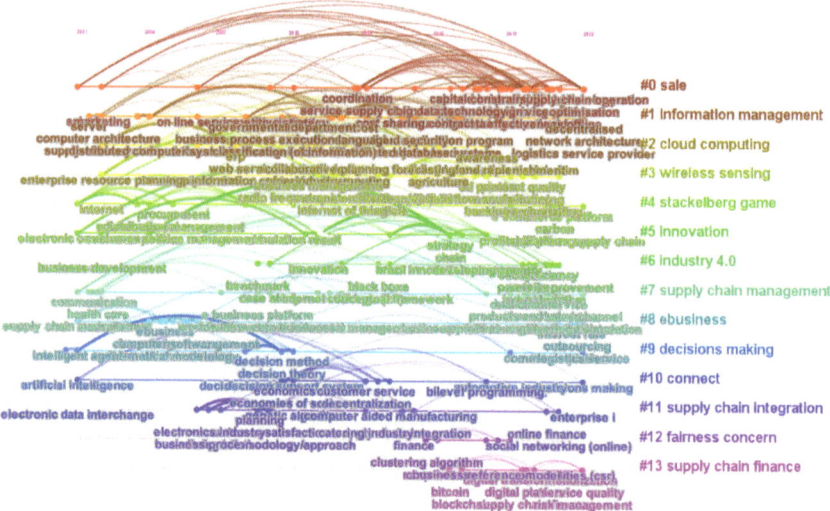

Figure 3. Keywords cluster.

3. Thematic Analysis

In this section, we examined all the articles in their entirety and retained only those articles that use mathematical modeling methods for PSSC's operational decision-making and optimization problems. After reading the title, abstract, and model, we generated a list of literature, for a total of 106 articles. Thereafter, we selected these research articles for the next steps of thematic analysis. To be specific, firstly, we will analyze the articles from their research focuses and research methods. After that, we will identify each paper's key research themes and cluster the related literature based on their thematic commonalities, that is, the topic the paper discussed.

We found that the literature we reviewed can be clustered into six groups according to their specific research topics and the problems they addressed characteristics. The six clusters are the E-commerce retailing platform, the online tourism platform, the sharing platform, the digital platform, the recycling and remanufacturing platform, and the financial service platform. The specific classification can be seen in Table 2. Among them, the E-commerce retailing platform has drawn the most attention, and the literature research on this topic accounts for more than 50% of our reviewed papers. Research on the online tourism platform, the sharing platform, and the digital platform is on the rise, which is inseparable from the development of information technology and the sharing economy. What is more, with the importance given to sustainable and corporate social responsibilities, the recycling and remanufacturing platform also attracted many scholars' interest. Meanwhile, financial service platforms are becoming a hot topic with the booming of supply-chain finance. In the following content, we will analyze the related literature in detail.

Table 2. Topic clusters.

Topic	Number of Papers	Percentage
E-commerce retailing platform	55	51.40%
Online tourism platform	13	13.08%
Sharing platform	13	12.15%
Digital platform	13	12.15%
Recycling and remanufacturing platform	6	5.61%
Financial service platform	6	5.61%

Through the analysis of the model part of the article, we find that the major methods that researchers adopted in their papers include game theory, optimal control theory, and mixed-integer linear programming. Among them, game theory is the most used in the research. During the modeling of game progress, the literature first defines the game objectives, power structure, and game events sequence. Among their models, consumer demand functions normally have three formats. The most common one is the linear function, which is related to the market size, retailing prices, merchants' efforts, etc. The inverse demand function is the second format adopted by some literature. Furthermore, some papers conducted consumer utility functions to consider consumer heterogeneity. In terms of the supply-chain members' profit functions, papers normally modeled merchants' service effort, advertising, and quality input, et al., as a quadratic cost function. Then they solved the models to obtain equilibrium optimal results to achieve the supply-chain members' profit maximization. When considering the uncertain demands or information values, the common format is to use a non-negative random variable to model, to assume it follows one distribution, and to conduct expected profit functions to analyze the equilibrium results. After obtaining the optimal results, researchers conducted numerical analysis to analyze the change trends of the optimal results and to visually compare the performance of the supply chain under different scenarios.

3.1. Cluster 1: E-Commerce Retailing Platform

3.1.1. Research Topic

In the past decade, online retailing has developed rapidly. Consumers are becoming more and more accustomed to purchasing online platforms and enjoying various services such as delivery. The cluster of papers that research the e-commerce retailing platform is reasonably large. At present, there are two main types of service platforms spawned by e-commerce: typical online sale platforms and on-demand service platforms.

- Typical Online Sale Platform

Typical online sale platforms are the business mode that retailers or manufacturers sell their products on online platforms that were previously sold only in physical stores. Through online sales platforms, like eBay, Amazon, JD.com, and Taobao, customers can purchase almost everything they need through the e-platform without time and space limitations. The platform will provide delivery services to customers according to their orders.

According to the research, there are two main operation modes in reality. The first one is that the platforms charge commission fees from merchants but do not own products, like eBay and Taobao. The second one is the platform that wholesales products from manufacturers and resells them to customers, like Amazon.com and JD.com [8,9].

Our review indicates that the pricing [10–12], quality [13,14], logistics [15,16], service [8,17,18], advertising [19–21], and return [22,23] strategies of retailers, suppliers, and online platforms are one of the main research issues in this field.

Research on pricing mainly concerns the setting of products' sales prices in different online and offline channels, like in [8,10,17,18]. Pricing strategy under bundling strategy and presales was also studied [8,11,12].

Research on product quality concerns quality control and quality information disclosure strategies. For example, Wen et al. (2021) researched online-shopping product quality control under government supervision [13]. Liu et al. (2021) analyzed ex ante blockchain-adoption and ex post voluntary-disclosure quality information strategies [14].

In terms of logistics, there are two kinds of logistics models within e-commerce platforms: self-built logistics of e-platforms and logistics outsourcing [15]. How to choose the optimal delivery service strategy is a crucial problem for e-tailers in practice [16]. Therefore, researchers analyzed different logistic strategies by considering different logistics models' costs, delivery service fees, commission rates, and so forth [15,16]. Wang et al. (2021) studied cooperation between third-party logistics service providers and e-platforms [15]. Tu et al. (2022) compared logistics service efforts under different contracts when green agriculture products are sold by online platforms [24]. He et al. (2022) researched logistics service integration issues in an e-commerce PSSC and proposed two coordination mechanisms [25].

Platforms' service investment strategy and sellers' service level are two main problems that related literature covers [8,17,18,26,27]. For example, Zhang et al. (2021) researched a platform's service investment strategy when a supplier encroaches on its retail market by opening a direct channel on the platform [27].

With the increase of fierce competition in the market, more merchants adopt advertising to attract consumers [20]. Therefore, many scholars are concerned with advertising equilibrium strategies under different conditions [19–21], like considering the delayed effort of advertising, platform goodwill, and brand goodwill [20,21].

In terms of return policy, Wang et al. (2021) analyzed different return policies when the platform retailer resells products or just provides a platform to suppliers [22]. Mondal et al. (2022) investigated refund and replacement policies for defective products and e-commerce platforms' exchange offers [23].

Apart from operational strategies, with the introduction of e-platforms, business modes and channel selection [3,26], and coordination [19,28,29] are e-platforms' major operation problems in both online and offline dual-channel operation modes.

The research on coordination proposed different contracts and other improvement strategies by considering fairness concerns [28] and altruistic preference [15,29], like revenue-sharing plus a fixed-fee contract, state-dependent contract, etc [3,19]. For example, Wang et al. (2020) studied the e-commerce supply chain's coordination when the platform provides extended warranty service and proposed a revenue-sharing joint commission contract [30]. Considering the showrooming effect, Wang et al. (2022) researched the interplay between the manufacturer's offline service effort strategy and the platform's online sales mode selection [26]. Wang et al. (2022) designed the Nash bargaining contract and Rubinstein bargaining contract to mitigate conflicts in the green supply chain that contains an e-commerce platform [31]. For more similar literature, we refer the readers to [8,9,17].

Besides, enterprises, especially small- and medium-sized enterprises, often face financial constraints. With the development of e-commerce, many platforms can provide financial services to capital-constrained suppliers or retailers, like JD Finance [32]. Many merchants face the problem of making financing decisions. The literature compared the performances of bank financing, credit financing, and financial services provided by e-commerce platforms and analyzed merchants' finance choices [33,34]. Tao et al. (2022) considered online retailers' risk-aversion and proposed revenue–cost-sharing contracts to coordinate [33]. Chang et al. (2022) studied the interaction between the retailers' financing strategies and the channel sales cooperation contracts [35]. Considering the seller's performance risk, Rath et al. (2021) analyzed optimal interest rates that the platform charge the seller and proposed contracts as an incentive [36]. For more references, we refer the readers to [37–41].

With the development of novel technology, the application of digital technology like blockchain and cloud computing in PSSC attracts many researchers' attention. Liu (2022) studied the operation of an agricultural products e-commerce platform based on cloud computing [42]. Wu et al. (2022) analyzed each supply-chain member's optimal blockchain strategy from the perspectives of information transparency and transaction cost. Besides, the development of the live streaming industry spawned by e-commerce platforms has also attracted the attention of some scholars [43]. Zhang et al. (2022) studied the e-commerce platform's decision-making problem of whether or not to introduce and how to introduce live streaming services [44].

- On-demand Service Platform

With the development of e-commerce, many offline merchants provide instant delivery services to customers according to their orders when they place orders on the online platform. This gave birth to the on-demand service platform, which is also known as online-to-offline (O2O) instant delivery service platform. Our review shows that the on-demand service platforms mainly include three categories. The first one is mainly for the distribution of daily necessities, fresh food, and other items by community supermarkets, such as Alibaba's Hema and JD's 7fresh [45]. Through these platforms, customers purchase various products, and platforms deliver orders by vehicles to customers within one hour or half an hour. The second one is the freight O2O platform mainly for goods delivery. The representatives include Lalamove, Yunniao, and Gogovan in China and Cargomatic, Convoy, and Loadsmart in the US [46]. The last one is the on-demand food delivery platform, i.e., the takeout platform. The representatives include Ele.me, Meituan, Grubhub, Postmates, and so forth [47]. With the increase in consumer demand, platforms simultaneously distribute medicines, flowers, etc., nowadays.

Different from a typical online sale platform, owing to the requirement of delivery time, more research on on-demand service platforms concern the design of instant delivery scheduling models that include order fulfillment and routine planning in order to minimize the delivery time, distances, and costs. In reality, these platforms only accept orders within a certain distance of the offline stores and deliver them to consumers within a specified time [45]. When designing different scheduling models, some scholars are concerned with order-picking and dispatch. For example, Zhang et al. (2019) considered multiple pickers' learning effects when studying the online integrated order picking and delivery problem [45]. Li et al. (2020) proposed an assignment matching strategy in freight O2O platforms [46]. Wang et al. (2020) proposed a three-stage order dispatch scheme [48]. Other research on order dispatching can be seen in [49,50]. Some scholars researched delivery routine plans and optimization, like [51,52]. Besides, He et al. (2020) analyzed the on-demand service platform's decisions about matching order volume with a self-scheduling delivery capacity [53]. Pachayappan and Sundarakani (2022) proposed sustainable drone delivery strategies [54].

Like normal PSSC, operational decision-making issues such as pricing [46,55], service [56], distribution fees [53], modes and logistics selections [57,58], and coordination [47] have received a lot of attention under this subject too. He et al. (2020) studied the O2O platform's pricing and market expansion strategy to attract grocery retailers, and they analyzed how to charge customers for delivery fees [53]. Tong et al. (2019) pointed out that dynamic pricing strategies are better than static pricing based on the two-sided market theory [55]. Other research about optimal pricing decisions can be seen in [46,56].

Research on modes, logistics selection, and coordination mainly focuses on O2O food delivery platforms. Scholars are concerned about the restaurants' decisions and coordination between them and platforms. The review shows that, first, restaurants face the choice of joining the platform or not [47]. Second, like typical online sale platforms, merchants or restaurants can choose platform logistics or self-logistics [58]. The results show that merchants' optimal decisions depend on customer demand, commission, and advertising effect, etc. [57,59].

In terms of coordination, research shows that there are profit conflicts between the restaurant and the platform due to the commission [60]. Therefore, many scholars are concerned about this problem and designed different contracts to coordinate, like the sales reward contract, the revenue-sharing contract with adding social responsibility, the one-way revenue-sharing contract with a price ceiling, and the two-way revenue-sharing contract, etc. [47,56,61].

3.1.2. Research Methods

Through our review, we find that the majority of research conducted analytical models based on game theory to study, especially when researching members' operational decisions under typical online sale platforms and on-demand service platforms. The models include the Stackelberg game, evolutionary game [12], and differential game [20].

In the literature about the typical online sale platform, the Stackelberg game model is the most used method. More than half of the literature we reviewed used typical Stackelberg game models and conducted numerical experiments [7–9,14,17,25,27–31,33]. For example, Fu et al. (2021) developed dynamic game models in four dual-channel e-retail structures [7]. Ma et al. (2022) conducted a multi-period game-theoretic model [38]. Zhang et al. (2021) considered the online retailer and a manufacturer facing a situation like the classical newsvendor problem [40].

Besides the Stackelberg game, part of the literature researched evolutionary game and differential game models. Wen et al. (2021) constructed an evolutionary game model to discuss the dynamic process of quality behaviors and analyze the key triggers of the evolutionary directions in online shopping [12]. Liu et al. (2021) built a three-party evolutionary game model including the service platform, the government, and the consumers to analyze governance mechanisms for preventing the service platform's discriminatory pricing behavior [13]. Wu et al. (2018) used differential game theory to give the optimal pricing and advertising strategies in decentralized and centralized scenarios [18]. Wu et al. (2020) used the optimal control method to discuss the consignment platform's advertising investment decisions [19]. Wu and Yu (2022) studied two suppliers who played a Bertrand game to analyze the blockchain's impact on PSSC [43]. In terms of the on-demand service platform, research on the design of instant delivery operation schemes adopted mixed-integer linear programming methods and design algorithms as a solution [45,46,54]. For example, Li et al. (2020) proposed an assignment matching strategy by using mixed-integer linear programming to jointly optimize the matching and pricing strategies with optimal delivery routes to multiple retailers [46]. Chen et al. (2022) abstracted the on-demand food delivery problem as a static generalized assignment problem with a rolling horizon strategy and proposed a limitation learning-enhanced iterated matching algorithm to solve the problem [50]. Yildiz and Savelsbergh (2019) studied the routing problem by considering the known order arrival information and used the method of generating columns and rows at the same time to solve the food delivery service and restaurant problem [52].

Research on the decision strategies of platforms and merchants used game models, such as research on typical online sale platforms. For some related works, we refer readers to [47,55–57,59,61].

3.2. Cluster 2: Online Tourism Platform

3.2.1. Research Topic

With the development of e-commerce, the online travel platform has become a novel development trend. Customers can purchase various tourism services through online travel platforms. For example, they can make hotel reservations and ticket bookings and gain tourist information through applications. Orbitz.com, Booking.com, Expedia, Travelocity, and Ctrip.com are some typical online tourism platforms [62–64]. Like typical online sale platforms, online tourism platforms also have two operating models: the agency model and the wholesale model (merchant model). The platform only charges commission fees from tourism service providers in the former mode and has the power to price in the latter mode [62,64]. Furthermore, hybrid online selling modes have been rising in recent years too [65].

The literature in this field mainly concerns the decisions of the platform, hotels, and scenic spots. The first strategy question they are concerned about is the choice between the agency model and the wholesale model [62,64,66–68]. The second topic is operation decisions, especially pricing and information sharing strategy [63,65,69]. Furthermore, much research concerned the coordination of the online tourism platform supply chain by contracts [70,71].

Our review shows that research analyzed the effects of prices, sales costs, commission rates, market demand, value-added service efficiency, demand forecast accuracy, altruism preference, and corporate social responsibility on the models' choices [62–64]. They discussed the effects of these different variables on platforms and tourism providers' mode decisions. We find that almost all literature did not point out which mode was the best.

Research on pricing mainly concerned optimal pricing, including analyzing different variables' effects and comparing different models' pricing strategies. For example, Yang et al. (2016) analyzed the online travel agency platform's pricing strategies when overbooking is allowed [65]. Mao et al. (2021) analyzed the optimal differential pricing strategy when information transparency can change by charging travelers [72]. For more similar research, we refer the readers to [65].

The online travel market's seasonal and random characteristics make research on demand and product information disclosure and sharing necessary [64]. Related literature analyzed platforms' information sharing decisions under different modes and discussed different methods to motivate sharing information to achieve Pareto improvement, like designing the transfer payment contract and the two-part tariff contract [62,64]. Besides, the application of blockchain in information disclosure has also been studied in recent years [73].

In terms of the coordination of the online tourism PSSC, scholars designed and compared different contracts to achieve channel coordination, like the fixed payment contract, the cost-sharing contract, the revenue-sharing contract, and the service commission contract, etc [70,74].

3.2.2. Research Methods

Game models are common models that researchers use to study. For example, Zhang et al. (2021) conducted a multistage game under demand uncertainty to analyze the selection of the cooperation model [64]. Yang et al. (2016) conducted Bertrand and Stackelberg game models when analyzing the online travel agency platform's pricing strategies [65]. Liao et al. (2017) consider a Stackelberg game and conducted the discount demand function [66]. He et al. (2021) researched the hotel and the platform's optimal service levels, advertising investment, and retail price in different modes by using differential equations to describe the dynamics of perceived service quality [69]. Taking the number of reserved rooms as a decision variable, Zha et al. (2015) used a newsvendor setting to depict the demands independently [70]. Mao et al. (2021) used a variation of the Hotelling model to study how to optimize online travel platforms' revenue [72]. Shi et al. (2021) established a principal-agent model when designing a service commission contract [74]. Other literature that used game models can refer to [62].

Besides, Wan et al. (2020) used variational inequalities to model the online travel agent platforms' altruistic preferences and the consumers' low-carbon preferences and used the improved projection gradient algorithm to obtain optimal results. They conducted a numerical case analysis to verify the effectiveness of the model [63].

3.3. Cluster 3: Sharing Platform

3.3.1. Research Topic

A significant economic model innovation brought by the PSSC is the sharing economy. Sharing platforms have been popular in recent years, especially with the improvement of mobile internet technology and the change in customers' life habits. People can share various products, like bicycles, boats, clothing, accessories, electronics, luxuries, cars, and apartments through different online sharing platforms [75]. Common examples include car-rental platforms like Turo, Zipcar, TOGO, GoFun, and EVCARD; carpooling platforms like Uber and Didi; and accommodation-sharing platforms like Airbnb [76–80]. In reality, business-to-consumer (B2C) and consumer-to-consumer (C2C) are two common sharing models owing to the differences in market participants, product ownership, and profit allocation [81]. These platforms are normally owned by manufacturers or third-party corporations [82].

The literature in this field mainly concerns the choices of sharing models and other economic operational decisions, including the pricing, service effort, dispatching plan, and so forth [78].

Our review shows that research on model choice mainly exists regarding car-sharing platforms. Manufacturers face the decision of making self-built platforms or collaborating with third-party platforms [75]. Research showed that costs, including product cost, sharing transaction and offline operating costs, commission rate, value perception factor, etc., will influence firms' optimal strategies [76,80,82,83]. Besides, Bian et al. (2021) explored whether a third-party C2C sharing platform firm launches its own sharing service by offering its own products [75]. Guo et al. (2022) discussed the third-party B2C car-sharing platform's value-added service investment strategy to compete with manufacturers when they provide the car-sharing services by themselves [80].

Other well-studied operational decisions focus on pricing strategies. For example, Bian et al. (2021) studied pricing decisions in a hybrid sharing model integrating both C2C and B2C sharing models [75]. Liang et al. (2021) compared the market pricing and platform pricing strategies' under B2C and C2C modes to obtain the car-sharing platforms' optimal pricing mechanism [78]. Chen et al. (2021) researched the accommodation-sharing platform Airbnb's dynamic pricing strategy by considering market conditions, quality, and risk preference [79]. Huang et al. (2022) examined the B2C car-sharing platform's optimal pricing and pricing policy selection during peak and off-peak hours. The platform can choose a fixed pricing policy or a dynamic pricing policy. Their results show that implementing a dynamic pricing policy can increase the sharing platform's profit and off-peak hours' demand but decrease the consumer surplus, social welfare, and peak hour demand [84]. For more related works, we refer the readers to [76,82,83,85].

Apart from the aforementioned operation strategies, Guo et al. (2022) researched platforms' dispatching strategy from the perspective of sustainability [77]. Cai et al. (2021) researched triple marginalization and hazard problems caused by the platform operation and proposed adopting blockchain technology and a "discounted" markdown sponsor contract to coordinate [81]. Wen et al. (2022) researched the sharing platforms' optimal product quality improvement efforts [85]. Sun et al. (2020) examined a free-floating sharing platform that owns a durable product and leases it to consumers and the platform's optimal product quality, input quantity, and dynamic advertising investment strategy [86]. Choi et al. (2020) analyzed rental-service platforms' product information disclosure strategy supported by blockchain technology [87].

3.3.2. Research Methods

According to our analysis, game models remain the most common approach. Most research was conducted on Stackelberg game models. For example, Guo et al. (2022) used a three-stage Stackelberg game model in which the original equipment manufacturer is the leader and the platform is the follower [80]. Cai et al. (2020) used the newsvendor product game model to explore the platform's operation [81]. For some related works, we refer the readers to [75,76,78,82,84].

Besides, Chen et al. (2021) developed a Hoteling model and extended the research into dynamic pricing decisions in the presence of Bayesian social learning that captures the interactions between social learning and platform strategies [79]. Wen et al. (2020) employed the mean-variance theory to model the risk-averse attitudes of decision-makers and analytically derive the platforms' optimal product quality improvement efforts and the optimal prices [85]. Sun et al. (2020) used an optimal control model and solved the problem via the maximum principle and an algorithm in their research [86]. Choi et al. (2020) constructed a stylized duopoly model to analyze the product information disclosure Nash game between two rental-service platforms [87].

Apart from the game model, Guo et al. (2022) conducted a holistic multi-objective mathematical model to study platforms' dispatching strategy. They proposed an effective method to solve the model and an approach to efficiently generate the Pareto front. Besides, they conducted extensive case studies of different scenarios with real data to validate the model [77].

3.4. Cluster 4: Digital Platform

3.4.1. Research Topic

In the last decade, the proliferation of digital platforms has generated substantial and growing revenues with the development of the internet [88]. Some digital platforms, such as Apple's App Store, Google Play, the Windows Phone Store, and BlackBerry App World are becoming hot research issues [89,90]. These digital platforms provide virtual-products-related services, and consumers can use applications or enjoy other services. Our analysis results show that research on this topic mainly concerns the operational decision-making and coordination between the digital platform and service distributors.

Through our review, we find that many scholars researched optimal pricing, quality effort service, and advertising strategies. For example, Liu et al. (2020) analyzed the optimal product quality and the platform's optimal advertising effort when considering the reference price and goodwill [90]. Xing et al. (2022) investigated the digital platform supply chain's optimal pricing and service quality strategies while considering the network externality's impact [91]. Ji et al. (2019) researched a mobile platform's joint advertising investment and in-app advertising adoption decisions [92]. Liu and Liu (2019) researched a dynamic advertising strategy model for one platform and multiple apps under decentralized and integrated conditions [93]. Besides, Avinadav et al. (2015) analyzed the effect of application developers' risk-sensitive behavior on supply-chain performance [94]. We refer the readers to references [95–98] for related research.

Besides, in reality, digital platforms and service developers have different access to information [89]. Therefore, many researchers studied the distribution platforms and application developers' private information disclosure strategy regarding whether to share information and how to share. Some coordinate mechanisms like different contracts were proposed. For example, Avinadav et al. (2021) found that the developer was not willing to voluntarily disclose his private information, and they designed mechanisms for platforms to motivate the developer to share information [88]. Avinadav et al. (2022) studied the value of information-sharing when the developer is risk-neutral or risk-averse [89]. Qu et al. (2022) pointed out that market structure will influence the information sharing strategy, and the distributor sharing information can weak the double marginalization [96]. Avinadav et al. (2022) investigated the information decisions under the conditions that the platform's owing demand information is hidden superiority or known superiority [99].

Our analysis results show that the coordination of digital PSSC also receives some attention. Researchers compared different contracts' roles in coordinating and increasing the total digital PSSC profits. For example, Li et al. (2017) compared the wholesale price contract and the two-part tariff contract, and they found digital platform's risk-averse degree will influence the optimal choice of contracts [100]. Similar research can refer to [88,94,95].

3.4.2. Research Methods

Among the literature that we review, game theory and optimal control theory are used in mathematical models as the common research method.

For example, Qu et al. (2022) used a Stackelberg and Nash games model to identify the digital platform's equilibrium conditions [96]. Both Wang et al. (2018) and Ji et al. (2019) conducted differential game models to analyze optimal advertising strategy [92,98]. Hao et al. (2017) conducted an N-shaped dynamic model by considering consumers' different perceived valuations for applications to research the game between the platform and the app developer [97]. Other research on using game theory to conduct models can be seen in [89,91,94,99].

Besides, some scholars adopted optimal control to analyze the digital platforms' operation strategies. For example, Avinadav et al. (2021) developed a menu of contracts based on optimal control theory [89]. Avinadav et al. (2020) applied the principal-agent framework to analyze the interaction between the platform and service provider and used optimal control to design the contract during their research [95]. Liu and Liu (2019) and Liu and Liu (2020) researched digital platforms and application distributors' quality and advertising strategies, respectively, by utilizing optimal control theory [90,93]. Apart from these, Li et al. (2017) used principal-agent models and used the mean-variance method when researching contract design [100].

3.5. Cluster 5: Recycling and Remanufacturing Platform
Research Topic

Apart from selling new products on platforms, out of consideration for environmental impact and profits, many manufacturers and retailers recycle and resell products to customers, especially electronics, on platforms [101]. Some research pointed out that coordination with third-party Internet service platforms like JD.com and Aihuishou makes the whole recycling and reselling progress more efficient [102]. Our review finds that research on remanufacturing has been widely investigated. However, research on recycling and remanufacturing platforms is not ample. The current research concerns pricing, marketing investment, and different members' coordination.

The literature on the recycling and remanufacturing platform researched the closed-loop supply chain (CLSC) that put new products and used or remanufactured products for sale on online platforms simultaneously. Research questions include the decision of channel choice and other operational decisions, like pricing, quality, and service.

Research on manufacturers' channel decisions concerned manufacturers' decisions on whether to recycle and sell remanufactured products on the platform as a trade-off of the profits from selling old and new products. Furthermore, whether recyclers will sell remanufactured products on self-built platforms or third-party agency platforms after they have decided to recycle and sell used has also attracted many researchers' attention [101,103]. For example, Jia et al. (2020) investigated the manufacturer and the e-retailer channel modes choices and found that determined by the order fulfillment cost and platform fee [101]. Zhong et al. (2021) considered the recycler's choice of selling remanufactured products through the e-retailer's platform or their own online platform while considering consumers' green education. They found that the e-retailer can benefit from the remanufactured goods' cannibalization in the agency channel when the consumer green education is under-developed, which is contrary to traditional opinions [103].

Besides, some research is concerned with operational decisions. For example, Xiang et al. (2019) analyzed supply-chain members' research and development investment, advertising investment, and Big Data marketing investment strategy [102]. Wang et al. (2021) analyzed the reward–penalty mechanism and the platform's altruistic preference's effect on the recycling service and the quality improvement decisions [104]. What is more, due to the uncertain qualities of secondhand or remanufactured products, some research analyzed the product information disclosure strategy. Shen et al. (2020) examined the value of blockchain for disclosing secondhand product quality, and they found that horizontal integration can improve the supply chain's total profit with blockchain [105]. Ma and Hu (2022) analyzed recycling platforms' blockchain adoption strategy and blockchain implementation effects on CLSC [106].

3.6. Cluster 6: Financial Service Platform
3.6.1. Research Topic

Nowadays, in the context of the demand for finance, many platforms provide rich financial services, such as mobile payment, online credit services, and funding [107–109]. Alipay and Wechat are two popular platforms in China that provide mobile payment services. The platforms that provide online credit finance for consumers include Jingdong pay and Huabei of Alipay, which make people able to consume in advance and pay later. The last mainly provides funding services, like JD Finance and some peer-to-peer (P2P) lending platforms, like PPmoney, PPDai, Hongling Capital, and Renrendai, etc. [110,111].

In terms of third-party payment platforms (3PP), Fan et al. (2020) researched the optimal decisions of the manufacturer, the retailer, and the 3PP under the non-information-sharing and information-sharing cases and analyzed the 3PP's effects on supply-chain performances [107].

In terms of online credit finance, researchers are concerned about whether platforms should provide credit services and how to make service-related decisions. Li et al. (2020) researched the platform's credit entry strategy when facing credit card competition. They found that the penetration rate of credit cards is vital for the platform's decision [108]. Wu et al. (2022) analyzed manufacturers' and platform retailers' credit payment service decisions and different scenarios' equilibrium results. Their results showed that the discount factor for credit payment service and the discount of cash opportunity cost will influence their decisions [112].

What is more, Luo et al. (2015) considered a firm with a financial services platform that pools the divisions' cash into a master account managed by the headquarters. They researched how to determine the optimal joint inventory replenishment and cash retention policy for the entire supply chain [109]. Wang et al. (2022) researched a P2P lending platform that connects individual investors and borrowers directly. They analyzed the P2P lending platform's information service fee rate, the credit guarantee company's guarantee service fee rate, etc., and compared the P2P lending platform's different credit guarantee types [111].

3.6.2. Research Methods

Almost all of the literature about the recycling and remanufacturing platform and the financial service platform that we reviewed used game models for analysis. Therefore, we will analyze the methods that the literature used in this section. The game models mainly include the Stackelberg game and the differential game.

In terms of the recycling and remanufacturing platform, Jia et al. (2020) conducted a single-period decision problem model to investigate CLSC members' optimal decisions [101]. Zhong et al. (2021) conducted a two-period game model to analyze [103]. Wang et al. (2021) developed three models to study and extended the models to multiple recycling periods [104]. Xiang et al. (2019) conducted a goodwill dynamic model based on the differential game theory [102]. Ma and Hu (2022) conducted a differential game model to analyze the market conditions that can incentivize the platform to adopt blockchain for waste-product recycling [106].

In terms of the financial service platform, Fan et al. (2020) built game-theoretic models when they researched 3PP's decision problems [107]. Luo et al. (2015) formulated a dynamic program for the cash pooling model that includes two inventory states and one cash state [109]. Wang et al. (2022) conducted a Stackelberg game model to analyze the P2P lending platform's optimal decision variables [111]. Mitra et al. (2022) used collaborative filtering technology and machine learning to identify defaulter borrowers in P2P platforms [110]. Wu et al. (2022) conducted analytical models based on game theory to analyze the problem of the manufacturer and retailer simultaneously deciding whether to implement credit payment service in their respective selling channels [112].

4. Conclusions

Platforms are playing an important role in enterprises' operations and people's daily lives. It is a broad research theme and involves many different subjects and activities. Extant research on this theme only concerns one specific area, and the research results are dispersed. Our review analyzed the research paper that was searched on the Scopus database and Web of Science comprehensively. The main findings of our review are concluded as follows.

Through our review, we find that research on the PSSC mainly concerns the e-commerce platform, especially online retailing platforms. Meanwhile, the development of O2O instant delivery services and online tourism services draws many researchers' attention now, and research trends are on the rise. What is more, with people's emphasis on environmental protection and sustainable development, manufacturers are paying more and more attention to recycling and remanufacturing platforms out of consideration for corporate social responsibility and economic profit. Therefore, a large amount of the literature showed interest in this theme, too.

In terms of the research context, our review shows that PSSC members' operational decisions, especially economically related, were researched comprehensively. Among them, pricing is a concern for almost all types of platforms. Information sharing strategy has attracted more researchers' attention recently, especially with the development of blockchain and other novel technologies. Different platforms make different decisions about what type of information to disclose. Research on typical online retailing platforms, sharing platforms, and recycling platforms is concerned with the merchants' and platforms' product quality information disclosure decisions. Research on online tourism platforms and digital platforms is concerned with the platforms' demand information disclosure decisions. Advertising strategies are mostly studied on typical online retailing platforms and digital platforms. Apart from these, many researchers are concerned about the merchants' channel and mode choices, especially in online retailing platforms, on-demand service platforms, and sharing platforms. What is more, the coordination of the PSSC is also a hot topic that the literature discussed. Many different coordination mechanisms were designed, like some contracts. Our review results demonstrate that there are still some challenges that one ought to pay more attention to. The first one is that research on food safety in on-demand food delivery platforms is not ample. The second one is that supply-chain finance is drawing more and more attention, but related research was also inadequate. In addition, supply-chain members' risk attitudes also need to be focused on during the research, which is seldom researched in the literature.

In terms of research methods, game theory is the most common and popular, and most of the literature used game theory models to analyze supply-chain members' behavior under different circumstances (e.g., collaborative and competition). Game models include the Stackelberg game, the differential game, and the evolutionary game. However, during mathematical modeling, the majority of the literature was concerned with certain demands. However, market demands are random in reality. Therefore, scholars can focus more on the uncertainness and the dynamics of demand in their future research. Besides, some research used optimal control theory in models for analysis. Apart from this, mixed-integer linear programming was used to analyze on-demand service platforms' instant delivery problems.

Our reviewed results describe the current research field of PSSC clearly and provide references for enterprises and platforms to optimize their operation progress and obtain more profits. Furthermore, our results provide future research direction and research innovation by recognizing gaps in the literature. For example, our review finds that, with consumers concerned with food safety, the research on takeout platforms' quality information disclosure is insufficient. Researchers can be more concerned about this problem in the future. What is more, the application of novel technology like blockchain and the Internet of Things in the PSSC can be researched deeper.

Author Contributions: Conceptualization, writing—review and editing, supervision, project administration, and funding acquisition, Y.H.; methodology, validation, formal analysis, resources, and data curation, Y.H. and X.G.; software, investigation, writing—original draft preparation, and visualization, X.G. All authors have read and agreed to the published version of the manuscript.

Funding: This research was supported by the National Natural Science Foundation of China (Nos. 72171047 and 71771053), the Key Project of Social Science Foundation of Jiangsu Province (No. 21GLA002), and the Natural Science Foundation of Jiangsu Province (No. BK20201144).

Institutional Review Board Statement: Not applicable.

Informed Consent Statement: Not applicable.

Data Availability Statement: Not applicable.

Conflicts of Interest: The authors declare no conflict of interest.

References

1. Song, M.; Fisher, R.; De Sousa Jabbour, A.B.L.; Santibañez Gonzalez, E.D.R. Green and sustainable supply chain management in the platform economy. *Int. J. Logist. Res. Appl.* **2022**, *25*, 349–363. [CrossRef]
2. Wulfert, T.; Woroch, R.; Strobel, G.; Seufert, S.; Möller, F. Developing design principles to standardize e-commerce ecosystems. *Electron. Mark.* **2022**, 1–30. [CrossRef]
3. Siqin, T.; Choi, T.M.; Chung, S.H. Optimal E-tailing channel structure and service contracting in the platform era. *Transp. Res. Part E Logist. Transp. Rev.* **2022**, *160*, 102614. [CrossRef]
4. Zhang, N.; Zhao, Y. Green supply chain management in the platform economy: A bibliometric analysis. *Int. J. Logist. Res. Appl.* **2021**, *25*, 639–655. [CrossRef]
5. Kuhzady, S.; Olya, H.; Farmaki, A.; Ertaş, Ç. Sharing economy in hospitality and tourism: A review and the future pathways. *J. Hosp. Mark. Manag.* **2021**, *30*, 549–570. [CrossRef]
6. Shroff, A.; Shah, B.J.; Gajjar, H. Online food delivery research: A systematic literature review. *Int. J. Contemp. Hosp. Manag.* **2022**, *34*, 2852–2883. [CrossRef]
7. Mody, M.A.; Hanks, L.; Cheng, M. Sharing economy research in hospitality and tourism: A critical review using bibliometric analysis, content analysis and a quantitative systematic literature review. *Int. J. Contemp. Hosp. Manag.* **2021**, *33*, 1711–1745. [CrossRef]
8. Fu, Y.; Gu, B.; Xie, Y.; Ye, J.; Cao, B. Channel structure and differential pricing strategies in dual-channel e-retail considering e-platform business models. *IMA J. Manag. Math.* **2021**, *32*, 91–114. [CrossRef]
9. Li, P.; Tan, D.; Wang, G.; Wei, H.; Wu, J. Retailer's vertical integration strategies under different business modes. *Eur. J. Oper. Res.* **2021**, *294*, 965–975. [CrossRef]
10. Yi, S.; Yu, L.; Zhang, Z. Research on pricing strategy of dual-channel supply chain based on customer value and value-added service. *Mathematics* **2021**, *9*, 11. [CrossRef]
11. Lan, C.; Zhu, J. New Product Presale Strategies considering Consumers' Loss Aversion in the E-Commerce Supply Chain. *Discret. Dyn. Nat. Soc.* **2021**, *2021*, 8194879. [CrossRef]
12. Guo, X.; Zheng, S.; Yu, Y.; Zhang, F. Optimal Bundling Strategy for a Retail Platform Under Agency Selling. *Prod. Oper. Manag.* **2021**, *30*, 2273–2284. [CrossRef]
13. Wen, D.; Yan, D.; Sun, X.; Chen, X. Evolutionary Game Analysis of Online Shopping Quality Control: The Roles of Risk Attitude and Government Supervision. *Complexity* **2021**, *2021*, 5531076. [CrossRef]
14. Liu, M.; Zhang, X.; Wu, H. The impact of platform restriction on manufacturer quality transparency in the blockchain era. *Int. J. Prod. Res.* **2021**, 1–17. [CrossRef]
15. Wang, Y.; Yu, Z.; Shen, L.; Fan, R.; Tang, R. Decisions and coordination in e-commerce supply chain under logistics outsourcing and altruistic preferences. *Mathematics* **2021**, *9*, 253. [CrossRef]
16. Yu, J.; Song, Z.; Zhou, C. Self-supporting or third-party? The optimal delivery strategy selection decision for e-tailers under competition. *Kybernetes* **2022**. [CrossRef]
17. Jia, X. Decision-making of online channels under three power structures. *Meas. Control* **2020**, *53*, 296–310. [CrossRef]
18. Hasiloglu, M.; Kaya, O. An analysis of price, service and commission rate decisions in online sales made through E-commerce platforms. *Comput. Ind. Eng.* **2021**, *162*, 107688. [CrossRef]
19. Wu, Z.; Feng, L.; Chen, D. Coordinating Pricing and Advertising Decisions for Supply Chain under Consignment Contract in the Dynamic Setting. *Complexity* **2018**, *2018*, 7697180. [CrossRef]
20. Wu, Z.; Liu, G.-P.; Chen, D. Advertising strategies and coordination for supply chain based on consignment platform with delayed effect. *Syst. Sci. Control. Eng.* **2020**, *8*, 162–174. [CrossRef]
21. Wu, Z. Optimal Control Approach to Advertising Strategies of a Supply Chain Under Consignment Contract. *IEEE Access* **2019**, *7*, 41454–41462. [CrossRef]
22. Wang, L.; Chen, J.; Song, H. Marketplace or reseller? Platform strategy in the presence of customer returns. *Transp. Res. Part E Logist. Transp. Rev.* **2021**, *153*, 102452. [CrossRef]
23. Mondal, C.; Giri, B.C. Analyzing strategies in a green e-commerce supply chain with return policy and exchange offer. *Comput. Ind. Eng.* **2022**, *171*, 108492. [CrossRef]
24. Tu, J.; Sun, Z.; Huang, M. Supply chain coordination considering e-tailer's promotion effort and logistics provider's service effort. *J. Ind. Manag. Optim.* **2022**, *18*, 2191–2220. [CrossRef]
25. He, P.; He, Y.; Tang, X.; Ma, S.; Xu, H. Channel encroachment and logistics integration strategies in an e-commerce platform service supply chain. *Int. J. Prod. Econ.* **2022**, *244*, 108368. [CrossRef]
26. Wang, X.; Chaolu, T. The Impact of Offline Service Effort Strategy on Sales Mode Selection in an E-Commerce Supply Chain with Showrooming Effect. *J. Theor. Appl. Electron. Commer. Res.* **2022**, *17*, 893–908. [CrossRef]
27. Zhang, X.; Li, G.; Liu, M.; Sethi, S.P. Online platform service investment: A bane or a boon for supplier encroachment. *Int. J. Prod. Econ.* **2021**, *235*, 108079. [CrossRef]
28. Wang, Y.; Fan, R.; Shen, L.; Jin, M. Decisions and coordination of green e-commerce supply chain considering green manufacturer's fairness concerns. *Int. J. Prod. Res.* **2020**, *58*, 7471–7489. [CrossRef]
29. Wang, Y.; Yu, Z.; Shen, L.; Dong, W. E-commerce supply chain models under altruistic preference. *Mathematics* **2021**, *9*, 632. [CrossRef]
30. Wang, Y.; Yu, Z.; Ji, X. Coordination of e-commerce supply chain when e-commerce platform providing sales service and extended warranty service. *J. Control. Decis.* **2020**, *7*, 241–261. [CrossRef]

31. Wang, Y.; Reivan Ortiz, G.G.; Dextre-Martinez, W.; Zhang, L. Green Supply Chain Coordination During the COVID-19 Pandemic Based on Consignment Contract. *Front. Environ. Sci.* **2022**, *10*, 899007. [CrossRef]
32. Yan, N.; Liu, Y.; Xu, X.; He, X. Strategic dual-channel pricing games with e-retailer finance. *Eur. J. Oper. Res.* **2020**, *283*, 138–151. [CrossRef]
33. Tao, Y.; Yang, R.; Zhuo, X.; Wang, F.; Yang, X. Financing the capital-constrained online retailer with risk aversion: Coordinating strategy analysis. *Ann. Oper. Res.* **2022**, 1–29. [CrossRef]
34. Zhen, X.; Shi, D.; Li, Y.; Zhang, C. Manufacturer's financing strategy in a dual-channel supply chain: Third-party platform, bank, and retailer credit financing. *Transp. Res. Part E Logist. Transp. Rev.* **2020**, *133*, 101820. [CrossRef]
35. Chang, S.; Li, A.; Wang, X.; Wang, X. Joint optimization of e-commerce supply chain financing strategy and channel contract. *Eur. J. Oper. Res.* **2022**, *303*, 908–927. [CrossRef]
36. Rath, S.B.; Basu, P.; Mandal, P.; Paul, S. Financing models for an online seller with performance risk in an E-commerce marketplace. *Transp. Res. Part E Logist. Transp. Rev.* **2021**, *155*, 102468. [CrossRef]
37. Wang, J.; Yao, S.; Wang, X.; Hou, P.; Zhang, Q. Analysis of sales and financing modes in a green platform supply chain with a capital-constrained manufacturer. *Kybernetes* **2021**. [CrossRef]
38. Ma, C.; Dai, Y.; Li, Z. Financing format selection for electronic business platforms with a capital-constrained e-tailer. *Transp. Res. Part E Logist. Transp. Rev.* **2022**, *162*, 102720. [CrossRef]
39. Cai, S.; Yan, Q. Online sellers' financing strategies in an e-commerce supply chain: Bank credit vs. e-commerce platform financing. *Electron. Commer. Res.* **2022**, 1–32. [CrossRef]
40. Zhang, J.; Li, X.; Kuo, Y.-H.; Chen, Y. Coordinating supply chain financing for e-commerce companies through a loan contract. *SAGE Open* **2021**, *11*, 21582440211065455. [CrossRef]
41. Wang, C.; Fan, X.; Yin, Z. Financing online retailers: Bank vs. electronic business platform, equilibrium, and coordinating strategy. *Eur. J. Oper. Res.* **2019**, *276*, 343–356. [CrossRef]
42. Liu, L. Research on the Operation of Agricultural Products E-Commerce Platform Based on Cloud Computing. *Math. Probl. Eng.* **2022**, *2022*, 8489903. [CrossRef]
43. Wu, J.; Yu, J. Blockchain's impact on platform supply chains: Transaction cost and information transparency perspectives. *Int. J. Prod. Res.* **2022**, 1–14. [CrossRef]
44. Zhang, X.; Chen, H.; Liu, Z. Operation strategy in an E-commerce platform supply chain: Whether and how to introduce live streaming services? *Int. Trans. Oper. Res.* **2022**. [CrossRef]
45. Zhang, J.; Liu, F.; Tang, J.; Li, Y. The online integrated order picking and delivery considering Pickers' learning effects for an O2O community supermarket. *Transp. Res. Part E Logist. Transp. Rev.* **2019**, *123*, 180–199. [CrossRef]
46. Li, J.; Zheng, Y.; Dai, B.; Yu, J. Implications of matching and pricing strategies for multiple-delivery-points service in a freight O2O platform. *Transp. Res. Part E Logist. Transp. Rev.* **2020**, *136*, 101871. [CrossRef]
47. Zhang, P.; Ju, S.; Huang, H. Can a Restaurant Benefit from Joining an Online Take-Out Platform? *Mathematics* **2022**, *10*, 1392. [CrossRef]
48. Wang, K.; Zhou, Y.; Zhang, L. A Workload-Balancing Order Dispatch Scheme for O2O Food Delivery with Order Splitting Choice. *J. Theor. Appl. Electron. Commer. Res.* **2022**, *17*, 295–312. [CrossRef]
49. Chen, J.; Fan, T.; Gu, Q.; Pan, F. Emerging technology-based online scheduling for instant delivery in the O2O retail era. *Electron. Commer. Res. Appl.* **2022**, *51*, 101115. [CrossRef]
50. Chen, J.-F.; Wang, L.; Ren, H.; Pan, J.; Wang, S.; Zheng, J.; Wang, X. An Imitation Learning-Enhanced Iterated Matching Algorithm for On-Demand Food Delivery. *IEEE Trans. Intell. Transp. Syst.* **2022**, *23*, 18603–18619. [CrossRef]
51. Wang, Z. Delivering meals for multiple suppliers: Exclusive or sharing logistics service. *Transp. Res. Part E Logist. Transp. Rev.* **2018**, *118*, 496–512. [CrossRef]
52. Yildiz, B.; Savelsbergh, M. Provably High-Quality Solutions for the Meal Delivery Routing Problem. *Transp. Sci.* **2019**, *53*, 1372–1388. [CrossRef]
53. He, B.; Mirchandani, P.; Wang, Y. Removing barriers for grocery stores: O2O platform and self-scheduling delivery capacity. *Transp. Res. Part E Logist. Transp. Rev.* **2020**, *141*, 102036. [CrossRef]
54. Pachayappan, M.; Sundarakani, B. Drone delivery logistics model for on-demand hyperlocal market. *Int. J. Logist. Res. Appl.* **2022**, 1–33. [CrossRef]
55. Tong, T.; Dai, H.; Xiao, Q.; Yan, N. Will dynamic pricing outperform? Theoretical analysis and empirical evidence from O2O on-demand food service market. *Int. J. Prod. Econ.* **2020**, *219*, 375–385. [CrossRef]
56. Guo, J.; Guo, Y. Optimal coordination and service level of the supply chain in the sharing economy: The perspective of social responsibility. *Complex Intell. Syst.* **2021**, 1–17. [CrossRef]
57. Du, Z.; Fan, Z.-P.; Gao, G.-X. Choice of O2O Food Delivery Mode: Self-built Platform or Third-Party Platform? Self-Delivery or Third-Party Delivery? *IEEE Trans. Eng. Manag.* **2022**, 1–14. [CrossRef]
58. Niu, B.; Li, Q.; Mu, Z.; Chen, L.; Ji, P. Platform logistics or self-logistics? Restaurants' cooperation with online food-delivery platform considering profitability and sustainability. *Int. J. Prod. Econ.* **2021**, *234*, 108064. [CrossRef]
59. Xing, P.; Yao, J.; Wang, M.; Zargarzadeh, H. Quality Effort Strategy of O2O Takeout Service Supply Chain under Three Operation Modes. *Complexity* **2022**, *2022*, 8177186. [CrossRef]
60. Feldman, P.; Frazelle, A.E.; Swinney, R. Managing Relationships Between Restaurants and Food Delivery Platforms: Conflict, Contracts, and Coordination. *Manag. Sci.* **2022**. [CrossRef]
61. Chen, M.; Hu, M.; Wang, J. Food Delivery Service and Restaurant: Friend or Foe? *Manag. Sci.* **2022**, *68*, 6355–7064. [CrossRef]

62. Liu, Y.; Zhang, X.; Zhang, H.; Zha, X. Competing tourism service provider introduction strategy for an online travel platform with demand information sharing. *Electron. Commer. Res. Appl.* **2021**, *49*, 101084. [CrossRef]
63. Wan, X.; Jiang, B.; Li, Q.; Hou, X. Dual-channel environmental hotel supply chain network equilibrium decision under altruism preference and demand uncertainty. *J. Clean. Prod.* **2020**, *271*, 122595. [CrossRef]
64. Zhang, X.; Liu, Y.; Dan, B. Cooperation strategy for an online travel platform with value-added service provision under demand uncertainty. *Int. Trans. Oper. Res.* **2021**, *28*, 3416–3436. [CrossRef]
65. Yang, L.; Ji, J.; Chen, K. Game Models on Optimal Strategies in a Tourism Dual-Channel Supply Chain. *Discret. Dyn. Nat. Soc.* **2016**, *2016*, 5760139. [CrossRef]
66. Liao, P.; Ye, F.; Wu, X. A comparison of the merchant and agency models in the hotel industry. *Int. Trans. Oper. Res.* **2017**, *26*, 1052–1073. [CrossRef]
67. He, P.; He, Y.; Xu, H.; Zhou, L. Online selling mode choice and pricing in an O2O tourism supply chain considering corporate social responsibility. *Electron. Commer. Res. Appl.* **2019**, *38*, 100894. [CrossRef]
68. Ye, F.; Yan, H.; Wu, Y. Optimal online channel strategies for a hotel considering direct booking and cooperation with an online travel agent. *Int. Trans. Oper. Res.* **2017**, *26*, 968–998. [CrossRef]
69. He, Y.; Yu, Y.; Wang, Z.; Xu, H. Equilibrium Pricing, Advertising, and Quality Strategies in a Platform Service Supply Chain. *Asia-Pac. J. Oper. Res.* **2021**, *39*, 2140031. [CrossRef]
70. Zha, Y.; Zhang, J.; Yue, X.; Hua, Z. Service supply chain coordination with platform effort-induced demand. *Ann. Oper. Res.* **2015**, *235*, 785–806. [CrossRef]
71. Chang, Y.W.; Hsu, P.Y.; Lan, Y.C. Cooperation and competition between online travel agencies and hotels. *Tour. Manag.* **2019**, *71*, 187–196. [CrossRef]
72. Mao, Z.; Liu, T.; Li, X. Pricing mechanism of variable opaque products for dual-channel online travel agencies. *Ann. Oper. Res.* **2021**, 1–30. [CrossRef]
73. Zhou, L.; Tan, C.; Zhao, H. Information Disclosure Decision for Tourism O2O Supply Chain Based on Blockchain Technology. *Mathematics* **2022**, *10*, 2119. [CrossRef]
74. Shi, P.; Hu, Y. Service commission contract design of online travel agency to create O2O model by cooperation with traditional travel agency under asymmetric information. *J. Destin. Mark. Manag.* **2021**, *21*, 100641. [CrossRef]
75. Bian, Y.; Cui, Y.; Yan, S.; Han, X. Optimal strategy of a customer-to-customer sharing platform: Whether to launch its own sharing service? *Transp. Res. Part E Logist. Transp. Rev.* **2021**, *149*, 102288. [CrossRef]
76. Pei, J.; Yan, P.; Kumar, S.; Liu, X. How to React to Internal and External Sharing in B2C and C2C. *Prod. Oper. Manag.* **2020**, *30*, 145–170. [CrossRef]
77. Guo, Y.; Zhang, Y.; Boulaksil, Y.; Qian, Y.; Allaoui, H. Modelling and analysis of online ride-sharing platforms–A sustainability perspective. *Eur. J. Oper. Res.* **2022**, *304*, 577–595. [CrossRef]
78. Liang, L.; Tian, L.; Xie, J.; Xu, J.; Zhang, W. Optimal pricing model of car-sharing: Market pricing or platform pricing. *Ind. Manag. Data Syst.* **2021**, *121*, 594–612. [CrossRef]
79. Chen, Y.; Zhang, R.; Liu, B. Fixed, flexible, and dynamics pricing decisions of Airbnb mode with social learning. *Tour. Econ.* **2021**, *27*, 893–914. [CrossRef]
80. Guo, D.; Fan, Z.P.; Sun, M. B2C car-sharing services: Sharing mode selection and value-added service investment. *Transp. Res. Part E Logist. Transp. Rev.* **2020**, *165*, 102836. [CrossRef]
81. Cai, Y.J.; Choi, T.M.; Zhang, J.Z. Platform Supported Supply Chain Operations in the Blockchain Era: Supply Contracting and Moral Hazards. *Decis. Sci.* **2021**, *52*, 866–892. [CrossRef]
82. Li, Y.; Bai, X.; Xue, K. Business modes in the sharing economy: How does the OEM cooperate with third-party sharing platforms? *Int. J. Prod. Econ.* **2020**, *221*, 107467. [CrossRef]
83. Tian, L.; Jiang, B.; Xu, Y. Manufacturer's Entry in the Product-Sharing Market. *Manuf. Serv. Oper. Manag.* **2021**, *23*, 553–568. [CrossRef]
84. Huang, C.-Y.; Fan, Z.-P.; Zhang, C. Optimal pricing and pricing policy selection for a B2C car-sharing platform during peak and off-peak hours. *Inf. Sci.* **2022**, *604*, 197–209. [CrossRef]
85. Wen, X.; Siqin, T. Wen, X.; Siqin, T. How do product quality uncertainties affect the sharing economy platforms with risk considerations? A mean-variance analysis. *Int. J. Prod. Econ.* **2020**, *224*, 107544. [CrossRef]
86. Sun, X.; Tang, W.; Chen, J.; Zhang, J. Optimal investment strategy of a free-floating sharing platform. *Transp. Res. Part E Logist. Transp. Rev.* **2020**, *138*, 101958. [CrossRef]
87. Choi, T.M.; Feng, L.; Li, R. Information disclosure structure in supply chains with rental service platforms in the blockchain technology era. *Int. J. Prod. Econ.* **2020**, *221*, 107473. [CrossRef]
88. Avinadav, T.; Chernonog, T.; Khmelnitsky, E. Revenue-sharing between developers of virtual products and platform distributors. *Eur. J. Oper. Res.* **2021**, *290*, 927–945. [CrossRef]
89. Avinadav, T.; Chernonog, T.; Meilijson, I.; Perlman, Y. A consignment contract with revenue sharing between an app developer and a distribution platform. *Int. J. Prod. Econ.* **2022**, *243*, 108322. [CrossRef]
90. Liu, H.; Liu, S. Research on Advertising and Quality of Paid Apps, Considering the Effects of Reference Price and Goodwill. *Mathematics* **2020**, *8*, 733. [CrossRef]
91. Xing, P.; Wang, M.; Yao, J. Optimal service quality and pricing for App service supply chain with network externality based on four different scenarios. *Kybernetes* **2022**. [CrossRef]

92. Ji, Y.; Wang, R.; Gou, Q. Monetization on Mobile Platforms: Balancing in-App Advertising and User Base Growth. *Prod. Oper. Manag.* **2019**, *28*, 2202–2220. [CrossRef]
93. Liu, H.; Liu, S. Considering In-App Advertising Mode, Platform-App Channel Coordination by a Sustainable Cooperative Advertising Mechanism. *Sustainability* **2019**, *12*, 145. [CrossRef]
94. Avinadav, T.; Chernonog, T.; Perlman, Y. The effect of risk sensitivity on a supply chain of mobile applications under a consignment contract with revenue sharing and quality investment. *Int. J. Prod. Econ.* **2015**, *168*, 31–40. [CrossRef]
95. Avinadav, T.; Chernonog, T.; Fruchter, G.E.; Prasad, A. Contract design when quality is co-created in a supply chain. *Eur. J. Oper. Res.* **2020**, *286*, 908–918. [CrossRef]
96. Qu, J.; Meng, C.; Hu, B. Pricing and quality decisions in virtual product supply chains with information sharing. *J. Oper. Res. Soc.* **2022**, 1–17. [CrossRef]
97. Hao, L.; Guo, H.; Easley, R.F. A Mobile Platform's In-App Advertising Contract Under Agency Pricing for App Sales. *Prod. Oper. Manag.* **2017**, *26*, 189–202. [CrossRef]
98. Wang, R.; Gou, Q.; Choi, T.M.; Liang, L. Advertising Strategies for Mobile Platforms with "Apps". *IEEE Trans. Syst. Man. Cybern. Syst.* **2018**, *48*, 767–778. [CrossRef]
99. Avinadav, T.; Levy, P. Value of information in a mobile app supply chain under hidden or known information superiority. *Int. J. Prod. Econ.* **2022**, *248*, 108467. [CrossRef]
100. Li, Z.; Li, B.; Lan, Y. Contract design on digital platform for the risk-averse retailer with moral hazard. *Kybernetes* **2017**, *47*, 716–741. [CrossRef]
101. Jia, D.; Li, S. Optimal decisions and distribution channel choice of closed-loop supply chain when e-retailer offers online marketplace. *J. Clean. Prod.* **2020**, *265*, 121767. [CrossRef]
102. Xiang, Z.; Xu, M. Dynamic cooperation strategies of the closed-loop supply chain involving the internet service platform. *J. Clean. Prod.* **2019**, *220*, 1180–1193. [CrossRef]
103. Zhong, L.; Nie, J.; Lim, M.K.; Xia, S. Agency or Self-Run: The effect of consumer green education on recyclers' distribution channel choice under platform economy. *Int. J. Logist. Res. Appl.* **2021**, *25*, 814–836. [CrossRef]
104. Wang, Y.; Yu, Z.; Shen, L.; Dong, W. Impacts of altruistic preference and reward-penalty mechanism on decisions of E-commerce closed-loop supply chain. *J. Clean. Prod.* **2021**, *315*, 128132. [CrossRef]
105. Shen, B.; Xu, X.; Yuan, Q. Selling secondhand products through an online platform with blockchain. *Transp. Res. Part E Logist. Transp. Rev.* **2020**, *142*, 102066. [CrossRef]
106. Ma, D.; Hu, J. The optimal combination between blockchain and sales format in an internet platform-based closed-loop supply chain. *Int. J. Prod. Econ.* **2022**, *254*, 108633. [CrossRef]
107. Fan, X.; Zhao, W.; Zhang, T.; Yan, E. Mobile payment, third-party payment platform entry and information sharing in supply chains. *Ann. Oper. Res.* **2020**, 1–20. [CrossRef]
108. Li, Q.; Zha, Y.; Dong, Y. Subsidize or Not: The Competition of Credit Card and Online Credit in Platform-based Supply Chain System. *Eur. J. Oper. Res.* **2022**, *305*, 644–658. [CrossRef]
109. Luo, W.; Shang, K. Joint inventory and cash management for multidivisional supply chains. *Oper. Res.* **2015**, *63*, 1098–1116. [CrossRef]
110. Mitra, R.; Goswami, A.; Tiwari, M.K. Financial supply chain analysis with borrower identification in smart lending platform. *Expert Sys. Appl.* **2022**, *208*, 118026. [CrossRef]
111. Wang, C.; Chen, X.; Jin, W.; Fan, X. Credit guarantee types for financing retailers through online peer-to-peer lending: Equilibrium and coordinating strategy. *Eur. J. Oper. Res.* **2022**, *297*, 380–392. [CrossRef]
112. Wu, H.; Zheng, H.; Zhang, M. Credit payment services and pricing strategy in the digital economy era. *Ann. Oper. Res.* **2022**, 1–18. [CrossRef]

Article
Strategic Licensing of Green Technologies to a Brown Rival: A Game Theoretical Analysis

Liu Liu, Ying Yuan, Xiaoya Wang and Hongfu Huang *

School of Economics and Management, Nanjing University of Science and Technology, Nanjing 210094, China
* Correspondence: huanghf@njust.edu.cn

Abstract: This paper studies a green manufacturer's strategic licensing of its green technology to a brown rival under the consideration of the green manufacturer's environmental concerns. Consumers in the market have green awareness. Adopting the green technology not only helps manufacturers to reduce carbon emissions, but also to increase market sizes. The green manufacturer can choose from three technology licensing strategies, i.e., no licensing (N), royalty licensing (R) or fixed-fee licensing (F). The equilibrium licensing strategy can be derived by comparing the respective payoff after adopting the three strategies. It is found that the green manufacturer should choose fixed-fee licensing strategy when the market size expansion effect is strong, and the competition intensity is moderate; otherwise, the green manufacturer should choose royalty licensing strategy. Furthermore, it is found that when the green manufacturer is more concerned about environmental impacts, it will be more willing to choose fixed-fee licensing strategy, rather than royalty licensing strategy. Through numerical tests, some interesting results are also found. For example, the brown manufacturer might be hurt even if the cost reduction effect of technology licensing is relatively stronger. Moreover, it is found that consumer surplus and social welfare nonmonotonically change with the substitution level. In summary, this research tries to provide some guidelines to the industry and the society on better managing green technology diffusions.

Keywords: green technology licensing; environmental concern; competition; consumer surplus; social welfare

MSC: 91A12

Citation: Liu, L.; Yuan, Y.; Wang, X.; Huang, H. Strategic Licensing of Green Technologies to a Brown Rival: A Game Theoretical Analysis. *Mathematics* 2022, 10, 4433. https://doi.org/10.3390/math10234433

Academic Editor: David Barilla

Received: 8 November 2022
Accepted: 23 November 2022
Published: 24 November 2022

Publisher's Note: MDPI stays neutral with regard to jurisdictional claims in published maps and institutional affiliations.

Copyright: © 2022 by the authors. Licensee MDPI, Basel, Switzerland. This article is an open access article distributed under the terms and conditions of the Creative Commons Attribution (CC BY) license (https://creativecommons.org/licenses/by/4.0/).

1. Introduction

With the sustained development of economy, environmental problems, such as energy over consumption or carbon emission, of the industry and the society has increased substantially at the same time. Despite the impacts of the COVID-19 pandemic, the global monthly peak amount of carbon emission rose by 417.2 parts per million in May 2020 [1]. The environmental problems pose a great threat to not only the global ecological environment, but also hinder the health and sustainable development of society and economy. As Pimentel et al., suggested, about 40% of world deaths are caused by environmental degradation [2]. Furthermore, in 2010, the pollution in China cost about USD 227 billion to the Chinese economy, which accounts for 3.5% of the gross domestic production [3]. Developing green economy is becoming a common responsibility of all mankind. Under the advocacy of international organizations and national governments, green and environmental protection have gradually become two major themes of today's social development.

The deeper problem of sustainable development lies in the change of production mode and business philosophy, which depends on the renewal and iteration of technology and the upgradation of industrial mode to balance economic development and natural environment protection. Many manufacturers are investing in green technologies so that they can produce low-carbon products with greener processes to gain competitive advantages.

For example, Lenovo has developed a kind of low-temperature solder manufacturing process which helps to reduce 35% carbon emissions compared to traditional manufacturing processes [4]. In Europe, about 900 firms have spent over EUR 125 billion in low-carbon technology research and development [5]. However, in actual operation, only a few firms have the key technologies of energy conservation or environmental protection. Taking new energy vehicles as an example, the solution to the problem of battery capacity and endurance is the core technology of leading enterprises, and this technical barrier is one of the key factors that affect energy conservation and environmental protection of enterprises.

Licensing of green technologies is a possible way to solve this problem, and it is also a scheme advocated by governments all over the world. In business practice, by green technology licensing, licensees can obtain such technologies, which help them to reduce environmental pollution or energy consumptions, and to achieve their goals of revenue gain and social responsibility improvement at the same time [6]. Furthermore, as licensors, green technology licensing can make up for the early R&D investments and improve the revenues by charging licensing fees.

However, in a competitive environment, although green technology licensing helps to improve environmental performance, it might not always be economically beneficial for the licensors. The reason is that licensing core green technologies might create powerful rivals that cannibalize their initial market shares. Therefore, the research question arises that

- (Q1) When should a manufacturer license the green technology to its rival under the consideration of both economic and environmental benefits?

According to technology licensing practices and theoretical researches, the licensors (the manufacturers who have the green technology) can either offer Royalty contracts or Fixed-fee contract to licensees (the manufacturers who do not have the green technology). In royalty licensing, the licensee (brown manufacturer) should pay a unit fee of all the products that produced by the licensor's (the green manufacturer's) technology, while in fixed-fee licensing, the licensee only needs to pay a lump-sum fee to the licensor and obtain the green technology. Therefore, two additional research questions arise that:

- (Q2) If technology licensing becomes an option, how to design the licensing contract, including the contract type (R or F) and licensing fee?
- (Q3) How will technology licensing affect the coopetition relationship between the licensors and licensees?

To answer the above research questions, game theoretical models are established for the three cases. The research findings can be summarized as follows. First, in this paper, it is found that technology licensing is always profitable for the green manufacturer. Second, comparing the two technology licensing contracts of F and R, it is found that higher cost saving effect, market expansion effect or environmental concern will incent the green manufacturer to implement strategy F. Otherwise, it is better for the green manufacturer to choose strategy R. Additionally, it is found that the impacts of competition intensity on the strategy choice is nonmonotonic. Only when competition intensity is moderate, will the green manufacturer implement strategy F; otherwise, for very high or very low level of competition intensity, strategy R will be chosen. Third, the sensitivity results of critical parameters on manufacturers' payoff, consumer surplus and social welfare are presented. It shows that more intense competition always hurts the green manufacturer, however, it may benefit the brown manufacturer when the technology licensing strategy switches from R to F. It also interesting that the maximum of consumer surplus or social welfare appears for moderate levels of substitution level.

This research aims to provide some guidelines to firms in the green product market about their green technology licensing strategies. The rest of the paper is organized as follows. In Section 2, the relevant prior literature is discussed. Section 3 develops the base model. In Sections 4 and 5, the manufacturers' equilibrium decisions and social welfare are analyzed, respectively. Section 6 summarizes the theoretical contributions of this paper. Section 7 concludes the paper, including the managerial implications and future research directions.

2. Literature Review

The research involves three research streams, namely, Coopetition strategies, Technology licensing, and Selling of green products.

2.1. Coopetition Strategies

Coopetition denotes a relationship between entities that compete and cooperate with each other at the same time. It appears in various management fields, such as outsourcing decisions [7,8], strategic alliances [9,10] and supply chain operations [11–13]. Take the automobile industry as example, [14–17] has investigated the external and internal driven forces of the coopetition between FV and NEV under the impacts of dual-credit policy. Among the factors, they demonstrate that the FV's negative credits pressure acts as the external driven force, while the technology R&D initiatives act as the internal driven force.

In addition, the advantages and disadvantages of coopetition strategies for participating firms, and the optimal choice of coopetition strategy have been investigated by scholars [18]. Venkatesh et al., show that, among three distribution strategies, co-optor strategy performs the best for manufacturers of proprietary component brands [19]. Chen et al., present the impacts of production substitution and interfirm power relationship on the optimal coopetition strategy for two manufacturers [20]. This paper regards horizontal green technology licensing as a type of coopetition between a green manufacturer and a brown one, which is different from the existing literature on coopetition theories.

2.2. Technology Licensing

The Second stream of literature is technology licensing strategies in supply chains. In existing literature, firms often face the trade-off on expected revenues and associated costs when determine whether to license their technologies. On one hand, technology licensing generates a channel of profit of licensing fee, however, on the other hand, licensing its technology will create another competitor and may cannibalize their market shares. How to deal with the trade-off is the main problem for firms when they determine the licensing strategies [21,22]. In the existing literature, an important decision for licensors is to design the technology licensing contracts. The contract types are varied, such as fixed-fee contract, royalty contract or two-part tariff contract. Many scholars have carried out research on the difference between different types of technology licensing contracts. Wang shows that when licensors participate in product competition, the fixed-fee contract is superior to the royalty contract when they have competitive market advantages over licensees [23]. A large number of scholars have done extensive research on the basis of [23] and verified the above conclusions. For example, Faul-Oller extended the product competition model to the price competition model [24]. Wang extended the homogeneous product model to the differentiated product model [25]. Kamien and Tauman established a technology licensing model with multiple licensees [26]. Heywood et al., introduced asymmetric information into the model [27].

In addition, many scholars also considered other factors, such as technology imitation behaviors, technology innovation degree, on the licensing contract design. Rockett studied the optimal technology licensing strategy in duopoly market. He found that in industries where imitation cost is lower and products are easier to imitate, fixed-fee licensing is dominant [28]. Kabiraj shows the impacts of technological innovation degree on the choice of licensing contracts among fixed-fee, royalty and auction [29]. From the above literature, it is found that most of the existing literature focuses on the research of normal technology licensing, while it has not analyzed the environmental benefits that generated by green technologies. Therefore, this paper tries to enrich the existing literature on technology licensing by considering the greenness property of the technology.

2.3. Marketing of Green Products

In recent years, more and more consumers are changing their consumption behaviors when facing the rising environmental issues in society. They are becoming more willing to purchase green products, which encourages firms to produce and sell eco-friendly products. In this stream of literature, scholars mainly concentrate on the studies of green products selling strategies considering consumers' environmental awareness (CEA), which help to improve firms' profits and social welfares. Some scholars have introduced consumer preference into the competition model of green and non-green products to study the influence of CEA. For example, Conrad constructed a duopoly model with greenness differentiation to analyze how CEA affects the pricing, product characteristics and market share of competing firms. The results show that the market share of green products increases with the enhancement of CEA. However, as the green products' production cost increases, the market share will drop [30]. Roberto analyzed the influence of different types of consumers on product sales and environment impacts in a duopoly competition model. It shows that the enhancement of CEA may lead to the increase of non-green products sales, and surprisingly generate negative environmental impacts [31].

In addition, some scholars have studied other aspects of market competition of green products. Zhang et al., analyzed the coordinated pricing strategy of green and brown manufacturers in two production modes: cooperative games and non-cooperative games. The results show that the system performance of a cooperative game is obviously better than that of a non-cooperative game [32]. Zhu and He analyze the impacts of important factors, including green product type, supply chain structure and competition type, on product greenness design [33]. From the above literature, it is found that at present, the literature on market competition of green products mainly focuses on the problems of pricing and quantity decisions, while how green technology licensing affect the competition and cooperation relationship among competing firms and the corresponding decisions has not been studied, which is the focus of this research.

3. Model Formulation

This paper establishes a game model with two competing manufacturers who produce and sell substitutable products in the same market. The key difference between the two manufacturers' products lies in their levels of production technology. Without loss of generality, it is assumed that Manufacturer 1 has a kind of green technology, while Manufacturer 2 does not have such a technology. This corresponds to the fact that some powerful manufacturers have abundant funds to support the research and development of green technologies, while some small manufacturers' funds are not enough, and they have no such ability to develop their own green technologies.

The adoption of such a green technology affects the manufacturers in two ways. Firstly, it has impacts on manufacturers' unit production costs. Adopting green technology may help to save unit production costs. For example, a brown manufacturer needs to pay for carbon emission tax if green technology is not implemented, while a green manufacturer can save such tax payment. Without loss of generality, it is assumed that a manufacturer's production cost is zero when green technology is implemented, while the production cost is $t(>0)$ when green technology is not implemented.

Secondly, it has impacts on consumers' purchasing behaviors. The inverse demand function of manufacturer i in the market is formulated as $p_i = \alpha_i - q_i - \beta q_{3-i}$ ($i = 1, 2$). In the function, q_i is the sales quantity of manufacturer i, and β ($0 \leq \beta \leq 1$) represents the substitutability of the two manufacturers' products [34–37]. It also denotes the competition intensity between two manufacturers. Higher β means higher substitutability or competition intensity of products produced by two manufacturers. The parameter of α_i represents the potential market size for manufacturer i. According to the relevant literature, green products have stronger market effect, that is, consumers are more inclined to buy green products than to buy brown products. In this model, adopting green technology generates higher market size, that is, $\alpha_i = 1$ when green technology is not adopted, while $\alpha_i = A > 1$ when green technology is adopted by manufacturer i.

In the market, manufacturer 1 can license the technology to manufacturer 2 to maximize its own payoff. Manufacturer 1 has three choices of licensing.

- Firstly, it can choose not to license the technology and maintain its competitiveness of selling green products exclusively. The market sizes for the two manufacturers are $(\alpha_1, \alpha_2) = (A, 1)$. This strategy is denoted as N (a benchmark).
- Secondly, it can license the technology to Manufacturer 2 with a royalty contract. Specifically, with the adoption of a royalty contract, manufacturer 2 should pay a unit fee of r to Manufacturer 1 for each sold product that produced by the green technology. The total payment can be expressed as rq_2. This strategy is denoted as R.
- Lastly, Manufacturer 1 can also offer a fixed-fee contract to Manufacturer 2. Specifically, Manufacturer 1 only charges a fixed amount of licensing fee f, which is independent of the sales quantities. This strategy is denoted as F.

In strategy R and F, manufacturer 2 also enjoys the market size expansion benefit, and the two manufacturers' market shares can be expressed as $(\alpha_1, \alpha_2) = (A, A)$. It also enjoys the production reduction benefits, i.e., its production costs drop to zero when green technology is implemented. The supply chain structures for the three cases are shown in Figure 1.

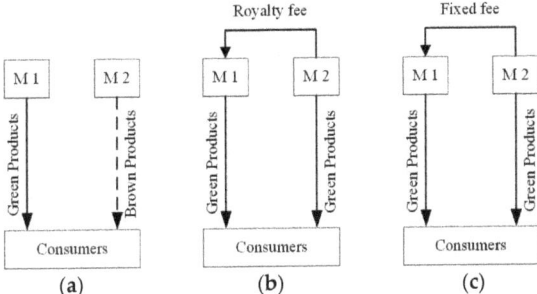

Figure 1. Supply chain structures. (**a**) Strategy N; (**b**) Strategy R; (**c**) Strategy F.

Then, the manufacturers' payoffs are formulated as follows. Different from previous literature on technology licensing which mainly concentrates on firms' economic gains, environmental benefits are incorporated into the green manufacturer's (i.e., manufacturer 1's) payoff functions. In other words, some leading manufacturers in the industry (such as Tesla) are not only caring about profits, but also about environmental benefits. Therefore, such a dual purpose for Manufacturer 1 is considered in its decision making. However, the brown manufacturer only cares about the maximization of profits, regardless of the environmental benefits.

Then, the environmental impacts of green technology adoption can be measured as follows. Assuming that, a unit green product generates e environmental benefits to the whole society, parameter e can be treated as the carbon emission reduction amount, or the energy saving amount during the lifecycle of the green products. It can also represent the greenness level of the technology. However, it is assumed that a unit brown product generates zero environmental benefits to the whole society. One may argue that brown products might have negative impacts on the environment. In this paper, to highlight the environmental benefits of green products, the impacts of brown products are normalized to zero for simplicity. In summary, the total environmental impact (positive) can be formulated as $ENVI = eQ^j$, where Q^j represents the total quantity of green products that sold to the market in strategy $j \in \{N, R, F\}$.

Then, Manufacturer 1's payoff that linked to the environmental benefit is formulated as $E^j = \delta(ENVI)^2/2, j \in \{N, R, F\}$. In this formulation, parameter δ characterized manufacturer 1's environmental benefit concern level. Furthermore, this formulation denotes that the total environmental payoff is quadratically increasing in the total sales of green products in the whole market (including its rival's sales quantities). To simplify the analysis and to focus on the analysis on manufacturer 1's environmental concern, the value of e is further normalized to 1. Other values of e do not affect the qualitative results in the following analysis. Therefore, the environmental payoff can be simplified as $E^j = \delta(Q^j)^2/2$, $j \in \{N, R, F\}$, which is used in the subsequent sections.

The formulation of both manufacturer's payoffs in the three scenarios will be expressed and explained in Section 4. The decision sequence of the model as follows:

- First, Manufacturer 1 decides whether to license the green technology to manufacturer 2. If technology licensing is allowed, it further makes decisions on the licensing contract (i.e., royalty or fixed-fee).
- Secondly, the two manufacturers make production and selling decisions at the same time to maximize their own payoffs.
- Lastly, the consumers make purchasing decisions and the market clears.

All the notations throughout the paper are summarized in Table 1.

Table 1. Notations.

Notations	Meanings
j	$j \in \{N, R, F\}$, denotes no licensing, royalty licensing and fixed-fee licensing.
i	$i \in \{1, 2\}$, denotes Manufacturer 1 and Manufacturer 2.
β	Substitution level of the two products, $0 \leq \beta \leq 1$.
e	Environmental benefit generated by unit green product, normalized to 1.
δ	Manufacturer 1's environmental concern level.
q_i^j	Manufacturer i's production quantity under licensing strategy j.
Q^j	Total production quantity of green products under licensing strategy j.
α_1	Manufacturer 1's market share, $\alpha_1 = A$.
α_2^j	Manufacturer 2's market share. $\alpha_2^j = 1$ for $j = N$, $\alpha_2^j = A$ for $j = \{F, R\}$.
p_i^j	Manufacturer i's selling price under licensing strategy j.
r	Royalty fee charged by Manufacturer 1 to Manufacturer 2 when $j = R$.
f	Fixed fee charged by Manufacturer 1 to Manufacturer 2 when $j = F$.
π_i^j	Manufacturer i's payoff under strategy j.
SW^j	Social welfare under strategy j.
E^j	Environmental payoff under strategy j, $E^j = \delta(Q^j)^2/2$.
CS^j	Customer surplus under strategy j.

4. Model Analysis

In this section, first, the two manufacturers' decisions for the three licensing strategies are analyzed. Second, the equilibrium payoffs are analyzed, and the equilibrium licensing strategy is derived.

4.1. Strategy N: No Licensing

In this strategy, Manufacturer 1 does not license the technology to Manufacturer 2. Therefore, the total sales quantity of green products is q_1^N. Considering Manufacturer 1's social responsibility level δ, the environmental payoff that Manufacturer 1 can gain by selling green products can be formulated as $E^N = \frac{\delta}{2} q_1^{N2}$. Considering both the economic and environmental payoffs, the two manufacturers' payoffs are formulated as follows:

$$\pi_1^N(q_1^N) = \underbrace{\left(A - q_1^N - \beta q_2^N\right) q_1^N}_{Economic\ Payoff} + \underbrace{\frac{\delta}{2} q_1^{N2}}_{Environmental\ Payoff}, \quad (1)$$

$$\pi_2^N(q_2^N) = \left(1 - \beta q_1^N - q_2^N - t\right) q_2^N \quad (2)$$

Then, the two manufacturers make quantity decisions of q_1^N and q_2^N simultaneously. The results are summarized as follows.

Proposition 1. *When strategy N is adopted,*

(1) *If* $1 < A < \frac{(1-t)(2-\delta)}{\beta}$, *the optimal sales quantities are* $q_1^{N*} = \frac{2A-\beta+t\beta}{4-\beta^2-2\delta}$, $q_2^{N*} = \frac{(1-t)(2-\delta)-A\beta}{4-\beta^2-2\delta}$.
The corresponding profits are $\pi_1^{N*} = \frac{(2A-(1-t)\beta)^2(2-\delta)}{2(4-\beta^2-2\delta)^2}$, $\pi_2^{N*} = \frac{((1-t)(2-\delta)-A\beta)^2}{(4-\beta^2-2\delta)^2}$.

(2) *If* $A \geq \frac{(1-t)(2-\delta)}{\beta}$, *the optimal sales quantities are* $q_1^{N*} = \frac{A}{2-\delta}$, $q_2^{N*} = 0$. *The corresponding profits are* $\pi_1^{N*} = \frac{A^2}{2(2-\delta)}$, $\pi_2^{N*} = 0$. *See the proofs in Appendix A.*

From Proposition 1, it shows that, in the scenario of technological monopoly, the payoffs of the manufacturers will be jointly influenced by the market size A of green products, the substitutability degree β of products, the environmental benefit indicator δ and the production cost t. Firstly, it shows the impacts of market size A on the equilibrium results. When A is relatively small, Manufacturer 2 can enter the market and earn positive profit. However, when A is relatively higher, Manufacturer 1 will set a higher sales quantity such that manufacturer 2 cannot enter the market due to its disadvantage of market size. Secondly, it shows that when the competition intensity is relatively small, Manufacturer 2 can enter the market successfully. However, when the competition intensity becomes relatively high, Manufacturer 1 will set a higher sales quantity to drive Manufacturer 2 out of the market. Thirdly, without technology licensing, if Manufacturer 1 is more careful about the environmental payoff, it will set a higher sales quantity to drive Manufacturer 2 out of the market. The reason is that, to maintain a higher level of environmental payoff, Manufacturer 2's goal is to increase the total sales quantity of green products, while to decrease the quantity of brown products in the market. Therefore, when the parameter of δ is higher, it will be more aggressive to drive Manufacturer 2 out of the market and achieve higher environmental payoffs. Conversely, when δ is lower, Manufacturer 1 cares less about the environmental payoffs. Therefore, it gives Manufacturer 2 a chance to enter the market. Lastly, when the brown manufacturer's production disadvantage t is higher, it will be more likely to be driven out of the market when the green manufacturer releases more products to the market, which conforms to intuition.

4.2. Strategy R: Licensing with Royalty Contract

In the case that Manufacturer 1 adopts the royalty licensing strategy, Manufacturer 2 pays a unit fee for its products that using the green technology to Manufacturer 1. At the same time, all the products in the market are green products, and Manufacturer 1's environmental payoff is not only linked to its own sales quantities, but also linked to Manufacturer 2's sales quantities. The environmental payoff can be expressed as $E^R = \frac{\delta}{2}\left(q_1^R + q_2^R\right)^2$. Moreover, considering the market size expansion effect, and production cost reduction effect, both manufacturers' payoff functions are formulated respectively as follow.

$$\pi_1^R\left(r, q_1^R\right) = \underbrace{\left(A - q_1^R - \beta q_2^R\right)q_1^R + rq_2^R}_{Economic\ Payoff} + \underbrace{\frac{\delta}{2}\left(q_1^R + q_2^R\right)^2}_{Environmental\ Payoff}, \quad (3)$$

$$\pi_2^R\left(q_2^R\right) = \left(A - \beta q_1^R - q_2^R\right)q_2^R - rq_2^R. \quad (4)$$

Manufacturer 1 first determines the royalty fee r. Then, the two manufacturers make quantity decisions of q_1^R and q_2^R simultaneously. The results are summarized as follows.

Proposition 2. *When strategy R is adopted,*

(1) *the optimal royalty fee is* $r^* = \frac{A(8-4\beta^2+\beta^3+(8\beta+\beta^2-16)\delta+(6-4\beta)\delta^2)}{(2-\delta)(8-3\beta^2-6\delta+4\beta\delta)}$.
The optimal sales quantities are $q_1^{R*} = \frac{A(2-\beta)(4+\beta-2\delta)}{(2-\delta)(8-3\beta^2-6\delta+4\beta\delta)}$, $q_2^{R*} = \frac{2A(1-\beta)}{8-3\beta^2-6\delta+4\beta\delta}$.
The corresponding profits are $\pi_1^{R*} = \frac{A^2(\beta^2+6(2-\delta)-4\beta(2-\delta))}{2(2-\delta)(8-3\beta^2-6\delta+4\beta\delta)}$, $\pi_2^{R*} = \frac{4A^2(1-\beta)^2}{(8-3\beta^2-6\delta+4\beta\delta)^2}$.

(2) $\pi_1^{R*} \geq \pi_1^{N*}$ and $\pi_2^{R*} \geq \pi_2^{N*}$. See the proofs in Appendix B.

In Proposition 2, it shows that in the case of royalty licensing, the optimal royalty fee r exists, which is determined by the values of market size A, substitutability degree β and social responsibility level δ. With simple calculation, it shows that the optimal royalty fee is increasing in A and β, while decreasing in δ. This denotes that when the market size expansion effect is strong, or the competition is more intense, Manufacturer 1 is more willing to license the technology to Manufacturer 2 without losing much of its market share, thus protecting its sales profits. However, when the parameter of δ increases, to induce more production of green products in the market, Manufacturer 1 will set a lower royalty level. In other words, a lower royalty fee reduces Manufacturer 2's unit product costs and enables Manufacturer 2 to produce more green products, which in turn contributes to Manufacturer 1's environmental payoffs. Comparing scenario R to scenario N, it is found that both manufacturers' profits in scenario R are becoming strictly higher. Therefore, it can be concluded that, royalty licensing benefits both manufacturers and result in a "win-win" outcome.

4.3. Strategy F: Licensing with Fixed-Fee Contract

When Manufacturer 1 adopts the fixed-fee licensing strategy, Manufacturer 2 should pay a fixed amount of money f to Manufacturer 1, in exchange for the green technology patent. In this scenario, the payment is independent of sales quantities. Like scenario R, in this scenario, all the products in the market will be green and Manufacturer 1's environmental payoff should be $E^F = \frac{\delta}{2}\left(q_1^F + q_2^F\right)^2$. Moreover, considering the market size expansion effect, both manufacturers' payoff functions are formulated respectively as follows.

$$\pi_1^F\left(q_1^F\right) = \underbrace{\left(A - q_1^F - \beta q_2^F\right)q_1^F + f}_{Economic\ Payoff} + \underbrace{\frac{\delta}{2}\left(q_1^F + q_2^F\right)^2}_{Environmental\ Payoff}, \quad (5)$$

$$\pi_2^F\left(q_2^F\right) = \left(A - \beta q_1^F - q_2^F\right)q_2^F - f. \quad (6)$$

Manufacturers 1 and 2 first negotiate on the determination of the fixed payment f. Assuming that, the two manufacturers have equal bargaining power. Then, the two manufacturers make quantity decisions of q_1^R and q_2^R simultaneously. The results are summarized as follows.

Proposition 3. *When strategy F is adopted, let*

(1) *If* $1 < A < \frac{(1-t)(2-\delta)}{\beta}$ *(Scenario F1), Manufacturer 1's optimal fixed fee is* $f_1^* = \frac{(1-t)^2(-2+\delta)}{4(4-\beta^2-2\delta)}$ $+ \frac{2A^2\left(\beta^3 + 2(-2+\delta)^2(-1+2\delta) + 2\beta^2(1+(-3+\delta)\delta) + \beta(-4+\delta^2)\right)}{4(4-\beta^2-2\delta)(-2+\beta)(2+\beta-\delta)^2}$.
The equilibrium quantities are $q_1^F = \frac{A(2-\beta+\delta)}{(2-\beta)(2+\beta-\delta)}, q_2^F = \frac{A(2-\beta-\delta)}{(2-\beta)(2+\beta-\delta)}$.
The corresponding profits are $\pi_1^F = \frac{A^2\left(4+(4-3\delta)\delta+\beta^2-2\beta(2-\delta)(1+\delta)\right)}{(2-\beta)^2(2+\beta-\delta)^2} + f_1$, $\pi_2^F = \frac{A^2(2-\beta-\delta)^2}{(2-\beta)^2(2+\beta-\delta)^2} - f_1$.

(2) *If* $A \geq \frac{(1-t)(2-\delta)}{\beta}$ *(Scenario F2), Manufacturer 1's optimal fixed fee is* $f_2^* = \frac{A^2(2-\beta-\delta)\left((2+\beta)^2-(10+3\beta)\delta+4\delta^2\right)}{4(2-\beta)(2+\beta-\delta)^2(2-\delta)}$.
The equilibrium quantities are $q_1^F = \frac{A(2-\beta+\delta)}{(2-\beta)(2+\beta-\delta)}, q_2^F = \frac{A(2-\beta-\delta)}{(2-\beta)(2+\beta-\delta)}$.
The corresponding profits are $\pi_1^F = \frac{A^2\left(4+\beta^2+(4-3\delta)\delta+2\beta(-2+\delta)(1+\delta)\right)}{(-2+\beta)^2(2+\beta-\delta)^2} + f_2$, $\pi_2^F = \frac{A^2(2-\beta-\delta)^2}{(2-\beta)^2(2+\beta-\delta)^2} - f_2$.

(3) $\pi_1^F \geq \pi_1^N$ *and* $\pi_2^F \geq \pi_2^N$. *See the proofs in Appendix C.*

In Proposition 3, it shows that under the strategy of fixed-fee licensing, there are also two situations. Specifically, when A, β, t and δ are small, Manufacturer 1 will set a lower fee and Manufacturer 2 can earn positive profit. However, when A, β, t and δ are relatively high, Manufacturer 1 becomes more powerful, and it will set a higher fee to extract more benefits of technology licensing. Therefore, Manufacturer 2's profit becomes lower. Notice that in the two situations, the two manufacturers have the same level of sales quantity, while the licensor's profit is higher than the licensee's profit because of the transferring of a fixed amount of licensing fee. Comparing scenario F with scenario N, it is found that both manufacturers' profits in scenario F are becoming higher than those in scenario N. Therefore, it can be concluded that, fixed-fee licensing benefits both manufacturers and results in a "win-win" outcome.

4.4. The Equilibrium Licensing Strategy

From the above analysis, it shows that technology licensing will always bring more profits to enterprises. This section will compare the payoffs of Manufacturer 1 under royalty licensing and fixed fee licensing to derive the equilibrium licensing strategy. (1) when strategy R is selected, the profits of Manufacturer 1 should satisfy $\pi_1^{R*} > \pi_1^{F*}$. (2) When strategy F is selected, the profits of Manufacturer 1 should satisfy $\pi_1^{F*} > \pi_1^{R*}$. By comparing the profits, the following proposition can be obtained.

Proposition 4. *(The equilibrium licensing strategy)*
(1) When $1 \leq A < \phi(t,\beta,\delta)$ and $0 \leq \beta < \widetilde{\beta}$, or $\widetilde{\beta} \leq \beta \leq 1$, the equilibrium licensing strategy is R.
(2) When $A > \phi(t,\beta,\delta)$ and $0 \leq \beta < \widetilde{\beta}$, the equilibrium licensing strategy is F. The expressions of $\phi(t,\beta,\delta)$ and $\widetilde{\beta}$ are provided in the Appendix D.

Proposition 4 shows that the choice of the optimal licensing strategy of the green technology depends on the market share A, the substitutability degree β, the production cost t and the social responsibility δ. The decision region is depicted in Figure 2. It can be seen from the figure that the region can be divided into three parts which are shaped by different ranges of parameters. For all the values of parameters, Manufacturer 1 can always earn higher profit when licensing technology, in comparison to no licensing. Therefore, strategy N does not exist in equilibrium. Manufacturer 1's can either choose to implement strategy F or strategy R.

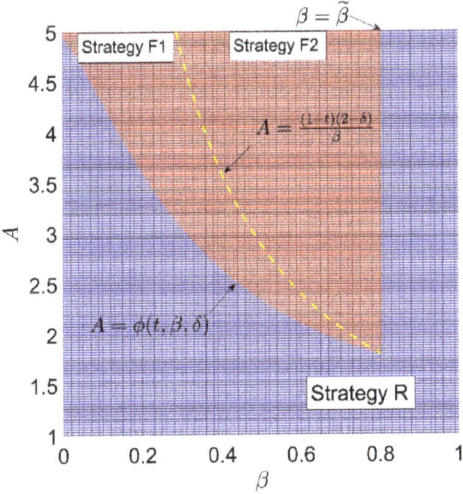

Figure 2. The decision region of technology licensing strategy.

First, when the substitutability of products is very high ($\tilde{\beta} < \beta \leq 1$), the equilibrium licensing strategy is royalty licensing (strategy R) for all the values of A. The reasons are as follows. When the technology is licensed to Manufacturer 2, Manufacturer 1's market size advantage disappears. If the substitutability level is high enough, in strategy F, the two manufacturers involve in direct competition in the final market, and this will hurt the benefits of Manufacturer 1. However, different to strategy F, strategy R makes the competition less fierce. In strategy R, the manufacturer has more power to directly control manufacturer 2's production cost and its sales quantities. Although in strategy R there would be losses caused by double marginalization effect, it is compensated by the gain due to the eased competition. Therefore, in this condition, Manufacturer 1 would always choose strategy R. This conclusion is also in line with real life cases. For example, in highly competitive industries such as high-tech electronic software products and new energy vehicles, most of the related licensing strategies such as chip technology and battery technology are royalty licensing.

Secondly, when the substitutability of products is not high ($0 < \beta \leq \tilde{\beta}$), the decision region of optimal licensing strategy will be divided into three parts based on different values of potential market share A. When the potential market size of green products is very small, the optimal strategy is royalty licensing. On one hand, when A is small, Manufacturer 1's profit increase under strategy F is not high, while royalty licensing can effectively defend the market share cannibalization from Manufacturer 2. Therefore, when A is relatively small, royalty licensing is preferred by Manufacturer 1. When the market size is large, enterprises will choose the fixed-fee licensing strategy. In this region, the market size expansion effect is strong while the competition effect is weak. The demand erosion effect of Manufacturer 2 to Manufacturer 1 is not strong. In this region, when fixed-fee licensing is adopted, the total supply chain efficiency will increase in comparison to royalty licensing (which generate double marginalization effect). Therefore, choosing the fixed-fee licensing strategy is more beneficial for manufacturer 1. At the same time, under this strategy, the output of both enterprises will be increased, which will also have a positive effect on environmental benefits and overall social welfare. Interestingly, combining (1) and (2), it is found that the impacts of substitution level on strategy choice is non-monotonic. When fixing the market size increment level A, the strategy switches from R to F, then back to R.

Lastly, it can be seen from Figures 3 and 4 about the impacts of t and δ on the decision regions. It is found that the shape of the decision region will not be affected by the level of δ and the production cost reduction t, but the size of the regions will change with the two parameters. A higher level of social responsibility weakens manufacturer 1's incentive to choose royalty licensing, while strengthen the incentive to choose fixed-fee licensing. This corresponds to the above analysis that fixed-fee licensing helps to achieve higher sales quantities of green products and achieve higher environmental payoffs for Manufacturer 1. Therefore, when Manufacturer 1 is more concerned about the environmental payoffs, fixed-fee licensing becomes more attractive. Moreover, when the cost saving effect is relatively strong, Manufacturer 1 becomes more willing to implement strategy F. From the results in Proposition 3, it can be observed that both parties' payoffs rise in t. Therefore, when t becomes higher, both manufacturers can benefit more from technology licensing, which makes strategy F more attractive for manufacturer 1.

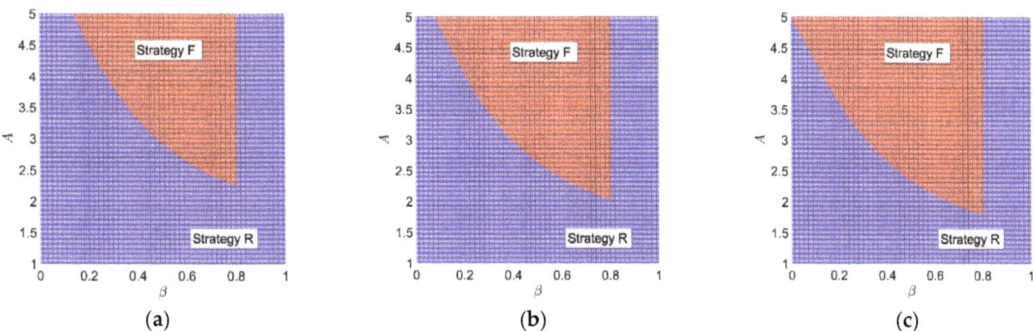

Figure 3. Impacts of t on the decision region when $\delta = 0.2$. (**a**) $t = 0$; (**b**) $t = 0.1$; (**c**) $t = 0.2$.

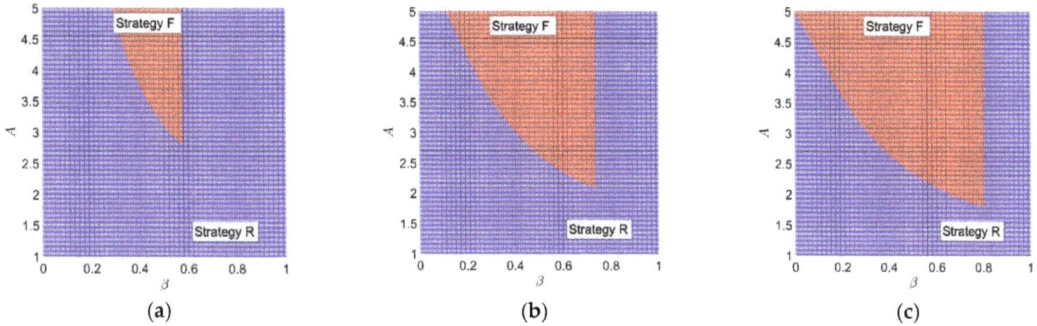

Figure 4. Impacts of δ on the decision region when $t = 0.2$. (**a**) $\delta = 0$; (**b**) $\delta = 0.1$; (**c**) $\delta = 0.2$.

To better illustrate the impacts of critical parameters, several numerical experiments are conducted, which are shown in Figure 5.

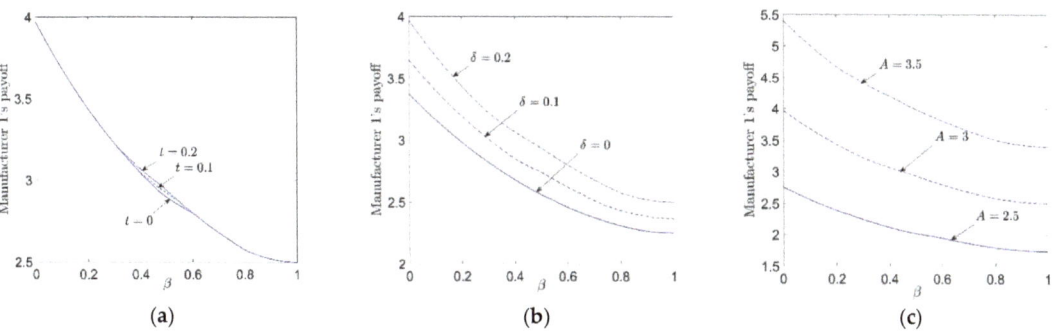

Figure 5. Impacts of β and (**a**) t (**b**) δ (**c**) A on Manufacturer 1's payoffs.

Observation 1. *(Impacts of t, A, δ and β on payoffs)*
In the equilibrium results,
(1) Manufacturer 1's payoff always decreases in β, while increases in t, A and δ.
(2) Manufacturer 2's payoff increases in A and δ, while can nonmonotonically change with t and β.

First, it is shown in Figures 5 and 6 that Manufacturer 1's payoff always decreases in the substitution level β. This conforms to intuition that intense competition always hurts Manufacturer 1's benefit. However, it is also presented that a manufacturer's payoff is nonmonotonic in β. When the strategy switches from R to F, a sudden rise appears. This provides an interesting result that Manufacturer 2 can benefit from the intensified competition when its competitor can switch the technology licensing strategy. Second, it shows the impacts of t on the two manufacturers' payoff in Figures 5a and 6a. It shows that manufacturer 1's payoff is weakly increasing in t, while Manufacturer 2's payoff can be nonmonotonic in t. This indicates that Manufacturer 1 can always benefit from the cost reduction effect generated by technology licensing. However, Manufacturer 2 does not always benefit from the cost reduction effect. Last, as one has expected, both manufacturers' payoffs increase in parameters A and δ which are shown in Figure 5b,c and Figure 6b,c. It is straightforward that Manufacturer 1's payoff increases when its environmental benefit concern rises. Then, when it is more concerned about the environmental benefit, it will be more willing to license the green technology and achieve higher sales quantities of green products in the whole market. This enables Manufacturer 2 to obtain such technology much easier (with lower license fee) and to generate higher payoff. Furthermore, it can be explained with similar reasons that higher market share A will induce Manufacturer 1's technology licensing, thus benefit both manufacturers.

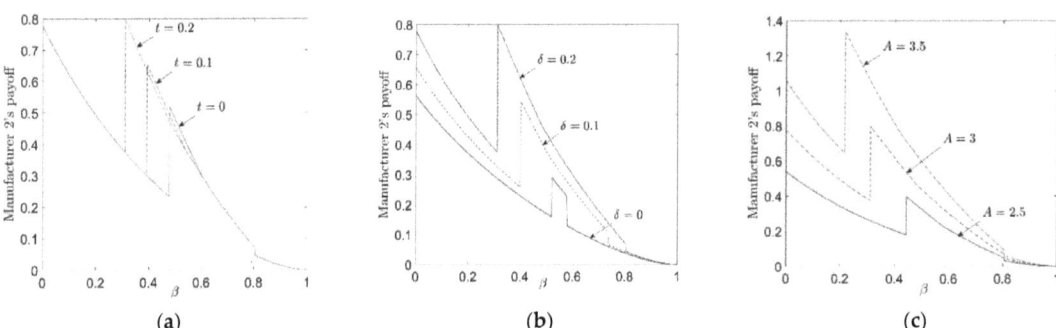

Figure 6. Impacts of β and (**a**) t (**b**) δ (**c**) A on Manufacturer 2's payoffs.

5. Welfare Implications

Following previous research of [34–37], social welfare can be formulated as follows. The social welfare consists of three parts, namely

$$SW^j = CS^j + \pi_1^j + \pi_2^j, \ j \in \{R, F\}. \tag{7}$$

The three parts on the right side of the formula represent: (i) consumer surplus, (ii) payoff (including economic benefits and environmental benefits) of Manufacturer 1, and (iii) payoff of Manufacturer 2, respectively. Following [34–37], and knowing the sales quantities, the consumer surplus can be formulated as

$$CS^j = \frac{\left[q_1^j\right]^2 + 2\beta q_1^j q_2^j + \left[q_2^j\right]^2}{2}, \ j \in \{R, F\}. \tag{8}$$

Under different licensing strategies, the expressions of social welfare are also different. Through calculation, social welfare for the two strategies can be expressed respectively as follows.

Proposition 5.

(1) When strategy R is adopted, the total social welfare in equilibrium is

$$CS^R = \frac{A^2\left[\beta^4(9-4\delta) + 20(-2+\delta)^2 - 8\beta(-2+\delta)\delta + 4\beta^3(3+2(-3+\delta)\delta) - 4\beta^2(19+2\delta(-9+2\delta))\right]}{(2(2-\delta)^2(8-3\beta^2-6\delta+4\beta\delta)^2)} \tag{9}$$

$$SW^R = \frac{A^2\left[\begin{array}{l}-\beta^4(-3+\delta)+4\beta^3(-5+2\delta)(-3+2\delta)-4(-2+\delta)^2(-19+9\delta)+\\ 8\beta(-2+\delta)(12+\delta(-19+6\delta))+4\beta^2(-25+\delta(7+(11-4\delta)\delta))\end{array}\right]}{(2(2-\delta)^2(8-3\beta^2-6\delta+4\beta\delta)^2)} \tag{10}$$

(2) When strategy F is adopted, the total social welfare in equilibrium is

$$CS^F = \frac{A^2(4+\delta^2+\beta((-3+\beta)\beta-\delta^2)}{(-2+\beta)^2(2+\beta-\delta)^2}. \tag{11}$$

$$SW^F = \frac{A^2((-2+\beta)^2(3+\beta)+(-1+\beta)\delta^2)}{(-2+\beta)^2(2+\beta-\delta)^2} \tag{12}$$

(3) $CS^F \geq CS^R$, $SW^F \geq SW^R$. See the proofs in Appendix E.

The expressions of CS and SW are presented in Proposition 4(1) and (2). Then, comparing CS and SW in the two cases, it is found that fixed fee licensing always generates higher CS and SW. The reason is as follows. When strategy F is adopted, the sales quantities are not dependent on the lump sum licensing fee, and the two manufacturers only have horizontal competition. However, in strategy R, the sales quantities are affected by the royalty licensing fee, and the two manufacturers have both horizontal and vertical competition. Comparing to strategy F, the existence of double marginalization effect in strategy R reduces the final sales quantities of the green products. Therefore, the total profits and environmental payoff in strategy R are lower than that in strategy F, which further result in lower consumer surplus and social welfare.

Next, the impacts of critical parameters on CS and SW are illustrated using numerical experiments, which are shown in Figure 6. The results are summarized in Observation 2.

Observation 2. *(Impacts of t, A, δ and β on SW and CS)*
(1) CS and SW increases in t, A and δ;
(2) CS and SW changes nonmonotonically in β.

In Observation 2, it first presents the impacts of parameters t, A and δ on consumer surplus and social welfare in Figures 7 and 8. It shows that both CS and SW increase in the three parameters. The results are straightforward, because higher t and A always generate higher profits for the two manufacturers, and higher δ stimulates technology licensing and results in higher environmental benefits.

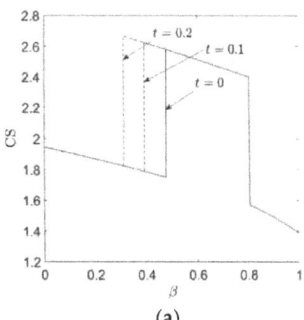
(a)

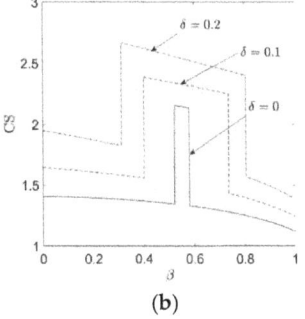
(b)

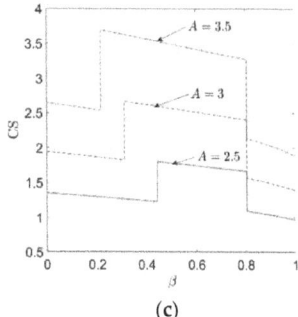
(c)

Figure 7. Impacts of β and (a) t (b) δ (c) A on CS.

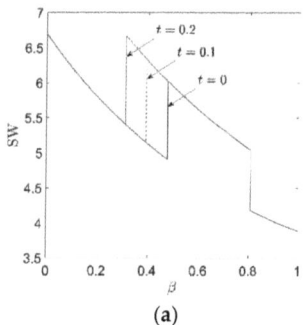 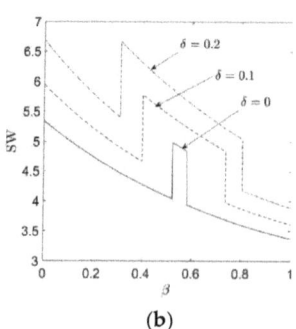 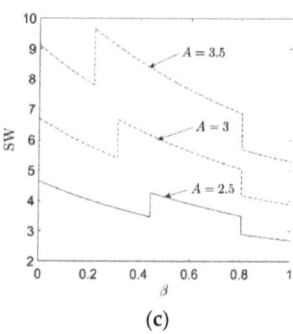

Figure 8. Impacts of β and (**a**) t (**b**) δ (**c**) A on SW.

Then, it shows the impacts of product substitution level β on CS and SW. Interestingly, it is found that both CS and SW are nonmonotonic in β. CS or SW experiences a sudden jump when the equilibrium strategy switches from R to F; then experiences a sudden drop when the equilibrium strategy switches from F to R. This provides a counterintuitive result that intense competition does not always benefit consumers and the society in a coopetition environment.

6. Theoretical Contributions

This research contributes to the existing literature in three aspects.

First, this paper contributes to the research of coopetition in supply chain management by incorporating horizontal green technology licensing strategies into the quantity and product greenness competition models. In existing research, coopetition between supply chain members mainly refers to outsourcing decisions in supply chains [7,8], strategic alliance formation [9,10], or coopetitive investments in quality or product greenness [11–13]. However, the notion that green technology licensing as a coopetative strategy between brown and green firms is seldom studied the existing literature. Therefore, this paper contributes to the theory of coopetition in supply chains. In the model analysis, we have highlighted the economical and environmental impacts of such coopetition.

Second, this paper has enriched the existing literature on technology licensing by considering the greenness property of the technology. In previous literature, researchers have considered various factors in technology licensing, such as product differentiation between licensors and licensees [25], multiple competition firms [25], imitation behaviours of technology [28], innovation degree of the technology [29], etc. However, none of them have realized the importance of factor of technology's green property. This paper fills this gap and has established new technology licensing models to study the new technology licensing problem. Additionally, some interesting and meaningful results concerning the technology's green property are also provided. These results not only contribute to firms' economic benefits (which is the focus of the existing literature), but also contribute to welfare implications (which provides important implications to the consumers and the governments).

Last, this paper has investigated how green technology licensing affect the selling strategies under competition. In the existing literature on green product selling, investing in greenness improvement is a good way to earn larger market coverage and more profits [32,33]. However, most of them focus on the cases that firms invest in greenness improvement by themselves. This paper provides a new way for firms to improve their product greenness, that is purchasing green technology license from green firms, which can avoid highly risky and expensive R&D of green technologies.

7. Conclusions

Green technology is becoming a driven force of sustainable development for the industry and society. In this paper, a green technology licensing problem between two manufacturers under the consideration of the licensor's environmental concerns is studied. Managerial implications and limitations and future research directions are presented as follows.

7.1. Managerial Implications

The managerial implications are as follows. First, in this model, it is found that the green manufacturer should always license its green technology to its rival with appropriate licensing contract design. Second, by comparing the two licensing contracts, i.e., royalty licensing and fixed-fee licensing, the equilibrium licensing strategy is obtained, which is shaped by critical factors in the model. It shows that higher cost saving effect, market expansion effect or environmental concern will incent the green manufacturer to implement strategy F. However, it shows that the impacts of product substitution on strategy choice is nonmonotonic. Specifically, only when the substitution level is moderate, the green manufacturer will implement strategy F; otherwise, for very high or very low level of substitution level, strategy R will be chosen. Third, it shows the sensitivity analysis results of critical parameters on manufacturers' payoff, consumer surplus and social welfare. Several interesting findings are presented. For example, more intense competition always hurts the green manufacturer, however, may benefit the brown manufacturer when the technology licensing strategy switches from R to F. Moreover, it is found that the maximum of consumer surplus or social welfare appears for moderate level of substitution level, which is counterintuitive.

7.2. Limitations and Future Research Directions

This paper has several limitations, which can be relaxed in future research. First, the production cost for the green manufacturer is not considered. In the future, the impacts of positive production cost on competing manufacturers' green technology licensing decisions can be further studied. Second, this paper only considers about two competing manufacturers. In the future, a more generalized case with multiple competing manufacturers can be studied, which is more realistic in business practice. Third, the formulation of the green technology licensor's environmental payoff is only linked to the green products. In the future, more generalized formulations of the environmental payoff can be considered. For example, in addition to the positive payoff incurred by green products, the negative payoff incurred by brown products could also be considered. Fourth, in the model, this paper has only considered the royalty and fixed fee licensing contract. In the future, other contracts can be considered in this model, such as revenue sharing, profit sharing and two-part tariff, etc. Fifth, in this paper, there exists one version of green technology. However, in real business, a licensor may have multiple versions of green technology. How will the adoption of each version of green technology alter the competition between the two firms and which one should be licensed to the brown firm is worth studying. Last, in this paper, the two manufacturers sell the products directly to the consumers. In the future research, we can extend the one-echelon supply chains to multiple-echelon supply chains. Therefore, how vertical and horizontal competition jointly affect manufacturers' technology licensing strategies needs to be carefully investigated in the future.

Author Contributions: Conceptualization, H.H.; methodology, validation, formal analysis, investigation, L.L. and Y.Y.; resources, writing—original draft preparation, writing—review and editing, visualization, H.H. and X.W.; supervision, H.H.; project administration, funding acquisition, H.H. All authors have read and agreed to the published version of the manuscript.

Funding: This work is supported by the National Natural Science Foundation of China (No. 72101117) and the Natural Science Foundation of Jiangsu Province (No. BK20200485).

Data Availability Statement: Not applicable.

Conflicts of Interest: The authors declare no conflict of interest.

Appendix A

Proof of Proposition 1. Solve the first order derivatives of

$$\frac{\partial \pi_1^N}{\partial q_1^N} = A - 2q_1^N - \beta q_1^N + \delta q_1^N = 0,$$

and $\dfrac{\partial \pi_2^N}{\partial q_2^N} = 1 - t - 2q_2^N - \beta q_1^N = 0,$

it can obtain the results of

$$q_1^{N*} = \frac{-2A + \beta - t\beta}{-4 + \beta^2 + 2\delta}, q_2^{N*} = \frac{-2 + A\beta - t(-2 + \delta) + \delta}{-4 + \beta^2 + 2\delta}.$$

Comparing the results, it is found that the results exist iff $1 < A < \frac{(1-t)(2-\delta)}{\beta}$. However, when $A > \frac{(1-t)(2-\delta)}{\beta}$, $q_2^{N*} \leq 0$ which is not a reasonable solution. Therefore, when $A > \frac{(1-t)(2-\delta)}{\beta}$, manufacturer 2 cannot enter the market. By setting $q_2^{N*} = 0$, and solve the problem of manufacturer 1, $q_1^{N*} = \frac{A}{2-\delta}$. Substituting the results into the payoff functions, we obtain the results in Proposition 1. □

Appendix B

Proof of Proposition 2. Solve the first order derivatives of

$$\frac{\partial \pi_1^R}{\partial q_1^R} = A - 2q_1^R - \beta q_2^R + \delta(q_1^R + q_2^R) = 0,$$

and $\dfrac{\partial \pi_2^R}{\partial q_2^R} = A - 2q_2^R - \beta q_1^R - r = 0,$

it can obtain the response functions of

$$q_1^R = \frac{2A - A\beta + r\beta + A\delta - r\delta}{(2-\beta)(2+\beta-\delta)}, q_2^R = \frac{2A - 2r - A\beta - A\delta + r\delta}{(2-\beta)(2+\beta-\delta)}.$$

Substitute the response functions into the payoff functions, it obtains

$$\pi_1^R = \frac{\begin{bmatrix} r^2(-2+\delta)(8-3\beta^2-6\delta+4\beta\delta) + 2Ar(8+\beta^3+\beta^2(-4+\delta)-16\delta-4\beta(-2+\delta)\delta+6\delta^2) \\ +2A^2(4+\beta^2+4\delta-3\delta^2+2\beta(-2-\delta+\delta^2)) \end{bmatrix}}{2(-2+\beta)^2(2+\beta-\delta)^2},$$

$$\pi_2^R = \frac{(r(-2+\delta) - A(-2+\beta+\delta))^2}{(-2+\beta)^2(2+\beta-\delta)^2}.$$

Then, manufacturer 1 determine the optimal royalty fee to maximize the payoff. Solving the first order derivative of

$$\frac{\partial \pi_1^R}{\partial r} = \frac{2r(-2+\delta)(8-3\beta^2-6\delta+4\beta\delta) + 2A(8+\beta^3+\beta^2(-4+\delta)-16\delta-4\beta(-2+\delta)\delta+6\delta^2)}{2(-2+\beta)^2(2+\beta-\delta)^2} = 0,$$

it obtains the optimal licensing royalty fee as

$$r^* = \frac{A(8 - 4\beta^2 + \beta^3 - 16\delta + 8\beta\delta + \beta^2\delta + 6\delta^2 - 4\beta\delta^2)}{(2-\delta)(8 - 3\beta^2 - 6\delta + 4\beta\delta)}.$$

Substituting the royalty fee into the above functions it obtains the equilibrium sales quantities and profits, which are summarized in Proposition 2. □

Appendix C

Proof of Proposition 3. Solving the first order derivatives of

$$\frac{\partial \pi_1^F}{\partial q_1^F} = A - 2q_1^F - \beta q_2^F + \delta\left(q_1^F + q_2^F\right) = 0,$$

and $\dfrac{\partial \pi_2^F}{\partial q_2^F} = A - 2q_2^F - \beta q_1^F = 0,$

it obtains the two manufacturers' sales quantities as

$$q_1^{F*} = \frac{2A - A\beta + A\delta}{(2-\beta)(2+\beta-\delta)}, q_2^{F*} = \frac{2A - A\beta - A\delta}{(2-\beta)(2+\beta-\delta)}.$$

Substitute the sales quantities into the payoff functions,

$$\pi_1^F = \frac{A^2\left(4 + \beta^2 + 4\delta - 3\delta^2 + 2\beta(-2 - \delta + \delta^2)\right)}{(-2+\beta)^2(2+\beta-\delta)^2} + f,$$

and $\pi_2^F = \dfrac{A^2(-2+\beta+\delta)^2}{(-2+\beta)^2(2+\beta-\delta)^2} - f.$

From the expressions of π_1^F, manufacturer 1's payoff function increases in f, however it should be constrained such that manufacturer 2 is profitable, i.e., $\pi_2^F - \pi_2^N \geq 0$. Therefore, the two manufacturers negotiate on the optimal f. According to the Nash bargaining model, the problem is to solve the target function of $Max\left\{\left(\pi_1^F - \pi_1^N\right)^\gamma \left(\pi_2^F - \pi_2^N\right)^{1-\gamma}\right\}$. In the function, γ denotes the bargaining power of manufacturer 1. In this model, it is assumed that the two manufacturers have equal bargaining power, i.e., $\gamma = 0.5$.

Consider the first scenario of $1 < A < \frac{(1-t)(2-\delta)}{\beta}$, and maximize the target function, it obtains the optimal fixed licensing fee as

$$f^* = \frac{(1-t)^2(-2+\delta)}{4(4-\beta^2-2\delta)} + \frac{2A^2\left(\beta^3 + 2(-2+\delta)^2(-1+2\delta) + 2\beta^2(1+(-3+\delta)\delta) + \beta(-4+\delta^2)\right)}{4(4-\beta^2-2\delta)(-2+\beta)(2+\beta-\delta)^2}.$$

Then, consider the second scenario of $A > \frac{(1-t)(2-\delta)}{\beta}$ and maximizing the target function, it obtains the optimal fixed licensing fee as

$$f^* = \frac{A^2(2-\beta-\delta)\left((2+\beta)^2 - (10+3\beta)\delta + 4\delta^2\right)}{4(2-\beta)(2+\beta-\delta)^2(2-\delta)}.$$

Substitute f^* into the payoff functions, the results can be obtained in Proposition 3. □

Appendix D

Proof of Proposition 4. The equilibrium is obtained by comparing the payoffs in the three strategies

(1) when $1 < A < \frac{(1-t)(2-\delta)}{\beta}$, the conditions that manufacturer 1 choose royalty contract are

$$\begin{cases} (1)\pi_1^{R*} = \frac{A^2(\beta^2+6(2-\delta)-4\beta(2-\delta))}{2(2-\delta)(8-3\beta^2-6\delta+4\beta\delta)} > \pi_1^{N*} = \frac{(2A-(1-t)\beta)^2(2-\delta)}{2(4-\beta^2-2\delta)^2} \\ (2)\pi_1^{R*} = \frac{A^2(\beta^2+6(2-\delta)-4\beta(2-\delta))}{2(2-\delta)(8-3\beta^2-6\delta+4\beta\delta)} > \pi_1^{F*} = \frac{A^2(4+(4-3\delta)\delta+\beta^2-2\beta(2-\delta)(1+\delta))}{(2-\beta)^2(2+\beta-\delta)^2} + f_1^* \\ (3)\pi_2^{R*} = \frac{4A^2(1-\beta)^2}{(8-3\beta^2-6\delta+4\beta\delta)^2} > \pi_2^{N*} = \frac{((1-t)(2-\delta)-A\beta)^2}{(4-\beta^2-2\delta)^2} \end{cases}$$

Solving the above inequalities, it obtains $A < \phi(t,\beta,\delta)$, where

$$\phi(t,\beta,\delta) = \frac{\sqrt{\frac{(-1+t)^2(-2+\delta)}{-4+\beta^2+2\delta}}}{\sqrt{\left(\begin{array}{c}\frac{4(-1+\beta)}{(-2+\beta)^2} + \frac{4\beta(-4+\beta(4+\beta))}{(-2+\beta)^2(2+\beta-\delta)^2} - \frac{8(-1+\beta)(2+\beta)}{(-2+\beta)^2(2+\beta-\delta)} \\ -\frac{2\beta^2}{(4-8\beta+3\beta^2)(-2+\delta)} - \frac{2}{-4+\beta^2+2\delta} + \frac{16(-1+\beta)^2(-3+2\beta)}{(-2+\beta)(-2+3\beta)(8-3\beta^2-6\delta+4\beta\delta)}\end{array}\right)}}.$$

(2) when $A \geq \frac{(1-t)(2-\delta)}{\beta}$, the conditions that manufacturer 1 chooses royalty contract are

$$\begin{cases} (1)\pi_1^{R*} = \frac{A^2(\beta^2-6(-2+\delta)+4\beta(-2+\delta))}{2(2-\delta)(8-3\beta^2-6\delta+4\beta\delta)} > \pi_1^{N*} = \frac{A^2}{2(2-\delta)} \\ (2)\pi_1^{R*} = \frac{A^2(\beta^2-6(-2+\delta)+4\beta(-2+\delta))}{2(2-\delta)(8-3\beta^2-6\delta+4\beta\delta)} > \pi_1^{F*} = \frac{A^2(4+(4-3\delta)\delta+\beta^2-2\beta(2-\delta)(1+\delta))}{(2-\beta)^2(2+\beta-\delta)^2} + f_2^* \\ (3)\pi_2^{R*} = \frac{4A^2(-1+\beta)^2}{(8-3\beta^2-6\delta+4\beta\delta)^2} > \pi_2^{N*} = 0. \end{cases}$$

Solving the above inequalities, it obtains $\tilde{\beta} \leq \beta \leq 1$, where $\tilde{\beta}$ is solved by the equation of $\frac{(\beta^4-2\beta^3\delta+\beta^2\delta^2+4(-2+\delta)^2(3+\delta)-4\beta(-2+\delta)(-4+\delta+\delta^2))}{4(-2+\beta)^2(2+\beta-\delta)^2(2-\delta)} + \frac{(-6(-2+\delta)+\beta(-8+\beta+4\delta))}{2(-2+\delta)(8-3\beta^2-6\delta+4\beta\delta)} = 0$. In summary, the condition that manufacturer 1 choose strategy R is

$$\left\{1 \leq A < \phi(t,\beta,\delta) \cap 0 \leq \beta < \tilde{\beta}\right\} \cup \left\{\tilde{\beta} \leq \beta \leq 1\right\}.$$

Following a similar fashion, it concludes that (1) strategy N is never optimal; (2) the condition that manufacturer 1 choose strategy R is

$$\left\{A > \phi(t,\beta,\delta) \cap 0 \leq \beta < \tilde{\beta}\right\}.$$

Therefore, the results can be obtained in Proposition 4. □

Appendix E

Proof of Proposition 5.

When strategy R is adopted, substitute the results in Proposition 2 into the social welfare function of

$$CS^R = \frac{\left[q_1^{R*}\right]^2 + 2\beta q_1^{R*} q_2^{R*} + \left[q_2^{R*}\right]^2}{2},$$

$$SW^R = \underbrace{\pi_1^{R*} + \pi_2^{R*}}_{\text{Manufacturers' Payoffs}} + \underbrace{\frac{\left[q_1^{R*}\right]^2 + 2\beta q_1^{R*} q_2^{R*} + \left[q_2^{R*}\right]^2}{2}}_{\text{Consumer Surplus}},$$

it obtains

$$CS^R = \frac{A^2\left[\beta^4(9-4\delta) + 20(-2+\delta)^2 - 8\beta(-2+\delta)\delta + 4\beta^3(3+2(-3+\delta)\delta) - 4\beta^2(19+2\delta(-9+2\delta))\right]}{\left(2(2-\delta)^2(8-3\beta^2-6\delta+4\beta\delta)^2\right)},$$

$$SW^R = \frac{A^2\begin{bmatrix}-\beta^4(-3+\delta) + 4\beta^3(-5+2\delta)(-3+2\delta) - 4(-2+\delta)^2(-19+9\delta) + \\ 8\beta(-2+\delta)(12+\delta(-19+6\delta)) + 4\beta^2(-25+\delta(7+(11-4\delta)\delta))\end{bmatrix}}{\left(2(2-\delta)^2(8-3\beta^2-6\delta+4\beta\delta)^2\right)}.$$

Likewise, substitute the results in Proposition 3 into the social welfare functions,

$$CS^F = \frac{\left[q_1^{F*}\right]^2 + 2\beta q_1^{F*} q_2^{F*} + \left[q_2^{F*}\right]^2}{2},$$

$$SW^F = \underbrace{\pi_1^{F*} + \pi_2^{F*}}_{Manufacturers'\ Payoffs} + \underbrace{\frac{\left[q_1^{F*}\right]^2 + 2\beta q_1^{F*} q_2^{F*} + \left[q_2^{F*}\right]^2}{2}}_{Consumer\ Surplus}.,$$

it obtains

$$CS^F = \frac{A^2\left(4+\delta^2+\beta((-3+\beta)\beta-\delta^2)\right)}{(-2+\beta)^2(2+\beta-\delta)^2}. \quad SW^F = \frac{A^2\left((-2+\beta)^2(3+\beta)+(-1+\beta)\delta^2\right)}{(-2+\beta)^2(2+\beta-\delta)^2}.$$

The results are shown in Proposition 5.

Then, compare the value of CS and SW of the two strategies.

$$CS^R - CS^F = \frac{A^2\left[\beta^4(9-4\delta) + 20(-2+\delta)^2 - 8\beta(-2+\delta)\delta + 4\beta^3(3+2(-3+\delta)\delta) - 4\beta^2(19+2\delta(-9+2\delta))\right]}{\left(2(2-\delta)^2(8-3\beta^2-6\delta+4\beta\delta)^2\right)} - \frac{A^2\left(4+\delta^2+\beta((-3+\beta)\beta-\delta^2)\right)}{(-2+\beta)^2(2+\beta-\delta)^2}.$$

Let $G(\beta,\delta) = \frac{\left[\beta^4(9-4\delta)+20(-2+\delta)^2-8\beta(-2+\delta)\delta+4\beta^3(3+2(-3+\delta)\delta)-4\beta^2(19+2\delta(-9+2\delta))\right]}{\left(2(2-\delta)^2(8-3\beta^2-6\delta+4\beta\delta)^2\right)} - \frac{(4+\delta^2+\beta((-3+\beta)\beta-\delta^2))}{(-2+\beta)^2(2+\beta-\delta)^2}$. Then, $CS^R - CS^F = A^2 G(\beta,\delta)$. Then, it only needs to prove $G(\beta,\delta) \leq 0$ for all the available values of β and δ. Here, using the numerical method to testify all the values of β and δ, which is shown in Figure A1 as follows. It shows that $G(\beta,\delta) \leq 0$ is always satisfied, therefore, $CS^R \leq CS^F$ holds. Follow the same fashion, $SW^R \leq SW^F$ can be proved. □

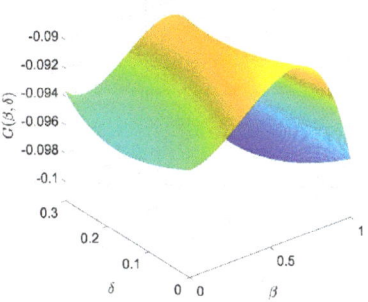

Figure A1. $G(\beta,\delta)$ with respect to β and δ.

References

1. Guardian, T. Atmospheric CO2 Levels Rise Sharply Despite COVID-19 Lockdowns. 2020. Available online: https://www.theguardian.com/environment/2020/jun/04/atmospheric-co2-levels-rise-sharply-despite-covid-19-lockdowns (accessed on 7 November 2022).
2. Pimentel, D.; Cooperstein, S.; Randell, H.; Filiberto, D.; Sorrentino, S.; Kaye, B.; Nicklin, C.; Yagi, J.; Brian, J.; O'Hern, J.; et al. Ecology of increasing diseases: Population growth and environ- mental degradation. *Hum. Ecol.* **2007**, *35*, 653–668. [CrossRef] [PubMed]
3. Larmer, B. What Does It Take to Stop Accepting Pollution as the Price of Progress? *The New York Times Magazine*, 23 January 2018.
4. Lenovo Newsroom. LenovoTM Announces Breakthrough, Innovative PC Manufacturing Process. 2017. Available online: http://news.lenovo.com/news-releases/lenovo-announces-breakthrough-innovative-pc-manufacturing-process.htm (accessed on 7 November 2022).
5. Bailey, B.; Yeo, J.; Koh, S.; Ferguson, A. Doubling Down: Europe's Low-Carbon Investment Opportunity. 2020. Available online: https://www.oliverwyman.com/our-expertise/insights/2020/feb/doublingdown.html (accessed on 7 November 2022).
6. Chen, X.; Wang, X.; Xia, Y. Low-carbon technology transfer between rival firms under cap-and-trade policies. *IISE Trans.* **2020**, *54*, 105–121. [CrossRef]
7. Chen, Y.; Shum, S.; Xiao, W. Should an OEM retain sourcing when outsourcing to a competing CM? *Prod. Oper. Manag.* **2019**, *28*, 1446–1464. [CrossRef]
8. Yan, Y.C.; Zhao, R.Q.; Lan, Y.F. Moving sequence preference in coopetition outsourcing supply chain: Consensus or conflict. *Int. J. Prod. Econ.* **2019**, *208*, 221–240. [CrossRef]
9. Rai, R.K. A coopetition-based approach to value creation in interfirm alliances construction of a measure and examination of its psychometric properties. *J. Manag.* **2016**, *42*, 1663–1699.
10. Bello, D.C.; Katsikeas, C.S.; Robson, M.J. Does accommodating a self-serving partner in an international marketing alliance pay off? *J. Mark.* **2010**, *74*, 77–93. [CrossRef]
11. Ge, Z.H.; Hu, Q.Y.; Xia, Y.S. Firms' R&D cooperation behavior in a supply chain. *Prod. Oper. Manag.* **2014**, *23*, 599–609.
12. Wilhelm, M.M. Managing coopetition through horizontal supply chain relations: Linking dyadic and network levels of analysis. *J. Oper. Manag.* **2011**, *29*, 663–676. [CrossRef]
13. Chen, P.P.; Zhao, R.Q.; Yan, Y.C.; Li, X. Promotional pricing and online business model choice in the presence of retail competition. *Omega* **2020**, *94*, 102085. [CrossRef]
14. Bengtsson, M.; Raza-Ullah, T. A systematic review of research on coopetition: Toward a multilevel understanding. *Ind. Marking Manag.* **2016**, *57*, 23–39. [CrossRef]
15. Ritala, A.; Golnam, A.; Wegmann, A. Coopetition-based business models: The case of amazon.com. *Ind. Marking Manag.* **2014**, *43*, 236–249. [CrossRef]
16. Gnyawali, D.R.; Park, B.J.R. Co-opetition between giants: Collaboration with competitors for technological innovation. *Res. Policy* **2011**, *40*, 650–663. [CrossRef]
17. Yin, P.Z.; Chu, J.F.; Wu, J. A DEA-based two-stage network approach for hotel performance analysis: An internal cooperation perspective. *Omega* **2020**, *93*, 102035. [CrossRef]
18. Xu, Y.; Gurnani, H.; Desiraju, R. Strategic supply chain structure design for a proprietary component manufacturer. *Prod. Oper. Manag.* **2010**, *19*, 371–389. [CrossRef]
19. Venkatesh, R.; Chintagunta, P.; Mahajan, V. Research note: Sole entrant, co-optor, or component supplier: Optimal end-product strategies for manufacturers of proprietary component brands. *Manag. Sci.* **2006**, *52*, 613–622. [CrossRef]
20. Chen, X.; Wang, X.J.; Xia, Y.S. Production coopetition strategies for competing manufacturers that produce partially substitutable products. *Prod. Oper. Manag.* **2019**, *28*, 1446–1464. [CrossRef]
21. Aulakh, P.S.; Jiang, M.S.; Pan, Y. International technology licensing: Monopoly rents, transaction costs and exclusive rights. *J. Int. Bus. Stud.* **2010**, *41*, 587–605. [CrossRef]
22. Khoury, T.A.; Pleggenkuhle-Miles, E.G.; Walter, J. Experiential learning, bargaining power, and exclusivity in technology licensing. *J. Manag.* **2019**, *45*, 1193–1224. [CrossRef]
23. Wang, X.H. Fee versus royalty licensing in a Cournot duopoly model. *Econ. Lett.* **1998**, *60*, 55–62. [CrossRef]
24. Faul-Oller, R.; Sandonis, J. Welfare reducing licensing. *Games Econ. Behav.* **2002**, *41*, 192–205. [CrossRef]
25. Wang, X.H. Fee versus royalty licensing in a differentiated Cournot duopoly. *J. Econ. Bus.* **2002**, *54*, 253–266. [CrossRef]
26. Kamien, M.; Tauman, Y. Patent licensing: The inside story. *Manch. Sch.* **2002**, *70*, 7–15. [CrossRef]
27. Heywood, J.S.; Li, J.; Ye, G. Per unit vs. ad valorem royalties under asymmetric information. *Int. J. Ind. Organ.* **2014**, *37*, 38–46. [CrossRef]
28. Rockett, K.E. Choosing the competition and patent licensing. *RAND J. Econ.* **1990**, *21*, 161–172. [CrossRef]
29. Kabiraj, T. Patent licensing in a leadership structure. *Manch. Sch.* **2004**, *72*, 188–205. [CrossRef]
30. Conrad, K. Price competition and product differentiation when consumers care for the environment. *Environ. Resour. Econ.* **2005**, *31*, 1–19. [CrossRef]
31. Roberto, R. Environmental product differentiation and environmental awareness. *Environ. Resour. Econ.* **2007**, *36*, 237–254.
32. Zhang, C.; Wang, H.; Ren, M. Research on pricing and coordination strategy of green supply chain under hybrid production mode. *Comput. Ind. Eng.* **2014**, *72*, 24–31. [CrossRef]

33. Zhu, W.; He, Y. Green product design in supply chains under competition. *Eur. J. Oper. Res.* **2017**, *258*, 165–180. [CrossRef]
34. Cai, G. Channel selection and coordination in dual-channel supply chains. *J. Retail.* **2010**, *86*, 22–36. [CrossRef]
35. Liu, B.; Cai, G.; Tsay, A.A. Advertising in asymmetric competing supply chains. *Prod. Oper. Manag.* **2014**, *23*, 1845–1858. [CrossRef]
36. Wu, H.; Cai, G.; Chen, J.; Sheu, C. Online manufacturer referral to heterogeneous retailers. *Prod. Oper. Manag.* **2015**, *24*, 1768–1782. [CrossRef]
37. Chen, J.; Liang, L.; Yao, D.; Sun, S. Price and quality decisions in dual-channel supply chains. *Eur. J. Oper. Res.* **2017**, *259*, 935–948. [CrossRef]

Article

Using Four Metaheuristic Algorithms to Reduce Supplier Disruption Risk in a Mathematical Inventory Model for Supplying Spare Parts

Komeyl Baghizadeh [1,*], Nafiseh Ebadi [2], Dominik Zimon [3] and Luay Jum'a [4]

1. Innovation and Technology Institute, University of Southern Denmark, 5230 Odense, Denmark
2. Department of Industrial Engineering, Iran University of Science and Technology, Tehran 46899, Iran
3. Department of Management Systems and Logistics, Rzeszow University of Technology, 35-959 Rzeszow, Poland
4. Department of Logistic Sciences, School of Management and Logistic Sciences, German Jordanian University, Amman 11180, Jordan
* Correspondence: kob@iti.sdu.dk

Abstract: Due to the unexpected breakdowns that can happen in various components of a production system, failure to reach production targets and interruptions in the process of production are not surprising. Since this issue remains for manufactured products, this halting results in the loss of profitability or demand. In this study, to address a number of challenges associated with the management of crucial spare parts inventory, a mathematical model is suggested for the determination of the optimal quantity of orders, in the case of an unpredicted supplier failure. Hence, a production system that has various types of equipment with crucial components is assumed, in which the crucial components are substituted with spare parts in the event of a breakdown. This study's inventory model was developed for crucial spare parts based on the Markov chain process model for the case of supplier disruption. Moreover, for optimum ordering policies, re-ordering points, and cost values of the system, four metaheuristic algorithms were utilized that include Grey Wolf Optimizer (GWO), Genetic Algorithm (GA), Moth–Flame Optimization (MFO) Algorithm, and Differential Evolution (DE) Algorithm. Based on the results, reliable suppliers cannot meet all of the demands; therefore, we should sometimes count on unreliable suppliers to reduce unmet demand.

Keywords: inventory policy; mathematical modeling; decision making; Markov chain

MSC: 90c40

1. Introduction

Any production system consists of different parts required to function well, to produce without losing performance. Over time, however, breakdowns might happen to any part of a system, which is unavoidable. These breakdowns might interrupt the production process and prevent meeting production goals, which might also lead to losing demand or profitability opportunities in the state where the product is demanded [1]. Accordingly, the malfunctioning time of systems must be minimized. To minimize system breakdown time, spare parts must be accessible. On the other hand, buying and storing spare parts is often costly, and these parts are especially vulnerable to obsolescence risk [2]. As a result, good spare part inventory management is critical in managing system costs. Furthermore, there are only a few suppliers of specialized spare parts. Indeed, if the main supplier does not provide spare parts or if supplies are disrupted, the part must be supplied by another supplier [3]. This issue raises the price considerably and lengthens the delivery time.

Since single sourcing is rigid and supplier reliance is high, supply chain managers employ multiple sourcing to reduce costs and mitigate operational risks by using different supplier characteristics. Additionally, since it is hard to find the best replenishment approach for a multi-supplier model, practitioners and academics have long been interested

in how to best execute and coordinate replenishment and inventory management with many varying supply alternatives [4].

Multiple sourcing is a broad term that may relate to any inventory system or replenishment decision issue in which two or more supply sources, transportation modes, delivery alternatives, or transit speeds must be chosen [5].

Many firms maintain many inventory items in practice, and scientific procedures and tools are required to efficiently handle such a large number of inventory items [6]. As a result, researching the multi-product inventory management issue has real-world implications and is still a difficult topic to solve today. The multi-product inventory issue is now receiving a lot of attention [7]. In most states, however, it is possible to purchase elsewhere, from an emergency supplier; for example, the desired part could be available in another company's warehouse. Accordingly, it is vital to consider supplier disruption as a critical component of inventory management [8]. As a result, one of the most important tools for dealing with supply disruptions is proper inventory management. For proposed and regular control of orders and inventories, obtaining values of two main parameters, including the amount of each order time and suitable date of order, is usually paramount [9]. Different orders and inventory control systems must be designed in a structure consistent with each industry's conditions to respond to the two factors mentioned above. It is evident that numerical values of the above parameters depend on several factors, including different inventory costs, consumption rate, certain or probabilistic (stochastic) consumption, and the required level of reliability to keep an inventory of any specific commodity [10,11]. They also depend on constraints acting on an industrial unit. Based on these factors and their impact on an industrial unit, different inventory control systems for various commodities at a time are defined.

As a result, order systems are classified into two categories: order point systems and periodic order systems. Several parameters, such as demand, demand locations, and the ability of centers to provide service and their usable capacity, were not accurately predictable due to the uncertain nature of some significant supply chain factors. As an outcome, effort is made to employ some techniques that take these uncertainties into consideration as much as possible while providing demanders with a high-quality response [12]. Efficient and perfect supply chains are more subject to disruption, and efficiency and risk are inversely correlated. Organizations cannot merely focus on cost reduction for a long time, and supply chain investors must pay attention to how these capitals and changes affect the disruption in the supply chain [13]. Besides, the studied disruptions are often general and do not take account of specific conditions and the reason behind the occurrence of disruption, while considering that these issues can significantly contribute to the selected strategy to reduce the effects and tackle the disruption [14].

Nowadays, according to current competitive conditions, companies try to reduce their inventory level to reduce their costs. In inventory management and control of organizations, there must be a balance between spare part inventory level and cost and risk imposed by lack of spare parts when demanded. It is obvious that this spare part inventory level is affected by the device's properties and reliability [15].

Most previous studies have considered inventory maintenance with an assumption of unlimited access to spare parts [10]. Considering that this assumption increases inventory costs, the costs can significantly be reduced by considering an optimal spare part inventory level [16].

Polito and Watson [17] developed a model that may be used to create a multi-echelon and multi-product distribution system. In a multi-product and multi-period inventory control, Moin and co-workers [18] looked at the optimum ordering amount. Pal [19] presented a stochastic inventory model with product recovery and inspection policy is incorporated for lot-sizing.

Murray et al. [20] studied a price-setting and multi-product newsvendor with moderate assets capacity. Choi and Ruszczyski [21] used a risk aversion hypothesis in their multi-product inventory model; however, their model also considered independent product requirements. Over the past few years, many researchers have prioritized the multi-product inventory model in their studies. Ramkumar and coworkers [22] suggested a mixed-integer linear programming explanation to unravel this problem. Hosseinifard [23] devised a linear penalty/bonus system to estimate optimal stocking resolution for choosing a strategic supplier by utilizing the stochastic dynamic programming technique.

Sokolinskiy [24] suggested a stochastic optimization method for endogenous demand and inventory management regarding the inspection of the function of client defections and referrals. Mjirda [25] presented a two-phase variable neighborhood technique for solving the problem, while Coelho [26] proposed a branch-and-cut approach. Even though the prior models have assisted in the evolution of the operation theory for the multi-product inventory control issue, their optimum policy for the multivariate Markov demand perspective is still missing. Sethi and Cheng [27] investigated the state-dependent policies of the inventory by using Markov-modulated lost and demand sales. Gharaei [28] offered a mathematical model utilizing mixed-integer nonlinear programming for minimizing the total costs of both buyers and the vendor and optimal batch-sizing policy by taking into consideration the algorithm of augmented penalty. Khaniyev and Aliyev [29] utilized their model in order to evaluate state-dependent policies with the asymptotic behavior of the ergodic distribution of the process. The optimum inventory model that has a limited capacity and rather observable Markov-modulated supply and demand procedures were investigated by Arifolu [30] and Ozer and Atali [31] using Markov-modulated production and demand quantity requirements to study a two-stage multi-item manufacturing system. Ahiska [32] investigated the case of an uncertain source and managed to develop a stochastic inventory approach based on a Markov decision processes. Parker and Olsen [33] devised a Markov equilibrium technique in inventory competition under dynamic circumstances while assuming that the equilibrium in a fixed infinite-horizon is a Markov perfect equilibrium. In addition, Barron [34] studied a make-to-stock inventory/production system that was exposed to accidental conditions with moderate storage capacity and restrained backlog chances, while supposing that the entry of demand pursues Markov additive processes guided through continuous-time Markov chains. However, the theory of the Markov chain is utilized in all the aforementioned literature, all of which solely deals with a single item or multiple items with independent demand. Luo [35] proposed a single-product mathematical model for controlling and predicting inventory systems, which includes a stable and unstable supplier. Asadi [36] investigated a stochastic model to control inventory with respect to the Markov chain. According to the complexities of the proposed model, they employed two approaches, including a heuristic benchmark policy and a reinforcement learning method, to solve their model. Ye [37] proposed an MINLP mathematical model for determining optimized inventory policy under disruption according to the Markov chain. They employed a two-stage algorithm to solve their complex model. Chin [38] used the Markov chain in MINLP mathematical model for determining optimized long-term policy. Patriarca [39] presented a Multi-Echelon Technique for inventory of Recoverable Item Control (METRIC) to investigate the potential use of a Weibull distribution for modelling items' demand in case of failure. Milewski [40] focused on the economic efficiency of decentralized and centralized inventory strategies of distribution products in terms of both internal efficiency of firms and external costs of logistics processes.

In line with the studies conducted over the past years in this field, research gaps in the studies carried out by researchers remain. Most of the research focused on one supplier and one product, while in real world cases, there are more suppliers considering their situations (reliable–unreliable) that provide a variety of products [36]. It is critical to include exploring the interdependencies between up/down probabilities for the unreliable supplier across periods. Moreover, investigating the performance of different optimization methods to find more suitable methods to solve inventory models is vital [38]. Uncertainty in demand and other parameters, which has an undeniable effect on the models, is not widely considered [35].

Therefore, this study aims to propose a multi-product mathematical model to determine optimal inventory policy by considering the Markov chain. Moreover, two reliable and unreliable suppliers with disruption probability in the supply chain were also taken into account. The demand for all products will also be uncertain. Given that the proposed model will be highly complex, several meta-heuristic methods will be proposed to solve the problem. In order to assess the model better, a state study is also implemented, and the best assessed meta-heuristic method is employed to solve it. More specifically, in this research, Grey Wolf Optimizer (GWO), Genetic Algorithm (GA), Moth–Flame Optimization (MFO) Algorithm, and Differential Evolution (DE) Algorithm are applied to solve the model faster and more accurately. To evaluate their efficiency, two factors including numbers of iterations and spent time are investigated to discover which solution method is more useful to solve the inventory models.

Table 1 shows this research's contributions in comparison to the most recently published articles which are completely relevant to this paper. Regarding all these gaps reviewed, the present research aims to cover these neglected concepts in mathematical inventory models. In what follows, some important innovations of the research are stated:

- Design of a mathematical model for determining optimized multi-product policy with the Markov approach, designing a novel mathematical model to optimize multi-product inventory control considering the Markov system under disruption and uncertainty;
- Considering lead time as an objective function;
- Considering two reliable and unreliable suppliers with different costs and delivery times;
- Using four meta-heuristic methods to estimate their performance to solve a real case inventory model;
- Considering uncertainty in demand;
- Proposing a state study in the production of automobile spare parts.

Table 1. Previous Articles.

Research	Year	Multiple Sourcing	Unreliable Supply	Multiple Periods	Optimality	Multi PRODUCT	Markov Chain	Disruption	Uncertainty
Sha Luo et al.	2021					-	-	-	-
Hon Huin Chin et al.	2021	-	-				-	-	-
Sha Luo et al.	2021					-	-	-	-
Patriarca et al.	2020	-	-	-	Scenario Based		-		
Yixin Ye et al.	2020	-	-	-	Two-phase algorithm			-	-
Asadi et al.	2020	-	-		Heuristic Method	-			
This Research					Four Meta Heuristics				

2. Materials and Methods

One retailer and two kinds of suppliers are assumed in this research; one is reliable, and the other one is unreliable, providing the demanded item at a lower price compared with the reliable supplier. The following method specifies an unreliable supplier's accessibility process. The status for an unreliable supplier can be "appropriate", which means they can take orders, or the status can be "inappropriate", which means they are not taking orders. Based on the inventory, the retailer demands the preferred price from a single supplier or both of them. The unreliable supplier's status and circumstances are dependent on the demands at the start of each time period. An order that was made at the start of a time period will be shipped at the end of that time period. A certain delivery and specified value at the end of the time period are guaranteed for the reliable supplier. An unreliable supplier cannot take orders from the retailer if it is not currently at an appropriate status. An unreliable supplier's status is specified after the demand. If the appropriate status changes to inappropriate at the final days of the time period, the order will be canceled, otherwise, the unreliable supplier will deliver the order. In the case of an order to an unreliable supplier, the fixed ordering fee (internal running cost of constructing an order) is reimbursed at the time of the delivery.

Demand during a period is independently and equally divided between distributers. Demand and system cost parameters are constant and do not change over time. Any unit in the inventory during a period has a maintenance cost. If the inventory is available, each required unit on the unit will be subtracted from the inventory. Otherwise, the demand is reordered and restored. Any demand higher than this limit is missed, and the missed selling cost is imposed on the retailer. The constraint that acts as the lowest limit in the inventory limits this problem to a Markov chain process model, which can be solved by overloading computation.

The activities that are carried out in a period are listed as follows:

- The system status depends on inventory at the beginning of the period;
- Making a decision regarding the amount of order;
- Demand is dispatched during the period and happens from the beginning of the inventory time period;
- The order dispatched to an unreliable supplier is received at the end of the period;
- The status of unreliable suppliers is determined at the end of the period;
- The cost of missed order demand is calculated.

2.1. Mathematical Modelingl

The presented mathematical model in this research aims to determine order strategy, such that the total expected cost for any period is minimized, which includes the following states:

- Order cost is fixed and is paid to each one of the suppliers for each dispatched order;
- The number of order units (number of buying); in the research problem, it is assumed that the number of made orders is a linear function;
- Maintenance cost; the cost of each unit for the unreliable supplier is less than the reliable supplier;
- The cost of missed sales is considered in the number of missed sales as a linear function;
- Shortage is not allowed;
- Products are not independent of each other;
- Preparation time is considered a uniform distribution function.

2.1.1. System Status

According to the mentioned states, the system status is displayed as $S = (I, J)$, where I indicates inventory level and J is supplier status. J has values equal to one or zero, which indicate appropriate or inappropriate supplier status, respectively. The inventory level of retailers is between $I_{min} \leq I \leq I_{max}$ and $I_{min} > 0$, and $+\infty > I_{max}$ indicates the capacity of the retailer's storehouse.

2.1.2. Decision Variables

Supposing that $K = (k_u, k_r)$ vector equals the order amount to two studied suppliers, and $S = (I, J)$ is the status of the system, the value of the order to two suppliers is indicated as A_s, whose value is determined according to the retailer's storage capacity and the status of the unreliable supplier, which is expressed as the following equation:

$$A_s = \begin{cases} (k_u, k_r) \; k_u \geq 0, \; k_r \geq 0, \; k_u + k_r \leq I_{max} - I \; if \; j = 0 \\ (k_u, k_r) \; k_u = 0, 0 \leq \; k_r \leq I_{max} - I \; if \; j = 1 \end{cases}$$

2.1.3. Transition Modes and Transition Probabilities

Two fundamental Markov chain processes describe the transition status. One is related to unreliable suppliers and the other is related to inventory status. The first is independent of the second.

k_u	:	The number of orders to the unreliable supplier
k_r	:	The number of orders to the reliable supplier

The status of an inappropriate supplier is controlled by a two-status Markov chain process with transition probability matrix, W, where W_{ij} indicates the probability of a transition status of an unreliable supplier from i to j during a period. In particular, we define α as the probability of an unreliable supplier from up to down (from an appropriate status to an inappropriate status in demand-supply), from one period to the next, and β is the probability of inappropriate status from down to up, from one period to the next.

$$W = \begin{matrix} 0 \\ 1 \end{matrix} \begin{bmatrix} \alpha & 1-\alpha \\ \beta & 1-\beta \end{bmatrix} \quad (1)$$

Demand at each period for each product equals D_m, whose occurrence probability is indicated by $P_{D_m}(d_m)$ probability function. According to the system status, which is $S(I, J)$ at the beginning of the period, the demand value is defined according to $K = (k_u, k_r)$, which equals d_m for each product. It is expressed as the following Equation when the system status changes to $S' = (I', J')$ demand for different products according to unreliable supplier status.

$J = 0$: Status of the inappropriate supplier is appropriate.

$$J' = \begin{cases} 0 \\ 1 \end{cases} \quad (2)$$

In Equation (2), if the supplier remains unreliable during the period, it equals 0. Otherwise, it equals 1.

$$I' \begin{cases} \max\{I-d, I_{min}\} + k_u + k_r & if\ up \\ \max\{I-d, I_{min}\} + k_r & if\ down \end{cases} \quad (3)$$

It is worth mentioning that when the status of the unreliable supplier changes from appropriate to inappropriate, the value of the order to the unreliable supplier is canceled (k_u).

$$J' = \begin{cases} 0 \\ 1 \end{cases} \quad (4)$$

In Equation (4), if the status of the unreliable supplier changes from appropriate to inappropriate during the period, it equals 0. Otherwise, it equals 1.

$$I' = \max\{I - d, I_{min}\} + k_r \quad (5)$$

2.1.4. Markov Process, Markov Chain, and Markov Property

The Markov property, often known as the non-aftereffect property, specifies that the process state is known at a certain time t. At the point $t_1 > t$, the state at time t_1 is unrelated to the conditional probability distribution and is only concerned with the condition at time t [41].

The conditional probability distribution (CPD) function, which can be represented as follows, is used to explain the Markov property [42]:

The random process $\{X(t), t \in T\}$ has a state-space of I. If, at any point n in time t, that is $t_1 < t_2 < \ldots < t_n$, $n \geq 3$, $t_i \in T$, and under the $X(t_i) = x_i$. $x_i \in I$. $i = 1, 2, \ldots, n-1$

condition, then the CPD function of $X(t_n)$ equals the conditional distribution function $X(t_n)$ under the $X(t_{n-1}) = x_{n-1}$ condition:

$$P\{X(t_n) \leq x_n | X(t_1) = x_1, |X(t_2) = x_2, \ldots, |X(t_{n-1}) = x_{n-1}\} = P\{X(t_n) \leq x_n | X(t_{n-1}) = x_{n-1}\}, x_n \in \mathbb{R} \quad (6)$$

The process $\{X(t), t \in T\}$ is known as a Markov process because it possesses the Markov property. A Markov chain is a Markov process with discrete state and discrete time in general. The following is how mathematical terminology describes it [43].

The random process $\{X(t), t \in T\}$ has a state-space of I. It meets the following criteria for all m non-negative integers $n_1, n_2, \ldots, n_m (0 \leq n_1 < n_2 < \ldots < n_m)$, any natural number k and any $i_1, i_2, \ldots, i_m, j \in I$:

$$P\{X(n_m + k) = j, | X(n_1) = i_1, X(n_2) = i_2, \ldots X(n_m) = i_m\} = P\{X(n_m + k) \leq j | X(n_m) = i_m\} \quad (7)$$

The stochastic process $\{X(t), t \in T\}$ is known as the Markov chain.

2.1.5. Transition Probability

The random process $\{X(t), t \in T\}$ has a state-space of I. Additionally, the probability of an n-step transition of the time m is defined as the likelihood that the model is moved to the state j via n steps when the system is in the state I at time m, as indicated below:

$$p_{ij}^{(n)}(m) = P\{X_{m+n} = j | X_m = i\}; i, j \in I \quad (8)$$

When $n = 1$, $p_{ij}^{(n)}(m)$ may be denoted as p_{ij}, and the transition probability of the Markov chain is called p_{ij}.

The transition probability $p_{ij}^{(n)}(n)$ satisfies the two features listed below:

$$p_{ij}^{(n)}(n) \geq 0; i, j \in I \quad (9)$$

$$\sum_{j \in I} p_{ij}^{(n)}(m) = 1; i \in I \quad (10)$$

The literature theorem proves that the Chapman Kolmogorov formula is satisfied by the n-step Markov chain transition probability, i.e., for each positive integer h, l:

$$p^{h+l}(n) = P^{(h)}(n) P^{(l)}(n+h) \quad (11)$$

A recursive technique may be used to generate the following equation:

$$p^{(h)} = (p)^h \quad (12)$$

A single-step transition matrix may be used to immediately create a matrix of Markov transition from Equation (7), offering a straightforward way of calculating the transition probability.

2.1.6. The Markov Chain's Ergodic Property

If there is a transition probability limit of the Markov chain which is unrelated to i, then the ergodic property of the Markov chain is

$$\lim_{k \to \infty} p_{ij}(k) = p_j; i, j \in I \quad (13)$$

Furthermore, it can be shown that for each $i, j \in I; j = 1, 2, \ldots, N$, there is $p_{ij}(k) > 0$, i.e., the Markov chain is ergodic. Moreover, the limit distribution $\pi = (\pi_1, \pi_2, \ldots)$ is the only solution to the equations $\pi_i = \sum_{i=1}^{N} \pi_i p_{ij}$ (namely $\pi = \pi P$) under the conditions of $\pi_j > 0$, $\sum_{j=1}^{N} \pi_j$ [42].

2.2. Solution Methods

In this section, four solution methods are presented and described briefly which are applied for solving the mathematical model. The solution methods include Genetic Algorithm (GA), Differential Evolution (DE) Algorithm, Grey Wolf Optimizer (GWO) and Moth–Flame Optimization (MFO) Algorithm.

2.2.1. GA Solution Method

Genetic algorithm is a natural-principles-based heuristic evolutionary solution approach that may be used to solve hybrid search and optimization problems. There are two types of GA: continuous and binary GA. The algorithm's whole set of rules may be found in [40].

2.2.2. DE Solution Method

Mutation, initialization, recombination, selection, and crossover are the five major processes in this method [41]. The starting parameter is haphazardly set in specific regions, containing lower bounds and upper bounds, to be optimized by the variables in the initialization process. Furthermore, both the recombination and mutation processes are aimed at producing a number of population vector trails. Additionally, the crossover aims to arrange a parameter value crossover vector that is replicated on two vectors, the mutation vector and the original vector. The next step, the selection process, is used to separate the vectors so that they may be utilized as the population for further iterations [44].

2.2.3. GWO Solution Method

The Grey Wolf method is based on the grey wolf's natural leadership hierarchy and hunting process. To imitate the leadership system, four sorts of grey wolves are used: delta, omega, beta, and alpha. Furthermore, the key processes of hunting are supposed to be seeking prey, surrounding the prey, and assaulting the prey in this algorithm. Mirjalili [34] goes into detail about this method. As a consequence, while configuring the algorithm, the agent's number is assumed to be 6, and the findings are verified using the benchmark test performer, which is specified in [45].

2.2.4. MFO Solution Method

The Moth Flame method is a night-time moth fly behavior-inspired optimization approach. Mirjalili [45] explains how this optimizer was inspired by transverse orientation. The benchmark test function, which is specified as F8 [35], is used to verify the findings, and the dimensions' number in this optimization is regarded to be six for this approach.

3. Results

The input values to the model are collected based on the case study of the South Pars Complex Company. The model we are discussing is a two-level supply chain under a vendor inventory management strategy. A number of retailers, each of which has a definite demand, at regular intervals, order a fixed amount of a type of product to the seller. In other words, the demand of retailers is discrete and the period that this demand is met at the beginning of each period. For direct delivery of these orders from the seller to the retailers, there are different schedules. The seller also orders a fixed amount to the main supplier at specified intervals to meet the retailers' demand. In Table 2, the input values of the parameters of each product are presented separately. In order to model the uncertainty in procurement time for eight products, procurement time is considered as the probability function in Table 3.

Table 2. Products and their input value.

Products	Tag	CU_m	Cr_m	f_m	h_m	I_m	L_m
Electromotor	E1	8500	9500	50	4	2	0
Right gearbox	E2	250	280	43	5	3	0
Turbocharger	E3	1400	1480	45	2	4	0
Left gearbox	E4	250	275	65	7	3	3
Controller	E5	15,000	16,500	55	6	5	5
Pressure measuring tool	E6	1400	1470	43	8	3	5
Flow intensity measuring tool (E7)	E7	780	820	48	4	5	0
Flow level measuring tool (E8)	E8	920	975	46	5	3	0

Table 3. Average and variance of products demand.

Products	Variance (Min)	Average (Min)
Electromotor (E1)	2	10
Right gearbox (E2)	1	15
Turbocharger (E3)	3	14
Left gearbox (E4)	2	13
Controller (E5)	1	5
Pressure measuring tool (E6)	1	7
Flow intensity measuring tool (E7)	1	10
Flow level measuring tool (E8)	6	13

For solving the presented mathematical model, a Dell laptop with 8Gig RAM, Intel Core i7 CPU and Microsoft Win10 is used. Moreover, coding and model solving by metaheuristic methods are performed in MATLAB software. Moreover, to achieve the exact and optimum solution, small size and medium size problems are solved by GAMS software and CPLEX solver. Before solving the real case study, which is a complex model, to validate the solving methods, the model is solved based on some small and medium size problems. To do so, the model is solved with small and medium problems by four mentioned meta-heuristic solution methods and the exact solution of CPLEX to compare their performance by the exact method. As shown in Table 4, all of metaheuristic methods run the problems with marginal variation. However, regarding the Figure 1, the GWO method was able to find the best answer with minimum variation.

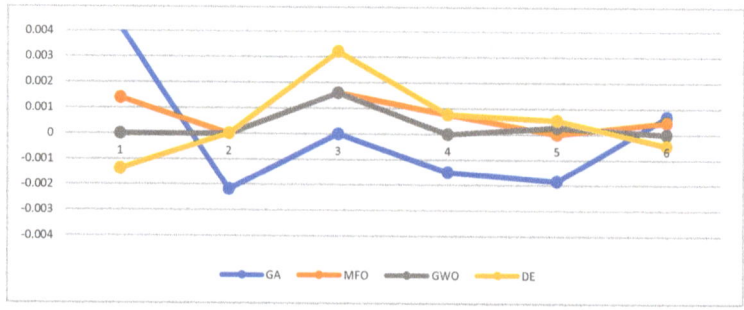

Figure 1. Variation of splution methods from exact solution method.

Table 4. Optimal value of meta-heuristics methods and exact methods.

Sample problem	Optimal Value and Variation								
	CPLEX	GA	Variation	MFO	Variation	GWO	Variation	DE	Variation
Small problem No. 1	722	719	0.004155	721	0.001385	722	0	723	−0.00139
Small problem No. 2	459	460	−0.00218	459	0	459	0	459	0
Small problem No. 3	625	625	0	624	0.0016	624	0.0016	623	0.0032
Medium problem No. 1	1335	1337	−0.0015	1334	0.000749	1335	0	1334	0.000749
Medium problem No. 2	3779	3786	−0.00185	3779	0	3778	0.000265	3777	0.000529
Medium problem No. 3	4403	4400	0.000681	4401	0.000454	4403	0	4405	−0.00045

After performance evaluation of the meta-heuristics methods, they are applied to solve the real case model to optimize a complex problem. Output data which are generated by the mentioned solution methods are investigated.

As can be seen in Figures 2 and 3, the GWO algorithm demonstrates a more proper answer compared to the other optimization methods. The preparation time and the financial costs have been considered in the optimization, where the optimization of each is not sufficient, and both factors should be taken into consideration together. The MFO, GWO and DE algorithms obtained the best cost function, but there is a difference in the lower convergence time of the GWO algorithm. The maximum passed the time for the executed algorithms is relevant to the GA with the maximum spent time.

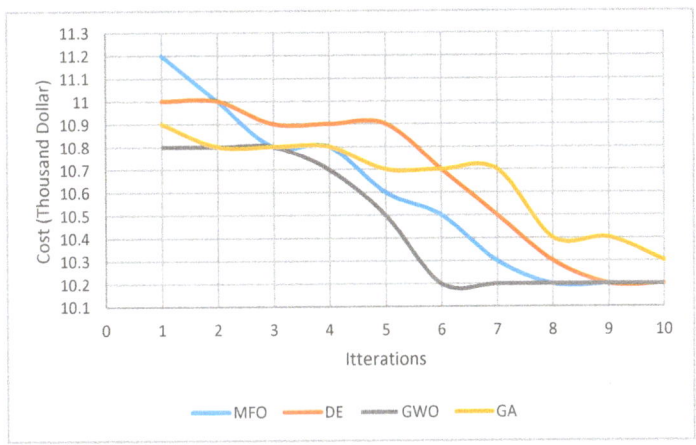

Figure 2. Convergence of the objective function in different iterations.

As can be seen from Figure 1, the convergence of the objective function for different solution methods is such that in the sixth iteration none of them were able to converge continuously. In the sixth iteration, the GWO algorithm was able to reach an acceptable level of convergence, and in the seventh iteration, it was also able to maintain this convergence. The MFO algorithm, which had the worst result of all the algorithms in the first iteration, converged very quickly in the next iterations, and finally in the eighth iteration, it converged faster than the other two algorithms. On the other hand, the two MFO and GWO algorithms, which performed better in convergence, recorded almost the same time in the first iteration. It was GWO that recorded the shortest convergence time. The GWO algorithm not only performed better in convergence, but was also able to do so in less time.

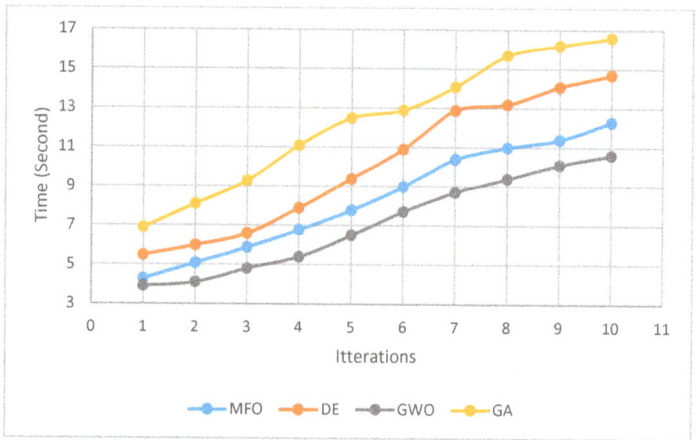

Figure 3. Time spent on the convergence of algorithms in each iteration.

Before providing the optimal value for each introduced product, defining some explanations regarding the different transition states is required. As discussed in the model of the research problem in Section 2, there are two states for ordering the products.

- First state: When the unreliable supplier state is improper, all demands are supplied by the reliable supplier in entire states. With respect to the policy, we have the following: The orders level is equal to the maximum inventory level of the products that the reliable supplier can supply; if the demand exceeds the supply capacity, the demands are retarded.
- Second state: When the unreliable supplier is in the proper situation, the four following states will occur:
   - State 1: With respect to the lower supply cost of the unreliable supplier, the demands are supplied merely from one supplier. With respect to the ordering policy, the maximum order level could be supplied.
   - State 2: The demand should be satisfied from both suppliers. In this state, if the demand is lower than the capacity of the reliable supplier, the remaining demands from the unreliable supplier are satisfied to the level.
   - State 3: The required demands are supplied from the two suppliers. In this state, before the demand, each supplier's inventory is investigated. Then, concerning the available inventory level, the two suppliers supply the required demand.
   - State 4: The demand is supplied merely from the reliable supplier.

With respect to the defined states above, Tables 5–12 demonstrate the results of investigating each aforementioned state.

With respect to Tables 5–12 addressing the optimal policies of each different state, we conclude the following from the indicated Tables.

- Given that the reliable supplier in the state four supplies all spare part demands, the demand is missed in several states, which imposes a cost on the system. This increase in the cost indicates its effect on the whole system, as shown in Table 11.
- In the third state, given that inventory of both suppliers is examined before making an order, the missed sale cost is zero. The total system cost is insignificant in this state compared to the fourth state. The only advantage of this state is the lack of missed sales.
- Since a reliable supplier first supplies the demands, maintenance cost is reduced in the second state. Accordingly, as indicated in Table 11, the system cost is reduced significantly compared to the third and fourth states.

- In this state, given that unreliable suppliers supply all demands, the probability of missed sales is increased. However, due to the low cost of buying from this supplier, the total cost of this state is significantly lower than the previous state.

Table 5. Optimal ordering policies for product (E1).

α		Proper				Improper		β		Proper				Improper	
	State	s_u	S_u	s_r	S_r	s_r	S_r		State	s_u	S_u	s_r	S_r	s_r	S_r
0/1	4	-	-	4	4	3	5	0/1	1	4	3	-	-	-	-
0/2	4	-	-	5	4	6	2	0/2	1	2	7	-	-	-	-
0/3	4	-	-	6	8	4	4	0/3	1	4	4	-	-	-	-
0/4	3	4	5	-	-	-	-	0/4	2	7	9	7	12	4	4
0/5	3	-	-	4	6	2	6	0/5	2	4	8	11	9	5	3
0/6	3	9	13	-	-	-	-	0/6	2	3	5	7	12	4	4
0/7	2	8	12	7	12	4	4	0/7	2	5	7	11	9	5	3
0/8	2	8	13	11	9	5	3	0/8	3	-	-	5	4	6	2
0/9	1	5	4	-	-	-	-	0/9	3	5	4	-	-	-	-
1	1	6	8	-	-	-	-	1	3	-	-	4	6	2	6
Cr		Proper				Improper		Cu		Proper				Improper	
	State	s_u	S_u	s_r	S_r	s_r	S_r		State	s_u	S_u	s_r	S_r	s_r	S_r
9500	1	7600	4500	-	-	-	-	8500	1			-	-	-	-
h		Proper				Improper		f		Proper				Improper	
	State	s_u	S_u	s_r	S_r	s_r	S_r		State	s_u	S_u	s_r	S_r	s_r	S_r
4	2	3	2	1	3	3	2	50	2	55	45	44	34	34	22

Table 6. Optimal ordering policies for product (E2).

α		Proper				Improper		β		Proper				Improper	
	State	s_u	S_u	s_r	S_r	s_r	S_r		State	s_u	S_u	s_r	S_r	s_r	S_r
0/1	4	-	-	4	3	5	4	0/1	1	6	9	-	-	-	-
0/2	4	-	-	4	6	2	4	0/2	1	5	9	-	-	-	-
0/3	4	-	-	8	4	4	8	0/3	1	1	3	-	-	-	-
0/4	3	6	7	5	7	7	10	0/4	2	2	8	12	7	12	4
0/5	3	7	9	-	-	-	-	0/5	2	2	8	13	11	9	5
0/6	3	4	8	-	-	-	-	0/6	2	2	8	12	7	12	4
0/7	2	4	3	6	9	4	12	0/7	2	2	8	13	11	9	5
0/8	2	4	6	5	6	4	9	0/8	3	-	-	4	8	3	7
0/9	1	8	4	-	-	-	-	0/9	3	-	-	3	6	4	8
1	1	4	3	-	-	-	-	1	3	3	6	-	-	-	-
Cr		Proper				Improper		Cu		Proper				Improper	
	State	s_u	S_u	s_r	S_r	s_r	S_r		State	s_u	S_u	s_r	S_r	s_r	S_r
280	1	255	240	-	-	-	-	250	1	220	215	-	-	-	-
h		Proper				Improper		f		Proper				Improper	
	State	s_u	S_u	s_r	S_r	s_r	S_r		State	s_u	S_u	s_r	S_r	s_r	S_r
5	2	5	8	5	9	4	7	43	2	44	67	34	41	25	35

Table 7. Optimal ordering policies for product (E3).

α	State	Proper s_u	Proper S_u	s_r	S_r	Improper s_r	Improper S_r	β	State	Proper s_u	Proper S_u	s_r	S_r	Improper s_r	Improper S_r
0/1	4	-	-	2	7	9	7	0/1	1	2	7	-	-	-	-
0/2	4	-	-	2	4	8	11	0/2	1	2	4	-	-	-	-
0/3	4	-	-	2	3	5	7	0/3	1	2	3	-	-	-	-
0/4	3	-	-	2	5	7	11	0/4	2	2	5	2	7	9	7
0/5	3	-	-	2	7	9	7	0/5	2	2	7	2	4	8	11
0/6	3	-	-	2	4	8	11	0/6	2	2	4	2	3	5	7
0/7	2	2	7	9	7	12	4	0/7	2	2	3	2	5	7	11
0/8	2	2	4	8	11	9	5	0/8	3	2	5	-	-	-	-
0/9	1	2	7	-	-	-	-	0/9	3	2	7	-	-	-	-
1	1	2	4	-	-	-	-	1	3	2	4	-	-	-	-

Cr	State	Proper s_u	Proper S_u	s_r	S_r	Improper s_r	Improper S_r	Cu	State	Proper s_u	Proper S_u	s_r	S_r	Improper s_r	Improper S_r
1480	1	1400	1470	-	-	-	-	1400	1	1270	1380	-	-	-	-

h	State	Proper s_u	Proper S_u	s_r	S_r	Improper s_r	Improper S_r	f	State	Proper s_u	Proper S_u	s_r	S_r	Improper s_r	Improper S_r
2	2	2	5	3	4	5	9	45	2	30	35	34	40	45	55

Table 8. Optimal ordering policies for product (E4).

α	State	Proper s_u	Proper S_u	s_r	S_r	Improper s_r	Improper S_r	β	State	Proper s_u	Proper S_u	s_r	S_r	Improper s_r	Improper S_r
0/1	4	-	-	3	7	9	3	0/1	1	3	7	-	-	-	-
0/2	4	-	-	3	4	8	3	0/2	1	3	4	-	-	-	-
0/3	4	-	-	2	4	3	2	0/3	1	2	4	-	-	-	-
0/4	3	3	7	-	-	-	-	0/4	2	2	4	3	7	9	3
0/5	3	3	4	-	-	-	-	0/5	2	1	8	3	4	8	3
0/6	3	2	4	-	-	-	-	0/6	2	1	4	2	4	3	2
0/7	2	2	7	9	7	12	4	0/7	2	3	7	2	4	6	2
0/8	2	2	4	8	11	9	5	0/8	3	3	7	-	-	-	-
0/9	1	3	7	-	-	-	-	0/9	3	-	-	3	7	9	3
1	1	3	4	-	-	-	-	1	3	-	-	3	4	8	3

Cr	State	Proper s_u	Proper S_u	s_r	S_r	Improper s_r	Improper S_r	Cu	State	Proper s_u	Proper S_u	s_r	S_r	Improper s_r	Improper S_r
275	1	3	7	-	-	-	-	250	1	-	-	-	-	-	-

h	State	Proper s_u	Proper S_u	s_r	S_r	Improper s_r	Improper S_r	f	State	Proper s_u	Proper S_u	s_r	S_r	Improper s_r	Improper S_r
7	2	3	7	9	3	7	9	65	2	35	45	34	44	51	55

Table 9. Optimal ordering policies for product (E5).

α	State	Proper s_u	Proper S_u	Proper s_r	Proper S_r	Improper s_r	Improper S_r	β	State	Proper s_u	Proper S_u	Proper s_r	Proper S_r	Improper s_r	Improper S_r
0/1	4	-	-	2	7	9	7	0/1	1	8	11	-	-	-	-
0/2	4	-	-	2	4	8	11	0/2	1	5	7	-	-	-	-
0/3	4	-	-	2	3	5	7	0/3	1	7	11	-	-	-	-
0/4	3	2	7	-	-	-	-	0/4	2	2	7	9	7	12	4
0/5	3	2	4	-	-	-	-	0/5	2	2	4	8	11	9	5
0/6	3	2	3	-	-	-	-	0/6	2	2	3	5	7	12	4
0/7	2	2	5	2	7	9	7	0/7	2	2	5	7	11	9	5
0/8	2	2	7	2	4	8	11	0/8	3	8	11	-	-	-	-
0/9	1	2	4	-	-	-	-	0/9	3	5	7	-	-	-	-
1	1	2	3	-	-	-	-	1	3	-	-	8	11	9	8

Cr	State	Proper s_u	Proper S_u	Proper s_r	Proper S_r	Improper s_r	Improper S_r	Cu	State	Proper s_u	Proper S_u	Proper s_r	Proper S_r	Improper s_r	Improper S_r
16,500	1	1600	16,500	-	-	-	-	15,000	1	13,500	15,000	-	-	-	-

h	State	Proper s_u	Proper S_u	Proper s_r	Proper S_r	Improper s_r	Improper S_r	f	State	Proper s_u	Proper S_u	Proper s_r	Proper S_r	Improper s_r	Improper S_r
6	2	4	6	3	6	5	8	55	2	50	55	42	50	55	55

Table 10. Optimal ordering policies for product (E6).

α	State	Proper s_u	Proper S_u	Proper s_r	Proper S_r	Improper s_r	Improper S_r	β	State	Proper s_u	Proper S_u	Proper s_r	Proper S_r	Improper s_r	Improper S_r
0/1	4	-	-	3	6	6	9	0/1	1	2	7	-	-	-	-
0/2	4	-	-	3	7	5	10	0/2	1	5	9	-	-	-	-
0/3	4	-	-	4	8	3	7	0/3	1	3	8	-	-	-	-
0/4	3	4	8	-	-	-	-	0/4	2	3	4	8	3	4	8
0/5	3	5	9	-	-	-	-	0/5	2	3	5	9	3	5	9
0/6	3	5	8	-	-	-	-	0/6	2	3	5	8	3	5	8
0/7	2	3	6	3	5	7	9	0/7	2	2	3	6	2	3	6
0/8	2	3	5	3	5	4	7	0/8	3	-	-	3	4	8	3
0/9	1	2	8	-	-	-	-	0/9	3	-	-	3	5	9	3
1	1	2	6	-	-	-	-	1	3	-	-	3	5	8	3

Cr	State	Proper s_u	Proper S_u	Proper s_r	Proper S_r	Improper s_r	Improper S_r	Cu	State	Proper s_u	Proper S_u	Proper s_r	Proper S_r	Improper s_r	Improper S_r
1470	1	1400	1470	-	-	-	-	1400	1	1365	1400	-	-	-	-

h	State	Proper s_u	Proper S_u	Proper s_r	Proper S_r	Improper s_r	Improper S_r	f	State	Proper s_u	Proper S_u	Proper s_r	Proper S_r	Improper s_r	Improper S_r
8	2	3	4	8	3	4	8	43	2	20	35	38	43	32	43

Table 11. Optimal ordering policies for product (E7).

α		Proper				Improper		β		Proper				Improper	
	State	s_u	S_u	s_r	S_r	s_r	S_r		State	s_u	S_u	s_r	S_r	s_r	S_r
0/1	4	-	-	3	4	8	3	0/1	1	3	6	-	-	-	-
0/2	4	-	-	3	5	9	3	0/2	1	3	7	-	-	-	-
0/3	4	-	-	3	5	8	3	0/3	1	4	8	-	-	-	-
0/4	3	-	-	2	3	6	2	0/4	2	3	6	6	9	3	6
0/5	3	-	-	2	3	5	2	0/5	2	3	7	5	10	3	7
0/6	3	-	-	1	2	8	1	0/6	2	4	8	3	7	4	8
0/7	2	3	6	1	2	6	1	0/7	2	3	6	6	9	3	6
0/8	2	3	7	3	4	8	3	0/8	3	3	6	-	-	-	-
0/9	1	4	8	-	-	-	-	0/9	3	3	7	-	-	-	-
1	1	5	9	-	-	-	-	1	3	4	8	-	-	-	-

Cr		Proper				Improper		Cu		Proper				Improper	
	State	s_u	S_u	s_r	S_r	s_r	S_r		State	s_u	S_u	s_r	S_r	s_r	S_r
820	1	800	820	-	-	-	-	780	1	700	780	-	-	-	-

h		Proper				Improper		f		Proper				Improper	
	State	s_u	S_u	s_r	S_r	s_r	S_r		State	s_u	S_u	s_r	S_r	s_r	S_r
4	2	3	6	6	9	3	6	48	2	40	42	38	42	28	39

Table 12. Optimal ordering policies for product (E8).

α		Proper				Improper		β		Proper				Improper	
	State	s_u	S_u	s_r	S_r	s_r	S_r		State	s_u	S_u	s_r	S_r	s_r	S_r
0/1	4	-	-	3	6	6	9	0/1	1	3	6	-	-	-	-
0/2	4	-	-	3	7	5	10	0/2	1	3	7	-	-	-	-
0/3	4	-	-	4	8	3	7	0/3	1	4	8	-	-	-	-
0/4	3	3	6	-	-	-	-	0/4	2	3	6	6	9	3	6
0/5	3	3	7	-	-	-	-	0/5	2	3	7	5	10	3	7
0/6	3	4	8	-	-	-	-	0/6	2	4	8	3	7	4	8
0/7	2	3	6	3	6	6	9	0/7	2	3	6	6	9	3	6
0/8	2	3	7	3	7	5	10	0/8	3	-	-	3	6	6	9
0/9	1	4	8	-	-	-	-	0/9	3	-	-	3	7	5	10
1	1	3	6	-	-	-	-	1	3	-	-	4	8	3	7

Cr		Proper				Improper		Cu		Proper				Improper	
	State	s_u	S_u	s_r	S_r	s_r	S_r		State	s_u	S_u	s_r	S_r	s_r	S_r
975	1	900	965	-	-	-	-	920	1	880	900	-	-	-	-

h		Proper				Improper		f		Proper				Improper	
	State	s_u	S_u	s_r	S_r	s_r	S_r		State	s_u	S_u	s_r	S_r	s_r	S_r
5	2	2	5	3	4	2	4	46	2	20	30	40	45	35	40

According to both the defined states at the beginning of the problem and the optimal values based on the ordering policies indicated in Tables 5–12, the optimal value for all of these products is indicated according to four states in Table 11. According to Table 13, it is evident that the fourth state imposes the maximum cost on the system since, as mentioned earlier, the orders are supplied by reliable suppliers in this state. Accordingly, due to the difference in costs between two suppliers (the cost of buying a product from a reliable supplier is greater than buying a product from an unreliable supplier), this cost is greater than other states.

Table 13. Optimal cost values for each spare part.

Product	State			
	1	2	3	4
E1	68,054	73,050	76,050	76,062
E2	2058	2133	2043	2293
E3	8449	8605	8445	8931
E4	1815	1915	1990	1999
E5	135,055	142,555	148,555	148,580
E6	11,243	11,523	11,243	11,818
E7	3948	4028	4148	4168
E8	3736	3891	3726	3951
Total sum	234,358	247,700	256,200	257,802

Based on the final reports, when it comes to reliable supplier disruption under uncertain conditions, there is no choice but to order from the unreliable supplier to meet demands. It is obvious that the cost of unreliable resources is higher that reliable one and the delivery time is less reliable. However, the company will consider these flaws and use the unreliable supplier to meet the demands of critical spare parts, since the waiting time for a comeback of the reliable supplier is not neglectable and the time lost due to the disruption causes the loss of demand.

4. Conclusions and Future Work

Planning and control of inventories are essential activities in supply chains and logistic systems. Hence, various studies and research have been conducted in this field. In terms of supply and demand, the issues in inventory planning are divided into two categories. The first category is inventory control, along with determining price. In conventional methods, determining price is the responsibility of the operational section, and pricing policies are separately determined by the marketing section. However, in order to maximize total profit, the policies and pricing must simultaneously be taken into account. Indeed, determining a suitable price is a complicated process, and organizations must have knowledge of operational costs, current customers, and future demand to be able to adjust and balance prices with minimum costs.

The second category is multi-objective models. Most of the inventory models cover the concept of different costs and services in one objective, and conventional methods are employed to solve them. On the other hand, one of the known features of trade in today's world is a variety of decision-maker wishes. In multi-objective problems, the decision-maker aims to simultaneously maximize or minimize two or several objectives. This type of model has been employed in various fields, while few multi-objective problems have addressed inventory control.

In this study, the inventory model is designed under the disruption condition of suppliers for supplying critical spare parts based on the Markov chain process model. Logistic time, time horizon, and shortage are considered probable, limitless, unallowed, and completely restored. Demand is considered as a function of price. The proposed model is complex. Accordingly, the optimal system cost, ordering policies, and reorder point must be determined. Moreover, a real state study and sensitivity analysis were carried out on the main parameters of the model. Since most of the previous research applied simple optimization methods, this paper decided to implement four different meta-heuristic algorithms to solve the mathematical mode. Based on the output, all four methods work well, though the GWO method was the best method to solve the inventory policy decision making model. Moreover, contrary to the articles that emphasized the use of reliable suppliers, outputs of this research show that under uncertain conditions and disruption of reliable suppliers, it is not possible to meet all demands just by relying on reliable suppliers, because the waiting time for a comeback of the reliable supplier is not neglectable and the time lost due to the disruption causes the loss of demand. Regarding the optimal value of variables in presented tables, it is clear that companies should consider the unreliable supplier when the reliable one is under disruption, even if this approach costs more.

This article attempted to cover neglected aspects to improve previous research; however, there were some barriers in addressing all of the neglected concepts. This research does not have access to long-term data to plan for long horizon planning. Considering uncertainty in some parameters such as delivery time of goods and transportation capacity requires a more comprehensive mathematical model. Moreover, four meta-heuristic methods are applied to solve the model which work well, however a heuristic method might be much useful to solve the mathematical optimization in this case.

In future research, other probability approaches can be employed. This combined Fuzzy and artificial intelligence approach can be employed, and the results can be compared. Moreover, a robust approach can also be used for allocation and consistency with uncertainty. In the present study, the correlation between uncertain demand and buying price is neglected. One of the essential problems in demand prediction is taking into account the interaction between demand and price. Given that demand is assumed uncertain, the assumed distribution parameters of demand can be included in the model as a function of the sales price. The function that expresses the demand distribution parameters in terms of price can be linear or non-linear. Moreover, modeling the problem as hierarchical and comparing weaknesses and strengths with an integrated approach. Modeling the problem with respect to other objectives, such a minimizing change in human force, minimizing greenhouse gas emission and industrial waste, can be considered in future research.

Author Contributions: Conceptualization, N.E.; Methodology, N.E.; Software, K.B.; Validation, K.B., N.E. and D.Z.; Formal analysis, K.B.; Investigation, N.E.; Data curation, K.B. and L.J.; Writing—original draft, K.B., D.Z. and L.J.; Visualization, K.B.; Project administration, D.Z. and L.J. All authors have read and agreed to the published version of the manuscript.

Funding: This research received no external funding.

Institutional Review Board Statement: Not applicable.

Informed Consent Statement: Not applicable.

Data Availability Statement: Data and optimal values of variables are available from the corresponding author upon reasonable request.

Acknowledgments: We had the pleasure of collaborating with our adviser in the company to collecting data in best way.

Conflicts of Interest: The authors declare no conflict of interest.

References

1. Malik, A.I.; Sarkar, B. Disruption management in a constrained multi-product imperfect production system. *J. Manuf. Syst.* **2020**, *56*, 227–240. [CrossRef] [PubMed]
2. Nnamdi, O. Strategies for Managing Excess and Dead Inventories: A Case Study of Spare Parts Inventories in the Elevator Equipment Industry. *Oper. Supply Chain Manag. Int. J.* **2018**, *11*, 128–138. [CrossRef]
3. Wallin Blair, C.; Rungtusanatham, M.; Rabinovich, E.; Hwang, Y.; Money, R.B. Managing Critical Spare Parts within a Buyer–Supplier Dyad: Buyer Preferences for Ownership and Placement. *J. Bus. Logist.* **2020**, *41*, 111–128. [CrossRef]
4. Svoboda, J.; Minner, S.; Yao, M. Typology and literature review on multiple supplier inventory control models. *Eur. J. Oper. Res.* **2021**, *293*, 1–23. [CrossRef]
5. Treber, S.; Benfer, M.; Häfner, B.; Wang, L.; Lanza, G. Robust optimization of information flows in global production networks using multi-method simulation and surrogate modelling. *CIRP J. Manuf. Sci. Technol.* **2021**, *32*, 491–506. [CrossRef]
6. Baghizadeh, K.; Zimon, D.; Jum'a, L. Modeling and optimization sustainable forest supply chain considering discount in transportation system and supplier selection under uncertainty. *Forests* **2021**, *12*, 964. [CrossRef]
7. Chen, J.; Chen, Z. A new optimal multi-product (Q, R, SS) policy with multivariate Markov stochastic demand forecasting model. *Int. J. Math. Oper. Res.* **2019**, *14*, 82–105. [CrossRef]
8. Saputro, T.E.; Figueira, G.; Almada-Lobo, B. Integration of Supplier Selection and Inventory Management under Supply Disruptions. *IFAC-PapersOnLine* **2019**, *52*, 2827–2832. [CrossRef]
9. Ghadimi, P.; Ghassemi Toosi, F.; Heavey, C. A multi-agent systems approach for sustainable supplier selection and order allocation in a partnership supply chain. *Eur. J. Oper. Res.* **2018**, *269*, 286–301. [CrossRef]
10. Baghizadeh, K.; Cheikhrouhou, N.; Govindan, K.; Ziyarati, M. Sustainable agriculture supply chain network design considering water-energy-food nexus using queuing system: A hybrid robust possibilistic programming. *Nat. Resour. Model.* **2022**, *35*, e12337. [CrossRef]
11. Trattner, A.; Hvam, L.; Forza, C.; Herbert-Hansen, Z.N.L. Product complexity and operational performance: A systematic literature review. *CIRP J. Manuf. Sci. Technol.* **2019**, *25*, 69–83. [CrossRef]
12. Baghizadeh, K.; Pahl, J.; Hu, G. Closed-Loop Supply Chain Design with Sustainability Aspects and Network Resilience under Uncertainty: Modelling and Application. *Math. Probl. Eng.* **2021**, *2021*, 9951220. [CrossRef]
13. Lin, S.S.C. Note on "The derivation of EOQ/EPQ inventory models with two backorders costs using analytic geometry and algebra". *Appl. Math. Model.* **2019**, *73*, 378–386. [CrossRef]
14. Woo, Y.-B.; Kim, B.S. A genetic algorithm-based matheuristic for hydrogen supply chain network problem with two transportation modes and replenishment cycles. *Comput. Ind. Eng.* **2019**, *127*, 981–997. [CrossRef]
15. Samal, N.K.; Pratihar, D.K. Joint optimization of preventive maintenance and spare parts inventory using genetic algorithms and particle swarm optimization algorithm. *Int. J. Syst. Assur. Eng. Manag.* **2015**, *6*, 248–258. [CrossRef]
16. Li, X.; Li, Y.; Cai, X. On a multi-period supply chain system with supplementary order opportunity. *Eur. J. Oper. Res.* **2011**, *209*, 273–284. [CrossRef]
17. Watson, K.; Polito, T. Comparison of DRP and TOC financial performance within a multi-product, multi-echelon physical distribution environment. *Int. J. Prod. Res.* **2003**, *41*, 741–765. [CrossRef]
18. Moin, N.H.; Salhi, S.; Aziz, N.A.B. An efficient hybrid genetic algorithm for the multi-product multi-period inventory routing problem. *Int. J. Prod. Econ.* **2011**, *133*, 334–343. [CrossRef]
19. Pal, B.; Sana, S.S.; Chaudhuri, K. A stochastic inventory model with product recovery. *CIRP J. Manuf. Sci. Technol.* **2013**, *6*, 120–127. [CrossRef]
20. Murray, C.C.; Gosavi, A.; Talukdar, D. The multi-product price-setting newsvendor with resource capacity constraints. *Int. J. Prod. Econ.* **2012**, *138*, 148–158. [CrossRef]
21. Choi, S.; Ruszczyński, A. A multi-product risk-averse newsvendor with exponential utility function. *Eur. J. Oper. Res.* **2011**, *214*, 78–84. [CrossRef]
22. Ramkumar, N.; Subramanian, P.; Narendran, T.T.; Ganesh, K. Mixed integer linear programming model for multi-commodity multi-depot inventory routing problem. *Opsearch* **2012**, *49*, 413–429. [CrossRef]
23. Hosseinifard, Z.; Shao, L.; Talluri, S. Service-Level Agreement with Dynamic Inventory Policy: The Effect of the Performance Review Period and the Incentive Structure. *Decis. Sci.* **2022**, *53*, 802–826. [CrossRef]
24. Sokolinskiy, O.; Sopranzetti, B.; Rogers, D.S.; Leuschner, R. Inventory Management and Endogenous Demand: Investigating the Role of Customer Referrals, Defections, and Product Market Failure. *Decis. Sci.* **2019**, *50*, 118–141. [CrossRef]
25. Mjirda, A.; Jarboui, B.; MacEdo, R.; Hanafi, S.; Mladenović, N. A two phase variable neighborhood search for the multi-product inventory routing problem. *Comput. Oper. Res.* **2014**, *52*, 291–299. [CrossRef]
26. Coelho, L.C.; Laporte, G. A branch-and-cut algorithm for the multi-product multi-vehicle inventory-routing problem. *Int. J. Prod. Res.* **2013**, *51*, 7156–7169. [CrossRef]
27. Sethi, S.P.; Cheng, F. Optimality of (s, S) policies in inventory models with markovian demand. *Oper. Res.* **1997**, *45*, 931–939. [CrossRef]
28. Gharaei, A.; Karimi, M.; Hoseini Shekarabi, S.A. An integrated multi-product, multi-buyer supply chain under penalty, green, and quality control polices and a vendor managed inventory with consignment stock agreement: The outer approximation with equality relaxation and augmented penalty algorithm. *Appl. Math. Model.* **2019**, *69*, 223–254. [CrossRef]

29. Aliyev, R.T.; Khaniyev, T.A. On the rate of convergence of the asymptotic expansion for the ergodic distribution of a semi-Markov (s, S) inventory model. *Cybern. Syst. Anal.* **2012**, *48*, 117–121. [CrossRef]
30. Arifoğlu, K.; Özekici, S. Optimal policies for inventory systems with finite capacity and partially observed Markov-modulated demand and supply processes. *Eur. J. Oper. Res.* **2010**, *204*, 421–438. [CrossRef]
31. Atali, A.; Özer, Ö. Stochastic multi-item inventory systems with markov-modulated demands and production quantity requirements. *Probab. Eng. Inf. Sci.* **2012**, *26*, 263–293. [CrossRef]
32. Ahiska, S.S.; Appaji, S.R.; King, R.E.; Warsing, D.P. A Markov decision process-based policy characterization approach for a stochastic inventory control problem with unreliable sourcing. *Int. J. Prod. Econ.* **2013**, *144*, 485–496. [CrossRef]
33. Olsen, T.L.; Parker, R.P. On markov equilibria in dynamic inventory competition. *Oper. Res.* **2014**, *62*, 332–344. [CrossRef]
34. Barron, Y.; Perry, D.; Stadje, W. A make-to-stock production/inventory model with MAP arrivals and phase-type demands. *Ann. Oper. Res.* **2014**, *241*, 373–409. [CrossRef]
35. Luo, S.; Ahiska, S.S.; Fang, S.C.; King, R.E.; Warsing, D.P.; Wu, S. An analysis of optimal ordering policies for a two-supplier system with disruption risk. *Omega* **2021**, *105*, 102517. [CrossRef]
36. Asadi, A.; Nurre Pinkley, S. A stochastic scheduling, allocation, and inventory replenishment problem for battery swap stations. *Transp. Res. Part E Logist. Transp. Rev.* **2021**, *146*, 102212. [CrossRef]
37. Ye, Y.; Grossmann, I.E.; Pinto, J.M.; Ramaswamy, S. Integrated optimization of design, storage sizing, and maintenance policy as a Markov decision process considering varying failure rates. *Comput. Chem. Eng.* **2020**, *142*, 107052. [CrossRef]
38. Chin, H.H.; Wang, B.; Varbanov, P.S.; Klemeš, J.J. Markov Decision Process to Optimise Long-term Asset Maintenance and Technologies Investment in Chemical Industry. *Comput. Aided Chem. Eng.* **2021**, *50*, 1853–1858. [CrossRef]
39. Patriarca, R.; Hu, T.; Costantino, F.; Di Gravio, G.; Tronci, M. A System-Approach for Recoverable Spare Parts Management Using the Discrete Weibull Distribution. *Sustainability* **2019**, *11*, 5180. [CrossRef]
40. Milewski, D. Total Costs of Centralized and Decentralized Inventory Strategies—Including External Costs. *Sustainability* **2020**, *12*, 9346. [CrossRef]
41. Xu, X.; Niu, D.; Qiu, J.; Wang, P.; Chen, Y. Analysis and Optimization of Power Supply Structure Based on Markov Chain and Error Optimization for Renewable Energy from the Perspective of Sustainability. *Sustainability* **2016**, *8*, 634. [CrossRef]
42. Katsigiannis, Y.A.; Georgilakis, P.S.; Karapidakis, E.S. Multiobjective genetic algorithm solution to the optimum economic and environmental performance problem of small autonomous hybrid power systems with renewables. *IET Renew. Power Gener.* **2010**, *4*, 404–419. [CrossRef]
43. Storn, R.; Price, K. Differential Evolution—A Simple and Efficient Heuristic for global Optimization over Continuous Spaces. *J. Glob. Optim.* **1997**, *11*, 341–359. [CrossRef]
44. Mirjalili, S.; Mirjalili, S.M.; Lewis, A. Grey Wolf Optimizer. *Adv. Eng. Softw.* **2014**, *69*, 46–61. [CrossRef]
45. Mirjalili, S. Moth-flame optimization algorithm: A novel nature-inspired heuristic paradigm. *Knowl. Based Syst.* **2015**, *89*, 228–249. [CrossRef]

Disclaimer/Publisher's Note: The statements, opinions and data contained in all publications are solely those of the individual author(s) and contributor(s) and not of MDPI and/or the editor(s). MDPI and/or the editor(s) disclaim responsibility for any injury to people or property resulting from any ideas, methods, instructions or products referred to in the content.

 *mathematics*

Article

Optimal Decision-Making of Retailer-Led Dual-Channel Green Supply Chain with Fairness Concerns under Government Subsidies

Lei Song [1], Qi Xin [1], Huilin Chen [1,*], Lutao Liao [1] and Zheyi Chen [2]

1. College of Economics and Trade, Fujian Jiangxia University, Fuzhou 350108, China
2. College of Computer and Data Science, Fuzhou University, Fuzhou 350116, China
* Correspondence: huilinchen626@fjjxu.edu.cn

Abstract: Green innovation is the inevitable trend in the development of the supply chain, and thus the government adopts subsidy policies for the relevant enterprises to enhance their enthusiasm for green development. In view of the manufacturers' fairness concerns in the dual-channel green supply chain that is composed of manufacturers and retailers, we propose a novel Stackelberg game model led by retailers and analyze the impact of manufacturers' fairness concerns on the decision-making of manufacturers and retailers in the dual-channel green supply chain under government subsidies. The results show that only the wholesale price of products, manufacturers' profits, and retailers' profits are affected by manufacturer's fair concerns. When manufacturer has fair concerns, product greenness and profits of supply chain members rise with the increase in government subsidies. The results can offer an effective reference for the dual-channel supply chain members with fairness concerns to make optimal decisions under government subsidies.

Keywords: government subsidies; dual-channel green supply chain; fairness concerns; retailer-led

MSC: 90B06

1. Introduction

With the rapid development of the economy, environmental degradation has become increasingly obvious, leading to the continuous depletion of natural resources. For example, carbon emissions are recognized as the leading cause of global warming. These environmental problems have attracted the attention of the international community, and many governments have issued a series of international conventions to protect the ecological environment, including the Kyoto Protocol in 1997 and the Climate Change Conference held in Copenhagen in 2010, which indicate that the international community attaches great importance to ecological protection [1]. Therefore, the sustainable green development mode with low consumption and emission has become an inevitable trend. As an effective and sustainable means to overcome resource and environmental constraints and promote sustainable development, green innovation has become the main determinant of green supply chain development [2]. Meanwhile, the implementation of the green supply chain can not only improve ecological problems but also increase the financial performance of supply chain enterprises and improve their competitiveness [3]. With the continuous development of the green supply chain, the sustainable management of the supply chain has become a concern of all walks of life, and the external pressure from the government, consumers, and the media is also growing [4]. For example, the supermarket industry in Britain and Japan, the aerospace industry in Britain and the convenience store industry in Japan are all implementing the green strategy, which reflected the improving environmental awareness and growing business types [5].

On one hand, as the main body of macro-control, the governments have paid more attention to improving the environmental awareness of enterprises and consumers. To

---

Citation: Song, L.; Xin, Q.; Chen, H.; Liao, L.; Chen, Z. Optimal Decision-Making of Retailer-Led Dual-Channel Green Supply Chain with Fairness Concerns under Government Subsidies. *Mathematics* 2023, 11, 284. https://doi.org/10.3390/math11020284

Academic Editor: Yong He

Received: 28 November 2022
Revised: 28 December 2022
Accepted: 3 January 2023
Published: 5 January 2023

Copyright: © 2023 by the authors. Licensee MDPI, Basel, Switzerland. This article is an open access article distributed under the terms and conditions of the Creative Commons Attribution (CC BY) license (https://creativecommons.org/licenses/by/4.0/).

encourage enterprises to develop and produce green products, some governments have introduced a series of incentives and subsidies for green manufacturing to ensure that economic growth is stable and environmental benefits are achieved at the same time. For example, the US Department of Energy implemented a management loan program to accelerate the commercial deployment of innovative new clean technologies and invested $30 billion to support more than 30 projects in different green industries [6]. In 2012, the European Commission invested 41.8 million euros in the green campaign for electric vehicles and funded energy technology research and development [7]. In 2016, the Scottish government spent 70 million pounds on subsidies to encourage the circular economy [8]. Moreover, in the Notice on Promoting the Green Development of E-commerce Enterprises [9] issued by the Ministry of Commerce in 2021, the Chinese government emphasized the importance and necessity of green development, which can ensure the high-quality development of e-commerce and also pointed out that building a modern economy should rely on green development. According to the above research, members of the supply chain can get incentives through various government subsidies. Therefore, to establish a system of sustainable green supply chain, it is necessary to bring government subsidies into the system for decision-making research.

On the other hand, due to the rapid development of e-commerce, customers' shopping behavior is changing, and people are getting used to online shopping. In 2021, the number of online-shopping users in China has reached 842 million, accounting for 81.6% of the total Internet users [10]. The way of purchasing products on e-commerce platform can increase the choice of customers, demonstrating that the online markets have a broad prospect. Some enterprises develop the online sale channel while maintaining the original offline sale channel, and thus the dual-channel supply chain development model arises spontaneously. For example, some manufacturers, such as Dell, Apple, Nike, and HP, have adopted a dual-channel supply chain structure to distribute their products. Meanwhile, some companies, such as Amazon, Alibaba, and JD, provide sale platforms for these manufacturers that choose the dual-channel strategy. As a giant enterprise in the household appliance, Suning only used offline sale mode at the beginning, but the development of e-commerce in recent years forced Suning to open up the online channel. The diversification of channels urges manufacturers to establish online sales to increase their market share, which also makes up for the defects of the traditional sale channel. However, in the case of the coexistence of dual channels, the difference in market share of manufacturers in each channel will affect consumers' choice, cause changes in channel demands, and thus affect the income of supply chain members. Under such an environment of the dual-channel supply chain, it is a realistic and urgent problem to explore the impact of the market share of manufacturers' online channel on the overall supply chain.

In the development process of green supply chain, although many enterprises take sustainable development as their future strategy, the core meaning is still to focus on their own interests. Manufacturers that are responsible for production and research development pay special attention to their own returns. When supply chain members think that their own investment is inconsistent with the return, they will pay extra attention to the fairness of channel profit distribution, resulting in manufacturers' fairness concerns [11]. Meanwhile, in the real business environment, due to the progress of information technology and familiarity with the market, some retailers have become powerful and gradually gained the leading position in supply chain channels, such as Suning, Vanguard, Gome, Wal Mart, and Home Depot, dominate the behavior decisions of members of the supply chain [12]. Therefore, when considering the governments' green innovation subsidies to supply chain members, it is necessary to pay attention to the fair concerns of manufacturers under the leadership of retailers in the supply chain. The manufacturers implementing green innovative technologies, especially small and medium-sized ones, have become a vulnerable group in cooperation with powerful retailers. For example, the "price war" between Gome and Gree continues to affect the relationship between the two. The "no gross loss" rule of Gome triggered Gree's fairness concerns. Gree realized that there was an uneven profit distribution between retailers and thus ended the cooperation. After reaching a fair deal, Gree and Gome started cooperation again. Nowadays, much research on green supply chains considers fairness concerns of members in the supply chain, but most only focus on the fairness of retailers, ignoring the fairness concerns of manufacturers. Moreover, in the dual-channel green supply chain, the pricing of products, terminal sales prices, and the prices of retailers' wholesale products from suppliers are different, and the online channel opened by manufacturers will compete with the offline channel dominated by retailers, which will affect the distribution decisions of channel profits and trigger the mechanism of manufacturer's fairness concerns. Therefore, it is of practical significance to consider the manufacturer's fair concerns.

Based on the above analysis, we construct a game model of dual-channel green supply chain under government subsidies and retailers' dominance with the consideration of the manufacturer's fairness concerns, which expands the traditional game model of single-channel green supply chain. Based on the situation of government green subsidies and retailers' dominance, we study the impact of manufacturer's fairness concerns on members' decision-making behaviors, in order to promote the green innovation of supply chain enterprises and the sustainable development, and meanwhile provides the government with theoretical support for making decisions.

Therefore, the following issues are mainly studied in this paper:

(1) Based on the situation that the government grants green subsidies to manufacturers, how do manufacturers' fairness concerns affect manufacturers' and retailers' optimal decisions and profits?

(2) What is the impact of different levels of government green subsidies to manufacturers on the supply chain?

(3) Under the green subsidies of the government, how do the optimal decisions and optimal profits of manufacturers and retailers change with the green efficiency of products?

(4) How will the change of market share for manufacturers' network channel affect the supply chain?

As there are few literatures related to the introduction of government subsidies and manufacturers' fairness concerns in the retailer-led dual channel green supply chain, the novelty of this paper lies in:

(1) The fairness concerns of manufacturers are introduced into the dual-channel green supply chain with government green subsidies, and the impact of government green subsidies, manufacturers' fair concern intensity and other factors on the decision-making of members in the dual-channel green supply chain is discussed.

(2) Retailers act as leaders in the dual-channel green supply chain with government green subsidies, while manufacturers act as followers in the supply chain. Under this structure of the supply chain, we discuss the impact of government green subsidies, manufacturers' fair concern intensity and other factors on the decision-making of members in the dual-channel green supply chain.

The rest of this paper is structured as follows. Section 2 reviews the related literature. In Section 3, the conditional assumptions and the model are established. Section 4 analyzes the model. Section 5 discusses the results. Finally, Section 6 gives the conclusion of this paper.

2. Literature Review

2.1. Dual-Channel Green Supply Chain

Green supply chain was first proposed by the Manufacturing Research Association of Michigan State University in 1996 in a study of "environmentally responsible of manufacturing", which is a modern supply chain management model that considers both resource efficiency and environmental impact. The dual-channel green supply chain is a supply chain structure combining green production and dual-channel operation. In other words, a network channel is established outside the original traditional offline channel.

In recent years, dual-channel green supply chain has attracted attention from all walks of life, and its abundant research has strong theoretical basis and practical guiding significance for policy makers. For supply chain enterprises, the dual channel supply chain model has a bright prospect [13].

He et al. [14] believed that compared with the traditional single-channel model, retailers adopting the dual-channel model can attract more consumers due to the diversity of choices. He et al. [15] studied the dual-channel green supply chain led by manufacturers and investigated the influence of retailers' efforts on the overall profit of the supply chain. Aslani et al. [16] analyzed the coordination between product pricing and product greenness in the dual-channel supply chain under the condition of channel interruption. Li et al. [17] studied the dual-channel green supply chain and analyzed the pricing and greening strategies of supply chain members under the centralized and decentralized conditions. Li et al. [18] discussed the pricing and greening strategies of supply chain members in different coordination modes based on the unified pricing strategy in the dual-channel green supply chain and concluded that the greening pricing strategies of supply chain are greatly affected by several factors: customer loyalty to retail channels, green cost and green sensitivity. Barman et al. [19] considered the double-echelon dual-channel green supply chain of a single manufacturer and retailer and concluded that both the demand degree of retail channel and network channel are affected by product price and product green degree. Gao J. et al. [20] considered the relationship between competition and coordination of dual-channel green supply chain with ecolabel policy, indicating that ecolabel policy can improve the economic and environmental performance of supply chain.

2.2. Government Green Subsidies

On the one hand, the production of green products requires a large amount of investment, resulting in a low profit margin of enterprises. On the other hand, the green innovation of products is limited by enterprise's technology, capital and other problems, and cannot meet the requirements of sustainable development [21]. Therefore, the government encourages enterprises to carry out green innovation through green subsidies.

Meng et al. [22] discussed the product coordination pricing policy in the dual-channel supply chain under the conditions of government subsidies and consumer preferences and came up with the optimal solution. Lou et al. [23] studied the government's green subsidies and the optimal strategies of manufacturers and retailers under the two-level supply chain. Li et al. [24] considered the impact of two types of government subsidies on green technology investment and green coordination under cap-and-trade mechanism. Yu et al. [25] discussed the decision-making problem of manufacturers in determining the level of green products and the production quantity of green products and considered the optimization model of manufacturers with green preference and government subsidies. Yang et al. [26] mainly studied the influence of channel leadership and government intervention on retail price, green level and expected profit with the condition of ambiguity and uncertainty. Madani et al. [27] discussed the product pricing, carbon tariff decision and green input of enterprises under government supervision. In the evolutionary game model, Sun et al. [28] considered three kinds of government subsidy cases and studied the evolution model of green investment in the two-tier supply chain based on the government subsidy mechanism. Liu et al. [29] studied the impact of government subsidies on the profits of green supply chain members by three-stage Stackelberg model.

2.3. Green Supply Chain with Fairness Concerns

Perfectly rational decision states are merely theoretical assumptions. In reality, decision makers not only consider the maximization of their own interests, but also consider the interests of the other side. Enterprises in the supply chain will inevitably have the problem of profit distribution. Manufacturers in charge of production will pay extra attention to their own costs, resulting in manufacturer's fair concern behavior, and pay attention to the fairness of supply chain channel distribution [30]. The theory of Fairness Concerns holds that when the partners think there is unfair distribution, they will punish the other side in some way even if it will harm their own interests.

Kim et al. [31] believe that the concept of equity plays a positive role in supply chain innovation, strengthening resource sharing among supply chain members and maintaining the stability of member relations. Zhang et al. [32] discussed how green preference of green suppliers affects product greenness and supply chain profit, and how to allocate supply chain surplus in the context of fair preference based on "cooperative game theory". Wang et al. [33] believed that manufacturers' fair preference would lead to the decline of product greenness and supply chain operation efficiency in green supply chain. Li et al. [34] believe that there is a negative relationship between the emission reduction cost of manufacturers and the fairness preference of retailers. Yang et al. [35] analyzed the influence of different fairness considerations on green supply chain and found that under the retailer-dominated structure, retail price, product greenness and total profit of supply chain would not be affected by fairness concerns. Jian et al. [36] consider the influence of manufacturers' fairness concerns on retailers' sales, product greenness, recovery rate and product pricing decision in green closed-loop supply chain. Li et al. [37] considered green product design in the supply chain and studied the influence of retailers' fairness concerns on green product design schemes under different circumstances.

2.4. Analysis

The existing literature has laid a good theoretical foundation for the research of this paper, but there are still some gaps in the current research which mainly includes the following points.

(1) On the study of dual-channel supply chain, many literatures focus on the influence of consumer behavior preference on supply chain channels and the pricing coordination problems existing in dual-channel supply chain. On the one hand, the profit distribution link in the supply chain is ignored. On the other hand, it is unreasonable to assume that all members in the green supply chain are in a completely rational state, and the fair concern behavior is not taken into account.

(2) Government subsidies play a positive role in supply chain decision-making, but the subsidy objects are mostly limited to supply chain members without dual-channel opening, and few pay attention to government green subsidies in dual-channel green supply chain.

(3) In the study of fairness concern, many scholars have discussed the fairness concern behavior of supply chain members from different perspectives. However, the existing studies on government subsidies only consider the fairness concerns of retailers in manufacturer-led supply chains and ignore retailers. With the development of modern business, the position of retailers in the supply chain is improving day by day. As the main body of supply chain, the fairness concern behavior of many small and medium-sized manufacturers is also worth to be investigated.

3. Model Description

3.1. Model Assumptions

This paper takes the two-channel and two-level green supply chain consisting of one manufacturer and one retailer as the research objects. The studies mainly focus on optimal decision of the two-channel green supply chain dominated by retailer considering fairness concerns under the government subsidy policy. After receiving the government green innovation subsidies, the manufactures supply green products to retailers through traditional retail channels (denoted as r), and on the other hand, they directly sell to consumers through online channels (denoted as d). Since retail giants such as Tesco, Costco and Aeon have great power of discourse and high user preferences in supply channels, this paper sets retailer as the dominant of Stackelberg game.

In the game model, the retailer's decision behavior depends on the manufacturer's decision behavior. First, manufacturers set direct and wholesale prices based on a given retail price in order to maximize their profits. Secondly, retailers can set their own optimal retail price according to the manufacturer's pricing to ensure that they can get the maximum profit. Figure 1 illustrates the structure of the dual-channel green supply chain.

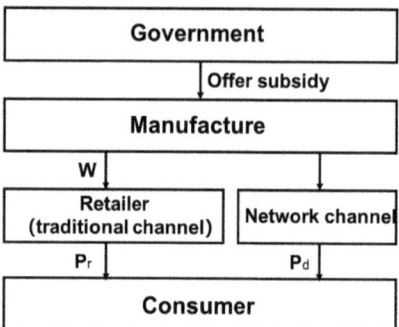

Figure 1. The structure of the dual-channel green supply chain.

Based on the above background, assumptions are made as follows.

(1) In the traditional channel, the wholesale price set by the manufacturer is w, the retail price set by the retailer is p_r ($p_r > w$), the price at which the manufacturer directly sells green products to consumers through the network channel is p_d, the carbon emission reduction in the production process (the product green degree) is g, and the sensitivity coefficient of consumers to product greenness is γ ($\gamma > 0$). The market demand for green products is jointly affected by p_r, p_d, and g.

(2) The R&D cost of green products produced by manufacturers is $c(g) = kg^2/2$ ($k > 0$) [11], where k is the cost coefficient. To facilitate the analysis and discussion, the product green efficiency is defined as $E_g = \frac{\gamma^2}{k}$. When products with the same green degree are produced, the lower the green cost or higher sensitivity to green products will lead to higher efficiency of product green.

(3) When a manufacturer has fairness concerns, its goal is to maximize its own utility, which is defined as U_m.

(4) The amount of subsidy given by the government to manufacturers per unit of carbon emission reduction is s.

Table 1 defines the model parameters.

Table 1. Model parameters and definitions.

Decision Variables	Implications
w	Wholesale price
δ	Retailer profit for single product in traditional channels
p_r	Retail price of retailers in the traditional channel
p_d	Direct selling price of manufacturers in the network channel
g	Product green degree
Relevant Parameters	**Implications**
c	Fixed cost of products
k	Cost coefficient of carbon emission reduction, $k > 0$
β	sales price sensitivity coeffificient, $\beta > 0$
θ	Coefficient of cross price sensitivity among different channels, $\theta > 0$
γ	Coefficient of consumer green preference, $\gamma > 0$
λ	Coefficient of manufacturer's fairness concerns, $\lambda > 0$
a	Market share of the online direct channel
Q	Potential market demand for green products
s	Government subsidies for unit carbon emission reduction
$*$	Optimum situation
Functions	**Implications**
D_r	Market demand of traditional retail channel
D_m	Market demand of network direct selling channel
π_r	Retailer profit
π_m	Manufacture profit
π_{sc}	Profit of supply chain
U_m	Manufacturer's utility function

Based on the above assumptions:
(1) The market demand of the traditional retail channel is defined as

$$D_r = (1-a)Q - \beta p_r + \theta p_d + \gamma g \tag{1}$$

(2) The market demand of the online direct channel [13] is defined as

$$D_d = aQ - \beta p_d + \theta p_r + \gamma g \tag{2}$$

(3) The manufacturer's profit is defined as

$$\pi_m = (w-c)D_r + (p_d - c)D_d + sg - kg^2/2 \tag{3}$$

(4) The retailer's profit is defined as

$$\pi_r = (p_r - w)D_r \tag{4}$$

(5) The utility of the manufacturer is defined as

$$U_m = \pi_m(1+\lambda) - \lambda \pi_r \tag{5}$$

3.2. Decision-Making Model of Dual Channel Green Supply Chain with Manufacturers' Fairness Concerns under Government Subsidies

The manufacturers have the negative effect of envy due to the unfair distribution of income. The retailer is the leader in the supply chain and can obtain a larger share of profits. Therefore, the variable $\delta = p_r - w$ is introduced, which is the retailer's profit per unit product. The retailer's decisions depend on the manufacturer's decisions.

The inverse induction method is used to solve the model. First, the partial derivatives of w, p_d and g of Equation (6) is calculated to obtain the Hessian matrix as follows.

$$H = \begin{bmatrix} \frac{\partial^2 U_m}{\partial w^2} & \frac{\partial^2 U_m}{\partial w \partial p_d} & \frac{\partial^2 U_m}{\partial w \partial g} \\ \frac{\partial^2 U_m}{\partial p_d \partial w} & \frac{\partial^2 U_m}{\partial p_d^2} & \frac{\partial^2 U_m}{\partial p_d \partial g} \\ \frac{\partial^2 U_m}{\partial g \partial w} & \frac{\partial^2 U_m}{\partial g \partial p_d} & \frac{\partial^2 U_m}{\partial g^2} \end{bmatrix} = \begin{bmatrix} -2\beta(1+\lambda) & 2\theta(1+\lambda) & \gamma(1+\lambda) \\ 2\theta(1+\lambda) & -2\beta(1+\lambda) & \gamma(1+\lambda) \\ \gamma(1+\lambda) & \gamma(1+\lambda) & -k(1+\lambda) \end{bmatrix} \tag{6}$$

When U_m exist the maximum, the above Hessian matrix should be a negative definite matrix. Thus, the first principal sub-formula $-2\beta(1+\lambda) < 0$, the second one $4(\beta-\theta)(\beta+\theta)(1+\lambda) > 0$, and the third one $-4(\beta+\theta)(\lambda+1)^3(\beta k - \gamma^2 - k\theta) < 0$. When $\beta > \theta$ and $\beta k - \gamma^2 - k\theta > 0$ are set, there exist an optimal solution (w^*, p_d^*, g^*) that can maximize the utility of manufacturers.

The first derivative of U_m with respect to w, p_d and g is calculated as

$$\frac{\partial U_m}{\partial p_d} = \theta \delta + (1+\lambda)(aQ + c\beta - 2\beta p_d - c\theta + g\gamma + 2\theta w)$$

$$\frac{\partial U_m}{\partial w} = -\beta \delta - (1+\lambda)((-1+a)Q - c\beta + 2\beta w + c\theta - g\gamma - 2\theta p_d)$$

$$\frac{\partial U_m}{\partial g} = -\gamma \lambda \delta + (1+\lambda)(s - gk + \gamma(w + p_d - 2c))$$

Next, the above variables are set to 0, and w, p_d and g can be calculated, respectively.

$$w = \frac{(-QA_2 + 2kA_5 + \gamma A_4)(1+\lambda) - B_1 \gamma^2 \delta(2\lambda - 1) - 2B_1 B_2 k\delta}{4B_1 B_3(\lambda+1)}$$

$$p_d = \frac{(QA_2 + 2kA_3 + \gamma A_4)(1+\lambda) - B_1 \gamma^2 \delta(2\lambda+1)}{4B_1 B_3(\lambda+1)}$$

$$g = -\frac{A_1(\lambda+1) - B_2 \gamma \delta(1+2\lambda)}{2B_3(\lambda+1)}$$

where
$$A_1 = Q\gamma - 2\beta\gamma c + 2\beta s + 2\gamma\theta c - 2\theta s$$
$$A_2 = 2a\beta k - 2a\gamma^2 - 2ak\theta + \gamma^2$$
$$A_3 = Q\theta + \beta^2 c - c\theta^2$$
$$A_4 = 2\beta s + 2\theta s - 4\beta\gamma c - 4\gamma\theta c$$
$$A_5 = Q\beta + \beta^2 c - c\theta^2$$
$$B_1 = \beta + \theta$$
$$B_2 = \beta - \theta$$
$$B_3 = \beta k - \gamma^2 - k\theta$$

Next, the above variables are substituted into Equation (4) and the first-order partial derivative of unit product profit is calculated as

$$\frac{d\pi_r}{d\delta} = -\frac{[-2A_1B_1\gamma - A_2B_1Q + 2A_3\beta k + A_4B_2\gamma - 2A_5k\theta + 4B_1B_3Q(a-1)](2\lambda+1)}{4B_1B_3(\lambda+1)} \\ \frac{-4B_1B_2\beta\delta k + 2B_1\delta\gamma^2(2\lambda+1)(2B_2+\theta) + 8B_1B_3\beta\delta(\lambda+1) - 2B_1\beta\delta\gamma^2(2\lambda-1)}{4B_1B_3(\lambda+1)}$$

Next, the above variable is set to 0, and the unit optimal product profit can be calculated as

$$\delta^* = \frac{(\lambda+1)(-A_2Q + 2A_6k + A_7)}{2B_4(2\lambda+1)}$$

where
$$A_6 = Q\beta - Q\theta - \beta^2 c + 2\beta c\theta - c\theta^2$$
$$A_7 = 2\gamma s(\beta - \theta)$$
$$B_4 = 2k\beta(\beta - \theta) - \gamma^2(\beta + \theta)$$

Next, the optimal product wholesale price w^*, online channel direct sale price p_d^*, and product green degree g^* can be obtained through elimination and simplification as

$$w^* = -\frac{2B_4(2\lambda+1)(A_2Q - 2A_3k - A_4\gamma) - [2B_1B_2k + B_1\gamma^2(2\lambda-1)](A_2Q - 2A_6k - A_7)}{8B_1B_3B_4(2\lambda+1)} \quad (7)$$

$$p_d^* = \frac{A_2B_1Q\gamma^2 + 2A_2B_4Q + 2A_4B_4\gamma + 4A_5B_4k - 2A_6B_1\gamma^2k - A_7B_1\gamma^2}{8B_1B_3B_4} \quad (8)$$

$$g^* = -\frac{-2A_1B_4 - A_2B_2Q\gamma + 2A_6B_2\gamma k + A_7B_2\gamma}{4B_3B_4} \quad (9)$$

By introducing the above optimal solution into Equations (1)–(4), the manufacturer's optimal profit π_m^*, the retailer's optimal profit π_r^* and the supply chain's profit π_{sc}^* can be obtained.

4. Model Analysis

Proposition 1. $\frac{\partial p_d^*}{\partial \lambda} = 0$, $\frac{\partial p_r}{\partial \lambda} = 0$, $\frac{\partial g^*}{\partial \lambda} = 0$, $\frac{\partial D_r^*}{\partial \lambda} = 0$, $\frac{\partial D_d^*}{\partial \lambda} = 0$.

Proof. It can be proved by derivation analysis.

Inference 1 indicated that, under the subsidies of green innovation provided by the government to manufacturers, the fair concerns of manufacturers do not affect the direct selling price of the online channel, the retail price of the traditional channel, the product greenness, and the market demand of the two channels. □

Proposition 2. $\frac{\partial^2 w}{\partial \lambda \partial a} < 0$.

Proof. $\frac{\partial^2 w}{\partial \lambda \partial a} = -\frac{Q(\beta k - \gamma^2 - k\theta)}{(2k\beta(\beta-\theta) - \gamma^2(\beta+\theta))(1+2\lambda)^2}$ and $\beta > \theta$, thus $\beta - \theta < \frac{2\beta(\beta-\theta)}{\beta+\theta}$.

Since $\frac{\gamma^2}{k} < \beta - \theta$, there must be $\frac{\gamma^2}{k} < \frac{2\beta(\beta-\theta)}{\beta+\theta}$, $2k\beta(\beta-\theta) - \gamma^2(\beta+\theta) > 0$.
Therefore, $\frac{\partial^2 w}{\partial \lambda \partial a} < 0$.
Inference 2 showed the sensitivity of wholesale prices to their fair concerns decrease with the increase in market share of the online channel. □

Proposition 3. $\frac{\partial \pi_m^*}{\partial \lambda} > 0$.

Proof. In $\frac{\partial \pi_m^*}{\partial \lambda} = \frac{\left(-2Qa\beta k + 2Qa\gamma^2 + 2Qak\theta + 2Q\beta k - Q\gamma^2 - 2Qk\theta - 2\beta^2 ck + 4\beta ck\theta + 2\beta\gamma s - 2ck\theta^2 - 2\gamma s\theta\right)^2}{16(2\lambda+1)^2(\beta k - \gamma^2 - k\theta)(2k\beta(\beta-\theta) - \gamma^2(\beta+\theta))}$, the numerator is always greater than 0. Since $\beta k - \gamma^2 - k\theta > 0$ and $2k\beta(\beta-\theta) - \gamma^2(\beta+\theta) > 0$, thus $\frac{\partial \pi_m^*}{\partial \lambda} > 0$.

Inference 3 proved that the manufacturers' profits increase with the enhancement of manufacturers' fairness concerns. □

Proposition 4. $\frac{\partial \pi_r^*}{\partial \lambda} < 0$.

Proof.

$$\frac{\partial \pi_r^*}{\partial \lambda} = -\frac{\left(-2Qa\beta k + 2Qa\gamma^2 + 2Qak\theta + 2Q\beta k - Q\gamma^2 - 2Qk\theta - 2\beta^2 ck + 4\beta ck\theta + 2\beta\gamma s - 2ck\theta^2 - 2\gamma s\theta\right)^2}{16(2\lambda+1)^2(\beta k - \gamma^2 - k\theta)(2\beta^2 k - \beta\gamma^2 - 2\beta k\theta - \gamma^2\theta)}$$

In this equation, the numerator is always greater than 0. Since $\beta k - \gamma^2 - k\theta > 0$ and $2k\beta(\beta-\theta) - \gamma^2(\beta+\theta) > 0$, $\frac{\partial \pi_r^*}{\partial \lambda} < 0$ always set up.
Inference 4 proved that the retailers' profits decrease with the enhancement of manufacturers' fairness concerns. □

5. Results and Discussions

To verify the inferences from Section 4, numerical examples are used to discuss the effects of government green subsidies and the degree of manufacturer's fairness concern on price and profit from different supply chain objects in this section. The relevant parameters were set as follows.

$$\beta = 1.5, \theta = 0.5, c = 20, Q = 100, k = 5, s = 1, a \in [0,1], \lambda \in [0,1).$$

5.1. The Impact of Manufacturers' Fairness Concerns on Supply Chain under Different Product Green Efficiency

According to the condition that Hessian matrix is negative definite matrix and the numerical setting in this section, we can assume that the range of product green efficiency is $0 < E_g < 1$, the value of product low green efficiency is $E_g = 0.2(\gamma = 1)$ and the value of product high green efficiency is $E_g = 0.8(\gamma = 2)$.

According to Figure 2, three characteristics can be found. First and foremost, when the product green efficiency and network market share are fixed, the wholesale price of the product will increase with the enhancement of the fairness concern intensity of the manufacturer. On the other hand, retailers' profit per unit product will decrease as manufacturers' fairness concerns increase. The reason is that the manufacturers, as the followers in the supply chain, will set higher wholesale prices in order to improve their own utility. What's more, When the product green efficiency is constant, the wholesale price of the product will decrease with the increase in the network market share. In order to stabilize the market demand, retailers need to maintain the same selling price, which can only reduce the sales profit per unit of product. Last but not the least, when the network market share is fixed, the wholesale price and the profit per unit product will rise along with the improvement of product green efficiency.

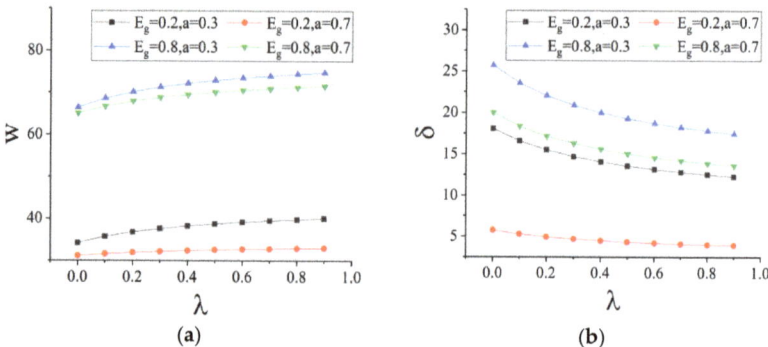

Figure 2. The impact of fairness concerns of manufacturer on the wholesale price and profit per unit of product. (**a**) The impact of fairness concerns of manufacturer on the wholesale price; (**b**) The impact of fairness concerns of manufacturer on profit per unit of product.

As can be seen from Figure 3a, first, when the product green efficiency is fixed, the direct selling price of the network channel is positively correlated with the market share of the network channel. It is generally believed that when a manufacturer's network market share is relatively large, the manufacturer will increase its profit by raising the selling price. Secondly, When the market share of the network channel is certain, the direct selling price of the network channel will also rise with the improvement of product green efficiency. At this point, consumers will increase their demand for green products, and the profit margin for manufacturers will increase by raising prices. Thirdly, when the product green efficiency and the network market share are fixed, the network channel direct selling price has nothing to do with the fairness concern coefficient of manufacturers. In combination with the above content, the reason for this phenomenon lies in the external factors that affect the manufacturers' decision on the direct price of products.

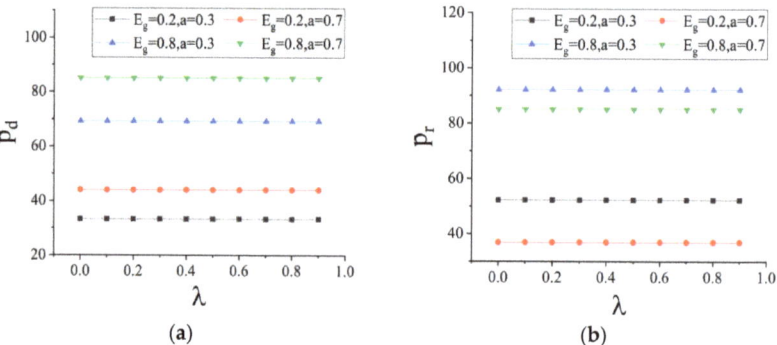

Figure 3. The impact of fairness concerns of manufacture on online direct selling price and offline direct selling price. (**a**) The impact of fairness concerns of manufacture on online direct selling price; (**b**) The impact of fairness concerns of manufacture on offline direct selling price.

As to Figure 3b, when product green efficiency is constant, the retail price of traditional channels is negatively correlated with the market share of network channels. This may be due to the fact that retailers need to improve their competitiveness by reducing their own prices when the market share of manufacturers' online direct sales channels is large. Meanwhile, when the market share of the network channel is fixed, the retail price of the traditional channel is higher under the condition of high green efficiency than under the condition of low green efficiency. What's more, when the product green efficiency and the network market share are fixed, the fairness concern behavior of the manufacturer will not affect the change of the traditional channel retail price.

Figure 4a shows that the manufacturer's profit is positively correlated with the market share of online direct sales channels under the condition of fixed product green efficiency. Next, when the market share of the network direct marketing channel is constant, the higher the efficiency of product greening, the greater the profit of the manufacturer. Therefore, in order to obtain higher profits, manufacturers can cultivate consumers' green preference for this type of products through certain marketing strategies or reduce the cost of carbon emission reduction through technological innovation, so as to improve the efficiency of product greening. Then, when the product green efficiency and the market share of the network direct selling channel are fixed, the manufacturer's profit will raise with the increase in its own fairness concerns, but its sensitivity to the change of its fairness concerns will decrease.

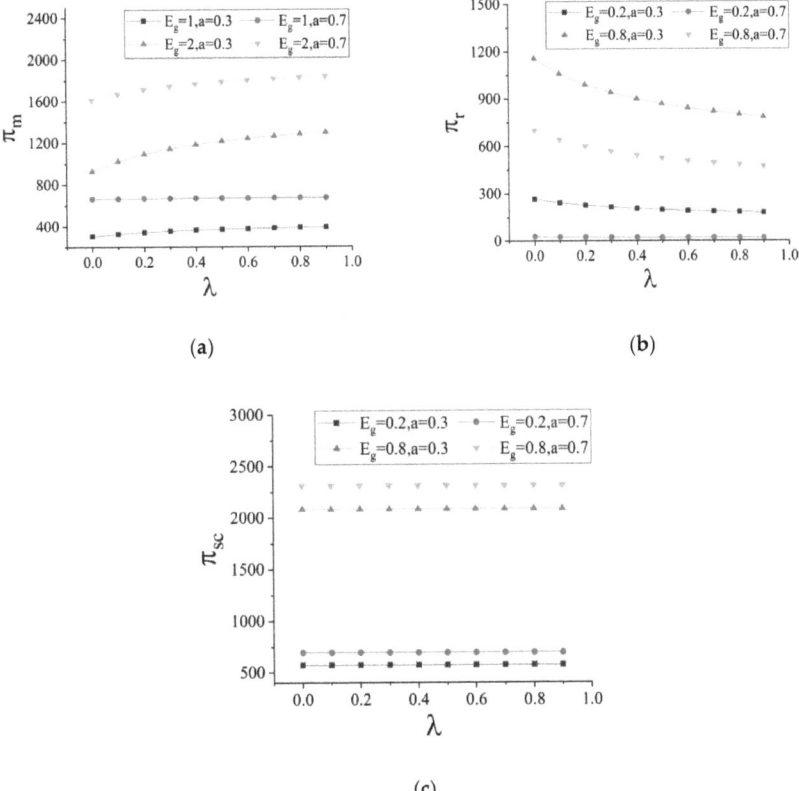

Figure 4. The impact of fairness concerns of manufacturer on the profits of manufacturer, retailer and supply chain. (**a**) The impact of fairness concerns of manufacturer on the profits of manufacturer; (**b**) The impact of fairness concerns of manufacturer on the profits of retailer; (**c**) The impact of fairness concerns of manufacturer on the profits of supply chain.

Figure 4b indicates that, first, the manufacturer's fairness concern behavior will affect the retailer's profit change, when the product green efficiency and network market share are fixed. The stronger the manufacturer's fairness concern is, the lower the retailer's profit will be. Secondly, under the condition of fixed product green efficiency, retailer's profits will decline with the increase in the market share of online direct sales channels. Finally, when the network market share is fixed, the retailer's profit will also go up with the improvement of product green efficiency.

According to Figure 4c, when the product green efficiency is constant, the overall profit of the supply chain will increase with the expansion of the market share of the network channel. The reason is that once the market share of the network opened by the manufacturer is relatively large, the manufacturer can increase its profit by raising the selling price. Furthermore, the overall profit of the supply chain will also rise with the improvement of the efficiency of product greening under the certain market share of network channel. At this time, consumers' preference for green products will expand the demand, and the manufacturer will increase the profit by raising the price. Finally, when product green efficiency and network market share are fixed, the overall profit of supply chain and the fairness concern coefficient of manufacturers are irrelevant.

As to Figure 5, first, when product green efficiency and network market share are fixed, manufacturer's fairness concern behavior will not affect product greenness. This is because the manufacturer will actively produce green products due to the green subsidies from the government even if the profit distribution in the supply chain is not ideal. Secondly, when the green efficiency of the product is constant, the greenness of the product will be improved with the increase in the network market share. Therefore, the network channel opened by manufacturers can effectively motivate them to produce green products if the market prospect is good. Thirdly, when the network market share is fixed, product greenness does not influence product green efficiency.

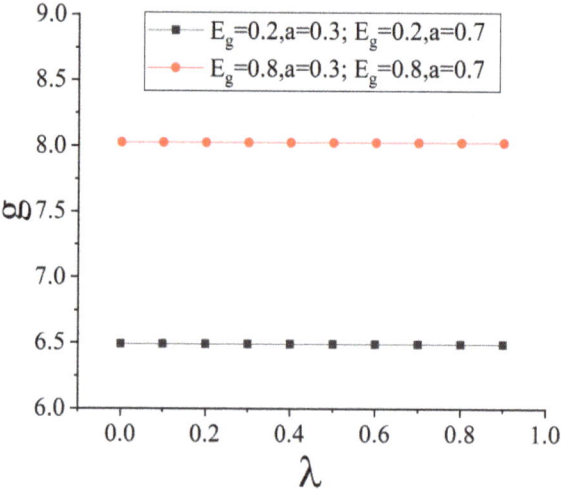

Figure 5. The impact of fairness concerns manufacturers on the product green degree.

5.2. The Impact of Manufacturers' Fairness Concerns on Government Subsidies

According to the above analysis, after comparing the situation of each decision variable in the two cases, it is found that the government will provide further subsidies only when the product green efficiency is low. According to the division of green efficiency of products mentioned above, this section assumes that $E_g = 0.2$ and the proportion of network market share is equal to that of traditional channels. The other parameters are set as follows. $\beta = 1.5, \theta = 0.5, c = 20, Q = 100, a = 0.5, \lambda = 1, \gamma = 1, k = 5, s \in [1, 10]$.

Table 2 describes the changes of supply chain decisions under different government green subsidies when manufacturers have fairness concerns. It can be seen that both the wholesale price and the price of two channels climb with the increase in the government's green subsidies. When the subsidy is fixed, the retailer's price will be slightly higher than the manufacturer's price.

Table 2. The optimal decision under different government subsidies.

s	w^*	p_d^*	p_r^*
0	36.11	38.03	43.8
1	36.21	38.15	43.96
2	36.32	38.27	44.12
3	36.43	38.39	44.27
4	36.54	38.51	44.43
5	36.64	38.63	44.59
6	36.75	38.75	44.75
7	36.86	38.87	44.91
8	36.96	38.99	45.07
9	37.07	39.11	45.23

Table 3 describes the changes of product greenness and supply chain profits under different subsidies when manufacturers have fairness concerns. With the increase in the subsidy value, the greenness of the product will increase. At the same time, profits for manufacturers, retailers and supply chains will rise. Moreover, at the same level of subsidies, manufacturers' profits would be higher than retailer.

Table 3. Product green degree and supply chain profit under different government subsidies.

s	g	π_r^*	π_m^*	π_{sc}^*
0	6.06	72.12	436.3	508.41
1	6.3	73.08	442.23	515.31
2	6.54	74.05	448.41	522.46
3	6.78	75.03	454.82	529.85
4	7.02	76.01	461.48	537.49
5	7.26	77	468.37	545.37
6	7.5	78	475.5	553.5
7	7.74	79	482.87	561.87
8	7.98	80.01	490.48	570.49
9	8.22	81.03	498.32	579.35

6. Conclusions

The shortage of resources and the deterioration of the environment make the demand for green products is growing. With the rapid development of e-commerce, many manufacturing enterprises have opened network channels. To gain a long-term advantage, companies must respond to the government's call to produce green products that meet the requirements for present society. The management of dual-channel green supply chain is an important embodiment of modern enterprise management in achieving sustainable development and responding to social demands. However, the decision-making process of the supply chain will be affected by the rational state of the decision-maker, leading to the difference between the actual result of the decision and the ideal optimal decision, which may bring damage to the supply chain members and enterprises.

Based on the comprehensive consideration of the government's green subsidies to manufacturers, this paper sets the retailer as the dominant player in the supply chain and constructs a dual-channel green supply chain model composed of a retailer and a manufacturer with fair concern behavior. A Stackelberg game model is established based on two cases of manufacturer with and without fairness concern behavior. Moreover, we further discuss the impact of manufacturers' fairness concerns on supply chain decision-making. The main research conclusions of this paper are listed as follows:

(1) Under government subsidies, only wholesale product prices, manufacturer's profits and retailer's profits are affected by manufacturer's fairness concerns. The change of manufacturer's profit and wholesale price is positively correlated with the change of manufacturer's fairness concern intensity, while the change of retailer's profit is negatively correlated with manufacturer's fairness concern intensity.

(2) When manufacturers have fairness concerns, wholesale prices, pricing of both channels (including traditional channel and network channel), product greenness, and supply chain profits all increase with the increase in government subsidies.

(3) The price among different channels, profit among manufacturer and retailers and the change of product greenness are all positively correlated with the change of product greenness efficiency.

(4) When the green efficiency of product remains unchanged, the direct selling price of network channel, manufacturer's profit, supply chain profit and product greenness go up with the increase in market share of network channel. Whereas, the retail price of traditional channels, wholesale price and profit of retailer will decline with the raise of market share of online channels.

Combined with the current situation and research results, several enlightenments can be obtained. First, from the perspective of the government, formulating a reasonable green subsidy policy not only encourages enterprises to produce green products that meet the demand, but also has great significance for promoting the development of green supply chain and sustainable development. Secondly, from the perspective of manufacturers, improving the green efficiency of products is conducive to reducing their own costs and improving corporate profits. Moreover, in a retailer-dominated supply chain, the fairness concern behavior of the manufacturer can increase its own profit and reduce the profit from the retailer, which contributes to improving the enthusiasm of producing green products. At the same time, the fair concern behavior of manufacturers also helps to reduce the retail price of products and improve the enthusiasm of consumers to buy green products.

However, there are still some omissions in this study, which can be improved in further research. First and foremost, this paper only considers the fairness concerns of manufacturers and ignores the fairness concerns of retailers. Therefore, further research can consider the influence of the supply chain when both objects have fairness concerns. What's more, only the decentralized decision model is used in this paper. The discussion among the coordination problem in the retailer-led dual-channel green supply chain considering fairness concern and government subsidies should be made by using the centralized decision-making model. Finally, examples or empirical evidence which are consistent with the conclusions of this study still need to be explored to increase the applicability of the paper.

Author Contributions: Conceptualization, L.S., Q.X. and H.C.; methodology, L.S., Q.X. and H.C.; validation, L.S. and L.L.; writing—original draft preparation, L.S., H.C., L.L. and Z.C.; writing—review and editing, H.C. and Z.C. All authors have read and agreed to the published version of the manuscript.

Funding: This research was supported by the Fuzhou Science and Technology Correspondent Project (JXH2022006).

Institutional Review Board Statement: Not applicable.

Informed Consent Statement: Not applicable.

Data Availability Statement: Not applicable.

Conflicts of Interest: The authors declare no conflict of interest.

References

1. Li, L. China's manufacturing locus in 2025: With a comparison of "Made-in-China 2025" and "Industry 4.0". *Technol. Forecast. Soc. Change* **2018**, *135*, 66–74. [CrossRef]
2. Johnson, T.M.; Alatorre, C.; Romo, Z.; Liu, F. *Low-Carbon Development for Mexico*; World Bank Publications; The World Bank: Washington, DC, USA, 2009.
3. He, P.; He, Y.; Tang, X.; Ma, S.; Xu, H. Channel encroachment and logistics integration strategies in an e-commerce platform service supply chain. *Int. J. Prod. Econ.* **2022**, *244*, 108368. [CrossRef]
4. Seuring, S. A review of modeling approaches for sustainable supply chain management. *Decis. Support Syst.* **2013**, *54*, 1513–1520. [CrossRef]
5. Hall, J. Environmental supply chain dynamics. *J. Clean. Prod.* **2000**, *8*, 455–471. [CrossRef]
6. Loan Programs Office. Available online: http://energy.gov/lpo/loan-programs-office (accessed on 20 February 2022).
7. Jung, S.H.; Feng, T. Government subsidies for green technology development under uncertainty. *Eur. J. Oper. Res.* **2020**, *286*, 726–739. [CrossRef]
8. Zhang, L.; Zhang, Z. Dynamic analysis of the decision of authorized remanufacturing supply chain affected by government subsidies under cap-and-trade policies. *Chaos Solitons Fractals* **2022**, *160*, 112237. [CrossRef]
9. Notice of the General Office of the Ministry of Commerce on Promoting the Green Development of E-commerce Enterprises. Available online: http://www.gov.cn/zhengce/zhengceku/2021-01/12/content_5579179.htm (accessed on 7 January 2021).
10. The 49th Statistical Report on Internet Development in China. Available online: http://www.cnnic.net.cn/hlwfzyj/hlwxzbg/hlwtjbg/202202/t20220225_71727.htm (accessed on 25 February 2022).
11. Rabin, M. Incorporating fairness into game theory and economics. *Am. Econ. Rev.* **1993**, *83*, 1281–1302.
12. Hu, B.; Meng, C.; Xu, D.; Son, Y.J. Supply chain coordination under vendor managed inventory-consignment stocking contracts with wholesale price constraint and fairness. *Int. J. Prod. Econ.* **2018**, *202*, 21–31. [CrossRef]
13. He, P.; He, Y.; Xu, H. Channel structure and pricing in a dual-channel closed-loop supply chain with government subsidy. *Int. J. Prod. Econ.* **2019**, *213*, 108–123. [CrossRef]
14. He, Y.; Huang, H.; Li, D. Inventory and pricing decisions for a dual-channel supply chain with deteriorating products. *Oper. Res.* **2020**, *20*, 1461–1503. [CrossRef]
15. He, C.; Zhou, H. A retailer promotion policy model in a manufacturer Stackelberg dual-channel green supply chain. *Procedia CIRP* **2019**, *83*, 722–727. [CrossRef]
16. Aslani, A.; Heydari, J. Transshipment contract for coordination of a green dual-channel supply chain under channel disruption. *J. Clean. Prod.* **2019**, *223*, 596–609. [CrossRef]
17. Li, M.; Mizuno, S. Dynamic pricing and inventory management of a dual-channel supply chain under different power structures. *Eur. J. Oper. Res.* **2022**, *303*, 273–285. [CrossRef]
18. Li, B.; Zhu, M.; Jiang, Y.; Li, Z. Pricing policies of a competitive dual-channel green supply chain. *J. Clean. Prod.* **2016**, *112*, 2029–2042. [CrossRef]
19. Barman, A.; Das, R.; De, P.K. Optimal pricing and greening decision in a manufacturer retailer dual-channel supply chain. *Mater. Today Proc.* **2021**, *42*, 870–875. [CrossRef]
20. Gao, J.; Xiao, Z.; Wei, H. Competition and coordination in a dual-channel green supply chain with an eco-label policy. *Comput. Ind. Eng.* **2021**, *153*, 107057. [CrossRef]
21. Ma, S.; He, Y.; Gu, R.; Li, S. Sustainable supply chain management considering technology investments and government intervention. *Transp. Res. Part E Logist. Transp. Rev.* **2021**, *149*, 102290. [CrossRef]
22. Meng, Q.; Li, M.; Liu, W.; Li, Z.; Zhang, J. Pricing policies of dual-channel green supply chain: Considering government subsidies and consumers' dual preferences. *Sustain. Prod. Consum.* **2021**, *26*, 1021–1030. [CrossRef]
23. Lou, Z.; Lou, X.; Dai, X. Game-Theoretic Models of Green Products in a Two-Echelon Dual-Channel Supply Chain under Government Subsidies. *Math. Probl. Eng.* **2020**, *2020*, 2425401. [CrossRef]
24. Li, Z.; Pan, Y.; Yang, W.; Ma, J.; Zhou, M. Effects of government subsidies on green technology investment and green marketing coordination of supply chain under the cap-and-trade mechanism. *Energy Econ.* **2021**, *101*, 105426. [CrossRef]
25. Yu, Y.; Han, X.; Hu, G. Optimal production for manufacturers considering consumer environmental awareness and green subsidies. *Int. J. Prod. Econ.* **2016**, *182*, 397–408. [CrossRef]
26. Yang, D.; Xiao, T. Pricing and green level decisions of a green supply chain with governmental interventions under fuzzy uncertainties. *J. Clean. Prod.* **2017**, *149*, 1174–1187. [CrossRef]
27. Madani, S.R.; Rasti-Barzoki, M. Sustainable supply chain management with pricing, greening and governmental tariffs determining strategies: A game theoretic approach. *Comput. Ind. Eng.* **2017**, *105*, 287–298. [CrossRef]
28. Sun, H.; Wan, Y.; Zhang, L.; Zhou, Z. Evolutionary game of the green investment in a two-echelon supply chain under a government subsidy mechanism. *J. Clean. Prod.* **2019**, *235*, 1315–1326. [CrossRef]
29. Liu, Y.; Quan, B.-T.; Xu, Q.; Forrest, J.Y.-L. Corporate social responsibility and decision analysis in a supply chain through government subsidy. *J. Clean. Prod.* **2019**, *208*, 436–447. [CrossRef]
30. Qin, Q.; Jiang, M.; Xie, J.; He, Y. Game analysis of environmental cost allocation in green supply chain under fairness preference. *Energy Rep.* **2021**, *7*, 6014–6022. [CrossRef]

31. Kim, K.T.; Lee, J.S.; Lee, S.Y. The effects of supply chain fairness and the buyer's power sources on the innovation performance of the supplier: A mediating role of social capital accumulation. *J. Bus. Ind. Mark.* **2017**, *32*, 987–997. [CrossRef]
32. Zhang, F.; Zhang, Z.; Xue, Y.; Zhang, J.; Che, Y. Dynamic Green Innovation Decision of the Supply Chain with Innovating and Free-Riding Manufacturers: Cooperation and Spillover. *Complexity* **2020**, *2020*, 8937847. [CrossRef]
33. Wang, Y.; Fan, R.; Shen, L.; Jin, M. Decisions and coordination of green e-commerce supply chain considering green manufacturer's fairness concerns. *Int. J. Prod. Res.* **2020**, *58*, 7471–7489. [CrossRef]
34. Li, Q.; Xiao, T.; Qiu, Y. Price and carbon emission reduction decisions and revenue-sharing contract considering fairness concerns. *J. Clean. Prod.* **2018**, *190*, 303–314. [CrossRef]
35. Yang, T.; Liu, G.; Wei, Y.; Zhang, X.; Dong, X. The Impact of dual fairness concerns under different power. structures on green supply. *Chain Decis.* **2019**, *15*, 1–26.
36. Jie, J.; Bin, L.; Nian, Z.; Su, J. Decision-making and coordination of green closed-loop supply chain with fairness concern. *J. Clean. Prod.* **2021**, *298*, 126779.
37. Li, Q.; Guan, X.; Shi, T.; Jiao, W. Green product design with competition and fairness concerns in the circular economy era. *Int. J. Prod. Res.* **2020**, *58*, 165–179. [CrossRef]

Disclaimer/Publisher's Note: The statements, opinions and data contained in all publications are solely those of the individual author(s) and contributor(s) and not of MDPI and/or the editor(s). MDPI and/or the editor(s) disclaim responsibility for any injury to people or property resulting from any ideas, methods, instructions or products referred to in the content.

Article

Are State-Owned Enterprises Equally Reliable Information Suppliers? An Examination of the Impacts of State Ownership on Earnings Management Strategies of Chinese Enterprises

Shan Lu [1], Peng Wu [1,*], Lei Gao [2] and Richard Gifford [2]

[1] School of Economics and Management, Southeast University, 2 Sipailou, Nanjing 211189, China
[2] School of Business, State University of New York at Geneseo, 1 College Circle, Geneseo, NY 14454, USA
* Correspondence: wupeng76@seu.edu.cn

Abstract: Earnings management refers to a company's use of either accounting techniques (accrual-based earnings management) or real economic activities (real earnings management) to manipulate reported earnings and mislead users of financial information. It often indicates serious ethical issues in a company's management, which will affect the reliability and sustainability of a firm's services in the supply chain. Using A-share listed Chinese firms on the Shanghai and Shenzhen Stock Exchanges, we investigated the impacts of state ownership on management's decision to select real or accrual-based earnings management strategies. We found that state-owned enterprises (SOEs) tend to favor real earnings management over accrual-based earnings management more than non-SOEs. Furthermore, those SOEs that are controlled by the central government engage in real earnings management more often than those controlled by local governments. We also examined whether media attention and litigation interact with state ownership to affect earnings management. We found that SOEs, especially central SOEs, with a high level of media attention or an incidence of litigation, are more likely to use real earnings management. Our research can assist firms in making better decisions in selecting business partners and service suppliers in an emerging market through the assessment of management integrity.

Keywords: state ownership; earnings management; supply chain; management integrity; media attention

MSC: 62J05

1. Introduction

In recent years, economic recession, pandemics, and regional conflicts have led to numerous business risks for organizations, making it more important for companies to enhance their risk governance processes [1]. Prior studies have found that companies prioritize suppliers' technical capabilities, cost, quality, delivery, and service when choosing suppliers [2]. Additionally, accounting information can help firms evaluate suppliers' operational efficiency, cost management, and profitability [3]. However, the question remains: can people trust the earnings information provided by suppliers? How could suppliers have manipulated reported earnings to mislead users of accounting information? This paper investigates how state ownership may have influenced the decision making of managers in Chinese listed companies with regards to the manipulation of reported earnings (referred to as earnings management in this study).

Currently, a large percentage of listed firms in China are still owned and controlled directly or indirectly by the Chinese government. As a developing and transitional economy, China is trying to balance centralization and decentralization. State-owned enterprises (SOEs) can be divided into central SOEs and local SOEs (Central SOEs represent companies that are ultimately controlled by the central government and its agencies, including the State Council, the State-Owned Assets Supervision and Management Committee, the

Ministry of Finance, the Ministry of Education, and other relevant government departments. Local SOEs are enterprises that are controlled by local governments, such as provincial or city governments and their agencies, e.g., the local finance bureau and local educational departments [4]). It is therefore important to analyze how the presence and the type of state ownership may affect managerial decisions. Extant literature has extensively investigated the effect of state ownership on earnings, but few studies have explored the differences in earnings management strategies among different types of SOEs. Our study performs an in-depth analysis of how state ownership type impacts a firm's decision to select a particular earnings management strategy in the China setting. In extending the literature on the impact of state ownership on earnings management, we also analyze whether other factors, e.g., media attention and litigation, interact with state ownership to impact managers' selection of earnings management strategies.

The Chinese government has been working to enhance stability and financial performance of SOEs to keep pace with the country's rapid economic growth. Over the last 20 years, it has implemented financial performance measures to evaluate the performance of executives in SOEs. Under this increased governmental pressure to improve financial performance, managers of SOEs may be more likely to use earnings management to reach their earnings goals. We believe that SOEs may choose an earnings management strategy that lowers the risk of being exposed, thereby avoiding the scrutiny and criticism of regulators and auditors. Furthermore, little is known about whether central SOEs and local SOEs may display distinct patterns in their selection of earnings management strategies. Our study will also attempt to examine this issue.

Extant accounting literature recognizes two major types of earnings management: accrual-based earnings management (referred to as "accruals management" hereafter) and real earnings management. Accruals management is used by managers to achieve earnings goals through the manipulation of accounting accruals, e.g., changing the estimates of bad debt expenses and depreciation expenses. In contrast, managers use real earnings management, e.g., reducing R&D expenditures or granting additional sales discounts, to achieve earning targets by manipulating the timing of investment and financing decisions [5,6].

There are only a few studies that examine the impact of state ownership on managers' selection of earnings management strategies. Fan and Song [7] find that Chinese central SOEs use real earnings management to help the government reduce GDP volatility. However, they base their findings on a small sample (100 central SOEs, 100 local SOEs, and 200 non-SOEs). Wang et al. [8] examine whether SOEs are more likely to use real earnings management than accruals management to achieve earnings goals, but they do not examine whether such strategy is impacted by other factors such as media attention and litigation. Li et al. [9] find the highly valued SOEs have lower levels of abnormal accruals than highly valued non-SOEs during periods of high valuation. Habib et al. [10] argue that ownership structure plays a crucial role in the determinants of real earnings management.

One major limitation of these prior studies is that they examine the two types of earnings management strategies separately instead of examining them within the same company. The high level of real earnings management in the results could be driven by some of the firms in the sample, while the low level of accruals management might be driven by other firms in that sample. Testing the two types of earnings management strategies separately may lead to incorrect conclusions from the regression results. To avoid this issue, we follow Braam et al. [11] to construct a set of measures for different combinations of earnings management strategies. This approach enables us to determine whether there is a substitution effect between accruals management and real earnings management at the firm level. In addition, we perform further analyses of whether media attention and litigation interact with state ownership to impact a firm's choice of earnings management strategies.

In this paper, we sample A-share companies listed on the Shanghai and Shenzhen Stock Exchanges during 2003 to 2018 to investigate the impact of state ownership on earnings management strategies. We find evidence to support our primary hypothesis that, although non-SOEs and SOEs both engage in the same level of earnings management, SOEs tend to favor real earnings management over accruals management. Furthermore, we find that, when compared with local SOEs and non-SOEs, central SOEs appear to prefer real earnings management to accruals management. To explore the reasons behind the trade-off issue of earnings management in SOEs, we also test whether media attention and litigation interact with state ownership to influence managers' selection of earning management strategies. We find that SOEs with high media attention are more likely to substitute real earnings management for accruals management. The impact is more prominent in central SOEs. Similar results are found in the joint effects of litigation and state ownership on earnings management. These results suggest that those firms that are most concerned with the exposure of earnings management appear to prefer real earnings management to accruals management.

This paper has two major contributions to the extant earnings management literature. First, prior studies that have investigated the relationship between state ownership and earnings management have focused on either accruals management [9,12,13] or real earnings management [14,15]. We believe that it is necessary to examine both types of earnings management strategies at the firm level to determine whether there is a substitution between real earnings management and accruals management in the same company. To examine the trade-off issue between the two strategies at the firm level, we construct a set of measures for different combinations of earnings management strategies. We find that SOEs, especially central SOEs, tend to favor real earnings management over accruals management. This finding indicates that top executives in firms with strong political connections appear to be more concerned with their job security and the loss of the privileges obtained from political connections when earnings management is exposed. Therefore, they prefer the more obscure real earnings management over accruals management to avoid being exposed and penalized, even though real earnings management harms a firm in the long term. Second, we analyze whether other factors, such as media attention and litigation, interact with state ownership to have joint effects on earnings management strategies. We find that SOEs, especially central SOEs, with high media attention are more likely to use real earnings management. Similar results are found in SOEs with litigation. These results indicate that those factors that affect the exposure risk (e.g., media attention) and the scrutiny level (e.g., litigation) of external reviewers increase the cost of accruals management and thus increase the chance that real earnings management will be used by firms with strong political connections. These findings suggest that companies should pay attention to the reliability of accounting information when choosing service suppliers in the supply chain. It is essential for information users to evaluate whether firms have engaged in earnings management to manipulate reported earnings in order to demand a greater share of profits in negotiations. The government should also strengthen regulations on financial reporting to prevent companies from taking short-sighted actions through real earnings management, such as granting significant sales discounts or cutting costs through overproduction, to satisfy the needs of large customers in the supply chain.

This paper continues with Section 2, where we discuss the prior literature and develop our hypotheses. In Section 3, we describe our data collection procedures and research methodology. In Section 4, we discuss our empirical results, and in Section 5, we summarize our conclusions.

2. Background and Hypothesis Development

2.1. Earnings Management Strategies: Accruals Management vs. Real Earnings Management

Prior studies suggest that the practice of earnings management is driven by capital market motivations, contracting motivations, and regulatory motivations [16]. Contracting motivations can be subdivided into those associated with lending contracts and management compensation contracts [16]. In China, access to economic resources and capital is limited. Managers of non-SOEs are motivated to engage in earnings management to more effectively compete for financing in the capital and debt (lending contracts) markets.

On the contrary, SOEs face less pressure from the capital markets and lending contracts because of their preferential access to capital and loans [4]. Nevertheless, Chinese SOEs' managers might be motivated to manage earnings in order to increase their compensation and to obtain other contracting benefits such as formal and informal promotions [17–19]. Therefore, both SOEs and non-SOEs have motives to manipulate earnings, but are they different in terms of strategies of earnings management?

As discussed previously, the extant literature recognizes two major types of earnings management: accruals management and real earnings management [6,20,21]. Managers will consider the relative costs and benefits between the two to determine the best strategy to achieve earnings targets [20,22]. While accruals management takes less effort and time, it is subject to more scrutiny from regulators and auditors because it often violates regulatory rules [20,22,23]. Liao and Zhang [24] note that the government can more easily recognize a company's accruals management, increasing the exposure risk of earnings management. When accruals management is exposed to the public, managers suffer severe reputational loss, litigation costs, and punishment [25]. Real earnings management, on the other hand, is less scrutinized by regulators and auditors [20]. It is also more difficult to identify since real earnings management uses actual transactions and associated cash flows to achieve earnings goals. However, real earnings management represents a deviation from the best business practices and may have a negative impact on the firm's future performance [26].

Prior studies have found that, when there is tightened oversight or a higher cost associated with using accruals management, managers may favor the use of real earnings management over accruals management [20,22,23,27]. In addition, Ding et al. [28] found that politically affiliated firms are more likely to engage in real earnings management than non-affiliated firms to manipulate earnings. SOEs have stronger political connections and receive more government subsidies than non-SOEs. They also face increasing scrutiny and criticism from the public because of their importance to society and the economy [29]. Furthermore, the managers of SOEs often have political rank and work in a relatively closed internal labor market. It is difficult for these managers to find other comparable job opportunities if they leave SOEs [30]. Accordingly, managers of SOEs face a higher cost of reputation loss and the associated loss of privileges when earnings management practices are detected by the government and announced to the public [11,31,32]. Thus, they are more concerned with the costs associated with the loss of privileges caused by the exposure of earnings management than managers of non-SOEs [33].

Once earnings management behaviors of SOEs are exposed, the political reputations of the executives involved as well as those of the relevant government bureaus, parties, and officials are damaged [11,33], which hurts the job security and the promotional opportunities for the people involved. Unlike non-SOEs, top executives in SOEs are not owners of the company. They may be more short-sighted and may neglect the long-term goals of the company in order to maximize their personal benefits [34,35]. As a result, although real earnings management will damage a company's long-term value, it meets the need of managers in the short run because it is less detectable. At the same time, when compared to non-SOEs, managers in SOEs receive less pressure and oversight from other shareholders in a firm when making business decisions, lowering the cost of using real earnings management [25]. Furthermore, the prior literature finds that suppliers in developing countries with large customers in developed countries are more inclined to align their performance measurement systems with the performance priorities of customers [2]. Companies that aim for a long-term stable position in the international supply chain, such as SOEs, may be more inclined to employ real earnings management techniques, such as providing additional discounts and reducing costs through overproduction, to meet the needs of customers. Thus, we put forward the first hypothesis as follows:

Hypothesis 1a. *Compared with non-state-owned enterprises, state-owned enterprises are more likely to substitute real earnings management for accruals management.*

2.2. Central SOEs vs. Local SOEs

A series of reforms in the 1980s enabled the central government of China to transfer certain responsibilities and authorities to local governments located in its provinces, cities, and counties. Since then, local governments have more power to oversee local SOEs independently. Overall, compared to central SOEs, local SOEs tend to have less complex organizational structures, fewer political assignments from the government, and fewer political connections.

We believe that central SOEs and local SOEs view earnings management and its associated costs differently. The administrative rank of a central SOE is higher than that of a local SOE; thus, its management has more privileges and promotional opportunities [36,37]. The reform in the performance evaluation system for central SOEs in the recent two decades has led to a much closer connection between the firms' financial performance and the compensation and promotional opportunities for senior management. On the other hand, local SOEs operations are closely aligned with local economic performance. Local governments, who are the ultimate controllers of local SOEs, pay close attention to local SOEs' performance since they affect the local GDP, a measure that is used by the central government to evaluate the performance of local governments and officials. Thus, both central SOEs and local SOEs have motives to engage earnings management, but the costs of using different types of earnings management may look different to central SOEs and local SOEs.

Compared to local SOEs, central SOEs have more political connections and privileges. Prior studies found that managers in central SOEs are more interested in pursuing "grey" money, such as company-funded trips and benefits, and non-monetary benefits, such as political promotions and connections [18,19,34]. Braam et al. [11] argue that firms with strong political connections suffer more when there is a damage to their reputation and public image. Meanwhile, central SOEs are in industries that are critical to the national safety and economic development. Thus, compared to local SOEs, central SOEs receive more attention and criticism from the public and media when these firms perform poorly [38]. This pressure from the public may affect managerial decisions regarding earnings management strategy. As discussed previously, managers are concerned with the costs associated with the loss of privileges caused by the exposure of earnings management [33]. Such concern will be more pronounced in central SOEs where the exposure of any illegal or wrong doings will attract more severe criticism from the public, which may lead to public anxiety and thus concern the central government. Therefore, managers of central SOEs are more likely to choose an earnings management strategy that is less likely to be scrutinized or detected. For this reason, we believe that central SOEs are more likely to substitute real earnings management for accruals management than local SOEs. We put forward the following hypothesis:

Hypothesis 1b. *Central SOEs are more likely to substitute real earnings management for accruals management than local SOEs.*

2.3. Impact of Other Factors: Media Attention and Litigation

Braam et al. [11] found that politically connected firms that are established in countries with high levels of public monitoring are more likely to substitute real earnings management for accruals management. The impact of public monitoring in China has not been examined in prior studies. In this study, we will use media attention to proxy for public monitoring and examine how it affects managerial decisions on earnings management strategies.

The extant Chinese literature on news media finds that the media has a positive monitoring effect on a firm's business decisions. Li and Shen [39] found that articles published by market-oriented media can push top management of a firm to take actions to correct their mistakes. Furthermore, the impact of the media is done through the intervention of government [39]. Chen [29] finds that the media has more positive governance effects on SOEs than on non-SOEs when the institutional environment is relatively weak. As discussed previously, managers of SOEs, especially central SOEs, are most concerned with their job security and all the privileges they receive from political connections. We believe that media attention will exacerbate the impacts of state ownership on earnings management. Thus, the managers in SOEs, especially central SOEs, would favor the use of real earnings management over accruals management in order to reduce the risk of exposure. For this reason, we propose the following two hypotheses:

Hypothesis 2a. *Compared with non-SOEs, SOEs with high media attention are more likely to substitute real earnings management for accruals management.*

Hypothesis 2b. *Compared with local SOEs, central SOEs with high media attention are more likely to substitute real earnings management for accruals management.*

The prior literature has found that tightened regulations and external reviews may lead to the substitution of real earnings management for accruals management [23,27]. Will an anticipated increase of scrutiny level also have a bigger impact on those firms, e.g., SOEs that are most concerned with an exposure of earnings management? To examine this issue, we use litigation as an extraneous factor to measure how an anticipated increase in scrutiny may affect managerial decisions of different types of companies. By analyzing debt-related lawsuits, Wang et al. [40] found that SOEs in litigation tend to reduce their accruals management. However, they did not examine whether there was an increase in the use of real earnings management in their study. On the other hand, Qian and Yu [41] found that there is an increase of accruals management in non-SOEs without political connections when there is an incidence of litigation, while it is not found in SOEs. Based on our previous discussions, we believe that those firms that are most concerned with exposure of earnings management are more likely to be affected when there is an anticipated increase of scrutiny level from external reviewers. For this reason, SOEs, especially central SOEs, may choose to use real earnings management over accruals management when they have ongoing litigations. Thus, we propose the following two hypotheses:

Hypothesis 3a. *Compared with non-SOEs, SOEs that are in litigation are more likely to substitute real earnings management for accruals management.*

Hypothesis 3b. *Compared with local SOEs, central SOEs that are in litigation are more likely to substitute real earnings management for accruals management.*

3. Sample and Methods

3.1. Data and Sample Selection

We used A-share companies listed on the Shenzhen and Shanghai Stock Exchanges from 2003 to 2018 to select our full sample according to the process described in Panel A of Table 1. We excluded all firms in the financial and insurance industries (944 firm-year observations) and those observations with missing data (8544 firm-year observations) from our sample. The final sample we used to test Hypothesis 1a, 1b and Hypothesis 3a, 3b totaled 11,905 firm-year observations. The financial data were obtained from the China Stock Market and Accounting Research (CSMAR) database and the iFinD database (iFinD is a financial database providing information of stocks, bonds, funds, futures, indexes, etc. of Chinese financial markets). To examine the joint effects of state ownership and media attention on earnings management (Hypothesis 2a, 2b), we selected a reduced sample from A-share companies listed on the Shanghai Stock Exchange from 2008 to 2012 according to the process described in Panel B of Table 1. We used a reduced sample for the test on media attention due to the concern that the impact of traditional media, such as newspaper, on earnings management may be diluted by that of social media in recent years. The final reduced sample included 1816 firm-year observations after excluding firms in the financial and insurance industries and firms with missing data.

Table 1. Sample Selection Process. Panel (A) Full Sample. Panel (B) Media Sample.

(A)	
A-share firms listed on Shanghai and Shenzhen Stock Exchanges (2003~2018)	21,393
Less: companies in financial and insurance industries	(944)
Less: companies with missing data	(8544)
Final full sample	11,905

(B)	
A-share firms listed on Shanghai Stock Exchange (2008~2012)	4451
Less: companies in financial and insurance industries	(133)
Less: companies with missing data	(2502)
Final media sample	1816

3.2. Methodology

3.2.1. Measure of Variables

- Accruals management

In this study, we used the modified Jones Model [42] to estimate discretionary accruals as the proxies for measuring accruals management. Researchers have proposed a variety of models to measure earnings management. The modified Jones Model [42] has been widely accepted and used in prior earnings management research [43,44]. While recent literature also uses a number of revised models to measure discretionary accruals, such as the performance-adjusted Jones Model [23,45], Chinese scholars have found that the modified Jones Model has better explanatory power in Chinese stock markets compared to other models [46,47]. Thus, we used it to estimate discretionary accruals.

Following Dechow et al. [43], we used the following model to estimate non-discretionary accruals:

$$NDA_{it} = \alpha_1 \left(\frac{1}{A_{i,t-1}}\right) + \alpha_2 \left[\frac{\Delta REV_{i,t} - \Delta REC_{i,t}}{A_{i,t-1}}\right] + \alpha_3 (PPE_{i,t}/A_{i,t-1}) \quad (1)$$

where NDA_{it} represents non-discretionary accruals; $A_{i,t-1}$ represents total assets at the end of year $t-1$; $\Delta REV_{i,t}$ represents the change of sales revenues; $\Delta REC_{i,t}$ represents the change of account receivables; $PPE_{i,t}$ is the year-end balance of gross property, plant, and equipment; α_1, α_2, and α_3 are estimated cross-sectionally based on the following model for industry-years with at least 15 observations:

$$\frac{TA_{i,t}}{A_{i,t-1}} = \beta_1 \left(\frac{1}{A_{i,t-1}}\right) + \beta_2 \left(\frac{\Delta REV_{i,t}}{A_{i,t-1}}\right) + \beta_3 \left(\frac{PPE_{i,t}}{A_{i,t-1}}\right) + \varepsilon_{i,t} \quad (2)$$

where $TA_{i,t}$ represents the total accruals measured by the difference between the earnings before extraordinary items and discontinued operations and cash flows from operations reported in the statement of cash flows. Discretionary accruals are the difference between actual accruals and non-discretionary accruals calculated as follows:

$$DA_{i,t} = \frac{TA_{i,t}}{A_{i,t-1}} - NDA_{i,t} \quad (3)$$

Consistent with prior literature, we generated three variables: the absolute value of DA (ABSDA), the income-increasing DA (DA+), and the income-decreasing DA (DA−) to measure accruals management (AM) [23].

- Real earnings management

Consistent with prior research [21–23], we used three measures to proxy for real earnings management (RM): abnormal production costs (A_PROD), related to the reduction of the cost of goods sold by overproducing inventory items; abnormal operating cash flows (A_CFO), related to the inflation of revenues through provisions of excessive sales discounts or extended payment periods; and abnormal discretionary expenditures (A_DISX), related to the abnormal decrease of expenses by reducing R&D, selling, and other general expenditures.

A_PROD, A_CFO, and A_DISX are residuals from the following three cross-sectional regressions:

$$\frac{PROD_t}{A_{t-1}} = \gamma_0 + \gamma_1 \frac{1}{A_{t-1}} + \gamma_2 \frac{S_t}{A_{t-1}} + \gamma_3 \frac{\Delta S_t}{A_{t-1}} + \gamma_4 \frac{\Delta S_{t-1}}{A_{t-1}} + \varepsilon_t \quad (4)$$

$$\frac{CFO_t}{A_{t-1}} = \delta_0 + \delta_1 \frac{1}{A_{t-1}} + \delta_2 \frac{S_t}{A_{t-1}} + \delta_3 \frac{\Delta S_t}{A_{t-1}} + \varepsilon_t \quad (5)$$

$$\frac{DISX_t}{A_{t-1}} = \lambda_0 + \lambda_1 \frac{1}{A_{t-1}} + \lambda_2 \frac{S_{t-1}}{A_{t-1}} + \varepsilon_t \quad (6)$$

where A_{t-1} is the total assets at the end of year $t-1$; S_t is the net sales in year t; ΔS_t is the change in net sales from year $t-1$ to t; $PROD_t$ is the sum of cost of goods sold in year t and the change in inventory from year $t-1$ to t; CFO_t is cash flows from operating activities in year t; $DISX_t$ is the discretionary expenditures (i.e., the sum of R&D, selling, and general and administrative expenditures) in year t.

Those companies that attempt to manipulate earnings through real transactions tend to have a higher A_PROD, a lower A_DISX, and a lower A_CFO. To avoid confusion, we multiply A_CFO and A_DISX by minus one to represent real earnings management in a consistent fashion as A_PROD, and we use NA_CFO and NA_DISX to represent them, respectively.

Following Cohen and Zarowin [22], we also generated two aggregate proxies of real earnings management by combining NA_CFO and NA_DISX to get RM1, and A_PROD and NA_DISX to get RM2, respectively, in order to capture the aggregate levels of real earnings management.

Finally, we followed Chan et al. and Badertscher [23,48] to measure the overall level of earnings management (EM) by summing accruals management (AM) and real earnings management (RM).

- Measure of earnings management combination strategies

To examine the impact of state ownership on a firm's selection of earnings management combination strategies, we followed Braam et al.'s approach [11]. We use two dummy variables to measure the major type of earnings management: real earnings management (RM_Dummy) and accruals management (AM_Dummy), respectively. RM_Dummy equals one if one of the real earnings management aggregate proxies (either RM1 or RM2) is above the industry-year median and zero otherwise [22]. AM_Dummy equals one if the company's ABSDA is above industry-year median and zero otherwise [22].

Rather than testing only on substitution between these two earnings management strategies, we examined how a firm selects different combinations of earnings management strategies. We created four indicator variables to measure the preference of a company's earnings management combination strategies: $RM_H\_AM_L$ (RM_dummy = 1, AM_dummy = 0), $RM_L\_AM_H$ (RM_dummy = 0, AM_dummy = 1), $RM_H\_AM_H$ (RM_dummy = 1, AM_dummy = 1), and $RM_L\_AM_L$ (RM_dummy = 0, AM_dummy = 0). We expect that SOEs, in particular central SOEs, will exhibit a significantly positive relationship with $RM_H\_AM_L$.

- Measure of state ownership

We classified the listed companies into SOEs and non-SOEs according to the nature of firms' ultimate shareholders [4,7]. Following Wang et al. [4], we further divided SOEs into central SOEs (CSOE) and local SOEs (LSOE). Central SOEs are those enterprises that are ultimately controlled by the central government or its agencies, including enterprises controlled by the State Council, the State Assets Supervision and Administration Commission, the Ministry of Finance, the Ministry of Education, and other relevant government departments. Local SOEs are those enterprises that are ultimately controlled by provincial and city governments or their agencies, including enterprises controlled by provincial/municipal's governments, the provincial/municipal State Asset Supervision and Administration Commission, provincial/municipal finance bureau, provincial/municipal Department of Education, and other local government departments.

- Measure of media attention and litigation

We used the total number of news reports on a firm to proxy for media attention to test the joint effects of statement ownership and media attention on a firm's selection of earnings management strategies. Following prior research, we took the natural logarithm of the total number of news report plus one to construct MEDIA [39,49,50]. To determine the number of news reports, we collected the data manually by reading articles in 14 newspapers (the 14 newspapers include the following: 21st Century Business Herald, China Securities Journal, Shanghai Securities News, Securities Daily, Securities Times, China Business News, China Business Journal, First Financial Daily, China Economic Times, China Times, Economy Daily, The Economic Observer, Financial Times, and Economic Information Daily). These selected newspapers are the most popular and the most influential media of financial and economic news in China. To control for the endogeneity issue, we use a one-year lag in the number of news reports ($MEDIA_{t-1}$) to measure the media's attention on a firm. We expect that SOEs, especially central SOEs, with high media attention are more likely to use real transactions rather than accruals to manage earnings.

To examine the joint effects of state ownership and litigation on earnings management, we used a dummy variable, LIT, to measure litigation [51,52]. LIT equals one when there is a lawsuit or a sanction against the firm and zero otherwise. We used the CSMAR database to obtain litigation data directly. We expect that SOEs, especially central SOEs, with an incidence of litigation are more likely to substitute real earnings management for accruals management.

- Control variables

Based on extant earnings management literature, we included a variety of control variables to control for the influence of other factors on earnings management. A stronger institutional environment in more developed stock exchanges may help monitor managerial behavior and decrease earnings management. Therefore, we included overseas listing (OL) in the model to indicate whether a company is also listed in foreign stock exchanges such as in NYSE, NASDAQ, or LSE. The percentage of institutional holdings (INST), using total shares held by institutions divided by total shares outstanding based on the year-end data, was used to control for the impact of institutional investors [20]. Asset size (LNA), which is the log of year-end total assets, controls for the impact of company size. A large firm's internal control might be stronger than that of small firms, reducing the opportunities for earnings management [53]. We used the leverage ratio (LEV) to control for the impact of debt covenants on earnings management. Watts [54] found that debt covenants can bring more accounting conservatism to firms, restricting the opportunistic behavior of managers. The cash to asset ratio (CA) was included due to the concern that free cash flows may affect how shareholders perceive a company's profitability and thus their investment plan, which in turn influences managerial decisions regarding earnings management. Ownership concentration (H10) was used to control for the impact of concentrated ownership structure on earnings management [55]. We also included the ROA ratio (ROA) in our models to control for the influence of earnings performance on earnings management. In addition, following Chan et al., Zang, and Krishnan et al. [20,23,56], we included the operating revenue growth ratio (MBG) and market to book ratio (MB) as control variables.

Prior research on Chinese enterprises has found that the earnings quality and management decisions of Chinese listed companies could be affected by the level of market and legal institutions' development and the degree of government power [4]. Considering that, we followed Wang et al. [4] to include three indexes: the credit market index (CMI), government decentralization index (GDI), and legal environment index (LEI), which were developed by Fan and Wang [57], to capture the impact of institutional environment on managerial behavior. Prior literature has also found that "tunneling", described as the transfer of assets and resources between related parties, is a major tool that has been used by Chinese state-owned firms to manage their earnings [58]. We included non-operating income to control for the tunneling effects [12,59]. To control for the differences between the Shanghai and Shenzhen Stock Exchanges, we included a dummy variable SZSH as a control variable, which equals one if a firm is listed on the Shanghai Stock Exchange.

Following Liu and Lu [58], we included the following three governance variables in our models: the dual role of CEO as the chairman of board (CEOCHR), percentage of independent directors (INDDIR), and management ownership (MO). We then included an audit-related variable, Big-10 auditors (Big10), to control for the cost associated with the use of accruals management. Big10 equals one when the firm's auditor is one of the top 10 auditors in China based on firm revenues (The market share of Big 4 international auditors in China is relatively small and thus is inappropriate to be used as a proxy for auditor quality. Considering that, we follow Wang et al. [4] to use Big10 as a control variable).

Finally, following prior studies that examine the issue of substitution between real earnings management and accruals management, we included AM (RM) as a control variable when the dependent variable was RM (AM) [23,27]. Because we obtained similar results using either RM1 or RM2 as control variables, we only present the results based on RM1.

We summarize our definitions of all variables in Table 2.

Table 2. Definition of Variables.

Variable	Definition
Dependent Variables:	
NA_CFO	The reversed level of abnormal cash flows from operations, as defined by Roychowdhury [21]
A_PROD	The level of abnormal production costs, where production costs are defined as the sum of the cost of goods sold and the change in inventories, as defined by Roychowdhury [21]
NA_DISX	The reversed level of abnormal discretionary expenses, where discretionary expenses are the sum of R&D expenses and SG&A expenses, as defined by Roychowdhury [21]
RM1	=NA_CFO + NA_DISX
RM2	=A_PROD + NA_DISX
ABSDA	The absolute value of the accruals management, with the discretionary accruals' values calculated by using the modified Jones Model (Dechow et al. [43])
DA(+)	Income-increasing discretionary accruals
DA(−)	Income-decreasing discretionary accruals
EM1	=ABSDA + RM1
EM2	=ABSDA + RM2
$RM_H\_DA_L$	=1 if RM_Dummy [a] = 1 and DA_Dummy [a] = 0, 0 otherwise
$RM_L\_DA_H$	=1 if RM_Dummy = 0 and DA_Dummy = 1, 0 otherwise
$RM_H\_DA_H$	=1 if RM_Dummy = 1 and DA_Dummy = 1, 0 otherwise
$RM_L\_DA_L$	=1 if RM_Dummy = 0 and DA_Dummy = 0, 0 otherwise
Independent Variables:	
SOE	=1 if government is the ultimate controller, 0 otherwise
CSOE	=1 if central government is the ultimate controller, 0 otherwise
LSOE	=1 if local government is the ultimate controller, 0 otherwise
MEDIA	=Log (1 + Number of total news report at year $t - 1$)
LIT	=1 if a company is in litigation or a sanction that year, 0 otherwise
Control Variables:	
ROA	=Net profit/year-end total assets
MBG	=(Operating sales of current year/operating sales of last year) − 1
LEV	=Year-end total liabilities/year-end total assets
LNA	Natural logarithm of year-end total assets
OL	=1 if the company is listed in both China stock exchanges and foreign stock exchanges
MB	=Market value/book value
NOI	=Non-operating income/sales
INST	=Total shares held by institutions/Total shares outstanding at year-end
H10	The sum of the square of the holding percentage of the ten largest shareholders
CEOCHR	=1 if firms' chairman and CEO are the same person, 0 otherwise
INDDIR	The proportion of the number of independent directors to the board of directors

Table 2. Cont.

Variable	Definition
MO	shares of common stocks held by top management
Big 10	=1 if the firm is audited by a big 10 audit firm, 0 otherwise.
CMI	Fan and Wang [57] credit market index
GDI	Fan and Wang [57] government decentralization index
LEI	Fan and Wang [57] legal environment index
SZSH	=1 if stock is listed on Shanghai stock exchange, 0 otherwise

[a] RM_Dummy equals 1 if the company's RM1 or RM2 is above the median of industry-year and 0 otherwise. DA_Dummy equals 1 if the company's ABSDA is above the median of industry-year and 0 otherwise.

3.2.2. Regression Models

To examine the effect of state ownership (SOEs vs. non-SOEs) on earnings management combination strategies (Hypothesis 1a), we developed the following logistic model:

$$\text{Earnings Management Strategy} = \zeta_0 + \zeta_1 SOE + \zeta_i \sum Controls + \text{Year Fixed Effects} + \text{Industry Fixed Effects} + \varepsilon \quad (7)$$

where Earnings Management Strategy is one of the following measures: $RM_H\_DA_L$, $RM_L\_DA_H$, $RM_H\_DA_H$, and $RM_L\_DA_L$. To examine the impact of state ownership on specific types of earnings management strategies, we developed the following model:

$$\text{Earnings Management} = \eta_0 + \eta_1 SOE + \eta_i \sum Controls + \text{Year Fixed Effects} + \text{Industry Fixed Effects} + \varepsilon \quad (8)$$

where Earnings Management is one of the following measures: ABSDA, DA(+), DA(−), NA_CFO, A_PROD, NA_DISX, RM1, RM2, EM1, and EM2. To further examine the differences between central SOEs and local SOEs (Hypothesis 1b) in their choices of earnings management strategies, we developed the following model:

$$\text{Earnings Management Strategy (Earnings Management)} = \theta_0 + \theta_1 CSOE + \theta_2 LSOE + \theta_i \sum Controls + \text{Year Fixed Effects} + \text{Industry Fixed Effects} + \varepsilon \quad (9)$$

To examine how media attention and litigation may interact with state ownership to impact earnings management strategies (Hypothesis 2a, 2b and Hypothesis 3a, 3b), we developed the following models:

$$\text{Earnings Management Strategy (Earnings Management)} = \iota_0 + \iota_1 SOE + \iota_2 MEDIA\,(LIT) + \iota_3 SOE * MEDIA(LIT) + \iota_i \sum Controls + \text{Year Fixed Effects} + \text{Industry Fixed Effects} + \varepsilon \quad (10)$$

$$\text{Earnings Management Strategy (Earnings Management)} = \kappa_0 + \kappa_1 CSOE + \kappa_2 LSOE + \kappa_3 MEDIA\,(LIT) + \kappa_4 CSOE * MEDIA(LIT) + \kappa_5 LSOE * MEDIA(LIT) + \kappa_i \sum Controls + \text{Year Fixed Effects} + \text{Industry Fixed Effects} + \varepsilon \quad (11)$$

Controls are the control variables from Table 2. Following Chan et al. and Cohen et al. [23,27], in Models (8)–(11), we included real earnings management (measured by RM1) in Controls when accruals management (e.g., ABSDA) is regressed, and vice versa.

4. Results

4.1. Descriptive Statistics

Table 3 presents descriptive statistics of all variables. To avoid the distortions caused by extreme values on our results, we winsorized the dependent variables and control variables at the top and bottom 1%.

Table 3. Summary Statistics.

Variable	Obs.	Mean	STD	Min.	Max.	25%	50%	75%
ABSDA	11,905	0.065	0.099	0.000	4.675	0.019	0.042	0.081
DA(+)	6406	0.070	0.117	0.000	4.675	0.020	0.044	0.086
DA(−)	5499	−0.059	0.071	−1.204	0.000	−0.076	−0.040	−0.017
NA_CFO	11,905	−0.003	0.115	−1.796	3.849	−0.049	−0.002	0.040
A_PROD	11,905	−0.004	0.432	−13.754	39.330	−0.063	0.006	0.064
NA_DISX	11,905	−0.001	0.152	−3.715	6.407	−0.018	0.012	0.041
RM1	11,905	−0.004	0.205	−3.725	6.845	−0.060	0.008	0.067
RM2	11,905	−0.005	0.471	−16.347	37.619	−0.076	0.019	0.101
EM1	11,905	0.061	0.241	−3.587	8.389	−0.015	0.048	0.120
EM2	11,905	0.060	0.482	−15.723	38.115	−0.031	0.067	0.162
$RM_H\_DA_L$	11,905	0.293	0.455	0.000	1.000	0.000	0.000	1.000
$RM_L\_DA_H$	11,905	0.180	0.384	0.000	1.000	0.000	0.000	0.000
$RM_H\_DA_H$	11,905	0.320	0.467	0.000	1.000	0.000	0.000	1.000
$RM_L\_DA_L$	11,905	0.206	0.405	0.000	1.000	0.000	0.000	0.000
SOE	11,905	0.634	0.482	0.000	1.000	0.000	1.000	1.000
CSOE	11,905	0.207	0.405	0.000	1.000	0.000	0.000	0.000
LSOE	11,905	0.428	0.495	0.000	1.000	0.000	0.000	1.000
MEDIA	1816	0.713	0.417	0.000	2.053	0.477	0.699	1.000
LIT	11,905	0.109	0.312	0.000	1.000	0.000	0.000	0.000
ROA	11,905	0.039	0.057	−0.775	0.477	0.013	0.033	0.062
MBG	11,905	0.354	4.909	−0.984	400.677	−0.022	0.108	0.274
LEV	11,905	0.507	0.191	0.007	1.352	0.372	0.516	0.649
LNA	11,905	22.480	1.345	17.641	28.509	21.573	22.327	23.263
OL	11,905	0.018	0.133	0.000	1.000	0.000	0.000	0.000
MB	11,905	4.210	21.543	0.182	2011.634	1.699	2.599	4.216
NOI	11,905	0.010	0.181	−15.122	7.824	0.000	0.003	0.010
INST	11,905	7.948	8.987	0.000	75.495	1.620	4.798	11.013
H10	11,905	0.175	0.128	0.001	0.810	0.075	0.142	0.246
CEOCHR	11,905	0.134	0.340	0.000	1.000	0.000	0.000	0.000
INDDIR	11,905	0.366	0.054	0.000	0.800	0.333	0.333	0.385
MO	11,905	0.007	0.052	0.000	1.578	0.000	0.000	0.000
Big10	11,905	0.495	0.500	0.000	1.000	0.000	0.000	1.000
CMI	11,905	6.175	1.758	1.270	11.930	4.740	6.870	7.450
GDI	11,905	8.762	1.461	−4.660	10.650	8.230	9.050	9.690
LEI	11,905	10.726	5.548	0.180	19.890	5.990	8.180	16.270
SZSH	11,905	0.652	0.476	0.000	1.000	0.000	1.000	1.000

All variables are defined in Table 2.

The minimum value of ABSDA is less than 0.001, while the maximum value reaches 4.675, with a mean of 0.065, which is lower than the value in prior research based on the earlier years' data of Chinese stock markets [12,13]. This may indicate that Chinese listed companies have reduced the use of accruals management in recent years. On the contrary, the mean values of three proxies of real earnings management are all higher than that of earlier years' data of Chinese stock market [14]. Table 4 reports the comparative results of the mean values of earnings management in central SOEs, local SOEs, and non-SOEs.

Consistent with our expectations, the mean values of accruals management of central SOEs and local SOEs are both lower than that of non-SOEs. As for real earnings management (including NA_CFO, A_PROD, NA_DISX, RM1, and RM2), central SOEs appear to be at the highest level, followed by the local SOEs and non-SOEs. From Table 4, we find that the mean value of $RM_H\_DA_L$, of both central SOEs and local SOEs, is significantly higher than that of non-SOEs, while the mean value of $RM_L\_DA_H$ is significantly lower than that of non-SOE, showing that SOEs tend to substitute for accruals management with real earnings management. Such a difference can also be observed between central SOEs and local SOEs.

Table 5 shows the correlation analysis of dependent variables and test variables. Most of the correlations are consistent with our previous estimations. We examine the variance inflation factors (VIFs) of the independent variables to check for multicollinearity. The VIF values for all variables do not exceed 4, indicating that there is no serious multicollinearity issue in our models.

4.2. Regression Results

4.2.1. SOEs vs. Non-SOEs

To test whether SOEs are more likely to engage real earnings management to substitute for accruals management (Hypothesis 1a), we followed Braam et al.'s [11] approach and compared the difference in the selection of earnings management strategies between SOEs and non-SOEs. The results are presented in Table 6.

From column (1), we can see that SOE is significantly positively associated with $RM_H\_DA_L$ (coefficient = 0.113, p value < 0.05), showing that SOEs are more likely to substitute real earnings management for accruals management, supporting our Hypothesis 1a. As expected, due to more scrutiny and criticism from outsiders, such as regulators, auditors, and the media, SOEs prefer to use real earnings management to avoid scrutiny and penalties.

To test Hypothesis 1a further, we examined the impact of state ownership on different types of earnings management strategies and on the overall level of earnings management. Table 7 presents the results.

The test results of the overall levels of earnings management are presented in columns (9) and (10), which show that there is no significant difference between SOEs and non-SOEs regarding the overall level of earnings management (coefficient = −0.003 for both, p value > 0.10). These results show that SOEs are as equally likely to engage in earnings management as non-SOEs. By looking further into the results, we found that SOEs are more likely to substitute real earnings management for accruals management to avoid scrutiny than non-SOEs.

Column (1) shows that SOEs are negatively associated with ABSDA (coefficient = −0.006, p value < 0.01), indicating that SOEs have lower accruals management than non-SOEs. Furthermore, compared with non-SOEs, SOEs have significantly less income-increasing discretionary accruals (coefficient = −0.005, p value < 0.01) but more income-decreasing discretionary accruals (coefficient = 0.003, p value < 0.05). Overall, SOEs are less likely to use accruals management than non-SOEs. As for real earnings management, with results presented in columns (4) to (8), SOEs seem to have more NA_CFO and A_PROD than non-SOEs (coefficient = 0.005 for both, p values < 0.05). These results provide further support to our Hypothesis 1a that SOEs are more likely to substitute real earnings management for accruals management than non-SOEs.

4.2.2. Central SOEs vs. Local SOEs

We performed an additional test to examine how the central SOEs differ from local SOEs in the trade-off or combination of earnings management strategies, with results presented in Table 8. We used CSOE to represent central SOEs and use LSOE to represent local SOEs, with non-SOEs as the default comparison.

Compared to other firms, central SOEs are more likely to use $RM_H\_DA_L$ strategy (coefficient = 0.240, p value < 0.01). At the same time, central SOEs are less likely to use $RM_L\_DA_H$ strategy. These results indicate that, compared with local SOEs and non-SOEs, central SOEs are more likely to substitute real earnings management for accruals management to reduce the risk of having earnings management exposed and to avoid the scrutiny and criticism from the public and media. This result supports our Hypothesis 1b.

Table 4. Mean Values Partitioned by Ownership Type.

	Mean CSOE	Mean LSOE	Mean NSOE	Mean Difference (CSOE-NSOE)	Mean Difference (LSOE-NSOE)	Mean Difference (CSOE-LSOE)
ABSDA	0.061	0.059	0.075	−0.014 ***	−0.016 ***	0.002
DA(+)	0.063	0.062	0.083	−0.021 ***	−0.021 ***	0.001
DA(−)	−0.058	−0.055	−0.065	0.007 ***	0.010 ***	−0.003
NA_CFO	0.004	−0.004	−0.006	0.010 ***	0.002	0.008 ***
A_PROD	0.017	−0.006	−0.014	0.031 **	0.008	0.023 ***
NA_DISX	0.017	−0.003	−0.009	0.026 **	0.005 **	0.021 ***
RM1	0.022	−0.007	−0.014	0.036 ***	0.007 *	0.029 ***
RM2	0.034	−0.010	−0.023	0.057 ***	0.013	0.044 ***
EM1	0.082	0.052	0.060	0.022 ***	−0.009 *	0.031 ***
EM2	0.095	0.049	0.052	0.042 ***	−0.003	0.046 ***
RM$_H$_DA$_L$	0.338	0.299	0.261	0.077 ***	0.038 ***	0.038 ***
RM$_L$_DA$_H$	0.158	0.179	0.194	−0.037 ***	−0.016 *	−0.021 **
RM$_H$_DA$_H$	0.330	0.307	0.331	−0.001	−0.024 **	0.023 **
RM$_L$_DA$_L$	0.175	0.215	0.214	−0.039 ***	0.001	−0.040 ***
MEDIA	0.793	0.705	0.673	0.121 ***	0.032	0.088 ***
LIT	0.120	0.101	0.113	0.008	−0.012 *	0.020 ***

*, **, *** represent significance at the level of 0.10, 0.05, and 0.01, respectively. All variables are defined in Table 2.

Table 5. Correlation Matrix.

	1	2	3	4	5	6	7	8	9	10	11	12	13	14	15	16	17
1. ABSDA	1	0.110	0.068	0.031	0.099	0.070	0.418	0.342	0.517	0.340	0.601	0.434	−0.013	−0.014	−0.001	0.029	0.020
2. NA_CFO	0.348	1	0.443	0.219	0.832	0.406	0.761	0.414	0.170	0.339	0.383	0.308	0.076	0.095	−0.005	−0.029	0.055
3. A_PROD	0.025	0.097	1	0.572	0.641	0.956	0.608	0.895	0.341	0.437	0.402	0.429	0.033	0.061	−0.019	0.074	0.022
4. NA_DISX	0.053	0.166	0.095	1	0.660	0.759	0.626	0.717	0.335	0.365	0.308	0.382	−0.033	0.012	−0.041	0.091	0.036
5. RM1	0.155	0.682	0.125	0.834	1	0.709	0.914	0.698	0.314	0.460	0.465	0.449	0.041	0.089	−0.035	0.071	0.065
6. RM2	0.006	0.143	0.947	0.410	0.384	1	0.671	0.936	0.373	0.455	0.417	0.463	0.010	0.056	−0.036	0.087	0.024
7. EM1	0.541	0.723	0.117	0.688	0.915	0.329	1	0.768	0.121	0.313	0.622	0.555	0.032	0.072	−0.029	0.055	0.062
8. EM2	0.210	0.211	0.931	0.390	0.407	0.979	0.433	1	0.199	0.355	0.566	0.536	0.017	0.054	−0.029	0.068	0.033
9. RM$_H$_DA$_L$	0.287	0.091	0.080	0.176	0.181	0.130	0.037	0.069	1	0.302	0.438	0.325	0.034	0.051	−0.009	−0.039	0
10. RM$_L$_DA$_H$	0.153	0.289	0.150	0.223	0.327	0.210	0.216	0.174	0.302	1	0.326	0.242	−0.008	−0.012	0.002	0.001	0.047
11. RM$_H$_DA$_H$	0.352	0.301	0.145	0.163	0.289	0.186	0.390	0.254	0.442	0.322	1	0.354	0.004	0.005	0	−0.005	0.031
12. RM$_L$_DA$_L$	0.229	0.174	0.114	0.174	0.227	0.161	0.287	0.204	0.328	0.239	0.350	1	−0.035	0.052	0.009	0.048	0.009
13. SOE	0.076	0.019	0.017	0.039	0.039	0.028	0.002	0.012	0.054	0.028	−0.017	−0.015	1	0.374	0.645	0.062	−0.016
14. CSOE	0.023	0.031	0.025	0.062	0.063	0.043	0.045	0.037	0.050	0.030	0.010	0.040	0.387	1	0.468	0.096	0.032
15. LSOE	0.056	−0.007	−0.004	−0.013	−0.014	−0.008	0.034	0.019	0.012	−0.003	0.025	0.018	0.656	0.441	1	−0.02	−0.042
16. MEDIA	0.038	−0.033	0.078	0.103	0.088	0.099	0.060	0.081	−0.040	0.003	0	0.042	0.069	0.100	−0.017	1	0.036
17. LIT	0.020	−0.001	0.006	0.021	0.015	0.013	0.021	0.016	0.004	−0.005	0.019	0.022	−0.009	0.018	0.024	0.034	1

Spearman (Pearson) correlation coefficients are above (below) the diagonal. Bold values are significant at 0.10 level or better (two-tailed). All variables are defined in Table 2.

Table 6. The Effect of State Ownership on Earnings Management Combination Strategies.

Dependent Variables	(1) $RM_H\_DA_L$	(2) $RM_L\_DA_H$	(3) $RM_H\_DA_H$	(4) $RM_L\_DA_L$
SOE	0.113 **	0.011	−0.120 ***	0.013
	(0.047)	(0.056)	(0.045)	(0.052)
ROA	−9.446 ***	10.957 ***	−6.330 ***	9.272 ***
	(0.548)	(0.614)	(0.497)	(0.592)
MBG	−0.283 ***	0.321 ***	0.104 **	−0.134 **
	(0.053)	(0.047)	(0.042)	(0.053)
LEV	−0.015	0.008	0.519 ***	−0.426 **
	(0.152)	(0.182)	(0.144)	(0.172)
LNA	0.169 ***	−0.105 ***	−0.043 *	−0.094 ***
	(0.027)	(0.031)	(0.025)	(0.030)
OL	−0.606 ***	0.258	−0.149	0.723 ***
	(0.174)	(0.200)	(0.167)	(0.168)
MB	−0.066 ***	0.047 ***	0.015 *	−0.054 ***
	(0.010)	(0.010)	(0.008)	(0.011)
NOI	4.037 ***	−4.665 ***	1.895 ***	−3.877 ***
	(0.756)	(1.063)	(0.721)	(0.997)
INST	−0.018 ***	0.017 ***	−0.010 ***	0.016 ***
	(0.003)	(0.003)	(0.003)	(0.003)
H10	−0.584 ***	0.037	0.249	0.331
	(0.194)	(0.233)	(0.184)	(0.215)
CEOCHR	−0.203 ***	−0.022	0.052	0.181 ***
	(0.066)	(0.076)	(0.061)	(0.069)
INDDIR	0.268	−0.430	0.145	−0.342
	(0.413)	(0.515)	(0.398)	(0.473)
MO	0.732	1.740 **	−1.895 **	−0.707
	(0.860)	(0.831)	(0.836)	(0.861)
Big10	−0.049	0.120 **	−0.122 ***	0.120 **
	(0.046)	(0.054)	(0.043)	(0.050)
CMI	0.054 ***	−0.062 **	0.007	−0.021
	(0.020)	(0.025)	(0.020)	(0.023)
GDI	−0.001	−0.034	0.047 *	−0.043
	(0.029)	(0.034)	(0.028)	(0.033)
LEI	−0.014 **	0.017 **	−0.007	0.018 **
	(0.007)	(0.008)	(0.006)	(0.008)
SZSH	0.066	0.009	−0.073 *	0.044
	(0.046)	(0.055)	(0.044)	(0.052)
YEAR Controls	Yes	Yes	Yes	Yes
Industry Controls	Yes	Yes	Yes	Yes
_cons	−4.072 ***	0.733	−0.280	0.875
	(0.608)	(0.730)	(0.584)	(0.689)
Obs.	11,905	11,905	11,905	11,905
pseudo R^2	0.061	0.080	0.029	0.050

***, **, and * indicate statistical significance at the 1%, 5%, and 10% levels, respectively. Standard errors are in parenthesis below the regression coefficients. All variables are defined in Table 2.

Moreover, our results indicate that central SOEs are more likely to use the combination strategy of $RM_H\_DA_H$ than local SOEs (CSOE and LSOE coefficients = −0.01 and −0.170, p value > 0.1 and <0.01, respectively) but less likely to use the strategy of $RM_L\_DA_L$ than local SOEs (CSOE and LSOE coefficients = −0.181 and 0.094, p value < 0.05 and <0.10, respectively). Prior research found that companies with severe financial problems might choose to increase earnings through both accruals and real earnings management [60,61]. As argued by Zhang et al. [37], compared with local SOEs, managers of central SOEs need to rely more on corporate performance to get promotional opportunities. The pressure on central SOEs to meet earnings goals might have pushed some managers to use extreme ways to manipulate their financial results. Such a finding should receive close attention from the regulators in China.

Table 7. The Effect of State Ownership on Real Earnings Management and Accruals Management.

Dependent Variables	(1) ABSDA	(2) DA(+)	(3) DA(−)	(4) NA_CFO	(5) A_PROD	(6) NA_DISX	(7) RM1	(8) RM2	(9) EM1	(10) EM2
SOE	−0.006 *** (0.001)	−0.005 *** (0.001)	0.003 ** (0.001)	0.005 *** (0.002)	0.005 ** (0.002)	−0.001 (0.002)	0.004 (0.002)	0.005 (0.004)	−0.003 (0.003)	−0.003 (0.004)
Year & Industry & Control Variables	Yes	Yes	Yes	Yes	Yes	Yes	Yes	Yes	Yes	Yes
_cons	0.072 *** (0.017)	0.067 *** (0.018)	−0.105 *** (0.017)	0.001 (0.021)	−0.258 *** (0.032)	−0.085 *** (0.020)	−0.082 ** (0.032)	−0.334 *** (0.047)	0.014 (0.039)	−0.239 *** (0.053)
Obs.	11,905	6406	5499	11,905	11,905	11,905	11,905	11,905	11,905	11,905
adj. R²	0.138	0.449	0.342	0.138	0.239	0.141	0.177	0.216	0.105	0.154

***, and ** indicate statistical significance at the 1% and 5% levels, respectively. Standard errors are in parenthesis below the regression coefficients. All variables are defined in Table 2.

Table 8. The Effect of State Ownership Type on Earnings Management Combination Strategies.

Dependent Variables	(1) RM$_H$_DA$_L$	(2) RM$_L$_DA$_H$	(3) RM$_H$_DA$_H$	(4) RM$_L$_DA$_L$
CSOE	0.240 ***	−0.130 *	−0.010	−0.181 **
	(0.061)	(0.075)	(0.059)	(0.071)
LSOE	0.055	0.073	−0.170 ***	0.094 *
	(0.051)	(0.060)	(0.048)	(0.055)
ROA	−9.366 ***	10.901 ***	−6.263 ***	9.178 ***
	(0.548)	(0.614)	(0.497)	(0.593)
MBG	−0.283 ***	0.322 ***	0.104 **	−0.134 **
	(0.052)	(0.047)	(0.042)	(0.053)
LEV	0.018	−0.008	0.544 ***	−0.453 ***
	(0.152)	(0.182)	(0.145)	(0.173)
LNA	0.160 ***	−0.100 ***	−0.050 *	−0.085 ***
	(0.027)	(0.031)	(0.025)	(0.030)
OL	−0.628 ***	0.283	−0.170	0.753 ***
	(0.174)	(0.200)	(0.168)	(0.169)
MB	−0.069 ***	0.049 ***	0.013	−0.050 ***
	(0.010)	(0.010)	(0.008)	(0.011)
NOI	4.091 ***	−4.735 ***	1.939 ***	−3.972 ***
	(0.757)	(1.062)	(0.721)	(0.997)
INST	−0.018 ***	0.017 ***	−0.010 ***	0.016 ***
	(0.003)	(0.003)	(0.003)	(0.003)
H10	−0.585 ***	0.039	0.250	0.332
	(0.195)	(0.233)	(0.184)	(0.215)
CEOCHR	−0.188 ***	−0.038	0.064	0.160 **
	(0.066)	(0.076)	(0.061)	(0.069)
INDDIR	0.265	−0.431	0.146	−0.344
	(0.413)	(0.515)	(0.398)	(0.474)
MO	0.731	1.755 **	−1.899 **	−0.676
	(0.860)	(0.831)	(0.836)	(0.860)
Big10	−0.064	0.136 **	−0.135 ***	0.141 ***
	(0.046)	(0.054)	(0.044)	(0.051)
CMI	0.051 **	−0.057 **	0.004	−0.014
	(0.020)	(0.025)	(0.020)	(0.023)
GDI	0.008	−0.044	0.055 **	−0.058 *
	(0.029)	(0.035)	(0.028)	(0.033)
LEI	−0.015 **	0.018 **	−0.008	0.020 ***
	(0.007)	(0.008)	(0.006)	(0.008)
SZSH	0.072	0.003	−0.069	0.036
	(0.046)	(0.055)	(0.044)	(0.052)
YEAR Controls	Yes	Yes	Yes	Yes
Industry Controls	Yes	Yes	Yes	Yes
_cons	−3.936 ***	0.682	−0.182	0.764
	(0.610)	(0.731)	(0.585)	(0.691)
Obs.	11,905	11,905	11,905	11,905
pseudo R^2	0.062	0.080	0.030	0.051

***, **, and * indicate statistical significance at the 1%, 5%, and 10% levels, respectively. Standard errors are in parenthesis below the regression coefficients. All variables are defined in Table 2.

Table 9 presents the results of different types of earnings management strategies with specifics. Column (1) shows that both central and local SOEs are significantly associated with lower discretionary accruals (CSOE and LSOE coefficients = −0.004 and −0.006, p value < 0.05 and <0.01, respectively). Our untabulated t-test result shows that the coefficient of central SOEs is not significantly different from that of local SOEs.

Columns (4) to (8) list the results of the effect of state ownership type on real earnings management. One can see that, compared with other firms, central SOEs are more likely to use all three types of real earnings management including: abnormal cash flows (NA_CFO coefficient = 0.010, p value < 0.01), abnormal overproductions (A_PROD coefficient = 0.017, p value < 0.01), and abnormal discretionary expenditures (NA_DISX coefficient = 0.008, p value < 0.01), showing that central SOEs engage more real earnings management than local SOEs and non-SOEs. All the real earnings management coefficients of central SOEs are higher than those of local SOEs, including both aggregate measures, providing further evidence to Hypothesis 1b that central SOEs are more likely to use real earnings management than local SOEs. Columns (9) and (10) present the results of the aggregate level of earnings management and show that central SOEs are more likely to manage earnings than local SOEs, which is primarily driven by the high level of real earnings management in central SOEs.

Overall, the results show that central SOEs are more likely to substitute real earnings management for accruals management than other firms. When choosing service suppliers or other business partners, firms should pay close attention to the real earnings management issue in central SOEs.

4.2.3. Joint Effects of State Ownership and Media Attention on Earnings Management

To look further into the reasons why SOEs, especially central SOEs, are more likely to use the trade-off strategy by substituting real earnings management for accruals management, we proposed Hypothesis 2a and 2b to examine whether SOEs, especially central SOEs, with high media attention are more likely to use real earnings management to reach earnings goals. Table 10 presents the results.

Panel A of Table 10 shows that those SOEs with high media attention are more likely to engage the trade-off strategy of $RM_H\_DA_L$ (coefficient = 0.787, p-value < 0.01). Consistent with our expectation in Hypothesis 2a, SOEs with high media attention might be more concerned with their reputation loss if their earnings management were exposed. Such a reputation loss will affect managers' compensations and hurt their chance of get political promotions [39,62]. Therefore, SOEs with high media attention are more likely to use the type of earnings management that receives less scrutiny from outside reviewers, e.g., real earnings management, even though it may harm the company in the long term. In specific, SOEs with high media attention exhibit higher levels of real earnings management in all three categories.

Panel B of Table 10 presents the test results of the difference between central SOEs and local SOEs in terms of earnings management strategies. Supporting our prediction in Hypothesis 2b, among central SOEs, local SOEs, and non-SOEs, those central SOEs that are with high media attention are most likely to use the trade-off strategy of $RM_H\_DA_L$ (coefficient = 0.999, p-value < 0.01), while they are less likely to use the $RM_L\_DA_H$ strategy (coefficient = -0.875, p-value < 0.01). Compared with local SOEs and non-SOEs, central SOEs have the strongest political connections, which provide more political promotion opportunities to their executives. They are also often the focus of the public criticism and the media coverage, making them more sensitive to the public exposure of earnings management. Thus, the central SOEs with high media attention are most likely to substitute real earnings management for accruals management to reduce the chance of getting caught while achieving their earnings goals.

4.2.4. Joint Effects of State Ownership and Litigation on Earnings Management

To examine whether there is a joint effect of state ownership and litigation on earnings management, we proposed Hypothesis 3a&b and anticipate that the SOEs, especially central SOEs, with an incidence of litigation are more likely to engage the trade-off strategy of using high real earnings management and low accruals management. Table 11 presents the results.

Table 9. The Effect of State Ownership Type on Real Earnings Management and Accruals Management.

Dependent Variables	(1) ABSDA	(2) DA(+)	(3) DA(−)	(4) NA_CFO	(5) A_PROD	(6) NA_DISX	(7) RM1	(8) RM2	(9) EM1	(10) EM2
CSOE	−0.004 **	−0.006 ***	−0.000	0.010 ***	0.017 ***	0.008 ***	0.019 ***	0.027 ***	0.016 ***	0.024 ***
	(0.002)	(0.002)	(0.002)	(0.002)	(0.003)	(0.002)	(0.003)	(0.005)	(0.004)	(0.005)
LSOE	−0.006 ***	−0.004 ***	0.004 ***	0.003 *	−0.000	−0.005 ***	−0.003	−0.006	−0.011 ***	−0.015 ***
	(0.001)	(0.002)	(0.001)	(0.002)	(0.003)	(0.002)	(0.003)	(0.004)	(0.003)	(0.004)
Year & Industry & Control Variables	Yes	Yes	Yes	Yes	Yes	Yes	Yes	Yes	Yes	Yes
_cons	0.073 ***	0.066 ***	−0.108 ***	0.004	−0.249 ***	−0.078 ***	−0.070 **	−0.316 ***	0.029	−0.218 ***
	(0.017)	(0.018)	(0.017)	(0.021)	(0.032)	(0.020)	(0.032)	(0.047)	(0.039)	(0.053)
Obs.	11,905	6406	5499	11,905	11,905	11,905	11,905	11,905	11,905	11,905
adj. R²	0.138	0.449	0.343	0.139	0.241	0.144	0.181	0.220	0.109	0.158

*, **, *** represent significance at the level of 0.10, 0.05, and 0.01, respectively. Standard errors are in parenthesis below the regression coefficients. All variables are defined in Table 2.

Table 10. The Joint Effects of State Ownership and Media Attention on Earnings Management. Panel (A) Regressions on SOEs, Panel (B) Regressions on CSOEs and LSOEs.

(A)

	(1) RM$_H$_DA$_L$	(2) RM$_L$_DA$_H$	(3) RM$_H$_DA$_H$	(4) RM$_L$_DA$_L$	(5) ABSDA	(6) DA+	(7) DA−	(8) NA_CFO	(9) A_PROD	(10) NA_DISX	(11) RM1	(12) RM2
SOE	−0.466 **	0.625 **	0.058	0.047	0.007	0.006	−0.003	−0.009	−0.024 **	−0.018 ***	−0.027 **	−0.044 ***
	(0.226)	(0.284)	(0.217)	(0.257)	(0.006)	(0.006)	(0.007)	(0.008)	(0.011)	(0.007)	(0.012)	(0.017)
MEDIA	−1.053 ***	0.586 *	0.242	0.524 *	0.010	0.015 **	0.003	−0.011	−0.047 ***	−0.036 ***	−0.048 ***	−0.086 ***
	(0.260)	(0.305)	(0.238)	(0.270)	(0.007)	(0.007)	(0.008)	(0.009)	(0.012)	(0.008)	(0.013)	(0.018)
MEDIA_SOE	0.787 ***	−0.723 **	−0.168	−0.163	−0.006	−0.004	0.009	0.022 **	0.034 **	0.016 *	0.038 ***	0.053 **
	(0.294)	(0.344)	(0.270)	(0.308)	(0.007)	(0.007)	(0.009)	(0.010)	(0.014)	(0.009)	(0.014)	(0.021)
Year & Industry & Control Var.	Yes	Yes	Yes	Yes	Yes	Yes	Yes	Yes	Yes	Yes	Yes	Yes
Obs.	1816	1816	1816	1816	1816	1024	792	1816	1816	1816	1816	1816
pseudo R² or adj. R²	0.090	0.117	0.038	0.054	0.134	0.529	0.317	0.176	0.313	0.212	0.255	0.302

151

Table 10. Cont.

(B)

	(1)	(2)	(3)	(4)	(5)	(6)	(7)	(8)	(9)	(10)	(11)	(12)
	RM$_H$_DA$_L$	RM$_L$_DA$_H$	RM$_H$_DA$_H$	RM$_L$_DA$_L$	ABSDA	DA+	DA−	NA_CFO	A_PROD	NA_DISX	RM1	RM2
CSOE	−0.510 *	0.717 *	0.150	−0.037	0.013	0.010	−0.000	0.008	−0.021	−0.017 *	−0.009	−0.041 *
	(0.310)	(0.370)	(0.296)	(0.357)	(0.008)	(0.008)	(0.010)	(0.011)	(0.015)	(0.010)	(0.016)	(0.023)
LSOE	−0.421 *	0.577 *	0.026	0.060	0.004	0.002	−0.004	−0.015 *	−0.023 *	−0.017 **	−0.032 ***	−0.042 **
	(0.242)	(0.307)	(0.233)	(0.276)	(0.006)	(0.007)	(0.007)	(0.009)	(0.012)	(0.007)	(0.012)	(0.018)
MEDIA	−1.042 ***	0.582 *	0.244	0.516 *	0.010	0.015 **	0.003	−0.011	−0.046 ***	−0.035 ***	−0.047 ***	−0.085 ***
	(0.260)	(0.305)	(0.238)	(0.270)	(0.007)	(0.006)	(0.008)	(0.009)	(0.012)	(0.008)	(0.013)	(0.018)
MEDIA_CSOE	0.999 ***	−0.875 **	−0.214	−0.333	−0.013	−0.014	0.001	0.013	0.048 ***	0.029 ***	0.042 **	0.079 ***
	(0.367)	(0.443)	(0.346)	(0.414)	(0.010)	(0.009)	(0.012)	(0.013)	(0.018)	(0.011)	(0.018)	(0.026)
MEDIA_LSOE	0.637 **	−0.647 *	−0.157	−0.065	−0.002	0.003	0.012	0.025 **	0.025	0.008	0.031 **	0.035
	(0.318)	(0.371)	(0.292)	(0.331)	(0.008)	(0.008)	(0.009)	(0.011)	(0.015)	(0.009)	(0.015)	(0.022)
Year & Industry &Control Var.	Yes	Yes	Yes	Yes	Yes	Yes	Yes	Yes	Yes	Yes	Yes	Yes
Obs.	1816	1816	1816	1816	1816	1024	792	1816	1816	1816	1816	1816
pseudo R^2 or adj. R^2	0.091	0.117	0.038	0.056	0.135	0.532	0.319	0.179	0.316	0.219	0.262	0.307

*, **, *** represent significance at the level of 0.10, 0.05, and 0.01, respectively. Standard errors are in parenthesis below the regression coefficients. All variables are defined in Table 2.

Table 11. The Joint Effects of State Ownership and Litigation on Earnings Management. Panel (**A**) Regressions on SOEs, Panel (**B**) Regressions on CSOEs and LSOEs.

(A)

	(1)	(2)	(3)	(4)	(5)	(6)	(7)	(8)	(9)	(10)	(11)	(12)
	RM$_H$_DA$_L$	RM$_L$_DA$_H$	RM$_H$_DA$_H$	RM$_L$_DA$_L$	ABSDA	DA+	DA−	NA_CFO	A_PROD	NA_DISX	RM1	RM2
SOE	0.079	0.058	−0.138 ***	0.043	−0.006 ***	−0.005 ***	0.003 **	0.005 ***	0.004	−0.001	0.003	0.003
	(0.050)	(0.059)	(0.047)	(0.054)	(0.001)	(0.001)	(0.001)	(0.002)	(0.003)	(0.002)	(0.003)	(0.004)
LIT	−0.215 *	0.251 **	−0.028	0.088	0.004	0.004	−0.001	−0.005	−0.005	0.003	−0.004	−0.005
	(0.118)	(0.125)	(0.105)	(0.123)	(0.003)	(0.003)	(0.003)	(0.004)	(0.006)	(0.004)	(0.006)	(0.009)
LIT_SOE	0.318 **	−0.421 **	0.145	−0.286 *	0.002	−0.003	−0.004	0.004	0.007	0.004	0.010	0.015
	(0.144)	(0.165)	(0.132)	(0.160)	(0.004)	(0.004)	(0.004)	(0.005)	(0.007)	(0.005)	(0.007)	(0.011)
Year & Industry &Control Var.	Yes	Yes	Yes	Yes	Yes	Yes	Yes	Yes	Yes	Yes	Yes	Yes
Obs.	11,905	11,905	11,905	11,905	11,905	6406	5499	11,905	11,905	11,905	11,905	11,905

Table 11. Cont.

(A)

	(1)	(2)	(3)	(4)	(5)	(6)	(7)	(8)	(9)	(10)	(11)	(12)
	$RM_H\_DA_L$	$RM_L\_DA_H$	$RM_H\_DA_H$	$RM_L\_DA_L$	ABSDA	DA+	DA−	NA_CFO	A_PROD	NA_DISX	RM1	RM2
pseudo R^2 or adj. R^2	0.061	0.080	0.029	0.050	0.138	0.450	0.342	0.138	0.239	0.141	0.178	0.217

(B)

	(1)	(2)	(3)	(4)	(5)	(6)	(7)	(8)	(9)	(10)	(11)	(12)
	$RM_H\_DA_L$	$RM_L\_DA_H$	$RM_H\_DA_H$	$RM_L\_DA_L$	ABSDA	DA+	DA−	NA_CFO	A_PROD	NA_DISX	RM1	RM2
CSOE	0.199 ***	−0.077	−0.036	−0.128 *	−0.004 **	−0.005 ***	0.001	0.010 ***	0.016 ***	0.008 ***	0.017 ***	0.024 ***
	(0.065)	(0.079)	(0.062)	(0.074)	(0.002)	(0.002)	(0.002)	(0.002)	(0.003)	(0.002)	(0.003)	(0.005)
LSOE	0.026	0.117 *	−0.183 ***	0.113 *	−0.006 ***	−0.004 ***	0.004 ***	0.003	−0.001	−0.005 ***	−0.004	−0.007 *
	(0.053)	(0.063)	(0.050)	(0.058)	(0.001)	(0.002)	(0.002)	(0.002)	(0.003)	(0.002)	(0.003)	(0.004)
LIT	−0.212 *	0.248 **	−0.026	0.083	0.004	0.004	−0.001	−0.005	−0.005	0.003	−0.004	−0.005
	(0.118)	(0.125)	(0.105)	(0.123)	(0.003)	(0.003)	(0.003)	(0.004)	(0.006)	(0.004)	(0.006)	(0.009)
LIT_CSOE	0.362 **	−0.436 *	0.155	−0.437 *	0.004	−0.001	−0.011 **	0.003	0.006	0.005	0.008	0.016
	(0.178)	(0.226)	(0.168)	(0.227)	(0.005)	(0.006)	(0.005)	(0.006)	(0.009)	(0.006)	(0.009)	(0.014)
LIT_LSOE	0.273 *	−0.395 **	0.123	−0.200	−0.000	−0.003	0.000	0.004	0.006	0.003	0.009	0.011
	(0.157)	(0.182)	(0.146)	(0.173)	(0.004)	(0.005)	(0.004)	(0.005)	(0.008)	(0.005)	(0.008)	(0.012)
Year & Industry &Control Var.	Yes	Yes	Yes	Yes	Yes	Yes	Yes	Yes	Yes	Yes	Yes	Yes
Obs.	11,905	11,905	11,905	11,905	11,905	6406	5499	11,905	11,905	11,905	11,905	11,905
pseudo R^2 or adj. R^2	0.062	0.081	0.030	0.051	0.138	0.450	0.343	0.139	0.241	0.145	0.181	0.220

*, **, *** represent significance at the level of 0.10, 0.05, and 0.01, respectively. Standard errors are in parenthesis below the regression coefficients. All variables are defined in Table 2.

Consistent with our expectation (Hypothesis 3a), SOEs in litigation are more likely to use real earnings management to substitute for accruals management ($RM_H\_DA_L$ coefficient = 0.318, p-value < 0.05). With an anticipated increase in scrutiny from regulators and auditors, managers in SOEs that are in litigation tend to use the earnings management strategy that has a lower exposure risk while achieving earnings goals. Moreover, based on the results in Panel B of Table 11, one can notice that central SOEs in litigation are more likely to use the $RM_H\_DA_L$ strategy (coefficient = 0.362, p value < 0.05) than other companies, supporting our Hypothesis 3b.

Overall, the test results of media attention and litigation show that both have more impacts on the earnings management strategies of SOEs, especially central SOEs, than on that of non-SOEs. Such impact might be related to the higher cost of the reputation loss caused by exposure of earnings management on SOEs than on non-SOEs. The government and regulators should pay close attention to the trade-off issue of earnings management strategies in SOEs with high media attention or litigation.

4.3. Robustness Tests

In this study, we used the modified Jones Model [43] to estimate discretionary accruals. This is based on the findings in prior literature [46,47] that the modified Jones model has a better explanatory power for Chinese enterprises compared to other models. To examine whether our results are robust to other commonly used estimation models for discretionary accruals, we used performance-adjusted discretionary accruals developed by Kothari et al. [45] to conduct our analyses. Our results stay the same.

To examine whether the substitution of real earnings management for accruals management is caused by the state ownership, we used a natural experiment setting and perform a difference-in-difference test on those firms that changed from non-SOEs to SOEs. Our test results show that a firm is more likely to use the strategy of high real earnings management and low accruals management after the firm changed from a non-SOE to a SOE. This result provides further evidence for our hypothesis.

When assessing a firm's use of real and accruals management and earnings management combination strategy, we followed Braam et al. [11] to use the industry-year median as cut-off point to determine the values of the dummy variables: RM_Dummy and AM_Dummy. To examine whether our results are robust to alternative cut-off points, we repeated our analyses by using the top and bottom 25% of the sample. Our untabulated results show that all the results are robust to the change of cut-off points.

Unlike Chan et al. [23], some prior literature does not include AM (or RM) as a control variable in the models for the test on the opposite earnings management strategy RM (or AM). In order to examine whether the omission of AM (or RM) in the models will affect our results, we repeated all our tests by removing the control variable from our regression models. Our results remain the same.

Fan and Song [7] found that central SOEs engage in real earnings management to reduce GDP volatility. In order to examine whether our results are affected by the GDP volatility, we included dummy variables of high and low GDP years in our models and repeated our analyses. We obtained the same results.

Prior literature has often used an earnings management suspect group to examine the trade-off issue of earnings management strategies [20,22,23]. We followed the prior literature and use only those firms that intended to use earnings management to manipulate earnings as the suspect group to examine how these firms choose earnings management strategies. We obtained similar results.

5. Conclusions

In recent years, financial crises, pandemics, and regional conflicts have led to significant uncertainties to business operations. In response, companies are placing greater emphasis on enhancing risk governance processes to ensure the safety and reliability of their supply chains. Selecting stable and reliable partners to work with has become an increasingly crucial question for organizations to answer. Previous research on supply chains has shown that accounting information is often used by firms to evaluate the profitability and operational efficiency of suppliers [3]. However, if such financial information has been manipulated by the providers, it can lead to a misjudgment of the credibility and reliability of suppliers by the users. Using A-share Chinese firms listed on the Shenzhen and Shanghai Stock Exchanges for the years 2003–2018, we performed an in-depth analysis of the impact of state ownership on earnings management strategies, particularly the trade-off issue between the two different types of earnings management: accruals management and real earnings management. We found that: first, in contrast with non-SOEs, SOEs prefer to substitute real earnings management for accruals management, indicating a trade-off between the two strategies. Moreover, when comparing central SOEs to local SOEs, we found that central SOEs are more likely to substitute real earnings management for accruals management. Second, we also performed analyses on the joint effects of media attention and state ownership on a firm's earnings management strategies and found that, when compared to SOEs with low media attention, the SOEs with high media coverage are more likely to use real transactions than accruals to manipulate earnings. In particular, this result is more salient in central SOEs. Third, we tested the joint effects of litigation and state ownership on earnings management strategies and found that SOEs, particularly central SOEs, with an incidence of litigation are more likely to favor real earnings management over accruals management.

Our study makes several important contributions to the earnings management literature in China. We use different methods to examine the trade-off issue of earnings management at the firm level. Furthermore, to our best knowledge, we are the first to examine how the interactions between state ownership and other factors such as media attention and litigation impact managers' selection of earnings management strategies. Compared with prior literature on earnings management studies using Chinese listed firms, our investigation uses a longer and more recent period, from 2003 to 2018, to study the effects of ownership structures on earnings management. In additional, unlike most prior research, we divide SOEs into central SOEs and local SOEs to examine the impact of different types of state ownership on earnings management.

Using a large data set of Chinese listed firms, our results provide additional empirical support to Braam et al.'s [11] argument that firms with strong political connections are more likely to substitute real earnings management for accruals management. By exploring the impact of media attention and litigation on how state ownership affects earnings management strategies, we provide evidence to explain why politically connected firms prefer to use real earnings management to accruals management. It appears that, compared to the management of non-SOEs, the management of SOEs are more concerned with the exposure of earnings management since they risk losing all their privileges when their reputation or public image is damaged. In other words, they have a higher cost of using accruals management since this method is under stricter public scrutiny and subject to more severe penalties from regulators. Furthermore, those factors that affect the exposure risk (e.g., media attention) and the scrutiny level (e.g., litigation) of external reviewers will have a significant impact on earnings management strategies. All these findings suggest that, when selecting suppliers, companies should be attentive to the credibility of the financial information they provide. In addition to accruals management, some firms may use real earnings management, which is more difficult to detect, to manipulate earnings. Such actions will harm the companies in the long term, making them less dependable partners to work with. Regulators should also pay more attention to real earnings management to investigate whether some firms have sacrificed the long-term interests of the company to meet the demands of customers. Furthermore, we suggest firms and regulators to pay close attention to real earnings management in companies with strong political connections, such as central SOEs, and to incorporate more comprehensive measures to assess the performances of these firms and the integrity of their executives.

Author Contributions: Conceptualization, P.W.; methodology, S.L. and L.G.; software, S.L.; validation, S.L., P.W. and L.G.; formal analysis, S.L. and L.G.; data curation, S.L.; writing—original draft preparation, S.L.; writing—review and editing, R.G.; supervision, P.W.; project administration, P.W.; funding acquisition, P.W. All authors have read and agreed to the published version of the manuscript.

Funding: This research was funded by National Social Science Fund Project (grant number 20BGL092).

Data Availability Statement: The data that support the findings of this study are available on request from the corresponding author. The data are not publicly available due to privacy or ethical restrictions.

Acknowledgments: We gratefully acknowledge the helpful comments received at the 2016 American Accounting Association Annual Meeting and 2017 China Accounting and Finance Conference. We would like to thank Xiao Li, Yiyang Gu, Tingting Gu, and Tianping Chen for their great help on our data collection.

Conflicts of Interest: The authors declare no conflict of interest.

References

1. Beasley, M.S.; Branson, B.; Braumann, E.; Pagach, D. Understanding the Ecosystem of Enterprise Risk Governance. *Account. Rev.* **2022**, *forthcoming*. [CrossRef]
2. O'Connor, N.G.; Schloetzer, J.D. Aligning Performance Measurement Systems across the Supply Chain: Evidence from Electronic Components Suppliers. *J. Manag. Account. Res.* **2022**, *forthcoming*. [CrossRef]
3. Chang, L.J. ABC Cost Driver Framing and Altering the Balance of Power in Customer-Supplier Negotiations. *Account. Rev.* **2022**, *97*, 149–171. [CrossRef]
4. Wang, Q.; Wong, T.J.; Xia, L. State Ownership, the Institutional Environment, and Auditor Choice: Evidence from China. *J. Account. Econ.* **2008**, *46*, 112–134. [CrossRef]
5. Schipper, K. Commentary on Earnings Management. *Account. Horiz.* **1989**, *3*, 91–102.
6. Kałdoński, M.; Jewartowski, T.; Mizerka, J. Capital Market Pressure, Real Earnings Management, and Institutional Ownership Stability-Evidence from Poland. *Int. Rev. Financ. Anal.* **2020**, *71*, 101315. [CrossRef]
7. Fan, H.; Song, X. Earnings Management of Chinese Central State-Owned Enterprises–The Effects of State Level Incentives. *Asia-Pac. J. Account. Econ.* **2019**, *26*, 643–658. [CrossRef]
8. Wang, Z.; Braam, G.; Reimsbach, D.; Wang, J. Political Embeddedness and Firms' Choices of Earnings Management Strategies in China. *Acc. Financ.* **2020**, *60*, 4723–4755. [CrossRef]
9. Li, L.; Monroe, G.S.; Wang, J.J. State Ownership and Abnormal Accruals in Highly-Valued Firms: Evidence from China. *J. Contemp. Account. Econ.* **2021**, *17*, 100223. [CrossRef]
10. Habib, A.; Ranasinghe, D.; Wu, J.Y.; Biswas, P.K.; Ahmad, F. Real Earnings Management: A Review of the International Literature. *Account. Financ.* **2022**, *62*, 4279–4344. [CrossRef]
11. Braam, G.; Nandy, M.; Weitzel, U.; Lodh, S. Accrual-Based and Real Earnings Management and Political Connections. *Int. J. Account.* **2015**, *50*, 111–141. [CrossRef]
12. Wang, L.; Yung, K. Do State Enterprises Manage Earnings More than Privately Owned Firms? The Case of China: Do State Enterprises Manage Earnings? *J. Bus. Financ. Account.* **2011**, *38*, 794–812. [CrossRef]
13. Bo, L.; Wu, X. The Governance Roles of State-Owned Controlling and Institutional Investors: A Perspective of Earnings Management. *Econ. Res. J.* **2009**, *2*, 81–91. (In Chinese)
14. Li, Z.F.; Zheng, Y.H.; Lian, Y.J. Equity Refinancing, Earnings Management and the Performance Decline of China Listed Companies: Viewpoint from Accruals and Real Activities Manipulation. *Chin. J. Manag. Sci.* **2011**, *19*, 49–56. (In Chinese)
15. Dong, N.; Wang, F.; Zhang, J.; Zhou, J. Ownership Structure and Real Earnings Management: Evidence from China. *J. Account. Public Policy* **2020**, *39*, 106733. [CrossRef]
16. Healy, P.M.; Wahlen, J.M. A Review of the Earnings Management Literature and Its Implications for Standard Setting. *Account. Horiz.* **1999**, *13*, 365–383. [CrossRef]
17. Capalbo, F.; Lupi, C.; Smarra, M.; Sorrentino, M. Elections and Earnings Management: Evidence from Municipally-Owned Entities. *J. Manag. Gov.* **2021**, *25*, 707–730. [CrossRef]
18. Li, Y.X.; Chen, K.J. Ultimate Controller, External Governance Environment and Earnings Management: Analysis Based on Dynamic Panel Data with System GMM Estimation. *J. Manag. Sci. China* **2014**, *9*, 56–71. (In Chinese)
19. Quan, X.F.; Wu, S.N.; Wen, F. Managerial Power, Private Income and Compensation Rigging. *Econ. Res. J.* **2010**, *45*, 73–87. (In Chinese)
20. Zang, A.Y. Evidence on the Trade-off between Real Activities Manipulation and Accrual-Based Earnings Management. *Account. Rev.* **2012**, *87*, 675–703. [CrossRef]
21. Roychowdhury, S. Earnings Management through Real Activities Manipulation. *J. Account. Econ.* **2006**, *42*, 335–370. [CrossRef]
22. Cohen, D.A.; Zarowin, P. Accrual-Based and Real Earnings Management Activities around Seasoned Equity Offerings. *J. Account. Econ.* **2010**, *50*, 2–19. [CrossRef]
23. Chan, L.H.; Chen, K.C.W.; Chen, T.Y.; Yu, Y. Substitution between Real and Accruals-Based Earnings Management after Voluntary Adoption of Compensation Clawback Provisions. *Account. Rev.* **2015**, *90*, 147–174. [CrossRef]

24. Liao, G.M.; Zhang, G.T. Earnings Management and the Efficiency of Executive Promotion in SOEs. *China Ind. Econ.* **2012**, *4*, 115–127. (In Chinese)
25. Li, Z.F.; Dong, Z.Q.; Lian, Y.J. Accruals Earnings Management or Real Activities Management? A study of the 2007 tax reform of China. *Manag. World* **2011**, *1*, 121–134. (In Chinese)
26. Gunny, K.A. The Relation Between Earnings Management Using Real Activities Manipulation and Future Performance: Evidence from Meeting Earnings Benchmarks*: Real Activities Manipulation and Future Performance. *Contemp. Account. Res.* **2010**, *27*, 855–888. [CrossRef]
27. Cohen, D.A.; Dey, A.; Lys, T.Z. Real and Accrual-Based Earnings Management in the Pre- and Post-Sarbanes-Oxley Periods. *Account. Rev.* **2008**, *83*, 757–787. [CrossRef]
28. Ding, R.; Li, J.; Wu, Z. Government Affiliation, Real Earnings Management, and Firm Performance: The Case of Privately Held Firms. *J. Bus. Res.* **2018**, *83*, 138–150. [CrossRef]
29. Chen, K.L. Media Supervision, Rule of Law and Earnings Management of Listed Companies. *Manag. Rev.* **2017**, *29*, 3–18. (In Chinese)
30. Bai, M.; Wang, R.; Yu, C.-F.; Zheng, J. Limits on Executive Pay and Stock Price Crash Risk: Evidence from a Quasi-Natural Experiment. *Pac. Basin Financ. J.* **2019**, *55*, 206–221. [CrossRef]
31. Faccio, M.; Masulis, R.W.; McCONNELL, J.J. Political Connections and Corporate Bailouts. *J. Financ.* **2006**, *61*, 2597–2635. [CrossRef]
32. Xu, L.P.; Xin, Y.; Chen, G.M. The Types of Controlling Shareholders and the Performance for China's Listed Companies. *J. World Econ.* **2006**, *29*, 78–89+96. (In Chinese)
33. Burton, F.G.; Wilks, T.J.; Zimbelman, M.F. The Impact of Audit Penalty Distributions on the Detection and Frequency of Fraudulent Reporting. *Rev Acc. Study* **2011**, *16*, 843–865. [CrossRef]
34. Li, L.; Gu, C.X.; Yu, J.Y. The Impact of Political Promotions of Top Executives in SOEs on Innovation Investment: Views from the Regulatory Independence and Marketization Process perspective. *Stud. Sci. Sci.* **2018**, *2*, 342–351. (In Chinese)
35. Wu, Y.B. The Dual Efficiency Losses in Chinese State-owned Enterprises. *Econ. Res. J.* **2012**, *3*, 15–27. (In Chinese)
36. Wang, X. Research on the Relationship between Executive Compensation Regulation in SOE and Information Transparency. Ph.D. Thesis, Southwestern University of Finance and Economics, Chengdu, China, 2010. (In Chinese).
37. Zhang, L.L.; Liu, F.; Cai, G.L. Regulatory Independence, Market-oriented Process and the Implementation of Executives' Promotion Mechanism in SOEs—Based on the SOE Executives Turnover Data from 2003 to 2012. *Manag. World* **2015**, *10*, 117–131. (In Chinese)
38. Song, T.B.; Wu, X.J. Diversification Strategy of Market Segmentation Conditions: Analysis of Central and Local State-owned Enterprises. *Reform* **2013**, *5*, 127–136. (In Chinese)
39. Li, P.G.; Shen, Y.F. The Corporate Governance Role of Media: Empirical Evidence from China. *Econ. Res. J.* **2010**, *45*, 14–27. (In Chinese)
40. Wang, Y.C.; Lin, B.; Xin, Q.Q. Institutional Environment, Civil Litigation and Earnings Management. *China Account. Rev.* **2008**, *1*, 21–40. (In Chinese)
41. Qian, A.M.; Yu, Z. Litigation Risk, State Ownership and Earnings Management. *Secur. Mark. Her.* **2017**, *7*, 16–24. (In Chinese)
42. Jones, J.J. Earnings Management during Import Relief Investigations. *J. Account. Res.* **1991**, *29*, 193. [CrossRef]
43. Dechow, P.M.; Sloan, R.G.; Sweeney, A.P. Detecting Earnings Management. *Account. Rev.* **1995**, *70*, 193–225.
44. Bartov, E.; Gul, F.A.; Tsui, J.S.L. Discretionary-Accruals Models and Audit Qualifications. *J. Account. Econ.* **2000**, *30*, 421–452. [CrossRef]
45. Kothari, S.P.; Leone, A.J.; Wasley, C.E. Performance Matched Discretionary Accrual Measures. *J. Account. Econ.* **2005**, *39*, 163–197. [CrossRef]
46. Xia, L.J. Application of Earnings Management Measuring Models in the Chinese Stock Market. *China Account. Financ. Rev.* **2003**, *2*, 94–154. (In Chinese)
47. Huang, M.; Xia, X.P. An Evaluation on Specification and Power of Discretionary Accruals Models in the Chinese Context. *Nankai Bus. Rev.* **2009**, *5*, 136–143. (In Chinese)
48. Badertscher, B.A. Overvaluation and the Choice of Alternative Earnings Management Mechanisms. *Account. Rev.* **2011**, *86*, 1491–1518. [CrossRef]
49. Wu, P.; Gao, L.; Li, X. Does the Reputation Mechanism of Media Coverage Affect Earnings Management? Evidence from China. *Chin. Manag. Stud.* **2016**, *10*, 627–656. [CrossRef]
50. Aharonson, B.S.; Bort, S. Institutional Pressure and an Organization's Strategic Response in Corporate Social Action Engagement: The Role of Ownership and Media Attention. *Strateg. Organ.* **2015**, *13*, 307–339. [CrossRef]
51. Zhao, K.S.; Zhou, P.; Liu, Y.B. Managers' Shareholding, Ownership Property and Firm Litigation Risk. *Soft Sci.* **2017**, *31*, 60–65. (In Chinese)
52. Zhang, X.H.; Chen, X.L. Special General Partnership, Potential Client Litigation Risk and Earnings Management. *Contemp. Financ& Econ.* **2015**, *7*, 108–117. (In Chinese)
53. Francis, J.; LaFond, R.; Olsson, P.; Schipper, K. The Market Pricing of Accruals Quality. *J. Account. Econ.* **2005**, *39*, 295–327. [CrossRef]
54. Watts, R.L. Conservatism in Accounting Part I: Explanations and Implications. *Account. Horiz.* **2003**, *17*, 207–221. [CrossRef]
55. Xu, X.N. Establishing Corporate Governance Mechanism and Capital Market with Legal Persons as Its Main Body. *J. Reform* **1997**, *5*, 28–30. (In Chinese)
56. Krishnan, J.; Su, L.; Zhang, Y. Nonaudit Services and Earnings Management in the Pre-SOX and Post-SOX Eras. *AUDITING A J. Pract. Theory* **2011**, *30*, 103–123. [CrossRef]
57. Fan, G.; Wang, X.L. *The Report on the Relative Rrocess of Marketization of Each Region in China*; The Economic Science Press: Beijing, China, 2003. (In Chinese)

58. Liu, Q.; Lu, Z. (Joe) Corporate Governance and Earnings Management in the Chinese Listed Companies: A Tunneling Perspective. *J. Corp. Financ.* **2007**, *13*, 881–906. [CrossRef]
59. Aharony, J.; Wang, J.; Yuan, H. Tunneling as an Incentive for Earnings Management during the IPO Process in China. *J. Account. Public Policy* **2010**, *29*, 1–26. [CrossRef]
60. García Lara, J.M.; Osma, B.G.; Neophytou, E. Earnings Quality in Ex-post Failed Firms. *Account. Bus. Res.* **2009**, *39*, 119–138. [CrossRef]
61. Campa, D.; Camacho-Miñano, M.-M. Earnings Management among Bankrupt Non-listed Firms: Evidence from Spain. *Span. J. Financ. Account. /Revista Española de Financiación y Contabilidad* **2014**, *43*, 3–20. [CrossRef]
62. Luo, J.H. Media Coverage and the Effectiveness of Executive Compensation Contracts. *J. Financ. Res.* **2018**, *3*, 190–206. (In Chinese)

Disclaimer/Publisher's Note: The statements, opinions and data contained in all publications are solely those of the individual author(s) and contributor(s) and not of MDPI and/or the editor(s). MDPI and/or the editor(s) disclaim responsibility for any injury to people or property resulting from any ideas, methods, instructions or products referred to in the content.

Article

Integrating Replenishment Policy and Maintenance Services in a Stochastic Inventory System with Bilateral Movements

Yonit Barron

Industrial Engineering and Management, Ariel University, Ariel 40700, Israel; ybarron@ariel.ac.il

Abstract: We study an inventory control problem with two storage facilities: a primary warehouse (PW) of limited capacity M, and a subsidiary one (SW) of sufficiently large capacity. Two types of customers are considered: individual customers arriving at (positive and negative) linear rates governed by a Markov chain, and retailers arriving according to a Markov arrival process and bringing a (positive and negative) random number of items. The PW is managed according to a triple-parameter band policy (M, S, s), $0 \leq s < S \leq M$, under a lost sales assumption. Under this policy, as soon as the stock level at the PW falls below s, a refilling to S is performed by a distributor after a random lead-time. However, if the stock exceeds level S when the distributor arrives, no refilling is carried out, and only maintenance services are performed. Items that exceed level M are transferred to the SW at a negligible amount of time for those used in related products. Our cost structure includes a fixed order cost, a variable cost for each item supplied by the distributor, a cost for the additional maintenance, a salvage payment for each transferred item from the PW to the SW, and a loss cost for each unsatisfied item due to demands. We seek to determine the optimal thresholds that minimize the expected overall cost under the discounted criterion. Applying first-passage time results, we present a simple set of equations that provide managers with a useful and an efficient tool to derive the optimal thresholds. Sensitivity analysis and fruitful conclusions along with future scope of research directions are provided.

Keywords: inventory; band policy; MAP; Markov chain; first-passage times

MSC: 90B05; 60J28; 60G51

Citation: Barron, Y. Integrating Replenishment Policy and Maintenance Services in a Stochastic Inventory System with Bilateral Movements. Mathematics 2023, 11, 864. https://doi.org/10.3390/math11040864

Academic Editor: Yong He

Received: 27 December 2022
Revised: 21 January 2023
Accepted: 28 January 2023
Published: 8 February 2023

Copyright: © 2023 by the author. Licensee MDPI, Basel, Switzerland. This article is an open access article distributed under the terms and conditions of the Creative Commons Attribution (CC BY) license (https://creativecommons.org/licenses/by/4.0/).

1. Introduction

An inventory model is characterized by an inconsistency and volatility in the flow of items in and out of the supply network. Inventory management has been studied for decades, and volatile market conditions have increased the complexity of modeling and analyzing supply chains. Components such as demands, returns, delivery times, and collaborative initiatives among partners have become more variable. This increasing uncertainty has a direct impact on the inventory level. Although most inventory models assume that the manager owns a storage facility of unlimited capacity, it has been observed that, in real life, this assumption may be unrealistic. When inventory capacity is limited, the on-hand inventory may exceed the warehouse's capacity and need to be transferred to an external warehouse of insufficient capacity. Managing integrated storage facilities effectively and efficiently is an increasingly important task for companies in order to gain competitive advantages [1].

In the present paper, we introduce an integrated inventory management problem with two types of storage facilities: a primary warehouse (PW) of limited capacity M, and a subsidiary warehouse (SW) of sufficiently large capacity. The main storage facility, the PW, is used for ongoing demands and returns. We consider two types of customers arriving to the PW, individual customers and retailers; both arrivals are characterized by a continuous-time Markov chain (CTMC). Each individual customer demands or returns a unit, and the inter-arrival times between successive arrivals are negligible. Thus, these arrivals can be naturally approximated by continuous linear rates, where negative rates represent demands, and positive rates represent returns. In addition, we consider a stream of retailers, each bringing a positive or negative number of items. Here, the stock level jumps down (for a demand) or up (for a return) at the arrival instances, and the batch sizes are independent and identically distributed (i.i.d.) random variables (r.v.s), having phase-type (PH) distributions (see [2] for more details on the phase-distributions).

We assume that the management of the PW is assisted by the services of an outsourcing partner (for our needs, called the *distributor*), and directly affects the inventory level of the SW. Specifically:

(a) *Management of PW.* (i) The PW is managed according to a triple-parameter band policy (M, S, s) $(0 \leq s < S \leq M)$, i.e., when the on-hand stock drops to some level s, an order is placed to purchase more stock from the manufacturer in order to raise the current level up to level S. As in practice, the order arrives by the distributor after some random time (called the lead time); nevertheless, it is assumed that, during that lead time, new orders are not allowed. Upon arrival, the PW is refilled up to level S; in addition, maintenance activities are provided by the distributor. It may happen that, when the distributor arrives, the stock exceeds S due to returns; in such a case, no refilling is performed at the PW (however, the distributor is still employed in these maintenance activities; see Point (c) below). Furthermore, (ii) any demand or part of the demand that is not satisfied is lost. (iii) The PW has a limited storage capacity of M items; each time the on-hand stock exceeds level M, the excess amount is transferred to the SW in a negligible amount of time.

(b) *Storage at the SW.* The SW has unlimited capacity. We assume that each unit of material that is transferred from the PW is processed as one unit of material to be used in the SW; the transferred material is accumulated and used to satisfied related products. Thus, the SW is not accessible to customers.

(c) *Inventory management.* Each time the distributor arrives, he provides some basic maintenance services, including cleaning, organizing, and emptying the SW, as needed, and the SW stores with zero items. We assume that these maintenance services are an integral part of the distributor's duties; therefore, no additional payment is due for this work. However, if the PW is not refilled, the distributor is rewarded (a kind of monetary compensation) for his services.

A schematic diagram of the relationship between the existing entities is presented in Figure 1.

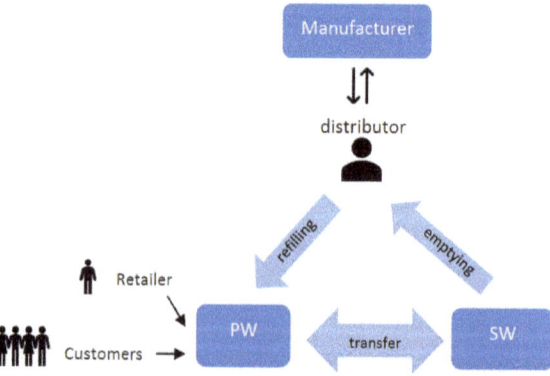

Figure 1. The relationship between the manufacturer, distributor, customers, and warehouses.

Our model is motivated by various practical settings. The first example is taken from the collaboration between firms and farms—specifically, the vegetable marketing firm

Chasalat Alei Katif (https://www.aleikatif.org) (27 December 2022), which specializes in growing insect-free, fresh cabbage without using pesticides. The firm markets products from several farms, each with several greenhouses for growing organic cabbage. The ripe cabbage is stored in the PW, which serves both individual customers and retailers. When the stock in the PW falls below a certain level, the farms supply the firm with additional stock, which is time-consuming. However, according to a special agreement, if the supplied cabbages cannot be stored in the PW (due to capacity constraints), they are sliced, and accumulated until they are sold privately by the farms.

The second example is taken from the collaboration between medical centers and university scientists [3]. Here, specialists are responsible for the operation and management of the blood bank. When a lack of blood donations is observed, the associated medical faculty is enlisted to help carry out a rapid and immediate blood donation campaign on campus. Since the capacity of the storage facility is limited, the surplus blood donations are transferred to the university faculty for academic use, after which it cannot be used by patients.

In this paper, we assume the following costs and rewards: (i) a fixed cost for each order; (ii) a cost for each item supplied by the distributor (this cost includes the payment to the distributor for his maintenance services). (iii) If the PW is not refilled due to a high inventory level, the distributor is rewarded for their maintenance services; (iv) a salvage payment for each item transferred from the PW to the SW; and (iv) a loss cost is charged for each unsatisfied item at the PW.

We seek to determine the optimal levels of s and S that minimize the overall discounted cost of managing the warehouses. We further assume a fixed cost to operate the PW and, thus, each item has a negligible storage cost. This assumption has many applications in reality, e.g., in blood inventory management and in organic food storage, where the cost of storing an item is negligible compared to the cost of cooling the storage facility. Moreover, we assume that the distributor arrives after an exponentially distributed lead time. This assumption is practical when the lead time depends on different logistics factors—for example, for a distributor that serves several independent companies that line up as an M/M/1 queue. The time it takes to prepare and deliver the items can be interpreted as a sojourn time that is exponentially distributed. Due to variable delivery times, the company may ask the distributor for a flexible contract that allows for delays or cancellations of outstanding orders.

The policy addressed here expands the band (S, s)-type policy. As far as we know, most of the existing studies under the (S, s) control policy consider continuous movements and allows at most unilateral jumps; there are no studies on inventory management that consider a Markov-modulated process with bilateral continuous and jump movements. However, when considering the significant increase in returns and the uncertainty in lead times, allowing double-side changes is more appropriate for modeling inventory management. Fluctuations in inventory levels, where the inventory level not only decreases due to demands but also increases due to returns, make the analysis much more challenging. From a managerial perspective, this difficulty becomes the main driving force behind for an integrated inventory management.

The main contributions of the paper are fourfold: (1) We differ from existing works in the inventory management literature by considering continuous and batch-type bilateral changes, which are both governed by the underlying Markov chain. We further assume phase-distributed batch amounts, given that any nonnegative continuous distribution can be approximated by a phase distribution. By that, we capture the uncertainty of customers' consumption habits impacted by a fluctuating environment. As a result, our framework can be adapted to a wide range of applications. (2) We extend classic inventory models to include a limited storage capacity and, thus, introduce a simple and practical (M, S, s)-type band policy. As in practice, we further assume that the fixed cost is paid at the time that the order is placed, and that the variable cost is paid at the time the PW is refilled. This difference in timing is significantly important and may lead to cost saving. (3) We also contribute to the inventory management literature by implementing the new business concept integrating partnerships for managing the warehouses. (4) Most existing papers employ analytic approaches, such as a dynamic programming approach [4,5] difference-differential equations approach [6] or scale function [7,8]; by contrast, we use a more probabilistic and intuitive approach. We combine the first-step conditioning technique for the expectation, renewal theory and the strong Markov property (which says that, for a Markovian process $X(t)$, conditioning on state at a given stopping time T, the probabilistic behavior of the process depends only on its value at time T and discards its past behavior; see [2]). By doing so, we build a relatively simple set of equations that provide managers with a useful and efficient tool to derive optimal thresholds. To the best of our knowledge, this is the first time that first-passage time results have been carried out in bilateral movements in the inventory management literature. We further note that many studies deal with the long-run average criterion, without taking timing into consideration [5,9]. Our results show that timing significantly impacts the system performance and is a crucial factor; therefore, it should be taken into account.

From our conclusions, we numerically glean some important insights. Firstly, the total cost seems to be convex in S and s (for a fixed M; see Figure 4). Although we cannot prove this result, it enables us to numerically obtain the optimal thresholds S^* and s^* using a linear search over the range $0 \leq s < S < M$. Secondly, we show the impact of the limited capacity of the PW on the optimal thresholds, especially when the transfer cost is high (see Figure 4a, Table 2, and the discussions thereafter). Thirdly, as demands become more frequent, it becomes worthwhile to order more frequently and for smaller quantities. In such a case, the impact on S^* is negligible and, surprisingly, the weight of the cost's components is relatively fixed (here, the transfer cost is negligible). By contrast, more returns prompt the manager to reduce the frequency of orders and enlarge their quantities. Here, the weight of the cost of the distributor's services increases relative to the weight of the loss cost (see Figures 5–8). Fourthly, investigating the impact of the timing, we observe that, when the discount factor is high, postponing the call for the distributor becomes economically profitable (see Figure 9). The outline of the paper is as follows: In Section 2, we review the related literature. Section 3 presents the mathematical structure of the stock levels at the PW and SW; the cost components are also detailed. The core preliminaries are given in Section 4. Section 5 derives the expected discounted cost components; a summary of the costs' derivation is given in Appendix A.2. Numerical examples, observations, and insights are provided in Section 6. Finally, Section 7 concludes. Technical parts of the proofs are relegated to Appendices B.1–B.3.

2. Literature Review

It is well established in the literature that customer flows can exhibit high variability and unpredictably [10,11], state dependency [12], and batch patterns [13,14]. Thus, modeling the behavior of customers has become a key challenge in inventory management. These modeling challenges are aggravated by the rapid spread of the home shopping phenomenon, which force retailers to incorporate the occurrence of returns on a daily basis [4]. Real-word examples of such variability include the introduction of new products, where the flow rates are obviously non-stationary and evolve throughout the stages of the product's life cycle [15,16], fluctuating environments, where economic conditions, extreme weather, technological advancements, competition, and dynamic events can perturb customer flows [17–19], home shopping and internet retailing, where a high return rate, particularly for electronic and computer devices, significantly changes customers' behavior [20,21]. Any of these sources of variability on its own impacts the on-hand stock level and, thus, complicates the analysis of the inventory model. Therefore, a considerable portion of the related literature usually uses Markov processes due to their versatility in matching key statistical properties of the customers' consumption needs [10,13,22,23].

In this study, the inventory level changes are the sum of continuous linear rates forming a likewise fluid process, and instantaneous big inflows and outflows governed by a Poisson process. For example, a company that sells its product through two channels, usual daily sell contracts and one-time opportunities [24], or a manufacturer who produces a component needed for few products, as well as a replacement [25]. Consequently, an excellent example of a return in batches policy is out-of-fashion products, and parts delivered to maintenance service engineers, particularly in isolated areas [4].

We assume that the batch sizes come from the family of phase distributions. The advantage of a PH distribution is that its Markovian nature allows for an exact analysis and performance evaluation; thus, they are often used [12,13,26,27]. When general distributions are appropriate, phase distributions can be taken into account in a natural way, as any nonnegative continuous distribution of the probability can be approximated with a phase-type distribution [2].

We note that incorporating continuous rates and instantaneous jumps is well studied also in economics and cash management (e.g., loads and withdrawals), in healthcare management (e.g., daily patients and unexpected disasters), in reliability models (e.g., parts delivered to maintenance service engineers in geographically spread out areas), and in chemical production systems and gas stations. More examples are available in [28–30].

In the literature, the (S,s) control policy is one of the most widely used [24]. The optimality of (S,s)-type policies has been investigated for various inventory models, including those with discrete and continuous time reviews, different time horizons, discounted or average cost criteria, and backlogging or lost-sales. Under continuous time, the underlying stochastic stock level governing the state variables is typically linked to either varying rates [4,31], fluid processes [32], Wiener processes [9,33–36], renewal processes [5,12,37,38], superposition of deterministic rates combined with a renewal process [25], and a one-sided Lèvy process [7,39,40]. Using batch-size patterns, Bensoussan et al. [41] consider two models: one model is a mixture of a diffusion process and a compound Poisson process with exponentially distributed jump sizes, and the second model, as in Presman and Sethi [25], is a mixture of constant demand governed by a compound Poisson process. Their work was generalized by Benkherouf and Bensoussan [6] to a general compound Poisson process. Yamazaki [8] tackled the inventory problem when the demand follows a Lèvy process with jumps having infinite activity/variation. Chakravarthy and Rao [42] assume that the customers arrive according to a Markovian arrival process (MAP) with demand of varying sizes. Along with this line, Barron [13,18] studies a mixture of a fluid process and a MAP demand process. For a comprehensive survey, see [24].

All papers cited above consider a one-dimensional inventory process. For the multi-dimensional process, several models used in the literature focus on the derivation of the Laplace transform of the first-passage time in a Markov-modulated process with bilateral random jumps, mostly for studying various financial problems (e.g., [26,39,43–45]).

Furthermore, the increasing environment uncertainty has been mitigated over the last few decades, the phenomenon of a gradual transition to collaborative and integrative approaches to achieving optimal supply chain performance. In this paper, we assume that the distributor also assists with the maintenance and upkeep of the storage. Particularly, it has become customary for managers to motivate high-quality relationships with their distributor. Research on marketing shows that most distributors also provide a range of services such as technical support, warranty, and other complex services [46–48].

To outline our position, an overview of the most relevant literature studies concerning the continuous-review base stock policy is given in Table A1 in Appendix A.1. To the best of our knowledge, the combination of random demands and returns (bilateral continuous and jump type) in supply chain collaboration under the (S,s) policy with cancellation has not been explored in literature of inventory management; hence, the model developed here significantly contributes to the literature.

3. The Stock Level Processes at PW and SW

In this section, we use similar notations to those of Breuer [27] (see also [18,26]).

Consider two storage facilities, the PW and the SW, and two types of customers, namely, individual customers and retailers. The demands (returns) of the individual customers form a likewise fluid process with linear rates, governed by a continuous-time Markov chain (CTMC) that is used as a background environment as follows. Let $\widetilde{\mathcal{J}} = \{\widetilde{J}(t) : t \geq 0\}$ be a CTMC with state space $\widetilde{E}$, initial probability vector $\eta = \left[\eta_1, \eta_2, \ldots, \eta_{|\widetilde{E}|}\right]$, and infinitesimal generator $\widetilde{\mathbb{Q}} = (\widetilde{q}_{ij})_{i,j \in \widetilde{E}}$. Let π be the stationary probability vector; π is the unique solution of the equation $\pi \widetilde{\mathbb{Q}} = 0$ such that $\pi e = 1$. When the state equals $i \in \widetilde{E}$, products are returned at rate r_i, and demand is observed at rate d_i by the individual customers. The growth rate is denoted by $c_i = r_i - d_i$, which can be positive or negative. Thus, the state space $\widetilde{E}$ is composed of two subsets $\widetilde{E} = E_p \cup E_n$, where E_p includes the increasing states, $E_p = \{i : c_i > 0\}$, and E_n includes the decreasing states, $E_n = \{i : c_i < 0\}$. Accordingly, we use the terms ascending (descending) environment when $i \in E_p$ (E_n).

Next, we describe the retailers' arrivals. The retailers arrive at random times and form a Poisson process of instantaneous big inflows (returns) or outflows (demands). Specifically, we assume that, when an ascending environment is observed, i.e., when there are more returns than demands, the manager offers retailers the opportunity to demand products, in order to balance the stock level. On the other hand, when a descending environment is observed, i.e., when there are more demands than returns, the manager offers retailers the ability to return products.

For the mathematical description, we define the process $\widehat{\mathcal{I}} = \{\widehat{I}(t) : t \geq 0\}$ as a special case of a Lèvy process $\widehat{\mathcal{I}}^{(i)}$ with a drift c_i (to describe the customers) and a Lèvy measure $\widehat{v}_i$ (to describe the retailers) during intervals when the phase equals $i \in \widetilde{E}$. We assume that $\widehat{v}_i$ takes the form

$$\widehat{v}_i(dx) = \lambda_i^{(+)} \mathbf{1}_{\{i \in E_n\}} \boldsymbol{\alpha}^{(i+)} \exp(\mathbb{T}^{(i+)}x)\boldsymbol{\eta}^{(i+)}dx + \lambda_i^{(-)} \mathbf{1}_{\{i \in E_p\}} \boldsymbol{\alpha}^{(i-)} \exp(-\mathbb{T}^{(i-)}x)\boldsymbol{\eta}^{(i-)}dx, \; x > 0 \qquad (1)$$

for all $i \in \widetilde{E}$. Here, $\lambda_i^{(\pm)} \geq 0$ is the retailers' arrival rates, and the retailers' batch amounts $U^{(i\pm)}$ are PH distributed r.v.s with initial probability vectors $\boldsymbol{\alpha}^{(i\pm)}$ and transition rate matrices $\mathbb{T}^{(i\pm)}$; i.e., the arrival process is a compound Poisson process with jump sizes $U^{(i+)} \sim PH\left(\boldsymbol{\alpha}^{(i+)}, \mathbb{T}^{(i+)}\right)$ of order m_i^+ when $i \in E_n$, and $U^{(i-)} \sim PH\left(\boldsymbol{\alpha}^{(i-)}, \mathbb{T}^{(i-)}\right)$ of order m_i^- when $i \in E_p$. Let $\boldsymbol{\eta}^{(i\pm)} = -\mathbb{T}^{(i\pm)}e$ be the exit vectors. Now, the process $\widehat{\mathcal{I}}$ is a MAP-modulated process with upward jumps and downward jumps. Let $\boldsymbol{\lambda}^{(+)}$ be a $(1 \times |E_n|)$ vector whose i component is $\lambda_i^{(+)}, i \in E_n$. Similarly, let $\boldsymbol{\lambda}^{(-)}$ be a $(1 \times |E_p|)$ vector whose i component is $\lambda_i^{(-)}, i \in E_p$. Finally, define the $\left(1 \times \sum_{i=1}^{|E_n|} m_i^+\right)$ vector $\boldsymbol{\alpha}^{(+)} = \left(\boldsymbol{\alpha}^{(1+)}, \ldots, \boldsymbol{\alpha}^{(|E_n|+)}\right)$, and the $\left(1 \times \sum_{i=1}^{|E_p|} m_i^-\right)$ vector $\boldsymbol{\alpha}^{(-)} = \left(\boldsymbol{\alpha}^{(1-)}, \ldots, \boldsymbol{\alpha}^{(|E_p|-)}\right)$.

The PW is controlled by a triple-parameter band policy $(M, S, s), 0 \leq s < S \leq M$, under a lost sales policy. Let $\widetilde{\mathcal{I}}_o = \{\widetilde{I}_o(t) : t \geq 0\}$ be the on-hand stock level at the PW. We assume that, as soon as $\widetilde{\mathcal{I}}_o$ drops to or below level s, a delivery is ordered and arrives by the distributor after an exponential lead time; during that lead time, new orders are not allowed. When the distributor arrives, if the on-hand stock increases to or above level S, no items are refilled; otherwise, the stock is refilled up to level S. Thus, the amount refilled at arrival time is random and is equal to $\max(S - \widetilde{I}_o(t), 0) \equiv \left[S - \widetilde{I}_o(t)\right]^+$ items. We further assume that the PW has a capacity of $M > S$ units. Every time the inventory exceeds level M, the excess items are transferred from PW to SW in a negligible amount of time and for some fee. Hence, $\widetilde{\mathcal{I}}_o$ lies in the range $[0, M]$.

Next, we describe the management of the SW. The SW has unlimited capacity. Each time the distributor arrives, he provides some basic maintenance activities and empties the SW; no additional payment is given to him for this work. However, if the PW is not refilled, the distributor is rewarded for his service. Let $\widetilde{\mathcal{I}}_R = \{\widetilde{I}_R(t) : t \geq 0\}$ be the on-hand stock level at the SW; Note that, in contrast to $\widetilde{\mathcal{I}}_o$, the process $\widetilde{\mathcal{I}}_R$ is not bounded from above. For simplicity, we further assume that $\widetilde{\mathcal{I}}_o(0) = S$ and $\widetilde{\mathcal{I}}_R(0) = 0$.

Let $\mathcal{L}_n, n \geq 1$ be a sequence of i.i.d. $exp(\mu)$-distributed r.v.s representing the lead times independent of $(\widetilde{\mathcal{I}}_o, \widetilde{\mathcal{J}})$. Let $\mathcal{Z}_1 = \inf\{t : t > 0, \widetilde{I}_o(t) \leq s\}$ be the first time that the stock level drops to or below level s, and thus a delivery is ordered. Let $K_1 = \mathcal{Z}_1 + \mathcal{L}_1$ be the first arrival time of the distributor. We define, recursively, the following stopping times:

$$
\begin{aligned}
\mathcal{Z}_n &= \inf\left\{t : t > \sum_{i=1}^{n-1} K_i, \widetilde{I}_o(t) \leq s\right\}, & n &= 2, 3, \ldots \\
K_n &= \mathcal{Z}_n + \mathcal{L}_n, & n &= 2, 3, \ldots
\end{aligned}
\tag{2}
$$

The r.v. $\mathcal{Z}_n, n = 1, 2, \ldots$, represents the n-th *ordering* time; the r.v $K_n, n = 1, 2, \ldots$ represents the n-th *arrival* time of the distributor. Recall that $\widetilde{I}_o(\mathcal{Z}_n) = s$ occurs only due to a continuous hitting linear rate, i.e., by a customer's demand, while $\widetilde{I}_o(\mathcal{Z}_n) < s$ occurs due to a downward jump, i.e., by a retailer's demand. At arrival times, $\left[S - \widetilde{I}_o(K_n)\right]^+$ items are refilled, such that, if $\widetilde{I}_o(K_n) < S$, then $\widetilde{I}_o$ is refilled with $S - \widetilde{I}_o(K_n)$ items and starts from level S; otherwise, no refilling is carried out. In addition, at times $K_n, n = 1, 2, \ldots$, the SW is emptied. Thus, we have $\widetilde{I}_o(K_n) \geq S, \widetilde{I}_R(K_n) = 0, n = 1, 2, \ldots$. Finally, we define J_i as

$$
J_i = \min\{K_n > J_{i-1} : \widetilde{I}_o(K_n-) < S\}, n = 1, 2, \ldots\}, i = 1, 2, \ldots, \text{with } J_0 = 0, \tag{3}
$$

to represent the i-th (actual) *refilling* time of the PW (and emptying time of the SW). Clearly, we obtain $\widetilde{I}_o(J_i) = S$ and $\widetilde{I}_R(J_i) = 0$ for $i = 1, 2, \ldots$. It is easy to verify that the processes $\widetilde{I}_o(t)$ and $\widetilde{I}_R(t), t \geq 0$ are semi-regenerative processes with regenerative points $J_i, i = 1, 2, \ldots$ Let $C_i = J_i - J_{i-1}, i = 1, 2, \ldots$ be the time between two consecutive (actual) refillings. A typical sample path of $\widetilde{I}_o(t)$ and $\widetilde{I}_R(t)$ is depicted in Figure 2.

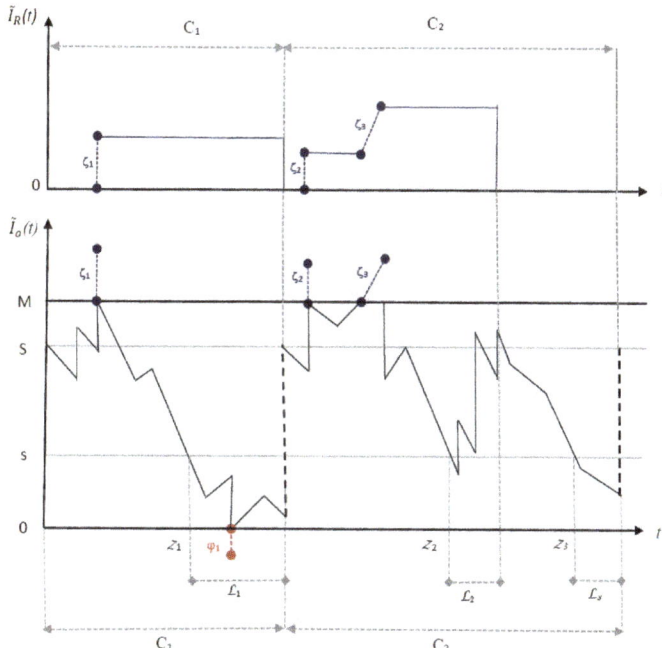

Figure 2. A typical sample path of $\widetilde{I}_o(t)$ and $\widetilde{I}_R(t)$.

The stock levels of PW and SW, $\widetilde{I}_o(t)$ and $\widetilde{I}_R(t)$, are depicted in the bottom and top parts of Figure 2, respectively. We start with the first cycle. At time $\mathcal{Z}_1$, we have

$\tilde{I}_o(\mathcal{Z}_1) < s$, and thus a delivery is ordered. After lead time $\mathcal{L}_1$, when the distributor arrives, $\tilde{I}_o(K_1 = \mathcal{Z}_1 + \mathcal{L}_1) < S$, and thus the refilling is carried out, the stock is raised up to level S, and the cycle ends. At that time, the SW is emptied by the distributor. Here, $J_1 = K_1$. By contrast, during the second cycle, a delivery is ordered twice. At the first time, $\mathcal{Z}_2$, the distributor arrives after lead time $\mathcal{L}_2$ when $\tilde{I}_o(K_2 = \mathcal{Z}_2 + \mathcal{L}_2) > S$, and thus no items are supplied and only maintenance service is performed, leading to $\tilde{I}_R(K_2) = 0$. The second order is placed at time $\mathcal{Z}_3$, when $\tilde{I}_o(\mathcal{Z}_3) < s$. Here, we see that $\tilde{I}_o(K_3 = \mathcal{Z}_3 + \mathcal{L}_3) < S$, and thus the PW is refilled, the SW is emptied, and the cycle ends. Here, $J_2 = K_3$ and we obtain $\tilde{I}_o(J_2) = S$ and $\tilde{I}_R(J_2) = 0$. Figure 2 also shows that level M is exceeded three times: once during cycle 1 with ζ_1 items (due to a return by a retailer), and twice during cycle 2 with ζ_2 (due to return by a retailer) and with ζ_3 items (due to a return by a customer); these overstocking events are represented by the blue segments. The excess items are accumulated in the SW and emptied at times K_1 and K_2 (we note that maintenance services are also provided at time $K_3 = \mathcal{Z}_3 + \mathcal{L}_3$; however, since $\tilde{I}_o(t) < M$ and $\tilde{I}_R(t) = 0$ for $t \in (K_2, K_3]$, no change in $\tilde{I}_R$ is depicted in the figure). In addition, we see one shortage event, with amounts of φ_1 (due to a demand by a retailer), represented by the red segment.

Our aim is to find the optimal parameters in order to optimize the expected discounted total cost. To that end, we let $\mathbb{E}_x(e^{-\beta C})$ be the $\left(\left|\tilde{E}\right| \times \left|\tilde{E}\right|\right)$ conditional Laplace transform matrix (LST) of the cycle length whose (i,j)-th component is:

$$\left(\mathbb{E}_x(e^{-\beta C})\right)_{i,j} = E(e^{-\beta C} 1_{\{\tilde{J}(C)=j\}} \mid \tilde{I}_o(0) = x, \tilde{J}(0) = i), i,j \in \tilde{E}.$$

Applying renewal theory, we can express all the cost functionals by using the first cycle.

(a) *Order cost* $OC(\beta)$. At ordering time, a fixed cost Y^+ is paid. This cost is non-refundable (even when no refilling is performed due to returns). Note that there may be multiple orders per cycle, each costing Y^+. Thus, we obtain

$$OC(\beta) = Y^+ \sum_n E_S(e^{-\beta \mathcal{Z}_n}) = Y^+ \eta \left(\mathbb{I} - \mathbb{E}_S(e^{-\beta C})\right)^{-1} OC_S(\beta), \quad (4)$$

where $OC_S(\beta)$ is the $(|\tilde{E}| \times 1)$ vector, representing the total expected discounted ordering times per cycle, given $\tilde{I}_o(0) = S, \tilde{J}(t) \in \tilde{E}$.

(b) *Distributor's service cost.* At times J_n, $n = 1, 2, \ldots$, the PW is refilled with $S - \tilde{I}_o(J_n-)$ items and the cycle ends; this amount is random depending on the stock level upon arrival. Let γ be the cost of each refilled item (and is charged when the distributor arrives). When no refilling is performed, the distributor is rewarded with Y^- for his maintenance services. Summarizing, we obtain

$$DC(\beta) = \gamma \sum_n E_S\left(e^{-\beta J_n}(S - \tilde{I}_o(J_n))\right) + Y^- \sum_n E_S\left(e^{-\beta K_n} 1_{\{\tilde{I}_o(K_n)>S\}}\right)$$

$$= \gamma \cdot S \sum_n E_S\left(e^{-\beta C_n}\right) + \sum_n E_S(e^{-\beta K_n})\left(Y^- 1_{\{\tilde{I}_o(K_n)>S\}} - \gamma \tilde{I}_o(K_n) 1_{\{\tilde{I}_o(K_n)<S\}}\right)$$

$$= \eta \left[\mathbb{I} - \mathbb{E}_S(e^{-\beta C})\right]^{-1} DC_S(\beta), \quad (5)$$

where $DC_S(\beta)$ is the expected discounted cost per cycle incurred by the distributor. Note that, while Y^- may be charged several times per cycle (due to maintenance services), γ is charged only once, at the end of the cycle, when the PW is refilled.

(c) *Transfer cost* $SC(\beta)$. When the on-hand stock in the PW exceeds level M, the excess amount is transferred to the SW. Let ν be the cost of transferring each item. Here, level M is exceeded either continuously by an individual customer at a linear rate $c_{\tilde{J}(t)}, \tilde{J}(t) \in E_p$, or by an upward jump due to a demand by a retailer. In the latter case, denote by Ξ_n the n-th time that level M is exceeded by an upward jump, and let ζ_n be the amount exceeding level M and transferred to SW at time Ξ_n. The overall discounted transfer cost is given by (see also Remark 1, Point 1):

$$SC(\beta) = v\left(\sum_{n=1}^{\infty} E(e^{-\beta \Xi_n}\zeta_n) + \int_0^{\infty} E(e^{-\beta t}c_{\widetilde{J}(t)}1_{\{\widetilde{I}_0(t)=M,\widetilde{J}(t)\in E_p\}})dt\right)$$
$$= \eta v\left(\mathbb{I} - \mathbb{E}(e^{-\beta C})\right)^{-1} SC_S(\beta), \tag{6}$$

where the $(|\widetilde{E}| \times 1)$ vector $SC_S(\beta)$ is the expected discounted amount exceeding level M per cycle. Note that the first (second) term of (6) refers to a jump (continuous linear rate).

(d) *Loss cost* $LC(\beta)$. Any demand or part of a demand that is not satisfied is lost. Similarly, we distinguish between customers and retailers. Level 0 is hit either continuously by an individual customer at a linear rate $-c_{\widetilde{J}(t)}$, $\widetilde{J}(t) \in E_n$, or by a retailer by a downward jump. Let Φ_n be the n-th time that level 0 is hit by a downward jump, and let φ_n be the number of unsatisfied demands at time Φ_n. Let ϕ be the cost of each unsatisfied demand. The expected discounted loss cost is given by (see also Remark 1, Points 1 and 2):

$$LC(\beta) = \phi\left(\sum_{n=1}^{\infty} E(e^{-\beta \Phi_n}\varphi_n) - \int_0^{\infty} E(e^{-\beta t}c_{\widetilde{J}(t)}1_{\{\widetilde{I}_0(t)=0,\widetilde{J}(t)\in E_n\}})dt\right)$$
$$= \eta\phi\left(\mathbb{I} - \mathbb{E}_S(e^{-\beta C})\right)^{-1} LC_S(\beta), \tag{7}$$

where the $(|\widetilde{E}| \times 1)$ vector $LC_S(\beta)$ is the expected discounted unsatisfied demands per cycle.

Remark 1.
1. *Regarding the individual customers. We emphasize that, when the on-hand stock level M is exceeding in an ascending state $i \in E_p$, demands are continuously satisfied by some of the returns (and the remaining returns are transferred to the SW at rate $c_i = r_i - d_i > 0$). Similarly, when the on-hand stock level 0 is hit in a descending state $i \in E_n$, some of the demands are continuously satisfied by returns (and the remaining unsatisfied demands are lost at rate $-c_i > 0$).*
2. *As in practice, here we assume that new arrivals (both customers and retailers) are willing to accept that only some of their demands are satisfied as long as they receive some compensation for the unsatisfied demands. Nowadays, such a policy is highly valued and and even considered by the customer as a high level of service.*

The expected total cost of integrated inventory management is therefore

$$TC(\beta) = OC(\beta) + DC(\beta) + SC(\beta) + LC(\beta).$$

In what follows, we denote by $(\mathbb{A})_{ij}$ the elements of a matrix $\mathbb{A}$, by $\mathbb{A}_{i,j}$ the submatrix of $\mathbb{A}$ with row indices in E_i and column indices in E_j; in particular, the matrix $\mathbf{0}_{i,j}$ represents the $(|E_i| \times |E_j|)$ zero matrix. Vectors are denoted by bold letters (e.g., $\mathbf{E}, \mathbf{P}$), and matrices by blackboard letters (e.g., $\mathbb{E}, \mathbb{P}$). The $(|E| \times |E|)$ conditional matrix expectation, given an initial state $(x, i \in E)$, is denoted by $\mathbb{E}_x(.) = \mathbb{E}(. \mid I(0) = x)$ (and, similarly, the $(|E| \times 1)$ conditional vector expectation $\mathbf{E}_x(.)$). Specifically, we use the notations $\overline{\mathbb{E}}_x(.)$ and $\underline{\mathbb{E}}_x(.)^T$ to denote the submatrices of $\mathbb{E}_x(.)$, of order $(|E_p| \times |E|)$ and $(|E_n| \times |E|)$, respectively, associated with the ascending and the descending states of $\mathbb{E}_x(.)$, i.e., $\mathbb{E}_x(.) = \left(\overline{\mathbb{E}}_x(.), \underline{\mathbb{E}}_x(.)\right)^T$. Following convention, we let $1_{\{A\}}$ be the indicator of an event A, $\mathbf{e} = (1,\ldots,1)^T$ be the unit column vector, and $(A\ B)$ be the matrix obtained by stringing the matrix B after the matrix A, all of the appropriate size.

4. Preliminaries
4.1. Markov-Modulated Fluid Flow Process for MAP

Following Breuer [27], let $\widetilde{\mathcal{J}} = \{\widetilde{J}(t), t \geq 0\}$ be a CTMC with state space $\widetilde{E}$ and infinitesimal generator $\widetilde{\mathbb{Q}} = (\widetilde{q}_{ij})_{i,j \in \widetilde{E}}$. Let $\widehat{\mathcal{I}} = \{\widehat{I}(t), t \geq 0\}$ be a real-valued process evolving like a Lévy process $\widehat{\mathcal{I}}^{(i)}$ with a drift c_i (negative or positive) and a Lévy measure $\widehat{v}_i$ (given by (1)) when $i \in \widetilde{E}$; here, we assume a compound Poisson jump. The jump sizes $U^{(i\pm)}$ are PH-distributed r.v.s $PH\left(\boldsymbol{\alpha}^{(i\pm)}, \mathbb{T}^{(i\pm)}\right)$ of order $m_i^{\mp}$ and depend on the phases $i \in \widetilde{E}$ prior to the jumps. The two-dimensional process $(\widehat{\mathcal{I}}, \widetilde{\mathcal{J}})$ is called a MAP. The main advantage of PH-distributed jumps is the possibility of lengthening the jumps into a succession of linear periods of exponential duration (having slopes 1 and -1 for the positive and negative jumps, respectively) and retrieving the original process via a simple time change. The transformation is conducted as follows. First, we partition the phase space $\widetilde{E}$ (without the jumps) into subspaces E_p (for positive drifts, i.e., $c_i > 0$) and E_n (for negative drifts, i.e., $c_i < 0$), $\widetilde{E} = E_p \cup E_n$. Then, we introduce two new phase spaces:

$$E_\pm := \{(i, k, \pm) : i \in \widetilde{E}, 1 \leq k \leq m_i^\pm\}, \tag{8}$$

to model the (positive and negative) jumps. Next, we define the enlarged state space $E \equiv \widetilde{E} \cup E_- \cup E_+$. The revised phase process $\mathcal{J}$ with state space E is determined by the generator matrix $\mathbb{Q} = (q_{ij})_{i,j \in E}$

$$q_{ij} = \begin{cases} \widetilde{q}_{ii} - \lambda_i, & j = i \in \widetilde{E}, \\ \widetilde{q}_{ij}, & j \neq i, h \in \widetilde{E}, \\ \lambda_i \alpha_k^{(i\pm)}, & j = (i, k, \pm), \end{cases} \tag{9}$$

for $i \in \widetilde{E}$ as well as

$$q_{(i,k,\pm),(i,l,\pm)} = T_{kl}^{(i\pm)} \text{ and } q_{(i,k,\pm),i} = \eta_k^{(i\pm)} \tag{10}$$

for $i \in \widetilde{E}$ and $1 \leq k, l \leq m_i^\pm$. By that, $\mathcal{J}$ tracks the states (phases) of the PH-type jumps in addition to the states in $\widetilde{\mathcal{J}}$. The revised process constructed by such a technique is denoted by $\{\mathcal{I}, \mathcal{J}\}$ and becomes a Markov-modulated fluid flow process (MMFF) without jumps. Accordingly, the infinitesimal generator $\mathbb{Q}$ can be written in block form with respect to the subspaces $E_1 = E_p \cup E_+$ (ascending states) and $E_2 = E_n \cup E_-$ (descending states):

$$\mathbb{Q} = \begin{pmatrix} \mathbb{Q}_{11} & \mathbb{Q}_{12} \\ \mathbb{Q}_{21} & \mathbb{Q}_{22} \end{pmatrix}.$$

Specifically, we modify the MAP $\{\widetilde{\mathcal{I}}_o, \widetilde{\mathcal{J}}\}$, with $\widetilde{\mathcal{I}}_o$ being the stock level at the PW, to the revised MMFF process $\{\mathcal{I}_o, \mathcal{J}\}$. Figure 3 illustrates the first cycle of $\widetilde{\mathcal{I}}_o$, presented in Figure 2, and its corresponding sample path $\mathcal{I}_o$; the jumps that are lengthened to linear segments are marked by the dotted black segments. Note that downward jumps below level 0 and upward jumps above level M are preserved in their original form and are not lengthened to linear segments (as we will show, these quantities require a special treatment). Next, we present the main tools used for the analysis of the MMFF process $\{\mathcal{I}_o, \mathcal{J}\}$.

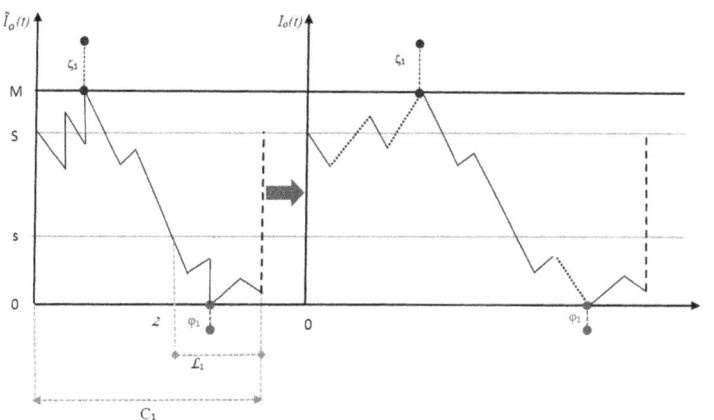

Figure 3. The MMFF process $\mathcal{I}_o$ for $\widetilde{\mathcal{I}}_o$.

4.2. First-Passage Times

In our analysis, the Laplace transform matrices of the first passage times play an essential component. Our first step is to obtain the LST matrix $\mathbb{A}(\beta)$ of the return time for the MAP $\{\widetilde{\mathcal{I}}_o, \widetilde{\mathcal{J}}\}$ process. Using $\mathbb{A}(\beta)$ as a key matrix, we then obtain the conditional LST matrices of the first passage times for the MMFF process.

4.2.1. Return Times for MAPs

Let $\{\widetilde{I}(t), \widetilde{J}(t), t \geq 0\}$ be a MAP process with phase-type jumps. Define $\widetilde{\tau}(x) = \inf\{t \geq 0, \widetilde{I}(t) > x\}$ for $x \geq 0$ to be the LST of the first passage time above x. Assume that $\widetilde{I}(0) = 0$ and let

$$E_{ij}(e^{-\widetilde{\tau}(x)}) = E(e^{-\widetilde{\tau}(x)}, J(\tau(x)) = j \mid \widetilde{I}(0) = 0, \widetilde{J}(0) = i), \quad i, j \in E. \tag{11}$$

Breuer [27] shows that the matrix $\mathbb{E}(e^{-\widetilde{\tau}(x)})$ can be written in a block form according to E_1 and E_2 as

$$\mathbb{E}(e^{-\widetilde{\tau}(x)}) = \begin{pmatrix} e^{\mathbb{U}(\beta)x} & 0 \\ \mathbb{A}(\beta)e^{\mathbb{U}(\beta)x} & 0 \end{pmatrix}, \tag{12}$$

for some matrices $\mathbb{U}(\beta)$ and $\mathbb{A}(\beta)$ of dimensions $|E_1| \times |E_1|$ and $|E_2| \times |E_1|$, respectively (note that, since a first passage to a level above cannot occur at a descending state, we have the zero matrices). Furthermore, the matrices $\mathbb{U}(\beta)$ and $\mathbb{A}(\beta)$ can be determined by successive approximation to the limits of the sequence $((A_n, U_n) : n \geq 0)$ with specific initial values (see Section 2.2 of Breuer [27] for the detailed algorithm). Setting $x = 0$ in (11) and (12), i.e., the return time to level 0 from below given $\widetilde{I}(0) = 0$, yields that $\mathbb{E}_{11}(e^{-\widetilde{\tau}(0)}) = \mathbb{I}$ and $\mathbb{E}_{21}(e^{-\widetilde{\tau}(0)}) = \mathbb{A}(\beta)$.

An important variant of the MAP process $\widetilde{\mathcal{I}}$, called the *image-reversed* process, is particularly useful in the analysis of our process. We define the *image-reversed MAP process* $\widetilde{\mathcal{I}}^r$ by reversing the roles of the up and down states; let $\widetilde{\mathcal{J}}^r(t)$ be the modulated state process for $\widetilde{\mathcal{I}}^r$. Then, $\mathbb{A}^r(\beta)$ is the matrix of order $(|E_1| \times |E_2|)$, whose (i, j)-th component is the LST of $\widetilde{\tau}^r(0)$, i.e., the time until a downward jump to level 0 for the process $\widetilde{\mathcal{I}}^r$ at state $j \in E_2$, given that $\widetilde{I}^r(0) = 0$ and $\widetilde{\mathcal{J}}^r(0) = i \in E_1$. As we show, these two LSTs, $\mathbb{A}(\beta)$ and $\mathbb{A}^r(\beta)$, are the key matrices used in our analysis; we further emphasize that these matrices are the return time for the original MAP process, meaning that the time spent in jump states $E_\pm$ does not account.

Next, to extend our LSTs and include upper and lower borders, we employ results from MMFF processes.

4.2.2. First Passage Times for MMFF Processes

Let ${}_u^v\tau(x,y)$ (for $x \geq 0, y \geq 0$) be the first passage time of $\mathcal{I}$ from level x to level y, with avoiding a visit to the levels in $[0, u] \cup [v, \infty)$ enroute (in the case of an unlimited visit, u and v are omitted). The notation ${}_u^v\widehat{f}(x, y,)$ denotes the LST matrix of the joint distribution of the first passage time ${}_u^v\tau(x,y)$ and the state of the phase process at that time, ${}_u^v\widehat{f}^r(x,y,)$ denotes the LST of the hitting time for $\mathcal{I}^r$. Ramaswami [49] shows that, once $\mathbb{A}(\beta)$ and $\mathbb{A}^r(\beta)$ are computed, the derivation of other LST matrices is straightforward; thus, all quantities of interest in this paper are characterized explicitly in terms of $\mathbb{A}(\beta)$ and $\mathbb{A}^r(\beta)$; the explicit expressions of the LST matrices and their probabilistic interpretations are summarized in [49]. To account for the jump-like nature of the additional movements, we substitute $\beta = 0$ in all entries of the form $(i, h), (h, i)$, or (h, h') for $i \in \widetilde{E}$ and $h, h' \in E_+ \cup E_-$. This means that the time is not discounted for all states associated with the jumps (i.e., at states E_+ and E_-). Henceforth, we assume that all LST matrices for hitting times ($\mathbb{A}(\beta)$, $\mathbb{A}^r(\beta)$, ${}_u^v\widehat{f}(x,y,)$ and ${}_u^v\widehat{f}^r(x,y,)$) are modified for the original process $\{\widetilde{\mathcal{I}}_o, \widetilde{\mathcal{J}}\}$.

4.3. MMFF at an Exponential Time

Corollary 1. *Let $\{\mathcal{I}, \mathcal{J}\}$ be an MMFF with state space E and $\mathbb{Q}$, and let $\mathcal{L}$ be an exponential r.v. with rate $\mu > 0$ independently of $\{\mathcal{I}, \mathcal{J}\}$.*

(1) *The LST matrix at time $\mathcal{L}$ with the (ij)-th component*

$$\left(\mathbb{E}(e^{-\beta\mathcal{L}})\right)_{ij} = E\left(e^{-\mathcal{L}}, J(\mathcal{L}) = j \mid J(0) = i\right), i \in E$$

is given by

$$\mathbb{E}(e^{-\beta\mathcal{L}}) = \mu((\beta + \mu)\mathbb{I} - \mathbb{Q})^{-1}. \tag{13}$$

In our analysis, the matrix form of (13) is required in order to track the initial and final states of the background CTMC. Here, we use the fact that, for a CTMC $\mathcal{J}$, the matrix $\mathbb{Q}$ satisfies $\left(e^{\mathbb{Q}x}\right)_{ij} = P(J(x) = j \mid J(0) = i)$ (see [2]). (Recall that the original state space is $\widetilde{E}$; thus, only rows in $\widetilde{E}$ are considered while other rows in (13) are set to zero.)

(2) *Applying the complete probability equation, it is easy to verify that, for a nonnegative generally distributed r.v. X,*

(i) $\mathbb{E}(e^{-\beta X}\mathbf{1}_{\{X<\mathcal{L}\}}) = \mathbb{E}(e^{-(\beta+\mu)X}). \tag{14}$

(ii) $\mathbb{E}(e^{\alpha I(\mathcal{L})-\beta\mathcal{L}}\mathbf{1}_{\{\mathcal{L}<X\}}) = \mu\mathbb{E}\left(\int_{t=0}^{X} e^{\alpha I(t)-(\beta+\mu)t}dt\right).$

Here, Equations (13) and (14) are used with respect to the lead time $\mathcal{L}$.

4.4. The Multidimensional Martingale

Let $\{\mathcal{X}(t), t \geq 0\}$ be a right-continuous Markov-modulated Lévy process with a modulating process $\{\mathcal{J}(t), t \geq 0\}$ that is an irreducible right-continuous Markov chain with a finite state space E. Let $\{Y(t), t \geq 0\}$ be an adapted continuous process with a finite expected variation on finite intervals and let $\mathcal{Z}(t) = \mathcal{X}(t) + Y(t)$. Asmussen and Kella [50] have shown that the matrix with elements $E_i\left[e^{\alpha \mathcal{X}(t)}; J(t) = j\right]$ has the form of $e^{t\mathbb{K}(\alpha)}$ for some matrix $\mathbb{K}(\alpha)$. Theorem 2.1 of Asmussen and Kella [50] yields that, under certain mild conditions on $\{\mathcal{Z}(t), t \geq 0\}$, the multidimensional process

$$M(\alpha, t) = \int_{u=0}^{t} e^{\alpha \mathcal{Z}(u)}\mathbf{1}_{J(u)}du\mathbb{K}(\alpha) + e^{\alpha \mathcal{Z}(0)}\mathbf{1}_{J(0)} - e^{\alpha \mathcal{Z}(t)}\mathbf{1}_{J(t)} + \alpha\int_{u=0}^{t}e^{\alpha \mathcal{Z}(u)}\mathbf{1}_{J(u)}dY(u) \tag{15}$$

is a (row) vector-valued zero mean martingale. Here, the indicator $\mathbf{1}_{J(t)}$ is an $|E|$-row vector mean $\{\mathbf{1}_{J(t)=i}, i \in E\}$. In our model, the process $I_o(t)$ has piecewise linear sample paths (at rate c_i for $i \in \widetilde{E}$, rate 1 for $i \in E_+$, and rate -1 for $i \in E_-$). Some of the cost functionals used are obtained by applying the optional stopping theorem (OST) to the multidimensional martingale process (15).

5. Derivation of the Expected Discounted Cost Functionals

We need to derive $E_S(e^{-\beta C})$, $OC_S(\beta)$, $DC_S(\beta)$, $SC_S(\beta)$, and $LC_S(\beta)$. The derivation of $DC_S(\beta)$ is more challenging and will be carried out at the end. To this end, we first derive two unique LSTs associated with hitting the boundaries, i.e., hitting level M from below, and dropping to level 0 from above.

Corollary 2.

(i) Assume that level M is hit from below at ascending state $J(t) \in E_1$. It is easy to verify that the $(|E_1| \times |E_2|)$ matrix $(\beta \mathbb{I} - \mathbb{Q}_{11})^{-1} \mathbb{Q}_{12}$ is the expected discounting time until exiting level M at a descending state (either continuously at a state in E_n or by a downward jump at a state in E_-). As we set $\beta = 0$ in all entries in $E_+ \in E_1$ due to the jumps, the matrix $(\beta \mathbb{I} - \mathbb{Q}_{11})^{-1} \mathbb{Q}_{12}$ has the block form

$$(\beta \mathbb{I} - \mathbb{Q}_{11})^{-1} \mathbb{Q}_{12} = \begin{pmatrix} (\beta \mathbb{I} - \widetilde{\mathbb{Q}}_{11})^{-1} \widetilde{\mathbb{Q}}_{12} & (\beta \mathbb{I} - \widetilde{\mathbb{Q}}_{11}) \lambda^{(-)} \alpha^{(-)} \\ \mathbb{I} \otimes e & 0 \end{pmatrix}$$

with respect to the subspaces $(E_p\ E_+) \times (E_n\ E_-)$. The matrix $\mathbb{I} \otimes e$ arises due to the zero time spent in E_+, and thereafter $I_o(t)$ immediately returns to its original state in E_n (recall that an upward jump is allowed only when $J(t) \in E_n$).

(ii) Similarly, assume that level 0 is hit from above at a descending state $J(t) \in E_2$. It is easy to verify that the $(|E_2| \times |E_1|)$ matrix $(\beta \mathbb{I} - \mathbb{Q}_{22})^{-1} \mathbb{Q}_{21}$ is the expected discounting time until exiting level 0 at ascending state E_n (either continuously at a state in E_p or by an upward jump at a state in E_+) Here, too, by setting $\beta = 0$ in all entries in $E_- \in E_2$, the matrix $(\beta \mathbb{I} - \mathbb{Q}_{22})^{-1} \mathbb{Q}_{21}$ has the block form

$$(\beta \mathbb{I} - \mathbb{Q}_{22})^{-1} \mathbb{Q}_{21} = \begin{pmatrix} (\beta \mathbb{I} - \widetilde{\mathbb{Q}}_{22})^{-1} \widetilde{\mathbb{Q}}_{21} & (\beta \mathbb{I} - \widetilde{\mathbb{Q}}_{22}) \lambda^{(+)} \alpha^{(+)} \\ \mathbb{I} \otimes e & 0 \end{pmatrix}$$

with respect to the subspaces $(E_n\ E_-) \times (E_p\ E_+)$.

5.1. Cycle Length and Order Cost

The cycle length is composed of two sequential periods: the time elapsed until level s is hit when a refilling is ordered, and the remaining cycle time. The next proposition summarizes the derivation of $E_S(e^{-\beta C})$ (recall that the superscript o indicates the stock-level evolution during lead time).

Proposition 1. The LST $(|E| \times 1)$ vector $\mathbf{E}_S(e^{-\beta C}) = (\overline{\mathbf{E}}_S(e^{-\beta C})\ \underline{\mathbf{E}}_S(e^{-\beta C}))^T$ satisfies the following set of equations:

(remaining cycle length with no upcoming refill)

(i) $\overline{\mathbf{E}}_S(e^{-\beta C}) = {}^{M-S}\mathbb{A}^r(\beta) \underline{\mathbf{E}}_S(e^{-\beta C}) + {}_s\hat{f}_{11}(S, M, \beta) \overline{\mathbf{E}}_M(e^{-\beta C})$,

(ii) $\underline{\mathbf{E}}_S(e^{-\beta C}) = {}^S\hat{f}_{22}(S, s, \beta) \underline{\mathbf{E}}_s^o(e^{-\beta C}) + {}^{S-s}\mathbb{A}(\beta) \overline{\mathbf{E}}_S(e^{-\beta C})$,

(iii) $\overline{\mathbf{E}}_M(e^{-\beta C}) = (\beta \mathbb{I} - \mathbb{Q}_{11})^{-1} \mathbb{Q}_{12} \underline{\mathbf{E}}_M(e^{-\beta C})$,

(iv) $\underline{\mathbf{E}}_M(e^{-\beta C}) = {}^M\hat{f}_{22}(M, S, \beta) \underline{\mathbf{E}}_S(e^{-\beta C}) + {}^{M-S}\mathbb{A}(\beta) \overline{\mathbf{E}}_M(e^{-\beta C})$, (16)

(remaining cycle length during lead time)

(v) $\underline{E}_S^o(e^{-\beta C}) = {}_0\hat{f}_{21}(s, S, \beta + \mu)\,\overline{E}_S^o(e^{-\beta C}) + {}^S\hat{f}_{22}(s, 0, \beta + \mu)\underline{E}_0^o(e^{-\beta C})$
$+ \dfrac{\mu}{\beta + \mu}\left[e - \left({}_0\hat{f}_{21}(s, S, \beta + \mu)e + {}^S\hat{f}_{22}(s, 0, \beta + \mu)e\right)\right],$

(vi) $\overline{E}_S^o(e^{-\beta C}) = {}^{M-S}\mathbb{A}^r(\beta + \mu)\underline{E}_S^o(e^{-\beta C}) + {}_S\hat{f}_{11}(S, M, \beta + \mu)\overline{E}_M^o(e^{-\beta C})$
$+ \left({}^{M-S}\mathbb{A}^r(\beta) - {}^{M-S}\mathbb{A}^r(\beta + \mu)\right)\underline{E}_S(e^{-\beta C})$
$+ \left({}_S\hat{f}_{11}(S, M, \beta) - {}_S\hat{f}_{11}(S, M, \beta + \mu)\right)\overline{E}_M(e^{-\beta C}),$

(vii) $\underline{E}_S^o(e^{-\beta C}) = {}^S\hat{f}_{22}(S, s, \beta + \mu)\underline{E}_0^o(e^{-\beta C}) + {}^{S-s}\mathbb{A}(\beta + \mu)\,\overline{E}_S^o(e^{-\beta C})$
$+ \dfrac{\mu}{\beta + \mu}\left[e - \left({}^{S-s}\mathbb{A}(\beta + \mu)e + {}^S\hat{f}_{22}(S, s, \beta + \mu)e\right)\right],$

(viii) $\underline{E}_0^o(e^{-\beta C}) = ((\beta + \mu)\mathbb{I} - \mathbb{Q}_{22})^{-1}\mathbb{Q}_{21}\,\overline{E}_0^o(e^{-\beta C})$
$+ \dfrac{\mu}{\beta + \mu}\left[e - ((\beta + \mu)\mathbb{I} - \mathbb{Q}_{22})^{-1}\mathbb{Q}_{21}e\right],$

(ix) $\overline{E}_0^o(e^{-\beta C}) = {}_0\hat{f}_{11}(0, S, \beta + \mu)\,\overline{E}_S^o(e^{-\beta C}) + {}^S\mathbb{A}^r(\beta + \mu)\,\underline{E}_0^o(e^{-\beta C})$
$+ \dfrac{\mu}{\beta + \mu}\left[e - \left({}_0\hat{f}_{11}(0, S, \beta + \mu)e + \left({}^S\mathbb{A}^r(\beta + \mu)e\right)\right)\right],$

(x) $\overline{E}_M^o(e^{-\beta C}) = ((\beta + \mu)\mathbb{I} - \mathbb{Q}_{11})^{-1}\mathbb{Q}_{12}\,\underline{E}_M^o(e^{-\beta C})$
$+ \left((\beta\mathbb{I} - \mathbb{Q}_{11})^{-1}\mathbb{Q}_{12} - ((\beta + \mu)\mathbb{I} - \mathbb{Q}_{11})^{-1}\mathbb{Q}_{12}\right)\underline{E}_M(e^{-\beta C}),$

(xi) $\underline{E}_M^o(e^{-\beta C}) = {}^{M-S}\mathbb{A}(\beta + \mu)\,\overline{E}_M^o(e^{-\beta C}) + {}^M\hat{f}_{22}(M, S, \beta + \mu)\underline{E}_S^o(e^{-\beta C})$
$+ \left({}^{M-S}\mathbb{A}(\beta) - {}^{M-S}\mathbb{A}(\beta + \mu)\right)\overline{E}_M(e^{-\beta C})$
$+ \left({}^M\hat{f}_{22}(M, S, \beta) - {}^M\hat{f}_{22}(M, S, \beta + \mu)\right)\underline{E}_S(e^{-\beta C}). \tag{17}$

Proof. The proof of Proposition 1 (and all subsequent proofs) is based on the first-step conditioning method and is obtained in Appendix B.1. □

Corollary 3. *The total number of expected discounted ordering times per cycle* $\mathbf{OC}_S(\beta) = \left(\overline{\mathbf{OC}}_S(\beta)\,\underline{\mathbf{OC}}_S(\beta)\right)^T$ *satisfy the set of Equations (16) and (17) with only three differences:*

(a) *The vector* $\mathbf{OC}$ *replaces the vector* $\mathbf{E}(e^{-\beta C})$ *(all of the appropriate sizes and with the same superscripts and subscripts).*
(b) *The first term of Case (ii) becomes* ${}^S\hat{f}_{22}(S, s, \beta)(e + \underline{\mathbf{OC}}_s^o)$ *(instead of* ${}^S\hat{f}_{22}(S, s, \beta)\,\underline{E}_s^o(e^{-\beta C})$*).*
(c) *The last terms in Cases* (v), (vii), (viii), *and* (ix) *are deleted.*

We emphasize that calling the distributor during lead time is not allowed. Thus, the order cost is charged only when dropping to s with no upcoming order explains Corollary 3(b). Accordingly, when $\mathcal{L} < T_S$, the distributor refills the PW at no additional order cost, and the cycle ends, which explains Corollary 3(c).

5.2. Transfer Cost

The derivation of $SC_S(\beta)$ includes two steps. First, Claim 1 below derives the expected discounted number of transferred items from hitting level M until exiting it for the first time. From that time, Proposition 2 derives the remaining number of transferred items until the end of the cycle. To see this, let $\zeta = \{\zeta_l, l \in E_1\}$ be the $(|E_1| \times 1)$ vector whose l-th component represents the expected discounted number of transferred items from hitting level M at state $l \in E_1$ until exiting M at a descending state.

Claim 1. *The vector $\zeta = (\zeta_l, l \in E_1)$ satisfies the following system of linear equations:*

$$\zeta_l = \begin{cases} -e_r^{(i+)}(\mathbb{T}^{(i+)})^{-1}e & l = (i, r, +) \in E_+, \\ \frac{c_l}{\beta - q_{ll}} + \sum_{k \neq l} \frac{q_{lk}}{\beta - q_{ll}} \zeta_k & l, k \in E_p. \end{cases} \quad (18)$$

Proof. Clearly, level M can be exceeded only at an ascending state in E_1. We distinguish between two situations. (i) Exceeding level M by an upward jump at state $l = (i, r, +)$, $i \in E_n$, $1 \leq r \leq m_i^+$, i.e., by a batch amount $U^{(i+)}$ at phase r (here, the timing is omitted due to the jump pattern). Thus, the exceeded amount is $U_r^{(i+)} \sim PH(e_r^{(i+)}, \mathbb{T}^{(i+)})$ of order m_i^+, where $e_r^{(i+)}$ is a $(1 \times m_i^+)$ vector equal to 1 at the r-th entry and to 0 otherwise. From that point, level M is left at a descending state i. (ii) Hitting level M continuously at a linear rate $c_l, l \in E_p$. First, the items are transferred to the SW at rate c_l at a random time $\delta_l \sim \exp(-q_{ll})$ and, thus, the expected discounted amount is $E\left(\int_{t=0}^{\delta_l} c_l e^{-\beta t} dt\right)$. Then, with probability $\frac{q_{lk}}{-q_{ll}}, k \neq l \in E_p$, the state changes to k, and the stock level $\mathcal{I}_R$ continues to accrue at rate c_k; otherwise (i.e., with probability $1 - \sum_{k \neq l \in E_p} \frac{q_{lk}}{-q_{ll}}$), level M is left at a descending state. Summarizing, we can express the vector ζ as

$$\zeta_l = \begin{cases} E(U_r^{(i+)}) & l = (i, r, +) \in E_+, \\ E\left(\int_{t=0}^{\delta_l} c_l e^{-\beta t} dt\right) + E_l(e^{-\beta \delta_l}) \sum_{k \neq l} \frac{q_{lk}}{-q_{ll}} \zeta_k & l, k \in E_p. \end{cases} \quad (19)$$

Substituting $E(U_r^{(i+)}) = -e_r^{(i+)}(\mathbb{T}^{(i+)})^{-1}e$, $E\left(\int_{t=0}^{\delta_l} c_l e^{-\beta t} dt\right) = \frac{c_l}{\beta}\left(1 + \frac{q_{ll}}{\beta - q_{ll}}\right) = \frac{c_l}{\beta - q_{ll}}$, and $E_l(e^{-\beta \delta_l}) = \frac{-q_{ll}}{\beta - q_{ll}}$ into (19) completes the proof. □

Proposition 2. *The expected discounted number of transferred items to the SW during a cycle $SC_S(\beta) = \left(\overline{SC}_S(\beta)\ \underline{SC}_S(\beta)\right)^T$ satisfies the following set of equations:*
(transferred items with no upcoming order)

(i) $\overline{SC}_S(\beta) = {}_S\hat{f}_{11}(S, M, \beta)\overline{SC}_M(\beta) + {}^{M-S}\mathbb{A}^r(\beta)\ \underline{SC}_S(\beta)$,

(ii) $\underline{SC}_M(\beta) = {}^{M-S}\mathbb{A}(\beta)\overline{SC}_M(\beta) + {}^M\hat{f}_{22}(M, S, \beta)\ \underline{SC}_S(\beta)$,

(iii) $\overline{SC}_M(\beta) = \zeta + (\beta\mathbb{I} - \mathbb{Q}_{11})^{-1}\mathbb{Q}_{12}\ \underline{SC}_M(\beta)$,   (20)

(iv) $\underline{SC}_S(\beta) = {}^S\hat{f}_{22}(S, s, \beta)\ \underline{SC}_s^o(\beta) + {}^{S-s}\mathbb{A}(\beta)\ \overline{SC}_S(\beta)$.

(transferred items during lead time)

(v) $\underline{SC_s^o}(\beta) = {}^s\mathbb{A}(\beta+\mu)\,\overline{SC_s^o}(\beta) + {}^s\hat{f}_{22}(s,0,\beta+\mu)\,\underline{SC_0^o}(\beta),$

(vi) $\overline{SC_s^o}(\beta) = {}_s\hat{f}_{11}(s,S,\beta+\mu)\overline{SC_S^o}(\beta) + {}^{S-s}\mathbb{A}^r(\beta+\mu)\,\underline{SC_s^o}(\beta),$

(vii) $\underline{SC_0^o}(\beta) = ((\beta+\mu)\mathbb{I} - \mathbb{Q}_{22})^{-1}\mathbb{Q}_{21}\overline{SC_0^o}(\beta),$

(viii) $\overline{SC_0^o}(\beta) = {}^s\mathbb{A}^r(\beta+\mu)\,\underline{SC_0^o}(\beta) + {}_0\hat{f}_{11}(0,s,\beta+\mu)\overline{SC_s^o}(\beta),$

(ix) $\underline{SC_S^o}(\beta) = {}^S\hat{f}_{22}(S,s,\beta+\mu)\underline{SC_s^o}(\beta) + {}^{S-s}\mathbb{A}(\beta+\mu)\,\overline{SC_s^o}(\beta),$

(x) $\overline{SC_S^o}(\beta) = {}_s\hat{f}_{11}(S,M,\beta+\mu)\overline{SC_M^o}(\beta) + {}^{M-S}\mathbb{A}^r(\beta+\mu)\,\underline{SC_S^o}(\beta)$
$+ \left({}_s\hat{f}_{11}(S,M,\beta) - {}_s\hat{f}_{11}(S,M,\beta+\mu)\right)\overline{SC}_M(\beta)$
$+ \left({}^{M-S}\mathbb{A}^r(\beta) - {}^{M-S}\mathbb{A}^r(\beta+\mu)\right)\underline{SC}_S(\beta),$

(xi) $\underline{SC_M^o}(\beta) = {}^{M-S}\mathbb{A}(\beta+\mu)\overline{SC_M^o}(\beta) + {}^M\hat{f}_{22}(M,S,\beta+\mu)\,\underline{SC_S^o}(\beta)$
$+ \left({}^{M-S}\mathbb{A}(\beta) - {}^{M-S}\mathbb{A}(\beta+\mu)\right)\overline{SC}_M(\beta)$
$+ \left({}^M\hat{f}_{22}(M,S,\beta) - {}^M\hat{f}_{22}(M,S,\beta+\mu)\right)\underline{SC}_S(\beta),$

(xii) $\overline{SC_M^o}(\beta) = \zeta + \left[(\beta+\mu)\mathbb{I} - \mathbb{Q}_{11}\right]^{-1}\mathbb{Q}_{12}\,\underline{SC_M^o}(\beta)$
$+ \left[(\beta\mathbb{I} - \mathbb{Q}_{11})^{-1}\mathbb{Q}_{12} - ((\beta+\mu)\mathbb{I} - \mathbb{Q}_{11})^{-1}\mathbb{Q}_{12}\right]\underline{SC}_M(\beta).$ (21)

Proof. The Proof is given in Appendix B.2. □

5.3. Loss Cost

Let $\Theta = (\Theta_l, l \in E_2)$ be the $(|E_2| \times 1)$ vector whose l-th component represents the expected discounted number of unsatisfied items when hitting level 0 at state $l \in E_2$ until exiting 0 for the first time.

Claim 2. *The vector $\Theta = (\Theta_l, l \in E_2)$ satisfies the following system of linear equations:*

$$\Theta_l = \begin{cases} -e_r^{(i-)}(\mathbb{T}^{(i-)})^{-1}e & l = (i,r,-) \in E_- \\ \frac{-c_l}{\beta+\mu-q_{ll}} + \sum_{k \neq l} \frac{q_{lk}}{\beta+\mu-q_{ll}}\Theta_k & l, k \in E_n. \end{cases} \quad (22)$$

Proof. Similar to Claim 1 with one exception, here, demand may be lost only during lead time. Thus, if level 0 is hit at a state $l \in E_n$, lost demand is accumulated at rate $-c_l$, as long as the distributor has not arrived or until leaving state l, i.e., the random time $\min(\delta_l, L)$ with $\exp(\precsim - q_{ll})$ distribution. A similar technique that used for Claim 1 completes the proof. □

Proposition 3. *The expected discounted number of unsatisfied items during a cycle $LC_S(\beta) = (\overline{LC}_S(\beta)\ \underline{LC}_S(\beta))^T$ satisfies the set of Equations (20) and (21) with the exception of three modifications:*

(a) *The vector LC replaces the vector SC (all of the appropriate sizes and with the same superscripts and subscripts).*
(b) *The first term of Cases (iii) and (xii), ζ, is deleted.*
(c) *The expected discounted loss Θ is added to Case (vii).*

5.4. Distributor's Service Cost

Recall that $K_n, n = 1, 2\ldots$ is the n-th arrival time of the distributor. Clearly, when $I_0(K_n) < S$, the stock is refilled at a cost γ for each refilled item. In addition, maintenance activities are conducted at no additional charge, and the cycle ends; in that case, $C = K_n$.

Otherwise, only maintenance activities are conducted at cost Y^-. Let N_C be the number of times that the distributor arrives during a cycle. Thus,

$$N_C = \min\{n : I_0(K_n) < S\}.$$

The distributor's service cost is therefore given by

$$DC_S(\beta) = \gamma E_S\left(e^{-\beta C}(S - I_0(K_{N_C}))\right) + Y^- \sum_{n=1}^{N_C-1} E_S(e^{-\beta K_n})$$

$$= \gamma\left(S\, E_S\left(e^{-\beta C}\right) - E_S(e^{-\beta C} I_0(C))\right) + Y^- \sum_{n=1}^{N_C-1} E_S(e^{-\beta K_n}). \quad (23)$$

The first term is the charge for to refilling the PW; the last term is the charge for maintaining the SW when no refilling is made. Note that the term $E_S(e^{-\beta C})$ is given by Equations (16) and (17). Let

$$\Delta_x(\beta) = Y^- \sum_{n=1}^{N_C-1} E_x(e^{-\beta K_n}) - \gamma E_x(e^{-\beta C} I_0(C)),$$

and let T_0^- be the time to exit level 0 (recall that T_0 is the time to enter level 0). The next proposition derives $\Delta_S(\beta)$ and the sequence of vectors to be used.

Proposition 4. *The cost functional $\Delta_S(\beta) = (\overline{\Delta}_S(\beta)\, \underline{\Delta}_S(\beta))$ satisfies the following set of equations: (cost with no upcoming order)*

(i) $\overline{\Delta}_S(\beta) =^{M-S} \mathbb{A}^r(\beta)\, \underline{\Delta}_S(\beta) + {}_S\widehat{f}_{11}(S, M, \beta)\overline{\Delta}_M(\beta),$

(ii) $\underline{\Delta}_S(\beta) = {}^M\widehat{f}_{22}(S, s, \beta)\, \Delta_s^o(\beta) +^{S-s} \mathbb{A}(\beta)\overline{\Delta}_S(\beta),$

(iii) $\overline{\Delta}_M(\beta) = (\beta\mathbb{I} - \mathbb{Q}_{11})^{-1}\mathbb{Q}_{12}\, \underline{\Delta}_M(\beta),$

(iv) $\underline{\Delta}_M(\beta) =^{M-S} \mathbb{A}(\beta)\overline{\Delta}_M(\beta) + {}^M\widehat{f}_{22}(M, S, \beta)\, \Delta_S(\beta).$

(cost during lead time)

(v) $\underline{\Delta}_S^o(\beta) = {}_0\widehat{f}_{21}(s,S,\beta+\mu)\overline{\Delta}_S^o(\beta) + {}^S\widehat{f}_{22}(s,0,\beta+\mu)\underline{\Delta}_0^o(\beta)$
$\quad - \gamma \underline{E}_s(e^{-\beta\mathcal{L}}I_0(\mathcal{L})\mathbf{1}_{\{\mathcal{L}<\min(T_S,T_0)\}})$,

(vi) $\overline{\Delta}_S^o(\beta) = {}^{M-S}\mathbb{A}^r(\beta+\mu)\underline{\Delta}_S^o(\beta) + {}_S\widehat{f}_{11}(S,M,\beta+\mu)\overline{\Delta}_M^o(\beta)$
$\quad + \left({}_S\widehat{f}_{11}(S,M,\beta) - {}_S\widehat{f}_{11}(S,M,\beta+\mu)\right)\left(\mathbf{Y}^- e + \overline{\Delta}_M(\beta)\right)$
$\quad + \left({}^{M-S}\mathbb{A}^r(\beta) - {}^{M-S}\mathbb{A}^r(\beta+\mu)\right)\left(\mathbf{Y}^- e + \underline{\Delta}_S(\beta)\right)$,

(vii) $\overline{\Delta}_M^o(\beta) = \left[(\beta+\mu)\mathbb{I} - \mathbb{Q}_{11}\right]^{-1}\mathbb{Q}_{12}\,\underline{\Delta}_M^o(\beta)$
$\quad + \left[(\beta\mathbb{I} - \mathbb{Q}_{11})^{-1}\mathbb{Q}_{12} - ((\beta+\mu)\mathbb{I} - \mathbb{Q}_{11})^{-1}\mathbb{Q}_{12}\right]\left(\mathbf{Y}^- e + \underline{\Delta}_M(\beta)\right)$,

(viii) $\underline{\Delta}_M^o(\beta) = {}^{M-S}\mathbb{A}(\beta+\mu)\overline{\Delta}_M^o(\beta) + {}^M\widehat{f}_{22}(M,S,\beta+\mu)\underline{\Delta}_S^o(\beta)$
$\quad + \left({}^{M-S}\mathbb{A}(\beta) - {}^{M-S}\mathbb{A}(\beta+\mu)\right)\left(\mathbf{Y}^- e + \overline{\Delta}_M(\beta)\right)$
$\quad + \left[{}^M\widehat{f}_{22}(M,S,\beta) - {}^M\widehat{f}_{22}(M,S,\beta+\mu)\right]\left(\mathbf{Y}^- e + \underline{\Delta}_S(\beta)\right)$,

(ix) $\underline{\Delta}_S^o(\beta) = {}^S\mathbb{A}(\beta+\mu)\overline{\Delta}_S^o(\beta) + {}^S\widehat{f}_{22}(S,0,\beta+\mu)\underline{\Delta}_0^o(\beta)$
$\quad - \gamma \underline{E}_S(e^{-\beta\mathcal{L}}I_0(\mathcal{L})\mathbf{1}_{\{\mathcal{L}<\min(T_S,T_0)\}})$,

(x) $\underline{\Delta}_0^o(\beta) = ((\beta+\mu)\mathbb{I} - \mathbb{Q}_{22})^{-1}\mathbb{Q}_{21}\overline{\Delta}_0^o(\beta))$,

(xi) $\overline{\Delta}_0^o(\beta) = {}_0\widehat{f}_{11}(0,S,\beta+\mu)\overline{\Delta}_S^o(\beta) + {}^S\mathbb{A}^r(\beta+\mu)\underline{\Delta}_0^o(\beta)$
$\quad - \gamma \overline{E}_0(e^{-\beta\mathcal{L}}I_0(\mathcal{L})\mathbf{1}_{\{\mathcal{L}<\min(T_S,T_0)\}})$. (24)

(We emphasize that $I_0(\mathcal{L})$ is the on-hand stock level at the PW just before the distributor arrives.)

Proof. We introduce only the key steps of the proof. Cases (i)–(iv) are straightforward. Cases $(v), (ix)$, and (xi) are based on the decomposition according to $\min(T_S, T_0, \mathcal{L})$. Similarly, Cases (vi)–$(viii)$ use similar techniques regarding the cost $\mathbf{Y}^-$. Regarding Case (x), note that $I_0(\mathcal{L})\mathbf{1}_{\{\mathcal{L}<T_0^-\}} = 0$ and, thus, only the event $\{\mathcal{L} > T_0^-\}$ (with LST $((\beta+\mu)\mathbb{I} - \mathbb{Q}_{22})^{-1}\mathbb{Q}_{21})$ should be considered. In order to complete the derivation, we need to obtain the last terms of Cases $(v), (ix)$, and (xi). We concentrate on Case (v); the derivations of Cases (ix) and (xi) are similar, and are given in Corollary 4(a) and 4(b), respectively. □

The ($|E_2| \times 1$) vector $\underline{E}_s(e^{-\beta\mathcal{L}}I_0(\mathcal{L})\mathbf{1}_{\{\mathcal{L}<\min(T_S,T_0)\}})$.
We shift the original time so that $I_0(0) = s$, $J(0) \in E_2$. Recall that $\varsigma = \min(T_S, T_0)$; we start by introducing the vector $\underline{E}_s(e^{\alpha I_0(\mathcal{L}) - \beta\mathcal{L}}\mathbf{1}_{\{\mathcal{L}<\varsigma\}})$. It is easy to see that

$$\underline{E}_s(e^{-\beta\mathcal{L}}I_0(\mathcal{L})\mathbf{1}_{\{\mathcal{L}<\varsigma\}}) = \frac{d}{d\alpha}\left(\underline{E}_s(e^{\alpha I_0(\mathcal{L}) - \beta\mathcal{L}}\mathbf{1}_{\{\mathcal{L}<\varsigma\}})e\right)\Big|_{\alpha=0}. \quad (25)$$

Applying (14)(ii) yields

$$\underline{E}_s(e^{\alpha I_0(\mathcal{L}) - \beta\mathcal{L}}\mathbf{1}_{\{\mathcal{L}<\varsigma\}}) = \mu\underline{E}_s\left(\int_0^\varsigma e^{\alpha I_0(t) - (\beta+\mu)t}\mathbf{1}_{J(t)}dt\right). \quad (26)$$

The basic tool to compute $\underline{E}_s\left(\int_0^\varsigma e^{\alpha I_0(t) - (\beta+\mu)t}\mathbf{1}_{J(t)}dt\right)$ is the OST to the Asmussen–Kella multidimensional martingale defined in Section 4.4. Consider the process $(\mathcal{X}(t))_{t\geq 0}$:

$$\mathcal{X}(t) = \mathcal{X}(0) + \int_{u=0}^t c_{J(u)}du \quad t \geq 0, \quad (27)$$

with $\mathcal{X}(0) = s, J(0) \in E_2$. It is not difficult to see that, by conditioning on $I_o(0) = s$, $J(0) \in E_2$, the process up to time ς, i.e., $(\mathcal{X}(t))_{0 \leq t < \varsigma}$, has the same distribution as $(I_o(t))_{0 \leq t < \varsigma}$. Let $\mathbb{C}$ be the rate matrix $\mathbb{C} = diag(\mathbb{C}_1, \mathbb{C}_2)$ with $\mathbb{C}_1 = diag(c_i : i \in E_1)$ and $\mathbb{C}_2 = diag(c_i : i \in E_2)$. It can be concluded from Chapter XI, p.311 of Asmussen [2] that $\mathbb{E}(e^{\alpha \mathcal{X}(t)} \mathbf{1}_{\{J(t)\}}) = e^{t\mathbb{K}(\alpha)}$, where $\mathbb{K}(\alpha) = \mathbb{Q} + \alpha \mathbb{C}$.

Claim 3. *The $(|E_2| \times |E|)$ matrix $\mathbb{E}_s \left(\int_0^\varsigma e^{\alpha I_o(t) - (\beta+\mu)t} \mathbf{1}_{J(t)} dt \right)$ is given by*

$$\mathbb{E}_s \left(\int_0^\varsigma e^{\alpha I_o(t) - (\beta+\mu)t} \mathbf{1}_{J(t)} dt \right) = \left[e^{\alpha S} \left({}_0\widehat{f}_{21}(s, S, \beta+\mu) \; \mathbf{0} \right) + \left(\mathbf{0} \; {}^S\widehat{f}_{22}(s, 0, \beta+\mu) \right) - e^{\alpha s} \left(\mathbf{0} \; \mathbb{I} \right) \right] (\mathbb{K}(\alpha) - (\beta+\mu)\mathbb{I})^{-1}. \quad (28)$$

Proof. The proof is given in Appendix B.3. □

Corollary 4.
(a) *The $(|E_2| \times 1)$ vector $\mathbb{E}_s(e^{-\beta\mathcal{L}} I(\mathcal{L}) \mathbf{1}_{\{\mathcal{L} < \varsigma\}})$ (Case (ix)) is given by*

$$\mathbb{E}_s(e^{-\beta\mathcal{L}} I_o(\mathcal{L}) \mathbf{1}_{\{\mathcal{L} < \varsigma\}}) = \frac{d}{d\alpha} \left[\mu \mathbb{E}_s \left(\int_0^\varsigma e^{\alpha I_o(t) - (\beta+\mu)t} \mathbf{1}_{J(t)} dt \right) e \right] \bigg|_{\alpha=0},$$

$$\mathbb{E}_s \left(\int_0^\varsigma e^{\alpha I(t) - (\beta+\mu)t} \mathbf{1}_{J(t)} dt \right) = \left[e^{\alpha S} \left({}^S\mathbb{A}(\beta+\mu) \; \mathbf{0} \right) + \left(\mathbf{0} \; {}^S\widehat{f}_{22}(S, 0, \beta+\mu) \right) - e^{\alpha S} \left(\mathbf{0} \; \mathbb{I} \right) \right]$$
$$\times (\mathbb{K}(\alpha) - (\beta+\mu)\mathbb{I})^{-1}. \quad (29)$$

(Applying (28) with S replacing s; note that ${}_0\widehat{f}_{21}(S, S, \beta+\mu) = {}^S\mathbb{A}(\beta+\mu)$.)
(b) *The $(|E_1| \times 1)$ vector $\overline{\mathbb{E}}_0(e^{-\beta\mathcal{L}} I(\mathcal{L}) \mathbf{1}_{\{\mathcal{L} < \varsigma\}})$ (Case (xi)) is given by*

$$\overline{\mathbb{E}}_0(e^{-\beta\mathcal{L}} I_o(\mathcal{L}) \mathbf{1}_{\{\mathcal{L} < \varsigma\}}) = \frac{d}{d\alpha} \left[\mu \overline{\mathbb{E}}_0 \left(\int_0^\varsigma e^{\alpha I_o(t) - (\beta+\mu)t} \mathbf{1}_{J(t)} dt \right) e \right] \bigg|_{\alpha=0},$$

$$\overline{\mathbb{E}}_0 \left(\int_0^\varsigma e^{\alpha I(t) - (\beta+\mu)t} \mathbf{1}_{J(t)} dt \right) = \left[e^{\alpha S} \left({}_0\widehat{f}_{11}(0, S, \beta+\mu) \; \mathbf{0} \right) + \left(\mathbf{0} \; {}^S\mathbb{A}^r(\beta+\mu) \right) - \left(\mathbb{I} \; \mathbf{0} \right) \right]$$
$$\times (\mathbb{K}(\alpha) - (\beta+\mu)\mathbb{I})^{-1}. \quad (30)$$

(Here, we apply (28) with $(0, E_1)$ replacing (s, E_2).)

A summary of the costs' derivation is given in Appendix A.2.

6. Numerical Examples

In this section, we illustrate the impact of the thresholds, the parameters, and the uncertainty of demands and returns on the system's performance. Clearly, our aim is to find the optimal (s^*, S^*, M^*) for different values of the parameters. The sets of equations in Propositions 1–4 show that it is difficult to provide an explicit expression for the discounted expected cost functions and, thus, it is difficult to obtain explicit terms for the optimal controllers. Hence, a numerical investigation is applied. Our base case assumes a CTMC with $n = 2$ states: $\widetilde{E}_p = \{1\}, \widetilde{E}_n = \{2\}, \widetilde{E} = \widetilde{E}_p \cup \widetilde{E}_n = \{1, 2\}$, i.e., one state with positive net rate and one state with negative net rate. The infinitesimal generator and the stationary probability vector are given by

$$\widetilde{\mathbb{Q}} = \begin{pmatrix} -0.03 & 0.03 \\ 0.05 & -0.05 \end{pmatrix}, \quad \pi = (0.625, 0.325), \quad (31)$$

where, for simplicity, we let the initial probability vector $\eta = \pi$. In states 1 and 2, demand occurs at rate $d_1 = 1$ and $d_2 = 2$, respectively, and return occurs at rate $r_1 = 1.5$ and $r_2 = 0.5$, respectively. The net growth is thus $c_1 = 0.5$ and $c_2 = -1.5$. Furthermore, in state 1, a downward jump may occur at rate λ_1 with a demand size $U^{(1-)} \sim PH(\alpha^{(1-)}, \mathbb{T}^{(1-)})$ of order $m_1^- = 2$; in state 2, an upward jump may occur at rate λ_2 with a return size $U^{(2+)} \sim PH(\alpha^{(2+)}, \mathbb{T}^{(2+)})$ of order $m_2^+ = 1$. We denote by ξ^+ (ξ^-) the average growth rate of states in E_1 (E_2); thus, $E(\xi^+) = \pi_1 c_1 + \pi_2 \lambda_2 E(U^{(2+)})$, and $E(\xi^-) = \pi_2 |c_2| + \pi_1 \lambda_1 E(U^{(1-)})$. Finally, let $\xi = \xi^+ - \xi^-$ be the net average rate (which can be positive or negative). We start with

$$\begin{array}{lll} \lambda_1 = 0.2, & \alpha^{(1-)} = (0.3, 0.7), & \mathbb{T}^{(1-)} = \begin{pmatrix} -0.25 & 0 \\ 0 & -0.5 \end{pmatrix}, \\ \lambda_2 = 0.161, & \alpha^{(2+)} = (1), & \mathbb{T}^{(2+)} = (-0.2). \end{array} \qquad (32)$$

(i.e., $U^{(2+)}$ is an exponentially r.v.). Here, $E(\xi^+) = E(\xi^-) = 0.614$ and $E(\xi) = 0$ (i.e., the system is considered to be *balanced*). Assume a discounted factor $\beta = 0.075$, an exponential lead time $\mathcal{L} \sim \exp(\mu = 0.1)$, and cost values

$$Y^+ = 50, \ Y^- = 50, \ \gamma = 10, \ \phi = 50, \ \nu = 0.5.$$

We start by studying the impact of the parameters S and s; then, we focus on the optimal policy and cost.

Example 1. *The impact of the parameters S and s on the system's performance. It is practically a commonplace that warehouses have limited and known capacity; thus, and without loss of generality, we assumed that $M = 35$ and study the changes of S and s. Table 1 summarizes the effect of changing S and s on the expected discounted cycle length and cost components; each line presents the effect of increasing only one parameter while keeping the other fixed. We use "↑" and "↓" to express increasing and decreasing functions of the parameter and "∪" to express a convex shape. The star "★" stands for a special behavior to be discussed further on.*

Table 1. The impact of the parameters on the system's performance.

Increasing the Parameter	Expected Discounted				
	Cycle Length EC	Order Cost OC	Transfer Cost SC	Loss Cost LC	Distributor's Service Cost DC
S ↑	∪	↓	↑	↓	∪
s ↑	↑	↑	★	↓	↑

- *The impact of S.* As expected, increasing S decreases the number of orders and shortages, and increases the number of transferred items; thus, OC and LC decrease and SC increases. However, the changes in EC and DC are more challenging and are explained as follows. At first, increasing S increases the cycle length (i.e., EC decreases), minimizes value for money (due to β), and thus decreases DC. However, a highly increasing S increases the number of refillings, shortens the cycle length, intensifies the impact of β, and thus increases DC.
- *The impact of s.* Clearly, increasing s shortens the cycle length-resulting in early ordering times, and intensifies the impact of β; thus, the changes in EC, OC, LC, and DC are as expected. By contrast, the change in SC is not straightforward. Figure 4a curves SC as a function of s, for $S = \{20, 25, 30, 34\}$ (recall that $s < S$ and $M = 35$). We see that SC increases and then decreases, and these changes become more dramatic with S. At first, increasing s increases the stock, level M is hit more frequently and, thus, SC increases. However, as s approaches S, the ordering time and the cycle length are significantly shortened and thus SC decreases.

To summarize, while the impact of S and s on OC and LC is as expected, their impact on SC and DC is not straightforward and difficult to predict. To illustrate the overall impact, Figure 4b displays the expected discounted total cost per time unit $TC(M = 35, S, s)$ as a function of S and s. We see that $TC(M = 35, S, s)$ is jointly convex in S and s; we note that this appears in all our examples (other values of M, S, and s,, which are not reported here, also exhibit a similar behavior). Thus, we assume that the cost is convex in S, s for a fixed M. Assuming convexity enables us to numerically obtain the optimal thresholds S^* and s^* quicker by using a line search.

It should be noted that convexity of the total cost for base-stock policy is a common supposition, and it has been proven by several researchers for both periodic and continuous review contexts, however, for simpler models and under restricted assumption [51]. Although we cannot give a formal proof of this, we give the following intuitive explanation. Table 1 shows that the cost components are influenced in a different fashion with S and s. For example, increasing S reduces the number of orders and decreases OC; it also reduces the penalty cost, LC. However, at the same time, increasing S increases SC and the cycle length, and minimizes the impact of β. This trade-off between potential savings is due to fewer orders and timing on the one side, and more transferred items from the other side yields convexity.

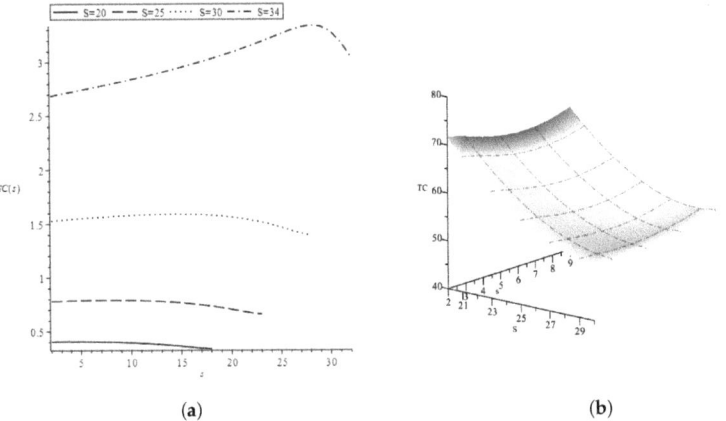

Figure 4. (a) $SC(s)$ for $S \in \{20, 25, 30, 34\}$, $M = 35$. (b) $TC(M = 35, S, s)$ as a function of S and s.

Example 2. *Sensitivity analysis of the optimal thresholds and cost. Here, we investigate the impact of the different parameters on the optimal thresholds and cost; we start with a balanced system. Following Example 1, we let $E(\xi) = 0$ (the specific values are given in (31) and (32)), $\beta = 0.075$, $\mu = 0.1, Y^+ = 50,$ and $M = 35$. We vary γ in $\{5, 10\}$, $Y^- \in \{50, 150, \}$, $\phi \in \{5, 25, 50, 100\}$, and $\nu \in \{0.5, 5, 15, 25, 100\}$. Table 2 summarizes the optimal (S^*, s^*) and the corresponding total cost $TC^* = TC(M = 35, S^*, s^*)$.*

Table 2 shows that increasing the lost cost ϕ increases S^* and s^* (to avoid shortage); increasing γ decreases s^*, probably to delaying the order time and, consequently, the refilling time. Additionally, S^* is increasing in Y^- when ν and ϕ are low in order to reduce the number of cancellations. We further see that, usually, increasing ν increases s^* and thus shortens the until ordering. However, Table 2 shows few exceptions particularly when Y^- is high ($Y^- = 150$); here, the distributor's service cost cost is very high and, thus, both S^* and s^* are kept low to reduce the number of cancellations. Additional numerical results (that are not reported here) further show that increasing Y^+ increases S^* and decreases s^*; thereby, $S^* - s^*$ increases and the number of orders decreases. Table 3 summarizes the changes in S^* and s^* when the costs are increasing; here, too, the star "★" stands for non-monotonic behavior.

Table 2. $S^*, s^*, TC^*(M=35, S^*, s^*)$ for $Y^- \in \{50, 150\}$, $\gamma \in \{5, 10\}$, $\phi \in \{5, 25, 50, 100\}$, and $\nu \in \{0.5, 5, 15, 25, 100\}$.

S^*, s^* TC^*	$\phi \setminus \nu$	0.5	5	15	25	100
$j^- = 50$ $\gamma = 5$	5	20, 2 27.133	24, 2 29.457	19, 2 38.748	17, 2 44.792	11, 2 69.150
	25	30, 2 30.153	26, 2 40.540	21, 4 53.402	19, 4 61.845	13, 4 96.876
	50	30, 7 37.363	26, 8 48.063	23, 8 62.386	21, 8 72.243	15, 8 114.098
	100	30, 11 44.696	27, 11 55.907	23, 8 62.386	22, 11 83.298	17, 11 133.019
$j^- = 50$ $\gamma = 10$	5	20, 2 38.039	24, 2 39.811	19, 2 49.818	17, 2 56.186	11, 2 81.156
	25	30, 2 40.785	26, 2 50.760	22, 2 64.027	20, 2 72.961	13, 2 108.709
	50	30, 4 51.595	27, 5 62.358	23, 6 77.256	21, 6 87.626	15, 7 130.449
	100	30, 9 62.397	27, 9 73.001	24, 10 89.145	22, 10 100.755	17, 10 151.083
$j^- = 150$ $\gamma = 5$	5	29, 2 21.328	24, 2 29.542	19, 2 39.043	17, 2 45.280	11, 2 71.492
	25	31, 2 30.170	26, 2 40.592	21, 4 53.706	19, 4 62.347	14, 2 98.084
	50	30, 7 37.430	26, 8 48.315	23, 8 62.921	21, 8 73.131	16, 7 117.311
	100	30, 10 44.878	27, 11 56.341	24, 11 72.911	22, 11 84.850	17, 10 137.497
$j^- = 150$ $\gamma = 10$	5	28, 2 1.728	24, 2 39.896	20, 2 50.062	17, 2 56.918	11, 2 83.498
	25	30, 2 40.812	26, 2 50.811	22, 2 64.167	20, 2 73.190	13, 5 115.468
	50	30, 4 51.640	27, 5 62.446	23, 6 77.569	21, 6 88.403	15, 6 133.090
	100	30, 8 62.871	27, 9 73.255	24, 10 89.856	22, 10 101.937	17, 9 155.096

Table 3. The impact of increasing costs on S^* and s^*.

	The Cost ↑				
The Effect on	Service Cost Y^-	Unit Cost γ	Loss Cost ϕ	Transfer Cost ν	Ordering Cost Y^+
S^*	↑	★	↑	↓	↑
s^*	★	↓	↑	★	↓

Our next goal is to study the effect of inflows and outflows (average demand and return) on the optimal thresholds S^* and s^*. To do so, we vary $E(\tilde{\zeta})$ in $\{-0.45, -0.41, -0.308, -0.24, -0.12, 0, 0.22, 0.43, 0.625\}$ by changing c_1 and $T^{(2+)}$ and fixing $c_2 = -1.5, \lambda_1 = 0.2$ and $\lambda_2 = 0.161$ (the specific pairs $\left(c_1, E(U^{(2+)})\right)$ corresponding to these values are (0.025, 2.5), (0.03, 3), (0.5, 1), (0.2, 3), (0.5, 3), (0.5, 5), (0.85, 5), (1, 7), and (1.5, 5), respectively). Recall that, when $E(\tilde{\zeta}) < 0$, demands arrive more frequently on average, and when $E(\tilde{\zeta}) > 0$, returns arrive more frequently (note that the results for $E(\tilde{\zeta}) = 0$ are given in

Table 2). We set $Y^+ = 50$, $Y^- = 150$, and $\nu = 5$, and focus on two scenarios: (1) $\gamma = 10$ and $\phi = 5$, and (2) $\gamma = 5$ and $\phi = 50$. Scenario 1 highlights the high cost of refilling; Scenario 2 highlights the high penalty cost of a shortage. Regarding Scenario 1, Figure 5 plots the pairs (S^*, s^*) (black and blue points, respectively) corresponding to $E(\xi)$, and Figure 6 shows the percentage of the cost components %OC, %LC, %SC, and %DC of TC^*. The blue-black scale depicts for cases where $E(\xi) \geq 0$, and the red-orange scale depicts cases where $E(\xi) < 0$; when $E(\xi) \leq 0$, the transfer cost percentage %SC becomes negligible and thus is omitted. Similarly, Figures 7 and 8 plot (S^*, s^*) and the cost percentages associated with Scenario 2, respectively. (Here, although %SC is low, it is reported).

Figures 5–8 show that:

The levels s^* and S^*. When the loss cost is low (i.e., Scenario 1), the level s^* is kept low; when the loss cost is high (i.e., Scenario 2), level s^* is significantly higher and is decreasing in $E(\xi)$. Consequently, it interesting to see that, despite the high loss cost, when $E(\xi) > 0$, s^* is set low, probably due to the more frequent returns that reduce the number of shortages (see Figure 7). When $E(\xi) > 0$, Figures 5 and 7 show similar values of S^*; we further see that S^* is increasing in $E(\xi)$. By contrast, when $E(\xi) < 0$, we see significantly higher values of S^* under Scenario 2. Here, when demands become more frequent, the impact of the high penalty cost dominates in increasing S^*. Nevertheless, the difference (S^*-s^*) is increasing in $E(\xi)$ under both scenarios, meaning that as demands become more frequent, the optimal policy is to call the distributor more frequently and for smaller quantities.

The cost components. Our results show that, as expected, when demands become more frequent ($E(\xi) < 0$) and S^* is low, the cost percentage of SC is negligible; this holds even when S^* is set higher due to a high penalty cost (Figure 8 showing that SC becomes a more significant but still meager component of the cost, less than 2%). Surprisingly, when $E(\xi) < 0$, the cost percentages remain generally similar in $E(\xi)$ under both scenarios. This can be explained by the relatively small changes in S^*. By contrast, when returns arrive more frequently, $E(\xi) > 0$, we see significant changes in the cost percentages as a function of $E(\xi)$. Figures 6 and 8 highlight the interplay between %DC and %LC. The percentage of the distributor's service cost %DC is significantly higher under Scenario 1 (which is directly impacted by γ); by contrast, under Scenario 2, the loss cost %LC forms the main component of the cost. Under both scenarios, when more returns arrive, SC (OC) becomes the more (less) dominant component of the cost. Moreover, comparing Figures 6 and 8 implies that, when $E(\xi) \geq 0$, we have %$SC_{\{Scenario\ 1\}} \approx$ %$SC_{\{Scenario\ 2\}}$ and %$OC_{\{Scenario\ 1\}} \approx$ %$OC_{\{Scenario\ 2\}}$. For example, we have %$SC_{\{Scenario\ 1\}} = \{0.17, 0.30, 0.64, 0.73\}$, and %$SC_{\{Scenario\ 2\}} = \{0.18, 0.33, 0.65, 0.71\}$ corresponding to $E(\xi) = \{0, 0.22, 0.43, 0.625\}$. When $E(\xi) < 0$, we have %$DC_{\{Scenario\ 1\}} \approx$ %$DC_{\{Scenario\ 2\}}$; here, we obtain %$DC_{\{Scenario\ 1\}} = \{0.37, 0.40, 0.41, 0.42\}$, and %$DC_{\{Scenario\ 2\}} = \{0.40, 0.40, 0.40, 0.38\}$ corresponding to $E(\xi) = \{-0.45, -0.41, -0.30, -0.12\}$. These observations emphasize the company's policy of balancing the cost components despite the different cost values. In general, when more returns arrive, and thus more items are transferred, the optimal policy aims to keep %SC relatively constant, whereas, when more demands arrive, and thus more orders are placed, the focus is to keep %DC relatively constant.

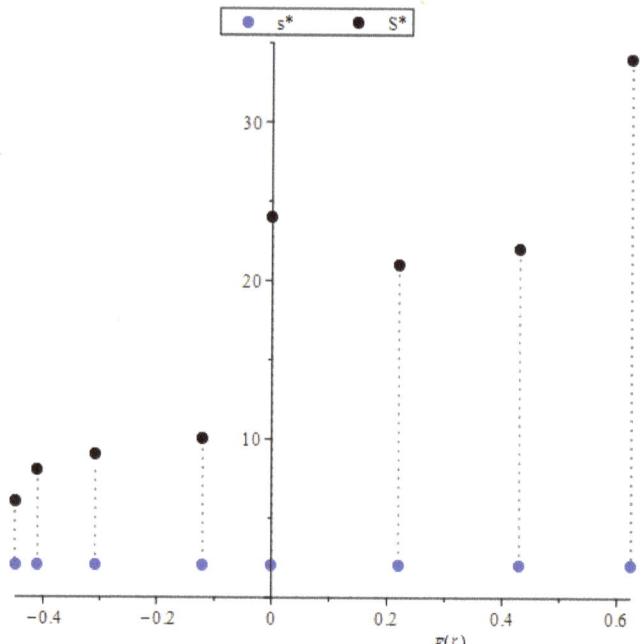

Figure 5. (S^*, s^*) corresponding to $E(\xi)$, Scenario 1.

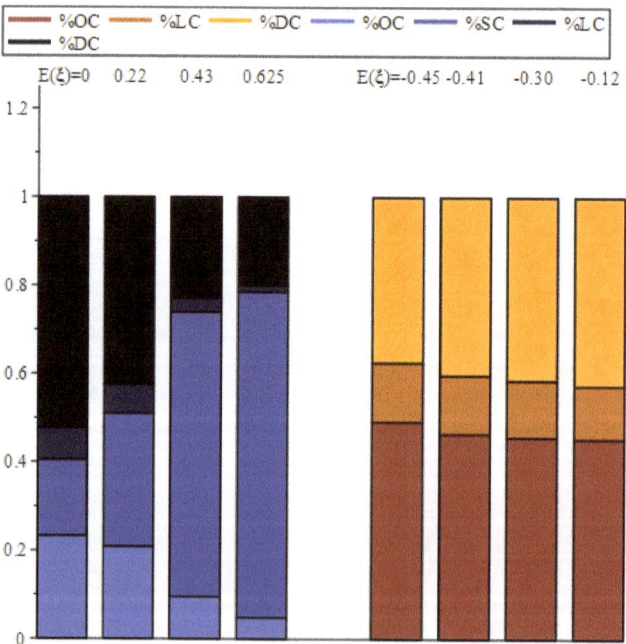

Figure 6. The %cost components, Scenario 1.

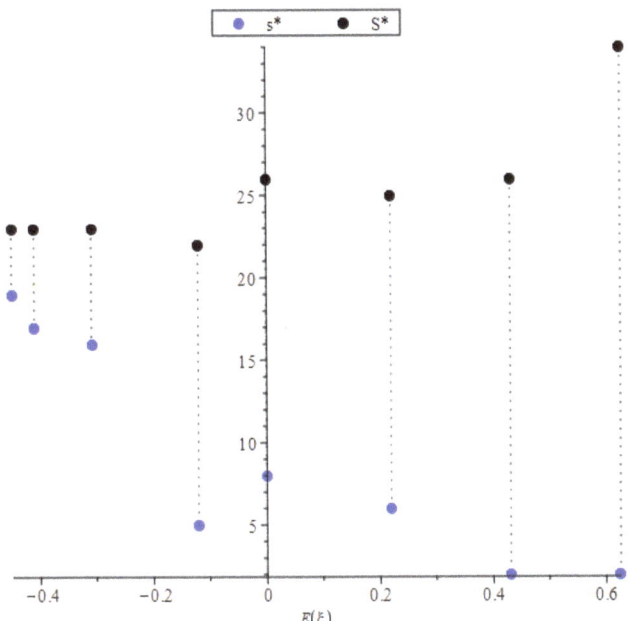

Figure 7. (s^*, S^*) corresponding to $E(\xi)$, Scenario 2.

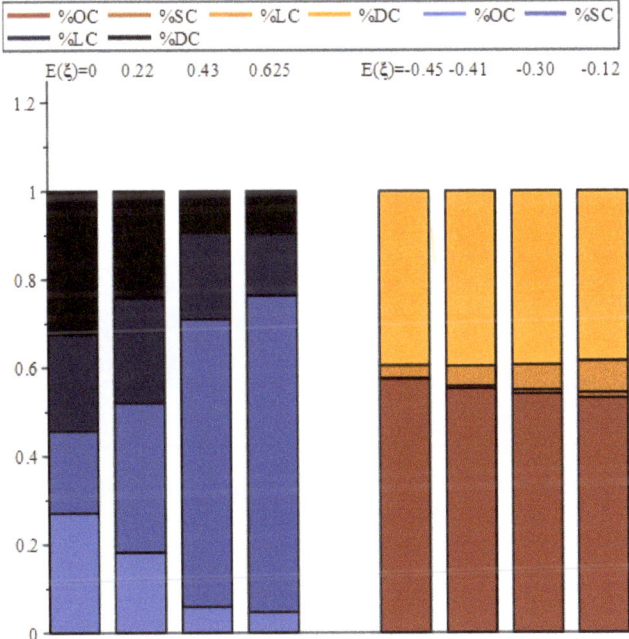

Figure 8. The %cost components, Scenario 2.

Example 3. *The impact of β. We next concentrate on the impact of the discounted factor β on the optimal thresholds and cost. To do so, we let $Y^- = 50$, $\nu = 25$, $\phi = 25$, $\gamma = 5$, $\mu = 0.1$, $Y^+ \in \{15, 25, 50, 100\}$, and vary β in $\{0.025, 0.05, 0.075, 0.1\}$. Table 4 presents the optimal policy and cost; it includes five subtables that differ in their $E(\xi)$. The top subtable corresponds to*

$E(\xi) = 0$, the two left-hand subtables correspond to the negative $E(\xi) = \{-0.308, -0.41\}$, and the two right-hand subtables correspond to the positive $E(\xi) = \{0.22, 0.43\}$. Each subtable presents the levels (S^*, s^*) and the cost $TC(S^*, s^*, M = 35)$ for different values of β; the entry $E(\xi) = 0$, $\beta = 0.075$, $Y^+ = 50$ is also given in Table 2. Figure 9a curves S^* and s^* as a function of β, for $E(\xi) = \{0, -0.308, -0.41\}$ (the black, blue, and gray curves, respectively); similarly, Figure 9b curves S^* and s^* for $E(\xi) = \{0, 0.22, 0.43\}$ (the black, blue, and gray curves, respectively). (Here, we take $Y^+ = 50$.) Note that both figures contain the case $E(\xi) = 0$, indicated by the black curves.

Table 4. (S^*, s^*), $TC(M = 35, S^*, s^*)$ as a function of β, $E(\xi)$, and Y^+.

	S^*, s^* TC^*		β						β		
	$E(\xi) = 0$	0.025	0.05	0.075	0.1						
$_i+$	15	13, 8 241.121	16, 9 92.529	17, 8 48.974	19, 5 29.221						
	25	12, 7 263.498	16, 8 102.091	18, 6 53.278	20, 4 31.282						
	50	12, 5 313.620	17, 7 122.909	19, 4 61.845	20, 2 34.708						
	100	13, 5 405.342	18, 2 155.221	21, 2 73.906	21, 1 40.932						
	$E(\xi) = -0.308$	0.025	0.05	0.075	0.1	$E(\xi) = 0.22$		0.025	0.05	0.075	0.1
$_i+$	15	14, 11 189.954	18, 16 98.580	20, 16 56.465	21, 14 35.679		15	15, 2 1193	13, 2 233.797	14, 5 83.106	15, 4 40.079
	25	13, 10 217.648	18, 15 117.955	21, 18 70.431	21, 13 42.855	$_i+$	25	21, 2 1145	14, 2 240.001	14, 2 86.883	16, 1 41.923
	50	12, 9 284.880	18, 15 165.584	20, 14 97.471	22, 11 59.143		50	21, 2 1188	15, 2 254.774	15, 1 94.634	17, 1 46.180
	100	12, 9 418.205	16, 13 259.948	19, 12 153.258	23, 8 87.600		100	21, 2 1274	17, 2 281.976	17, 1 108.364	18, 1 53.676
	$E(\xi) = -0.41$	0.025	0.05	0.075	0.1	$E(\xi) = 0.43$		0.025	0.05	0.075	0.1
$_i+$	15	16, 15 190.886	18, 16 104.637	20, 16 60.542	20, 14 38.376		15	34, 2 959.741	25, 2 417.673	15, 1 172.134	13, 1 76.027
	25	16, 15 223.120	18, 16 125.17	19, 15 73.465	21, 14 46.47	$_i+$	25	34, 2 963.969	25, 2 419.423	15, 1 174.239	13, 1 77.896
	50	14, 13 302.48	17, 15 176.372	19, 14 105.381	21, 11 64.951		50	34, 2 974.540	25, 1 423.796	16, 1 179.223	14, 1 82.263
	100	12, 11 454.858	16, 14 277.973	19, 13 167.416	23, 9 97.662		100	34, 2 995.681	26, 1 432.543	17, 1 197.933	15, 1 89.658

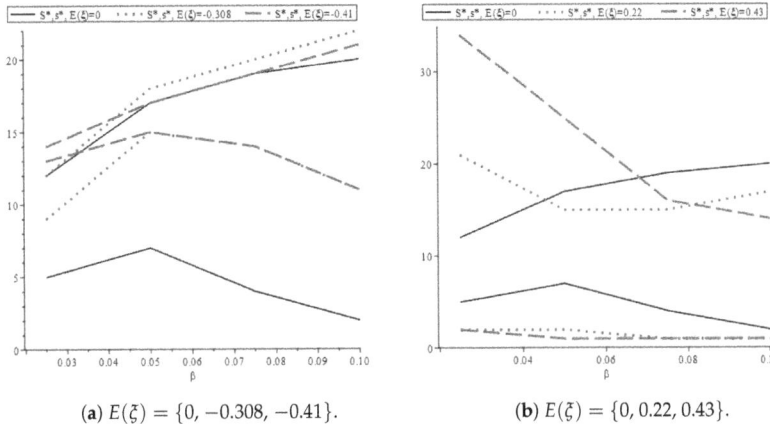

(a) $E(\xi) = \{0, -0.308, -0.41\}$. (b) $E(\xi) = \{0, 0.22, 0.43\}$.

Figure 9. The levels S^* and s^* as a function of β and $E(\xi)$.

From Table 4 and Figure 9, we derive the following conclusions:

- As expected, the cost TC^* is decreasing in β and is increasing in Y^+. We further see that, while increasing Y^+ decreases s^* (in accordance with Table 3), the changes of S^* in Y^+ are not monotone and are impacted also by β and $E(\xi)$ (in fact, S^* varies slightly in Y^+).
- When $E(\xi) \leq 0$, the level S^* is increasing in β, while s^* seems to be concave. Hence, increasing β increases the difference S^*-s^* (noted that a balanced system with $E(\xi) = 0$ is also included here; see Table 3). When the value of β is high, then, despite the fact that demands become more frequent, it is economically profitable for the company to postpone ordering and thereby increase the quantity of refilling.
- By contrast, when $E(\xi) > 0$, we see that S^* is convex in β, and s^* is decreasing. Here, the difference S^*–s^* is convex in β. In general, as more returns arrive, and for low values of β, the company's main motivation is to reduce the transfer cost by decreasing S^*, s^* and reducing S^*–s^*. However, as β increases, we see a slight increase in S^* (see Figure 9b, particularly the dotted blue curve when $\beta \geq 0.08$). The main implication is to postpone the distributor in order to achieve a full utilization of the discount factor.

Summarizing, we see that the discount factor, and the interplay between returns and demands, have a crucial impact on determining the optimal policy and obtaining a decisive economic advantage.

7. Conclusions

This paper studies an inventory control problem with two types of storage facilities that differ in purpose and capacity. We consider continuous and batch-type bilateral changes in the inventory level, where both types of changes are governed by the underlying Markov chain. Applying first passage time results, we build a relatively easy set of equations to derive the cost components under the discounted criterion and lost sales assumption. In doing so, we provide managers with a useful and efficient tool to derive, numerically, the optimal parameters. We show that the limited capacity yields lower thresholds, and as demands become more frequent, it is worthwhile to order more frequently and in smaller quantities. We further show that the timing has a significant impact on the optimal policy; for high values of β, it is worth considering postponing the distributor even at the risk of causing more shortage events.

For future research, it will be interesting to consider the case where each refilling order proceeds sequentially for a few stages, each of which has an independent exponential distributed time. Thus, the total time it would take to handle the order could be expressed by the phase-type distribution rather than by an exponential one. In particular, nowadays, when collaborative inventories and outsourcing services are widespread, it is practical to assume that each order has to go through several procedures, e.g., due to miscellaneous certificates, multiple managers, or different hierarchical ranks. Our approach in this study appears to be simple and easy to implement; thus, we believe that it can be applied as a powerful tool to address other inventory policies. For example, upon adding the option of backordering up to some fixed level, thereafter the unsatisfied demand will be lost. Another well-known policy is the (Q, r) policy, where a fixed order of size Q is placed whenever the on-hand stock level drops to or below level r. Finally, a combination of the above-mentioned policies can also be considered. Each of the discussed policy is worth studying and hence is left for future investigation.

Funding: This research received no external funding.

Conflicts of Interest: The authors declare no conflict of interest.

Appendix A

Appendix A.1. Selected Studies on Continuous Review Base Stock Inventory Policy

Table A1 presents the most relevant studies on continuous review base stock inventory policy and random demands and returns.

Table A1. Selected studies on continuous review base stock inventory policy.

Continuous-Review Base-Stock Inventory Models		Model Features				Optimization Approach
Authors	Arrival Pattern of Demand/Return	Movement Patterns (Conti., Jumps)	Lead Time	Base-Stock Policy	Additional Features	
Benkherouf, Bensoussan (2009) [6]	Com. Poiss. + diffusion/no returns	One-sided jumps	zero	(q_i, u_i)-band policy	Disc. criteria	A quasi-variational inequalities approach
Yamazaki (2016, 2017) [8,29]	Spectrally positive Lévy processes	One-sided jumps	zero	(S, s)	Disc. criteria	fluctuation theory of Lévy processes / The scale function
Perera, Janakiraman, Niu (2018) [5]	Renewal proc./no returns	One-sided unit jumps	zero/ constant	(S, s) (B)	Long run analysis	Renewal theory / Deterministic dynamic programming
Barron (2018) [18]	Fluid flow /MAP	One-sided jumps	zero	$(Q, 0)$ (LS)	Disc. criteria / Obsolescence + emergency	Martingales / Numerical investigation
Azcue, Muler (2019) [43]	Comp. Poiss./Comp. Poiss.	Two sided jumps	zero	Multi-band structure	Disc. criteria	Solution of HJB equation
Pérez, Yamazaki, Bensoussan (2020) [7]	Spectrally positive Lévy processes	One-sided jumps	zero	Periodical replenishments	Disc. criteria	The scale function / Guess and verify procedure
Barron, Dreyfuss (2021) [4]	Comp. Poiss./Comp. Poiss.	Two-sided jumps. No conti. movements	exp	(S, s) (LS)	Steady-state analysis	Markov chain / Numerical investigation
Chakravarthy, Rao (2021) [42]	MAP/no returns	One-sided jumps	zero	Random replenishments (LS, B)	Steady-state analysis	Matrix-analytic methods
Barron (2022) [13]	Fluid flow or jumps for demands/no returns	One-sided movements	exp	(S, s) + emergencies	Disc. Criteria / Immediate emergency	LSTs / Numerical investigation
This study	MAP/MAP	Bilateral linear rates. Two-sided-PH-Jumps	exp	(M, S, s) (LS)	Disc. Criteria / Joint management policy, two storages	Renewal set of equations / LSTs / Multidimensional / Martingales / Numerical investigation

187

It can be observed that, although numerous studies deal with the (S,s)-type inventory models with uncertainties, no study discusses cancellations, double-sided barriers, bilateral movements and integrated control policy. As we pointed out in Section 2, several models used in the literature focus on the derivation of the LSTs of the first-passage time in a Markov-modulated process with bilateral random jumps. However, they do not apply any replenishment policy or cost components; thus, they are not included in Table A1.

Appendix A.2. A Summary of the Cost' Derivation

Here, we summarize the algorithm for the derivation of the cost components. The algorithm is composed of three main parts. The first part includes the derivation of the matrices $\mathbb{A}(\beta)$ and $\mathbb{A}^R(\beta)$. In the second part, we derive the cost components. The third part is devoted to the optimal policy. The algorithm is demonstrated by applying the values of Scenario 1 and $E(\xi) = 0$, i.e., $\widetilde{\mathbb{Q}} = \begin{pmatrix} -0.03 & 0.03 \\ 0.05 & -0.05 \end{pmatrix}$, $\eta = (0.625, 0.325)$, $c_1 = 0.5$, $T^{(1-)} = \begin{pmatrix} -0.25 & 0 \\ 0 & -0.5 \end{pmatrix}$, $c_2 = -1.5$, $T^{(2+)} = -1/5$, $\lambda_1 = 0.2$, $\lambda_2 = 0.161$, $\beta = 0.075$, $\mu = 0.1$, $M = 35$, and the costs $Y^+ = 50$, $Y^- = 150$, $\nu = 5$, $\gamma = 10$ and $\phi = 5$.

Appendix A.2.1. Step 1 (Build the Modified Process)

- Define the enlarged state space $E \equiv \widetilde{E} \cup E_- \cup E_+$ where $E_\pm := \{(i,j,k,\pm) : i,j \in \widetilde{E}, 1 \le k \le m_{ij}^\pm\}$. Here, we obtain: $\widetilde{E} = \{1,2\}$, $E_+ = \{(2,1,+)\}$, $E_- = \{(1,1,-),(1,2,-)\}$. Thus, the enlarged state space E includes five states.
- Built the generator matrix $\mathbb{Q}$ of the modified MMFF process; use Equations (9) and (10). Here, we obtain:

$$Q = \begin{pmatrix} -0.23 & 0 & 0.03 & 0.06 & 0.14 \\ 0 & -1/3 & 1/3 & 0 & 0 \\ 0.05 & 0.1 & -0.15 & 0 & 0 \\ 0.25 & 0 & 0 & -0.25 & 0 \\ 0.5 & 0 & 0 & 0 & -0.5 \end{pmatrix}.$$

- Applying the algorithm of Section 2.2 of Breuer [27] for $((\mathbb{A}(\beta), U(\beta)) : n \ge 0)$ to obtain $\mathbb{A}(\beta)$. Built the process $\mathcal{X}^R$ by reversing the roles of the up and down movements; similarly, use the algorithm to obtain $\mathbb{A}^R(\beta)$. For our values, we obtain:

$$A(\beta) = \begin{pmatrix} 0.05582 & 0.5831 \\ 0.3808 & 0.1048 \\ 0.5516 & 0.07592 \end{pmatrix}, \quad A^R(\beta) = \begin{pmatrix} 0.08207 & 0.1981 & 0.4621 \\ 0.6229 & 0.03089 & 0.07207 \end{pmatrix}.$$

- Calculating the special LSTs given in Corollary 2(i) and (ii),

$$(\beta I - Q_{11})^{-1} Q_{12} = \begin{pmatrix} 0.175 & 0.563 \\ 1 & 0 \\ 1 & 0 \end{pmatrix}, \quad (\beta I - Q_{22})^{-1} Q_{21} = \begin{pmatrix} 0.098 & 0.197 & 0.459 \\ 1 & 0 & 0 \end{pmatrix}.$$

Appendix A.2.2. Step 2 (Derive the Cost Components)

For S and $0 \le s \le S - 1$, do the following:

- Apply the algorithm of [49] to derive the LSTs ${}_u^v \widehat{f}^r(x,y,)$ and ${}_a^b \widehat{f}^r(x,y,)$ to be used.
- Derive the expected discounted cycle-length matrix $\mathbb{E}_S(e^{-C})$; use Proposition 1.
- Apply Corollary 3 to obtain the expected discounted ordering times vector $OC_S(\beta)$.
- Use Proposition 2 and Claim 2 to derive the vectors $SC_S(\beta)$ and $LC_S(\beta)$, respectively.
- Derive the vectors $\mathbb{E}_s(e^{-\beta\mathcal{L}} I_0(\mathcal{L}) 1_{\{\mathcal{L} < \min(T_S, T_0)\}})$, $\mathbb{E}_S(e^{-\beta\mathcal{L}} I(\mathcal{L}) 1_{\{\mathcal{L} < \varsigma\}})$ and $\overline{E}_0(e^{-\beta\mathcal{L}} I(\mathcal{L}) 1_{\{\mathcal{L} < \varsigma\}})$; use Claim 3 and Corollary 4. Then, apply Proposition 4 to obtain $\Delta_S(\beta)$. Finally, substitute into Equation (23) to obtain the vector $DC_S(\beta)$.

- Use Equations (4)–(7) to calculate the expected discounted costs $OC(\beta), SC(\beta), LC(\beta),$ $DC(\beta)$ and the total cost $TC(S,s) = OC(\beta) + SC(\beta) + LC(\beta) + DC(\beta)$.

Appendix A.2.3. Step 3 (the Optimal Policy)

Choose the optimal value $TC^* = \min_{S,s}\{TC(S,s)\}$. For the values mentioned above, we obtain optimal thresholds $S^* = 24$, $s^* = 2$, $TC^* = 39.896$ (see Table 2), and costs

$$OC(\beta) = 9.295, \ SC(\beta) = 6.855, \ LC(\beta) = 2.910, \ DC = 20.836.$$

Appendix B. Proofs

Appendix B.1. Proof of Proposition 1

There is a significant difference between cases (i)–(iv), where a refilling has not been ordered yet, and the more challenging cases (v)–(xi) that occur during lead time (Recall that T_x denotes the time to hit level x.)

Cases (i)–(iv). We start with case (i); here, we assume an initial state (S, E_1), i.e., $I_o(0) = S$ at an ascending state. Applying decomposition according to T_S and T_M, we obtain

$$\overline{E}_S(e^{-\beta C}) = \overline{E}_S(e^{-\beta C}\mathbf{1}_{\{T_S < T_M\}}) + \overline{E}_S(e^{-\beta C}\mathbf{1}_{\{T_S > T_M\}}). \tag{A1}$$

The first term of (A1) is the LST to return to level S while avoiding level M ($^{M-S}\mathbb{A}^r(\beta)$); from that point, the expected discounted cycle length is $\underline{E}_S(e^{-\beta C})$. The second term of (A1) is the LST to hit level M while avoiding S ($_S\hat{f}_{11}(S,M,\beta)$), and thereafter the expected cycle length is $\overline{E}_M(e^{-\beta C})$. The proofs of cases (ii)–(iv) are similar and thus are omitted. Note that, by Corollary 2(i), the term $(\beta\mathbb{I} - \mathbb{Q}_{11})^{-1}\mathbb{Q}_{12}$ in case (iii) is the LST to exit level M at a descending state.

Cases (v)–(xi). Here, we need to track the stock level during lead time. We focus on the proofs of Cases (v) and (vi); other proofs use similar techniques and thus are omitted. Case (v) considers the situation of hitting level s and ordering a refill. We distinguish between three events that affect the continuity of the process: either the distributor arrives, or level S is hit, or level 0 is hit. Thus,

$$\underline{E}_s^o(e^{-\beta C}) = \underline{E}_s^o(e^{-\beta C}\mathbf{1}_{\{T_S < \min(\mathcal{L}, T_0)\}}) + \underline{E}_s^o(e^{-\beta C}\mathbf{1}_{\{T_0 < \min(T_S, \mathcal{L})\}}) + \underline{E}_s^o(e^{-\beta C}\mathbf{1}_{\{\mathcal{L} < \min(T_S, T_0)\}}). \tag{A2}$$

Applying the first passage times for MMFF, we obtain

$$\begin{aligned}\underline{E}_s^o(e^{-\beta C}\mathbf{1}_{\{T_S < \min(\mathcal{L}, T_0)\}}) &= {}_0\hat{f}_{21}(s, S, \beta + \mu)\overline{E}_S^o(e^{-\beta C}),\\ \underline{E}_s^o(e^{-\beta C}\mathbf{1}_{\{T_0 < \min(T_S, \mathcal{L})\}}) &= {}^S\hat{f}_{22}(s, 0, \beta + \mu)\underline{E}_0^o(e^{-\beta C}).\end{aligned} \tag{A3}$$

In the case of $\mathcal{L} < \min(T_S, T_0)$, the distributor arrives when $0 < I_o(\mathcal{L}) < S$, the refilling is made, the cycle ends and, thus, the remaining cycle length is $\mathcal{L}$. Formally,

$$\underline{E}_s^o(e^{-\beta C}\mathbf{1}_{\{\mathcal{L} < \min(T_S, T_0)\}}) = \underline{E}_s^o(e^{-\beta \mathcal{L}}\mathbf{1}_{\{\mathcal{L} < \min(T_S, T_0)\}}) = \underline{E}_s^o(e^{-\beta \mathcal{L}}) - \underline{E}_s^o(e^{-\beta \mathcal{L}}\mathbf{1}_{\{\mathcal{L} > \min(T_S, T_0)\}}). \tag{A4}$$

The first term of (A4) is given by $\underline{E}_s^o(e^{-\beta \mathcal{L}}) = \frac{\mu}{\beta+\mu}e$. For the second term, we use the memoryless property of the exponential distribution. Define the stopping time $\varsigma = \min(T_S, T_0)$. When $\mathcal{L} > \varsigma$, we can plug in $\mathcal{L} = \widetilde{\mathcal{L}} + \varsigma$, where $\widetilde{\mathcal{L}}$ is an independent exponential r.v. with rate μ. Altogether, we obtain

$$\begin{aligned}\underline{E}_s^o(e^{-\beta\mathcal{L}}\mathbf{1}_{\{\mathcal{L}>\varsigma\}}) &= \underline{E}_s^o(e^{-\beta(\widetilde{\mathcal{L}}+\varsigma)}\mathbf{1}_{\{\mathcal{L}>\varsigma\}}) = \underline{E}_s^o(e^{-\beta\varsigma}\mathbf{1}_{\{\mathcal{L}>\varsigma\}})E(e^{-\beta\widetilde{\mathcal{L}}})\\ &= \left({}_0\hat{f}_{21}(s,S,\beta+\mu)e + {}^S\hat{f}_{22}(s,0,\beta+\mu)e\right)\frac{\mu}{\beta+\mu}.\end{aligned} \tag{A5}$$

The second line of (A5) arises via the decomposition according to $\varsigma = T_S$ and $\varsigma = T_0$. Specifically, when $\varsigma = T_S$, we obtain $T_S < \mathcal{L}$, $T_S < T_0$ with LST ${}_0\hat{f}_{21}(s,S,\beta+\mu)$. When

$\varsigma = T_0$, we obtain $T_0 < \mathcal{L}$, $T_0 < T_S$ with LST ${}^S\hat{f}_{22}(s,0,\beta+\mu)$. Substituting (A3)–(A5) into (A2) proves Case (v).

Next, we prove Case (vi). Here, $\mathcal{I}_o$ hits level S from below during lead time (in contrast to Case (i), where no refilling is ordered). A similar decomposition yields

$$\overline{E}_S^o(e^{-\beta C}) = \overline{E}_S^o(e^{-\beta C}\mathbf{1}_{\{T_S<\min(\mathcal{L},T_M)\}}) + \overline{E}_S^o(e^{-\beta C}\mathbf{1}_{\{T_M<\min(\mathcal{L},T_S)\}}) + \overline{E}_S^o(e^{-\beta C}\mathbf{1}_{\{\mathcal{L}<\min(T_S,T_M)\}}). \tag{A6}$$

It is easy to verify that

$$\overline{E}_S^o(e^{-\beta C}\mathbf{1}_{\{T_S<\min(L,T_M)\}}) = {}^{M-S}\mathbb{A}^r(\beta+\mu)\,\underline{E}_S^o(e^{-\beta C}),$$
$$\overline{E}_S^o(e^{-\beta C}\mathbf{1}_{\{T_M<\min(L,T_S)\}}) = s\hat{f}_{11}(S,M,\beta+\mu)\,\overline{E}_M^o(e^{-\beta C}). \tag{A7}$$

The last term of (A6) describes the event where the distributor arrives when $\mathcal{I}_o > S$ and, thus, no refilling is carried out, and the cycle continues. Hence,

$$\overline{E}_S^o(e^{-\beta C}\mathbf{1}_{\{\mathcal{L}<\min(T_S,T_M)\}}) = \overline{E}_S^o(e^{-\beta T_S}\mathbf{1}_{\{\mathcal{L}<T_S<T_M\}})\underline{E}_S(e^{-\beta C}) + \overline{E}_S^o(e^{-\beta T_M}\mathbf{1}_{\{\mathcal{L}<T_M<T_S\}})\overline{E}_M(e^{-\beta C}).$$

Applying the first passage times to MMFF yields

$$\overline{E}_S^o(e^{-\beta T_S}\mathbf{1}_{\{\mathcal{L}<T_S<T_M\}}) = \overline{E}_S^o(e^{-\beta T_S}\mathbf{1}_{\{T_S<T_M\}}) - \overline{E}_S^o(e^{-\beta T_S}\mathbf{1}_{\{T_S<T_M,\mathcal{L}>T_S\}})$$
$$= \left({}^{M-S}\mathbb{A}^r(\beta) - {}^{M-S}\mathbb{A}^r(\beta+\mu)\right)\underline{E}_S(e^{-\beta C}). \tag{A8}$$

Similarly,

$$\overline{E}_S^o(e^{-\beta T_M}\mathbf{1}_{\{\mathcal{L}<T_M,T_M<T_S\}}) = \overline{E}_S^o(e^{-\beta T_M}\mathbf{1}_{\{T_M<T_S\}}) - \overline{E}_S^o(e^{-\beta T_M}\mathbf{1}_{\{T_M<T_S,\mathcal{L}>T_M\}})$$
$$= \left(s\hat{f}_{11}(S,M,\beta) - s\hat{f}_{11}(S,M,\beta+\not\geq)\right). \tag{A9}$$

Substituting (A7)–(A9) into (A6) completes the derivation of Case (vi). We further note that, by Corollary 2(ii), the term $((\beta+\mu)\mathbb{I} - \mathbb{Q}_{22})^{-1}\mathbb{Q}_{21}$ in Case $(viii)$ is the LST to exit level 0 at an ascending state. In addition, only in Cases $(v), (vii), (viii)$, and (ix) does the cycle end when the distributor arrives (represented by the last term in each case).

Appendix B.2. Proof of Proposition 2

We present only the key steps of the proofs of Cases (i)–(iv). It is easy to verify that Cases (i) and (ii) follow from the decomposition according to $\min(T_M, T_S)$; the only difference is due to the initial state (S, E_1) (in Case (i)) and (M, E_2) (in Case (ii)). Similarly, Case (iv) is derived with regard to S and s. Applying Claim 1 and Corollary 2(i) immediately yields Case (iii).

Next, we will address the impact of the lead time. Cases (v)–(ix) are straightforward since they include the event $I_o(\mathcal{L}) < S$, and thereafter the PW is refilled and the cycle ends. Cases (x)–(xii) are more complicated; here, the event $I_o(\mathcal{L}) > S$ may happen. We focus on case (x) and distinguish between four events. (a) Hitting level M during lead time and continue with $\overline{SC}_M^o(\beta)$. (b) The distributor arrives when $S < \mathcal{I}_o < M$ (with no refilling); thereafter, level M is hit. Using the decomposition yields

$$\overline{SC}_S^o(\beta)\mathbf{1}_{\{\mathcal{L}<T_M<T_S\}} = \overline{SC}_S^o(\beta)\mathbf{1}_{\{T_M<T_S\}} - \overline{SC}_S^o(\beta)\mathbf{1}_{\{T_M<T_S,\mathcal{L}>T_M\}},$$

where $\overline{SC}_S^o(\beta)\mathbf{1}_{\{T_M<T_S\}} = s\hat{f}_{11}(S,M,\beta)$ and $\overline{SC}_S^o(\beta)\mathbf{1}_{\{T_M<T_S,\mathcal{L}>T_M\}} = s\hat{f}_{11}(S,M,\beta+\mu)$. (c) Hitting level S during lead time and continues with $\underline{SC}_S^o(\beta)$. Finally, (d) the distributor arrives when $S < \mathcal{I}_o < M$ (with there is no refilling); thereafter, level S is hit; a similar technique to (b) is used for ${}^{M-S}\mathbb{A}^r(\beta) - {}^{M-S}\mathbb{A}^r(\beta+\mu)$. The proofs of Cases (xi)–(xii) are similar and thus are omitted.

Appendix B.3. Proof of Claim 3

Let $Y(t) = -(\beta+\mu)t/\alpha$ and $\mathcal{Z}(t) = \mathcal{X}(t) + Y(t)$. Applying Theorem 2.1 of Asmussen and Kella [50] yields that the process

$$M(\alpha, t) = \left(M^1(\alpha, t), M^2(\alpha, t), \ldots, M^{|E_2|}(\alpha, t)\right)^\top$$

$$= \int_0^t e^{\alpha \mathcal{Z}(u)} \mathbf{1}_{J(u)} du \mathbb{K}(\alpha) + e^{\alpha \mathcal{Z}(0)} \mathbf{1}_{J(0)} - e^{\alpha \mathcal{Z}(t)} \mathbf{1}_{J(t)} + \alpha \int_0^t e^{\alpha \mathcal{Z}(u)} \mathbf{1}_{J(u)} dY(u)$$

$$= \int_0^t e^{\alpha \mathcal{X}(u) - (\beta+\mu)u} \mathbf{1}_{J(u)} du (\mathbb{K}(\alpha) - (\beta+\mu)\mathbb{I}) + e^{\alpha \mathcal{X}(0)} \mathbf{1}_{J(0)} - e^{\alpha \mathcal{X}(t) - (\beta+\mu)t} \mathbf{1}_{J(t)} \quad \text{(A10)}$$

is an $|E_2|$-row vector-valued zero mean martingale. The OST yields $\mathbb{E}(M(\alpha,\varsigma)) = \mathbb{E}(M(\alpha,0)) = \mathbf{0}$, i.e.,

$$\mathbb{E}_s \left(\int_0^\varsigma e^{\alpha I_0(t) - (\beta+\mu)t} \mathbf{1}_{J(t)} dt \right) = \left[\mathbb{E}_s(e^{\alpha \mathcal{X}(\varsigma) - (\beta+\mu)\varsigma} \mathbf{1}_{J(\varsigma)}) - \mathbb{E}_s(e^{\alpha \mathcal{X}(0)} \mathbf{1}_{J(0)}) \right] (\mathbb{K}(\alpha) - (\beta+\mu)\mathbb{I})^{-1}. \quad \text{(A11)}$$

Since $\mathcal{X}(0) = s$ and $J(0) = i \in E_2$, we have that $\left[\mathbb{E}_s\left(e^{\alpha \mathcal{X}(0)} \mathbf{1}_{J(0)}\right)\right]_{i,i} = e^{\alpha s}, i \in E_2$; using an $(|E_2| \times |E|)$ matrix form yields

$$\mathbb{E}_s\left(e^{\alpha \mathcal{X}(0)} \mathbf{1}_{J(0)}\right) = e^{\alpha s} (\mathbf{0} \ \mathbb{I}). \quad \text{(A12)}$$

To derive the $(|E_2| \times |E|)$ matrix $\mathbb{E}_s(e^{\alpha \mathcal{X}(\varsigma) - (\beta+\mu)\varsigma} \mathbf{1}_{J(\varsigma)})$, we use the following decomposition (note that $\mathcal{X}(T_S) = S$ and $\mathcal{X}(T_0) = 0$):

$$\mathbb{E}_s(e^{\alpha \mathcal{X}(\varsigma) - (\beta+\mu)\varsigma} \mathbf{1}_{J(\varsigma)}) = \mathbb{E}_s(e^{\alpha \mathcal{X}(T_S) - (\beta+\mu)T_S} \mathbf{1}_{\{\varsigma = T_S, J(\varsigma)\}}) + \mathbb{E}_s(e^{\alpha \mathcal{X}(T_0) - (\beta+\mu)T_0} \mathbf{1}_{\{\varsigma = T_0, J(\varsigma)\}})$$

$$= e^{\alpha S} \mathbb{E}_s(e^{-(\beta+\mu)T_S} \mathbf{1}_{\{\varsigma = T_S, J(\varsigma)\}}) + \mathbb{E}_s(e^{-(\beta+\mu)T_0} \mathbf{1}_{\{\varsigma = T_0, J(\varsigma)\}})$$

$$= e^{\alpha S} \left(_0\widehat{f}_{21}(s, S, \beta+\mu) \ \mathbf{0}\right) + \left(\mathbf{0} \ {^S}\widehat{f}_{22}(s, 0, \beta+\mu)\right). \quad \text{(A13)}$$

Plugging (A13) and (A12) into (A11) yields (28).

References

1. Kuraie, V.C.; Padiyar, S.S.; Bhagat, N.; Singh, S.R.; Katariya, C. Imperfect production process in an integrated inventory system having multivariable demand with limited storage capacity. *Des. Eng.* **2021**, *2021*, 1505–1527.
2. Asmussen, S. *Applied Probability and Queues*, 2nd ed.; Springer: New York, NY, USA, 2003.
3. Rodríguez-García, M.C.; Gutiérrez-Puertas, L.; Granados-Gámez, G.; Aguilera-Manrique, G.; Mxaxrquez-Hernxaxndez, V.V. The connection of the clinical learning environment and supervision of nursing students with student satisfaction and future intention to work in clinical placement hospitals. *J. Clin. Nurs.* **2021**, *30*, 986–994. [CrossRef] [PubMed]
4. Barron, Y.; Dreyfuss, M. A triple (S, s, ℓ)-thresholds base-stock policy subject to uncertainty environment, returns and order cancellations. *Comput. Oper. Res.* **2021**, *134*, 105320. [CrossRef]
5. Perera, S.; Janakiraman, G.; Niu, S.C. Optimality of (s, S) inventory policies under renewal demand and general cost structures. *Prod. Oper. Manag.* **2018**, *27*, 368–383. [CrossRef]
6. Benkherouf, L.; Bensoussan, A. Optimality of an (s, S) policy with compound Poisson and diffusion demands: A quasi-variational inequalities approach. *SIAM. J. Control Optim.* **2009**, *48*, 756–762. [CrossRef]
7. Pérez, J.L.; Yamazaki, K.; Bensoussan, A. Optimal periodic replenishment policies for spectrally positive Lévy demand processes. *SIAM J. Control Optim.* **2020**, *58*, 3428–3456. [CrossRef]
8. Yamazaki, K. Inventory control for spectrally positive Lèvy demand processes. *Math. Oper. Res.* **2017**, *42*, 212–237. [CrossRef]
9. Yao, D.; Chao, X.; Wu, J. Optimal control policy for a brownian inventory system with concave ordering cost. *J. Appl. Probab.* **2015**, *52*, 909–925. [CrossRef]
10. Dbouk, W.; Tarhini, H.; Nasr, W. Re-ordering policies for inventory systems with a fluctuating economic environment—Using economic descriptors to model the demand process. *J. Oper. Res. Soc.* **2022**, 1–13. [CrossRef]
11. Germain, R.; Claycomb, C.; Dröge, C. Supply chain variability, organizational structure, and performance: The moderating effect of demand unpredictability. *J. Oper. Manag.* **2008**, *26*, 557–570. [CrossRef]

12. Barron, Y. A state-dependent perishability (s, S) inventory model with random batch demands. *Ann. Oper. Res.* **2019**, *280*, 65–98. [CrossRef]
13. Barron, Y. The continuous (S, s, S_e) inventory model with dual sourcing and emergency orders. *Eur. J. Oper. Res.* **2022**, *301*, 18-38. [CrossRef]
14. Lu, Y. Estimation of average backorders for an assemble-to-order system with random batch demands through extreme statistics. *Nav. Res. Logist.* **2007**, *54*, 33–45. [CrossRef]
15. Feng, L.; Chan, Y.L. Joint pricing and production decisions for new products with learning curve effects under upstream and down stream trade credits. *Eur. J. Oper. Res.* **2019**, *272*, 905–913. [CrossRef]
16. Hu, K.; Acimovic, J.; Erize, F.; Thomas, D.J.; Van Mieghem, J.A. Forecasting new product life cycle curves: Practical approach and empirical analysis: Finalist-2017 M&SOM practice-based research competition. *Manuf. Serv. Oper. Manag.* **2018**, *21*, 66–85.
17. Avci, H.; Gokbayrak, K.; Nadar, E. Structural results for average-cost inventory models with Markov-modulated demand and partial information. *Prod. Oper. Manag.* **2020**, *29*, 156–173. [CrossRef]
18. Barron, Y. An order-revenue inventory model with returns and sudden obsolescence. *Oper. Res. Lett.* **2018**, *46*, 88–92. [CrossRef]
19. Ozkan, C.; Karaesmen, F.; Ozekici, S. Structural properties of Markov modulated revenue management problems. *Eur. J. Oper. Res.* **2013**, *225*, 324–331. [CrossRef]
20. Ishfaq, R.; Raja, U.; Rao, S. Seller-induced scarcity and price-leadership. *Int. J. Logist. Manag.* **2016**, *27*, 552–569. [CrossRef]
21. Rudolph, S. E-commerce product return statistics and trends. *Bus. Community* **2016**.
22. Chen, L.; Song, J.S.; Zhang, Y. Serial inventory systems with Markov-modulated demand: Derivative bounds, asymptotic analysis, and insights. *Oper. Res.* **2017**, *65*, 1231–1249. [CrossRef]
23. Nasr, W.W. Inventory systems with stochastic and batch demand: Computational approaches. *Ann. Oper. Res.* **2022**, *309*, 163–187. [CrossRef]
24. Perera, S.C.; Sethi, S. A survey of stochastic inventory models with fixed costs: Optimality of (s, S) and (s, S)-type policies. *Prod. Oper. Manag.* **2022**, *32*, 154–169. [CrossRef]
25. Presman, E.; Sethi, S.P. Inventory models with continuous and Poisson demands and discounted and average costs. *Prod. Oper. Manag.* **2006**, *15*, 279–293. [CrossRef]
26. Ahn, S. Time-dependent and stationary analyses of two-sided reflected Markov-modulated Brownian motion with bilateral ph-type jumps. *J. Korean Stat. Soc.* **2017**, *46*, 45–69. [CrossRef]
27. Breuer, L. A quintuple law for Markov additive processes with phase-type jumps. *J. Appl. Probab* **2010**, *47*, 441–458. [CrossRef]
28. Dudin, A.; Dudina, O.; Dudin, S.; Samouylov, K. Analysis of single-server multi-class queue with unreliable service, batch correlated arrivals, customers impatience, and dynamical change of priorities. *Mathematics* **2021**, *9*, 1257. [CrossRef]
29. Yamazaki, K. Cash management and control band policies for spectrally one-sided Lèvy processes. *Recent Adv. Financ. Eng.* **2016**, *2014*, 199–215.
30. Zhang, Z. Dynamic Cash Management Models. Ph.D. Thesis, Lancaster University, Lancaster, UK, 2022.
31. Yan, K. Fluid Models for Production-Inventory Systems. Ph.D. Thesis, The University of North Carolina at Chapel Hill, Chapel Hill, NC, USA, 2006.
32. Kawai, Y.; Takagi, H. Fluid approximation analysis of a call center model with time-varying arrivals and after-call work. *Oper. Res. Perspect.* **2015**, *2*, 81–96. [CrossRef]
33. Cao, P.; Yao, D. Dual sourcing policy for a continuous-review stochastic inventory system. *IEEE Trans. Automat. Control* **2019**, *64*, 2921–2928. [CrossRef]
34. Gong, M.; Lian, Z.; Xiao, H. Inventory control policy for perishable products under a buyback contract and Brownian demands. *Int. J. Prod. Econ.* **2022**, *251*, 108522. [CrossRef]
35. He, S.; Yao, D.; Zhang, H. Optimal ordering policy for inventory systems with quantity-dependent setup costs. *Math. Oper. Res.* **2017**, *42*, 979–1006. [CrossRef]
36. Li, Y.; Sethi, S. Optimal Ordering Policy for Two Product Inventory Models with Fixed Ordering Costs. 2022. Available online: https://ssrn.com/abstract=4199040 (accessed on 26 December 2022).
37. Anbazhagan, N.; Joshi, G.P.; Suganya, R.; Amutha, S.; Vinitha, V.; Shrestha, B. Queueing-inventory system for two commodities with optional demands of customers and MAP arrivals. *Mathematics* **2022**, *10*, 1801. [CrossRef]
38. Vinitha, V.; Anbazhagan, N.; Amutha, S.; Jeganathan, K.; Shrestha, B.; Song, H.K.; Joshi, G.P.; Moon, H. Analysis of a stochastic inventory model on random environment with two classes of suppliers and impulse customers. *Mathematics* **2022**, *10*, 2235. [CrossRef]
39. López, D.M.; Pérez, J.L.; Yamazaki, K. Effects of positive jumps of assets on endogenous bankruptcy and optimal capital structure: Continuous-and periodic-observation models. *SIAM J. Financ. Math.* **2021**, *12*, 1112–1149. [CrossRef]
40. Noba, K.; Yamazaki, K. On stochastic control under Poisson observations: Optimality of a barrier strategy in a general Lévy model. *arXiv* **2022**, arXiv:2210.00501.
41. Bensoussan, A.; Liu, R.H.; Sethi, S.P. Optimality of an (s, S) policy with compound Poisson and diffusion demands: A quasi-variational inequalities approach. *SIAM. J. Control Optim.* **2005**, *44*, 1650–1676. [CrossRef]
42. Chakravarthy, S.R.; Rao, B.M. Queuing-inventory models with MAP demands and random replenishment opportunities. *Mathematics* **2021**, *9*, 1092. [CrossRef]

43. Azcue, P.; Muler, N. Optimal cash management problem for compound Poisson processes with two-sided jumps. *Appl. Math. Optim.* **2019**, *80*, 331–368. [CrossRef]
44. Deelstra, G.; Latouche, G.; Simon, M. On barrier option pricing by Erlangization in a regime-switching model with jumps. *J. Comput. Appl. Math.* **2020**, *371*, 112606. [CrossRef]
45. Kijima, M.; Siu, C.C. On the First Passage Time under Regime-Switching with Jumps. In *Inspired by Finance*; Springer: Cham, Switzerland, 2014; pp. 387–410.
46. Chew, A.; Mus, S.; Rohloff, P.; Barnoya, J. The Relationship between Corner Stores and the Ultra-processed Food and Beverage Industry in Guatemala: Stocking, Advertising, and Trust. *J. Hunger Environ. Nutr.* **2022**, 1–16. [CrossRef]
47. Mandi, E.; Chen, X.; Zhou, K.Z.; Zhang, C. Loose lips sink ships: The double-edged effect of distributor voice on channel relationship performance. *Ind. Mark. Manag.* **2022**, *102*, 141–152. [CrossRef]
48. Sato, K.; Yagi, K.; Shimazaki, M. A stochastic inventory model for a random yield supply chain with wholesale-price and shortage penalty contracts. *Asia-Pac. J. Oper. Res.* **2018**, *35*, 1850040. [CrossRef]
49. Ramaswami, V. Passage times in fluid models with application to risk processes. *Methodol. Computat. Appl. Probab.* **2006**, *8*, 497–515. [CrossRef]
50. Asmussen, S.; Kella, O. A multi-dimensional martingale for Markov additive processes and its applications. *Adv. Appl. Probab.* **2000**, *32*, 376–393. [CrossRef]
51. Bijvank, M.; Vis, I.A.F. Lost sales inventory theory: A review. *Eur. J. Oper. Res.* **2011**, *215*, 1–13. [CrossRef]

Disclaimer/Publisher's Note: The statements, opinions and data contained in all publications are solely those of the individual author(s) and contributor(s) and not of MDPI and/or the editor(s). MDPI and/or the editor(s) disclaim responsibility for any injury to people or property resulting from any ideas, methods, instructions or products referred to in the content.

Article

Decisions for a Retailer-Led Low-Carbon Supply Chain Considering Altruistic Preference under Carbon Quota Policy

Xiao Zhou [1] and Xiancong Wu [2,*]

[1] College of Business Administration, Fujian Jiangxia University, Fuzhou 350108, China
[2] Business School, Southwest University of Political Science & Law, Chongqing 401120, China
* Correspondence: wuxiancong@swupl.edn.cn

Abstract: With the release of the national energy-saving emission reduction policy and the improvement of consumers' awareness of environmental protection, the demand for low-carbon products is growing rapidly. In a retailer-led low-carbon supply chain, the increased cost of carbon emission reduction puts manufacturers at a disadvantage. Under the carbon quota policy, to improve manufacturers' profits as well as enhance carbon emission reduction, this paper studies the players' decisions in a low-carbon supply chain consisting of one dominant retailer and one manufacturer. To maintain the supply chain's stability and sustainability, the dominant retailer tends to employ altruistic preference policies towards the manufacturer. The optimal decision, carbon emission reduction and supply chain profit are compared and analyzed under three decision models: (i) centralized decision, (ii) decentralized decision without altruistic preference and (iii) decentralized decision with altruistic preference. The results indicate that the carbon emission reduction rate, market demand and profit in the centralized model are higher than in the decentralized model. The retailer's altruistic preference is beneficial to the improvement of carbon emission reduction, market demand and the profit of the manufacturer and the supply chain. Under certain conditions, carbon trading can effectively reduce the cost pressure of manufacturers and improve the level of carbon emission reduction and the overall profit of the supply chain. These results will guide low-carbon supply chain decision-making and provide insight into the research of irrational behaviors in supply chain decision-making under carbon policies.

Keywords: low-carbon supply chain; retailer-led; altruistic preference; carbon quota policy

MSC: 90B06

Citation: Zhou, X.; Wu, X. Decisions for a Retailer-Led Low-Carbon Supply Chain Considering Altruistic Preference under Carbon Quota Policy. *Mathematics* **2023**, *11*, 911. https://doi.org/10.3390/math11040911

Academic Editor: Andreas C. Georgiou

Received: 12 January 2023
Revised: 8 February 2023
Accepted: 9 February 2023
Published: 10 February 2023

Copyright: © 2023 by the authors. Licensee MDPI, Basel, Switzerland. This article is an open access article distributed under the terms and conditions of the Creative Commons Attribution (CC BY) license (https://creativecommons.org/licenses/by/4.0/).

1. Introduction

Extreme weather, such as high temperatures, droughts, rainstorms, and hurricanes, has grown increasingly regular in recent years, seriously threatening human survival and health and posing a challenge to all humanity. Many governments have enacted environmental policies to combat climate change, including carbon taxes and cap-and-trade. Particularly, carbon cap-and-trade can save more energy and reduce emissions by encouraging businesses to invest more resources in low-carbon supply chains for carbon emission reduction. For example, the European Union's emissions trading scheme [1] and China's cap-and-trade scheme [2] are both effective solutions. Moreover, as public awareness of environmental protection grows, consumers are increasingly willing to pay more for low-carbon and energy-saving products [3]. For example, from 2011 to 2015, the compound growth rate of the consumers who were willing to pay a higher price for green products on the Alibaba platform exceeded 80%, and the number of green consumers on the JingDong e-commerce platform climbed by 62% year-on-year in 2017 [4]. Numerous businesses have included environmental protection and sustainable development in their strategic decisions [5–7] in response to the growing demand for low-carbon products on the market. For instance, based on the "circular economy theory", Huawei implements an environmental strategy to continuously improve the use efficiency of resources and energy. Haier establishes the strategic goals of producing green products with an emphasis on energy-efficient product design, innovation, manufacturing, management, and recycling. However, the research and development, introduction, and implementation of low-carbon technologies commonly demand substantial financial support for manufacturing firms [8], which undoubtedly increases the production costs of enterprises. This situation is not conducive to the stability and long-term development of enterprises and their supply chain, especially in the retailer-dominated supply chain. For example, Wal-Mart and Jingdong are the leading enterprises in their respective supply chains, and most of their suppliers are small and medium-sized manufacturing enterprises in vulnerable positions. Under the green economy, in order to maintain the cooperative relationship with manufacturers, increase the sales volume of products, and stabilize their positions, the leading retailers must pay attention to the profit loss suffered by upstream manufacturing enterprises in order to achieve carbon emission reduction, and to some extent, adopt the behavior of "profit concession" to improve the profits of manufacturers. For example, Walmart supports suppliers in Central America, raises their bank loan limits, and provides farmers with technical training on sustainable agricultural practices, improving suppliers' profitability and product quality [9]. Jingdong has built large-scale new energy fleets in many cities and plans to gradually replace its partners' vehicles with new energy ones through incentive measures such as subsidies [10]. This type of attention and profit-giving behavior is known as altruistic preference. "Altruistic preference" is different from "fairness concern". Fairness concern behavior refers to the irrational egoistic decision-making taken by decision-makers to protect their rights and interests [11]. In contrast, the dominant enterprise in the supply chain prioritizes its interests while considering the benefits of other participants in the system. This irrational decision-making behavior increases the enthusiasm of other enterprises to cooperate by selling part of the profits of the dominant enterprise to maintain the supply chain's stability. In the supply chain operation mode, when enterprises take social responsibility as a part of corporate decision-making, most enterprises will consider altruistic preference to varied degrees to reflect their social value and enhance their competitiveness [12].

The government's carbon policy and consumers' low-carbon preference create external pressure, forcing manufacturers to transform production strategies, adopt technological innovations, or replace their equipment to control carbon emissions and reduce pollution [13]. As rational decision-makers, manufacturers would raise wholesale prices to offset the expense of reducing emissions, which would be detrimental to the interests of downstream retailers. However, manufacturers in a "weak" position are frequently exploited in a retailer-dominated supply chain. Thus, retailers, as supply chain leaders, should not only consider their profits but also pay attention to manufacturers' earnings, and create internal incentives for carbon emission reduction, to maintain the sustainable development of the supply chain. Therefore, it is of great significance to study retailer-led supply chain decisions considering altruistic preferences in the context of the carbon cap-and-trade policy. Currently, no relevant studies have integrated carbon quota policy and retailers' altruistic preferences into the supply chain decision-making process.

Recently, extensive research efforts have been devoted to the effects of the carbon cap-and-trade policy and altruistic preference behaviors on the low-carbon supply chain. However, most of the existing studies only consider the carbon cap-and-trade policy [14–18] or altruistic preference behaviors [11,19–22] on low-carbon supply chain decision-making. To the best of our knowledge, only a few papers have simultaneously studied the impact of the carbon cap-and-trade policy and the altruistic preference [23], which only discussed manufacturer-led supply chain decision-making. However, both carbon quota policy and retailers' altruistic preferences have not been studied yet in the retailer-led supply chain context. Facing the increasingly strict environmental protection requirements, manufacturers may have to adopt technological innovations or replace their equipment to control carbon emissions and reduce pollution, which means high costs of equipment replacement and technology improvement for those manufacturers. Therefore, considering the carbon cap-and-trade policy and the altruistic preference of the retailer, this study discusses the decisions of a low-carbon supply chain formed by a retailer and a manufacturer who is assumed to have less market power than the retailer. This study addresses the following three questions: (1) What are the optimal decisions when the leading retailer considers the altruistic preference under the carbon quota policy? (2) What is the relationship between the altruistic preference coefficient and system performance under the carbon quota policy, including pricing, carbon emission rate level, and profitability? (3) How do carbon trading price, carbon emission reduction cost, and consumers' low-carbon preferences affect system performance? To answer these questions, we construct three models of centralized decision, decentralized decision without altruistic preference, and decentralized decision with altruistic preference. Then, we calculate the equilibrium solutions for each model and compare them. The purpose of this study is to provide a theoretical basis and decision support not only for a low-carbon product supply chain but also for a low-carbon service supply chain.

Our study draws the following conclusions: (1) carbon trading under the carbon quota policy helps mitigate the manufacturer's cost pressures and improve carbon emission reduction levels; (2) retailer's altruistic preference contributes to carbon emission reduction, the demand for low-carbon products, and the manufacturer's profit and system profit, but decreases his interest; (3) factors such as carbon reduction cost, carbon trading price, and consumer's low-carbon preference affect the correlation between retailer's altruistic preference and price (including wholesale price and retail price).

This study contributes to the sustainability of low-carbon supply chains by helping members of retailer-led low-carbon supply chains better understand the impact of both carbon quota policies and altruistic preferences on their optimal decisions in the context of government-imposed carbon quota policies and retailers' altruistic preferences. This hitherto unexplored topic is expected to shed light on the study of irrational behavior in supply chain decision-making in the context of carbon policy.

The rest of the paper is organized as follows. Section 2 comprehensively reviews carbon quotas and altruistic preferences based on low-carbon supply chains. Section 3 describes the notation and assumptions of the model and analyzes different models. Section 4 presents a numerical analysis. The conclusion and research prospects are provided in Section 5.

2. Literature Review

The theory of the supply chain is well known, and numerous papers have reviewed it from various directions (such as [24,25]). Focus on carbon cap-and-trade policy and altruistic preference for low-carbon supply chain, the previous studies related to our research, can be classified into two categories. The first category is the impact of carbon quota policy on low-carbon supply chain management decisions. The second category is the impact of altruistic preferences on low-carbon supply chain management decisions.

2.1. The Impact of Carbon Quota Policy on Low-Carbon Supply Chain Decision-Making

In order to effectively reduce carbon emissions, many countries and regions have implemented a carbon tax and cap-and-trade policy. Compared with carbon tax control, the carbon cap-and-trade policy is more economical and realizable [26]. The carbon cap-and-trade policy has recently become a hot topic in academic research. Taking manufacturing enterprises as research objects, scholars have discussed the decision-making of production and carbon trading by using the classical newsvendor model [27], the economic order quantity model [28], and the duopoly model [2]. Some scholars studied the effect of consumers' low-carbon preference [18] and government low-carbon subsidy [19,20] on the optimal production and carbon emission reduction level. Although low-carbon production is the key factor to the sustainability of the economy and environment, it is not enough to achieve low-carbon goals only relying on manufacturing. The other players in the supply chain also needs to be considered [29,30]. Therefore, the different supply chains with different influencing factors are discussed under carbon cap and trade.

Du et al. [14] studied the impact of the carbon cap-and-trade system on the decisions and profits of emission-dependent supply chain players and the distributional equity of social welfare and also discussed the issue of supply chain coordination. For "make-to-order" supply chains, Xu et al. [31] studied the production- and emission-reduction decision-making of supply chain members and proposed optimal wholesale prices and cost-sharing contracts. Bai et al. [32] further investigated the optimal decision-making in the case of one manufacturer producing and selling two products under cap-and-trade regulation and designed a coordination contract based on revenue- and investment-sharing. Meanwhile, the rapid development of e-commerce has encouraged numerous companies to open online sales channels [33]. On this background, Ji et al. [15] investigated the effects of carbon cap-and-trade regulation on supply chain decision-making, profits, and social welfare, considering retailers with the dual-channel green supply chain. Xu et al. [34] studied the decision-making and coordination issues in the dual-channel supply chain where manufacturers added direct online sales under cap-and-trade control. Some scholars have also focused on the impact of the carbon cap-and-trade policy on the operation of supply chains with different power structures. Zhang et al. [16] studied the carbon reduction decisions of manufacturers and the changes of government's emission caps under three kinds of supply chain power structures. Jiang et al. [35] studied supply chain decisions simultaneously considering different supply chain power structures and flexible cap and trade. With the enhancement of consumers' environmental awareness, consumers' low carbon preference becomes an important factor influencing market demand. Mondal et al. [17] extended supply chain coordination, including both manufacturer and retailer environmental awareness, while using the revenue-sharing contract to coordinate the supply chain. To promote enterprises investing in green technology, the government usually provides subsidies to enterprises. Li et al. [18] studied and compared the effects of government subsidies on green technology investment and emission reduction amounts of supply chains under the carbon cap-and-trade mechanism. In business management, decision-makers' behavioral and cognitive factors cannot be ignored [36]. Therefore, in recent years, some scholars have introduced behavioral factors into the study of the supply chain under the carbon cap-and-trade policy. Considering the social preferences of supply chain members and consumers' low-carbon awareness, Xia et al. [37] explored the optimal decision and coordination of the supply chain. Meanwhile, Zou et al. [38] studied the impact of fairness on a sustainable low-carbon supply chain and analyzed the optimal decision of pricing and carbon emission reduction rate. Zhang et al. [23] studied the pricing and carbon emission reduction strategies of a supply chain wherein there is a retailer with corporate social responsibility and a manufacturer with altruistic preference.

2.2. The Influence of Altruistic Preference on Low-Carbon Supply Chain Decision-Making

Numerous psychological and behavioral economics studies have proven that policy-makers are not entirely rational in their self-interest but also consider the interests of other members [39,40]. In addition, the academic community has gradually acknowledged that it is insufficient to explain the behavior of enterprises from the perspective of external incentives. It is necessary to study behavior preference as the internal motivation of corporate decision-making [12]. Developing a low-carbon supply chain can help reduce total carbon emissions, excessive resource consumption, and environmental pollution [41]. In recent years, many scholars have been increasingly interested in studying the impact of altruistic preference on enterprises and society [42].

Considering consumers' low-carbon preferences, Fan et al. [11] incorporated retailers' altruistic behaviors into a low-carbon supply chain and explored the effects of retailers' altruistic preferences and consumers' low-carbon preferences on the optimal decision-making of a low-carbon supply chain. While Huang et al. [19] introduced consumers' green preferences and altruistic preferences into a cooperative supply chain with two cooperating manufacturers and one retailer, investigated the optimal greenness and pricing decision-making of a cooperative supply chain, and analyzed the impact of altruistic preference on the supply chain decision-making and profits. Considering carbon emission reduction and retailers' altruistic preferences, Wang et al. [20] studied the decision-making and coordination of a retailer-led low-carbon supply chain. In addition, Wan et al. [43] discussed the optimal pricing strategies and coordination contracts for providers of low-carbon tourism products and services and online travel agencies based on the altruistic preferences of decision-makers. Ma et al. [21] studied a low-carbon tourism online-to-offline (O_2O) supply chain and discussed the effects of big data empowerment, consumer preference effects, channel preferences, and corporate altruistic behaviors on optimal decision-making and performance. Wang et al. [44] and Liu et al. [45] studied altruistic preference behavior in the e-commerce supply chain including e-commerce platform. The government's low-carbon subsidy can increase enterprises' enthusiasm for low-carbon innovation [46]. Liu et al. [47] studied the impact of government subsidies and altruistic preferences on green supply chain innovation and analyzed enterprises' optimal decisions under different decision-making models. Xiao et al. [22] discussed the impact of altruistic preference and two types of government subsidies (eco-design subsidy and recycling subsidy) on the manufacturing–recycling system with eco-design. They explored rational altruism coefficients and subsidy strategies from the economy, environment, and social welfare perspectives.

In summary, considering altruistic preference in supply chain management decisions under the low carbon environment has become a hot topic in academic research. However, few studies have included carbon quota policy and altruistic preference in the decision-making process of low-carbon supply chains. No works have simultaneously considered the carbon quota policy and altruistic preference in a retailer-led low-carbon supply chain, and this study aims to fill this research gap. Fan et al. [11], Zhang et al. [16], Wang et al. [20], and Zhang et al. [23] are the most relevant papers to our study. Table 1 shows the differences between the existing research and our study.

Table 1. The differences between the existing literature and our study.

References	Cap-and-Trade	Retailer-Led	Low-Carbon Supply Chain	Altruistic Preference
[11]			✓	✓
[16]	✓	✓	✓	
[20]		✓	✓	✓
[23]	✓		✓	✓
This paper	✓	✓	✓	✓

3. Model and Analysis

We design a retailer-led low-carbon supply chain consisting of a manufacturer and a retailer, where the manufacturing process produces carbon emissions. At the beginning of each year, the government gives a free carbon quota to the manufacturer. If carbon emissions exceed the quota, the manufacturer must buy carbon credits from a carbon trading market, while if carbon emissions are lower than the quota, the manufacturer can sell the remaining carbon credits. To meet the low-carbon emission requirement and the growing low-carbon demand of consumers, the manufacturer has to accelerate the development of emission reduction technologies or update the equipment. This will increase the production costs of the manufacturer. In the low-carbon supply chain, the retailer buys the low-carbon products from the manufacturer at a wholesale price and sells them at a retail price.

According to the above low-carbon supply chain, three decision models, centralized, decentralized without altruistic preference, and decentralized with altruistic preference, are constructed to study the optimal pricing decision by considering the carbon quota policy. The main parameters and variables of the models are shown in Table 2.

Table 2. Main Parameters and Variables.

Parameters	
c	manufacturer's unit production cost
k	cost coefficient of carbon reduction investment
A	free carbon quotas provided by the government
e	unit initial carbon emissions of product
p_{ct}	unit carbon trading price
s	initial market demand for product
b	price sensitivity coefficient of consumer
λ	low-carbon preference coefficient of consumer
θ	altruistic preference coefficient of retailer
$(\ )_c^*$	centralized decision
$(\ )_d^*$	decentralized without altruistic preference decision
$(\ )_a^*$	decentralized with altruistic preference strategy
Decision Variables	
w	wholesale price of per unit product
p	sales price of per unit product
δ	per unit product profit of the retailer
β	carbon emission reduction rate per unit product
Functions	
q	market demand function of low-carbon product
π_r	the retailer's profit function
π_m	the manufacturer's profit function
π_s	profit function of the supply chain
U_r	the retailer's utility function

Among them, five functions are defined as follows:

(1) The market demand for low-carbon products is not only directly related to the retail or sales price of the products but also affected by consumers' low-carbon preference. Therefore, the market demand function (q) can be described by $q = s - bp + \lambda\beta$ ($b > 0, \lambda > 0$) [48].

(2) The retailer's profit depends on the wholesale price, retail price, and market demand for the product and can be described by $\pi_r = (p - w)q$.

(3) The manufacturer's cost consists of three parts: production cost, carbon trading cost, and carbon emission reduction cost. Therefore, the manufacturer's profit can be described by $\pi_m = (w - c)q + [A - e(1 - \beta)q]p_{ct} - \frac{1}{2}k\beta^2$, ($0 < \beta < 1$, $k > 0$), where $[A - e(1 - \beta)q]p_{ct}$ indicates carbon trading revenue, $\frac{1}{2}k\beta^2$ represents the cost of carbon emission reduction [49].

(4) The overall profit of the supply chain system is the sum of the retailer's profit and the manufacturer's profit, that is, $\pi_s = \pi_r + \pi_m$.

(5) In the retailer-led supply chain system, for the long-term development of the supply chain, retailers focus on their own benefits along with the benefits of the manufacture. Drawing on the literatures [20,50], the utility function under the retailer's altruistic preference is defined as $U_r = \pi_r - \theta(\pi_r - \pi_m)$, ($0 < \theta < 1$).

3.1. Centralized Decision-Making Model

In the centralized decision-making model, the retailer and the manufacturer face the sales market together and make decisions on sales or retail price and carbon emission reduction rate to maximize the overall profit of the supply chain. The profit of the supply chain can be expressed as:

$$\pi_s = (p-c)(s-bp+\lambda\beta) + [A - e(1-\beta)(s-bp+\lambda\beta)]p_{ct} - \frac{1}{2}k\beta^2 \quad (1)$$

According to Equation (1), the Hesse matrix of π_s (p,β) can be expressed as:

$$H_s(p,\beta) = \begin{bmatrix} -2b & \lambda - p_{ct}eb \\ \lambda - p_{ct}eb & 2p_{ct}e\lambda - k \end{bmatrix} \quad (2)$$

When $-2b < 0$ and $2bk - (\lambda + p_{ct}eb)^2 > 0$, $H_s(p,\beta)$ is a negative definite matrix and $\pi_s(p,\beta)$ has a maximum value. To ensure the practical significance of the model, we assume that the model satisfies $2bk - (\lambda + p_{ct}eb)^2 > 0$. Let $\frac{\partial \pi_s}{\partial p} = 0$ and $\frac{\partial \pi_s}{\partial \beta} = 0$, we can obtain the best decision in the centralized model:

$$p_c^* = \frac{k(s + bc + p_{ct}eb) - (\lambda + p_{ct}eb)(p_{ct}es + p_{ct}e\lambda + c\lambda)}{2bk - (\lambda + p_{ct}eb)^2} \quad (3)$$

$$\beta_c^* = \frac{(s - bc - p_{ct}eb)(\lambda + p_{ct}eb)}{2bk - (\lambda + p_{ct}eb)^2} \quad (4)$$

To ensure β_c^* is positive, it must be satisfied that $s - bc - p_{ct}eb > 0$. Then, the market demand and supply chain profit in a centralized decision model can be obtained:

$$q_c^* = s - bp_c^* + \lambda\beta_c^* = \frac{bk(s - bc - p_{ct}eb)}{2bk - (\lambda + p_{ct}eb)^2} \quad (5)$$

$$\pi_{sc}^* = (p_c^* - c)(s - bp_c^* + \lambda\beta_c^*) + [A - e(1-\beta_c^*)(s - bp_c^* + \lambda\beta_c^*)]p_{ct} - \frac{1}{2}k\beta_c^{*2}$$
$$= \frac{k(s - bc - p_{ct}eb)^2}{2[2bk - (\lambda + p_{ct}eb)^2]} + Ap_{ct} \quad (6)$$

3.2. Decentralized Model without Altruistic Preference

In decentralized decision-making, retailer and manufacturer seek to maximize their profits through the Stackelberg game. The retailer can be regarded as a Stackelberg leader who determines the sales profit of the unit product (δ), and the manufacturer can be regarded as a follower who determines the wholesale price of the unit product (w) and the carbon emission reduction rate (β). The optimal decisions and profits of the retailer and the manufacturer are obtained by backward induction.

The retailer sets the profit of per unit product δ; let the sales price $p = w + \delta$, market demand $q = s - b(w + \delta) + \lambda\beta$; at this time, the manufacturer's profit can be calculated:

$$\pi_m = (w - c)(s - b(w+\delta) + \lambda\beta) + [A - e(1-\beta)(s - b(w+\delta) + \lambda\beta)]p_{ct} - \frac{1}{2}k\beta^2 \quad (7)$$

According to Equation (7), the Hessian matrix of π_m (w,β) can be expressed as:

$$H_m(w,\beta) = \begin{bmatrix} -2b & \lambda - p_{ct}eb \\ \lambda - p_{ct}eb & 2p_{ct}e\lambda - k \end{bmatrix} \quad (8)$$

When $-2b < 0$ and $2bk - (\lambda + p_{ct}eb)^2 > 0$, $\pi_m(w,\beta)$ has the maximum value. Through $\frac{\partial \pi_m}{\partial w} = 0$ and $\frac{\partial \pi_m}{\partial \beta} = 0$, we can get:

$$w = -\delta + \frac{k(s + bc + b\delta + p_{ct}eb) - (\lambda + p_{ct}eb)(p_{ct}es + p_{ct}e\lambda + c\lambda + c\delta)}{2bk - (\lambda + p_{ct}eb)^2} \quad (9)$$

$$\beta = \frac{(\lambda + p_{ct}eb)(s - bc - b\delta - p_{ct}eb)}{2bk - (\lambda + p_{ct}eb)^2} \quad (10)$$

Taking Equations (9) and (10) into the retailer's profit function, we can get:

$$\pi_r = \delta\left[s - b\left(\frac{k(s+bc+b\delta+p_{ct}eb)-(\lambda+p_{ct}eb)(p_{ct}es+p_{ct}e\lambda+c\lambda+c\delta)}{2bk-(\lambda+p_{ct}eb)^2}\right)\right. \\ \left. + \lambda\left(\frac{(\lambda+p_{ct}eb)(s-bc-b\delta-p_{ct}eb)}{2bk-(\lambda+p_{ct}eb)^2}\right)\right] \quad (11)$$

Since $\frac{\partial^2 \pi_r}{\partial \delta^2} = \frac{-2b^2k}{2bk-(\lambda+p_{ct}eb)^2} < 0$, therefore, let $\frac{\partial \pi_r}{\partial \delta} = \frac{bk(s-bc-2b\delta-p_{ct}eb)}{2bk-(\lambda+p_{ct}eb)^2} = 0$, then we get:

$$\delta_d^* = \frac{s - bc - p_{ct}eb}{2b} \quad (12)$$

Substituting it into Equation (11), we can obtain the retailer's maximum profit under decentralized decision-making with altruistic preference:

$$\pi_{rd}^* = \frac{k(s - bc - p_{ct}eb)^2}{4\left[2bk - (\lambda + p_{ct}eb)^2\right]} \quad (13)$$

At the same time, substituting δ_d^* into Equations (9) and (10), we can obtain other decisions under a decentralized without altruistic preferences and the profits of the manufacturer and the supply chain system:

$$w_d^* = \frac{c + p_{ct}e}{2} + \frac{k(s + bc + p_{ct}eb) - (\lambda + p_{ct}eb)(p_{ct}es + p_{ct}e\lambda + c\lambda)}{2\left[2bk - (\lambda + p_{ct}eb)^2\right]} \quad (14)$$

$$\beta_d^* = \frac{(\lambda + p_{ct}eb)(s - bc - p_{ct}eb)}{2\left[2bk - (\lambda + p_{ct}eb)^2\right]} \quad (15)$$

$$p_d^* = w_d^* + \delta_d^* = \frac{s}{2b} + \frac{k(s + bc + p_{ct}eb) - (\lambda + p_{ct}eb)(p_{ct}es + p_{ct}e\lambda + c\lambda)}{2\left[2bk - (\lambda + p_{ct}eb)^2\right]} \quad (16)$$

$$q_d^* = s - bp_d^* + \lambda\beta_d^* = \frac{bk(s - bc - p_{ct}eb)}{2\left[2bk - (\lambda + p_{ct}eb)^2\right]} \quad (17)$$

$$\pi_{md}^* = (w_d^* - c)q_d^* + \left[A - e(1 - \beta_d^*)q_d^*\right]p_{ct} - \frac{1}{2}k\beta_d^{*2} \\ = \frac{k(s-bc-p_{ct}eb)^2}{8\left[2bk-(\lambda+p_{ct}eb)^2\right]} + Ap_{ct} \quad (18)$$

$$\pi_{sd}^* = \pi_{rd}^* + \pi_{md}^* = \frac{3k(s - bc - p_{ct}eb)^2}{8\left[2bk - (\lambda + p_{ct}eb)^2\right]} + Ap_{ct} \quad (19)$$

Proposition 1. $\pi_{md}^* = \pi_{rd}^*/2 + Ap_{ct}$.

Proof: See Appendix A. □

Unlike in [20], where the manufacturer's maximum profit is only half of the retailer's maximum profit, under the carbon quota policy in this paper, although the manufacturer bears the cost of carbon emission reduction, he can get extra gains by trading the remaining carbon quota, which can narrow the profit gap between the manufacturer and the retailer.

How much the gap narrowed depends on the carbon quota set by the government and the carbon trading price.

3.3. Decentralized Model with Altruistic Preference

As the leader in the supply chain, the retailer not only pays attention to his interests but also considers the profitability of the other members to form an altruistic preference for the stability and long-term development of the supply chain. By introducing the concept of utility in literature [20,50], the retailer's decision objective can be expressed as:

$$U_r = \pi_r - \theta(\pi_r - \pi_m) \tag{20}$$

Among them, $\theta(0 < \theta < 1)$ is the altruistic preference coefficient. The larger θ is, the stronger the retailer's altruistic preference is. For the supply chain leader, altruistic preference often occurs when the retailer's profitability is better than that of other members. Therefore, the constraint condition $\pi_r \geq \pi_m$ is added, and the optimal decision of the retailer's altruistic preference in the decentralized model can be defined as follows in this study:

$$\begin{cases} \max\limits_{\delta} \quad U_r = (1-\theta)\pi_r + \theta\pi_m \\ s.t. \quad \pi_r \geq \pi_m \end{cases} \tag{21}$$

Similarly to Section 3.2, the retailer and the manufacturer follow the Stackelberg game, where the retailer maximizes its utility through backward induction.

For the optimization problem shown in Equation (21), we calculate it by using the KKT condition. The Lagrangian function of Equation (21) is:

$$L = (1-\theta)\pi_r + \theta\pi_m + \eta(\pi_r - \pi_m) \tag{22}$$

The optimal solution of Equation (22) must satisfy the KKT condition as per the following:

$$\begin{cases} \frac{\partial L}{\partial \delta} = 0 \\ \pi_r \geq \pi_m \\ \eta(\pi_r - \pi_m) = 0 \\ \eta \geq 0 \end{cases} \tag{23}$$

Substituting Equations, take Equations (7) and (9)–(11) into the above equation, and we can get:

$$\delta = \frac{(1 - 2\theta + 2\eta)(s - bc - p_{ct}eb)}{(2 - 3\theta + 3\eta)b} \tag{24}$$

$$\pi_r - \pi_m = -\frac{k(s - bc - b\delta - p_{ct}eb)(s - bc - 3b\delta - p_{ct}eb)}{2\left[2bk - (\lambda + p_{ct}eb)^2\right]} - Ap_{ct} \tag{25}$$

When $\frac{\partial^2 L}{\partial \delta^2} = \frac{b^2 k(3\theta - 3\eta - 2)}{2bk - (\lambda + p_{ct}eb)^2} < 0$, $2bk - (\lambda + p_{ct}eb)^2 > 0$, so $3\theta - 3\eta - 2 < 0$, namely $0 < \theta < \frac{3\eta+2}{3}$, Equation (22) has an optimal solution.

According to Equations (23) and (24), when $\eta = 0$, $\delta = \delta_1 = \frac{(1-2\theta)(s-bc-p_{ct}eb)}{(2-3\theta)b}$, and $0 < \theta_1 < \frac{2}{3}$ can be obtained from $0 < \theta < \frac{3\eta+2}{3}$. From $\pi_r \geq \pi_m$ and $0 < \theta_1 < \frac{2}{3}$ we can get:

$$0 < \theta_1 \leq \frac{2}{3} - \frac{k(s - bc - p_{ct}eb)}{3\sqrt{k^2(s - bc - p_{ct}eb)^2 - 6Ap_{ct}k\left[2bk - (\lambda + p_{ct}eb)^2\right]}} < \frac{1}{3} \tag{26}$$

When $\eta > 0$, $\delta = \delta_2 = \frac{2(s-bc-p_{ct}eb)}{3b} + \frac{\sqrt{k^2(s-bc-p_{ct}eb)^2 - 6Ap_{ct}k[2bk-(\lambda+p_{ct}eb)^2]}}{3bk}$ and $\delta = \delta_3 = \frac{2(s-bc-p_{ct}eb)}{3b} - \frac{\sqrt{k^2(s-bc-p_{ct}eb)^2 - 6Ap_{ct}k[2bk-(\lambda+p_{ct}eb)^2]}}{3bk}$ can be obtained from $\pi_r - \pi_m = 0$. Substitute δ_2 and δ_3 into Equation (24) respectively, we can obtain:

$$\eta_2 = (\theta_2 - \frac{2}{3}) - \frac{k(s-bc-p_{ct}eb)}{3\sqrt{k^2(s-bc-p_{ct}eb)^2 - 6Ap_{ct}k[2bk-(\lambda+p_{ct}eb)^2]}} \quad (27)$$

$$\eta_3 = (\theta_3 - \frac{2}{3}) + \frac{k(s-bc-p_{ct}eb)}{3\sqrt{k^2(s-bc-p_{ct}eb)^2 - 6Ap_{ct}k[2bk-(\lambda+p_{ct}eb)^2]}} \quad (28)$$

$\eta > 0$, so:

$$\theta_2 > \frac{2}{3} + \frac{k(s-bc-p_{ct}eb)}{3\sqrt{k^2(s-bc-p_{ct}eb)^2 - 6Ap_{ct}k[2bk-(\lambda+p_{ct}eb)^2]}} \quad (29)$$

$$\theta_3 > \frac{2}{3} - \frac{k(s-bc-p_{ct}eb)}{3\sqrt{k^2(s-bc-p_{ct}eb)^2 - 6Ap_{ct}k[2bk-(\lambda+p_{ct}eb)^2]}} \quad (30)$$

Since $\frac{k(s-bc-p_{ct}eb)}{3\sqrt{k^2(s-bc-p_{ct}eb)^2 - 6Ap_{ct}k[2bk-(\lambda+p_{ct}eb)^2]}} > \frac{1}{3}$, $\theta_2 > 1$ can be obtained, which is not consistent with $0 < \theta < 1$, but θ_3 meets $0 < \theta < 1$. Comparing $U_r(\delta_1)$ and $U_r(\delta_3)$ under the two situations of $\theta = \theta_1$ and $\theta = \theta_3$, $U_r(\delta_1) > U_r(\delta_3)$ can be obtained. Therefore, when $\delta_a^* = \delta_1$, the retailer obtains the maximum utility. Here:

$$\delta_a^* = \frac{(1-2\theta)(s-bc-p_{ct}eb)}{(2-3\theta)b} \quad (31)$$

$$U_{ra}^* = \frac{(1-\theta)^2 k(s-bc-p_{ct}eb)^2}{2(2-3\theta)[2bk-(\lambda+p_{ct}eb)^2]} + Ap_{ct}\theta \quad (32)$$

Through the above analysis, the following proposition can be obtained:

Proposition 2: *In order for the retailer to realize higher profits than the manufacturer, the coefficient of altruistic preference must satisfy $0 < \theta \leq \frac{2}{3} - \frac{k(s-bc-p_{ct}eb)}{3\sqrt{k^2(s-bc-p_{ct}eb)^2 - 6Ap_{ct}k[2bk-(\lambda+p_{ct}eb)^2]}}$. Within this value range, the retailer can obtain maximum utility.*

When $\theta = \frac{2}{3} - \frac{k(s-bc-p_{ct}eb)}{3\sqrt{k^2(s-bc-p_{ct}eb)^2 - 6Ap_{ct}k[2bk-(\lambda+p_{ct}eb)^2]}}$, the retailer profit is equal to the manufacturer's profit. Since $\frac{k(s-bc-p_{ct}eb)}{3\sqrt{k^2(s-bc-p_{ct}eb)^2 - 6Ap_{ct}k[2bk-(\lambda+p_{ct}eb)^2]}} > \frac{1}{3}$, there is $0 < \theta < \frac{1}{3}$, where the range of the altruistic preference coefficient is less than the range of $\theta(0 < \theta \leq 1/2)$ in [45] and that of $\theta(0 < \theta \leq 1/3)$ in [20]. The government's carbon cap policy allows the manufacturer to earn profit through carbon trading, which will reduce the profit gap between the retailer and the manufacturer. The smaller profit gap between the retailer and the manufacturer will lead to a smaller value range for the retailer's altruistic preference coefficient.

Substitute δ_a^* into Equations (9) and (10); the following can be obtained:

$$w_a^* = \frac{(1-2\theta)(c+p_{ct}e)}{2-3\theta} + \frac{(1-\theta)[k(s+bc+p_{ct}eb)-(\lambda+p_{ct}eb)(p_{ct}es+p_{ct}e\lambda+c\lambda)]}{(2-3\theta)[2bk-(\lambda+p_{ct}eb)^2]} \tag{33}$$

$$\beta_a^* = \frac{(1-\theta)(\lambda+p_{ct}eb)(s-bc-p_{ct}eb)}{(2-3\theta)\left[2bk-(\lambda+p_{ct}eb)^2\right]} \tag{34}$$

The other optimal decisions in a decentralized model with altruistic preference are as follows:

$$p_a^* = w_a^* + \delta_a^* = \frac{(1-2\theta)s}{(2-3\theta)b} + \frac{(1-\theta)[k(s+bc+p_{ct}eb)-(\lambda+p_{ct}eb)(p_{ct}es+p_{ct}e\lambda+c\lambda)]}{(2-3\theta)[2bk-(\lambda+p_{ct}eb)^2]} \tag{35}$$

$$q_a^* = s - bp_a^* + \lambda \beta_a^* = \frac{(1-\theta)bk(s-bc-p_{ct}eb)}{(2-3\theta)\left[2bk-(\lambda+p_{ct}eb)^2\right]} \tag{36}$$

$$\pi_{ra}^* = \delta_a^* q_a^* = \frac{(1-\theta)(1-2\theta)k(s-bc-p_{ct}eb)^2}{(2-3\theta)^2\left[2bk-(\lambda+p_{ct}eb)^2\right]} \tag{37}$$

$$\pi_{ma}^* = (w_a^* - c)q_a^* + [A - e(1-\beta_a^*)q_a^*]p_{ct} - \tfrac{1}{2}k\beta_a^{*2}$$
$$= \frac{(1-\theta)^2 k(s-bc-p_{ct}eb)^2}{2(2-3\theta)^2[2bk-(\lambda+p_{ct}eb)^2]} + Ap_{ct} \tag{38}$$

$$\pi_{sa}^* = \pi_{ra}^* + \pi_{ma}^* = \frac{(1-\theta)(3-5\theta)k(s-bc-p_{ct}eb)^2}{2(2-3\theta)^2\left[2bk-(\lambda+p_{ct}eb)^2\right]} + Ap_{ct} \tag{39}$$

Proposition 3. (1) β_a^*, q_a^*, π_{ma}^*, π_{sa}^*, U_{ra}^* have positive correlations with θ, while δ_a^*, π_{ra}^* have negative correlations with θ. (2) When $bk > p_{ct}eb(\lambda + p_{ct}eb)$, w_a^* is positively correlated with θ, and when $bk < p_{ct}eb(\lambda + p_{ct}eb)$, w_a^* is negatively correlated with θ. (3) When $bk < \lambda(\lambda + p_{ct}eb)$, p_a^* is positively correlated with θ, and when $bk > \lambda(\lambda + p_{ct}eb)$, p_a^* is negatively correlated with θ.

Proof: See Appendix B. □

Proposition 3 shows that all optimal decisions are affected by the altruistic preference coefficient under the retailer's altruistic preference. Carbon emission reduction rate β_a^*, market demand for the product q_a^*, manufacturer's profit π_{ma}^*, and supply chain system profit π_{sa}^* are positively correlated with the altruistic preference coefficient θ. Although the retailer's unit product profit δ_a^* and total profit π_{ra}^* are negatively correlated with θ, the retailer's utility U_{ra}^* increases with the increase of θ, which is contrary to previous studies [38] where carbon reduction levels and manufacturer profits were negatively related to the equity concern coefficient while retailer profits were positively related to the equity concern coefficient. Moreover, different from the conclusion in the previous study that the wholesale price of the product w_a^* increases with the altruistic preference coefficient θ [20], under the carbon quota policy, the correlation between w_a^* and θ depends on b, k, λ, p_{ct}, e. When k is high, w_a^* is positively correlated with θ; when $p_{ct}e$ is high, w_a^* is negatively correlated with θ. The correlation between p_a^* and θ also depends on b, k, λ, p_{ct}, and e. When k is high, p_a^* is negatively correlated with θ; when λ is high, p_a^* is positively correlated with θ. Therefore, under the carbon quota policy, in addition to carbon emission reduction cost and consumer's low-carbon preference, the price of carbon trading is also an important factor to affect the product cost.

Propositions 4–7 are obtained by comparing the models of centralized decision, decentralized decision without altruistic preference, and decentralized decision with altruistic preference (altruistic preference coefficient satisfies

$$0 < \theta \leq \frac{2}{3} - \frac{k(s - bc - p_{ct}eb)}{3\sqrt{k^2(s - bc - p_{ct}eb)^2 - 6Ap_{ct}k\left[2bk - (\lambda + p_{ct}eb)^2\right]}}.$$

Proposition 4. *The relationship between retail prices of the three models satisfies: (1) When* $bk > \lambda(\lambda + p_{ct}eb)$, $p_c^* < p_a^* < p_d^*$, $(p_d^* - p_a^*) < (p_a^* - p_c^*)$; *(2) When* $bk < \lambda(\lambda + p_{ct}eb)$, $p_d^* < p_a^* < p_c^*$, $(p_a^* - p_d^*) < (p_c^* - p_a^*)$.

Proof: See Appendix C. □

Proposition 4 shows that, (1) when $bk > \lambda(\lambda + p_{ct}eb)$, the retail price in the centralized decision model is the lowest, and the retail price in the decentralized model without altruistic preference is the highest. Under decentralized decision-making, the manufacturer bears the cost of carbon emission reduction alone, so his profit is guaranteed by raising the wholesale price, which ultimately leads to a higher retail price. (2) When $bk < \lambda(\lambda + p_{ct}eb)$, the retail price under the centralized decision is the highest, and the retail price under the decentralized model without altruistic preference is the lowest. Under the decentralized model, the consumer's low-carbon preference expands market demand for green products, where the manufacturer can maintain a lower carbon emission cost at a lower level of carbon emission reduction. In this case, the manufacturer can obtain better profits without raising the product price. On the contrary, under the centralized decision, the manufacturer obtains profits by increasing the level of carbon emission reduction and the retail price of the product. (3) Under the decentralized model with the retailer's altruistic preference, the difference in retail prices between the centralized decision and the decentralized decision will be narrowed, but the reduction is limited.

Proposition 5. *When* $k > p_{ct}e(\lambda + p_{ct}eb)$, $w_a^* > w_d^*$; *when* $k < p_{ct}e(\lambda + p_{ct}eb)$, $w_a^* < w_d^*$.

Proof: See Appendix D. □

Proposition 5 shows that when $k > p_{ct}e(\lambda + p_{ct}eb)$, the wholesale price of products is higher in decentralized model with altruistic preference than in the decentralized model without altruistic preference. In this case, the cost of carbon reduction is higher. Under the decentralized model without altruistic preference, the manufacturer prefers a low level of carbon emission reduction to ensure profits. Under the decentralized model with altruistic preference, the retailer's altruistic preference motivates the manufacturer to improve the level of carbon emission reduction and increase the wholesale price to cover the increased cost of carbon emission reduction. When $k < p_{ct}e(\lambda + p_{ct}eb)$, the wholesale price of products is lower in the decentralized model with an altruistic preference than in the decentralized model without an altruistic preference. In this case, the carbon trading volume greatly impacts the manufacturer's profits. Under decentralized decision-making without altruistic preference, it is difficult for the manufacturer to profit from the carbon trading market, and he has to make a profit by raising the wholesale price. However, under decentralized decision-making with an altruistic preference, the manufacturer can obtain ideal profits at a lower wholesale price due to the increment of carbon trading revenue and product demand.

Proposition 6. *The relationship between emission reduction rates and market demands for the three models satisfies: (1)* $\beta_d^* = \frac{1}{2}\beta_c^*$, $\beta_a^* = \frac{1-\theta}{2-3\theta}\beta_c^*$, $\beta_d^* < \beta_a^* < \beta_c^*$, $(\beta_a^* - \beta_d^*) < (\beta_c^* - \beta_a^*)$; *(2)* $q_d^* = \frac{1}{2}q_c^*$, $q_a^* = \frac{1-\theta}{2-3\theta}q_c^*$, $q_d^* < q_a^* < q_c^*$, $(q_a^* - q_d^*) < (q_c^* - q_a^*)$.

Proof: See Appendix E. □

Proposition 6 shows that, among the three models, the carbon emission reduction rate under centralized decision-making is the highest, twice that of the decentralized decision-making without an altruistic preference model. So, there is the highest product demand under centralized decision-making, while the demand under decentralized decision-making without an altruistic preference is only half.

Retailers' altruistic preference can increase the carbon emission reduction rate, which in turn increases the demand for the products. However, because the retailer's altruistic preference is based on its profit being higher than the manufacturer's, it cannot greatly improve the carbon emission reduction rate and the market demand for the product. There is still a large gap between the optimal solutions in the centralized model and the decentralized model without an altruistic preference, which indicates that the decentralized model with an altruistic preference still cannot achieve the system profit of the centralized model.

Proposition 7. *In the three models, the relationships among manufacturer's profit, retailer's profit and the system profit satisfy:* (1) $\pi_{md}^* < \pi_{ma}^*$, $\pi_{rd}^* > \pi_{ra}^*$, $\pi_{sd}^* < \pi_{sa}^* < \pi_{sc}^*$; (2) $(\pi_{ra}^* - \pi_{ma}^*) < (\pi_{rd}^* - \pi_{md}^*)$.

Proof: See Appendix F. □

Proposition 7 shows that centralized decision-making has the highest system profit, while decentralized decision-making without altruistic preference has the lowest system profit. The retailer's altruistic preference will reduce its profit while increasing the profits of the manufacturer and the system, which will maintain the supply chain's stability by reducing the profit difference between the retailer and manufacturer. Altruistic preference helps to improve system efficiency, and this provides ideas for designing coordination contracts through altruistic preference. The findings of Propositions 6 and 7 are the same as those of the decentralized decision with altruistic preference in a low-carbon supply chain without carbon quota restrictions [20], which implies that the impacts of carbon quotas on the three models are consistent.

4. Numerical Simulation

To illustrate the above conclusions intuitively and further discover other unknown conclusions, this part will use numerical examples for simulation analysis. Referring to the relevant research [20], the parameter values of the examples all satisfy the requirements of the model descriptions and ensure that the optimal decision is positive.

4.1. Effects of Main Parameters on Optimal Decisions

Using the numerical analysis method, we discuss the influence of the retailer's altruistic preference coefficient, the manufacturer's carbon emission reduction cost, the consumer's low-carbon preference, and the carbon trading price on the optimal decision of the supply chain (including price, carbon emission reduction level, market demand, and profit). We give some estimated parameters as follows: $s = 1000$, $b = 5$, $c = 5$, $k = 65,000$, $A = 500$, $e = 100$, $p_{ct} = 1$, $\lambda = 10$, $\theta = 0.2$.

Figure 1 shows that the carbon emission reduction level β, market demand q, manufacturer's profit π_m, and the supply chain system profit π_s are positively correlated with the retailer's altruistic preference coefficient θ, while the retailer's profit π_r is negatively correlated with θ. Although the altruistic behavior sacrifices the retailer's interests, it is beneficial to the climate environment, consumers, manufacturer, and the whole supply chain. According to proposition 3, the influence of θ on wholesale price w and retail price p is closely related to b, k, p_{ct}, e, λ. According to the parameter values set, when $bk > p_{ct}eb(\lambda + p_{ct}eb)$ and $bk > \lambda(\lambda + p_{ct}eb)$, the wholesale price w is positively correlated with θ, and the sales price p is negatively correlated with θ. When the cost of carbon reduction is high, the manufacturer's cost pressure increases significantly. In this case, with the retailer's altruistic preference increases, the wholesale price rises, the retail price falls, and the market demand increases, which in turn ensures profits. On the contrary, when $bk < p_{ct}eb(\lambda + p_{ct}eb)$, w is negatively correlated with θ; when $bk < \lambda(\lambda + p_{ct}eb)$, p is positively correlated with θ. These will be discussed in detail in the next subsection

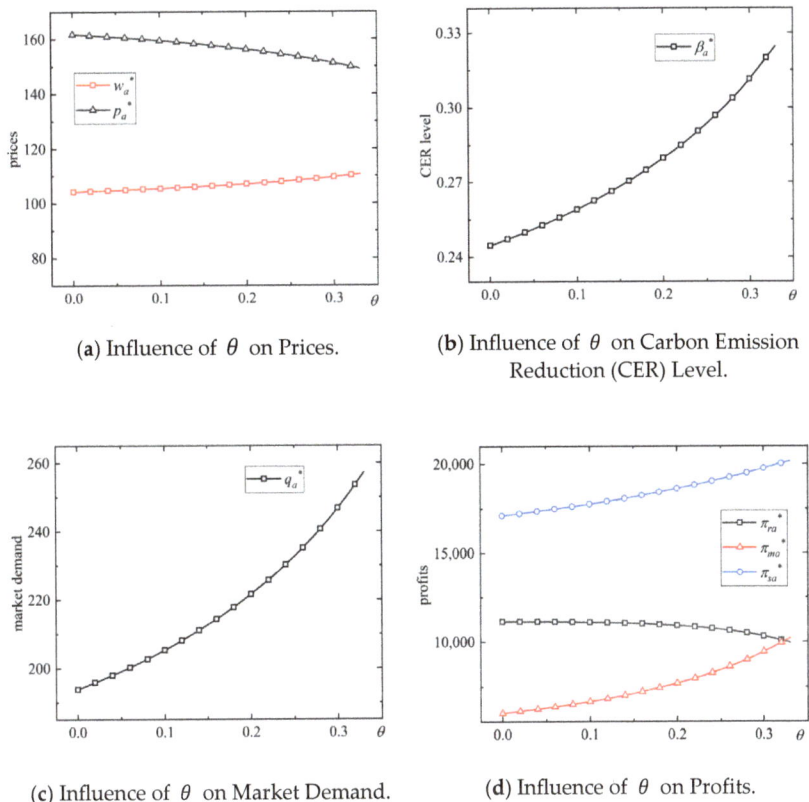

(a) Influence of θ on Prices.

(b) Influence of θ on Carbon Emission Reduction (CER) Level.

(c) Influence of θ on Market Demand.

(d) Influence of θ on Profits.

Figure 1. The Influence of Altruistic Preference θ on Supply Chain Decision.

Figures 2 and 3 shows that the impacts of carbon reduction cost k and consumers' low-carbon preference λ on each optimal decisions are completely contrary to Figure 1. Among them, the retail and wholesale prices are positively correlated with the carbon emission reduction cost, and negatively correlated with the consumers' low-carbon preference level. In contrast, the carbon emission reduction level and the market demand are negatively correlated with the carbon emission reduction cost and positively correlated with the consumers' low-carbon preference level. Meanwhile, the profit of the retailer, the manufacturer and the supply chain are negatively correlated with the carbon emission reduction cost and positively correlated with the consumers' low-carbon preference level.

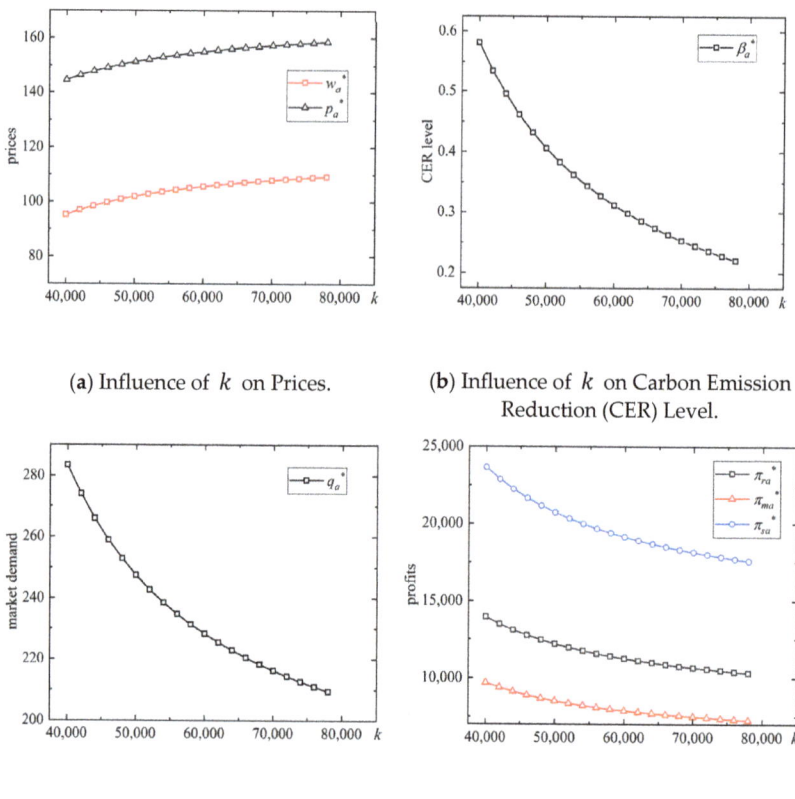

Figure 2. The Influence of Carbon Emission Reduction Cost k on Supply Chain Decision.

The cost of carbon emission reduction is the main factor to hinder the carbon emission reduction level. Usually, the players tend to ensure their profits by raising the price due to the increased production cost for carbon emission reduction. With the increase in the retail price, though, the market demand will decrease, ultimately affecting the profits of the retailer, the manufacturer, and the supply chain. Consumers' preference for low-carbon products expands the market size and motivates the manufacturer to reduce carbon emissions. With the growth of carbon trading and product demand, the players can earn good returns without raising or lowering prices.

In Figure 4, the sales price, the wholesale price, and the carbon emission reduction level are positively correlated with the carbon trading price, while the market demand and the profit of the retailer, the manufacturer, and the system are negatively correlated with the carbon trading price. As the carbon trading price rises, the manufacturer earns more profits in the carbon trading market, which promotes the level of carbon emission reduction. When the parameters satisfy $bk > p_{ct}eb(\lambda + p_{ct}eb)$, the wholesale price and retail price will rise inexorably due to the high carbon emission reduction cost borne by the manufacturer, which will affect the consumer's willingness to buy and ultimately reduce the profits of the manufacturer, retailer, and supply chain.

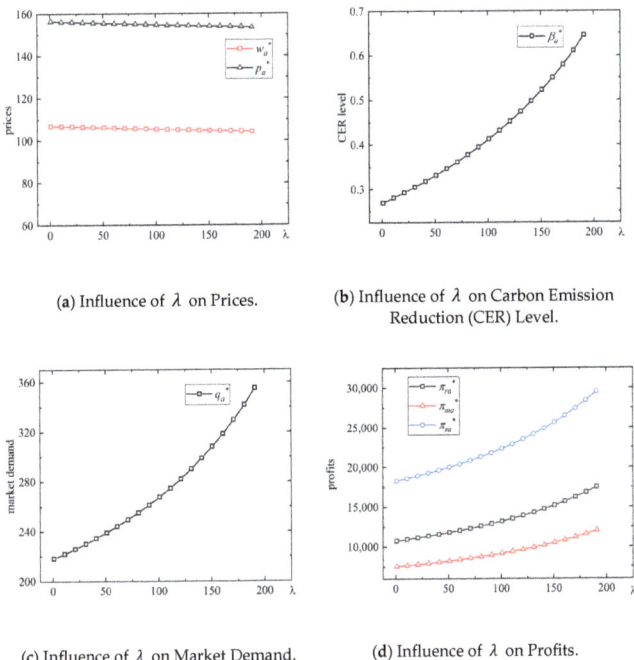

(a) Influence of λ on Prices.

(b) Influence of λ on Carbon Emission Reduction (CER) Level.

(c) Influence of λ on Market Demand.

(d) Influence of λ on Profits.

Figure 3. The Influence of Consumers' Low Carbon Preference λ on Supply Chain Decision.

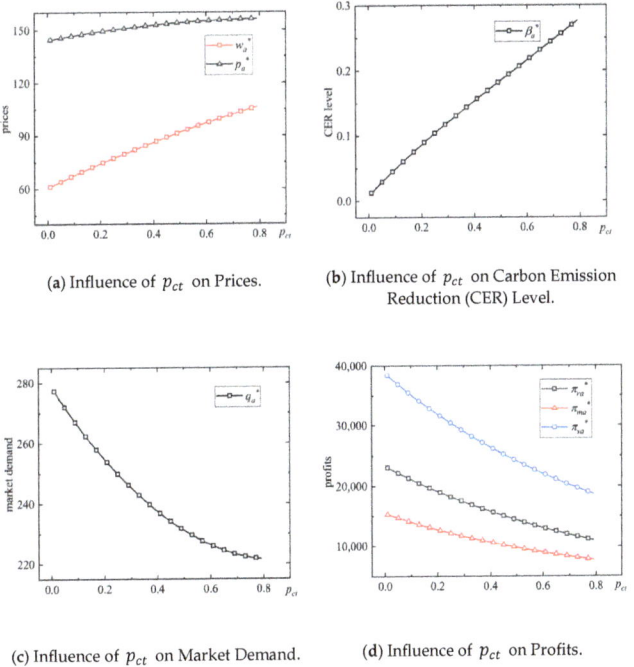

(a) Influence of p_{ct} on Prices.

(b) Influence of p_{ct} on Carbon Emission Reduction (CER) Level.

(c) Influence of p_{ct} on Market Demand.

(d) Influence of p_{ct} on Profits.

Figure 4. The Influence of Carbon Trading Price p_{ct} on Supply Chain Decision.

4.2. Comparison of The Optimal Decisions under The Three Models

The optimal decisions of the three models of the centralized decision, decentralized decision without altruistic preference, and decentralized decision with altruistic preference are compared and analyzed. We give some estimated parameters as follows: $s = 1000$, $b = 1, c = 5, k = 1,200,000, A = 500, e = 1, p_{ct} = 1, \lambda = 1080, \theta \in [0, 0.33]$.

The results show that among the three models, the centralized model has the highest carbon emission reduction level β, market demand q, and supply chain profit π_s, while the decentralized model without altruistic preference has the lowest β, q, and π_s. With the altruistic preference, the coefficient θ increases, the differences of β, q, and π_s between the two decentralized models gradually increase, and the three optimal values in the altruistic preference model are constantly approaching the ideal value of the centralized model (Figure 5d,e,h). Although the retailer's profit in the decentralized model with altruistic preference decreases as the altruistic preference coefficient θ increases (Figure 5f), the decrease is less than the increase in the manufacturer's profit (Figure 5g), which improves the overall benefit of the supply chain system. When $bk < \lambda(\lambda + p_{ct}eb)$, consumers have a higher low-carbon preference, the centralized model has the highest sales price, and the decentralized model without altruistic preference has the lowest sales price. When $bk > \lambda(\lambda + p_{ct}eb)$, the carbon emission reduction cost is higher, the decentralized model without altruistic preference has the highest sales price, while the centralized model has the lowest sales price (Figure 5a,b). When $k > p_{ct}e(\lambda + p_{ct}eb)$, compared to the case where there is no altruistic preference, the retailer's altruistic preference is conducive to the manufacturer earning more profits by increasing the wholesale price to compensate for carbon emission reduction costs. When $k < p_{ct}e(\lambda + p_{ct}eb)$, the high profits earned from the carbon trading market enables the manufacturer to ensure profits at a lower wholesale price. The retailer's altruistic preference can further encourage the manufacturer to set a lower wholesale price (Figure 5c).

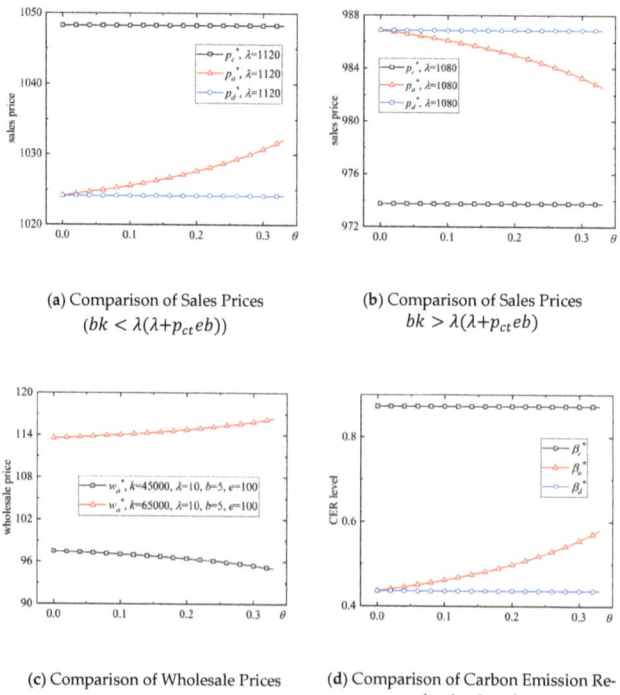

(a) Comparison of Sales Prices $(bk < \lambda(\lambda+p_{ct}eb))$

(b) Comparison of Sales Prices $bk > \lambda(\lambda+p_{ct}eb)$

(c) Comparison of Wholesale Prices

(d) Comparison of Carbon Emission Reduction Levels

Figure 5. Cont.

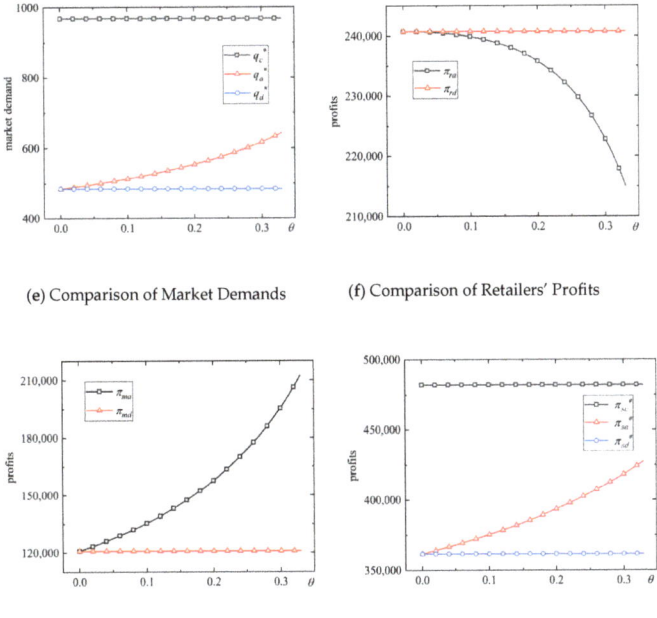

(e) Comparison of Market Demands (f) Comparison of Retailers' Profits

(g) Comparison of Manufacturer Profits (h) Comparison of Supply Chain Profits

Figure 5. Comparison of Optimal Decisions among the Three Models.

5. Conclusions

5.1. Conclusions

The increased awareness of low carbon has promoted the production of green products, while the increased cost of carbon emission reduction puts manufacturers at a disadvantage in the retailer-led supply chain. An important issue worth thoroughly inquiring about is how to incentivize manufacturers to reduce carbon emissions and maintain the sustainability of the low-carbon supply chain. This study investigates a retailer-led low-carbon supply chain problem by considering the government's carbon quota policy and the retailer's altruistic preference. Three models of centralized decision, decentralized decision without altruistic preference, and decentralized decision with altruistic preference are constructed. The main findings are as follows:

(1) Carbon trading under the carbon quota policy is important in improving the carbon emission reduction level. When the carbon price is high, the carbon trading revenue will effectively cover the cost of carbon emission reduction while the manufacturer's cost pressure decreases significantly. When the wholesale price remains low while improving the carbon emission reduction level, it is beneficial to expand market demand and increase the profit of the system.

(2) Retailers' altruistic preferences contribute to the sustainability of the low-carbon supply chain. The level of carbon emission reduction, the demand for low-carbon products, and the profits of manufacturers and systems are all positively related to the intensity of retailers' altruistic preferences. However, retailers' altruistic preferences will harm their interests. The improvement of retailers' altruistic preferences on decentralization decisions is limited due to the profit constraint.

(3) The effects of retailers' altruistic preferences on wholesale and retail prices are closely related to carbon reduction costs, carbon transaction prices, and consumers' low-carbon preferences. When carbon reduction costs are high, the wholesale price is positively related to the intensity of altruistic preference, while the retail price is negatively related to the intensity of altruistic preference; when carbon transaction prices and consumers'

low-carbon preferences are high, the wholesale price is negatively related to the intensity of altruistic preferences, and the retail price is positively related to the intensity of altruistic preferences.

5.2. Insights

Through the research of this paper, we can obtain the following theoretical and practical significance:

Theoretical significance: First, we consider the government's carbon quota policy and retailers' altruistic preferences in exploring retailer-led low-carbon supply chain decision-making and analyze the effects of retailers' altruistic preferences, manufacturers' carbon reduction costs, consumers' low-carbon preferences, and carbon trading prices on low-carbon supply chain decision-making, providing ideas for the study of irrational behaviors in low-carbon supply chain decision-making under carbon policies. Second, the research in this paper analyzes the impact of the carbon quota policy on the altruistic preference coefficient of the dominant supply chain player (retailers), which enriches the theoretical basis for studying the low-carbon supply chain and altruistic preferences. Subsequent scholars can conduct empirical studies based on this study to further verify the scope of altruistic preferences.

Practical significance: (1) The carbon quota policy positively relieves the cost pressure on manufacturers and improves the carbon emission reduction level. Therefore, while facing environmental problems and promoting carbon emission policies, the government should pay attention to the carbon emission reduction costs borne by manufacturers, improve the carbon trading market mechanism, and promote an increase in the carbon emission reduction rate of the whole society. (2) Retailers' altruistic preferences are conducive to improving profits in the retailer-led low-carbon supply chain. Therefore, retailers can provide service and support in finance, logistics, personnel training, and low-carbon product promotion to benefit manufacturers, enhance their willingness to cooperate, and promote the sustainable development of the supply chain system. (3) Consumers' low-carbon preferences contribute to improving carbon emission reduction levels and increasing profits in the low-carbon supply chain. Therefore, the government should strengthen environmental publicity and education and vigorously advocate green and low-carbon consumption. Enterprises should actively promote low-carbon products and cultivate a low-carbon consumption market. Although the input of carbon emission reduction costs will increase the price of products, popularizing the low-carbon consumption concept will bring great economic benefits and environmental improvement in the long run.

5.3. Directions for Future Research

Our study still has some limitations, which we will explore in the future.

(1) This study only considers the impact of the government's carbon quota policy and retailers' altruistic preferences on retailer-led low-carbon supply chain decisions. Other carbon policies (e.g., carbon tax policies) and social preferences (e.g., equity preferences, reciprocity preferences) can also have far-reaching effects on the decision-making and operation of the low-carbon supply chain, which will be our next research direction.

(2) This study is limited to the low-carbon supply chain with one dominant retailer and one manufacturer. Therefore, a future research direction is to extend this model and apply it to a more realistic supply chain system with one dominant retailer and multiple manufacturers. In this network configuration, the impact of the government's environmental policies and the social preferences of supply chain members on low-carbon supply chain decision-making is further explored.

(3) The low-carbon supply chain model in this study only considers the carbon reduction cost of manufacturers. However, as the dominant player in the supply chain, retailers should bear the responsibility of carbon reduction, which we will further explore based on this study.

Author Contributions: Conceptualization, X.Z. and X.W.; methodology, X.Z. and X.W.; validation, X.Z. and X.W.; writing—original draft preparation, X.Z. and X.W.; writing—review and editing, X.Z. and X.W. All authors have read and agreed to the published version of the manuscript.

Funding: This research was supported by the Chongqing Social Sciences Project (2021NDYB067).

Institutional Review Board Statement: Not applicable.

Informed Consent Statement: Not applicable.

Data Availability Statement: Not applicable.

Conflicts of Interest: The authors declare that they have no conflict of interest.

Appendix A

Proof of Proposition 1. $\pi_{md}^* = \frac{k(s-bc-p_{ct}eb)^2}{8[2bk-(\lambda+p_{ct}eb)^2]} + Ap_{ct} = \frac{1}{2} \cdot \frac{k(s-bc-p_{ct}eb)^2}{4[2bk-(\lambda+p_{ct}eb)^2]} + Ap_{ct}$, $\pi_{rd}^* = \frac{k(s-bc-p_{ct}eb)^2}{4[2bk-(\lambda+p_{ct}eb)^2]}$, so $\pi_{md}^* = \frac{1}{2} \cdot \pi_{rd}^* + Ap_{ct}$. □

Proposition 1 is demonstrated.

Appendix B

Proof of Proposition 3. When $0 < \theta \leq \frac{2}{3} - \frac{k(s-bc-p_{ct}eb)}{3\sqrt{k^2(s-bc-p_{ct}eb)^2 - 6Ap_{ct}k[2bk-(\lambda+p_{ct}eb)^2]}} < \frac{1}{3}$, $\frac{\partial \delta_a^*}{\partial \theta} = \frac{-(s-bc-p_{ct}eb)}{(2-3\theta)^2 b} < 0$, $\frac{\partial \beta_a^*}{\partial \theta} = \frac{(\lambda+p_{ct}eb)(s-bc-p_{ct}eb)}{(2-3\theta)^2[2bk-(\lambda+p_{ct}eb)^2]} > 0$, $\frac{\partial q_a^*}{\partial \theta} = \frac{bk(s-bc-p_{ct}eb)}{(2-3\theta)^2[2bk-(\lambda+p_{ct}eb)^2]} > 0$, $\frac{\partial \pi_{ma}^*}{\partial \theta} = \frac{2(1-\theta)k(s-bc-p_{ct}eb)^2}{2(2-3\theta)^3[2bk-(\lambda+p_{ct}eb)^2]} > 0$, $\frac{\partial \pi_{ra}^*}{\partial \theta} = \frac{-\theta k(s-bc-p_{ct}eb)^2}{(2-3\theta)^3[2bk-(\lambda+p_{ct}eb)^2]} < 0$, $\frac{\partial \pi_{sa}^*}{\partial \theta} = \frac{(1-2\theta)k(s-bc-p_{ct}eb)^2}{(2-3\theta)^3[2bk-(\lambda+p_{ct}eb)^2]} > 0$, $\frac{\partial U_{ra}^*}{\partial \theta} = \frac{(3+\theta)(1-\theta)k(s-bc-p_{ct}eb)^2}{2(2-3\theta)^2[2bk-(\lambda+p_{ct}eb)^2]} + Ap_{ct} > 0$. $\frac{\partial w_a^*}{\partial \theta} = \frac{(s-bc-p_{ct}eb)[bk-p_{ct}eb(\lambda+p_{ct}eb)]}{(2-3\theta)^2 b[2bk-(\lambda+p_{ct}eb)^2]}$; When $bk > p_{ct}eb(\lambda+p_{ct}eb)$, $\frac{\partial w_a^*}{\partial \theta} > 0$; when $bk < p_{ct}eb(\lambda+p_{ct}eb)$, $\frac{\partial w_a^*}{\partial \theta} < 0$. $\frac{\partial p_a^*}{\partial \theta} = \frac{(s-bc-p_{ct}eb)[-bk+\lambda(\lambda+p_{ct}eb)]}{(2-3\theta)^2 b[2bk-(\lambda+p_{ct}eb)^2]}$; when $bk < \lambda(\lambda+p_{ct}eb)$, $\frac{\partial p_a^*}{\partial \theta} > 0$; when $bk > \lambda(\lambda+p_{ct}eb)$, $\frac{\partial p_a^*}{\partial \theta} < 0$. □

Proposition 3 is demonstrated.

Appendix C

Proof of Proposition 4. $p_d^* - p_a^* = \frac{\theta(s-bc-p_{ct}eb)[bk-\lambda(\lambda+p_{ct}eb)]}{2(2-3\theta)b[2bk-(\lambda+p_{ct}eb)^2]}$, $p_a^* - p_c^* = \frac{(1-2\theta)(s-bc-p_{ct}eb)[bk-\lambda(\lambda+p_{ct}eb)]}{(2-3\theta)b[2bk-(\lambda+p_{ct}eb)^2]}$, Since $0 < \theta \leq \frac{2}{3} - \frac{k(s-bc-p_{ct}eb)}{3\sqrt{k^2(s-bc-p_{ct}eb)^2 - 6Ap_{ct}k[2bk-(\lambda+p_{ct}eb)^2]}} < \frac{1}{3}$, therefore, when $bk > \lambda(\lambda+p_{ct}eb)$, $p_c^* < p_a^* < p_d^*$, $(p_d^* - p_a^*) < (p_a^* - p_c^*)$; when $bk < \lambda(\lambda+p_{ct}eb)$, $p_d^* < p_a^* < p_c^*$, $(p_a^* - p_d^*) < (p_c^* - p_a^*)$. □

Proposition 4 is demonstrated.

Appendix D

Proof of Proposition 5. $w_d^* - w_a^* = \frac{\theta(s-bc-p_{ct}eb)[bk-p_{ct}eb(\lambda+p_{ct}eb)]}{2(2-3\theta)b[2bk-(\lambda+p_{ct}eb)^2]}$, since $0 < \theta \leq \frac{2}{3} - \frac{k(s-bc-p_{ct}eb)}{3\sqrt{k^2(s-bc-p_{ct}eb)^2 - 6Ap_{ct}k[2bk-(\lambda+p_{ct}eb)^2]}} < \frac{1}{3}$, therefore, when $k > p_{ct}e(\lambda + p_{ct}eb)$, $w_a^* > w_d^*$; when $k < p_{ct}e(\lambda + p_{ct}eb)$, $w_a^* < w_d^*$. □

Proposition 5 is demonstrated.

Appendix E

Proof of Proposition 6. $\beta_c^* = \frac{(\lambda+p_{ct}eb)(s-bc-p_{ct}eb)}{2bk-(\lambda+p_{ct}eb)^2}$, $\beta_d^* = \frac{(\lambda+p_{ct}eb)(s-bc-p_{ct}eb)}{2[2bk-(\lambda+p_{ct}eb)^2]}$, $\beta_a^* = \frac{(1-\theta)(\lambda+p_{ct}eb)(s-bc-p_{ct}eb)}{(2-3\theta)[2bk-(\lambda+p_{ct}eb)^2]}$, $\beta_a^* - \beta_d^* = \frac{\theta(\lambda+p_{ct}eb)(s-bc-p_{ct}eb)}{2(2-3\theta)[2bk-(\lambda+p_{ct}eb)^2]}$, $\beta_c^* - \beta_a^* = \frac{(1-2\theta)(\lambda+p_{ct}eb)(s-bc-p_{ct}eb)}{(2-3\theta)[2bk-(\lambda+p_{ct}eb)^2]}$, $q_c^* = \frac{bk(s-bc-p_{ct}eb)}{2bk-(\lambda+p_{ct}eb)^2}$, $q_d^* = \frac{bk(s-bc-p_{ct}eb)}{2[2bk-(\lambda+p_{ct}eb)^2]}$, $q_a^* = \frac{(1-\theta)bk(s-bc-p_{ct}eb)}{(2-3\theta)[2bk-(\lambda+p_{ct}eb)^2]}$, $q_a^* - q_d^* = \frac{\theta bk(s-bc-p_{ct}eb)}{2(2-3\theta)[2bk-(\lambda+p_{ct}eb)^2]}$, $q_c^* - q_a^* = \frac{(1-2\theta)bk(s-bc-p_{ct}eb)}{(2-3\theta)[2bk-(\lambda+p_{ct}eb)^2]}$, since $0 < \theta \leq \frac{2}{3} - \frac{k(s-bc-p_{ct}eb)}{3\sqrt{k^2(s-bc-p_{ct}eb)^2 - 6Ap_{ct}k[2bk-(\lambda+p_{ct}eb)^2]}} < \frac{1}{3}$, therefore, $\beta_d^* < \beta_a^* < \beta_c^*$, $(\beta_a^* - \beta_d^*) < (\beta_c^* - \beta_a^*)$; $q_d^* < q_a^* < q_c^*$, $(q_a^* - q_d^*) < (q_c^* - q_a^*)$. □

Proposition 6 is demonstrated.

Appendix F

Proof of Proposition 7. $\pi_{ma}^* - \pi_{md}^* = \frac{(4-5\theta)\theta k(s-bc-p_{ct}eb)^2}{8(2-3\theta)^2[2bk-(\lambda+p_{ct}eb)^2]}$, $\pi_{ra}^* - \pi_{rd}^* = \frac{-\theta k(s-bc-p_{ct}eb)^2}{4(2-3\theta)^2[2bk-(\lambda+p_{ct}eb)^2]}$, $\pi_{sa}^* - \pi_{sd}^* = \frac{(4-7\theta)\theta k(s-bc-p_{ct}eb)^2}{8(2-3\theta)^2[2bk-(\lambda+p_{ct}eb)^2]}$, $\pi_{sc}^* - \pi_{sa}^* = \frac{(1-2\theta)^2 k(s-bc-p_{ct}eb)^2}{2(2-3\theta)^2[2bk-(\lambda+p_{ct}eb)^2]}$, since $0 < \theta \leq \frac{2}{3} - \frac{k(s-bc-p_{ct}eb)}{3\sqrt{k^2(s-bc-p_{ct}eb)^2 - 6Ap_{ct}k[2bk-(\lambda+p_{ct}eb)^2]}} < \frac{1}{3}$, therefore, $\pi_{md}^* < \pi_{ma}^*$, $\pi_{rd}^* > \pi_{ra}^*$, $\pi_{sd}^* < \pi_{sa}^* < \pi_{sc}^*$, $(\pi_{ra}^* - \pi_{ma}^*) < (\pi_{rd}^* - \pi_{ma}^*) < (\pi_{rd}^* - \pi_{md}^*)$. □

Proposition 7 is demonstrated.

References

1. Chan, H.S.; Li, S.J.; Zhang, F. Firm competitiveness and the European Union emissions trading scheme. *Energy Policy* **2013**, *63*, 1056–1064. [CrossRef]
2. Wang, Z.; Wang, C. How carbon offsetting scheme impacts the duopoly output in production and abatement: Analysis in the context of carbon cap-and-trade. *J. Clean. Prod.* **2015**, *103*, 715–723. [CrossRef]
3. Adaman, F.; Karalı, N.; Kumbaroğlu, G.; Or, I.; Özkaynak, B.; Zenginobuz, Ü. What determines urban households' willingness to pay for CO_2 emission reductions in Turkey: A contingent valuation survey. *Energy Policy* **2011**, *39*, 689–698. [CrossRef]
4. Xia, L.; Liu, H.; Zhang, M.; Yuan, B.; Li, Y. Supply Chain Coordination Based on Incremental Profit-Sharing Contract of Carbon Emission Reduction under Mandatory Carbon Emissions Capacity Scheme. *J. Oper. Res. Manag. Sci.* **2019**, *28*, 92.
5. Benjaafar, S.; Li, Y.Z.; Daskin, M. Carbon Footprint and the Management of Supply Chains: Insights from Simple Models. *IEEE Trans. Autom. Sci. Eng.* **2013**, *10*, 99–116. [CrossRef]
6. Liu, Z.; Anderson, T.D.; Cruz, J.M. Consumer environmental awareness and competition in two-stage supply chains. *Eur. J. Oper. Res.* **2012**, *218*, 602–613. [CrossRef]
7. Shuai, C.; Ding, L.; Zhang, Y.; Guo, Q.; Shuai, J. How consumers are willing to pay for low-carbon products?—Results from a carbon-labeling scenario experiment in China. *J. Clean. Prod.* **2014**, *83*, 366–373. [CrossRef]
8. Wu, P.; Jin, Y.; Shi, Y.; Shyu, H. The impact of carbon emission costs on manufacturers' production and location decision. *Int. J. Prod. Econ.* **2017**, *193*, 193–206. [CrossRef]
9. Sun, Y.; Yuan, X.; Shi, K. Research on decision of supply chain of fresh agricultural product based on altruism preference. *J. Syst. Eng. Theory Pract.* **2017**, *37*, 1243–1253.

10. Shen, L.; FAN, R.; Wang, Y. Pricing Service Decision and Coordination Mechanism of Low-Carbon ECSC Based on Altruistic Preference. *J. Syst. Sci. Math. Sci.* **2022**, *42*, 1788–1804.
11. Fan, R.; Lin, J.; Zhu, K. Study of game models and the complex dynamics of a low-carbon supply chain with an altruistic retailer under consumers' low-carbon preference. *Phys. A Stat. Mech. Appl.* **2019**, *528*, 121460. [CrossRef]
12. Loch, C.; Wu, Y. Social preferences and supply chain performance: An experimental study. *Manag. Sci.* **2008**, *54*, 1835–1849. [CrossRef]
13. Guo, W.H.; Cheng, T.C.E.; Wang, S.Y. Managing Carbon Footprints in Inventory Control. *Int. J. Prod. Econ.* **2011**, *132*, 178–185.
14. Du, S.F.; Zhu, L.L.; Liang, L.; Ma, F. Emission-dependent supply chain and environment-policy-making in the 'cap-and-trade' system. *Energy Policy* **2013**, *57*, 61–67. [CrossRef]
15. Ji, J.N.; Zhang, Z.Y.; Yang, L. Comparisons of initial carbon allowance allocation rules in an O_2O retail supply chain with the cap-and-trade regulation. *Int. J. Prod. Econ.* **2017**, *187*, 68–84. [CrossRef]
16. Zhang, S.; Wang, C.; Yu, C.; Ren, Y. Governmental cap regulation and manufacturer's low carbon strategy in a supply chain with different power structures. *Comput. Ind. Eng.* **2019**, *134*, 27–36. [CrossRef]
17. Mondal, C.; Giri, B.C. Analyzing a manufacturer-retailer sustainable supply chain under cap-and-trade policy and revenue sharing contract. *Oper. Res.* **2022**, *22*, 4057–4092. [CrossRef]
18. Li, Z.; Pan, Y.; Yang, W.; Ma, J.; Zhou, M. Effects of government subsidies on green technology investment and green marketing coordination of supply chain under the cap-and-trade mechanism. *Energy Econ.* **2021**, *101*, 105426. [CrossRef]
19. Huang, H.; Zhang, J.; Ren, X.; Zhou, X. Greenness and Pricing Decisions of Cooperative Supply Chains Considering Altruistic Preferences. *Int. J. Environ. Res. Public Health* **2019**, *16*, 51. [CrossRef]
20. Wang, Y.; Yu, Z.; Jin, M.; Mao, J. Decisions and Coordination of Retailer-Led Low-Carbon Supply Chain under Altruistic Preference. *Eur. J. Oper. Res.* **2021**, *293*, 910–925. [CrossRef]
21. Ma, D.; Hu, J.; Yao, F. Big data empowering low-carbon smart tourism study on low-carbon tourism O_2O supply chain considering consumer behaviors and corporate altruistic preferences. *Comput. Ind. Eng.* **2021**, *153*, 107061. [CrossRef]
22. Xiao, S.; Chang, X.; Chen, M. Altruistic preference and government subsidies in a manufacturing-recycling system with eco-design. *J. Clean. Prod.* **2022**, *359*, 132095. [CrossRef]
23. Zhang, G.; Zhao, L.; Zhang, Q.; Zhang, Z. Effects of socially responsible behaviors in a supply chain under carbon cap-and-trade regulation. *Discret. Dyn. Nat. Soc.* **2021**, *2021*, 6218978. [CrossRef]
24. Asgari, N.; Nikbakhsh, E.; Hill, A.; Farahani, R.Z. Supply chain management 1982–2015: A review. *IMA J. Manag. Math.* **2016**, *27*, 353–379. [CrossRef]
25. Das, C.; Jharkharia, S. Low carbon supply chain: A state-of-the-art literature review. *J. Manuf. Technol. Manag.* **2018**, *29*, 398–428. [CrossRef]
26. Barragán-Beaud, C.; Pizarro-Alonso, A.; Xylia, M.; Syri, S.; Silveira, S. Carbon tax or emissions trading? An analysis of economic and political feasibility of policy mechanisms for greenhouse gas emissions reduction in the Mexican power sector. *Energy Policy* **2018**, *122*, 287–299. [CrossRef]
27. Song, J.; Leng, M. Analysis of the single-period problem under carbon emissions policies. In *Handbook of Newsvendor Problems*; Choi, T.-M., Ed.; Springer: New York, NY, USA, 2012; Volume 176, pp. 297–313. ISBN 9781461435990.
28. He, P.; Zhang, W.; Xu, X.Y.; Bian, Y.W. Production lot-sizing and carbon emissions under cap-and-trade and carbon tax regulations. *J. Clean. Prod.* **2015**, *103*, 241–248. [CrossRef]
29. Swami, S.; Shah, J. Channel coordination in green supply chain management. *J. Oper. Res. Soc.* **2013**, *64*, 336–351. [CrossRef]
30. Lee, J.Y.; Choi, S. Supply chain investment and contracting for carbon emissions reduction: A social planner's perspective. *Int. J. Prod. Econ.* **2021**, *231*, 107873. [CrossRef]
31. Xu, X.; Ping, H.; Hao, X.; Zhang, Q. Supply chain coordination with green technology under cap-and-trade regulation. *Int. J. Prod. Econ.* **2017**, *183*, 433–442. [CrossRef]
32. Bai, Q.G.; Xu, J.T.; Zhang, Y.Y. Emission reduction decision and coordination of a make-to-order supply chain with two products under cap-and-trade regulation. *Comput. Ind. Eng.* **2018**, *119*, 131–145.
33. Li, B.; Zhu, M.; Jiang, Y.; Li, Z. Pricing policies of a competitive dual-channel green supply chain. *J. Clean. Prod.* **2015**, *112*, 2029–2042.
34. Xu, L.; Wang, C.X.; Zhao, J.J. Decision and coordination in the dual-channel supply chain considering cap-and-trade regulation. *J. Clean. Prod.* **2018**, *197*, 551–561. [CrossRef]
35. Jiang, W.; Liu, M.; Gan, L.; Wang, C. Optimal Pricing, Ordering, and Coordination for Prefabricated Building Supply Chain with Power Structure and Flexible Cap-and-Trade. *Mathematics* **2021**, *9*, 2426. [CrossRef]
36. Gino, F.; Pisano, G. Toward a theory of behavioral operations. *Manuf. Serv. Oper. Manag.* **2008**, *10*, 676–691. [CrossRef]
37. Xia, L.; Hao, W.; Qin, J.; Ji, F.; Yue, X. Carbon emission reduction and promotion policies considering social preferences and consumers' low-carbon awareness in the cap-and-trade system. *J. Clean. Prod.* **2018**, *195*, 1105–1124. [CrossRef]
38. Zou, H.; Qin, J.; Dai, B. Optimal Pricing Decisions for a Low-Carbon Supply Chain Considering Fairness Concern under Carbon Quota Policy. *Int. J. Environ. Res. Public Health* **2021**, *18*, 556. [CrossRef]
39. Fehr, E.; Schmidt, K.M. A theory of fairness, competition, and cooperation. *Q. J. Econ.* **1999**, *114*, 817–868. [CrossRef]
40. Charness, G.; Rabin, M. Understanding Social Preferences with Simple Tests. *Q. J. Econ.* **2002**, *117*, 817–869. [CrossRef]

41. Nie, D.; Li, H.; Qu, T.; Liu, Y.; Li, C. Optimizing supply chain configuration with low carbon emission. *J. Clean. Prod.* **2020**, *271*, 122539. [CrossRef]
42. Fehr, E.; Schmidt, K.M. The economics of fairness, reciprocity and altruism—Experimental evidence and new theories. In *Handbook of the Economics of Giving, Altruism and Reciprocity*; Elsevier Science: New York, NY, USA, 2006; Volume 1, pp. 615–691.
43. Wan, X.; Jiang, B.; Qin, M.; Du, Y. Pricing decision and coordination contract in low-carbon tourism supply chains based on altruism preference. *Environ. Eng. Manag. J.* **2019**, *18*, 2501–2518.
44. Wang, Y.; Yu, Z.; Shen, L.; Dong, W. E-Commerce Supply Chain Models under Altruistic Preference. *Mathematics* **2021**, *9*, 632. [CrossRef]
45. Liu, J.; Zhou, L.; Wang, Y. Altruistic Preference Models of Low-Carbon E-Commerce Supply Chain. *Mathematics* **2021**, *9*, 1682. [CrossRef]
46. Wang, M.Y.; Li, Y.M.; Li, M.M.; Shi, W.Q.; Quan, S.P. Will carbon tax affect the strategy and performance of low-carbon technology sharing between enterprises? *J. Clean. Prod.* **2019**, *210*, 724–737. [CrossRef]
47. Liu, G.D.; Chen, J.G.; Li, Z.Y.; Zhu, H.G. Green supply chain innovation strategies considering government subsidy and altruistic preference. *Math. Probl. Eng.* **2022**, *2022*, 5495374. [CrossRef]
48. Bakal, I.S.; Akcali, E. Effects of random yield in remanufacturing with price-sensitive supply and demand. *Prod. Oper. Manag.* **2006**, *15*, 407–420. [CrossRef]
49. Nair, A.; Narasimhan, R. Dynamics of competing with quality-and advertising-based goodwill. *Eur. J. Oper. Res.* **2006**, *175*, 462–474. [CrossRef]
50. Nie, T.; Du, S. Dual-fairness supply chain with quantity discount contracts. *Eur. J. Oper. Res.* **2016**, *258*, 491–500. [CrossRef]

Disclaimer/Publisher's Note: The statements, opinions and data contained in all publications are solely those of the individual author(s) and contributor(s) and not of MDPI and/or the editor(s). MDPI and/or the editor(s) disclaim responsibility for any injury to people or property resulting from any ideas, methods, instructions or products referred to in the content.

Article

Strategy Analysis of Fresh Agricultural Enterprises in a Competitive Circumstance: The Impact of Blockchain and Consumer Traceability Preferences

Yuling Sun *, Xiaomei Song, Yihao Jiang and Jian Guo

College of Economics and Management, Nanjing Tech University, Nanjing 211816, China
* Correspondence: syl_nj@njtech.edu.cn; Tel.: +86-13705169239

Abstract: Blockchain technology allows fresh agricultural enterprises to share records stored on the chain, and the technology can benefit information management systems, such as decentralization and transparency. This study uses game theory to examine a blockchain introduction strategy for fresh agricultural enterprises in a competitive environment, considering consumer traceability preferences. We establish a pricing decision model in traditional and blockchain traceability modes and identify optimal solutions. Additionally, we analyze the impact of the blockchain introduction strategy, consumer preferences, and blockchain influence factor on optimal pricing decisions. The results indicate that the introduction of blockchain could improve the profits of enterprises under certain conditions. Moreover, consumer traceability preferences and the blockchain influence factor could significantly affect the blockchain introduction strategy. We also discover that when the blockchain influence factor meets a certain range, introducing blockchain technique in the traceability system could shift demand from traditional enterprises to blockchain enterprises. The total market demand for blockchain enterprises under the blockchain traceability mode will increase, whereas that of traditional enterprises under the blockchain traceability mode will decrease. Both consumer traceability preferences and the blockchain influence factor could significantly affect optimal pricing. Finally, some management suggestions are provided for the traceability of fresh agricultural enterprises based on the research conclusions.

Keywords: blockchain; consumer traceability preferences; fresh agricultural products; competitive environment

MSC: 91A80

1. Introduction

Fresh agricultural product traceability has always been a major concern for consumers. As consumers pay more attention to their health, they have higher requirements regarding the sensory quality of the products, such as taste, texture, color, and shape, and the internal quality and hygienic quality, such as ingredients, nutrients, harmful substances, pesticide residue, and mildew [1,2]. Based on experimental research, Dickinson and Bailey [3] showed that consumers are willing to pay more for the traceability and transparency of meat products. Recently, electronic trade among the supply chain members of agricultural products has become popular, which makes it more difficult to authenticate and track information in their production, processing, and distribution processes [4]. Dalian sea cucumber, Yangcheng Lake crab, Wuchang rice, and other branded agricultural products have been subject to information fraud incidents. Additionally, it is difficult for the consumer to trace accurate information about agricultural products. Food traceability is related to the behavior of all members in a supply chain, and information fraud committed by any member may reduce the authenticity and effectiveness of traceability.

In 1993, the Escherichia coli scare was the largest food crisis in the United States [5]. In 2011, bean sprouts contaminated with Escherichia coli caused many people to be infected in Germany [6]. From 2016 to 2019, many consumers complained on the Pinduoduo website because of rotting fruit. Some famous brands of agricultural products, such as Wuchang rice, Yangcheng Lake hairy crabs, Gannan navel oranges, West Lake Longjing tea, and Aksu apples, are often counterfeited [7]. Governments and enterprises have attempted to use various information technologies to solve the problems related to information opacity and authenticity in the agricultural product supply chain. For example, the European Union uses the RSS (Reduced Space Symbology) barcode system and the EAN/UCC (European Article Number/Uniform Code Council) identification system to track the quality of beef, vegetables, and other products. Some companies use the tracking system of the Internet of Things (IoT) to track the quality of products [8]. Other enterprises use the NetMES system based on a cloud platform to address information asymmetry in the supply chain. However, the above initiatives have failed because the traditional traceability systems are usually based on centralized information management systems, and information can be easily tampered with and forged [9,10]. As a result, the traditional traceability systems significantly damage consumers' trust in product authenticity. It is challenging to trace food effectively and ensure the authenticity of product traceability chain information.

Blockchain technology is feasible and has certain advantages in ensuring the traceability and authenticity of the food supply chain [11]. The traceability system based on blockchain technology is a decentralized database system with distinguishing features, such as credibility, security, and immutability [12]. In recent years, some fresh agricultural enterprises have joined the TAC platform (a traceability cloud platform based on blockchain technology) to trace agricultural products. Consumers can seek information on this platform concerning aspects such as the production date, batch, producer, and ingredients list. For example, Cainiao and Tmall Global enabled blockchain technology to trace the origin of cross-border imports in February 2018. By the end of 2019, more than 800 cooperative brands and more than 70,000 products joined JD Zhizhen Chain's anti-counterfeiting and traceability platform. According to "the report of Blockchain Traceability Service Innovation and Application in 2020," jointly released by Ceibs Supply Chain and Service Innovation Center and JD Digits, after brand owners adopted the blockchain anti-counterfeiting traceability service, the sales of nutritional health products and the visits of nutritional health products increased by 30%, while their repurchase rate increased by 44.8% and return rate decreased by 4.5%.

The traceability of fresh agricultural products is different from that of industrial products. Fresh agricultural products are perishable, and their shelf-life is considerably shorter. The value of fresh agricultural products rapidly drops to zero once the shelf-life is exceeded. It is impossible to resell these products once they have been returned. Therefore, the return loss may affect the decision of the supply chain members of fresh agricultural products. Simultaneously, the development cost of a blockchain project is hundreds of thousands up to millions, and this cost will fluctuate with the development difficulty. It is usually a huge expense for a business. The storage cost of wholly traceable data is another significant expense. Storing traceability data directly on the chain and backing up the stored data at all nodes will require a large amount of memory capacity and will increase the maintenance costs of a traceability system. The storage cost of a traceability database based on the blockchain technique is thousands of times higher than that of a traditional traceability database based on a distributed system or cloud storage technique. According to rough estimates, 1 KB of Ethereum storage costs about USD 1.58 [13]. In addition, the blockchain traceability system of the fresh products supply chain requires all nodes on the blockchain to be backed up and store data. This makes it easy to cause repetitive storage and increase memory consumption, thus increasing the maintenance cost of the traceability system. The costs related to blockchain are a colossal expense for enterprises. Additionally, Liu et al. [14] showed that consumers are more willing to pay for fresh agricultural products. The huge initial development and operating costs greatly reduce the willingness of companies in the food supply chain to adopt blockchain technology [15]. In reality, not all enterprises adopt blockchain technology; for example, Dalian sea cucumber brands such as Fortune Island and Sha Tuozi Island adopt blockchain traceability of sea cucumber products in various links, including breeding, seedling rearing, culture, and processing. Sea Star Island, Ocean Island, and other enterprises adopt the traditional traceability system to trace the origin of sea cucumber products.

In this study, we build a game model to investigate enterprise practice and the underexplored role played by blockchain in the traceability of fresh agricultural enterprises in competitive circumstances. We attempt to theoretically address the following research questions:

(1) In a competitive context, should fresh agricultural enterprises introduce blockchain technology?
(2) How does the blockchain influence factor affect the optimal pricing and profits of fresh agricultural enterprises?
(3) How would the traceability preferences of consumers affect the optimal pricing and profits of fresh agricultural enterprises?

Inspired by the observed management practice of the fresh agricultural product supply chain, this study first analyzed the optimal pricing and profits of enterprises of fresh agricultural products under a scenario where two enterprises adopt a traditional traceability mode considering consumers' traceability preferences in a competitive environment. Furthermore, we investigated the optimal pricing strategy and profits under a scenario where one enterprise adopts a blockchain traceability mode, and the other adopts a traditional traceability mode. We identify the condition of introducing blockchain traceability for the enterprise in a competitive environment and how blockchain influence factor and consumers' traceability preferences affect the optimal pricing of fresh agricultural enterprises. Unlike previous research, our study is theoretical. It explores the introduction strategy of blockchain technology to the traceability system of the agricultural product supply chain in two competitive enterprises. We examine the optimal pricing and profits of fresh agricultural enterprises under the traditional traceability mode and blockchain traceability mode with game theory. Furthermore, we examine the impact of the blockchain influence factor and consumers' traceability preferences. Novel insights and managerial implications are proposed.

Our paper is organized as follows. We review the related literature in Section 2. In Section 3, we build the basic theoretical model and explore the use of blockchain and government measures in Section 4. We formally conclude this study with suggestions for future research and management implications in Section 5. To improve readability, all technical proofs are presented in the Appendices A–F.

2. Literature Review

This study is closely related to the applications of blockchain in supply chain management, food traceability systems, and the impact of blockchain on operations management.

The literature concerning blockchain applications in supply chain management abounds. For example, Chod et al. [16] analyzed the application of blockchain in supply chain financing. Sander et al. and Tian et al. studied the feasibility of applying blockchain to operations management [17,18]. Azzi et al. [19] studied the challenges faced by the blockchain-based supply chain management ecosystem. Kshetri [20] further analyzed the impact of blockchain on supply chain objectives, such as cost, quality, speed and reliability, based on a case study. Ivanov et al. [21] studied the impact of digitalization and Industry 4.0 on supply chain reaction and disruption risk control analysis. Kamble et al. [22] developed a research model integrating the technology readiness index (TRI), technology acceptance model (TAM), and the theory of planned behavior (TPB) to examine the adoption of blockchain in the supply chain. They found that supply chain practitioners perceive BT adoption as effortless and believe it would help derive maximum benefits for improving supply chain effectiveness. Wang et al. [23] mainly used cognitive mapping and narrative analysis to evaluate people's cognitive complexity in understanding blockchain technology. They found that senior executives believe the blockchain can bring benefits such as improved tracking and traceability to the supply chain. Saberi et al. [24] studied how to use blockchain technology to design an intelligent signing mechanism in the sustainable supply chain. Duan et al., Li et al. and Pandey et al. [25–27] used content analysis to discuss the application, challenges, and future trends of blockchain in the food supply chain. Khan et al. [28] used the interview method to analyze the benefits and challenges of applying blockchain technology to agricultural supply chains during the COVID-19 pandemic and proposed solutions. Kouhizadeh et al. [29] discussed the cases and potential applications of blockchain technology in the supply chain. The above-mentioned literature discusses the feasibility, advantages, and challenges of different supply chains based on case studies, sense-making theory, and so on. We use game theory to investigate an introduction strategy for fresh agricultural enterprises in a competitive market.

The second study theme is a traceability system for fresh produce. Recently, some scholars focused on how blockchain affects the traditional traceability system. Deng et al. [30] analyzed the feasibility of using blockchain technology in food traceability. Behnke and Janssen [31] analyzed the boundary conditions when blockchain was applied to the food supply chain traceability through case analysis and interviews. Stranieri et al. and Wang et al. [32,33] found that the traceability system has a positive effect on the food market and enhances the consumer experience. Stuller and Rickard [34] investigated melon planting and processing enterprises in California, USA, and found that litigation concerns and firm reputation are the key drivers for maintaining traceability. Pouliot and Sumner [35] pointed out that food safety declines with rising numbers of farms and marketers, and imperfect traceability from consumers to marketers dampens farm liability incentives. Resende-Filho et al. [36] studied the supply chain composed of upstream and downstream food enterprises and discussed the quality improvement of upstream enterprises based on the accuracy of the traceability system. Gong and Chen [37] examined the impact of traceability on improving food safety levels in the supply chain and the profits of upstream and downstream enterprises. Aiello [38] used stochastic mathematical programming to evaluate the operational efficiency of the traceability system of the food supply chain. Cao et al. [39] designed a blockchain-based human–computer verification mechanism to strengthen consumers' trust in the traceability of the cross-border beef supply chain between Australia and China. Some scholars have studied traceability optimization decisions or incentive mechanisms under the influence of different factors. Dai et al. [40] analyzed the interactions of traceability and reliability optimization in a competitive environment with a product recall. Given the differences in the traceability of suppliers, Hastig and Sodhi [41] analyzed the need for implementing traceability systems in the cobalt mining and pharmaceutical industries and analyzed the key success factors of implementing the blockchain. This article extends the research on the traditional and blockchain traceability modes for fresh agricultural enterprises, focusing on the introduction strategy in the presence of demand competition, which is a further supplement to the above-mentioned literature.

Our third research stream relates to operational management based on the blockchain using a quantitative method model. Choi [42] assumed that the consumers' choice of products is related to the detection time of the product and the falseness of the product, and they analyzed the impact of blockchain technology on social welfare with uncertain demand. Zhang and Luo [43] proposed a traceability solution based on blockchain technology from the perspective of consumer rights. Yan et al. [44] analyzed the impact of blockchain technology on the upstream and downstream enterprises of the supply chain. Fan et al. [45] studied the optimal pricing strategies of the supply chain, considering the consumers' traceability awareness. Cao et al. [46] analyzed the impact of blockchain on the decisions of platforms in the agricultural product supply chain. He et al. [47] analyzed the impact of blockchain technology on the optimal decision for cross-order e-commerce platforms and foreign suppliers selling fresh products. As consumers pay increasing attention to product traceability, the verifiability and traceability of information are regarded as important standards for evaluating product quality, and product traceability is regarded as an important criterion for evaluating product quality. According to a report from IBM, 71% of consumers are willing to purchase traceable products at 37% higher prices. Zhou et al. [48] showed that consumers' organic preferences could affect the production and sales decisions of the fresh agricultural products supply chain. Closely related is blockchain introduction strategies for supply chains in a competitive market. Considering consumers' quality sensitivity, Feng et al. [49] analyzed the impact of blockchain technology on optimal pricing and quality decisions in the case of two competing platforms. Liu et al. [50] explore whether the E-platforms choose reselling or agency selling for fresh food in competition with different traditional retailers. They found that the competition between traditional and online channels could incentivize firms to invest more in product freshness and blockchain-enabled traceability goodwill. Assuming the consumers' traceability awareness as the sensibility to authentic and verifiable traceability information, Wu et al. [51] analyze a strategy for adopting blockchain technology in the fresh produce supply chain between two competitive supply chains. They find that when one supply chain adopts BT, the other may be a free rider. Different from the literature mentioned above, we focus on the introduction strategy of the blockchain between two competitive enterprises of fresh agricultural products. We extend the consumers' traceability preferences for fresh agricultural products to more realistic factors. We infer that consumers' traceability preferences relate to the consumers' sensitivity to the detection time of fresh agricultural products and to the falseness of the product and are also related to consumers' return loss and the probability of consumers' return. We also consider consumers' transfer cost and blockchain cost to investigate the interactive activities of enterprises in different traceability modes. Unlike Wu's conclusion, we find that under competitive circumstances, the enterprise adopting the blockchain traceability mode gains a competitive advantage, and the other enterprise adopting the traditional traceability mode is not a free rider when the blockchain influence factor is in a certain range.

In summary, the major contributions of this study lie in the following aspects. First, we identify the specific conditions needed for adopting blockchain technology to trace fresh agricultural products between two competitive enterprises, which has not been explored in previous studies. Second, we note that the blockchain influence factor has a significant impact on the introduction of blockchain technology. Third, extending the utility function of the consumers' traceability preference as information authenticity, product detection, and the falseness of the product, we prove that consumers' traceability preferences have a significant impact on the introduction of blockchain technology. Finally, we offer some important and valuable managerial insights for the literature and practice through this study. When consumers have a high preference for traceability and the blockchain influence degree is within a certain range, enterprises should adopt a blockchain traceability system. In a competitive market, enterprises that adopt the blockchain traceability system have a competitive advantage. The introduction strategy of blockchain is not only related to the consumers' traceability preference but also to the transfer cost of consumers and the input cost of blockchain. We also find that enterprises adopting blockchain traceability systems gain more customers than enterprises adopting traditional traceability systems.

3. Model Setting and Analysis

3.1. Competitive Decisions under the Traditional Traceability Mode

Suppose that two agricultural enterprises are selling similar agricultural products in a competitive market. The products provided by the two enterprises can be substituted for each other. The decision-making order of this article is that the enterprises first choose whether to introduce blockchain technology, and then consumers choose the enterprises' products. Assuming that enterprises use blockchain traceability, their entire supply chain also uses blockchain traceability.

Suppose that the market prices of enterprises 1 and 2 are p_1 and p_2, respectively, and their production costs are the same. To simplify the calculation, it can be assumed that the production cost is zero. Choi [42] assumed that the consumers' choice of products is related to the detection time of the product and the falseness of the product. Different from Choi's assumption, we suppose that consumers' traceability preference relates to the consumers' sensitivity to the detection time of fresh agricultural products and to the falseness of the product, and it is also related to consumers' return loss and the probability of consumers' return. Suppose that B represents the possibility of consumer return as a result of the disclosure of false information by traditional enterprises. ζ denotes the enterprise's return loss and τ denotes consumers' return loss. Assume that the total demand of the agricultural product market is one, and enterprises 1 and 2 cover the entire market. When neither enterprise 1 nor 2 joins the blockchain (that is, both enterprises are traditional enterprises), consumers' utilities of enterprises 1 and 2 are as follows.

$$U_1 = v - (p_1 + \beta t + (1-\alpha)\gamma - q) - kx - B\tau, \tag{1}$$

$$U_2 = v - (p_2 + \beta t + (1-\alpha)\gamma - q) - k(1-x) - B\tau, \tag{2}$$

where v represents consumers' retention value of the product, x represents the consumers' psychological position between the two enterprises, and k represents the unit transfer cost of consumers' purchases from one enterprise to the other. Here, t represents the checking time of fresh agricultural products, q represents the quality of the agricultural products, and α represents the possibility that consumers believe the information of the agricultural products is false. β and γ represent the consumers' sensitivity to the detection time of fresh agricultural products and to the falseness of the product, respectively [42].

Consumers will buy from enterprise1 only when $U_1 \geq U_2$, that is, $v - (p_1 + \beta t + (1-\alpha)\gamma - q) - kx - B\tau \geq v - (p_2 + \beta t + (1-\alpha)\gamma - q) - k(1-x) - B\tau$. We can obtain $x \leq \frac{p_2 - p_1 + k}{2k}$.

Therefore, the market demand of enterprises 1 and 2 is, respectively,

$$D_1 = \frac{p_2 - p_1 + k}{2k}, \tag{3}$$

$$D_2 = \frac{p_1 - p_2 + k}{2k}. \tag{4}$$

The profits of enterprise 1 and 2 are, respectively,

$$\pi_1 = p_1 \cdot \frac{p_2 - p_1 + k}{2k} - B\zeta \cdot \frac{p_2 - p_1 + k}{2k}, \tag{5}$$

$$\pi_2 = p_2 \cdot \frac{p_1 - p_2 + k}{2k} - B\zeta \cdot \frac{p_1 - p_2 + k}{2k}. \tag{6}$$

Let $\frac{\partial \pi_1}{\partial p_1} = 0, \frac{\partial \pi_2}{\partial p_2} = 0$, we can obtain Lemma 1.

Lemma 1. *In the traditional traceability mode, the optimal pricing for enterprises 1 and 2 is $p_1^* = p_2^* = k + B\zeta$, the total market demand for enterprises 1 and 2 is $D_1^* = D_2^* = \frac{1}{2}$, and the maximum profit for enterprises 1 and 2 is $\pi_1^* = \pi_2^* = \frac{k}{2}$.*

Since $\frac{\partial p_1^*}{\partial k} = \frac{\partial p_2^*}{\partial k} = 1, \frac{\partial \pi_1^*}{\partial k} = \frac{\partial \pi_2^*}{\partial k} = \frac{1}{2}$, the optimal pricing and the profit of both parties increase with an increase in the unit transfer cost.

$\frac{\partial p_1^*}{\partial B} = \zeta, \frac{\partial p_1^*}{\partial \zeta} = B, \zeta > 0, B > 0$, that is, the optimal pricing of both parties increases with an increase in the possibility of consumer return and the enterprise's return loss. Therefore, an optimal solution for both parties' pricing decisions exists when neither enterprise 1 nor 2 joins the blockchain. The unit transfer cost, the possibility of consumer return, and the enterprise's return loss could affect the optimal pricing and profit of both parties. The optimal pricing decision and profit of both parties increase as the switching cost increases. Additionally, the optimal pricing of both parties increases as the possibility of consumer return and the enterprise's return loss increase.

3.2. Competitive Decision-Making under the Blockchain Traceability Mode

Suppose that enterprise 1 uses blockchain technology to trace the quality of agricultural products, and enterprise 2 does not adopt blockchain technology. Compared with the traditional traceability system, the blockchain traceability system can ensure information security and maintain consumers' trust in the authenticity of product information. Therefore, when enterprise 1 uses blockchain technology to trace the source of agricultural products, consumers believe that the probability of agricultural product information fraud is zero; that is, $\alpha = 0$; the probability of consumer returns because of false information provided by enterprises is zero, that is, $B = 0$. The quality of the agricultural products becomes Q ($Q \geq q$), and the evaluation time becomes T ($T < t$). Enterprise 1's blockchain input cost is C.

Suppose that consumers have traceability preferences, such that the higher the degree of traceability preferences, the more likely consumers are willing to select products with blockchain traceability. Suppose that there are two types of consumers in the market, namely consumers with a high traceability preference (H) and those with a low traceability preference (L), where the proportion of the former in the market is θ. T and t represent the quality evaluation time for blockchain agricultural products and traditional agricultural products, respectively. Q and q denote the quality of blockchain agricultural products and traditional agricultural products, respectively. Consumers with a high traceability preference will buy agricultural products directly from enterprise 1 instead of enterprise 2. Consumers with a low traceability preference are likely to buy from enterprises 1 or 2. Enterprise 1 uses blockchain and is referred to as a blockchain enterprise, and Enterprise 2 does not use blockchain and is referred to as a traditional enterprise. The utility of consumers with a low traceability preference is, respectively,

$$U_1^L = v - (\overline{p}_1 + \beta T - Q) - kx, \tag{7}$$

$$U_2^L = v - (\overline{p}_2 + \beta t + (1-\alpha)\gamma - q) - k(1-x) - B\tau. \tag{8}$$

when $U_1^L > U_2^L$, consumers with a low traceability preference will buy agricultural products from the blockchain enterprise. The solution is $x < \frac{\overline{p}_2 - \overline{p}_1 + \beta \Delta t - \Delta q + (1-\alpha)\gamma + k + B\tau}{2k}$; therefore, the demand of consumers with a low traceability preference in the market for enterprises 1 and 2 are, respectively,

$$D_1^L = \frac{\overline{p}_2 - \overline{p}_1 + \beta \Delta t - \Delta q + (1-\alpha)\gamma + k + B\tau}{2k}(1-\theta), \tag{9}$$

$$D_2^L = \frac{\overline{p}_1 - \overline{p}_2 - \beta \Delta t + \Delta q - (1-\alpha)\gamma + k - B\tau}{2k}(1-\theta). \tag{10}$$

The total market demand of enterprises 1 and 2 are, respectively,

$$D_1^B = D_1^L + D^H = \frac{\overline{p}_2 - \overline{p}_1 + \beta \Delta t - \Delta q + (1-\alpha)\gamma + k + B\tau}{2k}(1-\theta) + \theta, \tag{11}$$

$$D_2^B = D_2^L = \frac{\overline{p}_1 - \overline{p}_2 - \beta \Delta t + \Delta q - (1-\alpha)\gamma + k - B\tau}{2k}(1-\theta). \tag{12}$$

The profit of enterprises 1 and 2 are, respectively,

$$\pi_1^B = \overline{p}_1 \cdot \left[\frac{\overline{p}_2 - \overline{p}_1 + \beta \Delta t - \Delta q + (1-\alpha)\gamma + k + B\tau}{2k}(1-\theta) + \theta \right] - C, \tag{13}$$

$$\pi_2^B = (\bar{p}_2 - B\xi) \cdot \frac{\bar{p}_1 - \bar{p}_2 - \beta\Delta t + \Delta q - (1-\alpha)\gamma + k - B\tau}{2k}(1-\theta). \tag{14}$$

Let $\frac{\partial \pi_1^B}{\partial \bar{p}_1} = 0$, $\frac{\partial \pi_2^B}{\partial \bar{p}_2} = 0$, we can obtain

$$\bar{p}_1 = \frac{\bar{p}_2}{2} + \frac{y + B\tau + k}{2} + \frac{k\theta}{1-\theta}, \tag{15}$$

$$\bar{p}_2 = \frac{\bar{p}_1}{2} + \frac{B(\xi-\tau) - y + k}{2}. \tag{16}$$

where $y = \beta\Delta t + (1-\alpha)\gamma + \Delta q$ represents the blockchain influence factor and reflects the comprehensive influence of blockchain technology on the quality traceability system of agricultural product supply chains. $\beta\Delta t + (1-\alpha)\gamma$ represents the unit net benefit for consumers who purchase products from enterprises using blockchain traceability technology. $\Delta q = Q - q(\Delta q \geq 0)$ represents quality improvement. In the blockchain traceability mode, the detection of fresh agricultural products belongs to multi-node detection. The reduction of detection time reduces the quality loss of fresh agricultural products [52]. In addition, the use of blockchain traceability will encourage suppliers to improve product quality [49]. The higher y is, the greater the positive effect of the blockchain traceability mode. This is because y is positively related to the unit net benefit of consumers who purchase products from enterprises using blockchain traceability technology and quality improvement.

From (15) and (16), we can obtain Lemma 2.

Lemma 2. *In a competitive environment, the optimal pricing of enterprises 1 and 2 are $\bar{p}_1^* = \frac{1}{3}\left(B\xi + y + B\tau + 3k + \frac{4k\theta}{1-\theta}\right)$ and $\bar{p}_2^* = \frac{1}{3}\left(2B\xi - y - B\tau + 3k + \frac{2k\theta}{1-\theta}\right)$, respectively.*

Substituting $\bar{p}_1^*$ and $\bar{p}_2^*$ into (11) and (12), the total market demand of enterprises 1 and 2 can be obtained as follows:

$$D_1^{B*} = \frac{1}{6k}(3k + B\xi + y + B\tau)(1-\theta) + \frac{2}{3}\theta,$$

$$D_2^{B*} = \frac{1}{6k}(3k - B\xi - y - B\tau)(1-\theta) + \frac{1}{3}\theta.$$

Substituting $\bar{p}_1^*$ and $\bar{p}_2^*$ into (13) and (14), the maximum profit of enterprises 1 and 2 are, respectively:

$$\pi_1^{B*} = \frac{1}{18k}\left(3k + \frac{4k\theta}{1-\theta} + B\xi + y + B\tau\right)^2(1-\theta) - C,$$

$$\pi_2^{B*} = \frac{1}{18k}\left(3k + \frac{2k\theta}{1-\theta} - B\xi - y - B\tau\right)^2(1-\theta).$$

Lemma 2 shows the optimal pricing decision when enterprise 1 adopts a blockchain traceability system and enterprise 2 insists on adopting a traditional traceability system. We obtained the optimal price, optimal total market demand, and maximum profit of enterprises 1 and 2 under the blockchain traceability mode.

4. Results

4.1. Analysis of the Influencing Factors of the Blockchain Introduction Strategy

Proposition 1. *In a competitive environment, the enterprise should adopt the blockchain traceability strategy when the blockchain influence factor satisfies $y > \frac{\sqrt{18k(1-\theta)\left(C+\frac{k}{2}\right) - 4k\theta}}{1-\theta} - 3k - B\xi - B\tau$.*

Proof. See Appendix A. □

Proposition 1 shows that enterprise 1 can obtain more profits than enterprise 2 when the blockchain influence factor is greater than a certain threshold. If the enterprise does not join the blockchain, it must bear the risk of losses arising from consumer returns. In this case, consumers must bear a longer quality evaluation time, a higher possibility of false quality information, and more loss of returns. If the enterprise chooses to join the blockchain, it may be subject to poor economic benefits (such as a slight reduction in consumer quality assessment time, excessive quality loss, and high costs), and consumers may be subject to an excessive loss of quality in agricultural products. Because $\frac{\partial y}{\partial \beta} = \Delta t$, $\frac{\partial y}{\partial \gamma} = 1 - \alpha$, $\Delta t > 0, 1 - \alpha > 0$, that is, the sensitivity of consumers to the detection time of the product and the sensitivity of consumers to the falseness of the product have a significant impact on the blockchain influence factor. The higher the sensitivity of consumers to the time of product detection and to the falseness of the product, the higher the blockchain influence factor.

The following numerical method is used to illustrate an introduction strategy for blockchain. Since the actual value is difficult to obtain, we assume $B = 0.14, \zeta = 0.8$, $\tau = 0.4, k = 1, C = 3, \theta = 0.5$.

Figure 1 shows the impact of blockchain influence factor y on the blockchain introduction strategy.

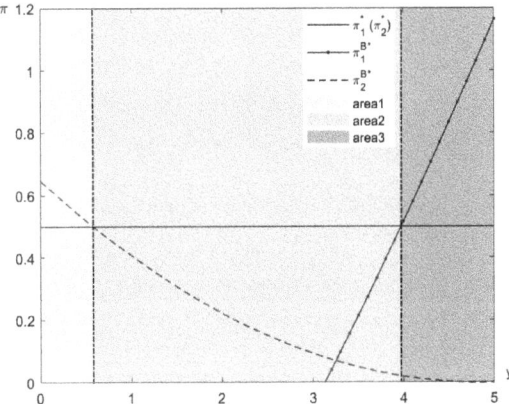

Figure 1. Impact of the blockchain influence factor y on the blockchain introduction strategy.

Figure 1 shows the influence of the blockchain influence factor on the blockchain introduction strategy. $\pi_1^*(\pi_2^*)$ represents the profit of enterprise 1 (enterprise 2) under the traditional traceability mode. Further, π_1^{B*} represents the profit of enterprise 1 under the blockchain traceability mode. π_2^{B*} represents the profit of enterprise 2 under the blockchain traceability mode. The different shaded areas in the figure represent different decisions. In a competitive environment, when the influence factor y is among [0, 3.972], enterprise 1 will not adopt blockchain. Because enterprise 1 had to invest a lot of money if enterprise 1 adopts a blockchain traceability system, its profits would be lower than that without blockchain. When the blockchain influence factor y is higher than 3.972, enterprise 1 will adopt a blockchain traceability system in a competitive environment because its profit under the blockchain traceability mode is higher than that in the traditional mode. The sensitivity of consumers to the detection time of the product and the sensitivity of consumers to the falseness of the product have a positive impact on the blockchain influence factor. As the sensitivity of consumers to the detection time of the product and the sensitivity of consumers to the falseness of the product increase, the blockchain influence factor will increase. At this time, the adoption of blockchain by enterprise 1 could significantly improve its profits, so enterprise 1 will adopt blockchain technology.

Figure 2 shows the critical conditions for introducing blockchain technology. Regional BTD (Blockchain Traceability Decision) denotes the strategy space of enterprise 1 adopting the blockchain traceability system, and regional TTD (Traditional Traceability Decision) denotes the strategy space of enterprise 1 adopting the traditional traceability system. Figure 2 shows that enterprise 1 adopting a blockchain traceability system can obtain higher profits when the blockchain influence factor is large enough and the proportion of consumers with a high traceability preference is relatively large. Therefore, when the blockchain influence factor is large enough, and the proportion of consumers with a high traceability preference is relatively large, enterprise 1 will be prompted to adopt the blockchain traceability strategy.

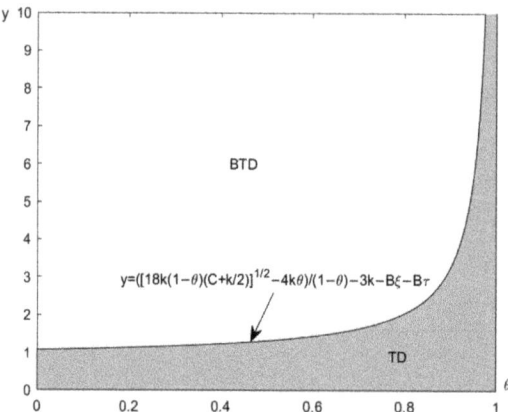

Figure 2. The impact of the proportion of consumers with a high traceability preference on the blockchain introduction strategy.

Based on proposition 1, we have $\frac{\partial \pi_1^{B*}}{\partial B} > 0$, $\frac{\partial \pi_1^{B*}}{\partial \xi} > 0$ and $\frac{\partial \pi_1^{B*}}{\partial y} > 0$, which results in Corollary 1.

Corollary 1. *In a competitive environment, the profits of enterprise 1 increase with an increase in the possibility of consumer returns as a result of the disclosure of false information by traditional enterprises (B), the enterprise's return loss (ξ), the sensitivity of consumers to the falseness of the product (γ), the sensitivity of consumers to the detection time of the product (β), and the quality improvement of the fresh agricultural products (Δq).*

Proposition 2. *Under a competitive environment, when the blockchain influence factor satisfies $y < 3k - \frac{3k\sqrt{1-\theta}-2k\theta}{1-\theta} - B\xi - B\tau$ or $y > 3k + \frac{3k\sqrt{1-\theta}+2k\theta}{1-\theta} - B\xi - B\tau$, the profit of enterprise 2 under the blockchain traceability mode will be higher than that under the traditional traceability mode.*

Proof. See Appendix B. □

Proposition 2 shows that the maximum profit of enterprise 2 under the blockchain traceability mode will be higher than under the traditional traceability mode when blockchain influence factor y is within a certain range. In a competitive environment, only when y satisfies this range can an enterprise with a traditional traceability system under the blockchain traceability mode gain more profit.

Based on the conclusion of Proposition 2, Corollary 2 can be obtained.

Corollary 2. *In a competitive environment, the maximum profit of enterprise 2 under the blockchain traceability mode increases with an increase in y when $y > 3k + \frac{2k\theta}{1-\theta} - B\xi - B\tau$. The maximum* profit of enterprise 2 under the blockchain traceability mode decreases with an increase in y when $y < 3k + \frac{2k\theta}{1-\theta} - B\zeta - B\tau$.

Proof. See Appendix C. □

Corollary 2 shows that when y is in a different range, the maximum profit of enterprise 2 under the blockchain traceability mode is different. $y = 3k + \frac{2k\theta}{1-\theta} - B\zeta - B\tau$ is the critical point of this range. The maximum profit of enterprise 2 under the blockchain traceability mode increases with an increase in y when $y > 3k + \frac{2k\theta}{1-\theta} - B\zeta - B\tau$. The maximum profit of enterprise 2 under the blockchain traceability mode decreases with an increase in y when $y < 3k + \frac{2k\theta}{1-\theta} - B\zeta - B\tau$.

Proposition 3. *When the blockchain influence factor satisfies $y \geq -B\zeta - B\tau - \frac{k\theta}{1-\theta}$, the introduction of blockchain in a competitive environment can lead to a shift of demand from the enterprise not adopting blockchain technology to the enterprise adopting blockchain technology.*

Proof. See Appendix D. □

According to proposition 3, when the blockchain influence factor satisfies $y \geq -B\zeta - B\tau - \frac{k\theta}{1-\theta}$, the total market demand of enterprise 1 under the blockchain traceability mode will be higher than that of enterprise 1 under traditional traceability mode, whereas the demand of enterprise 2 under the blockchain traceability model will be lower than that of enterprise 2 under the traditional traceability mode. That means that some consumers with a high traceability preference will be willing to buy fresh agricultural products and turn from enterprises using blockchain technology.

4.2. Analysis of the Influencing Factors of the Optimal Pricing Decision

Proposition 4. *Under a competitive environment, when the blockchain influence factor satisfies $y < \frac{B\zeta}{2} - B\tau - \frac{k\theta}{1-\theta}$, the optimal pricing of enterprise 1 under the blockchain traceability mode will be lower than that of enterprise 2 under the blockchain traceability mode.*

Proof. See Appendix E. □

Proposition 4 shows that if the optimal pricing of enterprise 1 under the blockchain traceability mode is lower than that of enterprise 2 under the blockchain traceability mode, the blockchain influence factor needs to satisfy $y < \frac{B\zeta}{2} - B\tau - \frac{k\theta}{1-\theta}$. That means, in a competitive environment, when y is less than a certain value, the price of a blockchain enterprise is less than that of an enterprise that does not use blockchain technology.

Proposition 5. *Under a competitive environment, the optimal pricing of enterprises 1 and 2 increases with an increase in the enterprises' return loss, the unit transfer cost, and the proportion of consumers with a high traceability preference. The optimal pricing of enterprise 1 increases with an increase in y, γ, β, τ, and Δq. Meanwhile, the optimal pricing of enterprise 2 decreases with an increase in y, γ, β, τ, and Δq.*

Proof. See Appendix F. □

Proposition 5 shows that the optimal pricing is related to the enterprises' return loss, the unit transfer cost, and the proportion of consumers with a high traceability preference. In the blockchain traceability mode, consumers' sensitivity to the detection time of the product β and the falseness of the product γ, blockchain influence factor y, consumers' return loss τ, and quality improvement could affect the optimal pricing for both blockchain enterprises and traditional enterprises. The optimal pricing of enterprise 1 increases with an increase in y, γ, β, τ, and Δq. Meanwhile, the optimal pricing of enterprise 2 decreases with an increase in y, γ, β, τ, and Δq.

5. Conclusions

Increasingly, consumers pay attention to the reliability and authenticity of agricultural product information. Traditional traceability systems are usually based on centralized information management systems, and information can be easily tampered with and forged. It is difficult for customers to verify the authenticity of the information. Assuming that the consumers' traceability preference is related to the detection time of the product and to the falseness of the product, this study examines the blockchain introduction strategy of fresh agricultural enterprises with two competitive enterprises based on non-cooperative game theory. In the traditional traceability mode, we consider two enterprises that do not use blockchain technology and derive the profit functions of the two enterprises. The optimal pricing and the maximum profits of the two enterprises are obtained through theoretical analysis. In the blockchain traceability mode, we consider the scenario where one enterprise uses blockchain technology and the other enterprise does not. Then, we construct the profit functions of the two enterprises. The optimal pricing and the maximum profits of the two enterprises are obtained through theoretical analysis. By comparing the profits in two different traceability modes, we obtained the specific conditions for the enterprise to introduce blockchain technology. Subsequently, we analyzed the impact of consumer traceability preference and blockchain influence factor. The results can be summarized as follows.

First, adopting blockchain technology is not always good for enterprises in a competitive environment. This conclusion is similar to that of Wu et al. [51]. However, we find that in specific conditions, the enterprise adopting blockchain technology as a traceability system will obtain a competitive advantage, and the enterprise not adopting blockchain technology as a traceability system will not be a free rider. Because the profit of an enterprise not adopting blockchain technology when its competitor adopts the blockchain technology is lower than the profit when the two enterprises do not adopt the blockchain technology, it is different from the view of Wu et al. [51], who found that when one supply chain adopts blockchain technology, the other may be a free rider. Furthermore, we found that the introduction strategy of blockchain technology relates to the transfer cost with consumers and the investment cost of blockchain technology. When the transfer cost with consumers and the investment cost is in a certain range, it is good for the enterprise to adopt blockchain technology. Moreover, in a competitive environment, the profit of blockchain enterprises increases with an increase in the possibility of consumer returns as a result of the disclosure of false information by traditional enterprises, the enterprise's return loss, the sensitivity of consumers to the falseness of the product, the sensitivity of consumers to the detection time of the product, and the quality improvement of the agricultural products.

Second, we observe that the decision to introduce blockchain technology in a competitive environment is related to the blockchain influence factor. Enterprises will introduce blockchain technology when the blockchain influence factor is greater than a certain value. When the blockchain influence factor is less than a certain value, the optimal price of blockchain enterprises under the blockchain traceability mode is lower than that of traditional enterprises under the blockchain traceability mode. We discovered that the blockchain influence factor has a significant impact on enterprise pricing. As the blockchain influence factor increases, the optimal pricing of blockchain enterprises will increase, whereas that of traditional enterprises under the blockchain traceability mode will decrease. This study also showed that the enterprises' return loss, unit transfer costs, and proportion of consumers with a high traceability preference could influence the optimal price of enterprises. With an increase in the enterprises' return loss, unit transfer costs, and the proportion of consumers with a high traceability preference, the optimal pricing of blockchain and traditional enterprises under the blockchain traceability mode will increase.

Thirdly, we discover that the consumers' traceability preferences could affect the optimal pricing and profits of enterprises. The profits of blockchain enterprises increase with an increase in the possibility of consumer returns as a result of the disclosure of false information by traditional enterprises, the sensitivity of consumers to the falseness of the product, and the sensitivity of consumers to the detection time of the product. The optimal pricing of blockchain enterprises increases with an increase in the proportion of consumers with a high traceability preference. The optimal pricing of blockchain enterprises increases with an increase in the consumers' sensitivity to the time of product detection, consumers' sensitivity to the falseness of the product and consumers' return loss. Our results also show that introducing blockchain into a competitive environment can lead to a shift in demand. We find that, in a competitive environment, the total market demand of enterprises applying the blockchain traceability system will increase, whereas that of traditional enterprises under the traditional traceability system will decrease. This means that some consumers with a high traceability preference will be willing to buy fresh agricultural products from enterprises using blockchain technology.

Based on our research results, we provide several implications for managers of fresh product enterprises. Enterprises should focus on two aspects when considering the introduction of blockchain technology. First, enterprises should consider the consumers' preference for the detection time of the product and the falseness of the product. If the proportion of consumers with a high traceability preference reaches a certain threshold, enterprises should adopt a blockchain traceability system. For example, enterprises should introduce a blockchain traceability system if consumers in the market become more concerned about food safety issues and are skeptical about the source of food and other information. Furthermore, enterprises should focus on the blockchain influence factor. Enterprises should introduce blockchain technology when the blockchain influence factor reaches a certain value. We found that the quality improvement caused by the use of the blockchain traceability mode will positively impact the blockchain influence factor. Enterprises should pay attention to the quality loss under the traditional mode. When the quality loss of fresh agricultural products is too significant, it is beneficial for enterprises to introduce blockchain technology to improve product quality. Moreover, enterprises should focus on the blockchain influence factor. Enterprises should introduce blockchain technology when the blockchain influence factor is in a certain range. This certain value is related to many factors, such as the possibility of consumer return as a result of the disclosure of false information by traditional processors, the processor's return loss, consumers' return loss, and so on. When consumers cannot bear the cost of return of goods due to the untrue information disclosed by some enterprises and the losses caused by the return of goods are large enough, enterprises in the same industry will be more willing to adopt blockchain technology.

Finally, we note some potential directions for future research. First, we assume that the quality and return costs are both exogenous parameters in the model; the situation where both or one of them are endogenous parameters is worthy of further study. Second, this study assumed that enterprises establishing blockchain traceability would trace the production process and analyze the introduction strategy of competitive enterprises. However, the cost of building a blockchain traceability system platform is high. Some enterprises probably choose blockchain traceability services provided by third-party trading platforms. It would be interesting to investigate the impact of blockchain on the interaction mechanisms between fresh agricultural enterprises and third-party trading platforms.

Author Contributions: Research framework, conceptualization, and model construction, Y.S.; model solving and simulation, X.S. and Y.J.; writing, Y.S., X.S. and Y.J.; review and editing, J.G. All authors have read and agreed to the published version of the manuscript.

Funding: National Natural Science Foundation of China (71301073, 71701093); National Social Science Foundation of China (22&ZD122); Humanities and Social Science Foundation Project of Ministry of Education (20YJC630142).

Data Availability Statement: Not applicable.

Conflicts of Interest: The authors declare no conflict of interest.

Appendix A Proof of Proposition 1

The maximum profit of enterprise 1 under the blockchain traceability mode is as follows:

$$\pi_1^{B*} = \frac{1}{18k}\left(3k + \frac{4k\theta}{1-\theta} + B\varsigma + y + B\tau\right)^2 (1-\theta) - C$$

In Section 2, we have $\pi_1^* = \pi_2^* = \frac{k}{2}$.

If the profit of enterprise 1 under the blockchain traceability mode is higher than that of enterprise 1 under the traditional traceability mode, it needs to meet:

$$\frac{1}{18k}\left(3k + \frac{4k\theta}{1-\theta} + B\varsigma + y + B\tau\right)^2 (1-\theta) - C > \frac{k}{2}$$

Let

$$Z = \frac{1}{18k}\left(3k + \frac{4k\theta}{1-\theta} + B\varsigma + y + B\tau\right)^2 (1-\theta) - C - \frac{k}{2}$$

Set

$$\varsigma = B\varsigma + y + B\tau + 3k,$$

Then

$$Z(\varsigma) = \frac{1}{18k}\left(\varsigma + \frac{4k\theta}{1-\theta}\right)^2 (1-\theta) - C - \frac{k}{2}$$

When

$$Z(\varsigma) > 0, \varsigma > \frac{\sqrt{18k(1-\theta)\left(C+\frac{k}{2}\right)} - 4k\theta}{1-\theta}$$

Substitute $\varsigma = B\varsigma + y + B\tau + 3k$ to obtain $y > \frac{\sqrt{18k(1-\theta)(C+\frac{k}{2})}-4k\theta}{1-\theta} - 3k - B\varsigma - B\tau$.

Therefore, when $y > \frac{\sqrt{18k(1-\theta)(C+\frac{k}{2})}-4k\theta}{1-\theta} - 3k - B\varsigma - B\tau$, $\frac{1}{18k}\left(3k + \frac{4k\theta}{1-\theta} + B\varsigma + y + B\tau\right)^2 (1-\theta) - C > \frac{k}{2}$.

Appendix B Proof of Proposition 2

The maximum profit of enterprise 2 under the blockchain traceability mode is as follows:

$$\pi_2^{B*} = \frac{1}{18k}\left(3k + \frac{2k\theta}{1-\theta} - B\varsigma - y - B\tau\right)^2 (1-\theta)$$

In Section 2, we have $\pi_1^* = \pi_2^* = \frac{k}{2}$.

If the profit of enterprise 2 under the blockchain traceability mode is higher than that of enterprise 2 under the traditional traceability mode, it needs to meet:

$$\frac{1}{18k}\left(3k + \frac{2k\theta}{1-\theta} - B\varsigma - y - B\tau\right)^2 (1-\theta) > \frac{k}{2}$$

Let

$$Z = \frac{1}{18k}\left(3k + \frac{2k\theta}{1-\theta} - B\varsigma - y - B\tau\right)^2 (1-\theta) - \frac{k}{2}$$

Set $\omega = 3k - B\varsigma - y - B\tau$, then $Z(\omega) = \frac{1}{18k}\left(\omega + \frac{2k\theta}{1-\theta}\right)^2 (1-\theta) - \frac{k}{2}$,

When $Z(\omega) > 0$, as $\omega > \frac{2k\theta}{\theta-1}$, then $\omega > \frac{3k\sqrt{1-\theta}-2k\theta}{1-\theta}$.

Substitute $\omega = 3k - B\varsigma - y - B\tau$ to obtain $y < 3k - \frac{3k\sqrt{1-\theta}-2k\theta}{1-\theta} - B\varsigma - B\tau$.

When $Z(\omega) > 0$, $\omega < \frac{2k\theta}{\theta-1}$, then $\omega < \frac{-3k\sqrt{1-\theta}-2k\theta}{1-\theta}$.

Substitute $\omega = 3k - B\xi - y - B\tau$ to obtain $y > 3k + \frac{3k\sqrt{1-\theta}+2k\theta}{1-\theta} - B\xi - B\tau$.

Therefore, when $y < 3k - \frac{3k\sqrt{1-\theta}-2k\theta}{1-\theta} - B\xi - B\tau$ or $y > 3k + \frac{3k\sqrt{1-\theta}+2k\theta}{1-\theta} - B\xi - B\tau$, $\frac{1}{18k}\left(3k + \frac{2k\theta}{1-\theta} - B\xi - y - B\tau\right)^2 (1-\theta) > \frac{k}{2}$.

Appendix C Proof of Corollary 2

The maximum profit of enterprise 2 under the blockchain traceability mode is as follows:

$$\pi_2^{B*} = \frac{1}{18k}\left(3k + \frac{2k\theta}{1-\theta} - B\xi - y - B\tau\right)^2 (1-\theta)$$

We have $1 - \theta > 0$ and $3k + \frac{2k\theta}{1-\theta} > 0$. Thus, we have the following two cases:

$y > 3k + \frac{2k\theta}{1-\theta} - B\xi - B\tau$. In this case, π_2^{B*} increases with the increase of y

$y < 3k + \frac{2k\theta}{1-\theta} - B\xi - B\tau$. In this case, π_2^{B*} decreases with the increase of y.

Appendix D Proof of Proposition 3

The total market demand of enterprise 1 under the blockchain traceability mode is:

$$D_1^{B*} = \frac{1}{6k}(3k + B\xi + y + B\tau)(1-\theta) + \frac{2}{3}\theta$$

In Section 2, we have $D_1^* = D_2^* = \frac{1}{2}$.

If the total market demand of enterprise 1 under the blockchain traceability mode is higher than that under the traditional traceability mode, it needs to meet:

$$\frac{1}{6k}(3k + B\xi + y + B\tau)(1-\theta) + \frac{2}{3}\theta \geq \frac{1}{2}$$

Therefore, $y \geq -B\xi - B\tau - \frac{k\theta}{1-\theta}$.

When $y \geq -B\xi - B\tau - \frac{k\theta}{1-\theta}$, $\frac{1}{6k}(3k + B\xi + y + B\tau)(1-\theta) + \frac{2}{3}\theta \geq \frac{1}{2}$.

The total market demand of the enterprise 2 under the blockchain traceability mode is:

$$D_2^{B*} = \frac{1}{6k}(3k - B\xi - y - B\tau)(1-\theta) + \frac{1}{3}\theta$$

In Section 2, we have $D_1^* = D_2^* = \frac{1}{2}$.

If the total market demand of enterprise 2 under the blockchain traceability mode is higher than that under the traditional traceability mode, it needs to meet:

$$\frac{1}{6k}(3k - B\xi - y - B\tau)(1-\theta) + \frac{1}{3}\theta \geq \frac{1}{2}$$

Therefore, $y \leq -B\xi - B\tau - \frac{k\theta}{1-\theta}$.

When $y \leq -B\xi - B\tau - \frac{k\theta}{1-\theta}$, $\frac{1}{6k}(3k - B\xi - y - B\tau)(1-\theta) + \frac{1}{3}\theta \geq \frac{1}{2}$.

When $y \geq -B\xi - B\tau - \frac{k\theta}{1-\theta}$, $\frac{1}{6k}(3k + B\xi + y + B\tau)(1-\theta) + \frac{2}{3}\theta \geq \frac{1}{2}$.

Since $y \geq -B\xi - B\tau - \frac{k\theta}{1-\theta}$ contradicts $y \leq -B\xi - B\tau - \frac{k\theta}{1-\theta}$, so when blockchain influence factor is positive, the total market demand of enterprise 1 will increase, and the total market demand of enterprise 2 under the blockchain traceability mode will decrease.

Appendix E Proof of Proposition 4

The optimal pricing of enterprise 1 under the blockchain traceability mode is as follows:

$$\overline{p}_1^* = \frac{1}{3}\left(B\xi + y + B\tau + 3k + \frac{4k\theta}{1-\theta}\right)$$

The optimal pricing of enterprise 2 under the blockchain traceability mode is as follows:

$$\bar{p}_2^* = \frac{1}{3}\left(2B\xi - y - B\tau + 3k + \frac{2k\theta}{1-\theta}\right)$$

If the optimal pricing of enterprise 1 under the blockchain traceability mode is lower than that of enterprise 2 under the blockchain traceability mode, it needs to meet:

$$\frac{1}{3}\left(B\xi + y + B\tau + 3k + \frac{4k\theta}{1-\theta}\right) < \frac{1}{3}\left(2B\xi - y - B\tau + 3k + \frac{2k\theta}{1-\theta}\right)$$

Therefore, $y < \frac{B\xi}{2} - B\tau - \frac{k\theta}{1-\theta}$.

When $y < \frac{B\xi}{2} - B\tau - \frac{k\theta}{1-\theta}$, $\bar{p}_1^* < \bar{p}_2^*$.

Appendix F Proof of Proposition 5

$$\bar{p}_1^* = \frac{1}{3}\left(B\xi + y + B\tau + 3k + \frac{4k\theta}{1-\theta}\right)$$

$$\bar{p}_2^* = \frac{1}{3}\left(2B\xi - y - B\tau + 3k + \frac{2k\theta}{1-\theta}\right)$$

Easy to know $\frac{d\bar{p}_1^*}{d\xi} > 0, \frac{d\bar{p}_1^*}{dk} > 0, \frac{d\bar{p}_2^*}{d\xi} > 0, \frac{d\bar{p}_2^*}{dk} > 0$.

From $0 < \theta < 1$, $\frac{d\bar{p}_1^*}{d\theta} > 0, \frac{d\bar{p}_2^*}{d\theta} > 0$.

Therefore, the optimal pricing of enterprise 1 and 2 under the blockchain traceability mode increases with the increase in the enterprise's return loss, the unit transfer cost, and the proportion of consumers with a high traceability preference.

Additionally, because $\frac{dp_1^*}{dy} > 0, \frac{dp_2^*}{dy} < 0, \frac{dy}{d\gamma} > 0, \frac{dy}{d\beta} > 0, \frac{dy}{d\tau} > 0, \frac{dy}{d\Delta q} > 0$,

Thus

$$\frac{dp_1^*}{d\gamma} = \frac{dp_1^*}{dy} \cdot \frac{dy}{d\gamma} > 0, \frac{dp_1^*}{d\beta} = \frac{dp_1^*}{dy} \cdot \frac{dy}{d\beta} > 0,$$

$$\frac{dp_1^*}{d\tau} = \frac{dp_1^*}{dy} \cdot \frac{dy}{d\tau} > 0, \frac{dp_1^*}{d\Delta q} = \frac{dp_1^*}{dy} \cdot \frac{dy}{d\Delta q} > 0;$$

$$\frac{dp_2^*}{d\gamma} = \frac{dp_2^*}{dy} \cdot \frac{dy}{d\gamma} < 0, \frac{dp_2^*}{d\beta} = \frac{dp_2^*}{dy} \cdot \frac{dy}{d\beta} < 0,$$

$$\frac{dp_2^*}{d\tau} = \frac{dp_2^*}{dy} \cdot \frac{dy}{d\tau} < 0, \frac{dp_2^*}{d\Delta q} = \frac{dp_2^*}{dy} \cdot \frac{dy}{d\Delta q} < 0.$$

References

1. Song, Y.J.; Lv, C.C.; Liu, J.X. Quality and safety traceability system of agricultural products based on Multi-agent. *J. Intell. Fuzzy Syst.* **2018**, *35*, 2731–2740.
2. Nie, W.J.; Li, T.P.; Hua, S.C. Consumer preference for quality attribute of fresh agricultural products and its influencing factors: A case study of Apple. *J. Agro. Econ.* **2016**, *257*, 60–71.
3. Dickinson, D.L.; Bailey, D. Meat traceability: Are US consumers willing to pay for it? *J. Agr. Resour. Econ.* **2002**, *27*, 348–364.
4. Pham, H.A.; Nguyen, D.H.; Tuong, N.H. Blockchain-based farming activities tracker for enhancing trust in the community supported agriculture model. In Proceedings of the The 11th International Conference on ICT Convergence, Jeju, Republic of Korea, 21–23 October 2020.
5. Seo, S.; Jang, S.S.; Miao, L.; Almanza, B.; Behnke, C. The impact of food safety events on the value of food-related firms: An event study approach. *Int. J. Hosp. Manag.* **2013**, *33*, 153–165. [CrossRef]
6. Marucheck, A.; Greis, N.; Mena, C.; Cai, L. Product safety and security in the global supply chain: Issues, challenges and research opportunities. *J. Oper. Manag.* **2011**, *29*, 707–720. [CrossRef]
7. Qian, F. Agricultural products to fight fake use a serial approach. *New Guangming Daily*, 21 September 2016.
8. Badia-Melis, R.; Mishra, P.; Ruiz-García, L. Food traceability: New trends and recent advances. A review. *Food Control* **2015**, *57*, 393–401. [CrossRef]
9. Abeyratne, S.A.; Monfared, R.P. Blockchain ready manufacturing supply chain using distributed ledger. *IJRET* **2016**, *5*, 1–10.

10. Sebastian, J.; Swaminath, S.; Nair, R.R.; Jakkala, K.; Pradhan, A.; Ajitkumar, P. De novo emergence of genetically resistant mutants of Mycobacterium tuberculosis from the persistence phase cells formed against antituberculosis drugs in vitro. *Antimicrob. Agents Chemother.* **2017**, *61*, e01343-16. [CrossRef]
11. Galvez, J.F.; Mejuto, J.C.; Simal-Gandara, J. Future challenges on the use of blockchain for food traceability analysis. *TrAC Trends Anal. Chem.* **2018**, *107*, 222–232. [CrossRef]
12. Swan, M. Blockchain thinking: The brain as a decentralized autonomous corporation [commentary]. *IEEE Technol. Soc. Mag.* **2015**, *34*, 41–52. [CrossRef]
13. Kumar, A.; Liu, R.; Shan, Z. Is blockchain a silver bullet for supply chain management? Technical challenges and research opportunities. *Decision. Sci.* **2020**, *51*, 8–37. [CrossRef]
14. Liu, H. Combating unethical producer behavior: The value of traceability in produce supply chains. *Int. J. Prod. Econ.* **2022**, *244*, 108374. [CrossRef]
15. Cao, B.B.; Zhu, M.F.; Tian, Q. Optimal operation policies in a cross-regional fresh product supply chain with regional government subsidy heterogeneity to blockchain-driven traceability. *Mathematics* **2022**, *10*, 4592. [CrossRef]
16. Chod, J.; Trichakis, N.; Tsoukalas, G.; Aspegren, H.; Weber, M. *Blockchain and the Value of Operational Transparency for Supply Chain Finance*; Working paper; Boston College: Chestnut Hill, MA, USA, 2018.
17. Sander, F.; Semeijn, J.; Mahr, D. The acceptance of blockchain technology in meat traceability and transparency. *Br. Food J.* **2018**, *120*, 2066–2079. [CrossRef]
18. Tian, Y.; Ma, J.; Xie, L.; Koivumäki, T.; Seppänen, V. Coordination and control of multi-channel supply chain driven by consumers' channel preference and sales effort. *Chaos Soliton Fract.* **2020**, *132*, 109576. [CrossRef]
19. Azzi, R.; Chamoun, R.K.; Sokhn, M. The power of a blockchain-based supply chain. *Comput. Ind. Eng.* **2019**, *135*, 582–592. [CrossRef]
20. Kshetri, N. 1 Blockchain's roles in meeting key supply chain management objectives. *Int. J. Inf. Manag.* **2018**, *39*, 80–89. [CrossRef]
21. Ivanov, D.; Dolgui, A.; Sokolov, B. The impact of digital technology and Industry 4.0 on the ripple effect and supply chain risk analytics. *Int. J. Prod. Res.* **2019**, *57*, 829–846. [CrossRef]
22. Kamble, S.; Gunasekaran, A.; Arha, H. Understanding the blockchain technology adoption in supply chains-Indian context. *Int. J. Prod. Res.* **2019**, *57*, 2009–2033. [CrossRef]
23. Wang, Y.; Singgih, M.; Wang, J.; Rit, M. Making sense of blockchain technology: How will it transform supply chains? *Int. J. Prod. Econ.* **2019**, *211*, 221–236. [CrossRef]
24. Saberi, S.; Kouhizadeh, M.; Sarkis, J.; Shen, L. Blockchain technology and its relationships to sustainable supply chain management. *Int. J. Prod. Res.* **2019**, *57*, 2117–2135. [CrossRef]
25. Duan, J.; Zhang, C.; Gong, Y.; Brown, S.; Li, Z. A content-analysis based literature review in blockchain adoption within food supply chain. *Int. J. Environ. Res. Public Health* **2020**, *17*, 1784. [CrossRef]
26. Li, K.; Lee, J.Y.; Gharehgozli, A. Blockchain in food supply chains: A literature review and synthesis analysis of platforms, benefits and challenges. *Int. J. Prod. Res.* **2021**, 1970849. [CrossRef]
27. Pandey, V.; Pant, M.; Snasel, V. Blockchain technology in food supply chains: Review and bibliometric analysis. *Technol. Soc.* **2022**, 101954. [CrossRef]
28. Khan, H.H.; Malik, M.N.; Konečná, Z.; Chofreh, A.G.; Goni, F.A.; Klemeš, J.J. Blockchain technology for agricultural supply chains during the COVID-19 pandemic: Benefits and cleaner solutions. *J. Clean. Prod.* **2022**, *347*, 131268. [CrossRef]
29. Kouhizadeh, M.; Sarkis, J. Blockchain practices, potentials, and perspectives in greening supply chains. *Sustainability* **2018**, *10*, 3652. [CrossRef]
30. Deng, W.; Jiang, X.S.; Bai, Q.L.; Sun, Y.J. The food safety traceability technology based on blockchain [OL]. *Big Data Time* **2018**, *12*, 30–36.
31. Behnke, K.; Janssen, M. Boundary conditions for traceability in food supply chains using blockchain technology. *Int. J. Inf. Manage.* **2020**, *52*, 101969. [CrossRef]
32. Stranieri, S.; Cavaliere, A.; Banterle, A. Do motivations affect different voluntary traceability schemes? An empirical analysis among food manufacturers. *Food Control* **2017**, *80*, 187–196. [CrossRef]
33. Wang, J.; Yue, H.; Zhou, Z. An improved traceability system for food quality assurance and evaluation based on fuzzy classification and neural network. *Food Control* **2017**, *79*, 363–370. [CrossRef]
34. Stuller, Z.J.; Rickard, B.J. Traceability adoption by specialty crop producers in California. *J. Agribus.* **2008**, *26*, 101–116.
35. Pouliot, S.; Sumner, D.A. Traceability, liability, and incentives for food safety and quality. *Am. J. Agric. Econ.* **2008**, *90*, 15–27. [CrossRef]
36. Resende-Filho, M.A.; Hurley, T.M. Information asymmetry and traceability incentives for food safety. *Int. J. Prod. Econ.* **2012**, *139*, 596–603. [CrossRef]
37. Gong, Q.; Chen, F. The impact of the supply chain traceability on food safety and corporate profits. *Nankai Econ. Stud.* **2012**, *6*, 30–48.
38. Aiello, G.; Enea, M.; Muriana, C. The expected value of the traceability information. *Eur. J. Oper. Res.* **2015**, *244*, 176–186. [CrossRef]
39. Cao, S.; Powell, W.; Foth, M.; Natanelov, V.; Miller, T.; Dulleck, U. Strengthening consumer trust in beef supply chain traceability with a blockchain-based human-machine reconcile mechanism. *Comput. Electron. Agric.* **2021**, *180*, 105886. [CrossRef]

40. Dai, B.; Nu, Y.; Xie, X.; Li, J. Interactions of traceability and reliability optimization in a competitive supply chain with product recall. *Eur. J. Oper. Res.* **2021**, *290*, 116–131. [CrossRef]
41. Hastig, G.M.; Sodhi, M.S. Blockchain for supply chain traceability: Business requirements and critical success factors. *Prod. Oper. Manag.* **2020**, *29*, 935–954. [CrossRef]
42. Choi, T.M. Blockchain-technology-supported platforms for diamond authentication and certification in luxury supply chains. *Transp. Res. Part E Logist. Transp. Rev.* **2019**, *128*, 17–29. [CrossRef]
43. Zhang, P.; Luo, X.X. A limited traceability method based on blockchain digital tokens. *Syst. Eng. Theom. Pract.* **2019**, *39*, 1469–1478.
44. Yan, Y.; Zhang, J. Research on supply chain risk aversion based on blockchaintechnology. *Ind. Eng. Manag.* **2018**, *23*, 33–42.
45. Fan, Z.-P.; Wu, X.-Y.; Cao, B.-B. Considering the traceability awareness of consumers: Should the supply chain adopt the blockchain technology? *Ann. Oper. Res.* **2022**, *309*, 837–860. [CrossRef]
46. Cao, Y.; Yi, C.; Wan, G.; Hu, H.; Li, Q.; Wang, S. An analysis on the role of blockchain-based platforms in agricultural supply chains. *Transp. Res. Part E Logist. Transp. Rev.* **2022**, *163*, 102731. [CrossRef]
47. He, Y.; Chen, L.; Xu, Q. Optimal pricing decisions for a global fresh product supply chain in the blockchain technology era. *Int. J. Logist. Res. App.* **2021**, 1981275. [CrossRef]
48. Zhou, L.N.; Zhou, G.G.; Ji, F.Z.; Cao, J. Research on fresh agricultural supply chain network equilibrium with consumers' preference for organic product. *Syst. Eng. Theom. Pract.* **2019**, *16*, 360–369.
49. Feng, T.; Wang, Y.Y.; Zhu, S.H. Impact of blockchain technology on the optimal pricing and quality decisions of platform supply chains. *Int. J. Prod. Res.* **2022**, 2050828. [CrossRef]
50. Liu, S.; Hua, G.; Kang, Y.; Cheng, T.E.; Xu, Y. What value does blockchain bring to the imported fresh food supply chain? *Transp. Res. Part E Logist. Transp. Rev.* **2022**, *165*, 102859. [CrossRef]
51. Wu, X.Y.; Fan, Z.P.; Li, G. Strategic analysis for adopting blockchain technology under supply chain competition. *Int. J. Logist. Res. Appl.* **2022**, 2058473. [CrossRef]
52. Gao, J.; Huo, H.; Zhang, X.Q. Application prospects and challenges of blockchain technology: Based on the perspective of information fidelity. *J. China Sci. Found.* **2020**, *34*, 25–30.

Disclaimer/Publisher's Note: The statements, opinions and data contained in all publications are solely those of the individual author(s) and contributor(s) and not of MDPI and/or the editor(s). MDPI and/or the editor(s) disclaim responsibility for any injury to people or property resulting from any ideas, methods, instructions or products referred to in the content.

Article

Robust Bi-Level Optimization for Maritime Emergency Materials Distribution in Uncertain Decision-Making Environments

Cong Wang [1,2], Zhongxiu Peng [2,*] and Wenqing Xu [2]

1. School of Economics and Management, Southeast University, Nanjing 211189, China; wangcong2017@dlmu.edu.cn
2. School of Maritime Economics and Management, Dalian Maritime University, Dalian 116026, China; xuwenqing1027@163.com
* Correspondence: pzxkadima@163.com

Abstract: Maritime emergency materials distribution is a key aspect of maritime emergency responses. To effectively deal with the challenges brought by the uncertainty of the maritime transport environment, the multi-agent joint decision-making location-routing problem of maritime emergency materials distribution (MEMD-LRP) under an uncertain decision-making environment is studied. First, two robust bi-level optimization models of MEMD-LRP are constructed based on the effect of the uncertainty of the ship's sailing time and demand of emergency materials at the accident point, respectively, on the premise of considering the rescue time window and priority of emergency materials distribution. Secondly, with the help of robust optimization theory and duality theory, the robust optimization models are transformed into robust equivalent models that are easy to solve. Finally, a hybrid algorithm based on the ant colony and tabu search (ACO-TS) algorithm solves multiple sets of numerical cases based on the case design of the Bohai Sea area, and analyzes the influence of uncertain parameters on the decision making of MEMD-LRP. The study of MEMD-LRP under uncertain decision-making environments using bi-level programming and robust optimization methods can help decision makers at different levels of the maritime emergency logistics system formulate emergency material reserve locations and emergency material distribution schemes that can effectively deal with the uncertainty in maritime emergencies.

Keywords: emergency logistics; location-routing problem; bi-level programming; uncertain decision-making environment; robust optimization

MSC: 90B06

1. Introduction

As trade activity between countries gradually resumes in the post-epidemic era, maritime transportation, which is responsible for more than 80% of world trade, has rebounded in 2021 with an estimated growth of 3.2% [1]. The increase in maritime transportation activities has also led to a high incidence of maritime accidents, thus posing significant safety risks [2–4]. When an accident occurs at sea, a rapid and efficient emergency response becomes a crucial part of the process, and in this process, the distribution of maritime emergency materials plays a key role. In the actual distribution process of maritime emergency materials, due to the suddenness and unpredictability of maritime accidents, and because maritime transportation is affected by complex meteorological and sea conditions and other factors, the emergency materials demand at the accident point and the ship's sailing time are usually highly uncertain. Research on emergency materials distribution in traditional deterministic decision-making environments is usually difficult to cope with the challenges brought by complex environmental changes, so it is urgent and important to investigate the maritime emergency materials distribution location-routing problem (MEMD-LRP) in uncertain decision-making environments.

Emergency responses to maritime emergencies is a multi-sectoral endeavor that requires different levels of decision-making bodies to participate in decision making. As a joint decision-making problem, MEMD-LRP involves locating shore-based emergency materials reserves and planning routes for emergency materials distribution. The location problem is solved at the strategic decision-making level, and the distribution route planning of emergency materials is determined at the tactical level or operation level. Bi-level programming can be used to solve the problem of joint decision making by different levels of decision makers, which can ensure that a global perspective is taken first, and the interests of the whole situation and each decision-making subject are considered at the same time.

For a long time, society has generally considered emergency rescue to be a matter of the country, thus neglecting the development of commercially operated rescue organizations. In the actual operation of emergency rescues, in addition to government departments, there are also public welfare rescue units and commercial rescue units. The emergence of public welfare rescue units and commercial rescue units not only improves the speed and efficiency of emergency rescues, but also helps to promote social participation. Among them, the interests represented by public welfare rescue units and government departments are consistent, usually taking the fairness of emergency rescue as the main consideration, and taking dissatisfaction, cost, time, and so on, as the goal [5,6]. On the other hand, commercial rescue units will consider the economy of emergency rescue, which is consistent with minimizing the total economic cost of emergency logistics in the literature [7,8]. The commercial rescue system's systematic network has yet to be expanded, and it should always be the government departments' responsibility in terms of the macro-unification of command and scheduling.

Therefore, from the perspective of multi-level decision makers that participate in joint decision making, it is necessary to adopt a method of bi-level programming and robust optimization based on the communication and cooperation between emergency management departments and commercial rescue units without considering public welfare rescue units. During the planning period, this paper studies the MEMD-LRP problem considering the rescue time window, the priority of distribution of different kinds of emergency materials, the uncertain emergency materials demand at the accident point, and the uncertain transportation time of emergency materials, and then optimizes the maritime emergency logistics system as a whole to ensure the demand of the accident points can be met, and the total cost of the emergency logistics system can be reduced in different cases. This paper is an extension of Peng et al.'s [9] study on MEMD-LRP in a deterministic decision-making environment. This study can provide optimal location selection and route planning solutions for MEMD-LRP in an uncertain decision-making environment within the planning period. It also offers decision makers a reference basis for addressing various emergency situations.

The following is the rest of the paper. The second part provides an overview of related studies, the third part describes the research problem, the construction, and the transformation of the model in detail, and the fourth part gives the solution analysis. Finally, the fifth part summarizes the paper.

2. Literature Review

The LRP proposal can be traced back to the 1980s [10]. This problem has aroused widespread concern and attracted many scholars to conduct in-depth research. At present, scholars at home and abroad have conducted a lot of research on the various extended models of general logistics LRP and the improvement of the solution methods [11–13]. In the innovation of solving methods, to solve the multi-objective chance-constrained programming model under an uncertain transportation time and cost, Lu et al. [14] changed the antennae search of a single beetle to multiple, embedded Dijkstra algorithms, and designed a hybrid beetle swarm optimization algorithm. Lu et al. [15] designed the ant colony system and improved the grey wolf optimization algorithm to solve the fourth party logistics routing problem model through the convergence factor and proportional weight in order to improve the grey wolf optimization algorithm. Şatir Akpunar and Akpinar [16] proposed a hybrid adaptive large neighborhood search algorithm (ALNS) to solve the LRP problem, which improves the performance of the algorithm by combining the variable neighborhood search (VNS) algorithm with the elite local search algorithm. Alamatsaz et al. [17] combines the progressive hedging algorithm (PHA) with a genetic algorithm (GA) to large-scale solve the green capacitated locating-routing problem. As scholars pay attention to the research of emergency logistics, the joint research of emergency logistics and LRP has become one of the hotspots. Earlier emergency logistics LRPs were considered in deterministic environments. Gan and Liu [18] designed a new multi-objective model based on multi-hazard and multi-supplier scenarios, and proposed an improved non-dominated sorting genetic algorithm (NSGA-II) to find the optimal scheduling scheme. Liu et al. [19] studied the location-routing problem in the early stage of an earthquake from a fair perspective, developed the multi-objective model by using a dictionary sequential object optimization method considering emergency window constraints and partial road damage, and designed a hybrid heuristic algorithm to solve the problem.

With the deepening of the research, the emergency logistics LRP problem gradually evolved from a problem in a deterministic decision-making environment to a more relevant problem in an uncertain decision-making environment, and methods such as stochastic programming, fuzzy functions, and robust optimization have gradually become mainstream tools for solving uncertain problems such as demand, time, and so on, in emergency logistics LRP. Ai et al. [20] constructed a discrete nonlinear integer programming model and solved it using a heuristic algorithm after transforming it into a two-stage model in the context of emergency resource distribution in maritime emergency response systems. Zhang et al. [21] studied sustainable multi-warehouse emergency facility LRP with information uncertainty; constructed multi-objective travel time, emergency response cost, and carbon dioxide emission model; designed a hybrid intelligent algorithm integrating an uncertainty simulation- and designed a genetic algorithm to solve it. Afshar and Haghani [22] proposed a comprehensive model for integrated supply chain operations in response to natural disasters that integrates details such as the optimal location of multi-level temporary facilities, vehicle routing, and pickup or delivery schedules in a dynamic environment. Zhang et al. [23] proposed a scenario-based mixed-integer planning model for reliable LRP with the risk of the stochastic disruption of facilities, designing meta-heuristic algorithms based on maximum likelihood sampling methods, route reallocation, a two-stage neighborhood search, and simulated annealing. Ghasemi et al. [24] proposed a mixed-integer mathematical planning model for the location assignment of a multi-objective, multi-commodity, multi-period, multi-vehicle, and modeled-by-scenario-based probabilistic approach for seismic emergency responses, which is solved using improved multi-objective particle swarm optimization, nondominated sequential genetic algorithm, and the epsilon constraint method. Long et al. [25] studied the multi-objective multi-periodic LRP of epidemic logistics considering stochastic demand, proposed a corresponding robust model, and proposed a preference-inspired co-evolutionary algorithm based on Tchebycheff decomposition (PICEA-g-td). Caunhye et al. [26] proposed a two-stage LRP that was transformed into a single-objective solution for the problem of risk management in the case of a disaster with an uncertain demand and infrastructure status. A nonlinear integer open location-routing model was constructed by Wang et al. [27] that considered travel time, total cost, and reliability when distributing post-disaster relief materials, and they proposed a non-dominated sorting differential evolution algorithm and a non-dominated sorting genetic algorithm to solve it. Raeisi et al. [28] constructed a robust fuzzy multi-objective optimization model to solve the hazardous waste management problem, which was solved using various heuristic algorithms and analyzed comparatively. Shen et al. [29] proposed a triangular fuzzy function to obtain the fuzzy demand considering the uncertainty of the demand in the disaster area, constructed a multi-objective model considering the carbon emissions, and used a two-stage hybrid algorithm to solve the problem. Zhang et al. [30] proposed a novel dynamic multi-objective split-delivery location-routing two-stage optimization model for the emergency logistics of offshore oil spill accidents, and developed a hybrid heuristic algorithm to solve it. Ghasemi et al. [31] proposed a scenario-based stochastic multi-objective location-allocation-routing model considering the existence of uncertainty before and after a disaster, which was solved using epsilon constraints and meta-heuristic algorithms.

Some scholars have also considered the problem of joint decision-making by multiple levels of decision makers in solving emergency LRPs in uncertain decision-making environments. Saeidi-Mobarakeh et al. [32] constructed a bi-level programming model with the government as the decision maker at the upper level and the government's followers as the decision makers at the lower level to solve a hazardous waste management problem under uncertainty, and a robust optimization was used in the multi-part solution methodology. Zhou et al. [33] addressed the uncertainty in the emergency logistics system, investigated the integration of the location of transit facilities and the transportation of relief materials, constructed a gray mixed-integer bi-level nonlinear program, and designed a hybrid genetic algorithm to solve the proposed model. Chen et al. [34] conducted a study on the robustness and sustainability of the port logistics system for emergency materials using a bi-level programming method to achieve coordinated optimization of emergency logistics infrastructure locations and emergency rescue vehicle routing planning, as well as simulation using statistical modeling.

This study comprehensively reviews 10 representative studies in related fields and compares them in several aspects, such as research background, model construction methods, types of emergency materials, time windows, and solution methods, as shown in Table 1. Overall, the research for emergency logistics LRPs is richer and deeper, and stochastic programming, fuzzy functions, robust optimization, and bi-level programming decision-making tools are beginning to be applied to emergency logistics LRPs in uncertain decision-making environments. The hybrid heuristic algorithms, which combine the ant colony algorithm, particle swarm algorithm, genetic algorithm, and other algorithms, are widely used in the solution of emergency logistics LRPs. To our limited knowledge, most of the existing studies are based on land-based disasters and emergencies, and even though the literature [20] has investigated the distribution of emergency resources in maritime emergency response systems, only the probability distribution of the demand has been considered. In addition, existing research has focused on the use of multi-objective models, and the bi-level programming method has not been applied to the marine accident LRP of multi-agent joint decision making under uncertain decision environments. Although the literature [34] studied the port logistics system for emergency materials, it did not address the distribution of maritime emergency materials. The purpose of this paper is to make a plan for different levels of decision makers in maritime emergency logistics systems under uncertain decision-making environments. To achieve this, a combination of a bi-level programming method and a robust optimization method is adopted.

Table 1. Comparison with related studies.

Author	Uncertainty	Maritime Emergency	Modeling Method	Emergency Materials	Time Window	Solution Method
Gan and Liu [18]	No	Yes	Multi-objective modeling	Multiple	Yes	Improved NSGA-II
Ai et al. [20]	Yes	Yes	Single-objective modeling	Single	No	Hybrid heuristic algorithm
Zhang et al. [21]	Yes	No	Multi-objective modeling	No	No	Hybrid intelligence algorithm
Zhang et al. [23]	Yes	No	Scenario-based Single-objective modeling	No	No	Metaheuristic approach

Table 1. *Cont.*

Author	Uncertainty	Maritime Emergency	Modeling Method	Emergency Materials	Time Window	Solution Method
Long et al. [25]	Yes	No	Multi-objective multi-stage robust modeling	Yes	No	Preference-inspired coevolutionary algorithm
Wang et al. [27]	Yes	No	Multi-objective modeling	Yes	No	Non-dominated sorting genetic algorithm Non-dominated sorting differential evolution algorithm
Shen et al. [29]	Yes	No	Fuzzy function Multi-objective modeling	No	No	Two-stage hybrid algorithm
Zhang et al. [30]	Yes	Yes	Dynamic multi-objective modeling	No	Yes	Hybrid heuristic algorithm
Zhou et al. [33]	Yes	No	Bi-level programming modeling	Yes	-	Hybrid genetic algorithm
Chen et al. [34]	Yes	Yes (Port)	Bi-level programming modeling	No	No	Statistical methods
This paper	Yes	Yes	Robust bi-level programming modeling	Yes	Yes	Hybrid heuristic algorithm

3. Mathematical Problem Formulation

3.1. Problem Description

The decision making of MEMD-LRP involves the location of shore-based emergency material reserves and maritime emergency material distribution route planning, which aims to distribute emergency materials with different priorities from the selected emergency material reserves to the accident point based on information such as the location of the potential accident point, and under constraints such as satisfying the time window. But due to the fact that in the actual MEMD-LRP, the ship's sailing time and the accident point emergency materials demand uncertainty, the location decision and routing planning decision can be significantly affected.

In uncertain decision-making environments, a joint decision-making model with multiple levels of decision makers becomes particularly important. The MEMD-LRP can be described from the perspective of bi-level programming, in which the upper-level decision maker (the emergency management department) integrates the location problem of the emergency reserves. Because the construction of the emergency reserve is required to be outsourced to the manufacturer [35], the emergency management department must consider the emergency reserve stockpile construction cost and accident point time satisfaction loss cost. Lower-level decision makers (commercial rescue units) independently plan emergency material distribution routes based on upper-level decisions to minimize distribution costs, ship transportation costs, ship dispatch costs, and time penalty costs. Rescue units will develop the distribution program feedback to the emergency management department, and according to the response of the rescue units here to make decisions, the interaction between the two is constantly carried out, forming an iterative decision-making process to develop the overall optimal decision to adapt to the maritime emergency's uncertainty.

The maritime emergency logistics system involving multi-level decision-making agents studied in this paper is shown in Figure 1.

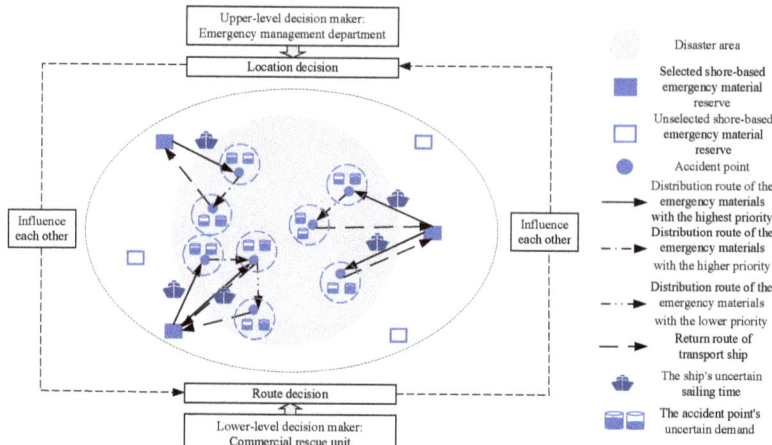

Figure 1. Schematic diagram of the maritime emergency logistics system involving multi-level decision-making agents.

The paper has the following assumptions:
(1) Commercial rescue units are taken, as the lower-level decision makers of this study and public relief units are not considered;
(2) Multiple candidates reserve with unrestricted capacity and known locations;
(3) Multiple potential accident points with known locations, without any consideration of drift spread;
(4) Emergency materials in multiple levels with known priorities for distribution; for different types of emergency materials, the transport of the materials should be in the order of priority, and there should be different distribution costs for each level of emergency materials;
(5) The number of ships is sufficient; they are of the same type and capacity, and emergency materials of different levels can be mixed under the limitation of the time window of the accident point;
(6) Each accident point receives assistance from a single emergency material reserve, and only one ship is permitted to visit the accident location during the allocation of each level of emergency materials, all within a specified time window;
(7) Each ship is affiliated with a specific emergency material reserve, commences its journey from that reserve, and upon completing the material delivery, returns to the same reserve. Furthermore, each ship can serve multiple accident points while adhering to the time window constraints;
(8) Because the study in this paper is in the preventive stage, which is the overall layout of the maritime emergency logistics system during the planning period, the wind speed, current speed, and the average still water speed of the ship between the nodes is assumed to be constant [20,36];
(9) To simplify the problem, the time of loading and unloading materials is not considered when calculating the arrival node time, and only the ship's sailing time at sea is considered;
(10) The numerical value and probability distribution information of ship sailing time and accident point demand for different levels of emergency materials are unknown, but only their respective upper and lower limits are known, and these two parameters do not influence each other and exist independently in their respective uncertain sets.

The variables and symbols in this paper are described in Table 2.

Table 2. Model sets, parameters, variables, and their descriptions.

Sets	Descriptions
$I = \{i \mid i = 1, 2, \cdots, \mid I \mid\}$	Candidate shore-based emergency reserves set
$J = \{j \mid j = 1, 2, \cdots, \mid J \mid\}$	Accident points set
$B = I \cup J$	Network nodes set
$K = \{k \mid k = 1, 2, \cdots, \mid K \mid\}$	Ships set
$W = \{w \mid w = 1, 2, \cdots, \mid W \mid\}$	Emergency material priority levels set
Parameters	**Descriptions**
F_i	The fixed construction cost for the i candidate shore-based emergency reserve (CNY)
S_k	The cost per unit distance for the k ship (CNY/nm)
C_0	The fixed dispatch cost per ship
G	The fixed capacity of the ship (unit/ship)
D_{jw}	The demand for emergency materials of level w at accident point j (unit)
C_{ijw}	The cost of transporting emergency materials of level w from reserve i to accident point j per unit of material (CNY/unit)
V_{pqk}	The actual average speed of the ship k when traveling from node p to q, accounting for the influence of wind and current speeds (kn)
V_{pqk}^A	The average speed of the ship k in still water from node p to q (kn)
V_1	The wind speed (kn)
V_2	The current speed (kn)
L_{pq}	The actual distance traveled from node p to q (nm)
T_{Ejw}	The expected arrival time of accident point j for emergency materials of level w (h)
T_{Ljw}	The latest arrival time of level w emergency materials that the accident point j can tolerate (h)
T_{jw}	The real-time delivery arrival of the emergency materials level w at the accident point j (h)
T_{pq}	The actual sailing time of the ship from point p to point q, where $T_{pq} = \frac{L_{pq}}{V_{pqk}}$ (h)
C_1	The time penalty cost coefficient caused by the arrival of emergency materials of level w at accident point j earlier than T_{Ejw}
C_2	The time-penalty cost coefficient incurred if the emergency materials of level w arrive at accident point j later than T_{Ejw} and earlier than T_{Ljw}
P_{jw}	The time penalty cost function for transporting the w level emergency materials to the incident point j
$F(T_{jw})$	The time satisfaction function of the accident point j during the conveyance of emergency materials of level w
$\phi(F(T_{jw}))$	The function representing the cost penalty coefficient for time satisfaction loss in transporting emergency materials of level w to accident point j
A	A sufficiently large positive number
Variables	**Descriptions**
x_i	If the emergency materials reserve is built at the location i, then 1; otherwise, 0
y_{ij}	If the accident point j is served by emergency reserve i, then 1; otherwise, 0
q_k	If the ship k is put into service, then 1; otherwise, 0
z_{pqk}	If the ship k sails from node p to node q, then 1; otherwise, 0
Auxiliary variable	**Descriptions**
u_{jw}	If the accident point j requires emergency materials of level ω, then 1; otherwise, 0

241

3.2. Model Construction

3.2.1. Description of Time Penalty Cost

Maritime emergency rescue is characterized by a strong time-sensitive rescue, so the time-penalty cost function in MEMD-LRP is constructed, and the relationship between time and time-penalty cost is shown in Figure 2, which is consistent with the authors' previous study [9].

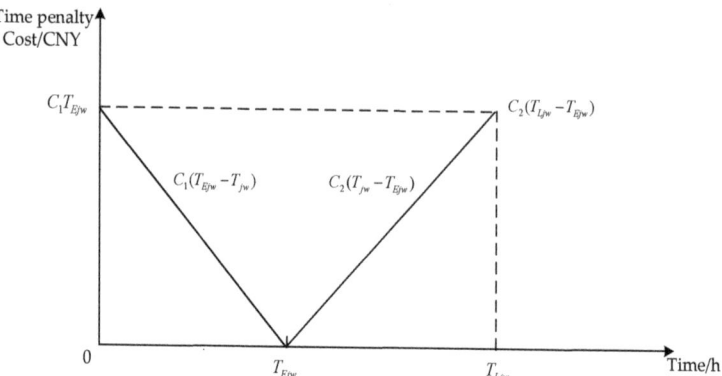

Figure 2. Time penalty cost curve.

The time penalty cost function expression is:

$$P_{jw} = \begin{cases} C_1(T_{Ejw} - T_{jw}), T_{jw} < T_{Ejw} \\ 0, T_{jw} = T_{Ejw} \\ C_2(T_{jw} - T_{Ejw}), T_{jw} > T_{Ejw} \end{cases}, \forall j \in J, w \in W \quad (1)$$

3.2.2. Description of Time Satisfaction Loss Cost at Accident Point

The upper-level emergency management decision makers face the challenge of balancing the cost of establishing shore-based emergency reserves with the time satisfaction at accident sites. To simplify calculations, time satisfaction is converted into a cost of time satisfaction loss integrated into the upper-level decision-maker's objectives. In this paper, a linear time satisfaction function is chosen. When a ship k delivers emergency materials of a certain level to accident point j but fails to meet the expected arrival time $T_{Ej\omega}$ at accident point j, time satisfaction is reduced at accident point j. The greater the deviation from the arrival time $T_{Ej\omega}$ of emergency materials w at accident point j, the more significant the reduction in time satisfaction. Furthermore, the cost associated with the loss of time satisfaction at accident point j is tied to the demand for emergency materials at that accident point. The penalty coefficient for the cost of time satisfaction loss at accident point j follows a segmented function corresponding to time satisfaction, with the functional relationship determined to be $\phi(F(T_{jw}))$ [9].

The expression representing the time satisfaction function of accident point j concerning the arrival time of a certain level of emergency materials is as follows:

$$F(T_{jw}) = \begin{cases} 1, T_{jw} = T_{Ejw} \\ \frac{T_{Ejw} - T_{jw}}{T_{Ejw}}, 0 \leq T_{jw} < T_{Ejw} \\ \frac{T_{Ljw} - T_{jw}}{T_{Ljw} - T_{Ejw}}, T_{Ejw} < T_{jw} \leq T_{Ljw} \\ 0, T_{Ljw} < T_{jw} \end{cases}, \forall j \in J, w \in W \quad (2)$$

The mathematical representation for the penalty coefficient associated with the loss cost of time satisfaction at accident point j is as follows:

$$\phi(F(T_{jw})) = \begin{cases} 0, F(T_{jw}) = 1 \\ 1, F(T_{jw}) = \frac{T_{Ejw}-T_{jw}}{T_{Ejw}}, \forall j \in J, w \in W \\ 1, F(T_{jw}) = \frac{T_{Ljw}-T_{jw}}{T_{Ljw}-T_{Ejw}}, \forall j \in J, w \in W \\ +\infty, F(T_{jw}) = 0 \end{cases} \quad (3)$$

The total cost resulting from the lost time satisfaction at accident point j can be expressed as follows:

$$\sum_{i \in I} \sum_{j \in J} \sum_{w \in W} x_i \phi(F(T_{jw})) y_{ij} D_{jw} \quad (4)$$

3.2.3. MEMD-LRP Robust Bi-Level Nominal Models

Based on the above assumptions and cost descriptions, the nominal model (denoted as BLNM) for constructing the robust bi-level model of MEMD-LRP is shown below.

(1) Upper level modeling:

$$\min f_1 = \sum_{i \in I} F_i x_i + \sum_{i \in I} \sum_{j \in J} \sum_{w \in W} x_i \phi(F(T_{jw})) y_{ij} D_{jw} \quad (5)$$

$$\text{s.t.} \quad 1 \leq \sum_{i \in I} x_i \leq I \quad (6)$$

$$y_{ij} - x_i \leq 0, \forall i \in I, j \in J \quad (7)$$

$$x_i \in \{0,1\} \quad (8)$$

The goal defined in objective function (5) is to minimize both the construction expenses of emergency reserves and the costs associated with time satisfaction losses at the accident point; constraint (6) restricts the actual count of emergency reserve constructions to not surpass the number of candidate shore-based emergency reserves; constraint (7) enforces that only when selected as an emergency material reserve can materials be transported; constraint (8) represents an upper-level decision variable.

(2) Lower level modeling:

$$\min f_2 = \sum_{i \in I} \sum_{j \in J} \sum_{w \in W} u_{jw} D_{jw} C_{ijw} y_{ij} + \sum_{p,q \in B} \sum_{k \in K} z_{pqk} L_{pq} S_k + \sum_{k \in K} C_0 q_k + \sum_{w \in W} \sum_{i \in I} \sum_{j \in J} y_{ij} P_{jw} \quad (9)$$

$$\text{s.t.} \sum_{i \in I} y_{ij} = 1, \forall j \in J \quad (10)$$

$$\sum_{k \in K} \sum_{j \in J} z_{ijk} \geq x_i, \forall i \in I \quad (11)$$

$$\sum_{i \in I} \sum_{j \in J} z_{ijk} \leq 1, \forall k \in K \quad (12)$$

$$z_{pqk} \leq q_k, \forall p, q \in B, p \neq q, k \in K \quad (13)$$

$$\sum_{k \in K} \sum_{p \in B} z_{pjk} u_{jw} = 1, \forall j \in J, w \in W \quad (14)$$

$$\sum_{p,q \in B} \sum_{i \in I} \sum_{j \in J} \sum_{w \in W} D_{jw} u_{jw} y_{ij} z_{pqk} \leq G, \forall k \in K \quad (15)$$

$$\sum_{k \in K} z_{pqk} = 0, \forall p, q \in I \tag{16}$$

$$\sum_{p \in B} z_{pqk} - \sum_{p \in B} z_{qpk} = 0, \forall k \in K, q \in B \tag{17}$$

$$\sum_{j \in J} z_{ijk} + \sum_{j \in J} z_{jrk} \leq 1, \forall i, r \in I, k \in K \tag{18}$$

$$y_{ij} D_{j(w+1)} \leq u_{jw} A, \forall w = 1, \cdots, |W|-1, i \in I, j \in J \tag{19}$$

$$T_{jw} \leq T_{j(w+1)}, \forall w = 1, \cdots, |W|-1, j \in J \tag{20}$$

$$\sum_{j \in J} T_{jw} \leq \sum_{j \in J} T_{j(w+1)}, \forall w = 1, \cdots, |W|-1, j \in J \tag{21}$$

$$y_{ij} T_{jw} \leq T_{Ljw}, \forall i \in I, j \in J, w \in W \tag{22}$$

$$T_{pw} + z_{pqk} T_{pq} \leq T_{Lqw}, \forall p, q \in J, w \in W, z_{pqk} = 1 \tag{23}$$

$$y_{ij} \in \{0,1\}, q_k \in \{0,1\}, z_{pqk} \in \{0,1\} \tag{24}$$

In a bi-level programming model, the upper model's constraints apply uniformly to the lower model. Objective function (9) aims to minimize the total costs encompassing different levels of emergency material distribution, ship transportation, ship dispatch, and time penalties; constraint (10) ensures that each incident point receives assistance from a single emergency reserve; constraint (11) ensures that each selected emergency materials reserve is assigned ships; constraint (12) ensures that each ship is linked to one selected emergency reserve; constraint (13) indicates that only operational ships are eligible for transportation; constraint (14) mandates that, during the distribution of each level of emergency materials, only one ship passes through each accident point; constraint (15) indicates that the demand for emergency materials at the accident point along a ship's route must not exceed the ship's capacity; constraint (16) indicates that there cannot be transportation between any two emergency materials reserves; constraint (17) indicates that ships entering from a point must also exit from that point; constraint (18) indicates that a ship leaving the emergency reserve is required to return to the same emergency reserve in the end; constraint (19) indicates that the transport of emergency materials from emergency reserve i to accident point j can commence for the next level only after the emergency materials of the previous level have been transported; constraints (20) and (21) denote that the actual delivery time of high-priority emergency materials is strictly less than the actual delivery time of low-priority emergency materials; constraint (22) denotes that the actual arrival time of level w emergency materials transported from emergency material reserve i to incident point j is less than or equal to the latest allowable delivery time for level w emergency materials at incident point j; constraint (23) accounts for the time window constraints on a ship while servicing multiple point points, and constraint (24) is the lower-level decision variable.

The time for the ship k to reach the accident point q is calculated by the following formula:

$$T_{qw} = T_{pw} + z_{pqk} T_{pq}, \forall p, q \in J, w \in W, z_{pqk} = 1 \tag{25}$$

The ship's k speed will be influenced by both the wind and current speed; consequently, the ship's k actual average speed is the vector superposition of the average still water speed, wind speed, and current speed of the ship k, which is calculated as follows:

$$V_{pqk} = V_{pqk}^A + V_1 + V_2, \forall p, q \in B, p \neq q \tag{26}$$

3.2.4. MEMD-LRP Robust Bi-Level Modeling

The upper-level objective function in the MEMD-LRP robust bi-level nominal model is first linearized by introducing the auxiliary variable CL, which leads to constraint (27) from constraints (2) and (3):

$$CL = \begin{cases} 0, T_{jw} = T_{Ejw} \\ 1, 0 \leq T_{jw} < T_{Ejw} \text{ or } T_{Ejw} < T_{jw} \leq T_{Ljw}, \forall j \in J, w \in W \\ +\infty, T_{Ljw} < T_{jw} \end{cases} \tag{27}$$

Continuing to linearize the upper objective function by introducing the auxiliary variable l_{ij} and making it equal to the product of two 0–1 variables, we have (28)–(32):

$$l_{ij} = x_i y_{ij}, \forall i \in I, j \in J \tag{28}$$

$$l_{ij} \leq x_i, \forall i \in I, j \in J \tag{29}$$

$$l_{ij} \leq y_{ij}, \forall i \in I, j \in J \tag{30}$$

$$l_{ij} \geq x_i + y_{ij} - 1, \forall i \in I, j \in J \tag{31}$$

$$l_{ij} \in \{0, 1\} \tag{32}$$

Function (5) is then transformed into function (33):

$$\min f_1 = \sum_{i \in I} F_i x_i + \sum_{i \in I} \sum_{j \in J} \sum_{w \in W} CL l_{ij} D_{jw} \tag{33}$$

In this paper, we consider that the uncertain parameter ship sailing time only appears in the constraints of the lower level, which has no direct influence on the upper and lower objective functions, whereas the uncertain parameter accident point demand for different levels of emergency materials has a direct influence on the upper and lower objective functions and constraints; the two uncertain parameters do not appear in the same constraints at the same time. The robust model proposed by Soyster [37] is optimized for the worst case scenario. Maritime emergency response has urgency and high requirements on rescue time when considering uncertainty in ship sailing time. The conservative Soyster robust model is used to construct a robust bi-level model containing uncertain parameters regarding the ship's sailing time. The Bertsimas and Sim [38] robust model is a gradual development of the Soyster robust model, introducing the budget of uncertainty (BoU) to regulate the degree of robust conservatism. Bertsimas and Sim's robust model is used to construct a robust bi-level model of emergency material demand at accident points containing uncertain parameters. The degree of conservatism of the whole robust bi-level model can be adjusted by introducing the uncertain budget of the emergency material demand, and the objective function and constraints of the emergency material demand containing uncertain parameters are transformed using the peer-to-peer transformation method of the Bertsimas and Sim robust model [39,40].

It is assumed that the uncertain ship sailing time $\tilde{T}_{pq}$ is perturbed in an interval uncertainty set; the different levels of emergency material requirements at the accident point $\tilde{D}_{jw}$ are perturbed in a box uncertainty set, and the decision-maker only knows the upper and lower bounds of the unknown parameters, which are distributed on their respective bounded symmetric intervals, and the distribution information is unknown:

$$\widetilde{T}_{pq} \in [T_{pq} - \hat{T}_{pq}, T_{pq} + \hat{T}_{pq}], \forall p, q \in B, p \neq q \tag{34}$$

$$\widetilde{D}_{jw} \in [D_{jw} - b_{jw}\hat{D}_{jw}, D_{jw} + b_{jw}\hat{D}_{jw}], \forall j \in J, w \in W \tag{35}$$

In constraints (34) and (35), T_{pq} represents the nominal value (NV) of the ship's sailing time between nodes, which is equivalent to the corresponding value in the deterministic model, and $\hat{T}_{pq} \geq 0$ is the amount of time perturbation. D_{jw} is the nominal value of the demand for different levels of emergency materials at the accident point, $\hat{D}_{jw} \geq 0$ is the amount of demand perturbation, and b_{jw} is a random variable taking values in the interval [0,1] and with an unknown distribution, notated as its uncertainty set $U_1 = \left\{ b_{jw} \mid \sum_w \sum_j b_{jw} \leq \Gamma_1, 0 \leq b_{jw} \leq 1, \forall j \in J, w \in W \right\}$. And Γ_1 is the uncertain budget of demand, controlling the uncertainty level of its uncertainty set, defining the box uncertainty set with the budget. The value of Γ_1 is related to the decision maker's preference: If the value of the uncertainty budget is larger, the more conservative the robust model is, the better the robustness of the solution, and the more satisfactory results can be obtained in the worst case scenario. However, if the value of the uncertainty budget is smaller, the less robust it is; however, better results may be obtained in the ideal case. Decision makers can adjust the values according to their preferences to obtain decision methods with different degrees of conservatism to achieve a compromise between optimality and robustness [40].

For the upper and lower bounds of the uncertain budget Γ_1, it is easy to see that $\Gamma_1 \geq 0$, by $\forall b_{jw} \in [0,1]$. By the definition of the uncertain set U_1, and constraint (35), we also obtain $\Gamma_1 \leq |J| \times |W|$.

MEMD-LRP Robust Bi-Level Model Based on Ship Sailing Time Uncertainty

(1) Robust bi-level modeling

Observing that the ship sailing time appears in (23) and (25) in the BLNM, the above equations are adjusted correspondingly when constructing the robust bi-level model to obtain the new robust constraints (60) and (63). The MEMD-LRP robust bi-level model based on the uncertainty of ship sailing time denoted as TRBLM is constructed according to the Soyster robust model as follows:

Upper level modeling:

$$\min f_1 = \sum_{i \in I} F_i x_i + \sum_{i \in I} \sum_{j \in J} \sum_{w \in W} CLl_{ij} D_{jw} \tag{36}$$

$$s.t. \ 1 \leq \sum_{i \in I} x_i \leq I \tag{37}$$

$$y_{ij} - x_i \leq 0, \forall i \in I, j \in J \tag{38}$$

$$x_i \in \{0, 1\} \tag{39}$$

$$CL = \begin{cases} 0, T_{jw} = T_{Ejw} \\ 1, 0 \leq T_{jw} < T_{Ejw} \text{ or } T_{Ejw} < T_{jw} \leq T_{Ljw}, \forall j \in J, w \in W \\ +\infty, T_{Ljw} < T_{jw} \end{cases} \tag{40}$$

$$l_{ij} = x_i y_{ij}, \forall i \in I, j \in J \tag{41}$$

$$l_{ij} \leq x_i, \forall i \in I, j \in J \tag{42}$$

$$l_{ij} \leq y_{ij}, \forall i \in I, j \in J \tag{43}$$

$$l_{ij} \geq x_i + y_{ij} - 1, \forall i \in I, j \in J \tag{44}$$

$$l_{ij} \in \{0,1\} \tag{45}$$

The objective function and constraints of the TRBLM upper model are changed, except that (37)–(39) are exactly the same as BLNM, but the meaning is exactly the same and will not be repeated.

Lower level modeling:

$$\min f_2 = \sum_{i \in I} \sum_{j \in J} \sum_{w \in W} u_{jw} D_{jw} C_{ijw} y_{ij} + \sum_{p,q \in B} \sum_{k \in K} z_{pqk} L_{pq} S_k + \sum_{k \in K} C_0 q_k + \sum_{w \in W} \sum_{i \in I} \sum_{j \in J} y_{ij} P_{jw} \tag{46}$$

$$\text{s.t.} \sum_{i \in I} y_{ij} = 1, \forall j \in J \tag{47}$$

$$\sum_{k \in K} \sum_{j \in J} z_{ijk} \geq x_i, \forall i \in I \tag{48}$$

$$\sum_{i \in I} \sum_{j \in J} z_{ijk} \leq 1, \forall k \in K \tag{49}$$

$$z_{pqk} \leq q_k, \forall p, q \in B, p \neq q, k \in K \tag{50}$$

$$\sum_{k \in K} \sum_{p \in B} z_{pjk} u_{jw} = 1, \forall j \in J, w \in W \tag{51}$$

$$\sum_{p,q \in B} \sum_{i \in I} \sum_{j \in J} \sum_{w \in W} D_{jw} u_{jw} y_{ij} z_{pqk} \leq G, \forall k \in K \tag{52}$$

$$\sum_{k \in K} z_{pqk} = 0, \forall p, q \in I \tag{53}$$

$$\sum_{p \in B} z_{pqk} - \sum_{p \in B} z_{qpk} = 0, \forall k \in K, q \in B \tag{54}$$

$$\sum_{j \in J} z_{ijk} + \sum_{j \in J} z_{jrk} \leq 1, \forall i, r \in I, k \in K \tag{55}$$

$$y_{ij} D_{j(w+1)} \leq u_{jw} A, \forall w = 1, \cdots, |W| - 1, i \in I, j \in J \tag{56}$$

$$T_{jw} \leq T_{j(w+1)}, \forall w = 1, \cdots, |W| - 1, j \in J \tag{57}$$

$$\sum_{j \in J} T_{jw} \leq \sum_{j \in J} T_{j(w+1)}, \forall w = 1, \cdots, |W| - 1, j \in J \tag{58}$$

$$y_{ij} T_{jw} \leq T_{Ljw}, \forall i \in I, j \in J, w \in W \tag{59}$$

$$T_{pw} + z_{pqk} \widetilde{T}_{pq} \leq T_{pqw}, \forall p, q \in J, w \in W, z_{pqk} = 1 \tag{60}$$

$$y_{ij} \in \{0,1\}, q_k \in \{0,1\}, z_{pqk} \in \{0,1\} \tag{61}$$

$$V_{pqk} = V^A_{pqk} + V_1 + V_2, \forall p, q \in B, p \neq q \tag{62}$$

where the time for the ship k to reach the accident point q is calculated as:

$$T_{qw} = T_{pw} + z_{pqk}\widetilde{T}_{pq}, \forall p, q \in J, w \in W, z_{pqk} = 1 \tag{63}$$

The objective function and constraints of the TRBLM lower model, except for (34) and (35), are identical to those of the BLNM, but have exactly the same meaning and will not be repeated.

(2) Robust equivalent model

According to references [37,41,42], the transformation of constraint (60) and (63) containing the equals sign yields constraints (64) and (65):

$$T_{pw} + z_{pqk}(T_{pq} + \hat{T}_{pq}) \leq T_{Lqw}, \forall p, q \in J, w \in W, z_{pqk} = 1 \tag{64}$$

$$z_{pqk}(T_{pq} - \hat{T}_{pq}) \leq T_{qw} - T_{pw} \leq z_{pqk}(T_{pq} + \hat{T}_{pq}), \forall p, q \in J, w \in W, z_{pqk} = 1 \tag{65}$$

The robust equivalent model TRBLM-RC of the model TRBLM is obtained:

Upper objective function (36) with constraints (37)–(39) and (40)–(45), and lower objective function (9) with constraints (10)–(22), (24), (26), (64), and (65).

When the amount of time perturbation is $\hat{T}_{pq} = 0$, the ship sailing time is equal to the corresponding value in the deterministic case, so the models TRBLM, TRBLM-RC, and BLNM are equivalent.

MEMD-LRP Robust Bi-Level Model Based on the Uncertainty of Emergency Material Demand at Accident Points

(1) Robust bi-level model

It is observed that the demand for emergency materials at the accident point appears in objective functions (36) and (9), and constraints (15) and (19) of the model. Thus, the above equations must be adjusted correspondingly when constructing the robust optimization model considering the uncertainty of the demand for emergency materials at the accident point to obtain the new robust upper and lower objective functions (66) and (76), and robust constraints (66) and (76). Other constraints are kept unchanged for the time being. Denote the robust bi-level model as DRBLM, as follows:

Upper level modeling:

$$\min f_1 = \min\left(\sum_{i \in I} F_i x_i + \max \sum_{i \in I} \sum_{j \in J} \sum_{w \in W}(D_{jw} + b_{jw}\hat{D}_{jw})CLl_{ij}\right) \tag{66}$$

$$\text{s.t. } 1 \leq \sum_{i \in I} x_i \leq I \tag{67}$$

$$y_{ij} - x_i \leq 0, \forall i \in I, j \in J \tag{68}$$

$$x_i \in \{0, 1\} \tag{69}$$

$$CL = \begin{cases} 0, T_{jw} = T_{Ejw} \\ 1, 0 \leq T_{jw} < T_{Ejw} \text{ or } T_{Ejw} < T_{jw} \leq T_{Ljw}, \forall j \in J, w \in W \\ +\infty, T_{Ljw} < T_{jw} \end{cases} \tag{70}$$

$$l_{ij} = x_i y_{ij}, \forall i \in I, j \in J \tag{71}$$

$$l_{ij} \leq x_i, \forall i \in I, j \in J \tag{72}$$

$$l_{ij} \leq y_{ij}, \forall i \in I, j \in J \tag{73}$$

$$l_{ij} \geq x_i + y_{ij} - 1, \forall i \in I, j \in J \tag{74}$$

$$l_{ij} \in \{0,1\} \tag{75}$$

Lower level modeling:

$$\min f_2 = \min \left(\sum_{p,q \in B} \sum_{k \in K} z_{pqk} L_{pq} S_k + \sum_{k \in K} C_0 q_k + \sum_{w \in W} \sum_{i \in I} \sum_{j \in J} y_{ij} P_{jw} + \max \sum_{i \in I} \sum_{j \in J} \sum_{w \in W} (D_{jw} + b_{jw} \hat{D}_{jw}) u_{jw} C_{ijw} y_{ij} \right) \tag{76}$$

$$\text{s.t.} \sum_{i \in I} y_{ij} = 1, \forall j \in J \tag{77}$$

$$\sum_{k \in K} \sum_{j \in J} z_{ijk} \geq x_i, \forall i \in I \tag{78}$$

$$\sum_{i \in I} \sum_{j \in J} z_{ijk} \leq 1, \forall k \in K \tag{79}$$

$$z_{pqk} \leq q_k, \forall p,q \in B, p \neq q, k \in K \tag{80}$$

$$\sum_{k \in K} \sum_{p \in B} z_{pjk} u_{jw} = 1, \forall j \in J, w \in W \tag{81}$$

$$\sum_{k \in K} z_{pqk} = 0, \forall p,q \in I \tag{82}$$

$$\sum_{p \in B} z_{pqk} - \sum_{p \in B} z_{qpk} = 0, \forall k \in K, q \in B \tag{83}$$

$$\sum_{j \in J} z_{ijk} + \sum_{j \in J} z_{jrk} \leq 1, \forall i,r \in I, k \in K \tag{84}$$

$$T_{jw} \leq T_{j(w+1)}, \forall w = 1, \cdots, |W| - 1, j \in J \tag{85}$$

$$\sum_{j \in J} T_{jw} \leq \sum_{j \in J} T_{j(w+1)}, \forall w = 1, \cdots, |W| - 1, j \in J \tag{86}$$

$$y_{ij} T_{jw} \leq T_{Ljw}, \forall i \in I, j \in J, w \in W \tag{87}$$

$$T_{pw} + z_{pqk} T_{pq} \leq T_{Lqw}, \forall p,q \in J, w \in W, z_{pqk} = 1 \tag{88}$$

$$y_{ij} \in \{0,1\}, q_k \in \{0,1\}, z_{pqk} \in \{0,1\} \tag{89}$$

$$T_{qw} = T_{pw} + z_{pqk} T_{pq}, \forall p,q \in J, w \in W, z_{pqk} = 1 \tag{90}$$

$$V_{pqk} = V_{pqk}^A + V_1 + V_2, \forall p,q \in B, p \neq q \tag{91}$$

$$\sum_{p,q \in B} \sum_{i \in I} \sum_{j \in J} \sum_{w \in W} D_{jw} u_{jw} y_{ij} z_{pqk} + \max \sum_{p,q \in B} \sum_{i \in I} \sum_{j \in J} \sum_{w \in W} b_{jw} \hat{D}_{jw} u_{jw} y_{ij} z_{pqk} \leq G, \forall k \in K \quad (92)$$

$$y_{ij} D_{j(w+1)} + \max y_{ij} \left(b_{j(w+1)} \hat{D}_{j(w+1)} \right) \leq u_{jw} A, \forall i \in I, j \in J, w = 1, \cdots, |W| - 1 \quad (93)$$

(2) Robust equivalent model

Upper and lower objective functions (66) and (76) of the DRBLM and constraints (92) and (93) of the DRBLM are nonlinear expressions containing inner maximization subterms, which are not convenient to solve directly. Using strong duality theory, it is possible to transform the DRBLM into a more easily solvable robust equivalent model, denoted as RBLM-RC.

The problem of maximizing the inner level of the objective function (66) is first decomposed to obtain Equation (94):

$$\max_{b_{jw} \in U_1} \sum_{i \in I} \sum_{j \in J} \sum_{w \in W} (D_{jw} + b_{jw} \hat{D}_{jw}) CLl_{ij} = \sum_{i \in I} \sum_{j \in J} \sum_{w \in W} D_{jw} CLl_{ij} + \max_{b_{jw} \in U_1} \sum_{i \in I} \sum_{j \in J} \sum_{w \in W} b_{jw} \hat{D}_{jw} CLl_{ij} \quad (94)$$

The linear programming problem with inner-level maximization is shown in constraints (95)–(97):

$$\max_{b_{jw} \in U_1} \sum_{i \in I} \sum_{j \in J} \sum_{w \in W} b_{jw} \hat{D}_{jw} CLl_{ij} \quad (95)$$

$$\text{s.t.} \quad \sum_{w} \sum_{j} b_{jw} \leq \Gamma_1 \quad (96)$$

$$0 \leq b_{jw} \leq 1 \quad (97)$$

Transformation according to the strong duality theory further yields duality problems (98)–(100) for problems (95)–(97), where ρ_{jw}, θ is a duality variable.

$$\min \rho_{jw} + \Gamma_1 \theta \quad (98)$$

$$\text{s.t.} \quad \rho_{jw} + \theta \geq \sum_{i \in I} \sum_{j \in J} \sum_{w \in W} \hat{D}_{jw} CLl_{ij}, \forall j \in J, w \in W \quad (99)$$

$$\rho_{jw}, \theta \geq 0 \quad (100)$$

Function (66) is then converted to function (101):

$$\min f_1 = \sum_{i \in I} F_i x_i + \sum_{i \in I} \sum_{j \in J} \sum_{w \in W} D_{jw} CLl_{ij} + \sum_{i \in I} \sum_{j \in J} \sum_{w \in W} \rho_{jw} + \Gamma_1 \theta \quad (101)$$

Similarly, objective function (41) is then transformed into function (102), which satisfies constraints (103) and (104):

$$\min f_2 = \sum_{p,q \in B} \sum_{k \in K} z_{pqk} L_{pq} S_k + \sum_{k \in K} C_0 q_k + \sum_{w \in W} \sum_{i \in I} \sum_{j \in J} y_{ij} P_{jw} + \sum_{i \in I} \sum_{j \in J} \sum_{w \in W} D_{jw} u_{jw} C_{ijw} y_{ij} + \sum_{i \in I} \sum_{j \in J} \sum_{w \in W} \rho_{jw1} + \Gamma_1 \theta_1 \quad (102)$$

$$\text{s.t.} \quad \rho_{jw1} + \theta_1 \geq \sum_{i \in I} \sum_{j \in J} \sum_{w \in W} \hat{D}_{jw} u_{jw} C_{ijw} y_{ij}, \forall i \in I, j \in J, w \in W \quad (103)$$

$$\rho_{jw1}, \theta_1 \geq 0 \quad (104)$$

The treatment of constraint (66) according to the strong duality theory leads to constraints (103)–(106):

$$\sum_{p,q \in B} \sum_{i \in I} \sum_{j \in J} \sum_{w \in W} D_{jw} u_{jw} y_{ij} z_{pqk} + \max_{b_{jw} \in U_1} \sum_{p,q \in B} \sum_{i \in I} \sum_{j \in J} \sum_{w \in W} b_{jw} \hat{D}_{jw} u_{jw} y_{ij} z_{pqk} \leq G, \forall k \in K \quad (105)$$

$$\sum_{p,q \in B} \sum_{i \in I} \sum_{j \in J} \sum_{w \in W} D_{jw} u_{jw} y_{ij} z_{pqk} + \min_{\rho_{jw2}, \theta_2} \sum_{p,q \in B} \sum_{i \in I} \sum_{j \in J} \sum_{w \in W} \rho_{jw2} + \Gamma_1 \theta_2 \leq G, \forall k \in K \quad (106)$$

$$\text{s.t.} \quad \hat{D}_{jw} u_{jw} y_{ij} z_{pqk} \leq \rho_{jw2} + \theta_2, \forall i \in I, j \in J, p, q \in B, w \in W \quad (107)$$

$$\rho_{jw2}, \theta_2 \geq 0, \forall j \in J, w \in W \quad (108)$$

where ρ_{jw2} and θ_2 are duality variables, the "min" sign in constraint (106) can be ignored, and constraint (106) is equivalent to (109).

$$\sum_{p,q \in B} \sum_{i \in I} \sum_{j \in J} \sum_{w \in W} D_{jw} u_{jw} y_{ij} z_{pqk} + \sum_{p,q \in B} \sum_{i \in I} \sum_{j \in J} \sum_{w \in W} \rho_{jw2} + \Gamma_1 \theta_2 \leq G, \forall k \in K \quad (109)$$

Similarly, constraint (76) can be transformed into (108)–(110):

$$y_{ij} D_{j(w+1)} + \rho_{jw3} + \Gamma_1 \theta_3 \leq u_{jw} A, \forall i \in I, j \in J, w = 1, \cdots, |W| - 1 \quad (110)$$

$$\text{s.t.} \quad y_{ij} \hat{D}_{j(w+1)} \leq \rho_{jw3} + \theta_3, \forall i \in I, j \in J, w = 1, \cdots, |W| - 1 \quad (111)$$

$$\rho_{jw3}, \theta_3 \geq 0, \forall j \in J, w \in W \quad (112)$$

The robust equivalent model DRBLM-RC of the model DRBLM is obtained:

Upper objective function (101) with constraints (6)–(8), (27)–(32), (99), and (100), and lower objective function (102) with constraints (10)–(14), (16)–(18), (20)–(26), (103), (104) and (107)–(112).

When the demand uncertainty budget is $\Gamma_1 = 0$, the demand for emergency materials is equal to the corresponding value in the deterministic scenario, so the models DRBLM, DRBLM-RC, and BLNM are equivalent.

3.3. Solution Method

The bi-level programming model is an NP-hard problem, and no exact solution algorithm exists [43]. Whether it is the robust bi-level nominal model constructed in this paper or the transformed robust equivalent model, due to the interaction between the upper level decision and the lower level decision, and many variables and constraints, this makes the solution more and more difficult. The following two algorithms should be combined; the ant colony algorithm, which has a strong global optimization search capability, and the tabu search algorithm, which has a strong local search capability, avoid falling into the local optimum, and obtains the global optimal solution [44,45]. The ACO-TS algorithm designed in this paper is the same as the one previously designed by the authors in the literature [9], except the corresponding parameters are adjusted according to the model when solving, which will not be repeated here. The specific solution flowchart is shown in Figure 3.

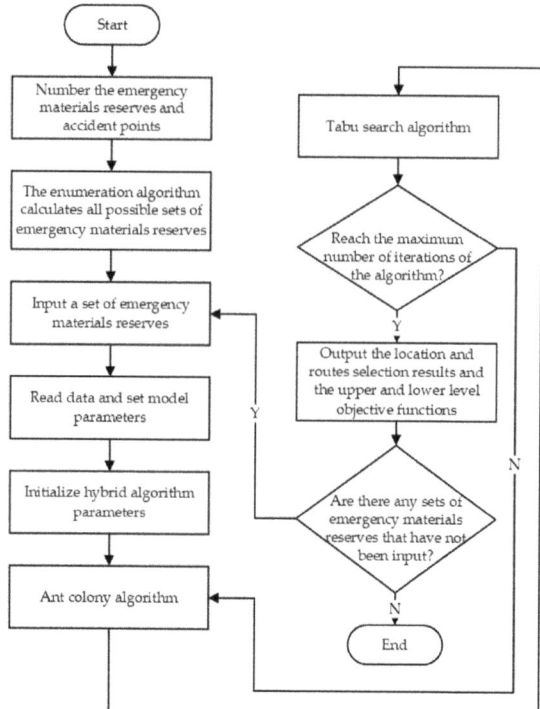

Figure 3. Flowchart for solving.

4. Solution Analysis

4.1. Example Information

Six ports in the Bohai Sea area were selected as alternative shore-based emergency material reserves, and 40 real historical cases in the Bohai Sea area were selected to design the arithmetic examples of this study according to the accident level, adding the emergency materials of different priority levels as well as the time window of the accident point and other related information. The example information of this paper is the same as that in study [9], which is shown in Appendix A.

The models and algorithms designed in this paper are solved using MATLAB R2017a and run on a computer with Intel(R) Core (TM) i7-10510U CPU @ 1.80 GHz CPU and 16 GB RAM. The key algorithmic parameters include the number of iterations N, number of ants m, ant crawling speed $speed$, the pheromone evaporation coefficient ρ, pheromone increase intensity Q, length of the taboo table L, and so on.

4.2. Analysis of the Algorithm and Solution Results

4.2.1. Algorithm Analysis

To verify the effectiveness of the algorithm in this paper, we compared the results of the ACO algorithm with the TS algorithm and the ACO algorithm without the TS algorithm in solving the BLNM model. During the experiment, we found that when the parameter is set to $N = 150$, $m = 150$, $speed = 0.05$, $Q = 1$, the ACO algorithm cannot obtain the feasible solution, while the ACO-TS algorithm can obtain the feasible solution. When the parameter is set to $N = 1000$, $m = 200$, $speed = 0.05$, $Q = 1$, ACO can obtain the feasible solution when the number of emergency material reserves is six. We set the parameter to $N = 150$, $m = 150$, $speed = 0.05$, $Q = 1$, $L = 20$, and use the ACO-TS algorithm to obtain the optimal solution under different emergency material reserve quantities, as shown in Table 3.

Table 3. The optimal solution of the BLNM model obtained by the ACO-TS algorithm.

Reserves	Upper Total Cost (CNY)	Time Satisfaction Loss Cost (CNY)	Lower Total Cost (CNY)	Emergency Materials Distribution Cost (CNY)	Ship Dispatch Cost (CNY)	Shipping Cost (CNY)	Time Penalty Cost (CNY)
(2,3,5)	560,621	621	90,486.35	2494	66,600	14,175.79	7216.56
(2,4,5,6)	760,621	621	90,479.06	2494	67,500	13,200.90	7284.16
(1,2,3,4,5)	96,0621	621	88,139.80	2494	63,000	15,402.78	7243.02
(1,2,3,4,5,6)	1,160,621	621	88,654.75	2494	64,800	14,397.99	6962.76

The decision-making process of the bi-level programming model is that the upper level gives priority to the decision-making, and the lower level makes independent decisions based on the upper level's decision-making, which is fed back to the upper level. Therefore, the solution when the number of emergency material reserves is three is the overall optimal solution of BLNM; that is, to establish emergency materials reserves in Yingkou Port, Tianjin Port, and Weifang Port. The service of all accident points can be satisfied when the total cost of the upper lever is 560,621. Ransikarbum and Mason [46] point out that geographic information system or maps are needed for emergency material distribution location-routing decision aiding; therefore, we used the software to convert the actual geographical coordinates of the emergency materials reserves and the accident points into Cartesian coordinates, and drew the location-routing map in Figure 4, which represents the actual geographical location. The part routes of emergency materials distribution are also shown in Table 4.

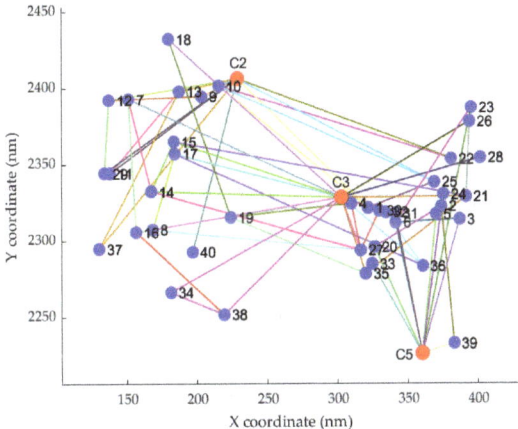

Figure 4. Location-routing map. The red dots represent the selected emergency materials reserves. The blue dots represent the potential accident points. The lines represent the route of the ship.

It can be seen that the emergency materials reserves have the situation of cross-regional distribution when serving the accident points, and it is not always based on the principle of giving priority to the nearest accident points. This is due to the higher priority and time satisfaction requirements of emergency materials distribution, such as reserve 2 in Figure 4. Table 4 is responsible for the distribution of emergency materials at accident points 22 and 25.

Table 4. Emergency materials distribution route (part).

Reserves	Accident Points of Reserves Service	Ship	Distribution Routes (Emergency Materials Level in Parentheses)
2	1, 9, 10, 11, 12, 13, 17, 22, 25, 29, 37, 40	1	0-37(1)-0
		2	0-11(1)-0
		3	0-1(1)-25(1)-0
		4	0-9(1)-12(1)-0
		5	0-22 (1)-0
		6	0-13(1)-37(2)-0
3	4, 7, 8, 14, 15, 16, 17, 18, 19, 21, 26, 27, 28, 30, 32, 34, 35, 36, 38	1	0-36(1)-17(2)-15(2)-21(3)-0
		2	0-18(1)-19(2)-4(2) -0
		3	0-17(1)-8(1)- 0
		4	0-21(1)-26(1)-0
		5	0-35(1)-19(1)-0
		6	0-27(1)-14(2)-7(3)-0
5	2, 3, 5, 6, 20, 23, 24, 31, 33, 39	1	0-23(1)-0
		2	0-20(1)-2(1)-0
		3	0-39(1)-0
		4	0-3(1)-0
		5	0-24(1)-0
		6	0-33(1)-0

Because our penalty cost function has high requirements for the timely arrival of emergency materials, to further analyze the ACO-TS and ACO algorithms, we increased the parameter of loading and unloading time of emergency materials to $T_k = 0.05$ h/unit, and set the algorithm parameter as $N = 200$, $m = 200$, speed $= 0.05$, $Q = 1$ to solve the problem. Equations (23) and (25) are transformed into:

$$T_{pw} + T_k D_{pw} z_{pqk} + T_{pq} \leq T_{Lqw}, \forall p, q \in J, w \in W, z_{pqk} = 1 \tag{113}$$

$$T_{qw} = T_{pw} + T_k D_{pw} z_{pqk} + z_{pqk} T_{pq}, \forall p, q \in J, w \in W, z_{pqk} = 1 \tag{114}$$

We have obtained the optimal solution of the two algorithms under different emergency material reserve construction numbers, as shown in Tables 5 and 6. When the number of emergency materials reserves constructed is one, neither of the two algorithms has an optimal solution. However, ACO-TS provides optimal solutions as the number of emergency supply depots increases from two to six, while the ACO algorithm only achieves optimal solutions when the number of reserves is three, five, and six. Furthermore, for the same number of emergency materials reserves constructions, ACO-TS yields a smaller optimal solution than ACO.

Table 5. The optimal solution of the BLNM model obtained by the ACO-TS algorithm.

Reserves	Upper Total Cost (CNY)	Time Satisfaction Loss Cost (CNY)	Lower Total Cost (CNY)	Emergency Materials Distribution Cost (CNY)	Ship Dispatch Cost (CNY)	Shipping Cost (CNY)	Time Penalty Cost (CNY)
(2,5)	360,621	621	89,078.47	2494	64,800	14,454.11	7330.37
(2,5,6)	560,621	621	91,609.56	2494	66,600	15,306.08	7209.48
(1,2,4,5)	760,621	621	86,400.66	2494	65,700	11,334.81	6871.74
(1,2,3,4,5)	960,621	621	85,884.94	2494	64,800	11,531.14	7059.79
(1,2,3,4,5,6)	1,160,621	621	84,288.8	2494	62,100	12,569.88	7124.91

Table 6. The optimal solution of BLNM model obtained by ACO algorithm.

Reserves	Upper Total Cost (CNY)	Time Satisfaction Loss Cost (CNY)	Lower Total Cost (CNY)	Emergency Materials Distribution Cost (CNY)	Ship Dispatch Cost (CNY)	Shipping Cost (CNY)	Time Penalty Cost (CNY)
(1,2,4)	580,621	621	99,227.50	2494	75,600	13,256.34	7877.16
(1,2,3,5,6)	960,621	621	103,418.47	2494	80,100	12,910.56	7913.90
(1,2,3,4,5,6)	1,160,621	621	87,991.54	2494	63,900	14,046.92	7550.63

It takes 64 times to run the algorithm through all emergency materials reserves, but there is no obvious rule in the number of iterations of the algorithm in each operation. To sum up, ACO-TS performs well in solving the problem, and can obtain more feasible solutions and optimal solutions, and the optimal solution is smaller than the corresponding optimal solution of the ACO algorithm.

4.2.2. Solution Results Analysis

To explore the impact of the uncertainty of ship sailing time on MEMD-LRP decision making in the planning period, examples with different values of the time disturbance ratio are set up. To explore the impact of the uncertainty of the demand for emergency materials at the accident point on the MEMD-LRP decision in the planning period, several sets of examples are set up, with different values for the demand uncertainty budget parameter Γ_1 and demand disturbance ratio. To verify the validity of the model constructed in this paper, the above arithmetic example is solved based on the ACO-TS algorithm described in detail in the literature [9], in which the number of algorithmic iterations N and number of ants m are set to 150, aiming at giving the optimal decision in different cases while exploring the influence of uncertain ship sailing times and uncertain emergency material demand at the accident point on the decision of MEMD-LRP.

1. The impact of ship sailing time uncertainty on MEMD-LRP decision making

To analyze the effect of uncertain ship sailing time on the MEMD-LRP decisions during the planning period, the model TRBLM-RC is solved using the ACO-TS algorithm, with the time disturbance ratios set to 0, 10%, 20%, 30%, 40%, and 50%. The optimal decision when the time disturbance ratio is equal to 0 is also equivalent to the optimal decision of the nominal model. Based on the decision-making principle that the upper level of bi-level programming prioritizes decision-making, and the lower level makes autonomous decisions on this basis, the optimal location-routing decisions under different time disturbance ratios are obtained. The results are shown in Table 3, and the cost curves under different time disturbance ratios are shown in Figure 4.

From the calculation results presented in Table 7 and illustrated in Figure 5, the following conclusions can be drawn:

(a) The optimal number of locations under different time perturbation ratios is the same—both are three—and the total cost of the upper level is the same, but the location results are different. It shows that different time disturbance ratios have a certain influence on the location scheme. The reason why the location results are different, but the total cost of the upper level is the same, is that the decision-maker of the upper level has the right to prioritize decision making and usually chooses the decision that maximizes its interests, so the location decision of the upper level always chooses the case where the total cost of the upper level is the smallest.

(b) With the upper level total cost remaining the same, the general trend in the lower-level total cost is to increase as the time disruption ratio increases. As the time disturbance ratio increases, the change in ship sailing time gradually increases, and the lower-level decision maker is affected in planning the route. When the disturbance ratio is 0 and 50%, the total cost of the lower-level increases by 4%, although the upper-level location decision is the same. When the disturbance ratios are 10%, 30%, and 40%, the upper-level decisions remain the same, but the total lower-level cost increases by about 2% for the latter two, indicating that the disturbance ratios do have an impact on route planning. When the disturbance ratio is 20%, the lower-level total cost exceeds the lower-level total cost under other disturbance ratios. This is because the lower decision maker is making decisions within the allowable range of the upper decision-maker; the upper decision maker prioritized to make the decision that is most beneficial to him/herself; and the impact of the lower decision-maker for the total cost of the system is less than the upper decision-maker. This kind of decision maker for the lower decision maker may not be the optimal decision, and at this time, the upper decision maker of the location scheme is different from the location scheme under all other perturbation ratios.

(c) Among the optimal solutions under different time disruption ratios, the choice of location (2,5,6) is the preferred selection. This suggests that establishing emergency materials reserves in Yingkou Port, Weifang Port, and Yantai Port is a more cost-effective option while ensuring the rescue of all accident points.

Table 7. The optimal location-routing decision under different time disturbance ratios.

Disturbance Ratio (%)	Location Decisions	Upper Total Cost/CNY	Lower Total Cost/CNY	Total Cost/CNY
0	(2,3,5)	560,621	90,486.35	651,107.35
10	(2,5,6)	560,621	91,645.96	652,266.96
20	(1,2,5)	560,621	96,984.13	657,605.13
30	(2,5,6)	560,621	93,874.88	654,495.88
40	(2,5,6)	560,621	93,984.37	654,605.37
50	(2,3,5)	560,621	94,678.47	655,297.47

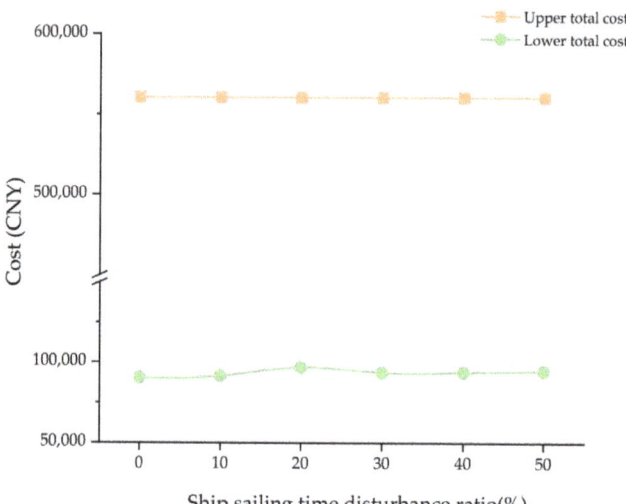

Figure 5. Cost profiles for different time perturbation ratios.

Through the above analysis, it can be found that the greater the uncertainty of ship sailing time—in most cases to distribute the emergency materials to the accident point in time under constraints such as meeting the time—the greater the total cost of the system, and the greater the cost of emergency rescue. By setting different time perturbation ratios, the upper- and lower-level decision makers can obtain the optimal decision that meets the interests under different sailing time conditions.

2. The impact of uncertain emergency material demands at accident points on MEMD-LRP decision making

To analyze the impact of the emergency material demands of the uncertain accident points on MEMD-LRP decision making in the planning period, the ACO-TS algorithm is used to solve the DRBLM-RC model. The uncertain budget parameters Γ_1 are 10, 20, 30, 30, 50, 60, 70, 80, and 90, and the ratio of demand disturbance is 10, 20, and 30. Based on the upper-level priority decision making of bi-level programming and the decision-making principle of lower-level independent decision making, the optimal location-routing decision under different uncertain budgets and different demand disturbance ratios is obtained. The results are shown in Table 8, and the results under different demand disturbance ratios are shown in Figure 6.

Table 8. The optimal location-routing decision under an uncertain budget and demand disturbance ratios.

Uncertain Budget	Demand Disturbance Ratio (%)	Location Decision	Upper Total Cost/CNY	Lower Total Cost/CNY	Total Cost/CNY
0	—	(2,3,5)	560,621	90,486.35	651,107.35
10	10	(1,2,5)	560,731	93,824.81	654,555.81
	20	(2,5,6)	560,791	93,759.10	654,550.10
	30	(1,2,5)	560,862	93,825.91	654,687.91
20	10	(2,5,6)	560,731	92,874.87	653,605.87
	20	(2,3,5)	560,791	92,301.58	653,092.58
	30	(2,4,5)	560,862	93,864.90	654,726.90
30	10	(2,5,6)	560,731	92,207.50	652,938.50
	20	(2,3,5)	560,791	96,484.78	657,275.78
	30	(1,2,5)	560,862	91,934.91	652,796.91
40	10	(2,5,6)	560,731	95,037.06	655,768.06
	20	(2,3,5)	560,791	91,663.90	652,454.90
	30	(1,2,5)	560,862	90,440.81	651,302.81
50	10	(2,5,6)	560,731	92,591.82	653,322.82
	20	(2,3,5)	560,791	91,275.81	652,066.81
	30	(1,2,5)	560,862	93,825.91	654,687.91
60	10	(1,2,5)	560,731	96,893.24	657,624.24
	20	(2,3,5)	560,791	97,588.78	658,379.78
	30	(2,4,5)	560,862	94,175.60	655,037.60
70	10	(1,2,5)	560,731	93,165.67	653,896.67
	20	(2,5,6)	560,791	94,173.81	654,964.81
	30	(2,4,5)	560,862	93,675.75	654,537.76
80	10	(1,2,5)	560,731	92,870.09	653,601.07
	20	(1,2,5)	560,791	96,044.88	656,835.88
	30	(1,2,5)	560,862	94,448.07	655,310.07
90	10	(2,5,6)	560,731	94,072.70	654,803.70
	20	(2,5,6)	560,791	99,535.75	660,326.75
	30	(2,5,6)	560,862	95,048.72	655,910.72

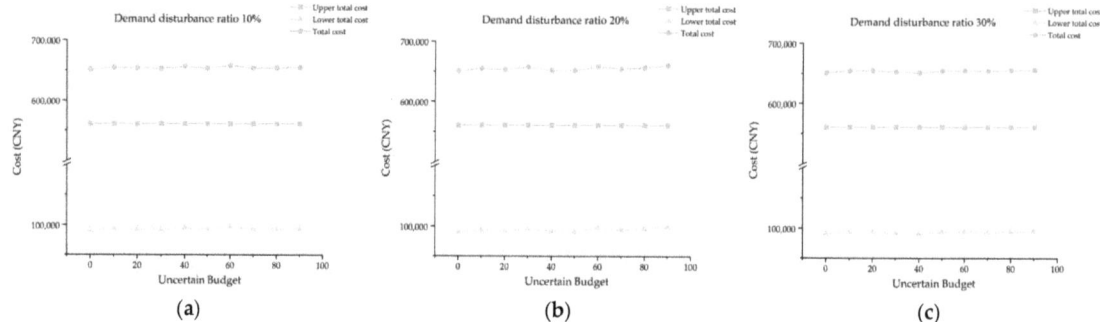

Figure 6. Cost curves for different demand-disruption ratios. (**a**) The demand disturbance ratio is 10%. (**b**) Demand disturbance ratio is 20%. (**c**) Demand disturbance ratio is 30%.

The following conclusions can be drawn from the computational results in Table 8 and Figure 6:

(a) When uncertain budget and demand-disruption ratios vary, the upper-level reserve locations remain constant at three, but the chosen location schemes differ, indicating a certain influence of uncertain budget and demand-disruption ratios on location selection. When the uncertain budget remains constant, the total upper-level cost exhibits a systematic increase with varying demand-disruption ratios. The reason for the increase in upper-level cost with increasing demand-disruption ratios lies in the fact that the cost of accident point time satisfaction loss in the upper-level objective function is demand-related. Whether in the DRBLM model or the DRBLM-RC model, the values of dual variables depend on the magnitude of demand-disruption. At this time, the impact of uncertain budget values on the upper-level objective function is relatively minimal.

(b) Once upper-level location decisions are determined, lower-level decision makers make decisions to maximize their interests based on these upper-level decisions. At this stage, the total lower-level cost is influenced by variations in uncertain budget and demand-disruption ratios. In cases where the uncertain budget equals 10, 20, 50, 70, 80, and 90, the overall trend of the total lower-level cost follows an increasing pattern with increasing demand-disruption ratios, but fluctuations occur in these scenarios. However, in cases where the uncertain budget equals 30, 40, and 60, this trend does not hold. In these instances, lower-level decision makers are constrained by the upper-level decisions, where the upper level prioritizes its maximization of interests. As a result, the total lower-level cost for scenarios with lower demand-disruption ratios can exceed that of scenarios with higher demand-disruption ratios. This phenomenon also explains the presence of fluctuations in cases with uncertain budgets of 10, 20, 50, and 90. When demand-disruption ratios are equal, the overall trend of the lower-level total cost generally increases with the increase of an uncertain budget.

(c) When the demand disturbance ratio is 10% and 20%, this change is not obvious when the demand ratio is 30%, and there are more volatility points. When uncertain budgets are smaller, the changing pattern is less distinct than when uncertain budgets are larger. This illustrates that greater demand uncertainty has a more substantial impact on location-routing decisions. The less distinct or irregular changing patterns can be attributed, on the one hand, to the upper-level's prioritization of minimizing the overall system cost at the expense of the lower-level's interests. On the other hand, it could also result from excessively small demand-disruption ratios, causing the influence of uncertain budget on location-routing decisions to be less pronounced.

(d) Among all the optimal decisions mentioned above, location decisions (1,2,5) and (2,5,6) perform well, and are the preferred choices among numerous decisions; namely, establishing emergency material depots in Dalian Port, Yingkou Port, and Weifang

Port, or Yingkou Port, Weifang Port, and Yantai Port. They exhibit resilience against uncertain factors.

Through the analysis presented above, it is evident that both the uncertain demand budget and demand disruption ratio impact the decisions of MEMD-LRP, but this impact heavily relies on their respective values. Decision makers can integrate the circumstances of maritime emergencies, adjusting the values of the uncertain demand budget parameter to subsequently fine-tune the model's robustness level. With consideration of their preferences, decision makers can flexibly make choices and devise emergency material reserve location and distribution plans, which can effectively address uncertainties in maritime emergencies and enable rapid responses.

5. Conclusions

Taking maritime emergency material distribution as the background, this paper explores the robust bi-level models of MEMD-LRP in uncertain decision-making environments from the perspective of joint decision making among multiple decision makers. Using a case study based on the Bohai Sea area, the research analyzes the optimal decision making of MEMD-LRP under conditions of uncertain sailing time and uncertain emergency material demand at accident points during the planning period. We have solved the problems raised in the introduction; under the constraints of the rescue time window and the priority of emergency materials allocation, a series of emergency material reserve locations and emergency material distribution schemes which can effectively deal with the uncertainty in maritime emergencies are developed for the upper and lower levels of decision makers. The optimal decision under different conditions can not only meet the needs of the accident point, but also reduce the total cost of the emergency logistics system within the prescribed rescue time window, thus realizing the overall optimization of the maritime emergency logistics system. The study yields the following managerial insights:

(a) Upper-level decision makers such as emergency management departments must possess prioritized decision-making authority. Their goal should be to maximize their own interests while considering the interests of lower-level decision-makers, such as commercial rescue units. When making decisions regarding the selection of emergency material reserve locations, it is necessary not only to evaluate the suitability of the number of reserve constructions but also to consider the feedback from commercial rescue units regarding the location decisions. For lower-level decision makers like commercial rescue units operating within the framework permitted by the emergency management department, these units should make decisions while fully considering their interests. Additionally, they should provide timely feedback on shipping route decisions to the emergency management department.

(b) Both uncertain ship sailing times and uncertain emergency material demands will influence the decisions of MEMD-LRP, and these decisions will be constrained by the managerial insights mentioned in (a). Upper- and lower-level decision makers can adjust the ratios of ship sailing time disruption and demand disruption, modify the values of the demand uncertainty budget parameter based on maritime emergencies, and make flexible decisions according to their preferences. By doing so, they can formulate emergency material reserve location and emergency material distribution decisions that not only address the uncertainties in maritime emergencies, but also respond rapidly.

(c) From the perspective of joint decision making among multiple decision makers, this study focuses on two crucial aspects of the maritime emergency logistics system under uncertain conditions: the selection of emergency material reserve locations and the planning of emergency material distribution routes. The aim is to ensure their mutual coordination, which can yield significant benefits in terms of achieving comprehensive decision making and enhancing decision adaptability. This study contributes to a more optimized and flexible emergency logistics system, ultimately improving the capability to respond to maritime emergencies.

This study discusses the impact of uncertain sailing times and uncertain emergency material demand at the accident point on decision maker choices. In the future, we can explore the impact of both on decision-makers simultaneously. In this study, the limited reserve capacity of emergency materials is not considered. In fact, the capacity of different emergency materials in different emergency material reserves may be limited, and the decision making in the case of limited capacity can be discussed in the future. Furthermore, this study did not account for the potential drift of accident points. In reality, maritime emergencies can lead to the drift of accident points due to the intricate marine environment, resulting in shifts in their geographical coordinates. Subsequent research could be undertaken to address the possibility of such accident point drift scenarios. The impact of uncertain delivery times, transportation costs, feasibility probability of transportation routes, and a combination of these factors on MEMD-LRP decision making can also be considered. More importantly, subsequent research will place a stronger emphasis on presenting practical viewpoints and exploring relevant issues in emergency rescue operations under an egalitarian policy framework.

Author Contributions: Conceptualization, C.W. and Z.P.; methodology, C.W. and Z.P.; writing—original draft preparation, C.W., Z.P. and W.X.; writing—review and editing, C.W., Z.P. and W.X. All authors have read and agreed to the published version of the manuscript.

Funding: This research was supported by Jiangsu Planned Projects for Postdoctoral Research Funds (2021K347C), the Fundamental Research Funds for the Central Universities (3132023288, 3132023296), the Humanities and Social Science Fund of Ministry of Education of China (No. 21YJC630186), the Natural Science Foundation of Guangdong Province (No. 2022A1515012034), and the Philosophy and Social Science Planning Project of Guangdong Province (No. GD20CGL19).

Institutional Review Board Statement: Not applicable.

Informed Consent Statement: Not applicable.

Data Availability Statement: Not applicable.

Conflicts of Interest: The authors declare that they have no conflict of interest.

Appendix A

Table A1. Information regarding candidate shore-based emergency materials reserves.

Reserve ID	Port	Longitude	Latitude	Construction Cost (CNY)
1	Dalian	121°39′17″	38°55′44″	200,000
2	Yingkou	122°06′00″	40°17′42″	180,000
3	Tianjin	117°42′05″	38°59′08″	200,000
4	Qinhuangdao	119°36′26″	39°54′24″	200,000
5	Weifang	120°19′05″	36°04′	180,000
6	Yantai	121°23′46.9″	37°32′51.8″	200,000

Table A2. Data of accident points.

Point ID	Longitude	Latitude	Accident Level	d_{j1}/Unit	T_{Ej1}/h	T_{Lj1}/h
1	118°06′1″	38°52′2″	Larger	8	1	7
2	119°13′.7	38°52′.3	General	6	2	8
3	119°29.6′	38°43.3′	General	6	2	8
4	117°51′.6	38°55′.5	General	5	2	8
5	119°08′.1	38°47′.3	Small	0	0	0
6	118°31′.9	38°42′.3	Small	0	0	0
7	120°25′.78	40°02′.95	Larger	7	1	7
8	120°50′.23	38°37′.44	Larger	8	1	7
9	121°33′15.54″	40°05′13.86″	Larger	7	1	7

Table A2. Cont.

Point ID	Longitude	Latitude	Accident Level	d_{j1}/Unit	T_{Ej1}/h	T_{Lj1}/h
10	121°48.80′	40°12.24′	Larger	6	1	7
11	120°10′.98	39°13′.0	Larger	8	1	7
12	120°07′.211	40°01′.560	Larger	7	1	7
13	121°12′.88	40°08′.59	General	5	2	8
14	120°48′00.96″	39°02′46.56″	General	6	2	8
15	121°08′49″.17	39°35′49″.18	General	5	2	8
16	120°35′48.42″	38°35′34.92″	General	4	2	8
17	121°09′	39°27′	General	5	2	8
18	121°01.08′	40°42.31′	General	5	2	8
19	122°01′.3	38°46′.2	General	6	2	8
20	118°11.39′	38°26.19′	Larger	8	1	7
21	119°36′.83	38°58′.26	Larger	7	1	7
22	119°23′.00	39°23′.00	General	7	1	7
23	119°42.84′	39°56.19′	General	5	2	8
24	119°15′.13	39°00′.14	General	5	2	8
25	119°07′.00	39°08′.60	Small	5	2	8
26	119°41′.83	39°47′.32	Small	6	2	8
27	117°59′.24	38°24′.81	Larger	5	2	8
28	119°50′31.95″	39°23′11.40″	Larger	5	2	8
29	120°05′.504	39°13′.716	Larger	0	0	0
30	118°16′.743	38°50′.206	Larger	3	3	8
31	118°31′860″	38°48′628″	Larger	0	0	0
32	118°22′.48	38°49′.71	Larger	0	0	0
33	118°09′217	38°15′177	General	8	1	7
34	121°08′.1	37°56′.3	General	6	1	7
35	118°03.103′	38°08.700′	General	6	1	7
36	118°55′.0	38°13′.3	General	7	2	8
37	120°02.204′	38°23.175′	General	6	2	8
38	121°56′	37°42′	General	6	2	8
39	119°22′	37°22′	General	2	3	8
40	121°27.1′	38°22.7′	Larger	0	0	0

Table A3. Specific parameters of the model.

Symbol	Value
G	30 unit/ship
V_{pqk}	25 kn
S_k	CNY/nm
c_0	900 CNY/ship
c_1	10 CNY/h
c_2	20 CNY/h
C_{ij1}	5 CNY/unit
C_{ij2}	4 CNY/unit
C_{ij3}	3 CNY/unit

Figure A1. Distribution map of candidate emergency materials reserves and potential accident points.

References

1. Review of Maritime Transport 2022. Available online: https://unctad.org/rmt2022 (accessed on 22 August 2023).
2. Annual Overview of Marine Casualties and Incidents. 2022. Available online: https://safety4sea.com/emsa-annual-overview-of-marine-casualties-and-incidents-2022/ (accessed on 22 August 2023).
3. Annual Report. 2022. Available online: https://www.bsu-bund.de/SharedDocs/pdf/EN/Annual_Statistics/Annual_Report_2022.pdf?__blob=publicationFile&v=1 (accessed on 22 August 2023).
4. Statistical Bulletin on the Development of Transportation Industry in 2022. Available online: https://xxgk.mot.gov.cn/2020/jigou/zhghs/202306/t20230615_3847023.html (accessed on 22 August 2023).
5. Ransikarbum, K.; Mason, S.J. A bi-objective optimisation of post-disaster relief distribution and short-term network restoration using hybrid NSGA-II algorithm. *Int. J. Prod. Econ.* **2022**, *60*, 5769–5793. [CrossRef]
6. Yan, T.; Lu, F.; Wang, S.; Wang, L.; Bi, H. A hybrid metaheuristic algorithm for the multi-objective location-routing problem in the early post-disaster stage. *J. Ind. Manag. Optim.* **2023**, *19*, 4663–4691. [CrossRef]
7. Qin, J.; Ye, Y.; Cheng, B.-R.; Zhao, X.; Ni, L. The Emergency Vehicle Routing Problem with Uncertain Demand under Sustainability Environments. *Sustainability* **2017**, *9*, 288. [CrossRef]
8. Tan, K.; Liu, W.; Xu, F.; Li, C. Optimization Model and Algorithm of Logistics Vehicle Routing Problem under Major Emergency. *Mathematics* **2023**, *11*, 1274. [CrossRef]
9. Peng, Z.; Wang, C.; Xu, W.; Zhang, J. Research on Location-Routing Problem of Maritime Emergency Materials Distribution Based on Bi-Level Programming. *Mathematics* **2022**, *10*, 1243. [CrossRef]
10. Laporte, G.; Nobert, Y. An exact algorithm for minimizing routing and operating costs in depot location. *Eur. J. Oper. Res.* **1981**, *6*, 224–226. [CrossRef]
11. Yang, J.; Sun, H. Battery swap station location-routing problem with capacitated electric vehicles. *Comput. Oper. Res.* **2015**, *55*, 217–232. [CrossRef]
12. Boccia, M.; Crainic, T.G.; Sforza, A.; Sterle, C. Multi-commodity location-routing: Flow intercepting formulation and branch-and-cut algorithm. *Comput. Oper. Res.* **2018**, *89*, 94–112. [CrossRef]
13. Yu, X.; Zhou, Y.; Liu, X.-F. A novel hybrid genetic algorithm for the location routing problem with tight capacity constraints. *Appl. Soft. Comput.* **2019**, *85*, 105760. [CrossRef]

14. Lu, F.; Chen, W.; Feng, W.; Bi, H. 4PL routing problem using hybrid beetle swarm optimization. *Soft Comput.* **2023**, *27*, 17011–17024. [CrossRef]
15. Lu, F.; Feng, W.; Gao, M.; Bi, H.; Wang, S. Corrigendum to "The Fourth-Party Logistics Routing Problem Using Ant Colony System-Improved Grey Wolf Optimization". *J. Adv. Transp.* **2022**, *2022*, 9864064. [CrossRef]
16. Şatir Akpunar, Ö.; Akpinar, Ş. A hybrid adaptive large neighbourhood search algorithm for the capacitated location routing problem. *Expert Syst. Appl.* **2021**, *168*, 114304.
17. Alamatsaz, K.; Ahmadi, A.; Mirzapour Al-e-hashem, S.M.J. A multiobjective model for the green capacitated location-routing problem considering drivers' satisfaction and time window with uncertain demand. *Environ. Sci. Pollut. Res.* **2022**, *29*, 5052–5071. [CrossRef]
18. Gan, X.; Liu, J. A multi-objective evolutionary algorithm for emergency logistics scheduling in large-scale disaster relief. In Proceedings of the 2017 IEEE Congress on Evolutionary Computation (CEC), Donostia, Spain, 5–8 June 2017; pp. 51–58.
19. Liu, C.; Kou, G.; Peng, Y.; Alsaadi, F.E. Location-Routing Problem for Relief Distribution in the Early Post-Earthquake Stage from the Perspective of Fairness. *Sustainability* **2019**, *11*, 3420. [CrossRef]
20. Ai, Y.-f.; Lu, J.; Zhang, L.-L. The optimization model for the location of maritime emergency supplies reserve bases and the configuration of salvage vessels. *Transp. Res. E-Log.* **2015**, *83*, 170–188. [CrossRef]
21. Zhang, B.; Li, H.; Li, S.; Peng, J. Sustainable multi-depot emergency facilities location-routing problem with uncertain information. *Appl. Math. Comput.* **2018**, *333*, 506–520.
22. Afshar, A.; Haghani, A. Modeling integrated supply chain logistics in real-time large-scale disaster relief operations. *Socio-Econ. Plan. Sci.* **2012**, *46*, 327–338. [CrossRef]
23. Zhang, Y.; Qi, M.; Lin, W.-H.; Miao, L. A metaheuristic approach to the reliable location routing problem under disruptions. *Transp. Res. E-Log.* **2015**, *83*, 90–110. [CrossRef]
24. Ghasemi, P.; Khalili-Damghani, K.; Hafezalkotob, A.; Raissi, S. Uncertain multi-objective multi-commodity multi-period multi-vehicle location-allocation model for earthquake evacuation planning. *Appl. Math. Comput.* **2019**, *350*, 105–132.
25. Long, S.; Zhang, D.; Liang, Y.; Li, S.; Chen, W. Robust Optimization of the Multi-Objective Multi-Period Location-Routing Problem for Epidemic Logistics System With Uncertain Demand. *IEEE Access* **2021**, *9*, 151912–151930. [CrossRef]
26. Caunhye, A.M.; Zhang, Y.; Li, M.; Nie, X. A location-routing model for prepositioning and distributing emergency supplies. *Transp. Res. E-Log.* **2016**, *90*, 161–176. [CrossRef]
27. Wang, H.; Du, L.; Ma, S. Multi-objective open location-routing model with split delivery for optimized relief distribution in post-earthquake. *Transp. Res. E-Log.* **2014**, *69*, 160–179. [CrossRef]
28. Raeisi, D.; Jafarzadeh Ghoushchi, S. A robust fuzzy multi-objective location-routing problem for hazardous waste under uncertain conditions. *Appl. Intell.* **2022**, *52*, 13435–13455. [CrossRef] [PubMed]
29. Shen, L.; Tao, F.; Shi, Y.; Qin, R. Optimization of location-routing problem in emergency logistics considering carbon emissions. *Int. J. Environ. Res. Public Health* **2019**, *16*, 2982. [CrossRef] [PubMed]
30. Zhang, L.; Lu, J.; Yang, Z. Dynamic optimization of emergency resource scheduling in a large-scale maritime oil spill accident. *Comput. Ind. Eng.* **2021**, *152*, 107028. [CrossRef]
31. Ghasemi, P.; Goodarzian, F.; Abraham, A. A new humanitarian relief logistic network for multi-objective optimization under stochastic programming. *Appl. Intell.* **2022**, *52*, 13729–13762. [CrossRef]
32. Saeidi-Mobarakeh, Z.; Tavakkoli-Moghaddam, R.; Navabakhsh, M.; Amoozad-Khalili, H. A bi-level and robust optimization-based framework for a hazardous waste management problem: A real-world application. *J. Clean Prod.* **2020**, *252*, 119830.
33. Zhou, Y.; Zheng, B.; Su, J.; Li, Y. The joint location-transportation model based on grey bi-level programming for early post-earthquake relief. *J. Ind. Manag. Optim.* **2022**, *18*, 45–73. [CrossRef]
34. Chen, Y.; Zheng, W.; Li, W.; Huang, Y. The Robustness and Sustainability of Port Logistics Systems for Emergency Supplies from Overseas. *J. Adv. Transp.* **2020**, *2020*, 8868533. [CrossRef]
35. Wei, X.; Qiu, H.; Wang, D.; Duan, J.; Wang, Y.; Cheng, T.C.E. An integrated location-routing problem with post-disaster relief distribution. *Comput. Ind. Eng.* **2020**, *147*, 106632. [CrossRef]
36. Ai, Y.; Zhang, Q. Optimization on cooperative government and enterprise supplies repertories for maritime emergency: A study case in China. *Adv. Mech. Eng.* **2019**, *11*, 1687814019828576. [CrossRef]
37. Soyster, A.L. Technical Note—Convex programming with set-inclusive constraints and applications to inexact linear programming. *Oper. Res.* **1973**, *21*, 1154–1157. [CrossRef]
38. Bertsimas, D.; Sim, M. The price of robustness. *Oper. Res.* **2004**, *52*, 35–53. [CrossRef]
39. Zhou, Y.; Yu, H.; Li, Z.; Su, J.; Liu, C. Robust Optimization of a Distribution Network Location-Routing Problem Under Carbon Trading Policies. *IEEE Access* **2020**, *8*, 46288–46306. [CrossRef]
40. Cheng, X.; Jin, C.; Yao, Q.; Wang, C. Research on Robust Optimization for Route Selection Problem in Multimodal Transportation under the Cap and Trade Policy. *Chin. J. Manag. Sci.* **2021**, *29*, 82–90.
41. Peng, C.; Li, J.; Ran, L.; Wang, S. Emergency Medical Service Station Robust Location Model and Algorithm Under Demand Uncertainty. *Oper. Res. Manag. Sci.* **2017**, *26*, 21–28.
42. Hatefi, S.M.; Jolai, F. Robust and reliable forward–reverse logistics network design under demand uncertainty and facility disruptions. *Appl. Math. Model.* **2014**, *38*, 2630–2647. [CrossRef]

43. Xu, J.P.; Wang, Z.Q.; Zhang, M.X.; Tu, Y. A new model for a 72-h post-earthquake emergency logistics location-routing problem under a random fuzzy environment. *Transp. Lett.* **2016**, *8*, 270–285. [CrossRef]
44. Chen, J.; Gui, P.; Ding, T.; Na, S.; Zhou, Y. Optimization of Transportation Routing Problem for Fresh Food by Improved Ant Colony Algorithm Based on Tabu Search. *Sustainability* **2019**, *11*, 6584. [CrossRef]
45. Li, Q.; Tu, W.; Zhuo, L. Reliable rescue routing optimization for urban emergency logistics under travel time uncertainty. *ISPRS Int. J. Geo.-Inf.* **2018**, *7*, 77. [CrossRef]
46. Ransikarbum, K.; Mason, S.J. Goal programming-based post-disaster decision making for integrated relief distribution and early-stage network restoration. *Int. J. Prod. Econ.* **2016**, *182*, 324–341. [CrossRef]

Disclaimer/Publisher's Note: The statements, opinions and data contained in all publications are solely those of the individual author(s) and contributor(s) and not of MDPI and/or the editor(s). MDPI and/or the editor(s) disclaim responsibility for any injury to people or property resulting from any ideas, methods, instructions or products referred to in the content.

Article

Self-Built or Third-Party Blockchain Traceability Strategy in a Dual-Channel Supply Chain Considering Consumers' Traceability Awareness

Yuling Sun *, Xiaomei Song, Xiang Fang and Jian Guo

College of Economics and Management, Nanjing Tech University, Nanjing 211816, China; 202161113019@njtech.edu.cn (X.S.); 201961213038@njtech.edu.cn (X.F.); 202161113008@njtech.edu.cn (J.G.)
* Correspondence: syl_nj@njtech.edu.cn

Abstract: Blockchain is widely used in the manufacturing industry. This paper establishes a dual-channel supply chain composed of a manufacturer and an e-retailer. A monopoly manufacturer conducts indirect online selling through retailers as well as direct offline selling. The manufacturer chooses to adopt a self-built blockchain traceability system (SBT) or a third-party blockchain traceability system (TBT). Game analysis is developed to depict the pricing decision for the manufacturer and e-retailer. The optimal pricing decisions of the supply chain between manufacturer and e-retailer for different blockchain traceability strategies are obtained. We explore the influence of consumers' traceability awareness on the decisions of dual-channel supply chain members when adopting different blockchain traceability strategies. The main results show that when the fee paid to the blockchain service provider is low, the manufacturer will prefer to adopt TBT. Moreover, we prove that consumers' traceability awareness, the cost of adopting TBT, the blockchain traceability technology level, and the research and development cost factor of blockchain technology could affect the decisions of supply chain members. Finally, some management suggestions are provided.

Keywords: dual-channel supply chain; blockchain technology; consumers' traceability awareness

MSC: 90B06

1. Introduction

With the rapid development of Internet technology, it is popular for consumers to purchase products via online channels. In particular, the continued outbreak of COVID-19 since 2020 has pushed more and more consumers to shop online. According to the Statistical Report on the Development Status of the Internet in China, by the end of December 2022, the number of China's netizens had reached 1.067 billion, and the Internet penetration rate reached 75.6% [1]. In 2022, China's e-commerce transactions reached CNY 4382.99 billion, an increase of 3.5% compared to 2021. According to the first-quarter financial statements released by Walmart in 2023, net e-commerce sales in the United States (Walmart) grew by 54%. More and more brand manufacturers are selling products via e-commerce platforms. At the same time, brand manufactures sell products offline via direct-sale stores. For example, the manufacturers LVMH, Nike, and Mengniu sell products in direct-sale stores and on Amazon, JD chaoshi, or Tmall chaoshi at the same time.

However, products sold on e-commerce platforms can be inauthentic because consumers cannot distinguish inauthentic from authentic products before purchasing them online. Even when products sold on e-commerce platforms are officially certified by the brand manufacturers, consumers still have doubts about their authenticity [2]. The authenticity of products sold on e-commerce platforms by brand manufacturers such as Apple, Gucci, and Kering can be difficult to determine. According to reports, nearly 90 percent of Apple product chargers sold on Amazon's U.S. website are fake. Brand manufacturers

Citation: Sun, Y.; Song, X.; Fang, X.; Guo, J. Self-Built or Third-Party Blockchain Traceability Strategy in a Dual-Channel Supply Chain Considering Consumers' Traceability Awareness. *Mathematics* **2023**, *11*, 4312. https://doi.org/10.3390/math11204312

Academic Editor: Yong He

Received: 24 July 2023
Revised: 12 October 2023
Accepted: 12 October 2023
Published: 16 October 2023

Copyright: © 2023 by the authors. Licensee MDPI, Basel, Switzerland. This article is an open access article distributed under the terms and conditions of the Creative Commons Attribution (CC BY) license (https://creativecommons.org/licenses/by/4.0/).

such as Kering and Gucci have sued a major Chinese online platform over fakes [3]. Online deceptive counterfeits have destroyed consumers' trust in brand manufacturers and e-commerce platforms.

Blockchain technology has been seen as one of the most promising technologies in providing information transparency and traceability [4]. Blockchain technology can effectively guarantee the reliability, authenticity, security, and timely feedback of transaction data, and can be used for the anti-counterfeit traceability of products [5]. It also helps all authorized businesses access information on the blockchain [6], allowing consumers to grasp information relating to product production and distribution. In reality, some manufacturers prefer third-party blockchain traceability systems to carry out product traceability. Alibaba provides blockchain traceability of products' originality for fashion brands [7]. JD provides a blockchain traceability service for brand companies such as Wuliangye, SK-II, and Yili based on an anti-counterfeiting blockchain traceability system. Amazon provides blockchain traceability for Nestlé's new coffee brand, Chain of Origin, to display information on where the coffee beans are grown, roasted, made, etc. Analogously, the products sold on anmo-malls such as Frog Prince and Runben are traced through third-party blockchain traceability. By scanning the QR code of product traceability, consumers can obtain information on the origin, batch, logistics, and distributors of products based on blockchain authentication.

Other manufacturers prefer to develop blockchain traceability systems to carry out product traceability. For example, Nike developed NFC + blockchain to carry out product traceability. By scanning NFC chips on the commodities, consumers can see the style, shipping warehouse, and shipping time of the commodities through blockchain authentication, which greatly improves the consumers' experience and protects their rights and interests. NFC+blockchain has been applied to nearly 130,000 pairs of Nike's 17 popular shoe models. De Beers established Tracr™ to track the journey of diamonds throughout the value chain, ensuring consumer trust in the origin of De Beers diamonds. Dalian Xinyulong also developed a blockchain traceability system for sea cucumbers. Consumers can trace detailed information on sea cucumbers regarding their breeding, release, fishing, processing, finished products, and other links.

Enterprises using the blockchain traceability services of third-party blockchain traceability systems may display limited traceability information because the traceability level is fixed and constrained by the third-party blockchain traceability platform. A self-built blockchain system could choose a more suitable traceability level and provide more comprehensive traceability information. This is helpful for attracting more customers. However, it requires significant research and development costs. It is an interesting question whether dual-channel manufacturers and e-retailers should adopt self-built or third-party blockchain traceability systems. The cost of self-built blockchain traceability systems is higher than that of third-party blockchain traceability systems, but the blockchain traceability level may be lower than that of the third party.

Some studies have shown that consumers have traceability awareness. Wu et al. [8] and Fan et al. [9] proved that consumer traceability awareness could affect the adoption of blockchain technology in the supply chain. However, the overall impact of consumers' traceability awareness for blockchain traceability strategies on the dual-channel supply chain is unclear.

Considering consumers' traceability awareness in a dual-channel supply chain, we will focus on the following research questions:

(1) What are the equilibrium decisions when adopting a third-party blockchain traceability system (TBT) and a self-built blockchain traceability system (SBT)?
(2) How do different blockchain scenarios in a dual-channel supply chain affect supply chain members' optimal decisions?
(3) Which kind of blockchain scenarios are beneficial for the e-retailer and the manufacturer?
(4) What is the impact of consumers' traceability awareness on supply chain members' decisions when adopting different blockchain traceability strategies?

To answer these questions, we develop a game model to describe a dual-channel supply chain. We consider a setting in which a brand manufacturer sells the same product through two channels: a direct offline channel and an online retail channel. In this setting, the brand manufacturer can adopt a self-built blockchain system or third-party blockchain system. We first simulate the equilibrium strategies of the two participants in two scenarios: (1) with an SBT and (2) with a TBT. Meanwhile, the effects of several parameters on optimal strategies are identified through sensitivity analysis. Finally, we obtain conditions under which the brand manufacturer should adopt an SBT by analyzing the impacts of consumers' traceability awareness on the optimal strategy and profit of both parties.

Our research shows that SBT does not always benefit the manufacturer and e-retailer using a dual-channel supply chain considering consumers' traceability awareness. When making the decision between SBT and TBT, a manufacturer should focus on the impact of consumers' traceability awareness on their traceability strategy. We find that a selection of blockchain technologies in an online indirect sales channel and an offline direct sales channel is associated with blockchain research and development cost, consumers' traceability awareness, consumers' channel preference, and the blockchain traceability level. These findings will provide useful managerial implications for dual-channel supply chains adopting the blockchain traceability strategy.

This paper is divided into the following five parts: the first part is the introduction, which introduces the research background and problems; the second part is the literature review, which summarizes the status of related research and presents the innovative points of this paper; the third part is the model construction, which puts forward the hypothesis of this paper and constructs a dual-channel supply chain model adopting a TBT and an SBT; the fourth part is the simulation analysis, which explores the influence of consumers' traceability awareness on dual-channel supply chain decisions; and the fifth part is the conclusion, which summarizes the main findings of this paper and puts forward corresponding management options.

2. Literature Review

We explore the impact of different blockchain traceability strategies on dual-channel supply chain decisions considering consumers' traceability awareness. The research is related to two steams of studies: the application of blockchain technology in the supply chain and dual-channel supply chain management.

For the application of blockchain technology in the supply chain, some of the literature has analyzed the application conditions and setting of blockchain on the supply chain via qualitative analysis or empirical analysis. Based on bibliometrics and network analysis methods, Moosavi et al. [10] pointed out that blockchain can improve the transparency, traceability, efficiency, and information security of supply chain management. Wang and Yang [11] proved that trust-building and supply chain flexibility in the supply chain can be affected by the information transparency and security of blockchain technology. Maher and Ashish [12] found that the most prominent drivers affecting blockchain adoption in the supply chain are the comparative advantages and external pressures of blockchain technology. Some scholars focus on the impacts of blockchain technology adoption and capture it with mathematical models. Niu et al. [13] analyzed the conditions for multinational companies to adopt blockchain technology. Pun et al. [14] studied the role of blockchain technology on optimal decisions and analyzed the conditions necessary to adopt blockchain technology in combating counterfeit products. Choi (2019) [15] analyzed the role of blockchain technology platforms in diamond certification. Dong et al. [16] studied the impacts of blockchain technology on the decisions of food supply chain members. Wu et al. [17] pointed out that the allocation ratio of blockchain traceability costs could affect blockchain technology adoption strategies in the fresh product supply chain. Wang et al. [18] analyzed the impact of blockchain technology in the port supply chain, considering blockchain technology costs. Orji et al. [19] found that technical factors, government policies, and the availability of specific blockchain tools affect blockchain application based on ANP modeling in the freight logistics industry. Choi and Ouyang [20] found that using a blockchain-based product-sourcing certification platform is beneficial for both firms and consumers, and that fixed service costs and fixed setup costs could affect a blockchain-based product-sourcing certification platform. Fan et al. [9] proved that the consumer awareness of traceability and blockchain costs affects the introduction of blockchain technology by supply chain members. There are also several studies focusing on the application of blockchain technology in government regulation and food traceability [21,22]. Our study expands this literature stream by analyzing the impacts of consumers' traceability awareness in SBT and TBT. We find that manufacturers will adopt SBT when consumers' traceability awareness is high enough.

Research on dual-channel supply chain management is popular. Some of the literature has focused on solutions to channel conflicts [23–25] or operational decisions in dual-channel supply chains [26,27]. Some studies have explored the impact of a dual-channel strategy [28–30]. Some scholars have explored the impact of channel price sensitivity, consumer loss aversion behavior, and government subsidies on supply chain decision making based on dual channels. For example, Pal and Sarkar [31] proved that channel price sensitivity could affect the profit of dual-channel supply chain members. Based on the reverse supply chain perspective, Xu et al. [32] analyzed the impact of consumer loss aversion behavior on the recycling pricing and profit of each node in the supply chain. Abhijit et al. [33] showed that government subsidies are beneficial for the suppliers and manufacturers of a three-layer green supply chain model with a dual-channel structure, and they can reduce the cost of green products. Song et al. [34] studied the impact of manufacturer fairness concerns on dual-channel supply chain members' decisions under government subsidies and showed that when manufacturers focus on equity, product greenness increases with government subsidies. Other scholars have also explored the issue of channel selection. Xiao et al. [35] proved that unit production cost, the marginal cost of product variety, and customer adaptation cost affect a manufacturer's choice of whether to adopt dual channels. Wang et al. [36] explored the opportunity for manufacturers to choose between a physical plus a direct electronic channel and a physical plus a consignment electronic channel. Differently from the above works, this paper investigates the impact of consumers' traceability awareness on the supply chain members' choice of dual channels between self-built blockchain traceability and third-party blockchain traceability. We find that consumers' traceability awareness has an impact on the decisions of members of a dual-channel supply chain.

In recent years, some scholars have analyzed dual-channel supply chains based on blockchain technology. Some scholars have explored the impact of factors such as production cost, premium effect, labeling cost, operating costs of blockchain, direct sales costs, and demand fluctuations on the adoption of blockchain technology [6,37]. Some scholars have explored the impact of blockchain technology on decisions in dual-channel supply chains. Xu et al. [38] discussed that blockchain technology can help products become greener and more profitable for manufacturers and platforms. Zhang et al. [39] found that applying blockchain technology is beneficial for manufacture and retailers of dual-channel supply chains. The longer a product is traceable, the lower the price of the online traceable product will be. Zhu et al. [40] studied a dual-channel supply chain dominated by brand manufacturers and showed that the adoption of blockchain technology is always beneficial for retailers; however, the adoption of blockchain technology is not always beneficial for brand owners. Only when the total market's potential improvement effect is sufficiently large is the brand owner willing to adopt blockchain technology. Other scholars have explored the interaction between blockchain technology adoption and channel selection. Li and Li [41] found that the online direct sales plus consignment sales approach is more suitable for manufacturers who introduce blockchain technology. Li et al. [42] found that genuine companies take the initiative to degenerate the established dual-channel sales model into a single-channel sales model due to the adoption of blockchain technology. Wang et al. [43] found that when the cost of blockchain and the service level of traditional channels are low, adopting a blockchain platform can incentivize manufacturers to open their online channel. Differently from the previous studies, we focus on the selection of a blockchain technology and the impact of this selection on the decisions of dual-channel supply chain members. We find that the selection of a blockchain technology in an online indirect sales channel and an offline direct sales channel is associated with blockchain research and development cost, consumers' traceability awareness, consumers' channel preference, and blockchain traceability level.

Our paper is closely related to the following works that consider blockchain adoption. Fan et al. [9] focused on the impact of consumers' traceability awareness on the introduction strategy of blockchain technology in a single-channel supply chain. They found that supply chains adopted blockchain technology when consumers' traceability awareness and the cost-sharing ratio of blockchain technology met certain conditions. Zhang et al. [39] explored the impact of blockchain introduction on pricing decisions in online direct channels and offline indirect channels. They found that with the increase of traceability sensitivity coefficient, the sales price of traceability products decreases, and the retail price of offline standard products increases. Similar to this article, Zhang et al. [6] studied the impact of blockchain technology introduction on the decisions of dual-channel supply chain members in offline direct sales and online indirect sales. Additionally, they found that unit blockchain operating costs, direct sales costs, and demand fluctuations could affect supply chain members' adoption of blockchain strategies. Different from the above works, this study explores the impact of consumers' traceability awareness on blockchain traceability strategy choice in online indirect sales and offline direct sales. This study constructs a dual-channel supply chain model based on SBT and TBT, respectively, and identifies the conditions for adopting SBT and TBT for dual-channel supply chains. Then, we analyze the impact of consumers' traceability awareness on the decision of dual-channel supply chain members to adopt one of two blockchain traceability strategies. We find that when the fee paid to the blockchain service provider meets a certain condition, the manufacturer adopts TBT; however, when consumers' traceability awareness is less than a certain value and the blockchain traceability technology level of TBT is less than a certain value, the online price of the e-retailer adopting SBT is higher than that of the e-retailer adopting TBT and the offline price and the wholesale price of the manufacturer adopting SBT are higher than those of the manufacturer adopting TBT. Consumers' traceability awareness could affect the equilibrium decision of supply chain members; that is, the online price of the e-retailer and the offline price of the manufacturer and the wholesale price of the manufacturer increase with consumers' traceability awareness when adopting TBT and SBT.

3. Model Construction

3.1. Problem Description

We consider a dual-channel supply chain consisting of a manufacturer M and an e-retailer R. In the supply chain of the branded product, the brand manufacturer usually plays the role of the leader, while the e-retailer plays the role of the followers of the same status [40]. The manufacturer is the leader of the dual-channel supply chain. The manufacturer sells a homogeneous product through a direct offline channel and an indirect online channel. The manufacturer and e-retailer use blockchain technology to trace the information of the product, and the cost of adopting the blockchain technology can be shared among the supply chain members. The manufacturer determines the wholesale price of the e-retailer w and the direct sales price of the offline channel p_M. Then, the e-retailer decides the sale price of the online channel. As the supply chain adopts the blockchain technique, consumers can scan the two-dimensional code on the product's package to check the traceability information and further judge the quality of the product. The structure of the benchmark model is shown in Figure 1.

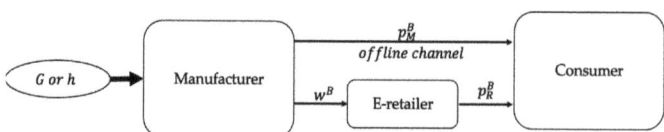

Figure 1. Decision-making process of dual-channel supply chain.

Table 1 shows all the notations in this paper.

Table 1. Parameter description.

Notation	Description
α	Potential market size, $\alpha > 0$.
c	Unit cost of producing the product, $0 < c < \frac{\theta\alpha}{1-b}$.
θ	Consumer preference for purchasing products through online channels (Consumers' channel preference), $0 < \theta < 1$.
b	Price elasticity coefficient between channels, $0 < b < 1$.
β	Consumers' traceability awareness, $0 < \beta < 1$.
G	Fee paid by the manufacturer to a third-party blockchain service provider, $G > 0$.
g_1	Blockchain traceability technology level provided by a third-party blockchain technology enterprise, $g_1 > 0$.
f_1	The unit verification fee paid by the e-retailer to the manufacturer in the TBT scenario.
f_2	The unit verification fee paid by the e-retailer to the manufacturer in the SBT scenario.
k	Research and development cost factor of blockchain technology, $k > 0$.
p_{R1}^B	The online price of the e-retailer when adopting TBT.
p_{R2}^B	The online price of the e-retailer when adopting SBT.
p_{M1}^B	The offline price of the manufacturer when adopting TBT.
p_{M2}^B	The offline price of the manufacturer when adopting SBT.
w_1^B	The wholesale price of the manufacturer when adopting TBT.
w_2^B	The wholesale price of the manufacturer when adopting SBT.
g_2	Blockchain traceability technology level of self-built blockchain system, $g_2 > 0$.
D_{R1}^B	The demand of the e-retailer when adopting TBT.
D_{R2}^B	The demand of the e-retailer when adopting SBT.
D_{M1}^B	The demand of the manufacturer when adopting TBT.
D_{M2}^B	The demand of the manufacturer when adopting SBT.
π_{R1}^B	The profits of the e-retailer when adopting TBT.
π_{R2}^B	The profits of the e-retailer when adopting SBT.
π_{M1}^B	The profits of the manufacturer when adopting TBT.
π_{M2}^B	The profits of the manufacturer when adopting SBT.
π_{S1}^B	The total profits of the supply chain when adopting TBT.
π_{S2}^B	The total profits of the supply chain when adopting SBT.

3.2. Adopting TBT

In the TBT scenario, the manufacturer and e-retailer adopt a third-party blockchain traceability service provided by a third-party professional blockchain technology research and development institution. The manufacturer and the e-retailer have a Stackelberg game relationship because the manufacturer dominates. When the manufacturer chooses to adopt TBT, the e-retailer follows and adopts TBT. Firstly, the manufacturer pays a fixed fee for the TBT service and determines its wholesale price and offline direct sales price to maximize its own profit. Referring to Fan et al. [9], the manufacturer and e-retailer pay a certain fixed fee, G, in exchange for the blockchain traceability service. Subsequently, the e-retailer shares the fixed fee for TBT with the manufacturer and determines its optimal retail price based on the manufacturer's decision. Referring to Li et al. [41], the e-retailer pays the unit verification fee, f_1, to the manufacturer in the TBT scenario. Referring to the assumptions of Cao et al. [44], the demand for the product in the dual-channel supply chain is assumed to be a function of the relevant selling price and the traceability level.

The demand functions of the indirect online channel D_{M1}^B and the direct offline channel D_{R1}^B can be obtained as follows:

$$D_{R1}^B = \theta\alpha - p_{R1}^B + bp_{M1}^B + \beta g_1 \qquad (1)$$

$$D_{M1}^B = (1-\theta)\alpha - p_{M1}^B + bp_{R1}^B + \beta g_1 \qquad (2)$$

The profits of the manufacturer and the online e-retailer using a third-party blockchain traceability service are as follows:

$$\pi_{R1}^B = \left(p_{R1}^B - w_1^B - f_1\right)D_{R1}^B \qquad (3)$$

$$\pi_{M1}^B = \left(w_1^B - c + f_1\right)D_{R1}^B + \left(p_{M1}^B - c\right)D_{M1}^B - G \qquad (4)$$

The total profits of the supply chain can be obtained as follows:

$$\pi_{S1}^B = \left(p_{R1}^B - c\right)D_{R1}^B + \left(p_{M1}^B - c\right)D_{M1}^B - G \qquad (5)$$

Lemma 1. *In the case of TBT, the optimal decisions for a manufacturer and e-retailer in a dual-channel supply chain are, respectively:*

$$p_{R1}^{B*} = \frac{(b+1)(b^2-1)c + (\theta\alpha + \beta g_1)(b^2-3) - ((1-\theta)2\alpha + 2\beta g_1)b}{4(b^2-1)} \qquad (6)$$

$$p_{M1}^{B*} = \frac{(b^2-1)c - (\theta\alpha + \beta g_1)b - (1-\theta)\alpha - \beta g_1}{2(b^2-1)} \qquad (7)$$

$$w_1^{B*} = \frac{(b^2-1)(c-2f_1) - ((1-\theta)\alpha + \beta g_1)b - \beta g_1 - \theta\alpha}{2(b^2-1)} \qquad (8)$$

Proof. See Appendix A. □

Substituting (6)–(8) into the profit functions of the e-retailer and the manufacturer, the optimal profits for the manufacturer and e-retailer and the total profits of the supply chain at this time can be found, respectively:

$$\pi_{R1}^{B*} = \frac{((b-1)c + \theta\alpha + \beta g_1)^2}{16}$$

$$\pi_{M1}^{B*} = \frac{1}{8(b^2-1)} \begin{pmatrix} -b^4c^2 - 2c(\theta\alpha + \beta g_1 + c)b^3 \\ +(-\alpha^2\theta^2 + (2c(\theta-2) - 2\theta\beta g_1)\alpha + 4c^2 - 6cg_1\beta - \beta^2 g_1^2)b^2 \\ +(4\theta(\theta-1)\alpha^2 + (-4\beta g_1 + 2\theta c)\alpha - 4g_1^2\beta^2 + 2c\beta g_1 + 2c^2)b \\ +(4\theta - 3\theta^2 - 2)\alpha^2 - 2(\theta-2)(-\beta g_1 + c)\alpha - 3(-\beta g_1 + c)^2 \end{pmatrix} - G$$

$$\pi_{S1}^{B*} = \pi_{R1}^{B*} + \pi_{M1}^{B*} = \frac{((b-1)c + \theta\alpha + \beta g_1)^2}{16}$$
$$+ \frac{1}{8(b^2-1)} \begin{pmatrix} -b^4c^2 - 2c(\theta\alpha + \beta g_1 + c)b^3 \\ +(-\alpha^2\theta^2 + (2c(\theta-2) - 2\theta\beta g_1)\alpha + 4c^2 - 6cg_1\beta - \beta^2 g_1^2)b^2 \\ +(4\theta(\theta-1)\alpha^2 + (-4\beta g_1 + 2\theta c)\alpha - 4g_1^2\beta^2 + 2c\beta g_1 + 2c^2)b \\ +(4\theta - 3\theta^2 - 2)\alpha^2 - 2(\theta-2)(-\beta g_1 + c)\alpha - 3(-\beta g_1 + c)^2 \end{pmatrix} - G$$

Lemma 2. *The impact of consumers' traceability awareness and channel preference on the online price of the e-retailer, the offline price of the manufacturer, and the wholesale price for the model in the TBT scenario is as follows:* $\frac{\partial p_{R1}^{B*}}{\partial \beta} > 0$, $\frac{\partial p_{M1}^{B*}}{\partial \beta} > 0$, $\frac{\partial w_1^{B*}}{\partial \beta} > 0$, $\frac{\partial p_{R1}^{B*}}{\partial \theta} > 0$, $\frac{\partial p_{M1}^{B*}}{\partial \theta} < 0$, $\frac{\partial w_1^{B*}}{\partial \theta} > 0$.

Proof. See Appendix B. □

Lemma 2 suggests that when a dual-channel manufacturer and e-retailer use third-party blockchain traceability services, consumers' traceability awareness has a positive impact on the offline price, online price, and wholesale price. As consumers' traceability awareness increases, the offline price, online price, and wholesale price increase. Consumers' channel preference has a positive effect on the online price and wholesale price. As consumers' channel preference increases, both the online price and wholesale price increase. However, consumers' channel preference has a negative effect on the offline price. As consumers' channel preference increases, the offline price decreases. This is because, as consumers' traceability awareness increases, both the e-retailer and manufacturer increase their profits by raising their retail prices, while the manufacturer also extracts profits from the e-retailer by raising their wholesale prices. Similarly, as consumers' channel preference increases, the e-retailer earns more profit by raising retail prices, while the manufacturer lowers their prices to attract more consumers and squeeze the e-retailer by raising their wholesale prices.

3.3. Adopting SBT

In the SBT scenario, the manufacturer builds their own blockchain system. In contrast to the TBT scenario, the manufacturer must decide the optimal level of blockchain traceability technology because the research and development input cost is related to the traceability level of the blockchain technology. Let the blockchain technology research and development input cost be h. According to the assumption of the previous literature [45], h is assumed to be a quadratic function of the blockchain technology traceability level $h = 1/2kg_2^2$; g_2 expresses the blockchain technology level; and k denotes the blockchain technology research and development cost coefficient. In the SBT scenario, the game sequence is as follows: first, the manufacturer decides the blockchain technology level, g_2, and then determines the product's online wholesale price and offline direct sale price to maximize its own profit. Subsequently, the e-retailer determines its optimal retail price based on the manufacturer's decision.

The demand functions for the manufacturer and the e-retailer are as follows:

$$D_{R2}^B = \theta\alpha - p_{R2}^B + bp_{M2}^B + \beta g_2 \quad (9)$$

$$D_{M2}^B = (1-\theta)\alpha - p_{M2}^B + bp_{R2}^B + \beta g_2 \quad (10)$$

The profits of the manufacturer and e-retailer are as follows:

$$\pi_{R2}^B = \left(p_{R2}^B - w_2^B - f_2\right) D_{R2}^B \quad (11)$$

$$\pi_{M2}^B = \left(w_2^B - c + f_2\right) D_{R2}^B + \left(p_{M2}^B - c\right) D_{M2}^B - \frac{1}{2}kg_2^2 \quad (12)$$

Thus, the total profits of the supply chain are as follows:

$$\pi_{S2}^B = \left(p_{R2}^B - c\right) D_{R2}^B + \left(p_{M2}^B - c\right) D_{M2}^B - \frac{1}{2}kg_2^2 \quad (13)$$

Lemma 3. *In the case of SBT, when $0 < \beta < 2\sqrt{\frac{k(1-b)}{b+3}}$, the optimal decisions for the manufacturer and the e-retailer are, respectively,*

$$p_{R2}^{B*} = \frac{2b^3ck + (2k(\theta\alpha + c) + 2\beta^2 c)b^2 + (((\theta-1)4\alpha - 2c)k + 2\beta^2((2\theta-1)\alpha + 4c))b - (6\theta\alpha + 2c)k + 6\beta^2\left(\left(\theta - \frac{1}{2}\right)\alpha + c\right)}{(b+1)\left(8k(b-1) + 2\beta^2(b+3)\right)} \quad (14)$$

$$p_{M2}^{B*} = \frac{\beta^2\left(2c(b^2+3) + 8bc + (1-2\theta)\alpha\right) - 4k\left((1-b^2)c + b\theta\alpha + (1-\theta)\alpha\right)}{(b+1)\left(8k(b-1) + 2\beta^2(b+3)\right)} \quad (15)$$

$$w_2^{B*} = \frac{(2\beta^2(c-f_2) + 4k(c-2f_2))b^2 + (((2\theta-1)\alpha + 8(c-f_2))\beta^2 + 4\alpha k(\theta-1))b + ((4\theta-2)\alpha + 6(c-f_2))\beta^2 - 4k(\theta\alpha + c - 2f_2)}{(b+1)\left(8k(b-1) + 2\beta^2(b+3)\right)} \quad (16)$$

$$g_2^* = \frac{\beta(-b^2 c - (\theta\alpha + 2c)b - (2-\theta)\alpha + 3c)}{4k(b-1) + \beta^2(b+3)} \quad (17)$$

Proof. See Appendix C. □

Substituting (14)–(17) into the profit functions of the e-retailer and the manufacturer, the optimal profits for manufacturer and e-retailer and the total profit of the supply chain in the TBT scenario can be found, respectively:

$$\pi_{R2}^{B*} = \frac{\left(k(b-1)(\theta\alpha + bc - c) + \alpha\beta^2\left(\theta - \frac{1}{2}\right)\right)^2}{8(4k(b-1) + \beta^2(b+3))^2}$$

$$\pi_{M2}^{B*} = \frac{1}{\left(16(b-1)k + 4\beta^2(b+3)\right)(b+1)}\left(\left(\left(-2b^2\theta^2 + (8\theta^2 - 8\theta)b - 6\theta^2 + 8\theta - 4\right)\alpha^2 - 4c(b-1)(b+1)(b\theta - \theta + 2)\alpha - 2c^2(b+3)(b+1)(b-1)^2\right)k + 2(4\theta - 2)^2\beta^2\alpha^2\right)$$

$$\pi_{S2}^{B*} = \pi_{R2}^{B*} + \pi_{M2}^{B*} = \frac{\left(k(b-1)(\theta\alpha + bc - c) + \alpha\beta^2\left(\theta - \frac{1}{2}\right)\right)^2}{8(4k(b-1) + \beta^2(b+3))^2}$$
$$+ \frac{1}{\left(16(b-1)k + 4\beta^2(b+3)\right)(b+1)}\left(\left(\left(-2b^2\theta^2 + (8\theta^2 - 8\theta)b - 6\theta^2 + 8\theta - 4\right)\alpha^2 - 4c(b-1)(b+1)(b\theta - \theta + 2)\alpha - 2c^2(b+3)(b+1)(b-1)^2\right)k$$
$$+ 2(4\theta - 2)^2\beta^2\alpha^2\right)$$

In order to explore the relationship between prices and profits when adopting TBT and SBT, we conduct a comparative analysis of the online price, offline price, wholesale price, manufacturer's profits, and retailer's profits when adopting TBT and SBT. Proposition 1 presents the comparison results between the optimal prices when adopting TBT and SBT. The relationships of the profits of the supply chain members when adopting TBT and SBT are presented in Propositions 2 and 3.

Proposition 1. *The comparative results for the prices of the e-retailer and the manufacturer are given as follows:*
(i) *when* $0 < \beta < 2\sqrt{\frac{k(1-b)}{b+3}}$ *and* $g_1 < g_2^*$, $p_{R1}^{B*} < p_{R2}^{B*}$, $p_{M1}^{B*} < p_{M2}^{B*}$;
(ii) *when* $0 < \beta < 2\sqrt{\frac{k(1-b)}{b+3}}$ *and* $g_1 < g_2^* - \frac{2(f_1 - f_2)(b-1)}{\beta}$ $w_1^{B*} < w_2^{B*}$.

Proof. See Appendix D. □

Proposition 1 indicates that when blockchain traceability technology level provided by a third-party blockchain technology enterprise is less than that of a self-built blockchain system (i.e., $g_1 < g_2^*$), the online price of the e-retailer in the SBT scenario is higher than that of the e-retailer in the TBT and the offline price of the manufacturer in the SBT scenario is higher than that of the manufacturer in the TBT scenario. When the blockchain traceability technology level provided by a third-party blockchain technology enterprise is less than a certain value (i.e., $g_1 < g_2^* - \frac{2(f_1-f_2)(b-1)}{\beta}$), the wholesale price of the manufacturer in the SBT scenario is higher than that of the manufacturer in the TBT scenario.

Proposition 2. *When $G \leq H$, the manufacturer should adopt TBT. Otherwise, the manufacturer should adopt SBT.*

Proof. See Appendix E. □

Proposition 2 indicates that the manufacturer should adopt blockchain traceability services provided by a TBT system when the fixed fee paid by the manufacturer to a third-party blockchain technology enterprise is low because the manufacturer can obtain more profits in the TBT scenario. When the fixed fee paid by the manufacturer to a third-party blockchain technology enterprise is high, the manufacturer will prefer to adopt SBT.

Proposition 3. *Compared with π_{R1}^{B*} and π_{R2}^{B*}, we have:*

(i) when $0 < \beta < 2\sqrt{\frac{k(1-b)}{b+3}}$, $k > \frac{(8\theta-4)\alpha\beta^2}{8(1-b)(\theta\alpha+bc-c)}$ and $g_1 \leq \frac{8(1-b)(\theta\alpha+bc-c)+(4-8\theta)\alpha\beta^2}{\beta((b+3)\beta^2+4k(b-1))}+g_2^*$ or $0 < \beta < 2\sqrt{\frac{k(1-b)}{b+3}}$, $k > \frac{(8\theta-4)\alpha\beta^2}{8(1-b)(\theta\alpha+bc-c)}$ and $g_1 \geq g_2^*$, e-retailer adopts TBT.

(ii) when $0 < \beta < 2\sqrt{\frac{k(1-b)}{b+3}}$, $k > \frac{(8\theta-4)\alpha\beta^2}{8(1-b)(\theta\alpha+bc-c)}$ and $\frac{8k(1-b)(\theta\alpha+bc-c)+(4-8\theta)\alpha\beta^2}{\beta((b+3)\beta^2+4k(b-1))}+g_2^* < g_1 < g_2^*$ or $0 < \beta < 2\sqrt{\frac{k(1-b)}{b+3}}$, $k \leq \frac{(8\theta-4)\alpha\beta^2}{8(1-b)(\theta\alpha+bc-c)}$ and $g_2^* < g_1 < \frac{8k(1-b)(\theta\alpha+bc-c)+(4-8\theta)\alpha\beta^2}{\beta((b+3)\beta^2+4k(b-1))}+g_2^*$, e-retailer always prefers to adopt SBT.

(iii) when $0 < \beta < 2\sqrt{\frac{k(1-b)}{b+3}}$, $k \leq \frac{(8\theta-4)\alpha\beta^2}{8(1-b)(\theta\alpha+bc-c)}$ and $g_1 \leq g_2^*$ or $0 < \beta < 2\sqrt{\frac{k(1-b)}{b+3}}$, $k \leq \frac{(8\theta-4)\alpha\beta^2}{8(1-b)(\theta\alpha+bc-c)}$ and $g_1 \geq \frac{8k(1-b)(\theta\alpha+bc-c)+(4-8\theta)\alpha\beta^2}{\beta((b+3)\beta^2+4k(b-1))}+g_2^*$, e-retailer prefers to adopt TBT.

Proof. See Appendix F. □

Proposition 3 indicates that when the research and development cost factor of blockchain technology is high and the blockchain traceability technology level provided by a third-party blockchain technology enterprise is low (i.e., $k > \frac{(8\theta-4)\alpha\beta^2}{8(1-b)(\theta\alpha+bc-c)}$ and $g_1 \leq \frac{8(1-b)(\theta\alpha+bc-c)+(4-8\theta)\alpha\beta^2}{\beta((b+3)\beta^2+4k(b-1))}+g_2^*$), the e-retailer should adopt TBT because the profits of an e-retailer adopting TBT are higher than those of an e-retailer adopting SBT. And when the research and development cost factor of blockchain technology is high and the blockchain traceability technology level provided by a third-party blockchain technology enterprise is relatively high (i.e., $k > \frac{(8\theta-4)\alpha\beta^2}{8(1-b)(\theta\alpha+bc-c)}$ and $g_1 \geq g_2^*$), the e-retailer should adopt TBT. Otherwise, the e-retailer should adopt SBT (i.e., $k > \frac{(8\theta-4)\alpha\beta^2}{8(1-b)(\theta\alpha+bc-c)}$ and $\frac{8k(1-b)(\theta\alpha+bc-c)+(4-8\theta)\alpha\beta^2}{\beta((b+3)\beta^2+4k(b-1))}+g_2^* < g_1 < g_2^*$). When the research and development cost factor of blockchain technology is low and the blockchain traceability technology level provided by a third-party blockchain technology enterprise is less than the blockchain traceability technology level of a self-built blockchain system (i.e., $k \leq \frac{(8\theta-4)\alpha\beta^2}{8(1-b)(\theta\alpha+bc-c)}$ and $g_1 \leq g_2^*$), the e-retailer should adopt TBT because the profits of the e-retailer adopting TBT are higher than those of the e-retailer adopting SBT. And when the research and development cost factor of blockchain technology is low and the blockchain traceability technology level provided by a third-party blockchain technology enterprise is relatively high (i.e., $k \leq \frac{(8\theta-4)\alpha\beta^2}{8(1-b)(\theta\alpha+bc-c)}$ and $g_1 \geq \frac{8k(1-b)(\theta\alpha+bc-c)+(4-8\theta)\alpha\beta^2}{\beta((b+3)\beta^2+4k(b-1))}+g_2^*$), the e-retailer should adopt TBT. Otherwise, the e-retailer should adopt SBT (i.e., $k \leq \frac{(8\theta-4)\alpha\beta^2}{8(1-b)(\theta\alpha+bc-c)}$ and $g_2^* < g_1 < \frac{8k(1-b)(\theta\alpha+bc-c)+(4-8\theta)\alpha\beta^2}{\beta((b+3)\beta^2+4k(b-1))}+g_2^*$).

4. Numerical Analysis

In order to observe the supply chain decision in different situations more intuitively, each parameter was assigned a value without violating the basic assumptions, and the correctness of the above proposition was further argued using numerical arithmetic examples. Based on the previous literature and without loss of generality [7,27], we set $\alpha = 200, b = 0.3, c = 1, g_1 = 5, G = 10, k = 6, f_1 = 1, f_2 = 1.2$, and $\theta = 0.5$.

4.1. Blockchain Technology Adoption

By comparing the profits of the manufacturer when adopting TBT and SBT, we determine the optimal strategies of blockchain technology adoption in Proposition 2. To investigate the impact of consumers' traceability awareness, β, and the research and development cost factor of blockchain technology, k, on blockchain technology adoption, we draw the impact of consumers' traceability awareness considering different research and development cost factors of blockchain technology, as shown in Figure 2.

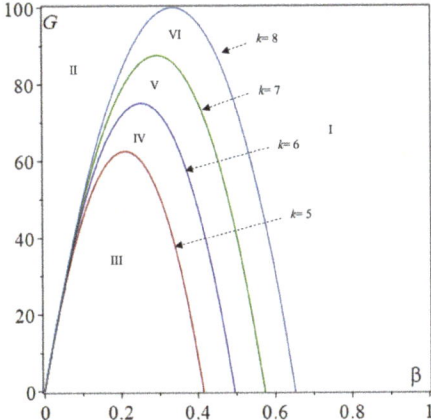

Figure 2. Blockchain technology adoption decisions of the manufacturer.

Figure 2 shows the interactive effect of the three parameters on the blockchain technology adoption decision of the manufacturer. Regions I and II indicate that the manufacturer should definitely adopt SBT. The remaining regions (regions III, IV, V, and VI) indicate that the manufacturer should adopt TBT. With the increase of the research and development cost factor of blockchain technology, the selection range of TBT increases. When the consumers' traceability awareness is greater, the manufacturer is more willing to choose SBT. Only when the consumers' traceability awareness is high enough, as the research and development cost factor of blockchain technology increases, is adopting SBT better for the manufacturer.

4.2. Consumers' Traceability Awareness Impact on e-Retailers

To investigate the impact of consumers' traceability awareness, β, on the e-retailer's profits and price, we draw the changes in the retailers' profits and price as consumers' traceability awareness increases, as shown in Figures 3 and 4.

As seen in Figure 3, the e-retailer's profits in both the TBT and SBT scenarios increase with consumers' traceability awareness. When the consumers' traceability awareness is higher than a certain value, scenario SBT outperforms scenario TBT because the e-retailer's profits in the SBT scenario are higher than those in the TBT scenario. In this case, adopting SBT could improve e-retailer's profits.

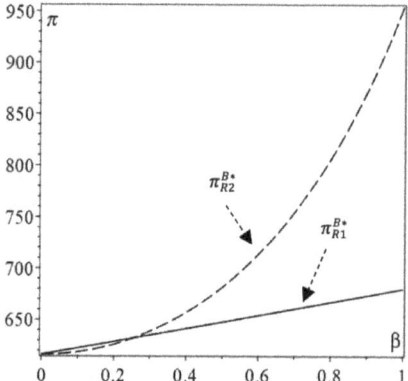

Figure 3. Impact of consumers' traceability awareness on e-retailer's profits.

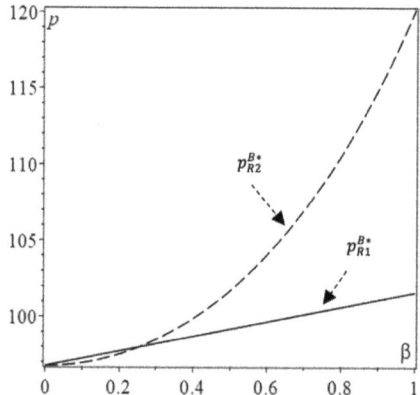

Figure 4. Impact of consumers' traceability awareness on e-retailer's online price.

In Figure 4, the online price of the e-retailer in both the TBT and SBT scenarios increases with consumers' traceability awareness. When the consumers' traceability awareness is higher than a certain value, the online price of the e-retailer in the SBT scenario is higher than that in the TBT scenario. A higher consumers' traceability awareness means that consumers will pay more attention to the traceability level of blockchain technology and the demand for the high traceability level of blockchain technology will increase. Therefore, products with a high traceability level will be more attractive to consumers. A higher consumers' traceability awareness prompts the e-retailer to invest more costs to improve the traceability level of blockchain technology. The e-retailer will charge a higher online price to obtain more profits. Comparing Figures 3 and 4, the online price of the e-retailer will increase with consumers' traceability awareness, thereby ensuring the increase of the e-retailer's profits.

4.3. Consumers' Traceability Awareness Impact on the Manufacturer

In order to study the impact of consumers' traceability awareness, β, on the manufacturer's decisions, we draw the changes in the manufacturer's decisions as consumers' traceability awareness increases, as seen in Figures 5 and 6.

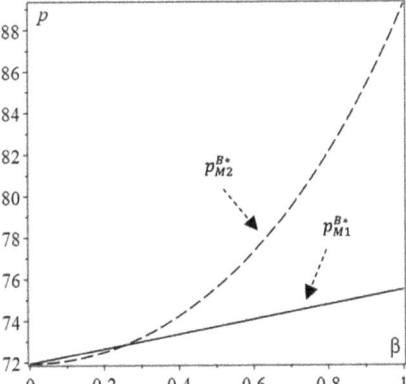

Figure 5. Impact of consumers' traceability awareness on manufacturer's offline price.

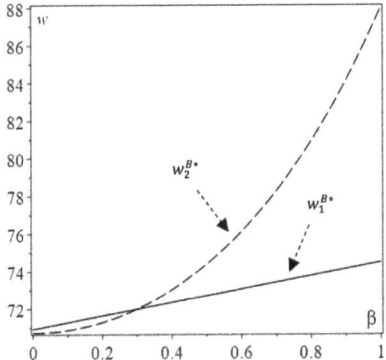

Figure 6. Impact of consumers' traceability awareness on manufacturer's online wholesale price.

Figure 5 shows the impact of consumers' traceability awareness on the manufacturer's offline price. The offline price of the manufacturer in both the TBT and SBT scenarios increases with the consumers' traceability awareness. When the consumers' traceability awareness is higher than a certain value, the offline price of the manufacturer in the SBT scenario is higher than that of the manufacturer in the TBT scenario. A higher consumers' traceability awareness prompts the manufacturer to invest more costs to improve the traceability level of blockchain technology. The manufacturer will charge a higher offline price to obtain more profits.

Figure 6 shows the impact of consumers' traceability awareness on the manufacturer's online wholesale price. The wholesale price of the manufacturer in both the TBT and SBT scenarios increases with the consumers' traceability awareness. When the consumers' traceability awareness is higher than a certain value, the wholesale price of the manufacturer in the SBT scenario is higher than that of the manufacturer in the TBT scenario. Comparing Figures 5 and 6, the offline price and the online wholesale price of the manufacturer will increase with consumers' traceability awareness, thereby ensuring that the manufacturer obtains more profits.

5. Conclusions

In this paper, we explore two blockchain adoption scenarios in a dual-channel supply chain consisting of a manufacturer and an e-retailer. The manufacturer not only sells their products through the e-retailer, but they also sell their products through a direct offline channel. The blockchain adoption scenarios include (a) the TBT scenario, in which the manufacturer and retailer adopt a blockchain technology service from a third-party platform, and (b) the SBT scenario, in which the manufacturer and retailer adopt the blockchain system provided by the manufacturer. By constructing game models, we derive the equilibrium wholesale price, offline price, online price, and the maximum profit of the manufacturer and the e-retailer in two scenarios. We compare the equilibrium solution of the supply chain members adopting SBT and TBT. Furthermore, we analyze the influence of consumers' traceability awareness on supply chain members' decisions. The main conclusions of our study can be summarized as follows:

First, the manufacturer should adopt blockchain traceability services provided by a third-party platform when the fee paid by the manufacturer to a third-party blockchain service provider is low. The manufacturer obtains more profit in the TBT scenario when the fixed fee paid by the manufacturer to a third-party blockchain technology enterprise is smaller than a certain value. Moreover, we find that with the increase of the research and development cost factor of blockchain technology, the selection range of TBT increases. When the consumers' traceability awareness is higher, the manufacturer is more willing to choose SBT.

Second, when consumers' traceability awareness is less than a certain value and the blockchain traceability technology level of TBT is less than a certain value, the online price of the e-retailer, the offline price of the manufacturer, and the wholesale price of the manufacturer in the SBT scenario are higher. When the research and development cost factor of blockchain technology and the blockchain traceability technology level of TBT meet certain conditions, the profits of the e-retailer in the TBT scenario are higher than those of the e-retailer in the SBT scenario.

Third, consumers' traceability awareness could affect the equilibrium decision of supply chain members in the dual-channel supply chain. The online price of the e-retailer, the offline price of the manufacturer, and the wholesale price of the manufacturer increase with consumers' traceability awareness in both the TBT and SBT scenarios. Fan et al. [9] found that the higher the consumer's traceability awareness, the higher the prices in the supply chain. However, when the manufacturer's and e-retailer's prices reach a certain threshold, consumers' traceability awareness has no effect on them. Different from Fan's conclusion, we find that consumers' traceability awareness always has an effect on the prices of supply chain members. A higher consumer traceability awareness will prompt members of the supply chain to charge higher prices in both the TBT and SBT scenarios.

Our findings provide insight into the supply chain members in a dual-channel supply chain with a choice in blockchain technology. We elucidate the following managerial insights: first, the manufacturer should pay attention to the cost of adopting a third-party blockchain traceability service and to consumers' traceability awareness when determining the optimal blockchain traceability system for dual-channel supply chains. When the fixed fee paid by the manufacturer to a third-party blockchain technology provider is relatively small, or when consumers' traceability awareness is comparatively small, the manufacturer can obtain more profit in the TBT scenario. Second, e-retailers should pay attention to the blockchain traceability technology level and the research and development cost factor of blockchain technology. When the dual-channel supply chain determines the blockchain traceability system, it is necessary to compare the blockchain traceability level of different traceability systems: for example, the completeness of information provided, including the origin information, production information, processing information, as well as logistics information. In addition, it is also important to focus on the research and development cost factor of blockchain technology. Third, supply chain members should pay more attention to consumers' traceability awareness. It is helpful for determining the key concern of consumers regarding product traceability. For example, for the traceability of meat, the key information that concerns consumers is feed information production information, processing information, logistics information, and so on. For luxury goods, consumers pay more attention to the origin information, production information, identification information, as well as logistics information.

Finally, we have highlighted some potential directions for future research. First, we focus on the dual-channel supply chain of a manufacturer-dominated system, in which the retailer is the follower. In reality, there are some retailers that dominate their dual-channel system. It would be interesting to study the blockchain choice strategies of a dual-channel supply chain that is retailer-dominated. Second, we only study a single manufacturer and a single supplier, and it is also a good idea to study the introduction of blockchain technology in a system with multiple manufacturers and multiple retailers. Third, it is popular for consumers to return products bought online. It may also be interesting to consider blockchain choice strategies for dual-channel supply chains considering returns behavior.

Author Contributions: Conceptualization, Y.S.; methodology, Y.S. and X.F.; formal analysis and visualization, X.S.; writing—original draft, Y.S. and X.S.; writing—review and editing, X.F. and J.G. All authors have read and agreed to the published version of the manuscript.

Funding: National Natural Science Foundation of China (71301073, 71701093, 71801125); National Social Science Foundation of China (22&ZD122); and Humanities and Social Science Foundation Project of Ministry of Education (20YJC630142).

Data Availability Statement: Not applicable.

Conflicts of Interest: The authors declare no conflict of interest.

Appendix A. Proof of Lemma 1

The second-order partial derivative of the e-retailer profit Function (3) with respect to p_{R1}^B is obtained as $\frac{\partial^2 \pi_{R1}^B}{\partial p_{R1}^{B2}} = -2$. Therefore, the e-retailer profit function is a concave function with respect to p_{R1}^B, and there exists an optimal solution. Calculating the first-order partial derivative of p_{R1}^B for π_{R1}^B and making it equal to 0, we obtain

$$p_{R1}^B = \frac{\theta\alpha + bp_{M1}^B + w_1^B + \beta g_1 + f_1}{2}$$

Substituting p_{R1}^B into the manufacturer's profit Function (4) and calculating the second-order partial derivatives of p_{M1}^B and w_1^B for π_{M1}^B, we can obtain the Hessian matrix for π_{M1}^B:

$$H\left(\pi_{M1}^B\right) = \begin{bmatrix} b^2 - 2 & b \\ b & -1 \end{bmatrix}$$

The Hessian matrix is negative definite, so the manufacturer's profit function is a concave function with respect to p_{M1}^B, w_1^B. The first-order partial derivatives of p_{M1}^B, w_1^B for π_{M1}^B are made equal to 0, and we can obtain:

$$p_{M1}^{B*} = \frac{(b^2 - 1)c - (\theta\alpha + \beta g_1)b - (1-\theta)\alpha - \beta g_1}{2(b^2 - 1)}$$

$$w_1^{B*} = \frac{(b^2 - 1)(c - 2f_1) - ((1-\theta)\alpha + \beta g_1)b - \beta g_1 - \theta\alpha}{2(b^2 - 1)}$$

Taking the above result back to p_{R1}^B again, we obtain:

$$p_{R1}^{B*} = \frac{(b+1)(b^2 - 1)c + (\theta\alpha + \beta g_1)(b^2 - 3) - ((1-\theta)2\alpha + 2\beta g_1)b}{4(b^2 - 1)}$$

Appendix B. Proof of Lemma 2

Calculating the first-order partial derivatives with respect to β and θ for p_{R1}^{B*}, p_{M1}^{B*}, w_1^{B*}, q_{R1}^{B*}, and q_{M1}^{B*}, respectively, we obtain $\frac{\partial p_{R1}^{B*}}{\partial \beta} = \frac{(b-3)g_1}{4(b-1)} > 0$, $\frac{\partial p_{R1}^{B*}}{\partial \theta} = \frac{\alpha(b+3)}{4b+4} > 0$, $\frac{\partial p_{M1}^{B*}}{\partial \beta} = \frac{-g_1}{2(b-1)} > 0$, $\frac{\partial p_{M1}^{B*}}{\partial \theta} = \frac{-\alpha}{2(b+1)} < 0$, $\frac{\partial w_1^{B*}}{\partial \beta} = \frac{-g_1}{2(b-1)} > 0$, $\frac{\partial w_1^{B*}}{\partial \theta} = \frac{\alpha}{2(b+1)} > 0$.

Appendix C. Proof of Lemma 3

The second-order partial derivative of the e-retailer profit Function (11) with respect to p_{R2}^B yields $\frac{\partial^2 \pi_{R2}^B}{\partial p_{R2}^{B^2}} = -2$, so the e-retailer profit function is a concave function with respect to p_{R2}^B and there exists an optimal solution. Finding the first-order partial derivative of p_{R2}^B for π_{R2}^B and making it equal to 0 yields:

$$p_{R2}^B = \frac{\theta\alpha + bp_{M1}^B + w_2^B + \beta g + f_2}{2}$$

Substituting p_{R2}^B into the manufacturer's profit Function (12) and calculating the second-order partial derivatives of p_{M2}^B, w_2^B, g for π_{M2}^B, the resulting Hesse matrix is

$$H(\pi_{M2}^B) = \begin{bmatrix} b^2 - 2 & b & \frac{1}{2}b\beta + \beta \\ b & -1 & \frac{1}{2}\beta \\ \frac{1}{2}b\beta + \beta & \frac{1}{2}\beta & -k \end{bmatrix}$$

Because $H(1) = b^2 - 2 < 0$ and $H(2) = 2(1 - b^2) > 0$, the Hessian matrix is negative definite when $H(3) = \frac{1}{2}(b+1)(4k(b-1) + \beta^2(b+3)) < 0$, so $0 < \beta < 2\sqrt{\frac{k(1-b)}{b+3}}$.

Let $\frac{\partial \pi_{M2}^B}{\partial p_{R2}^B}$, $\frac{\partial \pi_{M2}^B}{\partial p_{M1}^B}$, $\frac{\partial \pi_{M2}^B}{\partial g}$ be equal to 0; the joint cubic equation can be obtained as follows:

$$p_{M2}^{B*} = \frac{\beta^2\left(2c(b^2+3) + 8bc + (1-2\theta)\alpha\right) - 4k\left((1-b^2)c + b\theta\alpha + (1-\theta)\alpha\right)}{(b+1)\left(8k(b-1) + 2\beta^2(b+3)\right)}$$

$$w_2^{B*} = \frac{(2\beta^2(c-f_2) + 4k(c-2f_2))b^2 + \left(((2\theta-1)\alpha + 8(c-f_2))\beta^2 + 4\alpha k(\theta-1)\right)b + ((4\theta-2)\alpha + 6(c-f_2))\beta^2 - 4k(\theta\alpha + c - 2f_2)}{(b+1)\left(8k(b-1) + 2\beta^2(b+3)\right)}$$

$$g_2^* = \frac{\beta\left(-b^2c - (\theta\alpha + 2c)b - (2-\theta)\alpha + 3c\right)}{4k(b-1) + \beta^2(b+3)} \quad \left(0 < \beta < 2\sqrt{\frac{k(1-b)}{b+3}}\right)$$

Then, substituting p_{M2}^{B*}, w_2^{B*} into p_{R2}^B, we obtain:

$$p_{R2}^{B*} = \frac{2b^3ck + \left(2k(\theta\alpha+c) + 2\beta^2c\right)b^2 + \left(((\theta-1)4\alpha - 2c)k + 2\beta^2((2\theta-1)\alpha+4c)\right)b - (6\theta\alpha + 2c)k + 6\beta^2\left((\theta-\frac{1}{2})\alpha + c\right)}{(b+1)\left(8k(b-1) + 2\beta^2(b+3)\right)}$$

Appendix D. Proof of Proposition 1

The optimal price decisions for a manufacturer and e-retailer in a TBT scenario are, respectively:

$$p_{R1}^{B*} = \frac{(b+1)(b^2-1)c + (\theta\alpha + \beta g_1)(b^2-3) - ((1-\theta)2\alpha + 2\beta g_1)b}{4(b^2-1)}$$

$$p_{M1}^{B*} = \frac{(b^2-1)c - (\theta\alpha + \beta g_1)b - (1-\theta)\alpha - \beta g_1}{2(b^2-1)}$$

$$w_1^{B*} = \frac{(b^2-1)(c-2f_1) - ((1-\theta)\alpha + \beta g_1)b - \beta g_1 - \theta\alpha}{2(b^2-1)}$$

The optimal price decisions for a manufacturer and e-retailer in an SBT scenario are, respectively:

$$p_{R2}^{B*} = \frac{2b^3ck + \left(2k(\theta\alpha+c)+2\beta^2 c\right)b^2 + \left(((\theta-1)4\alpha-2c)k + 2\beta^2((2\theta-1)\alpha+4c)\right)b - (6\theta\alpha+2c)k + 6\beta^2\left(\left(\theta-\frac{1}{2}\right)\alpha+c\right)}{(b+1)\left(8k(b-1)+2\beta^2(b+3)\right)}$$

$$p_{M2}^{B*} = \frac{\beta^2\left(2c(b^2+3)+8bc+(1-2\theta)\alpha\right) - 4k\left((1-b^2)c+b\theta\alpha+(1-\theta)\alpha\right)}{(b+1)\left(8k(b-1)+2\beta^2(b+3)\right)}$$

$$w_2^{B*} = \frac{\left(2\beta^2(c-f_2)+4k(c-2f_2)\right)b^2 + \left(((2\theta-1)\alpha+8(c-f_2))\beta^2+4\alpha k(\theta-1)\right)b + ((4\theta-2)\alpha+6(c-f_2))\beta^2 - 4k(\theta\alpha+c-2f_2)}{(b+1)\left(8k(b-1)+2\beta^2(b+3)\right)}$$

$$p_{R1}^{B*} - p_{R2}^{B*} = \frac{\beta(b-3)\left(g_1((b+3)\beta^2+4k(b-1)) + (b^2c+(\theta\alpha+2c)b+(2-\theta)\alpha-3c)\beta\right)}{(b-1)\left(16k(b-1)+4\beta^2(b+3)\right)}$$

$$p_{M1}^{B*} - p_{M2}^{B*} = \frac{-\beta\left(g_1((b+3)\beta^2+4k(b-1)) + (b^2c+(\theta\alpha+2c)b+(2-\theta)\alpha-3c)\beta\right)}{(b-1)\left(8k(b-1)+2\beta^2(b+3)\right)}$$

$$w_1^{B*} - w_2^{B*} = \frac{-g_1\beta((b+3)\beta^2+4k(b-1)) - (b^2c+(\theta\alpha+2c)b+(2-\theta)\alpha-3c)\beta^2}{(b-1)\left(8k(b-1)+2\beta^2(b+3)\right)} - (f_1-f_2)$$

When $0 < \beta < 2\sqrt{\frac{k(1-b)}{b+3}}$, $(b+3)\beta^2+4k(b-1) < 0$, $8k(b-1)+2\beta^2(b+3) < 0$, $16k(b-1)+4\beta^2(b+3) < 0$.

Because $0 < b < 1$, $b-1 < 0$, $b-3 < 0$.

When $g_1 < \frac{(-b^2c-(\theta\alpha+2c)b+(\theta-2)\alpha+3c)\beta}{(b+3)\beta^2+4k(b-1)} = g_2^*$, $p_{R1}^{B*} < p_{R2}^{B*}$, $p_{M1}^{B*} < p_{M2}^{B*}$.

When $g_1 < \frac{(-b^2c-(\theta\alpha+2c)b+(\theta-2)\alpha+3c)\beta}{((b+3)\beta^2+4k(b-1))} - \frac{2(f_1-f_2)(b-1)}{\beta} = g_2^* - \frac{2(f_1-f_2)(b-1)}{\beta}$, $w_1^{B*} < w_2^{B*}$.

Thus, when $0 < \beta < 2\sqrt{\frac{k(1-b)}{b+3}}$ and $g_1 < g_2^*$, $p_{R1}^{B*} < p_{R2}^{B*}$, $p_{M1}^{B*} < p_{M2}^{B*}$.

When $0 < \beta < 2\sqrt{\frac{k(1-b)}{b+3}}$ and $g_1 < g_2^* - \frac{2(f_1-f_2)(b-1)}{\beta}$, $w_1^{B*} < w_2^{B*}$.

Appendix E. Proof of Proposition 2

The profits for a manufacturer in a TBT scenario are:

$$\pi_{M1}^{B*} = \frac{1}{8(b^2-1)} \begin{aligned}&(-b^4c^2 - 2c(\theta\alpha+\beta g_1+c)b^3 \\&+ (-\alpha^2\theta^2+(2c(\theta-2)-2\theta\beta g_1)\alpha+4c^2-6cg_1\beta-\beta^2g_1^2)b^2 \\&+ (4\theta(\theta-1)\alpha^2+(-4\beta g_1+2\theta c)\alpha-4g_1^2\beta^2+2c\beta g_1+2c^2)b \\&+ (4\theta-3\theta^2-2)\alpha^2-2(\theta-2)(-\beta g_1+c)\alpha-3(-\beta g_1+c)^2) - G\end{aligned}$$

The profits for a manufacturer in an SBT scenario are:

$$\pi_{M2}^{B*} = \frac{1}{(16(b-1)k+4\beta^2(b+3))(b+1)}(((-2b^2\theta^2+(8\theta^2-8\theta)b-6\theta^2+8\theta$$
$$-4)\alpha^2-4c(b-1)(b+1)(b\theta-\theta+2)\alpha$$
$$-2c^2(b+3)(b+1)(b-1)^2)k+2(4\theta-2)^2\beta^2\alpha^2)$$

$$\pi_{M2}^{B*} - \pi_{M1}^{B*} = \frac{1}{(16(b-1)k+4\beta^2(b+3))(b+1)}(((-2b^2\theta^2+(8\theta^2-8\theta)b-6\theta^2$$
$$+8\theta-4)\alpha^2-4c(b-1)(b+1)(b\theta-\theta+2)\alpha$$
$$-2c^2(b+3)(b+1)(b-1)^2)k+2(4\theta-2)^2\beta^2\alpha^2)$$
$$-\frac{1}{8(b^2-1)}(-b^4c^2-2c(\theta\alpha+\beta g_1+c)b^3$$
$$+(-\alpha^2\theta^2+(2c(\theta-2)-2\theta\beta g_1)\alpha+4c^2-6cg_1\beta-\beta^2g_1^2)b^2$$
$$+(4\theta(\theta-1)\alpha^2+(-4\beta g_1+2\theta c)\alpha-4g_1^2\beta^2+2c\beta g_1+2c^2)b$$
$$+(4\theta-3\theta^2-2)\alpha^2-2(\theta-2)(-\beta g_1+c)\alpha-3(-\beta g_1+c)^2)+G$$

When $\pi_{M2}^{B*} \leq \pi_{M1}^{B*}$, that is, $G \leq \frac{1}{8(b^2-1)}(-b^4c^2-2c(\theta\alpha+\beta g_1+c)b^3+(-\alpha^2\theta^2+(2c(\theta-2)-2\theta\beta g_1)\alpha+4c^2-6cg_1\beta-\beta^2g_1^2)b^2+(4\theta(\theta-1)\alpha^2+(-4\beta g_1+2\theta c)\alpha-4g_1^2\beta^2+2c\beta g_1+2c^2)b+(4\theta-3\theta^2-2)\alpha^2-2(\theta-2)(-\beta g_1+c)\alpha-3(-\beta g_1+c)^2) - \frac{1}{(16(b-1)k+4\beta^2(b+3))(b+1)}(((-2b^2\theta^2+(8\theta^2-8\theta)b-6\theta^2+8\theta-4)\alpha^2-4c(b-1)(b+1)(b\theta-\theta+2)\alpha-2c^2(b+3)(b+1)(b-1)^2)k+2(4\theta-2)^2\beta^2\alpha^2)$, let $H = \frac{1}{8(b^2-1)}(-b^4c^2-2c(\theta\alpha+\beta g_1+c)b^3+(-\alpha^2\theta^2+(2c(\theta-2)-2\theta\beta g_1)\alpha+4c^2-6cg_1\beta-\beta^2g_1^2)b^2+(4\theta(\theta-1)\alpha^2+(-4\beta g_1+2\theta c)\alpha-4g_1^2\beta^2+2c\beta g_1+2c^2)b+(4\theta-3\theta^2-2)\alpha^2-2(\theta-2)(-\beta g_1+c)\alpha-3(-\beta g_1+c)^2) - \frac{1}{(16(b-1)k+4\beta^2(b+3))(b+1)}(((-2b^2\theta^2+(8\theta^2-8\theta)b-6\theta^2+8\theta-4)\alpha^2-4c(b-1)(b+1)(b\theta-\theta+2)\alpha-2c^2(b+3)(b+1)(b-1)^2)k+2(4\theta-2)^2\beta^2\alpha^2)$.

Thus, when $G \leq H$, a manufacturer should choose to use blockchain traceability services provided by a TBT system.

Appendix F. Proof of Proposition 3

The optimal profit for an e-retailer in a TBT scenario is:

$$\pi_{R1}^{B*} = \frac{((b-1)c+\theta\alpha+\beta g_1)^2}{16}$$

The optimal profit for an e-retailer in an SBT scenario is:

$$\pi_{R2}^{B*} = \frac{\left(k(b-1)(\theta\alpha+bc-c)+\alpha\beta^2\left(\theta-\frac{1}{2}\right)\right)^2}{8(4k(b-1)+\beta^2(b+3))^2}$$

$$\pi_{R1}^{B*} - \pi_{R2}^{B*} = \frac{1}{2((b+3)\beta^2+4k(b-1))^2}(\beta(g_1((b+3)\beta^2+4k(b-1))$$
$$+(b^2c+(\theta\alpha+2c)b+(2-\theta)\alpha$$
$$-3c)\beta)\left(\frac{\beta}{8}(g_1((b+3)\beta^2+4k(b-1))\right.$$
$$+(b^2c+(\theta\alpha+2c)b+(2-\theta)\alpha+(8\theta-4)\alpha-3c)\beta)$$
$$+(b-1)(\theta\alpha+bc-c)k))$$

Let $Z = g_1((b+3)\beta^2+4k(b-1))+(b^2c+(\theta\alpha+2c)b+(2-\theta)\alpha-3c)\beta$,

Thus, $\pi_{R1}^{B*} - \pi_{R2}^{B*} = \frac{\beta Z\left(\frac{\beta}{8}(Z+(8\theta-4)\alpha\beta)+(b-1)(\theta\alpha+bc-c)k\right)}{2((b+3)\beta^2+4k(b-1))^2}$.

When $0 < \beta < 2\sqrt{\frac{k(1-b)}{b+3}}$, $4k(b-1)+\beta^2(b+3) < 0$.

When $Z \geq 0$ and $Z \geq \frac{8(1-b)(\theta\alpha+bc-c)k}{\beta}+(4-8\theta)\alpha\beta$, $\pi_{R1}^{B*} \geq \pi_{R2}^{B*}$.

Because $0 < c < \frac{\theta\alpha}{1-b}$, $\theta\alpha+bc-c > 0$.

If $k > \frac{(8\theta-4)\alpha\beta^2}{8(1-b)(\theta\alpha+bc-c)}$, when $g_1 \leq \frac{\frac{8(1-b)(\theta\alpha+bc-c)k}{\beta}+(4-8\theta)\alpha\beta-(b^2c+(\theta\alpha+2c)b+(2-\theta)\alpha-3c)\beta}{(b+3)\beta^2+4k(b-1)} = \frac{8k(1-b)(\theta\alpha+bc-c)+(4-8\theta)\alpha\beta^2}{\beta((b+3)\beta^2+4k(b-1))}+g_2^*$, $\pi_{R1}^{B*} \geq \pi_{R2}^{B*}$.

If $k \leq \frac{(8\theta-4)\alpha\beta^2}{8(1-b)(\theta\alpha+bc-c)}$, when $g_1 \leq \frac{(-b^2c-(\theta\alpha+2c)b-(2-\theta)\alpha+3c)\beta}{(b+3)\beta^2+4k(b-1)} = g_2^*$, $\pi_{R1}^{B*} \geq \pi_{R2}^{B*}$.

When $Z \leq 0$ and $Z \leq \frac{8(1-b)(\theta\alpha+bc-c)k}{\beta}+(4-8\theta)\alpha\beta$, $\pi_{R1}^{B*} \geq \pi_{R2}^{B*}$.

Because $0 < c < \frac{\theta\alpha}{1-b}$, $\theta\alpha + bc - c > 0$.

If $k > \frac{(8\theta-4)\alpha\beta^2}{8(1-b)(\theta\alpha+bc-c)}$, when $g_1 \leq \frac{(-b^2c-(\theta\alpha+2c)b-(2-\theta)\alpha+3c)\beta}{(b+3)\beta^2+4k(b-1)} = g_2^*$, $\pi_{R1}^{B*} \geq \pi_{R2}^{B*}$.

If $k \leq \frac{(8\theta-4)\alpha\beta^2}{8(1-b)(\theta\alpha+bc-c)}$, when $g_1 \geq \frac{\frac{8(1-b)(\theta\alpha+bc-c)k}{\beta}+(4-8\theta)\alpha\beta-(b^2c+(\theta\alpha+2c)b+(2-\theta)\alpha-3c)\beta}{(b+3)\beta^2+4k(b-1)} = \frac{8k(1-b)(\theta\alpha+bc-c)+(4-8\theta)\alpha\beta^2}{\beta((b+3)\beta^2+4k(b-1))}+g_2^*$, $\pi_{R1}^{B*} \geq \pi_{R2}^{B*}$.

If $k > \frac{(8\theta-4)\alpha\beta^2}{8(1-b)(\theta\alpha+bc-c)}$, when $\frac{8k(1-b)(\theta\alpha+bc-c)+(4-8\theta)\alpha\beta^2}{\beta((b+3)\beta^2+4k(b-1))}+g_2^* < g_1 < g_2^*$, $\pi_{R1}^{B*} < \pi_{R2}^{B*}$.

If $k \leq \frac{(8\theta-4)\alpha\beta^2}{8(1-b)(\theta\alpha+bc-c)}$, when $g_2^* < g_1 < \frac{8k(1-b)(\theta\alpha+bc-c)+(4-8\theta)\alpha\beta^2}{\beta((b+3)\beta^2+4k(b-1))}+g_2^*$, $\pi_{R1}^{B*} < \pi_{R2}^{B*}$.

Thus, when $0 < \beta < 2\sqrt{\frac{k(1-b)}{b+3}}$, $k > \frac{(8\theta-4)\alpha\beta^2}{8(1-b)(\theta\alpha+bc-c)}$ and $g_1 \leq \frac{8(1-b)(\theta\alpha+bc-c)+(4-8\theta)\alpha\beta^2}{\beta((b+3)\beta^2+4k(b-1))}+g_2^*$ or $0 < \beta < 2\sqrt{\frac{k(1-b)}{b+3}}$, $k > \frac{(8\theta-4)\alpha\beta^2}{8(1-b)(\theta\alpha+bc-c)}$ and $g_1 \geq g_2^*$, $\pi_{R1}^{B*} \geq \pi_{R2}^{B*}$.

When $0 < \beta < 2\sqrt{\frac{k(1-b)}{b+3}}$, $k > \frac{(8\theta-4)\alpha\beta^2}{8(1-b)(\theta\alpha+bc-c)}$ and $\frac{8k(1-b)(\theta\alpha+bc-c)+(4-8\theta)\alpha\beta^2}{\beta((b+3)\beta^2+4k(b-1))}+g_2^* < g_1 < g_2^*$ or $0 < \beta < 2\sqrt{\frac{k(1-b)}{b+3}}$, $k \leq \frac{(8\theta-4)\alpha\beta^2}{8(1-b)(\theta\alpha+bc-c)}$ and $g_2^* < g_1 < \frac{8k(1-b)(\theta\alpha+bc-c)+(4-8\theta)\alpha\beta^2}{\beta((b+3)\beta^2+4k(b-1))}+g_2^*$, $\pi_{R1}^{B*} < \pi_{R2}^{B*}$.

When $0 < \beta < 2\sqrt{\frac{k(1-b)}{b+3}}$, $k \leq \frac{(8\theta-4)\alpha\beta^2}{8(1-b)(\theta\alpha+bc-c)}$ and $g_1 \leq g_2^*$ or $0 < \beta < 2\sqrt{\frac{k(1-b)}{b+3}}$, $k \leq \frac{(8\theta-4)\alpha\beta^2}{8(1-b)(\theta\alpha+bc-c)}$ and $g_1 \geq \frac{8k(1-b)(\theta\alpha+bc-c)+(4-8\theta)\alpha\beta^2}{\beta((b+3)\beta^2+4k(b-1))}+g_2^*$, $\pi_{R1}^{B*} \geq \pi_{R2}^{B*}$.

References

1. China Internet Network Information Center. The 51st Statistical Report on the Development Status of China's Internet. Available online: https://www.cnnic.com.cn/IDR/ReportDownloads/202307/P020230707514088128694.pdf (accessed on 2 March 2023). (In Chinese).
2. Montecchi, M.; Plangger, K.; Etter, M. It's real, trust me! Establishing supply chain provenance using blockchain. *Business Horizons* **2019**, *62*, 283–293. [CrossRef]
3. Sun, J.; Zhang, X.; Zhu, Q. Counterfeiters in online marketplaces: Stealing your sales or sharing your costs. *J. Retail.* **2020**, *96*, 189–202. [CrossRef]
4. MacCarthy, B.L.; Ivanov, D. The digital supply chain—Emergence, concepts, definitions, and technologies. In *The Digital Supply Chain*; Elsevier: Amsterdam, The Netherlands, 2022; pp. 3–24. [CrossRef]
5. Saurabh, S.; Subhasis, T.; Shahid, H.; John, G.B.; Syed, M.J. Identification and Authentication in Healthcare Internet-of-Things Using Integrated Fog Computing Based Blockchain Model. *Internet Things* **2021**, *15*, 100422.
6. Zhang, T.Y.; Dong, P.W.; Chen, X.F.; Gong, Y. The impacts of blockchain adoption on a dual-channel supply chain with risk-averse members. *Omega* **2023**, *114*, 102747. [CrossRef]
7. Shen, B.; Dong, C.; Minner, S. Combating copycats in the supply chain with permissioned blockchain technology. *Prod. Oper. Manag.* **2022**, *31*, 138–154. [CrossRef]
8. Wu, X.Y.; Fan, Z.P.; Li, G.M. Strategic analysis for adopting blockchain technology under supply chain competition. *Int. J. Logist. Res. Appl.* **2022**, *26*, 1–24. [CrossRef]
9. Fan, Z.P.; Wu, X.Y.; Cao, B.B. Considering the traceability awareness of consumers: Should the supply chain adopt the blockchain technology? *Ann. Oper. Res.* **2022**, *309*, 837–860. [CrossRef]
10. Moosavi, J.; Naeni, L.M.; Fathollahi-Fard, A.M.; Fiore, U. Blockchain in supply chain management: A review, bibliometric, and network analysis. *Environ. Sci. Pollut. Res.* **2021**. [CrossRef]
11. Wang, M.M.; Yang, Y. An empirical analysis of the supply chain flexibility using blockchain technology. *Front. Psychol.* **2022**, *13*, 1004007. [CrossRef]
12. Maher, A.N.; Agi, A.K.J. Blockchain technology in the supply chain: An integrated theoretical perspective of organizational adoption. *Int. J. Prod. Econ.* **2022**, *247*, 108458.
13. Niu, B.; Mu, Z.; Cao, B.; Gao, J. Should multinational firms implement blockchain to provide quality verification? *Transp. Res. E Logist. Transp. Rev.* **2021**, *145*, 102121. [CrossRef]

14. Pun, H.; Swaminathan, J.M.; Hou, P. Blockchain adoption for combating deceptive counterfeits. *Prod. Oper. Manag.* **2021**, *30*, 864–882. [CrossRef]
15. Choi, T.M. Blockchain-technology-supported platforms for diamond authentication and certification in luxury supply chains. *Transport. Res. E Logist. Transport.* **2019**, *128*, 17–29. [CrossRef]
16. Dong, L.X.; Jiang, P.P.; Xu, F.S. Impact of traceability technology adoption in food supply chain networks. *Manag. Sci.* **2022**, *69*, 1324–1934. [CrossRef]
17. Wu, X.Y.; Fan, Z.P.; Cao, B.B. An analysis of strategies for adopting blockchain technology in the fresh product supply chain. *Int. J. Prod. Res.* **2021**, *61*, 3717–3734. [CrossRef]
18. Wang, J.; Liu, J.; Wang, F.; Yue, X. Blockchain technology for port logistics capability: Exclusive or sharing. *Transp. Res. Part B Methodol.* **2021**, *149*, 347–392. [CrossRef]
19. Orji, I.J.; Kusi-Sarpong, S.; Huang, S.F.; Vazquez-Brust, D. Evaluating the factors that influence blockchain adoption in the freight logistics industry. *Transp. Res. Part E Logist. Transp. Rev.* **2020**, *141*, 102025. [CrossRef]
20. Choi, T.M.; Ouyang, X. Initial coin offerings for blockchain based product provenance authentication platforms. *Int. J. Prod. Econ.* **2021**, *233*, 107995. [CrossRef]
21. Ding, Q.Y.; Gao, S.; Zhu, J.; Yuan, C. Permissioned blockchain-based double-layer framework for product traceability system. *IEEE Access* **2019**, *8*, 6209–6225. [CrossRef]
22. Mao, B.; He, J.; Cao, J.; Gao, W.; Pan, D. Food traceability system based on 3d city models and deep learning. *Ann. Data Sci.* **2016**, *3*, 89–100. [CrossRef]
23. Cattani, K.; Gilland, W.; Heese, H.S.; Swaminathan, J. Boiling frogs: Pricing strategies for a manufacturer adding a direct channel that competes with the traditional channel. *Prod. Oper. Manag.* **2006**, *15*, 40–56. [CrossRef]
24. Chen, J.; Zhang, H.; Sun, Y. Implementing coordination contracts in a manufacturer Stackelberg dual-channel supply chain. *Omega* **2012**, *40*, 571–583. [CrossRef]
25. Wu, H.; Cai, G.; Chen, J.; Sheu, C. Online manufacturer referral to heterogeneous retailers. *Prod. Oper. Manag.* **2015**, *24*, 1768–1782. [CrossRef]
26. Li, G.; Xue, J.; Li, N.; Ivanov, D. Blockchain-supported business model design, supply chain resilience, and firm performance. *Transport. Res. E Logist. Transport.* **2022**, *163*, 102773. [CrossRef]
27. Guan, X.; Liu, B.; Chen, Y.J.; Wang, H. Inducing supply chain transparency through supplier encroachment. *Prod. Oper. Manag.* **2020**, *29*, 725–749. [CrossRef]
28. Tsay, A.A.; Agrawal, N. Channel conflict and coordination in the e-commerce age. *Prod. Oper. Manag.* **2004**, *13*, 93–110. [CrossRef]
29. Guan, H.; Gurnani, H.; Geng, X.; Luo, Y. Strategic inventory and supplier encroachment. *Manuf. Serv. Oper. Manag.* **2019**, *21*, 536–555. [CrossRef]
30. Gao, L.; Guo, L.; Orsdemir, A. Dual-channel distribution: The case for cost information asymmetry. *Prod. Oper. Manag.* **2021**, *30*, 494–521. [CrossRef]
31. Pal, B.; Sarkar, A. Effects of green improvement and pricing policies in a double dual-channel competitive supply chain under decision-making power strategies. *RAIRO Oper. Res.* **2022**, *56*, 931–953. [CrossRef]
32. Xu, J.Y.; Meng, Q.F.; Chen, Y.Q.; Zhao, J. Dual-Channel Pricing Decisions for Product Recycling in Green Supply Chain Operations: Considering the Impact of Consumer Loss Aversion. *Int. J. Environ. Res. Public Health* **2023**, *20*, 1792. [CrossRef]
33. Barman, A.; De, P.K.; Chakraborty, A.K.; Lim, C.P.; Das, R. Optimal pricing policy in a three-layer dual-channel supply chain under government subsidy in green manufacturing. *Math. Comput. Simul.* **2023**, *204*, 401–429. [CrossRef]
34. Song, L.; Xin, Q.; Chen, H.; Liao, L.; Chen, Z. Optimal Decision-Making of Retailer-Led Dual-Channel Green Supply Chain with Fairness Concerns under Government Subsidies. *Mathematics* **2023**, *11*, 284. [CrossRef]
35. Xiao, T.; Choi, T.M.; Cheng, T.C.E. Product variety and channel structure strategy for a retailer-Stackelberg supply chain. *Eur. J. Oper. Res.* **2014**, *233*, 114–124. [CrossRef]
36. Wang, C.; Leng, M.; Liang, L. Choosing an online retail channel for a manufacturer: Direct sales or consignment? *Int. J. Prod. Econ.* **2018**, *195*, 338–358. [CrossRef]
37. Zhao, S.; Li, W.L. Blockchain-based traceability system adoption decision in the dual-channel perishable goods market under different pricing policies. *Int. J. Prod. Res.* **2023**, *61*, 4548–4574. [CrossRef]
38. Xu, X.P.; Zhang, M.Y.; Dou, G.-W.; Yu, Y.G. Coordination of a supply chain with an online platform considering green technology in the blockchain era. *Int. J. Prod. Res.* **2023**, *61*, 3793–3810. [CrossRef]
39. Zhang, R.; Xia, Z.W.; Liu, B. Optimal Pricing Decisions for Dual-Channel Supply Chain: Blockchain Adoption and Consumer Sensitivity. *Complexity* **2022**, *2022*, 4605455. [CrossRef]
40. Zhu, S.C.; Li, J.; Wang, S.Y.; Xia, Y.S.; Wang, Y.J. The role of blockchain technology in the dual-channel supply chain dominated by a brand owner. *Int. J. Prod. Econ.* **2023**, *258*, 108791. [CrossRef]
41. Li, Q.; Li, H.L. Pricing Decisions and Online Channel Selection Strategies in Dual-Channel Supply Chains considering Block Chain. *Discret. Dyn. Nat. Soc.* **2022**, *2022*, 3027249. [CrossRef]
42. Li, Z.W.; Xu, X.H.; Bai, Q.G.; Guan, X.; Zeng, K. The interplay between blockchain adoption and channel selection in combating counterfeits. *Transport. Res. E-Log.* **2021**, *155*, 102451. [CrossRef]
43. Wang, J.; Zhang, Q.; Hou, P.W.; Li, Q.H. Effects of platform's blockchain strategy on brand manufacturer's distribution strategy in the presence of counterfeits. *Comput. Ind. Eng.* **2023**, *177*, 109028. [CrossRef]

44. Cao, B.B.; Zhu, M.F.; Tian, Q. Optimal Operation Policies in a Cross-Regional Fresh Product Supply Chain with Regional Government Subsidy Heterogeneity to Blockchain-Driven Traceability. *Mathematics* **2022**, *10*, 4592. [CrossRef]
45. Dai, B.; Nu, Y.; Xie, X.; Li, J.B. Interactions of traceability and reliability optimization in a competitive supply chain with product recall. *Eur. J. Oper. Res.* **2021**, *290*, 116–131. [CrossRef]

Disclaimer/Publisher's Note: The statements, opinions and data contained in all publications are solely those of the individual author(s) and contributor(s) and not of MDPI and/or the editor(s). MDPI and/or the editor(s) disclaim responsibility for any injury to people or property resulting from any ideas, methods, instructions or products referred to in the content.

Article

Multi-Objective Green Closed-Loop Supply Chain Management with Bundling Strategy, Perishable Products, and Quality Deterioration

Golnaz Hooshmand Pakdel [1], Yong He [1,*] and Sina Hooshmand Pakdel [2]

[1] School of Economics and Management, Southeast University, Nanjing 211189, China; soniahosh1993@gmail.com

[2] Engineering Faculty, Science & Research Branch, Islamic Azad University, Tehran 1477893855, Iran; sina.houshmand.pakdel@gmail.com

* Correspondence: hy@seu.edu.cn

Citation: Pakdel, G.H.; He, Y.; Pakdel, S.H. Multi-Objective Green Closed-Loop Supply Chain Management with Bundling Strategy, Perishable Products, and Quality Deterioration. *Mathematics* **2024**, *12*, 737. https://doi.org/10.3390/math12050737

Academic Editor: Ripon Kumar Chakrabortty

Received: 31 January 2024
Revised: 25 February 2024
Accepted: 28 February 2024
Published: 29 February 2024

Copyright: © 2024 by the authors. Licensee MDPI, Basel, Switzerland. This article is an open access article distributed under the terms and conditions of the Creative Commons Attribution (CC BY) license (https://creativecommons.org/licenses/by/4.0/).

Abstract: This study presents a four-objective mathematical model to improve closed-loop supply chain (CLSC) management. The aim of this research is to reduce the costs of the entire chain, risk, emission of pollutants, and time to deliver the product to the customer in uncertain demand condition. In this paper, the NSGAII algorithm is used to solve the model. In this algorithm, among the answers of each generation, a number of them are selected using the two-run tournament selection method. In the binary selection method, the answers are randomly selected from the population, and then a comparison is made between these two answers, and whichever is better is finally selected. The selection criteria in NSGA-II are, firstly, the rank, and secondly, the crowding distance related to the answer. Also, the performance of the NSGA-II algorithm on the same model and data has been compared with the MOPSO algorithm. In the proposed algorithm, if it encounters an impossible solution, it exits the local mode and solves the problem in global conditions. The results show that the proposed method strikes a better balance between discovery and efficiency criteria and avoids falling into local optima. Therefore, in addition to its effectiveness in discovering optimal answers, the genetic-based method has high speed and subsequently, high convergence and diversity rates compared to the particle swarm method. Also, compared to previous methods in the green closed-loop supply chain, the proposed method is better than the modified genetic algorithm, reducing the costs of the chain by about 2.38%.

Keywords: bundling strategy; closed-loop supply chain management; green supply chain management; perishable products; quality deterioration

MSC: 90B06

1. Introduction

Supply Chain Management (SCM) represents the advancement of developing, implementing, and monitoring supply chain (SC) processes, professionally utilizing information and technology. SCM includes all operations that begin with the f raw material procurement, warehouses, work-in-process inventory, and finished goods, i.e., at consumption and origin points, and ensures organizational productivity while meeting customer demands and fulfilling and satisfying the customers (Alzoubi et al., 2022) [1]. However, in the past few decades, supply chains and their various stages have faced internal and external operational challenges, which may be in the environment, nature, or society. The increasing complexity and uncertainty of the environments in which supply chains operate double the significant role of adaptive planning and control, to guarantee delivery to end consumers with minimum delays and interruptions, avoiding unnecessary costs, and maintain business continuity. To implement compliance-based management principles, real-time coordination of production planning, inventory control, and delivery schedules will be essential, while system control parameters must be dynamically adjusted to minimize costs, maximize revenue, meet target service levels, or pursue any other measurable goals to account for dynamism, instability, and uncertainty (Rolf et al., 2022) [2]. Uncertainty of customer demand and unpredictable disturbances, such as short product life cycles and global sourcing, are challenges or problems that make supply chain management ineffective, unstable, vulnerable, and turbulent (Boskabadi et al., 2022; Chen et al., 2022; Roh et al., 2022) [3–5]. The application of supply chain design models has primarily failed to consider carbon emissions throughout cost minimization processes. However, many studies, including Zhu et al. (2015), Large et al. (2016), Abir et al. (2019), and Arani et al. (2020) [6–9], are among those recently taking into account eco-friendly production, hence considering carbon emissions and optimizing total costs.

The supply chain network has been known as a critically important aspect of supply chain management, affecting the chain's efficiency and effectiveness for many years. In a general classification, supply chain management is evaluated through two forward and reverse supply chain (FSC and RSC, respectively) approaches. The former includes a set of activities from the raw material to product conversion processes (Jabbarzadeh et al., 2018) [10], while the latter is defined as the returned products' collection and recovery within SCM. This FSC and RSC combination leads to CLSC formation (Devika et al., 2014) [11], which includes customers, collection centers, recycling, and destruction of used products. This chain focuses on collecting, inspecting, and sending the returned products from the customer to the relevant centers for recycling and destruction. Determining the location of the construction of recycling and destruction centers, along with operational variables such as the flow of returned materials, is one of the decision variables of these types of networks. The issue of integration in CLSC network design involves simultaneously determining the strategic and operational decisions of the two chain types (Farrokh et al., 2018) [12]. The reverse logistics order starts from the customer to first-class warehouses, then to second-class warehouses, and finally to the factory or other destinations. In this reverse logistics process, secondary warehouses play a role in recycling, classification, inspection, and transportation. First-class warehouses take responsibility for concentration, disposal, and transportation (Liu et al., 2018) [13]. The main goal in the CLSC network design problem is to maximize the profit of the entire supply chain by choosing the optimal number and location of facilities, their capacities, and the flow (direct and return) of products between facilities, while at the same time reducing environmental impact (through recycling or destruction of reciprocating products) and maximizing social benefits (Mohtashami et al., 2020) [14].

CLSC design comprises the location, number, and capacity determination of facilities and material flow through the network, all of which affect the flexibility, efficiency, and performance of the chains significantly (Rezae and Kheirkhah, 2017) [15]. Effectively designed CLSCs can help reduce adverse environmental effects caused by human intervention substantially (Garai et al., 2021) [16]. Through CLSC design, the chain of network processes helps reduce waste through reuse or recycling. In line with environmental priorities, economic savings also attract attention to the CLSC.

Considering the role of CLSC in improving the sustainable development process, this paper uses a supply chain model with four objective functions. Thus, the main contributions of the presented research paper include the following:

- Presenting a mathematical model of a CLSC encompassing the vectors of destruction and recycling of products under cost, time, pollutant, and risk reduction conditions.
- Considering the parts related to destruction and recycling under conditions of uncertainty, depending on the quality of the products, within a CLSC. Hence, the quality level of the returned products from the customer's side is evaluated, and based on the evaluation results, decisions are made regarding recycling or destruction.

This paper has been organized as follows: Section 2 discusses the literature review and research investigating CLSC management. Section 3 discusses the mathematical modeling and the developed method. In Section 4, we present the results obtained by implementing the presented method and compare the results with other methods. Ultimately, Section 5 provides the research conclusions.

2. Literature Review

To date, significant research has been allocated to the investigation of CLSC modeling and optimization. In this section, the most important articles from recent years are examined. Jerbiaa et al. (2018) investigated the CLSC network with multi-component recycling options, formulating deterministic problems with integer programming [17]. Their results showed that the solutions for stochastic problems are stable. Also, when using the stochastic model, the profit increased. Mohtashami et al. (2020) introduced a green CLSC design utilizing a queuing system to alleviate environmental impacts and energy consumption [14]. Their paper focused on designing a green supply chain under forward and reverse logistics and utilizing a queuing system to optimize transportation time and fleet network waiting, finally reducing environmental impacts. Santander et al. (2020) investigated a CLSC network for local and distributed plastic recycling for 3D printing [18]. Their research examined the economic and environmental dimensions of distributed plastic recycling from the perspective of logistics, validating their method. Goodarzian et al. (2020) introduced a novel mixed-integer multi-objective linear programming model in a drug supply chain network [19]. Their problem formulation of the Mixed Integer Linear Programming (MILP) model focused on minimizing economic costs and environmental impact while maximizing social outcomes. Zarbakhshnia et al. (2020) presented a multi-product, multi-stage, multi-period, and multi-objective MILP model for a forward and reverse logistics network problem [20]. Nasr et al. (2021) developed a multi-objective, multi-product, multi-period mathematical model within a sustainable CLSC, locating distribution, collection, recycling, and disposal centers while taking into account risk criteria [21]. The main objective of their study was to minimize total costs, along with reducing negative environmental outcomes and promoting social responsibility to provide more job opportunities. A fuzzy inference system was used to model and determine uncertainty in demand and parameters that are dependent on demand. Jian et al. (2021) introduced a green package SC comprising a manufacturer and a retailer and solved it using the Stackelberg game approach [22]. Their results showed that profit-sharing contracts improved the relationship between supply chain members, ensuring sustainable economic and environmental growth. Tavana et al. (2022) presented an inclusive framework for a sustainable CLSC network using the multi-objective MILP (MOMILP) model [23]. This study considered the design of stable CLSC networks with interconnection, location-inventory-routing, time window, supplier selection, order allocation, and transportation with simultaneous pickup and delivery in uncertain conditions. Cheng et al. (2022) examined optimal procedures regarding a CLSC network under economic constraints and greenhouse gas (GHG) emission control [24]. This paper investigated how related parameters, including carbon quotas, consumers' low carbon preferences, and recovery rates, affected the network status. Kouchaki Tajani et al. (2022) proposed a two-channel network of sustainable CLSC for rice, taking into account energy resources and consumption taxes [25]. Their paper sought to formulate an MILP model optimizing total costs, the number of pollutants, as well as job opportunities throughout the introduced SC network considering cost, supply, and demand uncertainties. Babaeinesami et al. (2022) developed a CLSC network considering the suppliers, assembly centers, retailers, customers, collection centers, refurbishing centers, disassembly centers, and disposal centers [26]. Their paper focused on designing a distribution network according to customer demands for simultaneous total cost and total CO_2 emission minimization. Alinezhad et al. (2022) presented a stable CLSC network under uncertainty according to fuzzy theory [27]. Their network was a multi-period multi-product problem formed utilizing a two-objective MILP model with fuzzy demand and return rates for SC profit and customer satisfaction maximization. Bathaee et al. (2023) developed an SLSC network, including used product collection as well as new product distribution [28]. The designed mathematical model included three objective functions: profit maximization, total risk minimization, and product scarcity. Wang et al. (2021) conducted a study on complex manufacturing planning (MP) tasks, aiming to optimize order fulfillment rates and minimize total costs [29]. To address the challenges of large-scale problems, they introduced a novel interactive multi-objective optimization-based MP system. This system utilizes a two-stage multi-objective optimization algorithm (TSMOA). Leung et al. (2020) addressed challenges faced by existing metaheuristic approaches like MOPSOs in solving problems with more than three objectives by introducing HGLSS, a Hybrid Global Leader Selection Strategy [30]. HGLSS incorporates two leader selection mechanisms for exploration and exploitation, enabling each particle to select its global best leader. Bahrampour et al. (2023) presented a novel nonlinear mathematical programming model using the mixed integer approach for sustainable CLSC design problem formulation [31]. Their article evaluated the CLSC model from three aspects of sustainability: social, environmental, as well as economic impacts. Wu et al. (2023) evaluated the choice of recycling channels in CLSCs, taking into account the retailer's competitive preferences [32]. The authors particularly considered the retailer's competitive preferences and made conclusions based on the three-channel structure of CLSC. They also examined the manufacturer's, the retailer's, and the third-party recycling channels (M, R, and T channels, respectively). Dey and Giri (2023) elaborated on a CLSC with two-channel waste recycling considering corporate social responsibility [33]. In their article, various game theory models were used to optimize design and reduce the economic costs of the model. In the following, the literature review summary is illustrated in Table 1.

Table 1. Literature review summary.

References	Objectives					Return System Type		Condition		Product Type	
	Cost	Time	Environment	Risk	Social	Recycling	Destruction	Certain	Uncertainty	Perishable	Imperishable
Jerbiaa et al. (2018) [17]	✓					✓		✓		✓	
Mohtashami et al. (2020) [14]		✓	✓			✓			✓		✓
Santander et al. (2020) [18]	✓		✓						✓		✓
Goodarzian et al. (2020) [19]	✓		✓		✓		✓	✓		✓	
Zarbakhshnia et al. (2020) [20]	✓	✓			✓	✓		✓			✓
Nasr et al. (2021) [21]	✓		✓		✓				✓		✓
Jian et al. (2021) [22]	✓		✓						✓	✓	
Tavana et al. (2022) [23]	✓	✓	✓						✓		✓
Cheng et al. (2022) [24]	✓		✓						✓		✓
Kouchaki Tajani et al. (2022) [25]	✓		✓	✓					✓	✓	
Babaeinesami et al. (2022) [26]	✓		✓			✓	✓		✓		✓
Alinezhad et al. (2022) [27]	✓			✓					✓	✓	
Bathaee et al. (2023) [28]	✓			✓				✓			✓
Bahrampour et al. (2023) [31]	✓		✓		✓				✓		✓
Wu et al. (2023) [32]	✓		✓			✓		✓			✓
Dey and Giri (2023) [33]	✓				✓	✓		✓			✓
Present Study	✓	✓	✓	✓		✓	✓		✓	✓	

3. Mathematical Modeling

Figure 1 highlights the schematic of the problem's mathematical model.

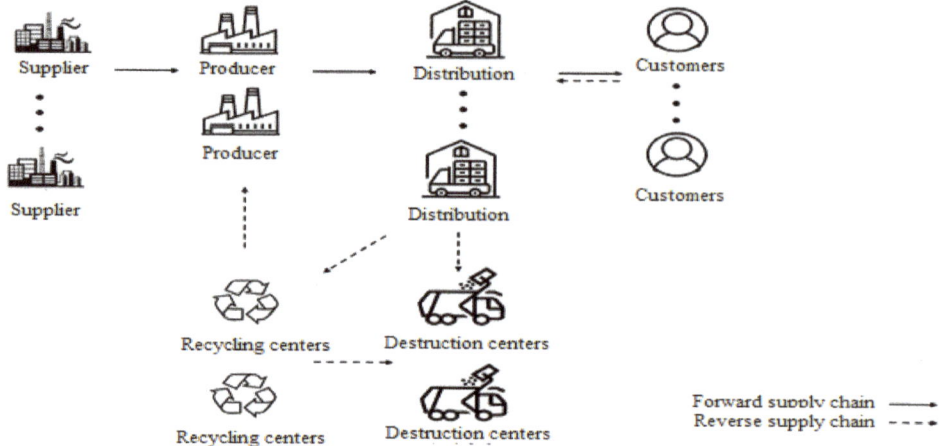

Figure 1. The schematic of the developed model.

3.1. Proposed Model Assumptions

The recent suppositions provided below formed the basis of the research model:

1. The problem represents a multi-objective, single-period, and multi-product model.
2. All customer demands must be met.
3. Material flow can only be established between two different levels of the network, and there is no material flow between facilities in one layer.
4. The capacity of the facility is limited.
5. The suppliers' location, production, distribution, collection, recycling, annihilation centers, and customers are known.
6. A part of returned products is recycled in the reverse supply chain and returned back into the chain, while part of it is excreted and removed from the network.
7. The packaging products' sales volume is usually greater than that of individual sold goods due to the lower price of packaging products than the total price of individual items combined.
8. The productive–technical risk considered in the proposed network model includes interruptions caused by equipment failure and a shortage of skilled labor.
9. Considering the uncertainties of demand in the real world, customer demand is uncertain in the model as well.
10. The amount of products returned from customers and the rates of recycling and destruction are considered uncertain. Disposal refers to the return of a product that enters the recycling stage, but destruction means returning the product to the destruction center. In fact, a product that cannot be recycled is transferred to the destruction center instead of the disposal center.

3.2. Notations and Formulations

The research model is introduced using the following related notations:

➢ **Sets:**

T	The entire sales period
s	Suppliers set $(s = 1, \ldots, N)$
i	Products set $(i = 1, \ldots, N)$
f	Production centers $(f = 1, 2)$
μ	Customers $(\mu = 1, \ldots, N)$
dc	Distribution-collection centers $(dc = 1, \ldots, N)$

di	Annihilation centers ($di = 1, 2$)
r	Recycling centers ($r = 1, 2$)
k	Staff ($k = 1, \ldots, N$)
l	Equipment set ($l = 1, \ldots, N$)
m	Vehicle types ($m = 1, \ldots, N$)
t	Decision cycle, pricing, and packaging phases ($t = 1, \ldots, N$)

➤ **Parameters:**

$n_{i,t}$	Number of type i products produced in period t
c_i	Inventory cost of type i product per decision period
$S_{i,t}$	Product i inventory in period t
q_i	Product i logistics cost
f_s	Purchasing costs for each raw material unit from supplier s
tr_{msf}	Raw material transportation costs from supplier s to production center f utilizing type m vehicle depending on distance
tr_{mfdc}	Product transportation costs from the production center f to the distribution-collection center dc by type m vehicle depending on distance
$tr_{mdc\mu}$	Product transportation costs from the distribution–collection center dc to customer μ by type m vehicle depending on distance
$tr_{m\mu dc}$	Transportation costs for the returned products from customer μ to the distribution–collection center dc by type m vehicle depending on distance
tr_{mdcr}	Transportation costs for the returned products from the distribution–collection center dc to the recycling center r by type m vehicle depending on distance
tr_{mdcdi}	Transportation costs for the returned products from the distribution–collection center dc to the annihilation center di by type m vehicle depending on distance
tr_{mrf}	Transportation costs for the recycled products from the recycling center r to the production center f by type m vehicle depending on distance
tr_{mrdi}	Transportation costs for the returned products from the recycling center r to the annihilation center di by type m vehicle depending on distance
C_h	Maintenance costs of type i products in the distribution–collection center dc
C_N	Equipment repair and maintenance costs
C_{tr}	Cost of staff training
C_{ri}	Recycling costs of type i products at the recycling center r
C_{di}	Costs of annihilating type i products in the annihilation center di
C_d	Delay costs per time
f_R	Inspection costs for each returned product unit in the distribution–collection center dc
f_H	Purchasing costs for each unit of type i product from customer μ
C_{rentm}	Renting costs for a car type m
C_{bm}	Purchasing costs for a car type m
T_{if_1d}	Person–hour needed to manufacture each type i product unit at the first production center
T_{if_2d}	Person–hour needed to manufacture each type i product unit at the second production center
T_{w_1}	Working hours during the order period at the first production center
T_{w_2}	Working hours during the order period at the second production center
k_{a_1}	Number of existing workers in the first production center
k_{a_2}	Number of existing workers in the second production center
k_{e_1}	Number of hired workers in the first production center
k_{e_2}	Number of hired workers in the second production center
e_{sf}	Transport-related CO_2 emission rates from supplier s to the production center of f per product unit
e_{fdc}	Transport-related CO_2 emission rates from the production center f to the distribution–collection center dc per product unit
$e_{dc\mu}$	Transport-related CO_2 emission rates from the distribution–collection center dc to customer μ per product unit
$e_{\mu dc}$	Transport-related CO_2 emission rates from customer μ to the distribution–collection center dc per product unit
e_{dcr}	Transport-related CO_2 emission rates from the distribution–collection center dc to the recycling center r per product unit

Symbol	Description
e_{rf}	Transport-related CO_2 emission rates from the recycling center r to the production center f per product unit
e_{rdi}	Transport-related CO_2 emission rates from the recycling center r to the annihilation center di per product unit
e_{dcdi}	Transport-related CO_2 emission rates from the distribution–collection center dc to the annihilation center di per product unit
e_i	CO_2 emission rates for producing each type i product unit
e_{ri}	CO_2 emission rates for the recycling process of each type i returned product unit
e_{dii}	CO_2 emission rates for the annihilation process of each type i returned product unit
e_{dc}	CO_2 emission rates for the returned product inspection process in the distribution–collection center dc
d_{sf}	Supplier s to the production center f distance
d_{fdc}	Production center f to the distribution–collection center dc distance
$d_{dc\mu}$	Distribution–collection center dc to client μ distance
$d_{\mu dc}$	Client μ to the distribution–collection center dc distance
d_{dcr}	Distribution–collection center dc to the recycling center r distance
d_{rf}	Recycling center r to the production center f distance
d_{rdi}	Recycling center r to the annihilation center di distance
d_{dcdi}	Distribution–collection center dc to the annihilation center di distance
Ca_s	Maximum capacity for supplier s
Ca_f	Maximum capacity for the production center f
Ca_{dc}	Maximum capacity for the distribution–collection center dc
Ca_r	Maximum capacity for the recycling center r
Ca_{di}	Maximum capacity for the annihilation center di
G	Maximum allowable CO_2 emissions from production
M_R	Maximum allowable production–technical risk
t_k	Maximum acceptable delivery time for customer μ
d_μ	Customer demand
d_f	Raw materials' demand of the production center f from supplier s
R_l	Device L failure risk
T_{ei}	CO_2 emission rate of total production at the production center
t_t	Total time from supplying raw materials from supplier s to sending final product to customer μ
t_{sf}	Length of time for supplying raw materials from supplier s to the production center f
t_{fdc}	Length of time for finished products to be sent from the production center f to the distribution–collection center dc
$t_{dc\mu}$	Length of time for sending the finished product from the distribution–collection center dc to customer μ
α	Product return rate
β	Product return rate from the distribution–collection center dc to the annihilation center di
γ	Product return rate from the distribution–collection center dc to the recycling center r
λ	Recycled product sending rate from the recycling center r to the production center f
τ	Recycled product sending rate from the recycling center r to the annihilation center di
$q_{s\mu}$	Customer μ expected quality
q_{sdcdi}	Quality level of the product that leads to transfer from the distribution–collection center dc to the annihilation center di
q_{sdcr}	Quality level of the product that leads to transfer from the distribution–collection center dc to the recycling center r
q_{srdi}	Quality level of the product level that leads to transfer from the recycling center r to the annihilation center di

Model's Decision Variables

The proposed mathematical model has two types of decision variables. The first category includes non-zero continuous decision variables to determine the material and product flow between different facilities and the number of employees in each production facility, while also determining the time period of product delivery between various facilities in the direct supply chain. The second category consists of zero and one variables, which are used to select facilities, automobiles, and equipment for production centers.

➢ **Continuous Decision Variables:**

$p_{i,t}$	Sale price of product i in cycle t
Y_{sf}	Raw material amounts sent from supplier s to the production center f
Y_{ifdc}	Type i product amounts sent from the production center f to the distribution–collection center dc
$Y_{idc\mu}$	Type i product amounts sent from the distribution–collection center dc to customer μ
$Y_{i\mu dc}$	Type i product amounts sent from customer μ to the distribution–collection center dc
Y_{idcr}	Type i product amounts delivered from the distribution–collection center dc to the recycling center r
Y_{irf}	Recycled product amounts delivered from the recycling center r to the production center f
Y_{irdi}	Product amounts delivered from the recycling center r to the annihilation center di
Y_{idcdi}	Returned product amounts delivered from the distribution–collection center dc to the annihilation center di
t_{sf}	Time to send raw materials from supplier s to the production center f
t_{fdc}	Time to send product from the production center f to the distribution–collection center dc
$t_{dc\mu}$	Time to send product from the distribution–collection center dc to customer μ
r_μ^i	Returned rate of product i with quality level qs from customer μ
$x_{\mu dc.q_s}$	Returned product amounts considering quality level q_s from customer μ to the distribution–collection center dc

➢ **Binary Variables:**

X_s	If supplier s is chosen, it is equal to 1; otherwise, it equals 0.
X_f	If the production center f is chosen, it is equal to 1; otherwise, it equals 0.
X_{dc}	If the distribution–collection center dc is chosen, it is equal to 1; otherwise, it equals 0.
X_μ	If customer μ is chosen, it is equal to 1; otherwise, it equals 0.
X_r	If the recycling center r is chosen, it is equal to 1; otherwise, it equals 0.
X_{di}	If the annihilation center di is chosen, it is equal to 1; otherwise, it equals 0.
X_v	If the vehicle type m is sent, it is equal to 1; otherwise, it equals 0.
X_{rm}	If the vehicle type m is rented, it is equal to 1; otherwise, it equals 0.
X_{im}	If the vehicle type m is purchased, it is equal to 1; otherwise, it equals 0.
X_l	If equipment l is used, it is equal to 1; otherwise, it equals 0.

3.3. Objective Functions

The study addresses a multi-objective, single-period, and multi-product model within a closed-loop supply chain network. The network design integrates environmental factors and imposes restrictions on material flow across different network levels. Facilities have limited capacities, and a dual-purpose location is implemented to minimize network costs for product distribution and collection. The locations of suppliers, production centers, distribution and collection centers, recycling centers, annihilation centers, and customers are known. The network consists of two production centers, two annihilation centers, two recycling centers, and various suppliers and distribution and collection centers. The reverse supply chain partially recycles returned products while removing the remaining ones from the network. Meeting specific inventory targets within a fixed sales period is crucial, particularly for perishable products. Packaging products have higher sales volumes due to their lower price compared to individual items. The total costs encompass several components, including sales, logistics, production, raw material procurement, transportation, delay, inventory, staff training, equipment maintenance, inspection, and recycling and annihilation costs. The model incorporates productive–technical risks associated with equipment failure and labor shortages. Uncertainty is considered in customer demand, product returns, recycling rates, and destruction. Greenhouse gas emissions are accounted for in production, transportation, and inspection processes throughout the supply chain network. The proposed model of the present study has four objective functions, all of which aim for minimization. Objective function (1) presented below, calculates and minimizes all network costs.

$$
\begin{aligned}
\text{Min } Z_1 = &\left(\sum_{t \in N} \sum_{i \in N} p_{i,t} n_{i,t} + \sum_{i \in N} S_{i,0} q_i + \sum_{t \in N} \sum_{i \in N} S_{i,t} - n_{i,t} c_i + \sum_{s \in S} \sum_{f \in F} f_s Y_{sf} X_s X_f \right) + \sum_{i \in N} \sum_{f \in F} c_i n_i X_f \\
&+ \sum_{i \in N} \sum_{\mu \in N} \sum_{dc \in DC} f_H Y_{i\mu dc} X_{dc} + \sum_{i \in N} \sum_{\mu \in N} \sum_{dc \in DC} f_R Y_{i\mu dc} X_{dc} + \sum_{i \in Nr} \sum_{Rdc \in DC} C_{ri} Y_{idcr} X_r \\
&+ \sum_{i \in N} \sum_{di \in i} C_{di} (Y_{idcdi} + Y_{irdi}) X_{di} + \sum_{l \in L} C_N X_l + \sum_{\mu \in N} \sum_{i \in N} \sum_{dc \in DC} C_d \max(0, t_t - t_k) Y_{idc\mu} \\
&+ \sum_{m \in M} \sum_{s \in S} \sum_{f \in F} tr_{msf} d_{sf} Y_{sf} X_s X_f + \sum_{m \in M} \sum_{i \in N} \sum_{dc \in DC} \sum_{f \in F} tr_{mfdc} d_{fdc} Y_{ifdc} X_{dc} X_f \\
&+ \sum_{m \in M} \sum_{i \in N} \sum_{\mu \in N} \sum_{dc \in DC} tr_{mdc\mu} d_{dc\mu} Y_{idc\mu} X_{dc} X_\mu + \sum_{m \in M} \sum_{i \in N} \sum_{\mu \in N} \sum_{dc \in DC} tr_{m\mu dc} d_{\mu dc} Y_{i\mu dc} X_{dc} X_\mu \\
&+ \sum_{m \in M} \sum_{i \in N} \sum_{r \in Nr} \sum_{Rdc \in DC} tr_{mdcr} d_{dcr} Y_{idcr} X_{dc} X_r + \sum_{m \in M} \sum_{r \in Ri} \sum_{i \in N} \sum_{f \in F} tr_{mrf} d_{rf} Y_{irf} X_r X_f \\
&+ \sum_{m \in M} \sum_{i \in N} \sum_{r \in Nr} \sum_{Rdi \in DI} tr_{mrdi} d_{rdi} Y_{irdi} X_{di} X_r + \sum_{m \in M} \sum_{i \in N} \sum_{r \in Nr} \sum_{Rdc \in DC} tr_{mdcdi} d_{dcdi} Y_{idcdi} X_{di} X_{dc} \\
&+ \sum_{i \in N} \sum_{dc \in DC} \sum_{f \in F} C_h Y_{idfc} X_{dc} + \sum_{m \in M} C_{rentm} X_{rm} + \sum_{m \in M} C_{bm} X_{im} + \sum_{k_{e_1} \in K} \sum_{k_{e_2} \in K} C_{tr}(k_{e_1} + k_{e_2})
\end{aligned}
\tag{1}
$$

The first statement represents the cost of sales and logistics of product *i* based on inventory levels, costs, and raw material purchasing costs from supplier *s*. The second statement represents the production costs of each product unit. The third and fourth statements represent the purchasing costs of each product unit returned from customers and the inspection costs of each returned product unit in the distribution–collection center, respectively. The fifth and sixth statements represent the recycling costs of each returned product unit and the annihilating costs of each returned and unrecyclable product unit, respectively. The seventh and eighth statements represent the cost of equipment repairs and maintenance, and the cost of delaying product delivery per unit of time, respectively. The ninth to sixteenth statements, respectively, represent the raw material transportation costs from suppliers to production centers, products transported from production to distribution–collection centers, products from distribution–collection centers to customers' locations, returned products transported from customers to distribution–collection centers, products from distribution–collection centers to recycling centers, products from recycling centers to production centers, products from recycling centers to annihilation centers, and products from distribution–collection centers to annihilation centers. The seventeenth statement represents maintenance costs in distribution–collection centers, and the eighteenth and nineteenth statements indicate the cost of renting and purchasing cars for transporting raw materials and products between facilities, respectively. Lastly, the twentieth statement is equivalent to the cost of training staff.

$$
\begin{aligned}
\text{Min } Z_2 = & \sum_{i \in N} n_i e_i + \sum_{i \in Nr} \sum_{r \in R} Y_{idcr} e_{ri} + \sum_{i \in N} \sum_{di \in DI} \sum_{r \in R} (Y_{idcdi} + Y_{irdi}) e_{dii} + \sum_{i \in N} \sum_{dc \in DC} Y_{i\mu dc} e_{dc} + \sum_{m \in M} \sum_{s \in S} \sum_{f \in F} Y_{sf} e_{sf} X_v \\
&+ \sum_{m \in M} \sum_{i \in N} \sum_{dc \in DC} \sum_{f \in F} Y_{ifdc} e_{fdc} X_v + \sum_{m \in M} \sum_{i \in N} \sum_{dc \in DC} \sum_{c \in C} Y_{idc\mu} e_{dc\mu} X_v \\
&+ \sum_{m \in M} \sum_{i \in N} \sum_{\mu \in N} \sum_{dc \in DC} Y_{i\mu dc} e_{\mu dc} X_v + \sum_{m \in M} \sum_{i \in N} \sum_{dc \in DC} \sum_{r \in R} Y_{idcr} e_{dcr} X_v + \sum_{m \in M} \sum_{i \in N} \sum_{r \in Nr} \sum_{f \in F} Y_{irf} e_{rf} X_v \\
&+ \sum_{m \in M} \sum_{i \in N} \sum_{r \in Nr} \sum_{Rdi \in DI} Y_{irdi} e_{rdi} X_v + \sum_{m \in M} \sum_{i \in N} \sum_{dc \in DC} \sum_{di \in DI} Y_{idcdi} e_{dcdi} X_v
\end{aligned}
\tag{2}
$$

Objective function (2) aims to minimize greenhouse gas emissions from different supply chain network processes. The first and second statements indicate the amount of emissions caused by the production process of products in production centers and the amount of emissions caused by the process of recycling, respectively. The third and fourth statements indicate the amount of emissions caused by the annihilation process and the amount of emissions caused by the inspection process of returned products in distribution–collection centers, respectively. The fifth to twelfth terms also represent the amount of emissions from the transportation process: from suppliers to production centers, from production to distribution–collection centers, from distribution–collection centers to customers, from customers to distribution–collection centers for transporting returned products, from distribution–collection centers to recycling centers, from recycling centers to production centers, from recycling centers to annihilation centers, and from distribution–collection centers to annihilation centers.

$$\text{Min } Z_3 = \sum_{l \in L} R_l X_l \qquad (3)$$

Objective function (3) aims to minimize the risk of device failure. This function is aimed at minimizing production–technical risk, which is the most critical risk in the green supply chain. As mentioned in the model assumptions, two factors of interruption, caused by equipment failure and a shortage of skilled labor, are considered as the main causes of production–technical risk. The repair and maintenance of network equipment seem necessary and inevitable to minimize the interruption caused by equipment failure. Therefore, the costs for repairing and maintaining equipment in the network to prevent equipment failure or reduce downtime are considered and modeled in objective function (1). Also, staff training is considered an effective solution to solve the problem of the shortage of skilled labor, so costs for training employees to compensate for this shortfall and increase the skills of employees are modeled in objective function (1):

$$\text{Min } Z_4 = \sum_{s \in S} \sum_{f \in F} t_{sf} X_f + \sum_{f \in F} \sum_{dc \in DC} t_{fdc} X_{dc} + \sum_{dc \in DC} \sum_{\mu \in N} t_{dc\mu} X_\mu \qquad (4)$$

The fourth objective function aims to minimize product delivery time. The first to last statements indicate time taken for raw materials to be sent from the supplier to the production center, the time taken for products to be sent from production to distribution–collection centers, and the time taken for products to be sent from distribution–collection centers to customers, respectively.

3.4. Constraints

In the following, the constraints of the whole system is described in detail.

$$\sum_{s \in S} X_s Y_{sf} \leq Ca_s \qquad (5)$$

The amount of raw materials sent from suppliers should be smaller than their capacity.

$$\sum_{f \in Fi} \sum_{i \in N} \sum_{dc \in DC} \sum_{\mu \in N} \left(Y_{ifdc} + Y_{i\mu dc} \right) X_{dc} \leq Ca_{dc} \qquad (6)$$

The amount of products entering distribution–collection centers should be smaller than their capacity.

$$\sum_{\mu \in N} \sum_{i \in N} \sum_{dc \in DC} Y_{idc\mu} X_{dc} \geq \sum_{\mu \in N} d_\mu \qquad (7)$$

All customer requests must be satisfied.

$$\sum_{i \in Nr} \sum_{r \in R} \sum_{dc \in DC} Y_{idcr} X_r \leq Ca_r \qquad (8)$$

The total amount of goods sent from distribution–collection to recycling centers should be smaller than the capacity of recycling centers.

$$\sum_{i \in Nr} \sum_{r \in R} \sum_{f \in F} Y_{irf} X_r \leq Ca_f \quad (9)$$

The total amount of products delivered from recycling centers to production centers must be smaller than the production center's capacity.

$$\sum_{i \in Ndc} \sum_{dc \in DC} \sum_{r \in R} \sum_{di \in DI} Y_{idcdi} X_{dc} X_{di} + Y_{irdi} X_{di} X_r \leq Ca_{di} \quad (10)$$

The total amount of goods sent to annihilation centers should be smaller than the capacity of annihilation centers.

$$\sum_{f \in Fs} \sum_{s \in S} X_s Y_{sf} \geq d_f \quad (11)$$

The amount of raw materials sent from the suppliers to the production centers should be large enough to meet the demands of the production center.

$$\sum_{i \in Ndc} \sum_{dc \in DC} \sum_{\mu \in N} Y_{i\mu dc} = \sum_{\mu \in N} \sum_{i \in Ni} \sum_{dc \in DC} \alpha Y_{idc\mu} \quad (12)$$

The total amount of returned products from customers to distribution–collection centers should be α% of the total products sent to customers.

$$\sum_{i \in Ndc} \sum_{dc \in DC} \sum_{f \in F} Y_{ifdc} = \sum_{i \in N} N_i \quad (13)$$

The total number of type i products delivered from the production centers to distribution centers must equal the total production of type i products.

$$\sum_{i \in Ndc} \sum_{dc \in DC} \sum_{di \in DI} Y_{idcdi} = \sum_{i \in N} \sum_{\mu \in N} \sum_{dc \in DC} \beta Y_{i\mu dc} \quad (14)$$

The total product delivered from the distribution–collection centers to annihilation centers can be represented as β% of the total returned products sent from customers to distribution–collection centers.

$$\sum_{i \in Ndc} \sum_{dc \in DC} \sum_{r \in R} Y_{idcr} = \sum_{i \in N} \sum_{\mu \in N} \sum_{dc \in DC} \gamma Y_{i\mu dc} \quad (15)$$

The total number of products sent from distribution–collection centers to recycling centers can be indicated as γ% of the total returned products sent from customers to distribution–collection centers.

$$\sum_{di \in DI} \sum_{i \in Nr} \sum_{r \in R} Y_{irdi} = \sum_{i \in Ndc} \sum_{dc \in DC} \sum_{r \in R} \tau Y_{idcr} \quad (16)$$

The total number of products sent from recycling centers to annihilation centers should be τ% of the total products sent from distribution–collection centers to recycling centers.

$$\sum_{i \in Ndc} \sum_{dc \in DC} \sum_{\mu \in N} \sum_{f \in F} Y_{ifdc} + Y_{i\mu dc} \geq \sum_{i \in Ndc} \sum_{dc \in DC} \sum_{\mu \in N} \sum_{r \in R} \sum_{di \in DI} Y_{idc\mu} + Y_{idcr} + Y_{idcdi} \quad (17)$$

The sum of products that enter distribution–collection centers must exceed the output sum from distribution–collection centers.

$$\sum_{i \in Nr} \sum_{r \in R} \sum_{f \in F} Y_{irf} = \sum_{i \in Ndc} \sum_{dc \in DC} \sum_{r \in R} \lambda Y_{idcr} \qquad (18)$$

The total product sent from recycling centers to production centers should be $\lambda\%$ of the total product amounts sent from distribution–collection centers to recycling centers.

$$\sum_{i \in Ndc} \sum_{dc \in DC} \sum_{r \in R} Y_{idcr} = \sum_{f \in Fi} \sum_{\in Nr} \sum_{r \in R} \sum_{di \in DI} Y_{irf} + Y_{irdi} \qquad (19)$$

The total product amounts entering recycling centers must equal the total output of recycling centers.

$$\sum_{i \in Ndc} \sum_{dc \in DC} \sum_{\mu \in N} Y_{idc\mu} = \sum_{i \in Ndc} \sum_{dc \in DC} \sum_{f \in F} Y_{ifdc} \qquad (20)$$

The sum of type i products delivered from distribution–collection centers to customers must equal the type i product total number sent from production centers to distribution–collection centers.

$$\sum_{m \in M} X_v \leq X_{rm} + X_{im} \qquad (21)$$

The total number of vehicles on the journey must be less than or equal to the total purchased and rental vehicles in the organization.

$$\sum_{l \in L} R_l \leq M_R \qquad (22)$$

Production–technical risk must be smaller than the maximum production–technical risk allowed.

$$\sum_{i \in N} T_{ei} \leq G \qquad (23)$$

The total CO_2 emission rate of production in production facilities should be less than the maximum allowable rate of CO_2 emissions from production.

$$t_t = t_{sf} + t_{fdc} + t_{dc\mu} \qquad (24)$$

The product delivery total time to the customer equals the total time for product transfer from the supplier to the production centers, the product transfer time from production centers to distribution–collection centers, and the product transfer time from distribution–collection centers to the customers.

$$\beta + \gamma + \lambda + \tau = 1 \qquad (25)$$

The above constraint ensures that the value of 1 is obtained for the sum of the returned products' coefficients.

$$\sum_{dc \in DC} \sum_{\mu \in N} x_{\mu dc.q_s} = r^i_\mu \qquad (26)$$

The above statement ensures the collection of all returned products from customer centers throughout the return process.

$$q_{sdcdi} + q_{sdcr} + q_{srdi} = q_{s\mu} \qquad (27)$$

The above statement ensures that the total product quality in the whole chain (except the product transfer stage from recycling centers to manufacturing centers) equals the original product quality.

$$\sum_{l \in Li} \sum_{i \in N} n_i X_l = \sum_{dc \in DC} \sum_{f \in Fi} \sum_{i \in N} Y_{ifdc} \qquad (28)$$

The total production of type i equipment in each production center equals the number of products delivered from the desired production center to distribution–collection centers.

$$\sum_{f \in Fi} \sum_{i \in N} T_{if_1 d} Y_{ifdc} \leq \sum_{k a_1 \in k} \sum_{k e_1 \in k} (k_{a_1} + k_{e_1}) T_{w_1} \qquad (29)$$

Person–hours needed to manufacture each product type i unit in the first production center should be supplied by the existing labor force and by hiring new labor in case of shortages.

$$\sum_{f \in Fi} \sum_{i \in N} T_{if_2 d} Y_{ifdc} \leq \sum_{k a_2 \in k} \sum_{k e_2 \in k} (k_{a_2} + k_{e_2}) T_{w_2} \qquad (30)$$

Person–hours needed to manufacture each product type i unit in the second production center should be supplied by the existing labor force and by hiring new labor in case of shortages.

$$Y_{sf}, Y_{ifdc}, Y_{idc\mu}, Y_{i\mu dc}, Y_{idcr}, Y_{irf}, Y_{irdi}, Y_{idcdi}, t_{sf}, t_{fdc}, t_{dc\mu}, r^i_\mu, x_{\mu dc.q_s} > 0 \qquad (31)$$

$$X_s, X_f, X_{dc}, X_\mu, X_r, X_{di}, X_v, X_{rm}, X_{im}, X_l \in \{0, 1\} \qquad (32)$$

These two constraints ensure that the mentioned parameters and variables are positive and between zero and one, respectively.

$$t_{sf.min} \leq t_{sf} \leq t_{sf.max} \qquad (33)$$

This constraint ensures that the time spent on raw material sending from supplier s to the production center f must be within the time frame set by the production center f.

$$t_{fdc.min} \leq t_{fdc} \leq t_{fdc.max} \qquad (34)$$

This constraint ensures that the time it takes to send final products from the production center f to the distribution–collection center dc must be within the time frame set by the distribution–collection center dc.

$$t_{dc\mu.min} \leq t_{dc\mu} \leq t_{dc\mu.max} \qquad (35)$$

This constraint ensures that the time it takes to send final products from the distribution–collection center dc to customer μ must be within the time frame set by customer μ.

$$\sum X_s, X_f, X_{dc}, X_r, X_{di}, X_v, X_{rm}, X_{im}, X_l \geq 1$$

$$\forall s \in S, \forall f \in F, \forall dc \in DC, \forall r \in R, \forall di \in DI, \forall m \in M, \forall l \in L \qquad (36)$$

This constraint ensures that at least one facility is used during the product transfer to the customer.

$$q_i + c_i \leq p_{i,t} \leq p_i^{max} \qquad (37)$$

This constraint ensures that pricing must be higher than the cost and below the maximum price reserved by consumers.

$$n_{i,t} \geq 0 \tag{38}$$

This constraint ensures that the volume of product sales in each decision cycle must be non-negative.

$$\sum n_{i,t} \leq S_i \tag{39}$$

This constraint is an indirect limiting condition to ensure that the sales volumes of the two types of products must be less than the total inventory.

$$max\{p_{1,t}, p_{2,t}\} < p_{3,t} < p_{1,t} + p_{2,t} \tag{40}$$

According to the bundling strategy, this constraint represents a package pricing that must be less than the sum of the separated pricing of two products and higher than the highest price of the two separate products sold. Otherwise, advertising through the bundling strategy is meaningless.

$$n_{3,t} < \min(S_{i,t}) \tag{41}$$

This constraint ensures that the sales volume of the bundling product must be less than the minimum inventory of two products.

$$\sum (n_{1,t} + n_{3,t}) \leq S_i, \sum (n_{2,t} + n_{3,t}) \leq S_i \tag{42}$$

This constraint is also a limited requirement to ensure that the sales volumes of two product types must be less than the total inventory.

4. Numerical Example and Results

4.1. Numerical Example

As a result of the NP-hard nature of the model and its computational complexity, it is not possible to solve it with exact methods. Hence, we will use a meta-heuristic algorithm to solve the model. Among multi-objective meta-heuristic algorithms, the NSGA-II algorithm has been selected in this research due to its significant advantages. The nature of this algorithm's random search in the problem space is considered a parallel search, because each of the random chromosomes generated by the algorithm is considered a new starting point for searching a part of the problem state space, and the search is conducted across all of them simultaneously. Also, due to the extensive dispersion of the points that are searched, it obtains favorable results for problems that have large search spaces. It is also considered a targeted random search and will reach different answers through different paths. In addition, it does not face any restrictions in the search and selection of random answers. Finally, due to competition among answers and selection of the best among the population, it will reach the global optimal point with a high probability. The proposed NSGA-II algorithm starts with a population initialization process that randomly generates populations with the values of each gene bounded by given values. Then, it uses a selection process to form a pool of parents to generate offspring using a crossover process. The genetic algorithm used in this research uses a simple crossover process that randomly selects two parents as parent1 and parent2 and then generates a random variable (r) from 0 to 1. The weight of this random variable is defined as R. We considered R as 0.8 and used $child = parent1 + r * R * (parent2 - parent1)$ to create each gene from a child. This is shown in Figure 2.

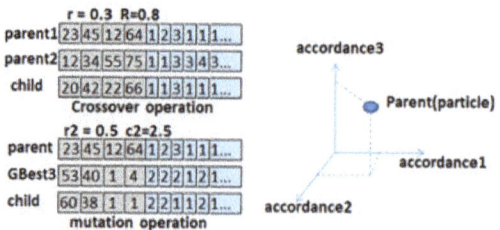

Figure 2. Crossover and mutation operators.

In the proposed NSGA-II algorithm, in order to improve population diversity and convergence speed, a combination of disorder mapping and conflict-based learning methods is used to generate the initial population. Also, an approach based on a penalty function is used for solutions that do not meet the time limit. This problem shows the differences between the proposed method and the classical NSGA-II and MOPSO methods.

The problem at hand is a multi-objective, single-period, multi-product green CLSC model. The settings for the NSGAII algorithm are presented in Table 2. It should be noted that the implementation of the proposed method was carried out using MATLAB version 2023 software, and the coding was performed on a system with a core i5 processor and 8 GB of RAM.

Table 2. Initial parameters of NSGA-II.

Parameter	Value
Population size	60
No. of generations	100
Selection method	Random
Non-dominant choice	Tournament DCD
Crossover method	Laplace
Probability of crossover	95%
Mutation method	Power
Probability of mutation	0.5%

Table 3 shows the initial values of some main parameters. These data were collected from a food packaging company in Tehran, Iran.

Table 3. Initial model parameters.

Parameter	Symbol	Value
Supplier	s	4
Production center	f	2
Distribution-collection center	Dc	5
Destruction center	Di	2
Recycling center	r	2
Customer	C	10
Staff	k	5
Set of products	p	3
Set of equipment	l	4
All vehicle types	m	3
Number of products produced	N_p	1000
Production costs per product unit	C_p	50,000
The costs of each raw material unit purchasing from the suppliers	f_s	10,000
The employee training costs	C_{tr}	1,200,000
Product recycling costs	C_{rp}	20,000
Product destruction costs	C_{di}	13,000
Inspection fee per returned product unit	F_{chp}	30,000

During the process of solving the model, some solutions were infeasible, which is due to the placement of the algorithm in local solutions. In order to overcome this issue, the proposed algorithm shifts from local mode and solves this problem under global conditions. The difference between feasible and infeasible solutions lies in establishing the necessary restrictions and conditions to solve the problem that is considered in the model.

Now, results related to all four objective functions have been obtained by setting the population number to 10, the operators' probability to 0.8, and the mutation operators' probability to 0.3. Nevertheless, as the developed model represents several different levels with 10 customers, five distributors, and two manufacturers (Table 3), the flow of products is determined considering the amount of customer demand. Hence, Table 4 illustrates the amount of demand for the 10 target customers separately.

Table 4. Customer demand values.

Customers	1	2	3	4	5	6	7	8	9	10
Demand	176	329	427	729	102	356	449	224	234	332

According to the above table, the first customer demands 176 pieces, the second demands 329 pieces, and so on until the end. It is necessary to note that the maximum time needed for product delivery to each customer without causing dissatisfaction is set at 120 h. Additionally, given the completely random determination of initial model values in problem-solving by the genetic algorithm (GA), unreasonable or infeasible solutions may arise, prompting the algorithm to promptly address the problem and find a practical answer. The above-mentioned process should be considered by the algorithm during 300 iterations. Table 5 presents the model implementation results with the genetic multi-objective algorithm for all four specific objectives.

Table 5. Problem-solving results with the genetic algorithm (NSGAII).

The Objective Function	Cost Objective Function ($)	Pollutant Emission Objective Function (PPM)	Risk Objective Function (%)	Time Objective Function (h)	Execution Time (s)
Value	10,981,185	11,744	0.27	117	14.5963

As shown in Table 5, the desired results are presented for the proposed model with a numerical example. The point that should be mentioned, regarding the presentation of results related to risk, is that in this research, supply chain risk assessment is related to two interruption factors: equipment failure and the lack of skilled labor, both considered the main factors contributing to production–technical risk. Any failure leads to an interruption in production of the product and increases the costs of the entire chain. Therefore, equipment maintenance costs and staff training costs are presented in the form of a cost model to compensate for this deficiency and increase the skills of employees. Therefore, by reducing risk, in addition to minimizing the delay in the production and shipping of the product, the costs of the entire chain are also reduced.

Tables 6 and 7 present the product transfer amounts from manufacturers to distributors and from distributors to customers to meet their expectations throughout the considered interval. The presented values highlight the desired figures to achieve the target functions' optimal amounts.

Based on Table 6, the first producer only transferred 1231 units of products to the fifth distributor, and the second producer only transferred 1853 units to the first distributor, 2 units to the third distributor, and 272 units to the fourth distributor. However, there have been no product deliveries to the second distributor. The issue that needs consideration is that the total customer demand, as indicated in Table 6, is 3358 units. As mentioned before, all demands should be answered. Therefore, the total amount of the provided products in Table 6 should equate to 3358 units as well. In addition, the maximum production capacities for the first and second producers were 1577 and 3071 units, adopting 1231 and 2127 units for each, respectively. In other words, the product amounts sent from manufacturers to distributors showed lower values than the manufacturers' maximum capacities. Table 7 presents the amounts of product transfers from each distributor to customers.

According to this table, the first customer takes all the demand of 176 units from the fourth distributor, and the ninth customer receives 9 and 225 product units from the first and second distributors, respectively, to satisfy its request of 234 units. As shown, each row's sum equals the total number of customer demands met.

Table 6. Transferring the products (units) from manufacturers to distributors.

	Distributors				
The first producer	0	0	0	0	1231
The second producer	1853	0	2	272	0

Table 7. Product transfer (units) from distributors to customers.

	Customers									
First Distributor	0	0	427	691	0	227	449	0	9	0
Second Distributor	0	0	0	0	0	0	0	0	0	0
Third Distributor	0	2	0	0	0	0	0	0	0	0
Fourth Distributor	176	0	0	0	96	0	0	0	0	0
Fifth Distributor	0	327	0	38	6	79	0	227	225	332

4.2. Different Sample Size Solution

Due to the complexity of the model and its limitations in the real world, this section aims to use different numerical multiples across different dimensions to make applications in the real world easier. So, in this section, we will examine the model's solution for various examples in small, medium, and large dimensions. Tables 8–10 highlight the findings for all four objective functions for all three problem dimensions.

Table 8. Objective function results for the problem in small dimensions.

Samples	1	2	3	4	5	6	7	8	9	10
Costumer No.	1	2	4	4	7	7	8	8	9	9
Distributer No.	2	2	2	3	3	4	4	4	5	5
Cost	103,813	104,190	104,938	109,889	110,440	120,444	133,912	145,530	145,838	147,781
Pollution (ppm)	350	384	399	450	459	632	885	935	1002	1027
Time (h)	7	8	10	13	19	25	39	44	68	75
Risk (%)	0.058	0.119	0.13	0.298	0.151	0.224	0.324	0.133	0.237	0.276

Table 9. Objective function results for the problem in medium dimensions.

Samples	1	2	3	4	5	6	7	8	9	10
Costumer No.	12	14	14	15	15	16	16	18	18	18
Distributer No.	6	6	7	7	8	8	9	12	13	14
Cost	1,086,833	1,180,532	1,209,745	1,222,165	1,232,836	1,295,891	1,302,785	1,339,529	1,344,999	1,377,401
Pollution (ppm)	1178	1208	1321	1342	1574	1622	1700	1765	1932	2120
Time (h)	50	51	52	62	64	69	73	77	80	84
Risk (%)	0.059	0.341	0.367	0.228	0.309	0.23	0.399	0.202	0.217	0.389

Table 10. Objective function results for the problem in large dimensions.

Samples	1	2	3	4	5	6	7	8	9	10
Costumer No.	30	45	50	50	60	65	65	70	70	70
Distributer No.	20	20	25	30	32	38	41	45	50	60
Cost	1,520,398	2,026,527	2,142,370	2,165,451	2,255,848	2,257,946	2,342,930	2,411,260	2,412,817	2,595,378
Pollution (ppm)	13,526	13,658	14,002	14,230	15,200	16,210	16,890	17,532	18,050	19,850
Time (h)	112	114	123	129	135	139	145	160	175	191
Risk (%)	0.177	0.346	0.443	0.303	0.391	0.408	0.479	0.587	0.599	0.631

Figures 3–6 are presented to compare the objective functions of cost, time, pollutant emission, and risk level, respectively, to better understand the results.

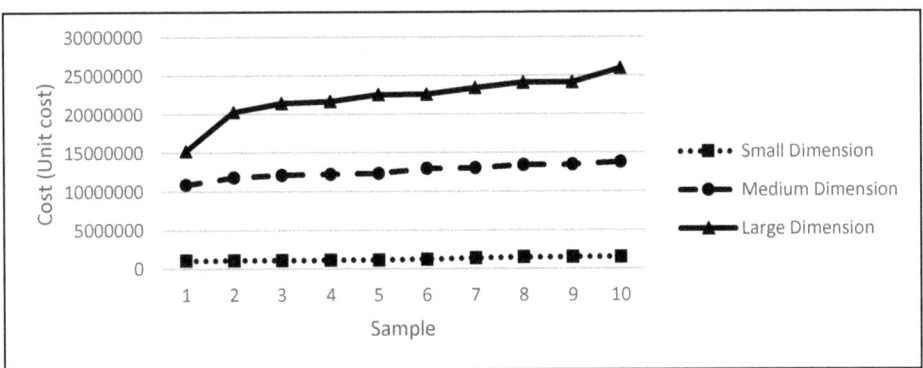

Figure 3. Comparison of costs in each dimension.

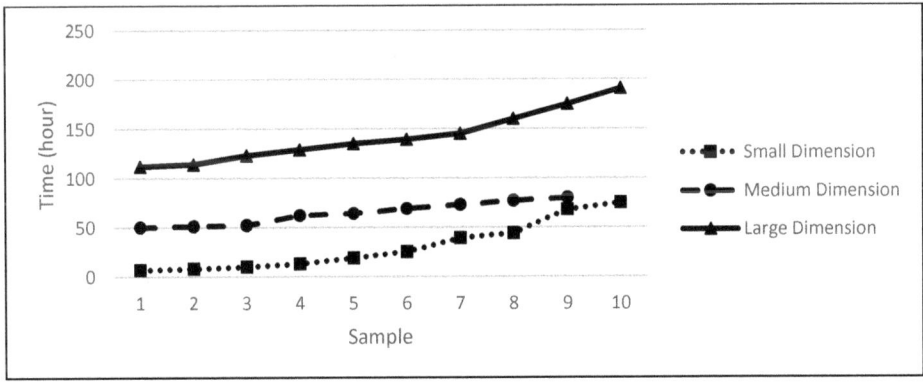

Figure 4. Comparison of times in each dimension.

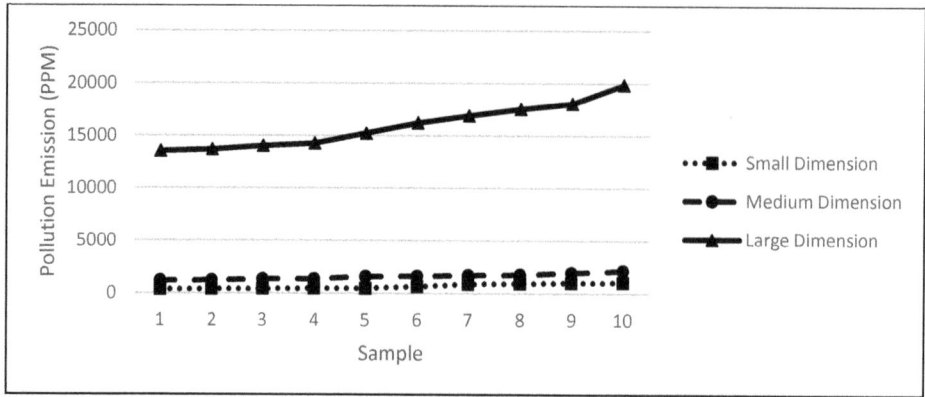

Figure 5. Comparison of pollution emissions in each dimension.

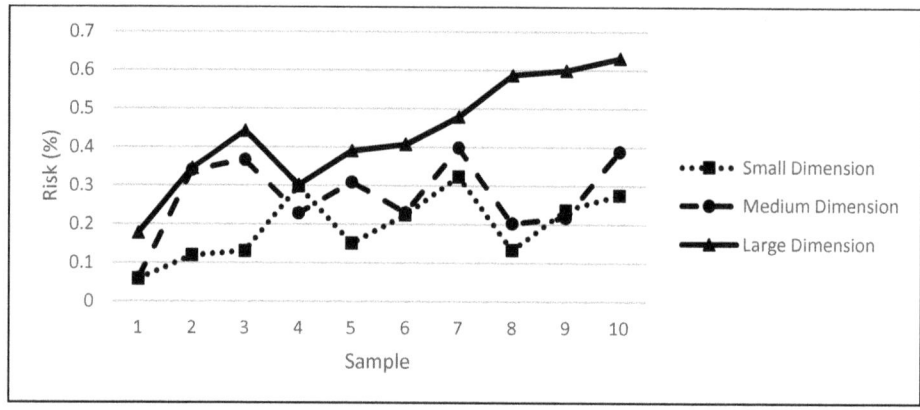

Figure 6. Comparison of risks in each dimension.

4.3. Sensitivity Analysis

Sensitivity analysis is a topic that can provide proper insight into solving problems. In other words, sensitivity analysis determines how much the dependent variable will change if the value of an independent variable changes in a specific and defined situation, assuming that other variables are constant. Here, the values presented in Table 3 are changed to find out how an increase or decrease in each parameter affects the final cost of the model. Based on sensitivity analyses performed on the main model parameters, the supplier, collection–distribution center, and producer numbers have the greatest impact on the target functions. It should be noted that the time required for product delivery to customers has an inverse relationship with the increase in these parameters. Hence, increased supplier, collection–distribution center, and producer numbers would lead to a decrease in the time required to transfer products to customers. Additionally, parameters related to destruction and recycling centers only have an effect on pollutant levels and chain costs, with no effects on objective functions related to time and risk. Thus, with an increase in destruction centers, the amount of pollutants increases more, while an increase in recycling centers results in a higher chain costs. The increased number of customers and produced products does not affect risk. Since the impact of other problem parameters, such as the costs of producing each product unit, purchasing raw materials, training, recycling, destruction, and inspection, as presented in Table 3, only affect chain costs and have no effects on other objective functions, they were not investigated in the sensitivity analysis section.

4.4. Comparison

We also use the MOPSO algorithm and compare its performance with the NSGA-II algorithm in solving large-scale problems to evaluate the developed methodology. Table 11 presents the comparison results.

Table 11. Comparing the performance of NSGA-II and MOPSO in model solving.

Distribution No.	Costumers No.	NSGA-II				MOPSO			
		Cost	Pollution (ppm)	Risk (%)	Time (h)	Cost	Pollution (ppm)	Risk (%)	Time (h)
20	30	15,203,980	13,526	0.177	112	15,878,009	15,321	0.201	122
20	45	20,265,270	13,658	0.346	114	16,508,714	16,807	0.359	126
25	50	21,423,701	14,002	0.443	123	21,046,485	17,243	0.481	131
30	50	21,654,514	14,230	0.303	129	21,245,259	17,296	0.329	135
32	60	22,558,487	15,200	0.391	135	22,857,772	17,633	0.405	141
38	65	22,579,460	16,210	0.408	139	23,429,838	18,828	0.415	154
41	65	23,429,301	16,890	0.479	145	23,968,083	19,309	0.502	161
45	70	24,112,607	17,532	0.587	160	24,099,886	19,655	0.592	167
50	70	24,128,172	18,050	0.599	175	25,479,452	19,738	0.621	181

As revealed by comparisons, the genetic optimization method (NSGA-II) has higher diversity in discovering solutions due to its ability to identify local and global optimal solutions and its continuity. Compared to MOPSO, a better balance is established between discovery and efficiency criteria to prevent the risk of falling into local optima. Therefore, in addition to its high power in discovering optimal answers, the genetics-based method shows higher speed and subsequently a higher convergence rate and diversity than MOPSO.

In the following analysis, we use the MGA, as employed by Gholizadeh and Fazlollahtabar (2020), to maximize the single objective model associated with the CLSC total costs [34]. The objective function presented here seeks to maximize the total profit of the closed-loop green SC. Gross profit equals the difference between income and expenses. Revenue sources are products sold to customers in both Tier 1 and Tier 2. The company's total costs also comprise operational and transportation costs. Thus, each period's operating costs within the future flow are equal to raw material purchasing costs, production of grade 1 products, assembly of grade 1 and 2 products, and the distribution centers' operating costs. A reverse supply chain also involves paying for the purchase of used products from customers, separation costs of returned products, quality checking of separated parts in the parts separation center, and waste disposal costs in the reverse flow. Hence, Table 12 presents the modeling results of the modified GA and the proposed model.

Table 12. Comparison of the developed algorithm (NSGA-II) and MGA, proposed by Gholizadeh and Fazlollahtabar (2020) [34].

Problem No.	1	2	3	4	5	6	7	8	9	10
Modified GA	11,005,413	10,363,216	15,344,758	20,483,956	16,050,510	28,996,989	20,668,679	22,790,123	23,998,908	14,999,575
Present Study	11,152,821	10,852,524	15,817,908	20,854,215	16,642,758	29,528,210	21,217,931	23,269,604	24,752,042	15,241,798
Diff. (%)	1.34	4.72	3.08	1.81	3.69	1.83	2.66	2.10	3.14	1.61

Based on Table 12, among the 10 examples of the solved problem, the algorithm introduced in this research has favorable performance in determining chain costs and enhacing profits, with the highest difference equal to 4.72% and the average difference equal to 2.38% compared to MGA.

The Non-dominated Sorting Genetic Algorithm II (NSGA-II) outperforms the modified genetic algorithm due to several key factors inherent in its design and operational mechanisms. NSGA-II's enhanced performance, which led to a 2.38% reduction in costs, can be attributed to its superior handling of multiple objectives, preservation of diversity among solutions, and efficient sorting and selection process.

5. Discussion and Conclusions

In this paper, the multi-objective genetic optimization method was used to find the optimal answer to the four-objective closed-loop supply chain nonlinear programming problem. The study involved comparing and analyzing the optimal values obtained from each method across different dimensions. The proposed algorithm was performed in several phases. In the first phase, the problem was modeled and initialized, encoding the supply chain network in question with a string of real numbers. Each solution (chromosome) in the genetic algorithm is equivalent to the components of suppliers, distribution centers, producers, repair centers, collection, renovation, destruction, and recycling, and the values of each sub-component of these parameters are randomly initialized within the intervals determined for each. Genetic algorithms usually use a higher quality population to speed up convergence. In the second phase, a criterion must be defined to evaluate the members of the population and enable the recognition of the better organisms in the population. This work, i.e., determining the suitability of an entity, is called the evaluation of that entity. The fitness function is equivalent to the planning problem discussed in Section 3, which deals with profit maximization and environmental impact minimization. The determined values for each of the components of suppliers, distribution centers, producers, and other investigated centers are placed in the objective function to calculate the objective functions and solve the problem according to the considered limitations. In the next step, Pareto solutions are extracted depending on the genetic algorithm model, representing the optimal values of regulatory parameters, including the number of disposals, renovation, repair, recycling, distributor, and supplier centers. The experimental results showed that the genetic algorithm had a favorable performance in finding solutions in all three dimensions, small, medium, and large, in finding the optimal solution, maximizing profit, and reducing the effects on the environment, risk and product transfer time. It was also determined by sensitivity analysis that the parameters related to the number of suppliers, collection–distribution centers, and manufacturers have the greatest impact on the performance of the proposed model's objectives. It was also found that the product delivery time to the customer will have the opposite effect with the increase in these parameters, and with the increase in the number of suppliers, collection–distribution centers, and manufacturers, the product transfer time to the customer will decrease. The results of the comparison of the proposed method with the MOPSO algorithm showed that the genetic optimization method has more diversity in discovering solutions due to finding local and global optimal solutions and its continuous nature, and a better balance is established between the discovery and efficiency criteria to avoid failing to local optima. It was also found that compared to the MOPSO method, it has a high speed and subsequently higher convergence and diversity in achieving optimal solutions. In other words, the advantage of the proposed method compared to other methods is in automatic subset creation and finding global optima and local optima to consciously maximize the profit from each stage of the supply chain. In addition, the proposed method has wider applicability, and we intend to focus on the design of supply chain systems with other objectives in the uncertain and ambiguous periods in the future. Also, in the future, the authors will attempt to perform a quantitative assessment of the environmental benefits resulting from pollutant reduction strategies, possibly including life cycle assessments (LCAs) and economic analyses of cost-saving measures, potentially incorporating a break-even analysis to assess financial feasibility.

Author Contributions: Conceptualization, G.H.P. and Y.H.; Methodology, G.H.P.; Software, G.H.P.; Validation, G.H.P.; Formal analysis, G.H.P.; Investigation, G.H.P.; Resources, G.H.P. and Y.H.; Data curation, G.H.P.; Writing—original draft, G.H.P.; Writing—review & editing, Y.H. and S.H.P.; Visualization, G.H.P.; Supervision, Y.H.; Project administration, Y.H.; Funding acquisition, Y.H. All authors have read and agreed to the published version of the manuscript.

Funding: The current work received support from the National Natural Science Foundation of China (No. 72171047).

Data Availability Statement: The data presented in this study are available on request from the corresponding author.

Conflicts of Interest: The authors declare no conflict of interest.

References

1. Alzoubi, H.M.; Ghazal, T.M.; Sahawneh, N.; Al-kassem, A.H. Fuzzy assisted human resource management for supply chain management issues. *Ann. Oper. Res.* **2022**, *326*, 125004644.
2. Rolf, B.; Jackson, I.; Müller, M.; Lang, S.; Reggelin, T.; Ivanov, D. A review on reinforcement learning algorithms and applications in supply chain management. *Int. J. Prod. Res.* **2022**, *61*, 7151–7179. [CrossRef]
3. Boskabadi, A.; Mirmozaffari, M.; Yazdani, R.; Farahani, A. Design of a distribution network in a multi-product, multi-period green supply chain system under demand uncertainty. *Sustain. Oper. Comput.* **2022**, *3*, 226–237. [CrossRef]
4. Chen, J.; Wang, H.; Fu, Y. A multi-stage supply chain disruption mitigation strategy considering product life cycle during COVID-19. *Environ. Sci. Pollut. Res.* **2022**, 1–15. [CrossRef]
5. Roh, T.; Noh, J.; Oh, Y.; Park, K.S. Structural relationships of a firm's green strategies for environmental performance: The roles of green supply chain management and green marketing innovation. *J. Clean. Prod.* **2022**, *356*, 131877. [CrossRef]
6. Abir, A.S.; Bhuiyan, I.A.; Arani, M.; Billal, M.M. Multi-Objective Optimization for Sustainable Closed-Loop Supply Chain Network Under Demand Uncertainty: A Genetic Algorithm. *arXiv* **2020**, arXiv:2009.06047.
7. Arani, M.; Liu, X.; Abdolmaleki, S. Scenario-based simulation approach for an integrated inventory blood supply chain system. In Proceedings of the 2020 Winter Simulation Conference (WSC), Orlando, FL, USA, 14–18 December 2020; pp. 1348–1359.
8. Large, R.O.; Thomsen, C.G. Drivers of Green Supply Management Performance: Evidence from Germany. *J. Purch. Supply Manag.* **2016**, *17*, 176–184. [CrossRef]
9. Zhu, Q.; Sarkis, J.; Lai, K.H. Green Supply Chain Management Practices and Sustainability Performance. *J. Purch. Supply Manag.* **2015**, *19*, 106–117. [CrossRef]
10. Jabbarzadeh, A.; Haughton, M.; Khosrojerdi, A. Closed-loop Supply Chain Network Design under Disruption Risks: A Robust Approach with Real World Application. *Comput. Ind. Eng.* **2018**, *116*, 178–191. [CrossRef]
11. Devika, K.; Jafarian, A.; Nourbakhsh, V. Designing a sustainable closed-loop supply chain network based on triple bottom line approach: A comparison of metaheuristics hybridization techniques. *Eur. J. Oper. Res.* **2014**, *235*, 594–615. [CrossRef]
12. Farrokh, M.; Azar, A.; Jandaghi, G.; Ahmadi, E. A novel robust fuzzy stochastic programming for closed loop supply chain network design under hybrid uncertainty. *Fuzzy Sets Syst.* **2018**, *341*, 69–91. [CrossRef]
13. Liu, M.; Liu, R.; Zhu, Z.; Chu, C.; Man, X. A bi-objective green closed loop supply chain design problem with uncertain demand. *Sustainability* **2018**, *10*, 967. [CrossRef]
14. Mohtashami, Z.; Aghsami, A.; Jolai, F. A green closed loop supply chain design using queuing system for reducing environmental impact and energy consumption. *J. Clean. Prod.* **2020**, *242*, 118452. [CrossRef]
15. Rezae, S.; Kheirkhah, A. A comprehensive approach in designing a sustainable closed-loop supply chain network using cross-docking operations. In *Computational and Mathematical Organization Theory*; Springer Science + Business Media: New York, NY, USA, 2017.
16. Garai, A.; Chowdhury, S.; Sarkar, B.; Roy, T.K. Cost-effective subsidy policy for growers and biofuels-plants in closed-loop supply chain of herbs and herbal medicines: An interactive bi-objective optimization in T-environment. *Appl. Soft Comput.* **2021**, *100*, 106949. [CrossRef]
17. Jerbiaa, R.; Kchaou Boujelbenb, M.; Amine Sehlia, M.; Jemaia, Z. A stochastic closed-loop supply chain network design problem with multiple recovery options. *Comput. Ind. Eng.* **2018**, *118*, 23–32. [CrossRef]
18. Santander, P.; Sanchez, F.A.C.; Boudaoud, H.; Camargo, M. Closed loop supply chain network for local and distributed plastic recycling for 3D printing: A MILP-based optimization approach. *Resources. Conserv. Recycl.* **2020**, *154*, 104531. [CrossRef]
19. Goodarzian, F.; Hosseini-Nasab, H.; Fakhrzad, M.B. A Multi-objective Sustainable Medicine Supply Chain Network Design Using a Novel Hybrid Multi-Objective Metaheuristic Algorithm. *Int. J. Eng.* **2020**, *33*, 1986–1995. [CrossRef]
20. Zarbakhshnia, N.; Kannan, D.; Mavi, R.K. Annals of Operations Research A novel sustainable multi-objective optimization model for forward and reverse logistics system under demand uncertainty. *Ann. Oper. Res.* **2020**, *295*, 843–880. [CrossRef]
21. Nasr, A.K.; Tavana, M.; Alavi, B.; Mina, H. A novel fuzzy multi-objective circular supplier selection and order allocation model for sustainable closed-loop supply chains. *J. Clean. Prod.* **2021**, *287*, 124994. [CrossRef]

22. Jian, J.; Li, B.; Zhang, N.; Su, J. Decision-making and coordination of green closed-loop supply chain with fairness concern. *J. Clean. Prod.* **2021**, *298*, 126779. [CrossRef]
23. Tavana, M.; Kian, H.; Nasr, A.K.; Govindan, K.; Mina, H. A comprehensive framework for sustainable closed-loop supply chain network design. *J. Clean. Prod.* **2022**, *332*, 129777. [CrossRef]
24. Cheng, P.; Ji, G.; Zhang, G.; Shi, Y. A closed-loop supply chain network considering consumer's low carbon preference and carbon tax under the cap-and-trade regulation. *Sustain. Prod. Consum.* **2022**, *29*, 614–635. [CrossRef]
25. Kouchaki Tajani, E.; Ghane Kanafi, A.; Daneshmand-Mehr, M.; Hosseinzadeh, A.A. A Robust Green Multi-Channel Sustainable Supply Chain based on RFID technology with considering pricing strategy and subsidizing policies. *J. Ind. Eng. Int.* **2022**, *18*, 43–78.
26. Babaeinesami, A.; Tohidi, H.; Ghasemi, P.; Goodarzian, F.; Tirkolaee, E.B. A closed-loop supply chain configuration considering environmental impacts: A self-adaptive NSGA-II algorithm. *Appl. Intell.* **2022**, *52*, 13478–13496. [CrossRef]
27. Alinezhad, M.; Mahdavi, I.; Hematian, M.; Tirkolaee, E.B. A fuzzy multi-objective optimization model for sustainable closed-loop supply chain network design in food industries. *Environ. Dev. Sustain.* **2022**, 1–28. [CrossRef]
28. Bathaee, M.; Nozari, H.; Szmelter-Jarosz, A. Designing a new location-allocation and routing model with simultaneous pick-up and delivery in a closed-loop supply chain network under uncertainty. *Logistics* **2023**, *7*, 3. [CrossRef]
29. Wang, Z.; Zhen, H.L.; Deng, J.; Zhang, Q.; Li, X.; Yuan, M.; Zeng, J. Multiobjective optimization-aided decision-making system for large-scale manufacturing planning. *IEEE Trans. Cybern.* **2021**, *52*, 8326–8339. [CrossRef]
30. Leung, M.F.; Coello, C.A.C.; Cheung, C.C.; Ng, S.C.; Lui, A.K.F. A hybrid leader selection strategy for many-objective particle swarm optimization. *IEEE Access* **2020**, *8*, 189527–189545. [CrossRef]
31. Bahrampour, P.; Najafi, S.E.; Edalatpanah, A. Designing a Scenario-Based Fuzzy Model for Sustainable Closed-Loop Supply Chain Network considering Statistical Reliability: A New Hybrid Metaheuristic Algorithm. *Complexity* **2023**, *2023*, 1337928. [CrossRef]
32. Wu, Z.; Qian, X.; Huang, M.; Ching, W.K.; Wang, X.; Gu, J. Recycling channel choice in closed-loop supply chains considering retailer competitive preference. *Enterp. Inf. Syst.* **2023**, *17*, 1923065. [CrossRef]
33. Dey, S.K.; Giri, B.C. Corporate social responsibility in a closed-loop supply chain with dual-channel waste recycling. *Int. J. Syst. Sci. Oper. Logist.* **2023**, *10*, 2005844. [CrossRef]
34. Gholizadeh, H.; Fazlollahtabar, H. Robust optimization and modified genetic algorithm for a closed loop green supply chain under uncertainty: Case study in melting industry. *Comput. Ind. Eng.* **2020**, *147*, 106653. [CrossRef]

Disclaimer/Publisher's Note: The statements, opinions and data contained in all publications are solely those of the individual author(s) and contributor(s) and not of MDPI and/or the editor(s). MDPI and/or the editor(s) disclaim responsibility for any injury to people or property resulting from any ideas, methods, instructions or products referred to in the content.

MDPI AG
Grosspeteranlage 5
4052 Basel
Switzerland
Tel.: +41 61 683 77 34

Mathematics Editorial Office
E-mail: mathematics@mdpi.com
www.mdpi.com/journal/mathematics

Disclaimer/Publisher's Note: The statements, opinions and data contained in all publications are solely those of the individual author(s) and contributor(s) and not of MDPI and/or the editor(s). MDPI and/or the editor(s) disclaim responsibility for any injury to people or property resulting from any ideas, methods, instructions or products referred to in the content.

www.ingramcontent.com/pod-product-compliance
Lightning Source LLC
LaVergne TN
LVHW070206100526
838202LV00015B/2010